More praise for *The American Play: 1787–2000*

"*The American Play* is a searching and elegant study of ~~ by one of its foremost critics." — Martin Puchner, Harvard University

"Rarely has such a good writer on drama undertaken such a project, and even more rarely executed it with such panache." — Don B. Wilmeth, Editor, *Cambridge Guide to American Theatre*

"Both a rich, revealing archaeology and an inspired and startling remapping of the American dramatic landscape, this brilliant, synoptic work will influence the shape of American drama and cultural studies for generations to come." — Una Chaudhuri, author of *Staging Place: The Geography of Modern Drama*

"Marc Robinson is one of the most astute and sensitive critics of American drama, and *The American Play* is his major work to date. . . . Powerful and persuasive. . . . Essential reading for any serious student of U.S. drama." — Stephen Bottoms, *New Theatre Quarterly*

"[An] inspired reassessment of this nation's theatrical history." — *Dramatics*

"Revelatory . . . Robinson's essays fulfill the lofty goal of giving close, interdisciplinary readings that liberally dip into new developments in American literature, dance, and visual art." — Randy Gener, *American Theatre*

"Robinson has mapped a new field guided by his passions, and his readings will set the standard for works to come. . . . *The American Play* stands as an important achievement." — Alan Ackerman, *Theater*

MARC ROBINSON

The American Play

1787–2000

Yale University Press
New Haven &
London

Published with the assistance of the Frederick W. Hilles Publication Fund of Yale University.

Set in Sabon Roman type by Keystone Typesetting, Inc.
Printed in the United States of America.

The Library of Congress has cataloged the hardcover edition as follows:

Robinson, Marc, 1962–
    The American play : 1787–2000 / Marc Robinson.
        p. cm.
    Includes bibliographical references and index.
    ISBN 978-0-300-11649-6 (alk. paper)
        1. American drama — History and criticism. 2. Theater — United States — History. I. Title.
PS332.R63 2009
812′.009 — dc22
2008042926

ISBN 978-0-300-17004-7 (pbk.)

A catalogue record for this book is available from the British Library.

10 9 8 7 6 5 4 3 2 1

For Henry

Contents

Acknowledgments

I am grateful to the many friends who have offered advice and encouragement over the last several years. Stanley Kauffmann, Alexander Nemerov, April Bernard, and Tom Sellar responded to individual chapters with their customary insight and generosity. Another acute reader, Joseph Roach, steered me from proposal to book; his enthusiasm for the project helped me finish it. Still other colleagues provided assistance at crucial junctures. Thank you to Emily Coates, Elizabeth Dillon, Langdon Hammer, Audrey Healy, David Joselit, Charles Musser, George Nicholson, Matthew Regan, Gordon Rogoff, and Don Wilmeth. Students in my seminars on American theater have been indulgent listeners as I tried out many ideas in these pages. Their responses and alternative readings urged me toward greater clarity.

I wrote part of this book at the MacDowell Colony on a Thornton Wilder Fellowship. Thank you to Cheryl Young, Tappan Wilder, and the colony's staff for this much-needed retreat. Yale's Americanist Colloquium and Whitney Humanities Center allowed me to present research in convivial settings. No less welcoming was a Hunter College symposium on Suzan-Lori Parks (organized by Jonathan Kalb), where I delivered an early version of part of the last chapter.

Librarians at several institutions helped me track down texts, recordings, photographs, and drawings. At Yale, I am indebted to Tobin Nellhaus of Sterling Memorial Library, Pam Jordan of the School of Drama Library, Patricia Willis of the Beinecke Rare Book and Manuscript Library, and Richard Warren of the Historical Sound Recordings Collection. The staffs of the Harvard Theatre Collection of the Houghton Library (especially Elizabeth Falsey), the Theater Collection of the Museum of the City of New York, and the Billy Rose Theatre Division of the New York Public Library for the Performing Arts were also tolerant of my many queries. Finally, I have been lucky in my editors at Yale University Press. Lara Heimert and, later, Keith Condon were imaginative and resourceful allies, keeping faith in a long-gestating manuscript. Eliza Childs was a sensitive copy editor. Jonathan Brent's support of drama and dramatic criticism has been gratifying. The Press's two anonymous, attentive readers made invaluable suggestions for improving the manuscript.

My largest debt is to Erika Rundle. Erika sent me back to plays I thought I knew, responded deeply to drafts, and put up with many neurotic flare-ups. Her investment in this book is only one of her many gifts to me.

Introduction

The American Play traces the development of American theater from the end of the eighteenth century, when Royall Tyler and William Dunlap produced the first stageworthy native-born dramas, to the end of the twentieth century, when Wallace Shawn and Suzan-Lori Parks were among the many writers overturning long-held ideas of "drama" and "stageworthiness." As these names suggest, my history is not exhaustive. Hoping to fulfill the purpose but elude the limits of the genre, I have instead aimed to create a hybrid of panoramic overview and close textual criticism. In each of the book's self-contained chapters, I map the landscape of an era's thematic preoccupations and formal procedures and then zero in on a small number of selected plays, paying attention to how their writers either embody ambitions shared by a generation or launch the art beyond existing conventions. Some of the most important figures in my narrative are the least representative. *The American Play* reads deeply in well-known dramatic literature but also, I hope, makes the case for assigning a secure place in our theater history to hitherto marginal work. If the case is persuasive, American theater will appear at once more integrated and more heterogeneous than is commonly assumed. Its "minor" writers will make us newly responsive to the unsteadying challenges posed by canonical playwrights; the canon, in turn, will provide a welcoming context for work ordinarily discussed as merely "experimental."

The development of American theater, in this light, may seem guided by a nourishing form of ecology. The very idea that such an ephemeral art in fact conserves, continuously returns to, and revises modes of performance once thought obsolete is itself jarring; even more so is the realization that some of the most radical of dramatists are the most observant of tradition. Among the many backward reachings and recoveries in our theater history (some deliberate, some unwitting) are Gertrude Stein's acknowledged debt to the melodramas *Uncle Tom's Cabin* and *Secret Service;* Eugene O'Neill's career-long absorption in his father's theater; T. S. Eliot's and E. E. Cummings's sincere engagement of music-hall idioms and other popular-culture structures; Adrienne Kennedy's return to the psychological landscapes of Marita Bonner and Jean Toomer; and Suzan-Lori Parks's purposefully ambiguous interest in minstrelsy, Barnumesque spectacle, and melodramatic dramaturgy. Nowhere is the American theater's historical consciousness more profound than among the artists of the so-called avant-garde. In their work, our theater comes full circle in the least expected ways. Robert Wilson (as he himself says) restores the shocking clarity of nineteenth-century illusionist stagecraft and gesturally emphatic acting. Richard Foreman acknowledges the anxiety beneath melodrama's tableaux and stock plots.[1] Elizabeth LeCompte and the Wooster Group offer a short course in the landmarks of American theater, releasing the repressed appetites (and exposing the subsequent disorder and abjection) in Stein, O'Neill, Thornton Wilder, and Arthur Miller.

Extending the spirit of these linkages, *The American Play* also attempts to integrate drama more fully with the surrounding culture. Developments in the other arts, in particular, cast strong, clarifying light on similar initiatives in theater. Whenever possible, I try to suggest how individual playwrights apply models of expressive candor or restraint, or execute strategies for harnessing or liberating a spectator's attention, available in American literature, visual art, and dance. No less suggestive are the frequent instances when theater itself serves as a plausible source for nontheater artists' experiments in lyrical tension, spatial composition, narrative stasis, or visual density.

The nineteenth-century interest in the modes and morality of spectatorship, for instance, acquires personal force when considered alongside the theatergoing memories Henry James records in *A Small Boy and Others* (1913). As he testifies to the erotic pull of the embodied image and the no less intense pressure to stand back and organize what he sees into rational scenes, he helps us understand how the era's plays, formulaic in their design and stereotypical in their characterization, in fact reveal the far more intricate patterns of our own ambivalent attention. Another companion text, Walt Whitman's *Specimen Days* (1882), contains no explicit commentary on the theater, but when read alongside contemporaneous Civil War dramas it trains spectators in a skeptical mode of attention, enabling us to imagine the subversiveness of seemingly normative sentiment, to register the self-aware theatricality in apparently sincere and transparent characters, and to detect the desperation powering superficially effortless narratives. Stephen Crane provides the same service to readers approaching the early realistic drama of the late nineteenth and early twentieth centuries. His novel *Maggie: A Girl of the Streets* (1893), which argues that melodramatic performance can seem like "transcendental realism" to spectators who disregard the border between lived and sought experience, and his short story "Manacled" (1899), a bitterly funny lampoon of realistic theater, help defamiliarize theatrical notions of naturalness, making visible the effort of artists claiming neutrality.[2]

Visibility itself is an unreliable quality in the American theater. My chapters on late eighteenth- and nineteenth-century drama examine what by the twentieth century reveals itself to be a futile effort to achieve visual mastery over landscape, behavior, and thought. With modernist skepticism still unfelt, early American playwrights return over and over to sites of transformative sight — sentimental characters scrutinizing one another's styles of self-display for evidence of sincerity or insincerity; other characters nominating themselves as witnesses to projects of moral reform; a roaming eye presiding over plays that replicate the rhythms of city life and thereby overturn hierarchies of station and virtue; the same panoramic appetites, stimulated further, enacting visions of national grandeur. All these ambitions depend upon a stagecraft that instructs spectators in vigorous, even intrusive forms of attention. My readings of nineteenth-century drama examine the era's protocinematic dramaturgy, the emphasis on gesture and physical prowess in the dominant modes of acting, the tableau as legible expression of emotion and key to the distribution of narrative power, the symbolic meanings assigned to stage space, and, late in the century, the obsession with objects in early realism.

Yet these approaches begin to falter even before the nineteenth century ends. When Steele MacKaye fails to realize his plan for a Spectatorium — a massive theater planned for the 1893 Chicago World's Fair and intended, as its name suggests, to mark the triumph of seeing — many assumptions sustaining the century's imagistic theater also collapse. The Spectatorium survives *only* as a vision. The lives and landscapes it meant to body forth — the whole visible nation itself, for MacKaye's inaugural production, *The World Finder,* would have told the story of Columbus — allow only a false sense of sovereignty, its ephemeral simulacra veiling a lived history inaccessible to even the most persistent attention.

Stanley Cavell lays the groundwork for our engagement with this and later American theater by reminding us of a self-evident but still disturbing truth:

"We can no more confront a character in a play than we can confront any fictitious being. The trouble is, there they are. . . . We know we cannot approach him, and not because it is not done but because nothing would count as doing it. Put another way, they and we do not occupy the same space; there is no path from my location to his."[3] The strictest twentieth-century American playwrights measure that distance and stress its unbridgeable permanence. Their plays, inward-turning and aloof even at their liveliest, demand a mode of spectatorship responsive to unresponsiveness, one neither expectant nor invasive, the attitude, rather, of a spectator whose own discretion matches that of the art — patient seeing directed toward the insight available only to those with partial or obstructed views. "Let the dark come upon you," writes T. S. Eliot in "East Coker," " . . . as, in a theatre, / The lights are extinguished, for the scene to be changed / With a hollow rumble of wings, with a movement of darkness on darkness."[4] Eliot's vision of a recessive theater, serving a religious project in the poem, can also be read literally, as an image of a severe interiority that dissents from the faith in revelation sustaining much performance. (The theater imagined here would replace the "continual impact / Of external events," as Eliot puts it in *The Family Reunion* [1939], with the "smell untraceable in the drains, / Inaccessible to the plumbers.")[5] On a fundamental level, this shuttered dramatic structure also answers Virginia Woolf's complaint about theater, countering it with an alternative found within theater itself. "What is it that we are coming to want so persistently?" she asks, after duly appreciating the "passionate intensity," "sublimity," and "extravagant laughter, poetry, and splendour" of the Elizabethan play. "It is solitude," she concludes. "There is no privacy here. . . . All is shared, made visible, audible, dramatic" — a judgment that condemns all theater only if one expects an unavoidably public art to affirm habits of public thinking.[6] As modernist American theater resists national, cultural, and aesthetic biases toward the "shared," it prompts the audience to "explore its own darkness" (to borrow Woolf's phrase for properly fearless thought), "not the bright-lit-up surfaces of others," an act of self-confrontation tougher and more extreme than mere privacy.[7]

These priorities sit in uneasy dialogue with many commonplaces about twentieth-century American drama. Its central figures are usually praised for asserting the force of candor or commitment (as well as for deploying the flexible dramatic languages they require) against myriad forms of cultural inhibition and aesthetic caution — the complacency of previous eras that settled too early on standards of authenticity. The ruthless psychological exposures in drama after World War I, the political engagement and ethical clarity of plays from the 1930s, the lyrical reach and emotional lability of much drama after World War II, the scrutiny of individual and national hubris in other postwar plays, or the renegotiation, in domestic drama, of the larger social contract — all these initiatives culminate in our own era, in the still bolder gestural languages, visual allure, and presentational confidence of theater exposing the means of theater itself.

My own readings acknowledge the vitality of all these ambitions. But I also track their accomplishment against an equally strong pull in the opposite direction: a formal and narrative undertow complicating one's confidence in such confrontational stances and explicit emotions. Some of the seemingly most declarative playwrights when read with different stresses can in fact appear the most diffident. Those readers who value *Death of a Salesman* (1949) as a large-voiced public statement on various national mythologies (to take only the best known of many possible examples) may be ignoring the first words in its crucial subtitle: "Certain Private Conversations in Two Acts and a Requiem." (The play's original title — "The Inside of His Head" — insists upon the recessiveness.) The modesty, contingency, and opacity enforced by Miller's subtitle surface earlier in American drama and persist up to the present. They affect more than narrative or characterization. Speech itself refuses to serve expository or confessional ends in plays in which language's own materiality obscures the people using it. This is clearest in *Long Day's Journey into Night* (1941) when, near the end, the Tyrone men hide behind blocks of quotation, the verbal equivalent of the fog shrouding their home. The same impulse is behind the coded epitaph on Simon Stimson's tombstone in *Our Town* (1938), unattributed musical notes signaling the deceased's equally unreadable passion. Other examples include the preverbal "Knock's" and "Hoo's" that open up abysses of dread and menace in Eliot's *Sweeney Agonistes* (1926–27); the self-protective, baroque idiom of plays by Cummings, Djuna Barnes, and Edward Albee; and more recently, the theatricalized footnotes and precisely shaped silences in Suzan-Lori Parks — linguistic signs pointing to her theater's other, more obvious hiding places.

Once acknowledged, these hollows and recesses seem to be everywhere on the American stage, pockmarking its deceptively smooth and secure surfaces. Elsewhere are real bunkers and hideaways, newly attractive as relief from arenas that now seem brutal in their exposures. One's sense of what is sufficiently "dramatic" also changes, as habits of evasion and self-abnegation, as well as of perverse inscrutability and ordinary shyness, become the form of, rather than the impediment to, action. Such behavior helps enforce an overall compositional austerity, one that refuses to temper the challenge posed by stillness to impatient viewers or to tease unambiguous opinions from characters guarding their uncommitted reserve.

The monastic sound of these priorities is not inappropriate. Gertrude Stein's

Four Saints in Three Acts (1927) details Saint Therese's passage from the distracting outside world to an "interior castle" (as the real Teresa of Avila called it), with its seven chambers nested within one another, leading her toward a frighteningly intimate communion with God. Her inward progress has its secular equivalent in the many other plays whose characters seek the kind of poise available only when it is unacknowledged. In doing so, they stimulate spectators' own claims on stage space, thereby directing attention to the very sites designed to elude it. One could point to the twin solitudes of a dance hall's backstage and a one-room shack in Zora Neale Hurston's *Color Struck* (1925) or to the pitch-black, edgeless cellar — repository of repressed history — in Jean Toomer's *Kabnis* (1923). Other, similar sites are the apartment fortified by the inward-looking sisters in Djuna Barnes's *The Dove* (1926), the onstage cottage to which Molly retreats in Jane Bowles's *In the Summer House* (1953), several bedrooms in Albee, and a bathroom in Shawn. All serve as architectural support to characters battling the pressure to account for themselves; declare their intentions; and render transparent the impure solution of recollection, ambition, and aversion that, in privacy, buoys the self. Only by refusing to make an appearance can they prolong the state of hesitation in which perception and thought are at their keenest — a period in which they are uncoerced toward the ordinary actions seemingly predicted by their impulses. Such charged restraint requires a dramatic structure as purposefully opaque as the architectural structures. Even those plays with the most eventful plots seem to rescind as many invitations to intimacy as they issue. Their narratives recoil even as they unspool, pulling incidents and individuals back from scenes where they risk becoming mere symbol, statement, or object — the degraded matter of the known world. "I like my human experience served up with a little *silence* and Restraint," writes Djuna Barnes in an admiring review of Marlene Dietrich, a passage that describes the taste of many American playwrights. "Silence makes experience go further and, when it does die, gives it that dignity common to a Thing one has touched but not RAVISHED."[8]

To call this approach antitheatrical implies an ideological stance no less public and explicit, and thus no more welcome to these writers, than theatricality itself (although Martin Puchner's important *Stage Fright: Modernism, Anti-Theatricality, and Drama* [2002] names several practices that also inform this strain of interiority, one unembarrassed by its psychological origins). Neither does this theater achieve the tranquility implicit in the idea of absorption (although Michael Fried's promotion of this quality in painting, a corrective to theatrical pandering, can seem the idealized, unneurotic resolution of a related ambivalence in theater itself). The confidence of both ideas is absent from modernist American theater, as its characters, indifferent to the culture's broader debates over genre, hunt for inviolate settings, durable masks, and a diction hard enough to deflect intrusive questions from other characters or ourselves. The plays themselves seem chronically doubtful of the compromises they strike between presence and absence. They demand sustained attentiveness only so they can foil it. Ezra Pound names this ambivalence precisely in *The Classic Noh Theatre of Japan,* a book published in the United States in 1917, one year after the Provincetown Players' first productions of O'Neill broke with nineteenth-century theater practice. Pound's only direct proposal for a new theater is easy to miss: in a brief note to one translation, Pound asserts, "Our own art is so much an art of emphasis, and even of over-emphasis, that it is difficult to consider the possibilities of an absolutely unemphasized art."[9]

The "possibilities" Pound envisions would not be fully discovered until the 1960s and 1970s, in the so-called Theater of Images—a development that forces us to confront the contradictions in the war between visibility and invisibility in two centuries of American theater. When nineteenth-century staging procedures recur in the post-1960 theater, only someone inattentive to the spectatorial challenges earlier in the modernist era can treat them as a belated vindication of visuality. Every image, here, acknowledges vaster experiences that the artist cannot, or will not, render. These stage pictures are less icons than shields, diversions, memorial stones, screens. The alluring surfaces and virtuoso displays of poise in Robert Wilson, for instance, uphold a prohibition on less shapely emotion. The dense layering and continuously shifting focus in a typical Wooster Group production prevent the numbness of ordinary visual enchantment—an antihypnotic strategy the group shares with Richard Foreman, whose characters (speaking for Foreman himself) further worry that their addiction to material pleasure, including that of art itself, postpones spiritual epiphanies. In Meredith Monk's work, objects and landscapes, addressed with a fetishistic wonder last seen among the realists, compensate for the untouchable, unapproachable regions of individual and cultural memory. In all this work, time's passage is especially obvious, its acid-like effect on stage pictures crueler than in other theater, if only because these pictures persuade us they are not mere replicas of real-world originals (the stock of so much other theater) but irreplaceable artifacts themselves.

This theater, like all recessive theater of American modernism, recalls Richard Poirier's well-known interest in the "reinstatement of the vague." William James's phrase, and his preference for "signs of direction" and "dumb psychic states" over explicit images and "substantive parts" of existence, are the starting points for Poirier's exploration (in *Poetry and Pragmatism* [1992]) of what he calls the "beneficial" "gaps" and "abysses" in American literature

— "gaps in what [language] only pretends already to have settled" — a linguistic project that leads to a moral conclusion: in the beneficial gap thrives a radical individualism that "can withhold itself from the over-defining appeals of ideologies, meanings, images, ideas that are making the rounds at any given moment. Such individualism can keep in touch with an idea without letting itself be possessed by it."[10] But it is a sentence from Djuna Barnes's *Nightwood* (1936), a novel unconcerned with theater per se, that most simply restores our awareness of everything that, in our pursuit of the theater's opportunities for visual pleasure, we try to ignore: "An image is a stop the mind makes between uncertainties."[11] In twentieth-century American theater, the uncertainties loom as large and grow as vivid as the images. Spectators are asked to scan the stage's uncharted territory as much as "stop" upon its attractions, to inhabit ambiguities no tableau can relieve, and to let their attention dilate in order to mark the boundaries keeping them from all they cannot see.

A related uncertainty determines the critical temperament of this book as a whole. The movement that I've described from sight to blindness, or from image to lacuna, may be the only clear trajectory in a theater that neither treats its forms as stable nor progresses rationally through them. (Even the argument over vision is, as we'll discover, dependent on paradox: we see prohibitions on seeing.) From the American theater's earliest days, dramatists have discouraged spectators from trusting any assertion in an art nourished by transience. We learn to shift agnostically between equally persuasive polarities or, more often, enter an arena with so many competing claims on belief that it's impossible to favor a single pair of opposing voices. This spectatorial flexibility may at first seem counterintuitive. An American theater in which the first professionally produced comedy is called *The Contrast* (Royall Tyler's 1787 satire of European manners among the native-born) and the earliest actable tragedy concerns treason (William Dunlap's *André*, from 1798) seems always to have tended toward a single correct style, ideology, or code of conduct. The reality is more ambiguous. In these two plays, and in many later works, few orthodoxies survive a self-arguing, multivoiced style. What Dunlap calls "wildering passions" (the phrase, from *André*, describes one character's competing loyalties) connotes the productive, theatrically vibrant disorder of American theater in general.[12] The outrageous is always unseating the earnest, then subsiding before it, too, becomes doctrine. Genuine pathos emerges from seeming parody but dissipates just when we begin to romanticize it. Codes of sensibility never entirely conceal darker, primal instinct.

Sacvan Bercovitch, in *The Puritan Origins of the American Self* (1975), teaches us to recognize the "psychic uncertainty" that prompts the "rhetorical self-assertion" in many colonial-era theological and secular narratives — a compensatory equation that, by implication, continues to play a central role in the national culture.[13] (One source he cites, the Separatist William Bradford, tries simultaneously to acknowledge and arrest "the mutable things of this unstable world" in his eyewitness history of Plymouth Plantation.)[14] Although Bercovitch doesn't discuss drama, the tension that he treats as generative is, if anything, even stronger in a temporal art, where "mutability" is necessary and "self-assertion" is enacted gesturally and aurally before witnesses. Heroic posturing, declarative speechifying, effortless narratives, and decorous discussion attest less to national confidence, in this view, than to individual fear. Any discussion of American drama must acknowledge the roiling anxiety beneath the placid surfaces.

Such turbulence is, predictably, strongest in the raw first decades of the American theater, but it continues to be felt in the mature plays of the middle and late nineteenth century. By the twentieth century, it has become the dominant mode of our dramaturgy. *The American Play* maps theater's own "unstable worlds" and locates the liveliest, most stimulating expression where dissolution is a constant possibility. Here are hybrid, pliant forms, able to accommodate seemingly incompatible languages and rhythms. Sophisticated melodrama (an oxymoron that, I hope, will prove justified) allows its sentiment to falter and its schematism to blur before righting itself. (These threats are more thrilling than any narrative turn.) A generation later, visionary realists manage to be at once retrograde and radical, betraying a hard-to-shake attraction to melodrama while looking dubiously at their new ism's assurances of "truth."[15] The truth that their twentieth-century successors pursue is equally remote. Those writing convincingly about psychology manage to win our deepest sympathy when they show how they manipulate us. Still other works take such theatrical self-consciousness to a seemingly self-destructive extreme. These writers, prominent in the twentieth century but active even in the nineteenth, exploit the possibilities of theater's fundamental element — time — and its inescapable status — temporariness — so vigorously as to dismantle character, mise-en-scène, plot, and argument. The spectacle of continuous change itself demands our attention instead, a shift that Bert O. States recommends, in a different context, in *The Pleasure of the Play* (1994): "We should think of the theatrical *now* not as a point or an interval that is succeeded by another point or interval (as in Zeno's paradox of the arrow) but as the window of our consciousness on the temporal flux taking place in the space before us."[16] The ascendancy of flux argues for principles as pertinent to life offstage as onstage. Fluid thought able to slip past codified ideas, capacious feeling unconstrained by textbook emotions, flexible morality mistrustful of dogma—all of these are impossible to recommend when theater is beholden to representation and aspires to permanence.

To find a figure who exemplifies American drama's fidelity to impermanence —one who in his brazen theatricality primes us to recognize other artists' subtler experiments in disequilibrium—we must look to the culture's margins and recuperate a delinquent figure. No one should be surprised that John Brougham's burlesques have proven perishable. (Only one remains in print after his heyday in the 1840s and 1850s.) The Irish-born writer who skewered the normative, catechistic pretensions of the literary theater would have sacrificed much of his authority if mainstream American culture had wholly assimilated him. The popularity he enjoyed in his day is deceptive. His ingratiating writing and acting convinced audiences that they were his allies, as if being in on the joke ensured other kinds of inclusion. Yet even on the page, Brougham exudes a manic impatience with anyone else's sense of limits. His subtitles alone betray his appetite. To read his "new and audaciously original historico-plagiaristic, ante-national, pre-patriotic, and omni-local confusion of circumstances, running through two acts and four centuries" (*Columbus el Filibustero!!* 1857) or his "original aboriginal erratic operatic semi-civilized and demi-savage extravaganza" (*Po-ca-hon-tas; or, The Gentle Savage,* 1855) is to test one's ability simply to keep up with him.[17]

The burlesques heralded by these snowballing, seemingly infinite titles seek to break through still other norms. Brougham's plots, such as they are, unfold with unsentimental haste. They exist to justify the many topical allusions—so varied and deployed so rapidly that not even the savviest spectator will catch them all—and the punning, which is compulsive and execrable. No less exhausting are the play's musical interludes, which often upstage the narrative and, in their willfully inconsistent style, one another. In *Po-ca-hon-tas,* English airs compete with children's songs until both give way to mongrel opera buffa ("Grand Scena Complicato in the Anglo-Italiano Style"), which in time collapses into "Ethiopian" minstrel tunes and, finally, a "Tyrolean" "exhibition of tracheotomous gymnastics" (408, 416). *Columbus el Filibustero!!* attempts even greater and more compressed multiplicity. In a single number, performers move through arias and choruses appropriated from *Robert le Diable, Rigoletto, The Poor Soldier, The Quaker's Wife,* and other works. Every Brougham burlesque contains at least one "concerted piece of antagonistic harmonies."[18]

It's only a matter of time before the plays erupt in open conflict and spin toward a breakdown. "The Curtain Falls to Babylonish Confusion," Brougham writes at the end of *Columbus*'s first act (18). *Po-ca-hon-tas* begins with all the characters getting high on a peace pipe (the resulting distractedness suggests a dramaturgical strategy for much Brougham) and is soon overtaken with rows, "mad intoxication," and "vociferous irruption[s] of Juvenile Squaw-lers" (411). As we can see, the wordplay alone in many burlesques is so frenetic as to threaten intelligibility, with words fracturing into syllables to enable a bad joke. All these risks are of course contrived to allow the ever-nimble Brougham to survive them, escaping disaster as well as our expectations. The wisest spectators acquiesce to a world shaped by contingency, obedient only to temporary rules. Audiences may enter Brougham's theater feeling superior to the targets he satirizes, but they leave humbled by an artist who has moved on while they were still laughing at his jokes.

On reentering the broader culture, the most engaged of Brougham's audiences will likely regard it, too, as far less secure, far less confident in its own mores, narratives, and aesthetic forms than its guardians would have us believe. Admirers of *Columbus el Filibustero!!* can no longer treat their national origin story as anything other than a parable of greed, political ambition, and related forms of self-interest. *Po-ca-hon-tas*—along with the earlier *Metamora; or, The Last of the Pollywogs* (1847)—lampoons the stirring narratives and somber atmospheres of the so-called Indian play, freeing the history it draws on from the romanticizing effects of culture. On a smaller scale, the piety in the new nation's embrace of Shakespeare looks foolish, if not unsustainable, in Brougham's 1869 *Much Ado About a Merchant of Venice* ("From the Original Text—a Long Way"). So, too, with other representatives of high culture. After one evening of his happily obnoxious rhymed couplets, it's impossible to stomach the century's proliferating verse dramas with Roman settings and "classical" diction. For every form the American theater puts forward—heroic tragedy, romance, history play, melodrama—Brougham counters with plays less poised, less linear, less respectful of polarities of good and evil. (That Brougham also writes plays that conform to the styles he burlesques makes it even harder to assign him a stable identity.) His closest descendent in the American theater may be Charles Ludlam, who, like him, mastered an array of performance and literary customs so that he would be bound by none. (What Ludlam says about his acting, that he plays "with the character, *at* the character" rather than embodies it, neatly describes Brougham's attitude to forms of drama.)[19] When all Brougham's targets are taken together with his burlesques—and he most significantly affects our view of American theater by insisting we do take them together—readers can't help but concede that, in these developmental years of the American theater, the regressive elements of the culture are more alive than those claiming immortality.

After an encounter with Brougham, the mortality of the American play—any American play—is unignorable. One needn't have a burlesque sensibility to regard plays as poor sources of moral authority or even of aesthetic doctrine. In the best works, norms and deviations continuously trade places, as writers keep changing their angle of vision on subjects too large and various for a single viewing. Spectators who emulate the playwrights' restlessness treat plays as acts (rather than artifacts) of writing, as still-mutating scenes of work rather than their compact and impersonal souvenirs. *The American Play* finds the richest meaning in a play's fragmentary utterances and fractured images, partial rather than comprehensive narratives, spasmodic impulses rather than accomplished actions. It values the idiosyncratic, charged expressiveness of characters plagued by indecision or stopped by obsessiveness.

When playwrights don't disguise their own self-doubts, their work is especially disarming. The texts that reward the closest scrutiny retain the memory of their composition. Otherwise dissimilar writers scattered across the last two centuries dramatize the stop-and-start of writing itself with an immediacy and at times excruciating precision far beyond what they bring to their ostensible subjects. This work is more than merely metatheatrical. Eschewing the egotism that often mars self-referentiality, they explore inadequacy so openly and exhaustively as to press us even beyond the details of their personal struggles. Their plays, in varying degrees of explicitness, allow us to imagine the debilitating ordeal (or addictive pleasure) of revision, the cold contemplation of error, and the temptation to renounce work that has veered fatally off course. Here, too, Brougham is an early touchstone figure. His many manufactured lapses ("I've made a small mistake," he says as Metamora. "These lines are in *The Lady of the Lake*.") differ only in tone from the complex admission of fallibility by later writers.[20] An incomplete list includes Bronson Howard and William Gillette dramatizing their inability to write unself-consciously about the Civil War; Cummings embedding in *Him* a critique of his jocular aesthetics; Stein calling attention to her difficulties in ordering action and getting characters onstage; Wilder theatricalizing error in his two major plays; Tennessee Williams visibly working to control his innate sentimentality; Bowles seeking to prevent her idiosyncrasy from dooming her to isolation; Kennedy lingering in the shame that comes with autobiographical candor; and David Mamet, Shawn, and Parks seeming to atone for every writer's presumptuousness toward his or her subject.

These and many other artists, exceptions in a culture crowded with speakers insisting upon their authority, allow us to imagine the aesthetic and ethical possibilities of humility. They return us to every writer's first encounter with the unmarked page and, by seeming to dispute each sentence before our eyes, prolong their experience of waiting for warring instincts to coalesce into imagery. All expressive possibilities, regardless of their compatibility, remain open to them; nothing is indelible. It doesn't take much effort to predict the larger applications of this style. If we position writers loath to stop revision at the center of any era's artistic life, they help delay the moment when the vital, surprising, experimental play of thought must settle into mere culture. The surrounding society may also benefit from their example. Plays that seem like drafts are the models for flexible civic structures. A still-gestating body politic, its citizens welcoming rather than suppressing doubt, prevents any proposition from becoming an oppressive fixed idea.

If one rereads Royall Tyler and William Dunlap with this aesthetic of confusion in mind, their status as "first" playwrights seems irrelevant to their actual value, if not outright misleading.[21] They don't devise new forms secure enough to be the foundation for later drama — or rather, they won't seem to have done so unless we value the theatrical possibilities of insecurity. Of these, they are masters. Readers who withstand their sharp turns in perspective, emulate their ability to argue on behalf of opposed philosophies, and join them in anticipating the collapse of seemingly inviolate codes of behavior are well prepared for the productive instability often overlooked in later, deceptively "mature" theater. A brief look at each writer's major play primes us for the no less tentative drama to come.

A famous scene in *The Contrast* shows us to ourselves, exposing (even burlesquing) the confusion that we usually repress before a new play. If we distance ourselves from the reflection — the conventional response — we miss a chance to see how any spectator, even the most cultured, negotiates tentatively among a theater production's impossibly multifarious appeals for attention and analysis. In Tyler's scene, a credulous, roughhewn servant named Jonathan — Yankee Jonathan, as historians call his many epigones — describes his first trip to a theater. Drama wasn't his intended diversion. He saw "a great crowd of folks going into a long entry that had lanterns over the door," he says, and followed them expecting to see "the *hocus pocus* man" who "could eat a case knife."[22] Instead, he sat in the balcony, disoriented by the noise, the light, and the talkative, jostling crowd, until "they lifted up a great green cloth and let us look right into the next neighbour's house." The family to whose intimacies he had become an unwilling voyeur was "pretty much like other families; — there was a poor, good-natured, curse of a husband, and a sad rantipole of a wife." Also a "youngster" named Mr. Joseph: "He talked as sober and as pious as a minister; but, like some ministers that I know, he was a sly tike in his heart for all that." Jonathan is most taken with "a little round plump face like mine, only not altogether so handsome," belonging to a man called "Wig — Wag — Wag-all, Darby Wag-all." At this, the other, more sophisticated servants listening to Jonathan can contain themselves no longer. They break it to him that he has in fact been to the theater, seen the American Company's production of *The School for Scandal,* and like so many before him, fallen under the spell of the real-life actor Thomas Wignell. "Mercy on my soul! did I see the wicked players?" he exclaims, his anger rising as he realizes he "paid . . . money to see sights, and the dogs a bit of a sight have I seen, unless you call listening to people's private business a sight" (34–35).

Tyler's short scene is thick with in-jokes introducing themes that will recur over the next century of American drama. The theater with the "lantherns" and "long entry" is New York's John Street Theatre, where *The Contrast* premiered in an American Company staging. In that production, the Jonathan complimenting Wignell was played by Wignell himself. As the frame breaks around Tyler's play, and audiences attend instead to their own story, the cultural ambiguities and aesthetic challenges of all theatergoing — and theater-making — in the new nation become clearer. Jonathan's after-the-fact aversion to the "wicked players" (only on learning that he had been to the theater does he imagine that Wignell had a cloven foot and that the stage candles smelled of brimstone) would of course amuse spectators wearied by the longstanding Puritan antitheatrical prejudice. Yet, in a further turnabout, Jonathan isn't unaware of Puritan hypocrisy. This paradox his eighteenth-century audience would also recognize — the bargain struck by one who still honors the minister even as he sees the "sly tike" beneath the false piety.

Tyler's scene exposes other, less topical contradictions as well. Jonathan practices a kind of attention that mirrors, in its fractured focus, the practices of his own spectators. In a hectic, relentlessly social playhouse, they, too, veer back and forth between the stage and the house, experiencing a seemingly impossible blend of escapism and self-consciousness. (One character describing her own night at the theater ranks "the sentimental charms of a side-box conversation" as equal to the sentimental drama onstage [23].) Even if the typical audience could direct its attention exclusively to the play, it would face further challenges to concentration. Jonathan came to the theater expecting "a sight" and instead was made to "listen to people's private business." Articulating, unwittingly, the tense relation between the visual and the verbal in any performance, and seduced, unwillingly, by sensibility while he awaits a sensation (the hoped-for knife-swallower), Jonathan expands the meaning of Tyler's title by identifying two of the many formal conflicts in early American drama. Well into the nineteenth and twentieth centuries, American theater artists resist imposing hierarchies on the relations between spectacle and discourse and between high and low culture. The phenomenon prompting these discoveries, a production of Sheridan, implies a third source of uneasiness: the issue of influence, vexing to many fledgling American playwrights in Tyler's era and to many theater historians in our own.

The proliferation of performative styles alluded to in this scene — English comedy of manners, American comedy of types, domestic drama, fairground spectacle, Puritan preaching, and the effusive posturing of the body politic — suggests a theater culture that fosters rather than resolves argument; that elevates disorder over legibility; that depends on centrifugal rather than centripetal force; and that purposefully effaces images, gestures, or propositions just when they reach full strength. For all the proselytizing ambitions and normative loyalties of early American play-texts, the stages they appear on cultivate a readiness to be disoriented. As was the custom until the mid-nineteenth century (as David Grimsted shows in *Melodrama Unveiled*), two or more plays, along with numerous self-contained interludes, formed a typical evening at the theater. Jonathan hasn't yet learned to distinguish the parts from the whole. He blends two roles in Wignell's repertory into one figure, part Darby, the comic relief from John O'Keeffe's Anglo-Irish operetta *The Poor Soldier,* and part Joseph Surface from *The School for Scandal.* His error recommends an interpretive strategy, suggesting to less naive spectators (and especially to critics) a way to perceive the energizing agitation beneath much eighteenth- and nineteenth-century theater. Jonathan corrects present-day assumptions about the self-sufficiency of any early American play, implicitly encouraging us to consider the parts of a mixed bill with multiple national origins as composing a single production, its various full-length dramas and farcical afterpieces, original and inherited works, song recitals and specialty acts as extending, complicating, or commenting on one another as do the scenes within individual works themselves. The most agile and engaged spectators may find themselves assimilating, or at least moving easily among, seemingly incompatible emotions, motivations, and tones ordinarily segregated in critical readings intent on tragic or comic consistency. (The playwright John Howard Payne, in an 1811 letter cited by Grimsted, calls a typical night at the theater a "motley mixture of amusements that can never harmonize."[23] He neglects to consider that other forms of union, indifferent to harmony, might be a possibility.)

Audiences who arbitrate among heterogeneous forms competing for sovereignty quickly become shrewd analysts of theatrical procedures and properly skeptical of the authority of any single style. This sophistication — taken for granted in later eras of metatheatrical American drama — deepens at plays in which characters learn to see through other kinds of seduction. When Jonathan can't tell whether or not people at the John Street Theatre are acting, he mirrors a difficulty troubling other, supposedly less foolish characters in *The Contrast*. They, in turn, help us recognize that Tyler dramatizes nothing so vividly as his own struggle to manage his responses to other people's art. How can he, too, distinguish original insight from its artistic precedent? The American theater's obsessive inquiry into writing begins, as we'll see, as a consideration of reading and misreading. Tyler's heroine Maria Van Rough spends her days buried in Richardson, Sterne, and the poet William Shenstone, consulting them as she scripts her own romantic narrative. Her fiancé, Billy Dimple, does the same with literature of his own, as "masculine" as hers is "feminine" — Chesterfield's *Letters* to his son. Billy's text, embraced as an etiquette manual by playboys and cavaliers, mediates between his public and private selves: he refers his every self-serving action to "my lord's" precedent. Maria's own reading helps her recognize her unhappiness with such behavior: she measures Billy's caddishness by Lovelace's standard. Even when she encounters Billy's opposite, the upright Colonel Henry Manly, a patriot scornful of borrowed manners and performed virtues, she can't see him as other than a character in a story. "No," she says when pressed to confess her love for him. "I only wished that the man I shall marry may look, and talk, and act, just like him" (43).

This dependence on fiction and other literature will of course be familiar to readers of sentimental fiction itself. Transferred to the stage, such self-reflexivity has the potential to turn delirious and hallucinatory. There is no ground in *The Contrast* that is not a literary or theatrical landscape, no terra firma. Characters confront a seemingly endless array of simulacra — embodied literary styles, rehearsed sentiment, hypocrisy, and even (when Dimple confesses he's only playing the Chesterfieldian to provoke Maria to leave him) hypocritical performances of hypocrisy. The characters' — and our own — vertigo grows acute as more and more utterances spring from sources beyond the self. Nothing makes sense, or even reaches the senses, without reference to something else.

Tyler's easy satirical targets — one person evaluating fashions by French standards, another referring vistas and manners to English precedent — are only the most overt symptoms of a persistent discomfort with unmediated, primary experience. Charlotte Manly, Henry's sister and another object of Dimple's promiscuous affections, is herself an obedient reader — the "grave *Spectator*" ratifies her instincts in social intercourse — yet the wit with which she makes such secondhand pronouncements her own can't wholly tamp down her underlying anxiety. It breaks through at the least expected moment, when she must name the unique qualities of someone she knows intimately. "I feel the rage of simile upon me," she says while describing her brother. "I can't talk to you in any other way." But when she falters in her comparisons, the deliberate emptiness of all Tyler's figures is suddenly (and perhaps, in a radical staging, shockingly) apparent: "it is like — it is like — Oh! . . . you have deranged all my ideas," she complains to a friend who had asked for "particular" description (19). She resembles an actor forgetting her lines, or more provocatively, a writer suffering a block. The scene is a fleeting instance of Tyler confessing to the insecurities plaguing his characters and thereby making us insecure, too.

For all the sharpness with which Tyler caricatures his rogues, flirts, and gossips, his more subversive achievement is to render ambiguous the characters expected to correct them. Manly of course seems transparent, and the plot positions him to step away from distorting literature into real life. (Literally so: he is hiding in Charlotte's library when he overhears Dimple's true intentions and emerges to stop him.) Yet he, along with the "natural" Jonathan, proves just as receptive to influence and just as helpless without the support of chosen codes, languages, and frames of reference. It can't be accidental that two scenes after Charlotte suffers the "rage of simile," Jonathan refers everything he sees in the John Street Theatre to something outside its doors: "just like meeting-house gallery . . . just like father's corn-cribs . . . like so many mad cats . . . just like our Peleg threshing wheat . . . just like the nation" (34). Wielding the tools of analogy, he writes his way out of confusion (and, in his last simile, toward the most broadly reassuring context). The seemingly unpretentious and patriotic Manly is no more able to take landscapes, conditions, or even himself as they are. He compares America to ancient Greece before foreign corruption; proudly displays a sword "presented me by that brave Gallic hero, the Marquis de Lafayette"; and (as Jeffrey H. Richards notes) borrows from the British writer Edward Wortley Montagu for his own attack on "luxury." As Richards puts it, "Manly is American by residence, his regimental coat, and his love for his country — and not much more."[24]

The coat itself communicates ambiguous meanings. As Manly dresses for the theater in one scene, he refuses to exchange his drab uniform for something smarter, thereby unwittingly acknowledging how he, no less than his fashionable sister, depends upon appearance to express social value. He also declares, "I have humbly imitated our illustrious WASHINGTON," a strange boast from one celebrated for his self-sufficiency (21). Even his authenticity turns out to be secondhand, an irony Charlotte seems to catch when she pointedly calls him "a player run mad, with your head filled with old scraps of tragedy" (22). With his every self-contradictory utterance and act, Manly's presence blurs. Charlotte may deem him "solid" (19), but he proves to be just as notional, just as much a creation of other people's imaginations, as those around him.

Such slipperiness should give pause to those spectators eager to cast Manly as Tyler's spokesman. The playwright, who is listed on the title page of the 1790 first edition only as "A Citizen of the United States," seems to embody the unaffected and nationalistic aspirations of his hero. In fact, Tyler mirrors only Manly's inconsistency. He is most compelling when he is the least sententious, securing our interest when he retracts the points he makes so passionately. In his prologue, he attacks "imitative sense" just before the curtain rises on an evening of mimesis. He also praises "native themes" against "Europe" but in the play that follows is candid about his sources (7). Manly may exalt the "laudable partiality" of "ignorant, untravelled men" and of those who, given the chance to see foreign "exhibitions," stay away (45). But Tyler welcomes into his play numerous continental predecessors, drawing particular attention to his most obvious source when Jonathan attends "The School for Scandalization" (35). (Kenneth Silverman, in *A Cultural History of the American Revolution*, lists other possible links to Wycherley, Farquhar, Hugh Kelly, and Isaac Bickerstaffe.)[25] The contradiction is far from fatal. We can enjoy, rather than turn tactfully away from, the interplay between supposedly opposed national literatures. This calculated act of self-subversion — "a piece which we may fairly call our own," as the prologue calls it, turns out to belong to everyone else — brings rewards greater than originality: Tyler escapes stultifying ideas of aesthetic nationalism and the equally rigid morality that often accompanies them. As Gordon S. Wood notes in *The Radicalism of the American Revolution*, cosmopolitanism is hardly a betrayal of the new nation's declaration of independence. "The American Revolution may have divided the British empire," he writes, citing Benjamin Rush, "but it 'made no breach in the republic of letters.' "[26]

In Tyler's case, the transatlantic dialogue is subtler than we may initially suspect. While the links to Sheridan (in character types, situations, and verbal rhythm) are obvious, more important are the less remarked differences. The older writer models a worldly, flexible understanding of the same principles promoted by the younger writer's more doctrinaire characters. To Sheridan, the values of sincerity, charity, and repentance are at once noble and vulnerable — vulnerable to distortion by the moralist most insistent upon their nobility. Unlike their American cousins, Sheridan's objects of reform — Charles Surface and Snake — refuse to be exemplary and instead direct attention to the more complicated facts of lives spent below the comforts of patriotic rhetoric. Snake can't afford to be good all the time, and all Charles will say "as to reforming" is "I'll make no promises. . . . I intend to set about it."[27] If Tyler's own spectators recall this pragmatism as *The Contrast* glides to its affirmative conclusion (and it's tempting to think that in a New York where *The School for Scandal* was a fixture of the repertoire, many did), they will approach it critically, delaying their assent to Tyler's uplifting platitudes until they have considered his and his play's broad cultural context. Some may still embrace Tyler as a corrective to continental relativism; others may weigh both sides dispassionately or allow the seemingly opposed philosophies to temper one another; and still others may emerge distressed at the spectacle of still fragile American principles challenged by both the borderless theater culture and the texts themselves. Even if they don't, *The Contrast* still asks much of us. A play in which all the characters, even the most ingenuous, are constantly fashioning selves, and in which the playwright himself openly thinks his way toward a comfortable writerly identity, requires audiences to think for themselves as well. Such candor on the page and stage denies early American spectators the passivity and anonymity that their inherited theater tradition led them to expect—Tyler's most shocking achievement.

The attempt to identify, much less to legislate, a dominant style—national or aesthetic—in the fledgling American theater seems especially futile when one turns to William Dunlap. In the 1790s and early 1800s, he was the nation's main conduit for contemporary French and German dramas, adapting their conventions to American sensibilities in more than twenty-five translations. His versions of Kotzebue created and then regularly fed the appetite for sentimental comedies about a reliably moral middle class. Schiller's emergence from Sturm und Drang, Iffland's domestic tearjerkers, and Zschokke's "grand dramatic romances" (as he calls them) also found an American idiom in Dunlap's versions of *Don Carlos, The Good Neighbor,* and *Abellino, the Great Bandit.* His concurrent enthusiasm for the writers on Paris's Boulevard du Crime stimulated demand for a theater that relieves still other forms of psychological distress. When, in 1803, he presented his adaptation of Caigniez's *Judgment of Solomon* (retitled *The Voice of Nature* for marketing to American believers in innate virtue), he introduced continental melodrama to the United States— arguably his most influential act if not his most important play—and in his later versions of Pixérécourt (*The Wife of Two Husbands*) and Goubaux and Ducange (*Thirty Years; or, The Gambler's Fate*), he codified character types, narrative patterns, and a moral orientation from which few later American playwrights would dare deviate. Finally, he also succumbed to the widespread eighteenth-century infatuation with the Gothic, adapting Ann Radcliffe's novel *Romance of the Forest* as *Fontainville Abbey* (1795), and, in a further blurring of stylistic loyalties, improving George Coleman's *Blue Beard* by adding original songs—a lighthearted touch that, remarkably, makes even more unnerving the atmosphere of sexual menace.

As Dunlap took up residence in all these forms and spoke in the voices of their most accomplished practitioners, he was both everywhere and nowhere to be seen in the American theater. Refusing to ally himself exclusively with a single genre, he instead mimicked all the passing fascinations in the culture at large. Such chameleon-like responsiveness is to be expected from a successful translator and adaptor. Yet it also determined his ambitions as a playwright. His twenty-eight original plays, taken together, attest to an omnivorous but dispersed imagination, a fluid temperament that grows claustrophobic upon assuming an "identity," an experimentalist whose interest in a particular form fades the moment he masters it. Dunlap's first produced play, *The Father of an Only Child* (1789), is a comedy written from within the cult of sensibility. (Its original title was *The Father; or, American Shandyism.*) Later works include a lurid, sexually frank tragedy, a gothic drama, a satirical musical, and an opera. At its most disarming, Dunlap's variousness is evident within a single play. After the moralizing of *The Father,* an actress delivers an epilogue attacking didactic drama: "Does any author . . . think stale morality can help him write?"[28] The same reversal occurs in the epilogue (Dunlap's original contribution) to *The Voice of Nature.* In one of the most unsettling passages in early American drama, Dunlap's lead actress renounces the character she has just finished playing: My "female heart . . . revolts whene'er I read the part," she says. "I am a mother — can I represent one who could steal the mother's best content? . . . O, no! — I cannot feel a part like this! . . . Yet I'll do my best, / To represent a being — *I detest.*"[29]

Dunlap's most enduring play envisions the broad implications of his self-arguing, even self-escaping nature. Here, the playwright's capacity for double-ness (and for negotiating among seemingly incompatible influences) is especially well suited to his subject. *André* tells the familiar story of Benedict Arnold's British handler, arrested on leaving West Point disguised as a peasant and executed on General George Washington's orders. In a series of scenes alternating between Major John André's cell and the encampment where his defenders plead for his life, Dunlap takes a critical look at the ideals elevated in earlier Revolutionary War dramas. The need for moderation in the face of political chaos; honor as both personal prize and civic obligation; the many synonyms of a mythic quality — fortitude — passed down through generations of soldiers; the utility of reason and the consolations of duty: most characters in American drama before Dunlap either wholly upheld or wholly flouted these qualities. Rarely did they confess ambivalence or conduct themselves in unclassifiable ways. Never did they openly doubt the value of "noble" attributes without also forsaking our sympathy. Without himself doubting their value, Dunlap does acknowledge how difficult they are to maintain. *André*

depicts the often clumsy effort to be honorable — and temperate and coura-
geous — and shows that, even to the character who succeeds, moral clarity
remains elusive. "His tide of passion," says Washington of "the virtuous man,"
is "struggling still with Reason's / Fair and favorable gale" (76). Struggling
still. Dunlap refreshes a classical idea of valor by naming the price his characters pay to embody it.

Such a milieu requires Dunlap to judge his characters stringently. No one in
André wins approval for merely observing a code of conduct. Instead, while
spectacular acts of espionage and war remain in the background (nothing is
heard from or seen of Benedict Arnold himself), the protagonists engage in
continuous self-monitoring and self-testing, sharpening their already acute
awareness of how far instinct can lead them from exemplary behavior. As if in
sympathy with his characters' analytic habit, Dunlap constructs his play di-
alectically, only to show the impossibility of choosing sides in any debate over
changeable thought and feeling. (The simultaneous embrace and subversion of
polarities reminds us that Dunlap was inspired to become a playwright after
seeing *The Contrast*.)[30] He asks spectators to subscribe to competing interpretations of every principle, character, and action. At the most fundamental
level, as Richards and other critics have noted, the "villain," André, is heroic,
or at least sympathetic, without diminishing his villainy. The "heroes" —
Washington especially — are cold-hearted, without diminishing their heroism.[31] Yet no sooner does the general's stoicism coalesce than it dissolves into
sentiment, weakening with it our ability to anchor this or any stage figure to
coherent identity.

Other attributes are just as fluid. Honor is an internal, private matter to one
man; to another equally persuasive character, it is a distant ideal that one
approaches as a "votary" (95). Excessive attention to appearances is shallow
in one soldier's estimation, yet to another it is the only guarantee of dignity.
(André is exercised over the manner of his execution more than by the questions of fairness it raises.) Even Dunlap's setting combines seemingly irreconcilable meanings. The war zone is first presented as a scene of unrestrained,
shapeless malevolence, wearying in its monotony. Later it offers a model of
restraint and prudence. "By the laws of war we will abide," says Washington,
optimistically believing that aggression can be orderly (86).

The quality his characters take for granted — duty — attracts Dunlap's liveliest scrutiny. To audiences schooled in the history from which Dunlap draws
his plot, *André* seems only to demonstrate the superior claim that one's country, and the idea of nation to which one's country aspires, has on one's duty — a
claim that transcends any obligation incurred from friendship, family, or other
merely personal loyalties. The least equivocal spokesman for this position, the

officer M'Donald, reins in the individualism that many other characters believe they are fighting a revolution to defend. "How self intrudes, delusive, on man's thoughts," he says to one Captain Bland (94). Yet Dunlap is careful not to let such rhetoric sound decisive. Bland delivers his own equally forceful argument on behalf of experience resistant to the simplifications of patriotism, justifying his loyalty to André by citing a principle no less potent in eighteenth-century America: gratitude. Dunlap tracks its shifting value. To M'Donald, gratitude may be behind "that selfish rule of action . . . misleading reason," but to Bland, it is "that first, that best of virtues, — / Without the which man sinks beneath the brute" (94).

The seesawing doesn't stop here. Duty to oneself makes its own demands, as does, more particularly, duty to one's chosen ideal of conduct. In a notorious bit of stage business, Bland throws his cockade at the feet of Washington, an act by which the young soldier pledges allegiance to personal rather than national principles. Yet Dunlap is ambivalent about such theatricality: after the cockade scene caused an unwelcome stir at the play's first performance, Dunlap added lines later in the play that restore reason to its place above passion. In deploying speech against gesture, Dunlap underscores another tension that prevents any single moment of performance or aspect of narrative from seeming central. Running alongside the characters' arguments is Dunlap's implicit, self-directed argument about his own practices. (It occasionally becomes explicit: "The Author has added the following lines," Dunlap writes in his preface, "which the reader is requested to insert, page 55, between the 5th and 15th lines instead of the lines he will find there, which were printed before the piece was represented" [65].) How effective are his words on this or any stage, he seems to ask, when image and action reach audiences more directly? Dunlap's self-interrogatory stance, as we'll see, will be mimicked by the many later writers who also let theatrical gestures backfire and verbal surfaces rupture. In 1798, these measures may have been especially necessary, as American drama attempts to emerge from inherited tradition and as this prolific playwright-translator himself begins to distinguish between his own and other writers' voices.

Within *André,* the scrutiny of a speaker's efficacy is unrelenting. The very showiness and frequency with which his characters declare their valor suggest that Dunlap mistrusts mere duty toward duty. Oratory is both exalted and mocked every time characters deliver stirring speeches on patriotic subjects only to cede the floor to others no less passionate (but far more economical) in their understanding of rhetoric's limits. "Be less profuse of words," says Washington to a digressive Bland (84). Bland himself lashes out, elsewhere, at another speaker: "Curst be thy sophisms!" (94) Soon all language seems able to express only its insufficiency. "Vain is my entreaty," says one of André's defenders, "All unmov'd / [Washington] hears my words" (96). Writing to his wife from prison, André himself laughs at how weak his own "blotted paper" must seem alongside the gestures of a "gallant Knight . . . / Of Coeur de Lion's day" (97).

If one sees Dunlap admitting the weakness of his own blotted paper in these scenes, one can't help imagining that he also doubts the expressiveness of other engines of narrative. Gestural speech, visual rhetoric, and ordinary "action" in *André* do not coalesce any more easily, nor carry meanings any more stable or legible, than the words accompanying them. This recognition of theater's limited ability to make things happen — and as they happen, to conform to established codes of meaning — results in the play's understated *coup de théâtre*: Washington crying on the eve of André's execution. The famous scene is unsettling only partly because the admirer of Cato suddenly seems more sentimental than stoic.[32] Dunlap had already upset his audience's assumptions a scene earlier when Bland is caught blushing — another index of feminine sentimentality — while at the same moment his mother declares that she will cry no more. "War hath made men rocks," she explains (101). When no less a man than Washington proves her wrong, he suggests that the war he now fights is internal, fated to an inconclusive outcome. It's this private struggle to assert ideological clarity in the face of experience, more than the tears that relieve its tension, that Dunlap asks us to study most closely. As Washington simultaneously allows and reins in his emotion, the many variations on ambivalence that Dunlap has worked throughout *André* gather into one faltering speech. "My heart is torn in twain," Washington confesses. He then exacerbates the play's turbulence by voicing uncertainty about the purpose of uncertainty. "Why, why, my country, did I hesitate?" (103–4). (Another character, in an unrelated context, utters a phrase that, in its juxtaposed opposites, captures concisely the era's temperament. "Uncertainty — man's bane and solace!" [101].)

The play eventually emerges from this pause — André is executed, as we knew he would be all along — but that ending is anticlimactic in more than just a narrative sense. A profound cultural change was taking place when it seemed that nothing was happening dramatically. Washington's embarrassed paralysis enables Dunlap to restore the human being to the offices he occupies: the military one Washington holds in the play and the political one he held until a year before the play's premiere.[33] But even more important, Dunlap restores humanity to himself. Washington's "hesitating" stands for Dunlap's own. Yet what the general treats as an agonizing state is to the playwright the site of exquisite arousal and intense sensation. We can, if we choose, hear in *André*'s every ideological debate the playwright hovering over choices he himself must make—between two alluring routes at a fork in his plot (say), or between competing but mutually exclusive motives for a character's behavior, or among equally effective speakers with which to begin a scene's dialogue. For Dunlap, such indecision is not a mere phase to push through, nor does one rejoice when it passes. (In 1803, Dunlap rewrote *André* as *The Glory of Columbia: Her Yeomanry!*—a change that was not, incidentally, for the better.) Instead, like an actor who resists the security of rehearsed sentiment the better to respond to a performance's present-tense signals, Dunlap strives to stay just on the verge of expression, able to say more by knowing less. The prolific playwright writes a pause into the opening of American theater history—a carefully shaped nonstart that, vibrating with more life than our theater's accredited beginnings, persuades fellow and future artists to resist the narrowing effects of any style, doctrine, dramaturgy, or still young tradition of resistance. If readers of *The American Play* delay their own emergence from this pause, they themselves can resist the narratives every theater historian forces upon imaginations indifferent to precedent or legacy.

Envisioning the Nineteenth Century

There is a property in the horizon which no man has but he whose eye can integrate all the parts.

— *Ralph Waldo Emerson, "Nature"*

My art is about just paying attention — about the extremely dangerous possibility that you *might be art.*

— *Robert Rauschenberg, in* Rauschenberg: An Interview, *by Barbara Rose*

Among eyewitnesses to nineteenth-century American theater, Henry James has few rivals in appreciating the stage's visual pleasures. The first volume of his autobiography, *A Small Boy and Others* (1913), is in fact a chronicle of theatergoing in the 1850s, less valuable for its descriptions of plots and interpretations (of these there are few) than for its record of this particular spectator's consciousness as he anticipates, admires, and memorializes a series of pictures animated by time. James's implicit conviction that theater is a visual art before it is a literary or even a performing art grows more persuasive as he betrays how completely he remains under the spell of images a less enthralled spectator would have soon forgotten or ignored in the first place. Even as he is watching a play, it seems, its narrative breaks apart for him, leaving a residue of a few compelling sequences — often silent, in memory if not in fact, and marginal to the action — saved from oblivion by their clarity and kinetic force. James remembers whole plays only by an actor's sudden rush up a mountainside, for instance, or the pace at which the light darkens, or the patterns made by the lengthening shadows. The most striking pictures allow a long look at a performer's face and body. James studies the angles formed by a hero's arms and legs when he falls dead, more expressive of loss than any valedictory speech. In other passages, he strings together adjectives both to rekindle and to control his passion for what he remembers. As Leon Edel notes, James is a connoisseur of actors' surfaces. Sixty years on, the novelist still treasures a Hermia for her "short salmon-coloured peplum over a white petticoat," a Walter Scott huntress for her kilt and velvet leggings, one actress's "broad brown face" framed in "tight black curls" and another's crowned in a gold tiara trailing a gold scarf, someone's "pendulous cheek," someone else's "protuberance of bosom."[1]

Elsewhere in *A Small Boy,* James defines the particular kind of attention this theater cultivates as a combination of "fascination" and "fear" (47). Such ambivalence seems no less inevitable before these performers, not only because the James viewing them is a sexually unorganized eleven-year-old. How should anyone respond to a figure neither wholly real nor wholly fictional, at once inviting and prohibiting intimacy, his or her flesh-and-blood presence bound by imaginary circumstances? The procedures of fantasy preoccupy James throughout *A Small Boy,* helping him to understand why his era's theater takes flight even when its jury-rigged plots and prosy dialogue should, by rights, keep it grounded. The spectator's role in that success, James shows, begins long before the performance does, as the force of his expectation generates images vivid enough to compete with those in the theater. He remembers conjuring whole performances as he stands transfixed before theater posters and, after taking his seat in an auditorium, treating the lowered stage curtain as a screen inviting him to project still more scenes from an ideal theater, as well as other images from memory, dreams, and barely acknowledged longings. By delaying the start of the production, this pleasurable "torment of the curtain" (61) ensures that when the stage is finally revealed, it is seductive less because of any particular sight than because the eye, frustrated for so long, can at last give itself up to someone else's reverie.

Yet James obeys a rigorous idea of fantasy, and it has important implications for an understanding of the visual appeals made by the era's theater. As James describes them, the theater's gaslit dioramas are not alternatives to or renunciations of reality. Rather, they reveal to him reality's psychological nodal points, the dreads and desires that one might not notice away from the theater, in the blur of everyday preoccupations. They permit him to experience life from both the inside and the outside — feeling, by means of identification, with greater intensity and precision than anywhere else, but also removing himself to a distance from which, unseen himself, he can see freely, identifying the causes and consequences of his emotions. Fantasy, in other words, is the arena in which James learns the skills of analysis. Even when his memoir takes him away from the playhouse, James reveals how much his sensibility has been formed by the theater. On the avenues and in drawing rooms, he pulls back to frame their inhabitants, turning everyday life into a succession of scenes before which he reads the code of glances and movements that often contradict what is said.

Such free play over the surface of experience enlarges his understanding of its depths. James recalls accompanying his family one night, "quite as if going to the theatre," to a gallery exhibiting *Washington Crossing the Delaware*, Leutze's monumental canvas as yet undiminished by familiarity. Gaslight illuminated the painting, he writes, "but Mr. Leutze's drama left behind any paler proscenium" (152) — its life-size scale, almost palpable wintry weather, and most of all, the protagonists' attitude of visionary self-confidence affecting James more deeply than could any ordinary, nontheatricalized exhibition of the painting. By the force of its presentation, a well-known episode from history reentered his life as urgent, still unfolding fact, demanding a more self-aware kind of engagement than he once brought to the legend it cites.

Shortly after this experience, James began writing plays. If he hadn't already intuited the value of theatrical pictorialism, the happy accident of his materials would have shown the way. He used a brand of paper that came folded in four pages, three of which were ruled. On these he wrote dialogue, reserving every fourth, blank sheet of the quarto for an illustration of the scene. From the very start, playwriting was inseparable from drawing. Only by experimenting with the placement of actors could he release the full implications of their conduct. One imagines James controlling psychological tension with the height and width of his stage, and centering attention on the essential narrative transaction by fixing the location of the vanishing point. "I panted toward the canvas on which I should fling my figures," he writes in *A Small Boy*, "which it took me longer to fill than it had taken me to write what went with it, but which . . . must have helped me to believe in the validity of my subject" (148–49).

"The validity of my subject." James's concern for the truth, or at least the credibility, of what he writes hints at the reasons — deeper than mere pleasure-seeking — for his interest in theatrical spectatorship. Is seeing believing? It seems to be, but in the theater itself James experiences a more complicated form of belief. It should come as no surprise that the author of *The Golden Bowl* is attentive to the cracks in stage illusion. In one production, James spots "the leg of a trouser and a big male foot" belonging to the performer playing the heroine (63). A wooden board creaks when Eliza steps on an ice floe in *Uncle Tom's Cabin.* Later in the same production, Little Eva emerges still dry and ironed after falling into the Mississippi River. In these and other sightings, theatrical illusion survives the betrayal. The flaws prompt James to check the seams of his engagement with the stage and to find them secure: he realizes that, in fact, his capacity for emotional and mental involvement depends neither on the scene's perfection nor its credibility. Far from feeling superior when the boards creak, James refuses to be disillusioned, thus learning, perhaps for the first time, how great is his need for faith.

That need — not for excitement, sensory or sensual — is what this era's theater of images tries to satisfy. Before long, this war between faith and doubt has become a spectacle in itself, fascinating James (he admits) more than the one onstage. He goes to the theater to await the moment when his resistance to a fiction breaks down, the moment he shifts from skepticism to belief or, more often, learns to be skeptical and trusting at the same time, a feat in which his cultural sophistication plays no part. "We had all intellectually condescended," he concludes after a theater outing with some friends, "and . . . we had yet had the thrill of an aesthetic adventure . . . this was a brave beginning for a consciousness that was to be nothing if not mixed" (95).

Any study of mid-nineteenth-century American theater must come to terms with this "mixed consciousness" — the experience of being both inside and outside the performance, and the process by which a spectator's surrender to visual pleasure, a surrender that typically involves self-forgetting, results in self-recognition of the kind James describes. (This is a version of what Whitman calls being "both in and out of the game, and watching and wondering at it.")[2] Such an experience enlarges one's sense of the purpose of theatrical seeing. Instead of being passive and anonymous, spectatorship in the nineteenth century is often a form of intervention, as audiences are invited to become witnesses, analysts, historians, and even reformers, able by the care with which they observe a production to practice the skills of self-scrutiny and social diagnosis necessary outside the theater as well. Yet this kind of looking isn't clinical: it also depends on the enchantment James longs for, if the scrutiny and diagnosis are to maintain their urgency. William Wells Brown speaks for many of his peers when he precedes his autobiographical 1858 abolitionist play, *The Escape,* with an epigraph from the closet scene in *Hamlet*: "Look here upon this picture, and on this," says Hamlet to his mother.[3] Brown omits but hopes we'll supply lines later in the speech that specify the responsibility of such vision. Hamlet chastises Gertrude for having "eyes without feeling, feeling without sight" (3.4.78), a divorce that Brown, too, resists as he leads his own audience from vision to empathy — sense to sensibility — and from sensibility to action.

Any theater culture in which the first theater historian and professional playwright is also its first art historian — William Dunlap, an active if undistinguished painter as well — is perhaps fated to care about how seeing affects thinking and feeling, and to take a lexicographic interest in the languages of gesture, posture, and facial expression. A pair of Dunlap's paintings on theatrical themes confirms the point. In one, depicting a performance of *The School for Scandal* at the moment when Lady Teazle is discovered hiding behind a screen in Joseph Surface's rooms, a set of pillars frames the alcove containing the eavesdropper, turning it into a stage within a stage, to which the other actors point with an astonishment mirroring that of their own spectators — a diagram making us conscious, if we weren't already, of our own presence before Dunlap's painting. Those who remember Sheridan's play might reasonably conclude that Dunlap is asking for *theater* spectators to adopt these characters' motives as well: to see their way to truth and, by such seeing, to force long-overdue change.

Even more suggestive, if no more formally accomplished, is Dunlap's *The Artist Showing a Picture from* Hamlet *to His Parents* (1788). Here, Dunlap depicts himself leaning against a canvas almost as tall as he is while his father directs Mrs. Dunlap's attention to the murky characters from the play's first act. In the painting-within-the-painting, two faceless figures are standing under moonlight on the Elsinore ramparts. The "real" Dunlap's own scene is theatrical — his spectator-mother is seated before his canvas-stage — and by reducing Shakespeare's action to an image he seems to ready us, as well, for the kind of seeing appropriate to the coming American theater. The scene from *Hamlet* is itself about seeing, its perils and responsibilities embodied as "the Watch." After Horatio has warned Hamlet that looking at the Ghost will "deprive your sovereignty of reason /And draw you into madness" (1.4.73–74), Hamlet insists on seeing for himself, hoping, rather, to bolster his reason. For him, as for Dunlap's ideal theater spectator, vision is both a seizing and a sacrificing of control, a form of inquiry with otherwise unavailable knowledge, even self-knowledge, the reward for its risks.

Dunlap pursued his interest in the link between vision and reason when he began adapting French and German melodramas in the 1790s and early 1800s, in particular the work of Pixérécourt, inventor of the genre. When

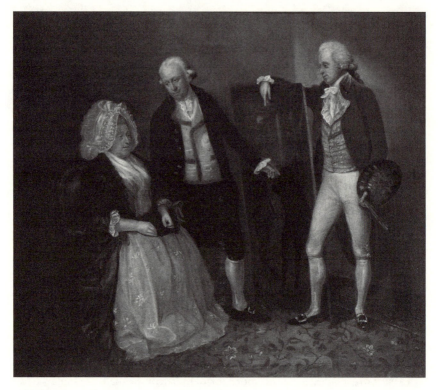

Figure 1: William Dunlap, *The Artist Showing a Picture from* Hamlet *to His Parents* (also known as *The Dunlap Family*), (1788). Collection of the New-York Historical Society.

Pixérécourt claimed that he wrote for the illiterate, he established the precedent for American artists' own efforts to enlist visual theater in the cause of populism.[4] The links in France between the audience sought for melodrama and the populace committed to revolution have been extensively chronicled by Peter Brooks, among others.[5] The relation was just as firm and perhaps more intuitive in the new American nation, as it met the obligation to free all civic ideals — justice, faith, virtue — from the dogma, tradition, and in many cases the very language of the Old World. In a theater unmarked by the borders maintained by language, where the intricacies of argument and nuances of psychology, such as they are, are telegraphed openly and thus rendered legible to all, spectators enjoy both access and autonomy, spared not only the humbling sense of their dependence on characters telling them what to think but also untroubled by the worry that someone sitting nearby can better understand what is onstage. Indeed, American melodrama at its height grants as much power to the spectator as to the artist, encouraging us to recognize the full generative potential of our sight. At the most basic level, one need only consider the melodramatic actor's vast repertoire of gestures of indication — "it often seems," writes Michael Booth, "as if [a] speaker cannot refer to another person on the stage without pointing at him"[6] — to discover a theater that enlists us as collaborators in the action. The pointing actor suggests that only when we consent to look upon a scene does it come to life.

Dramatists and the theorists who shadow them have of course been trying to fix the proper relation between theater and painting ever since Diderot called for "an arrangement of characters onstage so natural and true that if it were faithfully rendered by a painter it would please on canvas."[7] As Michael Fried reminds us, Diderot evaluated productions of well-known plays by sitting at the back of the theater and covering his ears.[8] The distance enabled him to see the scene whole, its proscenium frame as essential to its effect as anything depicted, while the silence exposed weaknesses in stage composition and imprecision in actors' gestures. In his preference for painterly tableaux over *coups de théâtre* (and for introspective rather than presentational performance), Diderot implied that vision should be as controlled as the action onstage. The most responsible audience members learn to think of seeing as itself a form of disciplined performing rather than merely a surrender to curiosity and fantasy. One looks with the same logic that informs the work of the rational theater artist.

Early American theater, insofar as it fosters the same ideal of careful attention, offers the same rewards. The theater's visual priorities (and the culture's awareness of its own theatricality) promise legibility and regularity against the sprawling experience, volatile feeling, and uncertain thought outside the theater. Once-submerged emotions surface in the body of an actor as reproducible emblems. Individual behavior and collective history obey simple patterns. Both emblem and pattern seem unassailable because empirically verified.

Such a promise unifies in a single grand design many otherwise unrelated aspects of American civic and cultural life. The theater's pictorialism can be seen, in this view, as the inevitable extension of the visual emphases of the developing nation — an application, in a controlled milieu monitored by artist and audience, of procedures already instrumental in forging and securing the social contract. As Garry Wills shows in *Inventing America,* Thomas Jefferson reknit a nation divided against itself in part by promoting Francis Hutcheson's belief that citizens maintain their capacity for benevolence — the crucial quality ensuring social interdependence — only by regularly seeing and imitating acts of benevolence performed by others. (Wills calls this the "spectacle of American virtue.")[9] Also in eighteenth-century America, the oratorical revolution, so influential upon the lyrical ambitions and acting styles of nineteenth-

century theater, begins, tellingly, with the lesson that "the eye is the best avenue to the heart," as Lord Kames put it in 1762, and that persuasive speakers
"transform us . . . into spectators" of what they describe, thus offering the
illusion that we can enter and even participate in such a verbal world, sharing
responsibility for its well-being.[10] Jay Fliegelman, who in citing Kames restores him to his proper place in American visual culture, sees the same conviction dictating Jefferson's writing of the Declaration of Independence. In a now
well-known piece of detective work, he points to Jefferson's markings on a
personal copy — slashes between words that denote pauses — as evidence not
only of the Declaration's relevance to oral culture but also of oral culture's link
to visual art. The slashes serve as frames around words and phrases, he suggests, helping listeners see the significance of what they hear.

The private emotions behind these public ideas are no less dependent on
scrutiny for their authority. Readers of early American fiction, of course, expect vision to crack codes of sensibility, as characters study the surfaces that
confirm or correct their inferences about one another's virtue, even as they
remember that appearances can be deceiving. The eye's testimony is even more
conclusive in the theater. It is indicative of the close kinship between social and
artistic display that popular acting manuals of the early nineteenth century
read like etiquette manuals, offering strict guidelines for reducing such emotions as dread, joy, and even anger to pleasing arrangements of limbs and
facial muscles.[11] When passion can be thus scripted, it can be read, monitored
by its victims and viewers alike. Later in the century, such systematic display
would be no less essential in conferring heroic status on bodies that, offstage,
are merely human, thereby turning individuals into icons. The virtuoso of this
technique, Edwin Forrest, began rehearsals of his vehicles only after designing
and mastering a series of poses appropriate to each important point in the
action. (His biographer describes him as favoring roles that allow him to
showcase his impressive calves and biceps.) Such an antipsychological approach to acting — the external prized over the internal — enables the performer to simultaneously abstract and particularize his role. A character's
personal history of heroism — or grief, or defiance — enlarges to become the
era's own, even as (say) American triumphalism or self-sacrifice shrinks to fit
the physical contours of a single citizen. We identify the general political
principle contained within the gesture — each pose seems to put forward a
moral or ethical attitude and is held long enough for spectators to consider all
its applications — but perhaps more important, we also see what such a stance,
literal and figurative, costs its passionate exemplars.[12]

The most elaborate expression of this practice — and the element of style by
which nineteenth-century theater is most recognized and often parodied — is

the tableau. A violation of many principles that distinguish theater from the other arts, the tableau resists time, reduces actors to objects, and banishes language and narrative in favor of compositions that give voice to silence and release the energy of stillness. Tableaux provide visual codas to the ends of scenes, as actors arrange themselves in ways that indicate their individual importance to the narrative (and to one another) and direct attention to the decisive events in their shared history. A representative example: the first act of *The Poor of New York* (1857) ends with a triangular tableau introducing the themes of gullibility, self-interest, and depravity that the playwright, Dion Boucicault, will develop over the next four acts. The triangle's base is formed by the prostrate body of a wealthy sea captain, killed by a stroke upon learning he has deposited his fortune in a failing bank. His face, with eyes bulging and mouth agape, is frozen into a mask of horror. Above him on one side looms Bloodgood, the unscrupulous bank manager, his own body arranged in what Boucicault describes only as "an attitude of cunning."[13] The egotism in his pose, however, is visually, if not verbally, countered by the remaining element of the tableau. A low-level bank clerk, Badger, completes the triangle by folding in on himself and turning away from the others, clutching the captain's deposit receipt to his chest. We first learn of Badger's own capacity for cunning — he will later blackmail Bloodgood — as we explicate his pose.

The almost classical tautness of such a composition is as significant and as eloquent as its individual elements. Although the nineteenth-century repertory is full of tableaux consisting only of a villain exulting over a victim or of lovers collapsing into one another's arms, the most satisfying involve more figures arranged in more intricate relationship to one another, inviting the same kind of close readings we do on texts. One actor's concave pose of cowardice rhymes with another's convex pose of pride. A third, frozen in an attitude of longing, begins a visual dialogue completed by a fourth actor turning away. These visual poetics control even subtler forms of expression. The articulation of the hands (signifying warning, benediction, or gratitude, for instance) or an actor's place in the hierarchy of the tableau are all codified to stimulate the viewers' desire to seek out meaning. What Roland Barthes says about photography's invitation to "pensiveness" applies even more directly to theatrical tableaux. To Barthes, the photograph is an antidote to the hectic procession of images at the cinema, where (he complains) he has no time to "add" his own thought to the images on screen. "Constrained to a continuous voracity," he writes, he cannot pause over an image, much less "shut his eyes." Before he opens them, the image he ponders will have been replaced by others he will never see.[14]

Few elements of a theatrical tableau do as much service as the actor's own eyes. Like his or her limbs, eyes bind together areas of the stage by the force with which a character looks in a particular direction, captures someone's attention, or responds to the attentions of others. Cueing our own looking, these characters ensure that we acknowledge the parts of a tableau in a sequence and rhythm that support its didactic purposes: our attention contracts or dilates to fit the arena marked out by the tableau. We move purposefully through a composition or worry a single element according to the style of looking set by the frozen characters themselves.

A scene from a famous production of *Uncle Tom's Cabin* — a play that is an archive of memorable tableaux — underscores the importance of the eyes in even the grandest stage composition. As Little Eva lies dying at the end of act 3, she is surrounded by her guardian, St. Clare, who kneels by her side; Ophelia and Marie, who stand above him, one draped in lace, the other holding a Bible; and, at the foot of the white-shrouded daybed, Uncle Tom. In any production of *Uncle Tom's Cabin,* this arrangement would itself serve as an appropriate tableau, but in a turn-of-the-century staging by William Brady, it is enclosed in a much larger tableau consisting of more than fifty supernumeraries: the slaves on St. Clare's plantation. They kneel around Eva's bed, spreading in concentric circles out to the perimeter of the room and beyond; a dozen more performers look in from outside the windows and French doors lining the upstage wall. Like so many arrows, all eyes direct us to the dying girl engulfed by this spectacle of spectatorship.

Yet if Brady doubted we'd know what's most important in this scene, his concern has unintended consequences. The onlookers' presence expands the meaning of the scene, shifting the emphasis from Eva's plight to its effect on her survivors. What on the page suggests a tableau of Eva's saintliness becomes in performance a tableau of her witnesses' awe, and of the confusion and reorientation that follow when awe recedes. The staging, moreover, clarifies racial meanings left unspoken or, at least, unstressed in the scene's text. The stark contrast between the white center of Brady's tableau — Eva's marble pallor, her cotton gown and bedclothes — and the black frame of observers restores a proper proportion between Eva's domestic scene and the larger surrounding society. It returns her to a world from which her otherworldly goodness and visionary spirituality seem, on the page, to exempt her.

It is through this kind of crack in an otherwise formulaic dramatic structure that the typical nineteenth-century play touches its more sympathetic spectators. For all their didactic truth-telling ambitions, the best tableaux suggest truth's variability. This is true even of those stereotypical tableaux — someone, say, lifting a chair over the cowering body of his enemy — in which the playwrights, like lucky photojournalists, preserve tension as it crests, locating the beginnings of passions usually remembered only for their ends and thus fixing

Figure 2: The death of little Eva in William Brady's 1901 production of *Uncle Tom's Cabin*. The Byron Collection, Museum of the City of New York.

responsibility for action. They also open up the play to our own acts of imagination. After stopping a narrative episode before the climax happens (we don't see the chair come crashing down on its victim's head), the playwrights ask us to consider, in the silence that the tableau creates, some of the possible alternatives to an event that would otherwise seem inevitable. Just the fact that other routes through such a crisis exist, this theater implies, is important to recognize, even if this narrative and these particular characters aren't going to take them.

As these examples suggest, the duration of a tableau shapes its meaning as much as the actors' bodies do. While time seems to stop, in fact its passage is felt more intensely during tableaux than at any other point in a production. Indeed, the comparison between tableaux and photographs, while inevitable, needs qualifying. A more precise comparison would be to the experience of sitting for a daguerreotype. Henry James, as ever, not only describes the latter well but unwittingly suggests its implications for theatrical seeing. As a boy he posed with his father for Mathew Brady, an experience he remembers as both trying and "beautiful." The "exposure" was "interminably long," he writes in *A Small Boy*, but it resulted in "a facial anguish far less harshly reproduced than my suffered snapshots of a later age" (52). James implies that time, passing slowly in stillness, has brought to the surface the person beneath the personality—a truth deeper than that of the image alone and available only when the photographer's intrusion is delayed. In *The House of Mirth*, Edith Wharton describes a similarly revelatory contest between visual stability and change in the famous scene of tableaux vivantes—that "boundary world between fact and imagination." Lawrence Selden, watching Lily Bart impersonate a Joshua Reynolds portrait, feels he is at last seeing "the real Lily Bart, divested of the trivialities of her little world." "In the long moment before the curtain fell," Wharton writes of the deceptively decorous scene, "he had time to feel the whole tragedy of her life."[15]

Both James and Wharton recognize the visual world's ambiguous promise: the "real" emerges only when artificial means of seeing control one's access to the image. The American theater's latent anxiety about the same ambiguity surfaces at its surprisingly frequent moments of metatheatricality. Indicative of this tension are scenes from two otherwise unrelated plays that depict the making of daguerreotypes and in the process stake out opposing positions in a debate over theater's visual truth. Dion Boucicault, a true believer in the authority of the image who once famously declared that the public wants "the actual, the contemporaneous, the photographic," sets out in *The Octoroon* (1859) to erase any distance between "actuality" and visuality.[16] In the play's crucial episode, a camera set up for portraiture instead captures the villain implicating himself in a murder and extortion plot. For a long minute, he stands motionless over his victim's body, engrossed in a stolen letter, while unbeknownst to him the camera is taking a perfectly exposed daguerreotype, later used to expose his villainy. "The apparatus can't mistake," an amateur photographer had said in a different context earlier in the scene, marveling at how well the camera corrects vanity and asserts the truth about status.[17] Boucicault invites us to reach the same unequivocal conclusion about his own visual honesty.

Such complacency lasts only until spectators register the implications of a later, more debased theatrical artifact, an anonymous minstrel-show afterpiece called *Scenes at Gurney's* (c. 1870), that reaches an opposite conclusion about the manufactured image. In the sketch, a "black" man, Gumbo, refuses to sit still for his portrait, much less to comprehend the rituals of photography. Told to "take a chair," he picks one up; once seated, he twists and turns, first distracted by the goings-on, then shaking off an assistant's attempts to pose him, until he has to be forcibly restrained. After he moves a last time, the photographer loses patience—"How dare you, sir, when I had you in position!"—to which Gumbo replies, "it's an imposition altogether!"[18] The photograph that finally results is blurred, of course. In a graphic acknowledgement of blackface's own procedures, Gumbo is shown with two faces. (Earlier, he had also expressed skepticism that any picture could be authentic: "A poor-Trayt — ain't dat what you call a curicature?" [5].)

As an image of the spectator's own proprietary ambitions and as a comment on the gulf between minstrel "black" and actual African-American, *Scenes at Gurney's* could hardly be clearer. All minstrel shows may be predicated on the belief that, as Eric Lott puts it, " 'black' figures were there to be looked at . . . screens on which audience fantasy could rest," but the playwright of *Scenes at Gurney's* devises a scenario that a present-day observer may read as unwittingly subverting such a process.[19] Gumbo's resistance to the photographer's (and spectator's) attempts to fix, frame, and limit his identity shifts the focus onto an unexpected target. With nothing clear or stable to look at, spectators are left to consider the motives behind and consequences of any assertion of visual authority — to look, in other words, at themselves.

This preoccupation with an image's truth and one's ability to recognize it — everything James had in mind when writing of "the validity of my subject" — becomes in certain midcentury plays as integral to their dramaturgy as any event or character. Such drama systematically argues for the authority of its imagery, making strenuous a visuality that is effortless in other modes of theater. No midcentury dramatic form counts on this kind of critical and, necessarily, self-critical spectator more than the temperance play. A typical text forms only one half of a spectacle that casts the viewers in crucial roles, demanding that they see themselves as pitilessly as they judge the pathetic characters onstage. A concise introduction to this collaborative dramaturgy is D. W. Griffith's *The Drunkard's Reformation*.[20] The 1909 silent film is only twelve minutes long, but nonetheless it sums up the ambitions of every reform-minded dramatist, depicting its hero's fall and rise less to warn others away from such a fate than to demonstrate theater's indispensability in the campaign for moral renewal. The film is both an example of and an advertisement for temperance drama.

The synopsis of *The Drunkard's Reformation* is taken from the thin catalogue of appropriate plots for its genre. An alcoholic abuses his devoted wife, neglects his precocious child (as in all temperance dramas, it's a girl), falls prey to opportunistic and two-faced friends, and humiliates himself until, bottoming out, he acquires a conscience unavailable earlier and in an instant sobers up. Art causes his turnaround. After he recovers from a particularly abject day of drinking, his daughter persuades him to take her to the theater: on the bill is a temperance drama, of course, its plot deviating from his own situation only

Figure 3: *The Drunkard's Reformation* by D. W. Griffith (1909). The drunkard (Arthur Johnson) watches a temperance drama with his daughter and decides to change his ways. Frame enlargement from paper print in the Library of Congress.

at its conclusion. When the fictional drunk dies, his real-life counterpart completes a process of self-reproach begun when the curtain rose. He returns home to throw away his liquor bottles and preside over a hearthside scene of recovered domestic stability.

For all the lurid behavior of its "real" and fictional protagonists, *The Drunkard's Reformation* finds the greater charge in the seemingly passive business of being a spectator. Griffith returns over and over to the alcoholic in the audience, framing his pale, raccoon-eyed face so as to track his reaction to the stage production. We see him looking into a horrifying mirror: at the first moment of self-recognition, he clutches his daughter, tightening his protective grip as his onstage surrogate fails to resist the temptations that hours earlier claimed his observer. The man in the audience recoils every time the stage-drunk berates his wife or beats his daughter; only by looking at his own daughter can this spectator relieve the agony of spectatorship. Debilitated by the end, he taps his chest and mouths the words "that's me" — a pitiable attempt to recover control over a spectacle whose lacerating images strike beneath the consolations of language.

In Griffith's imaginary theater, such vision is the common property of the tempters, the family members, and the protagonist whose soul they fight over. Characters — and audience members — cultivate, condemn, or atone for sin by looking at it. (In the film, the stage-drunk never opens a bottle without someone looking on, often from the shadows.) This understanding of vision's power derives from many of the actual temperance dramas produced before 1880. The most accomplished, William Henry Smith's *The Drunkard* (1844), tells a story that in its broad outlines is identical to Griffith's, with the more intricate drama in the watching of it. The drunkard's suffering allows Smith to address the less hackneyed subject of suffering's allure. His everyman hero, appropriately named Middleton, is the writhing center of concentric circles of attention: his worrying wife; his obsessed tormenter; a reformer trailing him to the end; the villagers by turns scornful, embarrassed, compassionate, and nosy; and not least, the theater audience, evaluating one man so to later evaluate themselves. In this regard, those of us in this outermost circle match those in the innermost, for the drunkard's own conscience watches him, scripting the self-indictments he delivers within hearing, he hopes, of a forgiving God and family.

The prosecutorial analogy is inevitable and sharpens the interplay between the watcher and the watched in Smith's theater. The showing of events in *The Drunkard* follows the form, if not the rules, for presenting evidence, and viewing them ends in judgment. (Jeffrey Mason calls this same style "exegetical.")[21] So central is the act of demonstration to *The Drunkard* — more important than the drunkenness, villainy, or recovery demonstrated — that the narrative seems to unfold in retrospective calm. Lines of dialogue that would be throwaways in a less austere play here are potent declarations: "Gaze on . . . that child." "Look!" "There!" "She comes." These and many other directives, urging logic upon the wayward attention of character and spectator alike, are matched by the equally frequent instances of characters encircling or pulling into view a subject in need of scrutiny. The play's first line sets the tone: "It was in that corner, Mary, where your poor father breathed his last."[22] The business of accurately identifying the significant place — the corner — matters more than any grieving over what happened there.

Most of all, like all moralizing dramatists, Smith hopes to expose the mechanics of influence: good and bad, the angel's and the devil's. While Smith voices this concern directly — too directly — in frequent pauses for catechism, he is more persuasive when he speaks a theatrical language. A careful production, following Smith's stage directions, displays Middleton's decline in light that begins "half-dark," moves to a single lamp "burning dimly," and ends in blackness before brightening again on his recovery. Smith matches this pattern in his use of space. For much of the play, Middleton's observers are hidden: the theater is densest in the wings, its atmosphere charged with the expectation of ambush or timely rescue. When the ensemble finally emerges in the daylight at the end, Smith's point is clear: one can resist dangerous influences only when they are in plain sight.

Smith expects us to emulate Middleton's reform, but he also recommends a style of deliberation, and of responding to experience in general, that goes beyond the issue of intemperance. Of the play's first production, Smith writes, "In the representation it was a powerful and living picture, and all that saw it, felt it, for IT WAS TRUE. No one who had not seen it would feel inclined, from the mere reading, to believe the very powerful effect produced" (250). Smith's bullying insistence on his fidelity to what's "TRUE" betrays his anxiety. If belief is the condition for reform, the vice-obsessed artist must first confront the skepticism—James's "mixed consciousness"—that even the most sympathetic spectator feels in the presence of a fiction, especially the fiction of theatrical illusion. It is not enough, Smith implies, to attest to the story's basis in fact, as so many novelists of the era did, nor is it enough to address a spectator's reason, for the thinking spectator will tend to question, and thus unravel, even his own conclusions, leaving all reform vulnerable to dissolution. Such a tendency must be squelched by a deeper conviction, rooted in feeling—belief achieved only with vision: "all that saw it, felt it." *The Drunkard*'s declarative sentences, graphic action (including a famous scene of delirium tremens), and bright lights banish darkness from the stage only to stimulate our own aversion to the no less frightening shadows of ambiguity and ambivalence in interpretation. We leave Smith's theater knowing less about his subject than when we entered, but we know it aggressively, our understanding of this diminished subject so visceral that it enlarges our sense of ourselves. This prize—the viewer consolidated by looking—would be even more attractive, and seem even more necessary to win, as stage landscapes fragment and disperse in other nineteenth-century playhouses.

＊　＊　＊

When a culture invests seeing with so much power, it is bound to fret over where to look. The same theater that shelters audiences from the bustling outside world, enabling them to negotiate competing claims on their attention, also forces them to recognize when such negotiations fail, the spectators swept up by the spectacle. Such a crisis (if that is what it is) forces viewers to rethink their definition of visual mastery. Reading through nineteenth-century chronicles of theatergoing, one encounters passage after passage about the difficulties of seeing—the confessions of spectators ready to exert their analytic power over theatrical imagery but unable to see their way to the stage, much less become enthralled by its action. Only rarely do these accounts sound bitter or rueful. More often, their writers are unsentimental about the reach of possessive vision and eager to develop a more flexible style of attention.

Washington Irving's testimony is characteristic. In his Jonathan Oldstyle letters of 1802–3, he describes nights at a New York theater in which novice spectators may be forgiven for thinking that their first duty is to resist or exclude objects of attention. Chandeliers drip hot wax on one's head. Inscrutable codes control the intercourse in the lounges and lobbies. Many spectators whistle, yell, and talk back to the stage. Others just as noisily eat apples, nuts, and gingerbread (when they aren't throwing them at one another). These and other unscripted distractions ensure that Irving's attention is always embattled, fractured, and mobile. The wisest spectators adapt to their environment. Only one of Irving's nine theater letters discusses an actual performance. The others concede and then implicitly celebrate the impossibility of concentration. Irving sees as much as he can, regardless of its location in the theater building. Only "dull souls . . . go for the sake of the play," he concludes.[23] The man turned away from the stage and scanning the audience with his opera glasses is the protagonist of Irving's many scenes that dramatize unplanned, digressive, and opinionated looking — as well as looking at looking. They form an endlessly mirrored spectacle for which the play itself is merely the socially acceptable excuse.

So irrelevant is drama to this kind of spectatorship that when a play does seize and retain a spectator's attention it deserves special mention. Fanny Trollope, in *Domestic Manners of the Americans* (1832), ends a series of descriptions of the same hectic, omnivorous form of spectatorship by remarking of one play, with astonishment, that "the interest must have been great, for till the curtain fell, I saw not one quarter of the queer things around me."[24] In such a multifocused culture, it is inevitable that Henry James himself would have to establish a viable relationship with the other spectators before he finds a channel for his own theatrical attention. Recalling a night at the Bowery Theatre in *The American Scene* (1907), he at first laments having to bridge the "queer chasm" between his box and the stage, a chasm teeming with a multi-ethnic crowd so unlike the audiences he remembers from his boyhood visits to the same theater.[25] Eventually, however, he admits that this arrested and alienating form of spectatorship has its own appeal, more ambiguous and thus able to unlock responses deeper and more unsettling than those prompted by the formulaic entertainments on the chasm's far side. (James's interest in what he calls the Bowery's "exotic" audience is a reminder that some chasms yawn wider than others — perhaps before no one more than African-American spectators, relegated to the back gallery of most theaters. When the African Company—the nation's first all-black theater, founded in 1821—restricted white spectators to a similarly remote section, it was merely affirming the custom of a culture already intensively aware that visual access and structures of attention shape the spectator as much as they control the spectacle.)[26]

These are the century's representative spectators. They are invested with the authority to engage the stage's visual propositions, versed in the gestural languages that convey emotion and thought, and aware that spectatorship confirms or prefigures the acts of recognition by which one joins the surrounding culture. Yet they are also uneasy. They fear that they may not be seeing the most important action or actors, or not seeing accurately and comprehensively enough. They also worry that sight, even if aggressive, won't be able to penetrate the thickest moral or psychological ambiguities. James's cool, equable recollections may radiate confidence that he can bridge the widest theatrical chasm and resolve his "mixed consciousness" in memories that have all the unity lacking in the original scene. But his approach seems idealistic and compensatory in the face of a theater shaken by a more severe centrifugal force. This performance challenges spectators to check their desire for legible patterns in favor of truer irregularity, or at least to remember that, with a temporal art, they must continuously renew their mastery of the compositions that flatter their interpretive skill. An image for this kind of spectatorship—less decorous than James's, hungrier for sensation, restless rather than systematic—can be found in an otherwise labored verse play by Robert Montgomery Bird, *The Gladiator* (1831). "My eyes /Seem parting from their sockets," says a character driven to look at staged combat and then to look at her own visual appetite in self-stimulating, self-absorbed fervor.

> My brain reels,
> While I look on; and while I look, each time,
> I swear I ne'er will look again. But when
> They battle boldly, and the people shout,
> And the poor creatures look so fearless. . . .
> I have to see them. These are your own shows:
> Oh, I must see them.[27]

"These *are* your own shows" indeed. The line is out of key with the rest of the speech, and one wants to imagine that it jolted a nineteenth-century audience out of Bird's Roman fantasy and returned them to themselves, making them see the erotic compulsion and self-disordering consequences of their own vision. Yet even plays less self-aware than *The Gladiator* can keep spectators on guard against the presumptions of their addiction to images. Throughout the century, the American theater moves audiences back and forth between the pleasure to be had in dominating the objects of their attention (as occurs in the presence of the typical temperance play) and their confusion (no less pleasurable) before scenes whose density and centerless variety invite surrender — a shift, in other words, between analytic and ecstatic seeing.

One can best begin measuring the dilation of the American theater's field of view, as well as its effects on the spectatorial ego, by returning to William Dunlap. His last play, *A Trip to Niagara; or, Travellers in America* (1828), is an explicit meditation on spectatorship, in which Dunlap argues that spectators are both enlarged and humbled by the act of seeing. The playwright's self-dismissive preface acknowledges only a far more limited goal: "The following Farce," Dunlap writes, "makes pretensions to no higher character. . . . [It] was written at the request of the Managers, and intended by them as a kind of running accompaniment to the more important product of the Scene-painter."[28] Its sole purpose, he claims, is to keep the audience "in good humour while the scenery and machinery was in preparation" (178). In fact, the relation between text and decor — and between the spectators and the spectator-characters on stage (a group of tourists) — is more complex than Dunlap admits. The visual splendor of *A Trip to Niagara,* far from seeming merely decorative, is active and potent, its didacticism offset by the playwright's short attention span. Midway through the play, the action stops to allow the background to become the foreground, and scenery to become character, as we join the tourists in beholding the passing sights on a Hudson riverboat cruise. No dialogue interrupts a silent procession of eighteen panels depicting, among other subjects, a storm, a rainbow, a sunset, other boats passing through fog or at anchor, and vistas in New York and New Jersey. The visual stimulation doesn't stop when the ship drops anchor near the Catskills. Looking remains the primary action in rural and urban landscapes designed to correct the nationalist myopia, if not total cultural blindness, of one resistant spectator-character in particular. An English-born traveler, George Wentworth, begins with the "obstinate determination to see nothing" except the verbal landscapes in books (as his sister complains) and ends, many backdrops later, by proclaiming, "I see it all" — a move from secondhand sight to panoramic vision (181, 196). The limited meaning of Wentworth's declaration indicates only that he has seen through his sister's scheme to correct his ignorance, but Dunlap welcomes the line's blurring of literal and figurative seeing, convinced that the study of nature encourages closer and more benevolent scrutiny of human nature. "When the film of prejudice is removed from the eye," says Wentworth, "man sees in his fellow man of every clime a brother" (197). (Another foreign-born traveler simultaneously sheds his own skepticism of American culture and says, in his native Irish accent, "I've sane liberty" [197].)

Dunlap's ideal form of attention also restores onstage and offstage spectators to their proper scale. He allows his travelers, like his audiences, to enjoy the illusion that they are sovereigns of all they see — the central figures occasioning the spectacle, around whom are arranged "wonders" in a circle that widens as their attention deepens. Yet the very strength of Dunlap's visuality checks any hubris in the beholder, a diminishment of character confirmed every time one of Dunlap's travelers declares a sight "sublime." As they seek opportunities to be dwarfed, engulfed, or even rendered irrelevant by the landscape, they discover the deferential form of attention that will in fact shore up individual dignity and ensure a harmonious relation to both natural and social landscapes. At least such an outcome is Dunlap's hope. He pursues it, and drives home his argument, by contrasting the travelers' method of surveying nature — ocular, distanced by a boat or promontory — with the more intrusive form of mastery associated with modernity, what Dunlap's version of James Fenimore Cooper's Leatherstocking has in mind when he says of the wilderness, "Fit to look on — but it's spoilt now. What has housen and bridges to do among the wonders of heaven?" (191). (Richard Poirier memorably identifies a similar argument made in contemporaneous and subsequent American fiction: "To take possession of America in the eye, as an Artist, is a way of preserving imaginatively those dreams about the continent that were systematically betrayed by the possession of it for economic and political aggrandizement.")[29]

Dunlap's play coincides with the rise of the panorama as a medium occupying the shifting ground between theater and visual art, a space where its patrons can experiment with forms of spectatorship unavailable in either the playhouse or the gallery and with forms of citizenship unavailable in either city or country. Such flexibility ensures the panorama's firm grip on the imagination. Naive in its methodology and imagery (most obey realist convention in reproducing a limited number of appropriate subjects — cityscapes, river journeys, battlefields, frontier vistas), the panorama nonetheless occasions complex and uncodified modes of spectatorship. After visitors to a typical panorama ascend to a circular platform set back from and seeming to float like a disc before all-encompassing painted scenery, they command the landscape with a confidence impossible in the outside world.[30] At the same time, however, spectators are swallowed up by the panorama, closed in by representation, able to walk around the platform freely but nonetheless made claustrophobic by the very plentitude of visible "space."

Whether or not one feels master or victim of the panorama's landscape depends on one's vision of oneself. Here, too, the panorama enables one to maintain contradictory views of the spectator's role. When visitors look back from the panorama to themselves, they may opt, with equal justification, to see themselves as central — as, in strictly architectural terms, they are — or anonymous, unreflected in a scene that emulates nature's own indifference to its admirers. Indeed, panoramas never single out individual "characters" for glory or opprobrium. Their focus is collective — armies, tribes, urban populations — when they are not obscuring human presence and responsibility altogether. Even so, here spectators may seize opportunities for self-assertion less available in the outside world. The empty streets and desolate fields in many panoramas are the backdrop for a crowded, shifting spectatorial landscape where, as Stephan Oettermann points out, democratic principles of equal access and continuous reform (every "seat" as good as every other, every arrangement of the viewing society subject to change) replace traditional hierarchies of seeing.[31]

The same vision of spectatorial authority lends urgency and seriousness to the deceptively passive pleasures of a related form, the moving panorama, especially popular in the United States in the late 1840s. (*A Trip to Niagara* can be seen as a moving panorama with dialogue, perhaps the only one of its kind. Dunlap recognized the form's egalitarian possibilities: panoramas, he wrote, "captivate all classes of spectators. . . . No study or cultivated taste is required fully to appreciate" them.)[32] Audiences at a moving panorama sit in conventional rows to watch a huge scroll of scenery unfurl behind the proscenium; as it does so, a narrator may describe the sights, tutoring viewers in the appropriate sentiments of nationalist pride and awe — ownership mixed with reverence, the same mix of dominance over and subordination to the visible world as in other panoramas. But the stationary audience at a moving panorama need not be any less active than the moving audience at a stationary panorama. If anything, with less authority to choose what to look at (and for how long), they have more opportunity to consider other, less purely practical modes of engaging the national landscape. Charles Dickens proposes one particularly ambitious approach in his detailed account of John Banvard's *Geographical Panorama of the Mississippi and Missouri Rivers* (1846). After praising the "plain and simple truthfulness" of the obviously illusionistic view, and encouraging audiences to go beyond mere curiosity toward "thorough understanding" of the American geography, Dickens asks audiences to forge an even stronger bond with the object of their attention. In the act of seeing so much of America, he writes, "our sense of immense responsibility may be increased."[33] With no characters shouldering that burden for us (as at a play) and no social structures to distribute obligations across the citizenry (as in the real nation), each spectator is left to imaginatively map, settle, and sustain the landscape by himself or herself. Or to confront the landscape's sometimes obscured history: in 1850, a sharper idea of Dickens's "sense of immense responsibility" awaited those who saw Henry "Box" Brown's *Mirror of Slavery,* a panorama that places Brown's experience of slavery and escape in landscapes prohibiting merely neutral, much less uncritically patriotic spectatorship.[34] In all cases, the moving panorama's form of presentation itself invites spectators to assume an interrogatory (and even self-interrogatory) rather than merely contemplative attitude, regardless of the banality or originality of the panorama's subjects. The scroll of canvas unspooling horizontally makes communal seeing seem like solitary reading — an illusion satisfying to those accustomed to intervening imaginatively with other texts.

Reading the landscape in panoramic culture coincides with American playwrights' attempts to write it — or rather, to claim it in writing and thus inspire spectators' own acts of taking possession. Whether or not such attempts succeed (and, as we've seen, panoramic breadth often ensures they don't) matters less than the vigor of the spectators' exploratory energies as they meet the theater's visual challenge. Seeing, at this theater, involves them in naming, measuring, cataloguing, or merely covering space, all acts by which they also seek knowledge about the individual and collective history that such spaces have witnessed. The theater's visual discipline literally grounds such abstractions. When William Dunlap, in *A Trip to Niagara,* provides captions-in-dialogue to a series of painted panels — first illustrating, then annotating the new nation — he is codifying efforts that preceded and would outlive him. As early as such Revolutionary War–era plays as John Leacock's *The Fall of British Tyranny* (1776) — a panoramic chronicle-play making stops at London, Boston, Charlestown, Lexington, Virginia, upstate New York, and Montreal — and stretching through such post–Civil War expressions of American expansionism as James J. McCloskey's *Across the Continent; or, Scenes from New York Life and the Pacific Railroad* (1870) to the early stirrings of realism in Edward Sheldon's streetscape *Salvation Nell* (1908), playwrights of otherwise primitive technique understand individual, local, and national experience in terms of cartography (rather than only in terms of ideals and actions), then subject those maps to the turbulence of theatrical performance, restoring the uncertainty of lived life to its representations.

This desire rises to a jubilant, fevered pitch in the many midcentury plays — they could form a school — that traverse and extol the city. Such plays resemble tours for wide-eyed newcomers, some streetsmart, others naive and easily humiliated, all of whom embody our own avid sightseeing. Their flanerie structures the narrative and sets its tempo. The typical play of this school, Benjamin A. Baker's *A Glance at New York* (1848), is crowded with representatives of the classes and vocations, as well as of the dangers and temptations, in any given urban setting. In its panoramic and resolutely public orientation — away from the nuanced affairs of the heart common to the century's sentimental drama — this theater affirms a vision of self as the reflection of the surrounding society. At the same time, it checks the desire stimulated by the era's heroic drama to cast any one character as the voice of the times. While certain cityscape plays have come to be associated with their liveliest flaneurs (Baker's play is usually remembered only for its hero, Mose the Fireman), such an impression distorts the true centerless, egalitarian shape they have in performance. Here, an individual's emotional and moral conduct is inseparable from and thus illegible apart from that of everyone else. No single character holds the stage for long, despite the larger-than-life stature of some of them, and few encounters flower into full-fledged relationships. This network of affiliation revises standards of the theater's emotional depth. A series of quick liaisons, epitomized in the con man's encounter with his mark or the cab-driver's with his fare, reveals more of a character's affective range than an exclusive and thus necessarily less demanding engagement.

The social perspective of the flaneur-playwrights has, in part, a social source: the communal self-consciousness stirring in what Whitman called the "best average of American-born mechanics," the mostly male, working-class audience concentrated, after 1826, at the newly built Bowery Theatre in New York and by the 1840s typed inside and outside the theater as the Bowery B'hoys.[35] Their restiveness peaked, notoriously, in the Astor Place riot of 1849, one year after the premiere of *A Glance at New York*. The rioters did more than protest the imperialist arrogance of an English actor, William Macready, and the presumed snobbery of those attending his *Macbeth* at the Astor Place Opera House. By the very location of their demonstration — the street — they also asserted, if only implicitly, the supremacy of a dramatic structure flexible enough to accommodate the world *outside* this or any theater. Such dramaturgy would restore the individual, heroic or not, to the world, and would reflect the same urban mastery and fellowship that the protesters experienced as they circulated through the city spreading word about the protest, convened in small groups merging toward the Opera House, and finally jostled one another on the square.

Indeed, in the flaneur-plays, character and plot have little independent value apart from their service as mapping instruments and placeholders. Their psychological or narrative interest is secondary to their role as devices by which to observe the changing identities and uses of a particular site. The shift in priorities is evident in the long list of plays that compensate for the limited interest of their interchangeable protagonists, situations, and stories with vibrant settings that depend for their power on our recognition, awe, and even intoxicated disorientation. In an effort to establish their urban authenticity, these playwrights lavish attention on environmental landmarks, create locally specific minor types, and acquire an insider's fluency with the talk of the town. Audiences accustomed to identifying or at least investing emotionally with characters must instead direct those energies to landscapes no less insistent about securing one's pledge of allegiance.

Plays of this sort had found an audience as early as the 1820s, when William Thomas Moncrieff's *Tom and Jerry; or, A Life in London,* a stage adaptation of an English serial, proved so popular that it spawned dozens of American variations. Some playwrights merely added locally relevant scenes to Moncrieff's original — the African Company's version even included a slave auction — while others dispensed with all but the flanerie structure as they created panoramas of their own. John Brougham's *Life in New York* (1843) is the best known of a series of *Life*s set in Philadelphia (1836), New Orleans (1837), and Brooklyn (1857). After Mose the Fireman and his girlfriend Lize appeared first in *A Glance at New York,* they became a franchise: Mose went to Philadelphia, California, and China in 1849 alone. Other years saw *Mose in France, Mose's Visit to the Arab Girl's,* and *Mose in a Muss.*

Many of these and other, related titles were never published, a fate that seems appropriate for drama that celebrates transitoriness. Indeed, the loss of so many texts helps readers of the surviving plays keep in mind their true language: movement itself communicates their meaning. More than most theater of the period, these plays rely on the unreliability of performance for their vitality and even for their value. Their lyrical range is narrow and their structural complexity nonexistent. Each play's incidents, emotions, and issues (such as they are) have no significance beyond the time they are enacted or engaged. (The insufficiency of a purely literary analysis of Baker's work is obvious when one looks to where its influence has been felt. Its closest descendent in recent theater isn't another play but a ballet — Jerome Robbins's *Fancy Free.*) Moreover, as spectators fall into sync with the playwright's accelerations and decelerations, his lulls and jolts, this new rhythm unsteadies earlier, once-dominant modes of attention. The change is clear in Baker's title. *A Glance at New York* is meant to be seen as it is acted — on the run. Like all flaneur-plays, it promotes a mode of spectatorship adjusted for the unreliability and incompleteness of vision. We move quickly in the face of a situation's perishability. There is no time for the long view, the analytic examination, the contemplative appraisal, or the comprehensive scan. The work of vision, instead, must be conducted in short, sharp bursts — glancing attacks — as the eye checks off a sight, and a site, before being called off to something else demanding attention.

Figure 4: Frank Chanfrau as Mose the Fireman in Benjamin A. Baker's *A Glance at New York* (1848). The Harvard Theatre Collection, Houghton Library.

The consciously superficial way of seeing causes a profound shift in a spectator's authority. By exalting the glance, Baker disabuses us of the illusion that sight ensures even minimally adequate knowledge, much less ownership, of what's seen. The spectator's grasp of the visible world, despite its empirical grounding, remains provisional. There is always more to look at, unreachable even by the fastest, most impatient eye; more, too, under the surfaces that the flaneur won't wait or doesn't care to penetrate. Baker sustains his play by sustaining paradoxes: only the skimming spectators do justice to their object — a city of multiple centers, simultaneous narratives, and proliferating heroes draining and replenishing their energy in a continuous cycle. Moreover, audiences succeed in absorbing the action only when they allow themselves to be absorbed. The spectacle is forever larger (at least in its field of reference) than the spectators.

Baker's interest in the partial view, a consequence of his kinetic theatricality, is evident in his play's erosion of narrative beginnings and ends. Everything in *A Glance at New York* is already underway when we encounter it. An action that seems like a beginning is in fact the sequel to an offstage event. An apparent conclusion is only a pause before the start of a new cycle of activity. Baker's first speaker — a taxi driver calling out, "Hire a cab to ride through the city, sir?" — helps us both to perceive and to enter this continuous action.[36] More than merely announcing the play's touring rhythm and postcard tone, the character functions like a relay runner, picking up as if they were batons a pair of tourists disembarking from a British steamship. The couple's voyage isn't over yet. The life on the pier also refuses to rest. Baker surrounds the protagonists with a vast, seemingly improvised, ever-transforming network in which money, objects, words, and people circulate so fluidly that we can't keep track of every exchange, much less decide which one deserves our closest attention. Suitcases bob from person to person in the crowd. More taxi drivers compete for fares. Con men distract their prey. Hosts search for guests. Tour guides promote their services. Ringing out over the scene, newspaper boys hawk the latest edition, their product the perfect emblem of the kind of play we're watching. Like the journalist, Baker is loyal to immediate experience, nourished by change, and able to integrate individual incidents with the day's — or the scene's — other events, all of which are rendered disposable by subsequent episodes.

What doesn't change is the topography. Much of Baker's action happens outdoors, on sidewalks and piers and in public gardens, all with transient populations. When the play moves indoors, it favors places also designed for congregation and circulation: a saloon, a dance hall, a bowling alley, an auction house, and other places of amusement. Despite their chronic impatience in these places, Baker's characters do stop to name them as well as to report where they have been and are going. One hears them take sensual pleasure in merely saying the words: Front Street, New Street, Spruce Street, Broadway; Bleecker, Bayard, and Barclay Streets; Chatham and Chrystie Streets; 300 Robinson Street. The characters are just as fastidious in naming the buildings and other attractions that draw them to these parts of town, even when they are not as sonorous: Astor House, the Bowery Theatre, Christy's Minstrels, the Elephant, and Loafer's Paradise, among others.

Not all, or even many, of these streets and sites are visible. There is a vast unseen city enveloping the stage, accessible only in speech but nonetheless vital to the characters' sense of themselves. People in Baker's world are defined in large part by their loyalties to and history in particular parts of town. These attachments go beyond the country and city stereotypes dividing Baker's ensemble. The urbanite Mose, one character tells us, has long "held Broadway in such contempt . . . [he] couldn' be persuaded even to cross it" (172). The same observer reminds Mose of their long friendship dating back to Bayard Street. Another character spells out his address as if it told his life story. The details are incidental to Baker's plot but not to his cartographer's idea of psychology, his larger concern. As Baker studies how space shapes character, he also, in turn, studies how character shapes space. Each site mentioned in *A Glance at New York* stands for the people it attracts, shelters, or expels. The Bowery Theatre entertains the classes shunned by the elegant Opera House. The Ladies' Bowling Saloon appeals to those unwelcome at the Loafer's Paradise. The latter itself is an "abode of many worthies who would not be at home in any other place" (179). (Its fragile calm is carefully guarded: a self-appointed bouncer takes care of all "foo-foos," the loafers' term for outsiders.) Such places cultivate more than self-esteem. As Baker's peripatetic characters identify with the city's communal spaces, they can see themselves as more permanent than a force of energy, able to transcend the limits of biography.

This merger with the landscape is so complete that memory itself is no longer private. Whenever a character reminisces, he or she begins with an obligatory setting of the scene. "I was walking on the Battery . . ." (176). " Last night . . . down in Front Street . . ." (171). "Don't you remember the chap we did at the foot of Barclay Street?" (179). "Dis puts me in mind when . . . down in Spruce Street . . ." (183). These and other prefaces argue that a character's past can acquire meaning and stave off obsolescence only when set against the city's timeless present. Yet these backward glances, however fond, are deliberately never sustained. Baker's characters remain nervous about nostalgia, treating memory as an invitation to idleness if allowed to run unchecked.

There is, in fact, very little substantive history beneath the lively doings of *A*

Glance at New York: no old stories working themselves out, no earlier en-tanglements so serious as to inhibit the characters' present dealings with one another, and few ideals demanding their acquiescence. These omissions pose an implicit challenge to the era's cult of sincerity. Here, every self-declaration is functional and situational rather than definitive; characters are known only by their changes. They enjoy a holiday from old versions of themselves as much as from home and its conventions, customs, and morality — a release especially apparent in John Brougham's *Life in New York,* whose tourist-characters have deceived their spouses about their true whereabouts. The air of illicitness is essential to most plays of this school. It underscores the playwrights' own interest in alternative, dissenting ideas of character and structure. While Baker and his peers do play happily with inherited types and even add new ones to the catalogue, their work is more important for envisioning a churning milieu capable of eroding typology, revealing flexible, not fated, characters seizing opportunities for self-reinvention. The same spirit of revisionism affects dra-matic structure. By deemphasizing, if not eradicating, the past, these plays do more than reinvigorate the theatrical present. They also claim the future as a plausible scene of dramatic action. "Where shall we go next?" says one man in *A Glance at New York* (177) — this theater's poetics in a sentence.

At the end of *A Glance at New York,* after Baker satisfies conventional taste with one character securing her fiancé's promise to "give up roaming" and another character confessing he's "tempted to remain" near his own beloved, the play spins away from its expected resolution as Mose disengages from Lize to rescue a friend in a "muss." He's on his way offstage as the curtain falls. The ending does more than reaffirm the ethos of a culture in which ambition matters more than achievement, and of a community in which permanent commitment is the anomaly, not the ideal. The ensemble's final centrifugal movements, coming after their many forward-looking exclamations of "let's be off!," also force spectators to rethink their idea of stage space. The play's settings, in retrospect, seem like mere thresholds, insufficient stages of their own. Under the pressure of anticipation, visible landscapes demand less of their inhabitants than potential, theoretical ones. Time, in this view, begins to diminish the importance of space. It also diminishes the power typically at-tributed to our attention to space. Even as Baker invites us to salute characters seizing their "right to the city" (in Henri Lefebvre's inevitable phrase), he prohibits us from claiming the same victory over the city's theatricalization.[37] We cannot keep what we see. Baker's characters, in moving offstage, widen the field of action until it is larger than the field of view, preserving a vision of autonomy by exercising their right to invisibility.

The story of mid-nineteenth-century theater thus far has been one of the eye's gradual assumption of more and more power — its analytic skills boring into tableaux and emerging with codes of conduct, its dilating interest granting it sovereignty over expanding territory, its agility and fondness for surprise ensuring that the spectator keeps up with and matches the spontaneity of the performer. Convention demands that such a triumphant ascent bring about a fall. In one of the many signs that nineteenth-century theater is not as formulaic as one expects, this pattern is honored in a play that simultaneously celebrates ardent seeing. George L. Aiken's *Uncle Tom's Cabin* (1852) invites viewers to synthesize modes of attention stimulated separately in earlier plays. It rewards close reading of visual structures and patterned imagery — the kind of systematic study by which viewers master didactic temperance plays and coded tableaux — and at the same time it encourages the ambulatory, panoramic seeing they bring to the city plays. Yet Aiken is also so honest about the pressure of performance on these visual arrangements that he calls their clarity into doubt. Time — the theatrical element that, as it works upon a scene, causes a spectator to see with ever more flexibility and vigor — also threatens the legibility of the composition, eroding, if not erasing, the objects of our attention, shaking our confidence in vision's hermeneutic reach. Our conclusions are as subject to revision as is the changing stage landscape. Insights disappear along with sights.

Once again, Henry James offers a useful, if ambiguous, point of reference. In a discussion of Harriet Beecher Stowe's novel, he famously calls it "much less a book than a state of vision" (elsewhere he refers to it as "Mrs. Stowe's picture") and argues that "appreciation and judgment . . . were thus an effect for which there had been no process" (92). The aura of vague spirituality — attention as prayer — is appropriate and inevitable to Stowe's evangelical project. But when such seeing is literal, as it is in the theater, a visionary narrative must become visible, and perceiving it involves us not in an atemporal, suspended "state" but in a series of active, variable approaches. We don't just see; we see in time. Aiken's interest in how performance makes and unmakes images restores the "process" that James doesn't recognize in the novel. The experience of watching Aiken's play, unlike that of witnessing the transcendental epiphanies embodied in and stimulated by Stowe's novel, is wholly secular.

Reading can be, too, of course — as Jane Tompkins demonstrates when she forestalls her own Jamesian surrender to the novel's blandishments by clinging to its "sensational design," the vast and mathematically elegant network of correspondences and antitheses that supports the narrative.[38] Her now canonical appreciation of Stowe (she doesn't discuss the play) helps one recognize that Aiken doesn't merely distill the novel in his adaptation; he also multiplies its modes of interconnection, tries out new imagistic patterns, and strengthens its symmetries. Despite the play's episodic form, Aiken ensures that no scene stands alone. Even characters traveling on storylines that never intersect forge relationships by repeating or meaningfully reversing one another's pattern of behavior. As a result, characters are measured not only against their own previous or potential selves but also against others facing similar situations.

Aiken's first act is typical. It consists of five scenes set in disparate worlds, all united by the single action they have in common: negotiation leading to a decision. Each scene's repetitive shape, growing more insistent as Aiken accelerates his pace, makes its own threat to Eliza's freedom. She seems ever more trapped in a world that in all its arenas, even those far from power, falls into the same habit of deal-making. Yet as Aiken heightens her emotional crisis, he also encourages spectators to step back and consider its formal priorities. Aiken's structural economy—he is ecological in his desire to exhaust all the possibilities of a conceit before moving on—is at odds with his sentimental excess. One can't identify with a character's plight or recoil from another's seemingly incomparable cruelty without also noting the dramatic structure they uphold. Each protagonist, in pursuing his or her ambition, directs us back to Aiken's own strategy. In the process, our style of spectatorship changes. We begin to see comparatively, learning to keep in mind the sequence of scenes even as we respond to separate events, and to defer our conclusions, as well as repeatedly to qualify our emotions, until the process is complete.

The strategy affects more than narrative, and in fact Aiken's richest pleasures derive from his manipulation of purely theatrical materials. Using the novel's narrative sequence, character typology, and even dialogue, Aiken elaborates Stowe's system of interrelated public and private histories, as well as the ideologies they stand for, in three dimensions. He makes visual and aural rhymes that complement Stowe's narrative ones, works out variations on a single gestural or choreographic theme, and manipulates the stage itself as one might turn shapeless nature into a cultivated, symbolically coded landscape. In what seems an implicit acknowledgment of medieval scenography (an inevitable kinship, given that melodrama shares with medieval drama a readiness to subordinate characters and events to moral types and homiletic patterns), Aiken stages many scenes on small playing spaces enclosed by larger, less defined areas, the latter used for observation, travel, and the give-and-take of everyday life. This variation on the cycle-play's tension between the locus and the platea shapes scenes in a tavern, its island-like security set against the menacing darkness outside, and later on a real island, the first of many ice floes carrying Eliza across the Ohio River. It can also be seen in two tableaux formed by Tom and Eva when they retreat from the play's larger landscape to a lakeside idyll and, later, to a cloistered garden. The latter scene is especially significant: here Aiken underscores his compositional methods and our own spectatorial habits by placing St. Clare and Ophelia before the garden hideaway. They stand gazing at Tom and Eva as if at a diorama or play-within-a-play, setting a standard of seriousness for our own attention. Numerous other compositions—Eva and St. Clare on their deathbeds, George Harris standing atop a rock to defy his pursuers, Tom on the auction block—derive their power from a similar understanding of space, each miniature stage-within-a-stage no larger than its occupant (like Eliza's ice floe, which each picture quotes). The compositions ensure the legibility of emotions that in a less austere mise-en-scène would be merely ordinary, overfamiliar, or insufficiently didactic.

The repetitiveness of this visual theme, for all its cumulative power, matters less than its variations. When George stands atop his rock to declare "I am George Harris!," Aiken lets the audience thrill to the moment's romanticism but then questions its promise in the very next scene, when Topsy echoes his words in a different key: "I's nothin' but a nigger."[39] The stage directions underscore the contrast. Whereas George steps out of the shadows and "rises on the rock," Topsy merely "goes up," receding upstage after her own pitiable self-declaration. Later, in the scenes leading to Eva's deathbed vigil, Aiken effects a violent shift in the characters' relation to their landscape. The stage space contracts as act 3 ends, moving from the outdoors to a corridor and then to Eva's bedroom, but her scene's intimate reassurances fritter away when the curtain rises next on the play's most public, anonymous space—a New Orleans street. With equal abruptness, Aiken moves from St. Clare's deathbed, and his scene's own celebration of the heavenly assumption of souls, to the slave auction, a vulgar exchange of bodies.

Without diminishing the formalist pleasure to be had in detecting these symmetries, Aiken establishes a broad cultural context for them. The interlocking narratives and mirror images illustrate his conviction that no private desire is without consequence in the public world—its effects are shown to ripple through communities far from its origin—nor can any act be excused as arbitrary. Aiken's characters assert their individuality only to see it dissolve under the pressure of both a history and a theology that stress the limits and disappointments they have in common. Indeed, the Christian ideal of mutuality that motivates Aiken's integrated dramatic structure (like much else, it is an ideal he adopts from Stowe) confirms the republican ideal of civic interdependence. The same mechanism that Garry Wills identifies as sustaining postrevolutionary American culture — citizens knowing themselves only insofar as they see (and see themselves in) one another — survives in the mirrored imagery of this nineteenth-century dramatic structure.

Uncle Tom's Cabin is an essential coda to any study of mid-nineteenth-century American spectatorship not simply because Aiken assents to this belief. He simultaneously admits — and theatricalizes — his doubt. It would be misleading to suggest that the playwright, in applying and extending the novelist's design, makes it definitive. Far from it. The metatheatrical frame in which he encloses so many scenes — characters watching other characters on stages within stages — implies skepticism, or at least sober curiosity, about the persuasive capabilities of his medium. He seems to be conceding, then probing, the differences between theater and fiction, and more particularly between seeing and reading Stowe's narrative. Does her plot exert the same catechistic, normative power in the less contained, less intimate, and less predictable arena of performance? Looking to answer such a question, Aiken tests the imagistic structures he inherits. He first recognizes that theater's temporality threatens the narrative's cohesion, even as it makes its action more immediate and its imagery more vivid. Since Stowe's "sensational design" has inevitably less durability in performance, it acquires more urgency. It seems less a workmanlike pattern than an uncertain bulwark against chaos and loss.

James Baldwin helps a spectator recognize the desperation of these symmetries. His hostile response to Stowe, "Everybody's Protest Novel" (1949), may no longer be representative of the critical literature, so sensitive have her serious modern-day readers grown to the psychological and political subversiveness of the best sentimental fiction. Yet Aiken's own readers dismiss Baldwin's reasoning at their peril. His principal complaint — that the novel feeds our "passion for categorization" by succumbing to the "terror of the human being, the determination to cut him down to size" — identifies, accurately, the play's overt tension between the longing for clarity and the reality of ambiguity.[40] One may even read Aiken as dramatizing the "passion," "terror," and "determination" as much as the cooler forms they inspire. Theological dialectics that seem impersonal and permanent in Stowe — what Baldwin calls the "brutal criteria" of "black, white, the devil, the next world . . . heaven and the flames" (9, 17) — regain in performance their human scale, sources, and fallibility.

From this perspective, melodramatic decorum itself can be seen as expressing the desire to resist the theater's own changeability, to say nothing of the less controlled reality beyond the stage's magic circle. Such a goal, unreachable in life or theater, charges with unspoken anxiety those scenes in which characters form compositions aspiring to the permanent value of the icon, the reassuring security of the shrine, and the clarity and containment of the diorama. The same longing for stability and invulnerability prompts them to fetishize props, since inanimate objects won't dissolve with the passing minutes of performance, and to obey logical choreography, their artificiality and stiffness standing in deliberate contrast to the plot's volatile passions and suspenseful action. Aiken's interest in the emotional needs behind theater's formal structures doesn't stop at the stage's edge. He ensures that his spectators are aware of their own efforts to control the production's fluid action and visual landscape. As audiences watch a narrative about the slaveowner's surveillance, the fugitive's fear of being seen, the bounty hunter's invasive, pursuing vision, and the ingenue's spiritual insight, they can no longer experience their own seeing as neutral. Attention, before the stage no less than onstage, acts upon rather than merely beholds its object. In this play, it can expose the spectator as much as it sustains the spectacle.

Aiken's self-conscious approach to Stowe's doctrine and design is nowhere more evident than in the settings he chooses for the play's most significant scenes. He favors sites that themselves test the relationships among their inhabitants, or that force characters to negotiate a relationship where none existed. Here, too, emotional contracts long taken for granted are adjusted, contested, or even violated. These redistributions of power go on in all public spaces, of course, and *Uncle Tom's Cabin* abounds in them—the tavern, the New Orleans street, the slave market: sites where individuals once protected by domestic familiarity must remake themselves in more fluid circumstances. But no space is more ambiguous—and more expressive of Aiken's double vision of interdependence and of the watchfulness needed to maintain it— than a border, versions of which stripe his theatrical landscape.

These borders are geographical and cultural, physical and metaphysical. (They are also functional, underscoring or framing stage pictures.) The Ohio River separating slave-owning Kentucky from free Ohio is only the most memorable in a series of dividing lines that include a path between two cliffs separating George Harris from his bloodthirsty pursuers ("whoever comes here has to walk single file" [403]); the corridor where Tom hopes to catch a glimpse of God as he waits outside the dying Eva's bedroom; and the Vermont property line on which Cute, a gold-digging confidence man, sets his sights as he pursues Ophelia. All of these lines (Aiken need not stress) are emblems of the largest border shaping the entire play—that between heaven and earth.

Daniel C. Gerould, in an influential essay on American melodrama, stresses the social significance of what he calls the "topographical" organization of *Uncle Tom's Cabin*.[41] As he shows, the play's itinerary—Kentucky, Ohio,

Pennsylvania, Louisiana, and Vermont — reminds viewers that Aiken's domestic drama plays out on a national scale, the narrative's betrayals, hungers, and efforts toward justice affecting the country more than they do any single character. Yet action that Gerould sees as syncopated (he describes it as a "dynamic spatial progression" [16], anticipatory of cinematic montage) can just as easily be seen as repetitive and futile, the borders remaining strong despite the determination of the characters crossing them. Aiken controls the action on his borders with the same preference for symmetry he shows elsewhere. Act 1 ends with a border breached — Eliza's escape across the river — but act 2 ends with its own border preserved: George successfully fends off the bounty hunters between the cliffs. The same spatial dialogue occurs in the last two acts. St. Clare crosses the border to heaven when he dies in act 4 (just as Eva did at the rhapsodic end of act 3), but the prose-world inversion of this action occurs an act later when Ophelia defends her border from Cute's own longing for paradise. Aiken draws attention to the contrast between surface motion and deeper stasis in more general ways as well. Eliza's and George's frenzy does not trouble the stoic landscape they cover. Tom's own relocation changes nothing but the degree of his humiliation. The visionary buoyancy of Eva is grounded by her incurable illness, itself an image of a societal disease against which she is ultimately just as powerless.

This tension between stasis and change, rendered tangible in the recurring imagery of borders, affirms Aiken's commitment to a rigorous present tense. Although Stowe and Aiken both keep their eye on an idealized future — emancipation, the afterlife, a family's reunification — Aiken alone demands of his audience a close monitoring of the theatrical here-and-now as well, one that, as in all performance, is always falling apart, giving way to new "here's" and new "now's" just when they seem strongest. The change also requires audiences to adjust their critical criteria. Baldwin, more eloquent than most of Stowe's detractors, determines the novel's value by measuring the force of its legacy, its effectiveness as an agent of change in the reader's future. So, too, does Jane Tompkins (this may be all she has in common with Baldwin). She sees a progressive motive in Stowe's aggressive patterning. The play, however, complicates such speculation. This is an *Uncle Tom's Cabin* of this world as much as the next, no sooner airing a character's prophesies and visions than it shakes them off, directing our attention to embodied experience. It can't be only for reasons of economy that Aiken chooses not to dramatize — nor even mentions — the journey to Liberia with which Stowe ends her novel. Throughout the play, Aiken's longing for utopia contends with his equally strong pragmatism.

Aiken's candor about all these contradictory impulses accounts for the pivotal importance of *Uncle Tom's Cabin* in American theater history. More interesting as a transitional work than as the apex of nineteenth-century theater, the play looks forward to the unsteady, fragmented theatrical landscapes of American modernism. It doesn't reach them, but neither does it rest on the certainties of melodrama. Here, too, the border is an apt image for Aiken's dramaturgy. The tension between melodrama and modernism is evident both on a narrative level, as characters respond to the appeals of both domesticity and flight, and on a structural level, as the play asserts visual geometries and character hierarchies only to dismantle them. (This dialogue between fixity and flux anticipates the dichotomies in Baudelaire's own, near contemporaneous definition of modernity: "the ephemeral, the fugitive, the contingent, the half of art whose other half is the eternal and the immutable.")[42] Aiken provides a concise image for his deliberately contradictory ambitions in the plot's most famous sequence. When Eliza steps off the solid Kentucky riverbank—looking back toward the melodramatic bloodhounds and mustachioed villains chasing her—and onto the first of a series of wobbly ice floes speeding her down the river she's trying to cross, the play's own troubled transition between aesthetic principles comes into clearer focus. Like Eliza, it too exists in unsettled space.

Although she never says so, the playwright who will do the most to push American theater into modernism, Gertrude Stein, seems to have been attuned, if only intuitively, to this aspect of *Uncle Tom's Cabin* when she writes that her sole memory of seeing the play as a child in California is of "the blocks of ice moving up and down."[43] Stein's simplest definition of her own theater—"it moves but it also stays" (131)—could also describe Aiken's attempt to maintain two seemingly self-canceling ideas of theatrical time. With only a slight shift in our way of looking at Aiken's play, we can pay more attention to its modernist flux than we do to its melodramatic fixity. As we do so, a temporality that used to be adhesive and sustaining—duration balancing the play's images against one another, progression moving the action steadily forward—now seems disordering. The "here" of *Uncle Tom's Cabin* becomes, from this perspective, a space of eruption and collapse, and its "now" becomes a force that taunts, opposes, or dishevels its characters—time's inexorable progress seeming as brutal, in some cases, as any villain or unjust social condition.

Spectators open to this variability in perception must rethink the conclusions they reach about every aspect of Aiken's seemingly cohesive dramatic structure. The many island-like spaces that anticipate or quote Eliza's ice floe, for instance, can of course be seen less as refuges from than confirmations of the current of activity surrounding them—the storm outside the tavern, the trading around the auction block, and the biological inevitability surrounding the spiritual idylls at the lakeside and Eva's deathbed. All these remind spectators that the more secure areas of the stage, and the worldview they symbolize, in fact represent only brief or finite victories over contingency. Aiken's stage is equidistant from hell's mouth and heaven's gate — a no-man's land. The same tension informs the way characters move. In many scenes, Aiken asks actors to obey a strictly horizontal arrangement: anchoring either end of a table, entering from opposite sides of the stage and staking themselves to strategic positions (as if preparing to play a match), or lining themselves up in a row upon a sofa, all facing forward like the parts of a mechanical toy. Yet Aiken establishes these patterns only to sabotage them. Not the least shocking moment in a play studded with reversals occurs when George lifts a trapdoor in the tavern floor, hoping to escape through the cellar. The surprise has little to do with the plot. Its deepest interest is formal: in a production that has already accustomed us to a strict horizontality, Aiken suddenly discovers depth. Characters who had relied on stable structures — of belief, identity, and domesticity — experience the floor literally falling out from under them.

Aiken's world fractures further at the very moments when characters are subject to scrutiny and their identities assume the burden of symbolic value. Just when they are most anxious to maintain their physical and moral integrity, Aiken's narrative reduces them to separate body parts. Tom experiences the most extreme form of this dissolution, of course, when he endures the invasive examinations from potential buyers at the slave auction. But even in less extreme circumstances, Aiken depicts characters breaking apart, as if the force of their experience — and of Aiken's teleological narrative momentum, made more emphatic by the treacherous linearity of performance — were eroding the integuments keeping the layers of identity together. In the tavern, a disguised George Harris reluctantly takes off a glove to reveal his marked hand, dwindling to the single image of his servitude. With less humiliating consequences, St. Clare experiences a related scattering of self. In his first scene, he presents himself in the diminished form of a daguerreotype, a gift to his no less immobilized convalescent wife, as well as an image of photography's equivocal promise that a truthful version of the self can be detached from its living subject. The burlesque version of this process occurs later in the same scene, as a kleptomaniacal Topsy separates Ophelia from her gloves and the ribbon she wears around her waist. The new mistress literally falls to pieces just when she needs her presence to be most imposing. At the opposite end of the emotional spectrum, the splintering of bodily identity reveals a concentration of spiritual meaning to those who fall under Eva's spell. As she nears death, Eva cuts off a lock of her hair for Tom. It sustains him at Legree's, where he suffers the greatest threat to his own wholeness, and later triggers Legree's memory of his mother's own hair, reviving her reproachful ghost and impelling him to treat Tom more humanely. (These diminishments of individuality have one benefit, which Aiken's covert antisentimentality allows: an unchanging and empirically verifiable thing takes the place of such fluctuating abstractions as goodness, love, nobility, and selflessness.)

All these dismemberings and dislocations of character are the most visceral expression of the uprooting that occurs throughout Aiken's narrative. It is the rare character (the invalid Marie may be the only one) who does not exist in some form of suspension, exile, transience, or, as with Topsy, perpetual motion. For all their dissimilarities, Aiken's characters share this sense of being out of place — Eliza on the run, Tom in Louisiana, Cute's vagabonding, Ophelia's southern discomfort, and Eva's belief that all earthly residence is temporary. Of course, this series of dispersals is meant to make the nineteenth-century cult of domesticity appear irresistible, but as Aiken accelerates the pace of action, home seems an ever more impossible ideal. Here, too, *Uncle Tom's Cabin* occupies the ambivalent middle ground, on the page asserting the value of domestic stability while in performance measuring its limits. The title and Aiken's own one-line description of the play ("A Domestic Drama in Six Acts") take that value for granted. But once a performance gets underway, Aiken, as if in spite of himself, exposes the ease with which his culture romanticizes domestic comfort and naively trusts it to endure. George, Eliza, and Harry Harris may knit themselves together with a determination they wouldn't have felt if they weren't homeless, yet Aiken tempers this reassuring storyline by synchronizing it with the dissolution of St. Clare's own family. His plantation as overseen by Marie is a place of decay and indulgence, as if the immoral foundation on which it was built has leached the vitality from all who live there. And so it has: Eva dies, her mother disappears, St. Clare dies, and Ophelia heads North — a scattering that leaves the house empty except for those never fully welcome in it, the slaves. Other characters must accustom themselves to only temporary residences: the Quaker household that briefly shelters the Harris family, the tavern cellar hiding George, Eva's garden retreat where Tom enjoys momentary peace and autonomy, and of course the ice floe — spaces whose safety derives from Aiken's ability to limit their visibility. They are pushed beneath or to the back of the stage, quickly slide out of view, or shape only a single scene before the play itself moves on. More possibilities than real places, these playing areas recall Tom's cabin. In its only appearance (itself a significant choice), Aiken is careful to keep his characters outside its walls, as if the cabin promises comforts neither it nor the play it names can in fact provide.

The "heavenly mansion," of course, still stands after Aiken's relentless dismantling of earthly, visible versions of home — a result true to Stowe's intent. "It is coming *home* at last!" says a dying St. Clare when Ophelia worries that his fevered mind is wandering (420). Tom echoes the sentiment exactly on his own deathbed. When Shelby rescues Tom from Legree, he says, "I have come to buy you, and take you home" (443). Yet Shelby's, and the play's, aspirations to close the circle on suffering end no further along than where he began and thus collapse with Tom's reply. "Oh, Mas'r George, you're too late. The Lord has bought me, and is going to take me home" (443). Coming at the end of a play that has been swinging between flux and fixity — Stein's "moving" and "staying" — Tom's response does more than mark the demise of the narrative's most oppressive form of stasis, the slavery that reduces bodies to "buys" and imposes repetition on lives stripped of free will. Tom also speaks to an entire sentimental culture that sees home (and being taken home by a rescuing hero) as a prize of unquestioned value and desirability, the only possible destination after such an ordeal (as it was in *The Drunkard* and countless other nineteenth-century morality plays). Shelby's plantation is of course no home for its black residents. Yet *any* image of settling, accepted uncritically, would look false, or at least facile, after six acts of continual deracination. The two-line exchange between Tom and Shelby, masterful in its economy, inverts definitions of purchase, rescue, home, servant, and master. As seen here and elsewhere, Aiken's symmetries don't only have the capacity to confirm his narrative's didactic and normative intentions; they also subvert them.

"You're too late." When heard at their most resonant, Tom's words return us to the uncertainty inherent in theater itself. The line (as much of a touchstone here as the related line "where shall we go next?" is in *A Glance at New York*) encapsulates Aiken's simultaneous obedience to and assault on the here-and-now of performance. The narrative design may take for granted all the characters' seamless interconnectedness, but in Aiken's version they are always out of sync with one another, plagued by a chronic sense of either belatedness or prematurity, or of the irrelevance of the secular clock in a world oriented toward Christian timelessness. Shelby's late arrival is only the most pathetic in a series of scenes depicting the difficulty of mastering time, beginning with the slave catchers just missing Eliza on the banks of the Ohio River and ending with St. Clare waiting too long to free Tom, the master dying before he signs the necessary papers. (He is associated with lateness even before his first entrance: "What can possibly detain St. Clare?" asks Marie. "He should have been here a fortnight ago" [386].) One hears time's nagging presence in other characters' speech, as they begin many scenes at the peak of distress or enthusiasm. Eliza's first word to George, "Ah!" (the important first word of the play as well), ignites an anxiety burning through the entire play, as characters hope that by speaking they can control and even turn back an impersonal current eroding their connection to the landscape, their fellow characters, and themselves. (Although

Aiken's dialogue is quoted almost verbatim from Stowe, it nonetheless sounds starker, more emphatic than it does in the novel, shorn of the descriptive language and leisurely pacing with which fiction cushions speech.)

Still other characters are ahead of time — Eva, sprung by her visionary optimism — or indifferent to its laws. Topsy "does not know what a year is, [nor] even . . . her own age" (392). Ophelia's all-purpose denunciation of her charge's irresponsibility, and that of anyone else she dislikes, is in fact unwittingly perceptive: "shiftless" denotes precisely the majority's experience of time. They are equally incapable of progress and tranquility, caught in a circular pattern that drains the purpose from all activity. The character with the most intimate, productive relation to time is the least powerful. When Tom says "*I can die!*" (442), he turns inside out his apparent passivity, revealing the force latent in submission. Alienating himself from the temporal world, he masters it.

Or does he? Tom's triumph seems glorious and definitive in the play's closing tableau, a dazzling picture of the afterlife revealed when painted clouds open on a triangle of virtuous souls, Tom and St. Clare at its base gazing up admiringly at Eva at its apex. After a production troubled by contingency from its first word, the scene promises relief. It leaves behind the buckling, riven ground as its characters rise toward heaven. It scorns time in the flush of immortality. Even the very act of their ascension seems indifferent to the demands of progress. The characters don't rise so much as fill the space. A huge dove, Eva's chariot, is in fact fixed in position, its wings extended but unmoving — a renunciation of the temporal pressures of performance in favor of the timeless certainties of visual art. (If early photographs are representative, the scene's artificiality was unapologetic: this "heavenly mansion" is unavoidably terrestrial.)

Yet more significant is the true final image of the play, what Aiken's last stage direction describes as a "slow curtain." It is necessarily an integral part of a production this self-conscious about time's effect on vision. As the curtain descends, closing us off from both visionary and visible realms, our own time and space reassert themselves. "The bright eternal doors have closed after thee," St. Clare had said two acts earlier upon Eva's death. "Oh! Woe for them who watched thy entrance into heaven, when they shall wake and find only the cold gray sky of daily life" (412). He could be speaking of ourselves. Lasting transcendence is no more available at the end of *Uncle Tom's Cabin*. The audience watches the closing of the stage's curtain — its own "eternal doors" — on "gorgeous clouds tinted with sunlight" (as the final tableau's stage direction describes it) and is left facing its own "cold gray sky of daily life," all the earthbound doubts and contingencies Aiken's characters had fled. The experience returns mid-nineteenth-century spectators, in a less sanguine mood, to what Henry James had said about the "torment of the curtain" in *A Small Boy and Others*. Shifting and shiftless themselves, spectators ruled by the curtain's schedule have come full circle, from emulating the pleasurable mood of expectation in which James dreamed about the stage's illusions to, now, acknowledging plain fact. What had been a screen for his projected fantasy is, here, a mirror of a world one never really left. Spectators will be asked to look at that world without flinching in the decades ahead, as melodrama frays even more severely than it does in *Uncle Tom's Cabin*, exposing sights that owe their allure and sensationalism to their deliberate banality.

2

Staging the Civil War

Present fears / Are less than horrible imaginings.

— *William Shakespeare*, Macbeth

In "Years of the Modern," published just after the Civil War's last battle flared and died, Walt Whitman turns to the theater for an image of the country's mood of mournful anticipation. The poem also has something to teach those who take its metaphor literally. Both the nation and the nation's theater, Whitman recognizes, have exhausted traditional structures and mythologies without discovering replacements appropriate to the disorienting new times. His opening lines are animated by his typical oracular exuberance, as he envisions a post-1865 America of "august dramas" and "force advancing with irresistible power on the world's stage."[1] But after scripting "tremendous entrances and exits, new combinations, the solidarity of races"—all part of a conventional heroic drama about a godlike protagonist whose "daring foot is on land and sea everywhere . . . / With the steamship, the electric telegraph, the newspaper"—Whitman seems unable to sustain the mood and allows his drama to slide into a minor key. Modernity is as much a source of anxiety as it is of hope, he concedes, almost in spite of himself. The echo of every rallying cry is a nervous question: "Have the old forces, the old wars, played their parts?" he asks. "Are the acts suitable to them closed?" The unknowability of a future full of "whispers," "phantoms," and inchoate "shapes" causes a fever as "strange" as it is "ccstatic," impeding the otherwise confident progress toward deliverance. By Whitman's final lines, a gothic menace has enveloped his symbolic stage. "The perform'd America and Europe grow dim, retiring in shadow behind me, / The unperform'd, more gigantic than ever, advance, advance upon me." One can choose to hear such lines as optimistic — several commentators have — but a deeper, darker resonance emerges if one listens for the undertone of fear.[2]

During these same years, in the war sketches that would later be published in *Specimen Days* (1882), Whitman's uncertainty was already hardening into skepticism. This least manipulative of literary responses to the Civil War (even its title recommends scientific restraint) begins on an uncharacteristically melodramatic note. "Secession slavery," he writes, "the arch-enemy person-ified."[3] Such theatrics are soon rendered irrelevant by Whitman's scrupulous reporting, but the very obsessiveness with which he accumulates details about the battlefields and hospitals, and the vigor with which he underscores the dailiness of suffering, suggest how strong remains the temptation to romanti-cize the war. One of the secondary fascinations of *Specimen Days*, in fact, is this successful struggle in Whitman to unlearn the narrative habits that his culture and even his own earlier self expect of him. The work's famous pro-nouncement — "the real war will never get in the books" (778) — is qualified, if never contradicted, by his own efforts to find a narrative rhythm flexible enough to pause over incidents other writers would deem insufficiently dra-matic. For despite the automatic pathos of Whitman's subject, *Specimen Days* drains emotion from its incidents to reveal a starker, colder image of pain. The most expressive characters are silent, awkward, and solitary. The most alarm-ing scenes are frozen, their action resisting the suspense-driven structure of typical war stories. At climactic moments in this narrative — the start of a great battle or the end of an anonymous soldier's life — Whitman's camera-eye zooms in to the seemingly neutral detail just off center from the protagonist's ordeal.

In Fredericksburg, for instance, a soldier whose arm has just been ampu-tated is seen "munching away at a cracker" with his remaining hand, seem-ingly indifferent to his loss. Another soldier lies in the dirt near Atlanta, dying from a head injury, but Whitman looks away from the shattered skull to where the man's heel had been "going night and day" for three days, digging a hole "big enough to put in a couple of ordinary knapsacks" (745). True to his aversion to histrionics, Whitman puts his first mention of Lincoln's assassination in parentheses and then quickly shifts focus to those far from the tragic scene. When Whitman's family hears of the murder, he writes, they try to maintain routine — "Mother prepared breakfast . . . as usual" — but instead of eating, they sit all day in silence, passing newspaper pages back and forth (711–12). The family's recourse to quotidian ritual and objective reportage when they are most vulnerable to disabling emotion is typical of Whitman's approach throughout *Specimen Days*. "Notice," he writes at the beginning of yet another sketch, the gently didactic command implicit in all these passages. Here, as he directs attention away from a wounded midwestern lieutenant and toward the water pail filling with blood at his bedside, Whitman also asks his readers, and himself, to change their methods of interpretation. "That tells the story," he writes, framing his still life of the water pail but also cutting off any indulgent lingering over the suffering it signifies. "It is useless to expend emotions," he concludes (735–36). From this most self-absorbed of poets comes the startling admission that what he feels doesn't matter.

To his contemporaries in the theater, Whitman's example must have been chastening. The typical nineteenth-century performance, with its ample space for emotional display inevitably stamped by the force of an actor's personality, sustains itself only as long as its spectators feel their own sympathies burning along with those of the characters. Whitman's rejection of the sentimentalism with which most writers and readers forge that kinship puts a strong challenge to dramatists and spectators. Even in those plays and playhouses that subvert as many opportunities for escapism as they offer — the burlesques of John Brougham, George L. Fox, and others — no nineteenth-century dramatist before or after the war makes this complete an admission of the inadequacy of his or her own materials.

It's not just emotion that is "useless." When it comes to capturing this opaque, unprecedented reality, language itself no longer seems able to compel awareness, much less understanding, of what Whitman has seen. It is as if the very vocabulary of grief, horror, or mere compassion has lost its elasticity from overuse. "Reader, did you ever try to realize what *starvation* actually is?" Whitman asks (765), interrupting a description of the Andersonville Prison to check whether his prose is having any effect and, fearing it isn't, squeezing the key word itself, as if hoping to get from it some last untapped reserve of meaning. Not for this Whitman the confident flow of language so nourishing to his poems. When the Homeric catalogues appear here, they convey only the cataloguer's weariness, his acknowledgement that no mere naming of a soldier, battle, or scorched landscape can account for the devastation, much less make us see it in our mind's eye. Often, the passionless, disembodied language of accounting takes the place of description, checking the poet's theatricalizing habits and frustrating a reader's voyeuristic appetites. In place of full-fledged characters are "bed 37," "bed 6," "bed 24," or, slightly more personalized, "bed 52, ward I . . . company B, 7th Pennsylvania" (750, 725). In place of action, boatloads of wounded arrive at 7:30 p.m.; it rains at 8:00; an enemy attack lasts until 3:00 in the morning. Where he elsewhere might have itemized carefully chosen gifts for the sick, here he doles out 25, 30, or 50 cents. When one might expect narrative climaxes, now there is only the news that "5,000 drown'd," 15,000 were "inhumed by strangers," and 25,000 were "never buried at all" (776). Eventually, Whitman gives up on even this half-accurate tabulating in favor of exhausted generalization: "the dead, the dead, the dead — *our* dead — or South or North, ours all, (all, all, all, finally dear to me)" (777).[4]

Whitman's threnody derives only part of its poignancy from the magnitude and commonality of loss. More comes from the mourner's confusion before the task of memorializing it — the task of representation. Language grinds in circles throughout these passages, milling to dust a subject it cannot master. When silence does come in *Specimen Days,* as it occasionally does, it offers both relief and reproach. The peacefulness lasts only until the reader realizes that, in this inverted world, silence marks the spot where an unconfronted drama is raging beneath the surface. Or just offstage: The "painful absence of demonstration" among the soldiers is ringed by the "unending, universal, mourning wail" of the spouses, parents, and orphans we never see (779). Whitman rarely even mentions them in *Specimen Days,* by their absence confirming that pathos is most convincing in its suppression.

Here, by the grace with which Whitman combines an indictment and a model of expression in a single absent image, *Specimen Days* deepens its relevance to readers of Civil War drama. Those contending with the book's challenges before rewarding themselves with the far smoother pleasures of the contemporaneous theater develop more than skepticism about emotive or effortlessly lyrical responses to the war. They also receive ear- and eye-training that enables them to recognize the revealing structural tensions in any writing about the subject — a prerequisite to reseeing plays that otherwise might beguile them with stirring narratives and characters. Such reseeing arguably defuses, if not distorts, the plays' more spectacular effects — a consequence justified only by the expansion of one's field of view. Students of *Specimen Days* master principles of a dramaturgy that relies for its own subtler but sharper effects on silence, impassivity, deflected passion, tonal instability, and often perverse contradictions between action and sentiment.

The reader following Whitman as he draws close to the least inflected elements in his tableaux of dying soldiers, for instance, learns also to veer from a

play's narrative center (where, typically, the action confirms a war-torn society's ability to heal all wounds and absorb all dissension) and instead to scan
the background and margins of the plot, where other characters, following
other patterns, may undo these conclusions. Larger compositional tensions
available to our peripheral vision are no less revelatory—a value Whitman
implicitly recognizes as, throughout *Specimen Days,* he dilates his attention to
admit scenes attractive precisely for their inappropriateness to the tragedy his
readers may think they are reading. Writing about the Washington Patent
Office, where the wounded lie about in a makeshift infirmary, he observes that
glass cases still display the inventions of a more optimistic, idealistic era, its
promise of a better future now a freakish artifact. On a nearby street, a hale
and hearty cavalry regiment marches up one side while down the other comes
a line of ambulances. A checkers game played by joking soldiers is no less
diverting for occurring in an otherwise grim hospital. Hardest to reconcile,
Whitman implies, are the conflicting images in the natural landscape, the
brutally exposed days seemingly unacknowledged by the "draperied," merely
"melancholy" nights (723). Pastoral charms remain seductive, somehow, despite the continuous insult. "The odor of blood mix[es] with"—but, it is
important to note, does not overwhelm—"the fresh scent of the night, the
grass, the trees" (723). Nature adjusts the writer's temperament as well, showing the temporariness of a mood that, inside a hospital, is so intense as to exclude all others. In all these passages, Whitman welcomes distraction, knowing that his understanding of the war deepens as his mind and eye wanders.
(He often mentions his actual wandering, too.) If the word "Notice" teaches
an attitude of careful scrutiny when we might otherwise mythologize suffering, the Whitman of these sentences resorts to a strategy signified by another
word—it appears later in the same passage—to prevent us from lingering too
long or prematurely reaching conclusions: "Meantime."

There are other such directional signs planted throughout his text—"meanwhile," "opposite," "neighboring," "near here," "off in a side place"—all of
which eject us from a scene just when we might become enthralled and accustom us to a mode of reading (and, by extension, seeing) conditioned by
permanent instability. For Whitman, enchantment marks the end of engaged or
even usefully compassionate thinking. That such a process seems an expository
version of theatrical alienation is a valuable confusion of genres. Theater-
minded readers who make these pivots of attention, resisting the urge to reconcile unrhymed juxtapositions of imagery, outgrow their dependence on narrative in general—a milestone that prepares them to see a play's figures, gestures,
and even language stripped of their often softening, trivializing contexts. (By
reading against a familiar plot, or at least apart from it, one can recover and do

justice to the full disarming force of its imagery.) Just as Whitman can't stamp his observations with a single emotion, his readers get nowhere in trying to impose a dramatically satisfying arc on their presentation. The literally fractured layout of Whitman's typical page, a sequence of separately titled entries, is an image of his prismatic sensibility. Whitman's war, as he dramatizes it, obeys no law of momentum; its acts don't build, peak, and subside; its lessons don't gather into a systematic course for future study. Instead, as the sketches refuse all unity and probability — save the unity of collective sacrifice and the probability of death — readers learn a more rigorous way to see, think about, and remember the war. They reengage with it at the start of each new entry, looking with fresh shock and disbelief even at scenes well known from other writers' narratives, and postpone indefinitely the moment when scattered experiences reveal a pattern capable of accommodating all of Whitman's dramatis personae. Those figures, along with their specimen days, are kept purposefully remote from the curatorial intelligence that would establish a definitive logic of display and interpretation.

The reader's productive ignorance of such ultimate meanings matches that of the writer himself, and it is for his candor about such helplessness that *Specimen Days* is, finally, an indispensable prefatory text to postbellum American drama. Every time Whitman lets stand dissonance in his description, or stresses the inconsistencies that test the integrity of a tableau, he concedes the futility of imposing the logic of craft — fictional, historical, or melodramatic — upon a resistant past. The war goes on and on in these pages, but in Whitman's telling such repetitiveness doesn't dull the senses. Instead, he (and we) sharpen our skepticism of the teleologies that most writers who engage history have taught us to expect. Conclusiveness of any sort seems not just remote but phony: an unearned consolation. It's more than merely an irresistible irony that Whitman refuses to satisfy the need for such comfort in a book recording the comforts he offers his soldier-patients. As the writer mirrors his subject, he pulls focus yet again in a work continually asserting new centers, a shift that, as before, only enhances the emotional authority of scenes the writer's attention seems to flee. Readers still hungering for traditional emotional involvement even after the many deflections of sentiment in *Specimen Days* need only imagine the performance of Whitman himself. In the work's torn unities and vertiginous tonal shifts, the consciously raw surfaces of its sentences, and the fragility of its overall structure, Whitman betrays the strain of confronting a subject so vast it won't submit even to an imagination used to containing multitudes.

The severity of this strain leaves his style marked by trial and error, as this "wound-dresser" seeks lyrical forms with which to treat extremities of experience unseen and unfelt before the war, and withstands a confusion unsedated by familiar techniques of explanation. To the reader seeing Whitman-the-writer alongside Whitman-the-nurse, even the many dispassionate passages in *Specimen Days* seem to enjoy only a temporary victory over disabling feeling. They cannot assert a norm before Whitman doubts their poise: omniscience is just as suspect as emotionalism. In one of his few points of contact with the era's playwrights, he joins them in wondering whether close-cropped analysis or panoramic vision will best capture and render visible to others a fast-degrading society. (Should he look at specimen days or democratic vistas?)

Perhaps neither approach will enable him to do so. Seeking greater authenticity, Whitman sometimes writes from a position of undefended intimacy with his subject, his senses excruciatingly responsive to what they encounter, as if he filtered every sound and sight through a membrane so delicate that the slightest irregularity disturbs even his syntax. Whitman's own word for this style is "convulsiveness" (775). The description suggests not only how completely he internalizes the spasmodic rhythm of the war and its effect on the surrounding society — something he acknowledges — but also how his very body seems to mimic the seizures and sudden desperation of the wounded as he takes pen to paper. (It is a style we will see reach theatrical fruition in a late Civil War play, *Secret Service*.) The thoroughness with which Whitman surrenders to this self-contradictory ordeal over style, preserving it for us to experience ourselves as we move across the choppy surfaces of his text, results in an antimelodrama notable for more than its unsentimentality. Whitman's uncertainty so pervades the text that his protagonists won't settle into two opposing camps. Their morality muddies when one seeks from them unequivocal allegiance to good or evil. Their denouement, depriving us of catharsis, ensures that our attention outlasts even Whitman's own.

As a standard by which to measure the achievements and failings of the contemporaneous drama about the Civil War, *Specimen Days* is unforgiving but not unique. The many playwrights who fell short of Whitman's lucidity or who never aspired to his level of radical, controlled compassion would look smaller still alongside other writers who, for all their differences, share a bracing antitheatricality. Students of Civil War drama should consult them not simply to be humbled — it takes nothing to say that the era's best prose and poetry are more sophisticated than the era's best drama — but to learn how, when it comes to this subject, an author's moral and aesthetic honesty depends in large part on how consistently he or she resists the conventions of display inherent in the theater. There are qualities more dangerous than sentimentality. The nineteenth-century theater's taste for declarative, unequivocal thought; its readiness to enclose disorderly events in explanatory frames; its habit of nominating individuals to represent ideals or embody cultural moments; its sheer will to expressiveness itself: the upholder of all these articles of theatrical faith risks a naiveté and presumptuousness that the self-aware Civil War writer guards against.

Stephen Crane identifies, with typical restraint, the theatricality he and many of his peers reject in an otherwise unremarkable sentence from *The Red Badge of Courage* (1895). "The officers, at their intervals, rearward, neglected to stand in picturesque attitudes."[5] Crane indulges his readers' spectatorial habits only to correct them: he moves our eye slowly down the line, building expectation with every comma, until, at the end, he shows us nothing. So, too, Ulysses S. Grant, who disappoints those expecting a melodramatic finale to his *Personal Memoirs* (1885) when he famously says of his surrendering antagonist, "What General Lee's feelings were I do not know."[6] (No actor, the Confederate general shows only an "impassible" face.) Grant prefers to study the phenomena that keep their meaning on the surface. The *Memoirs* are so dense with battle detail that a reader cannot easily pull back from the narrative to locate high points, narrative cruxes, definitive triumphs — the arc of drama — much less hypothetical psychology and remote ideals. (Grant looks at the trees because he sees through the romance of forests.) It is a discipline that the war's two most uncompromising writers, Ambrose Bierce and Herman Melville, perfect in their own antitheatrical descriptions. No playwright tempted to ennoble suffering would dare do so if he or she paused over Bierce's astringent depiction of soldiers "dead upon the field of honor, yes; but the field of honor was so very wet! It makes a difference."[7] And so it does, a difference tabulated definitively — for all the war's writers and readers — in *Battle-Pieces* (1866), where Melville discredits Civil War imagery dependent on emotion ("No passion," he writes of the ironclad *Monitor,* "all went by on crank, / Pivot, and screw"), nostalgia ("Does the elm wood / Recall the haggard beards of blood?"), and finally, directly, the habits of performance, if not theater, itself ("War shall yet be, and to the end; / But war-paint shows the streaks of weather").[8]

To audiences turning next to drama, all these passages — blunt, decisive, pruning back a reader's imagination in order to stimulate it — oppose an inventory of sins few Civil War playwrights are strong enough to resist. But to dismiss the period's drama as mere hackwork would be to miss a chance to learn something about the American playwright's growing pains on the road to modernism. The lesson forces an important adjustment to master narratives of American theater history. The much-heralded shift with Eugene O'Neill away from mechanical plotting and superficial characterization has tended to minimize the importance of the theatrically viable pressure building up in the works of his predecessors, plays in which writers voice their growing self-consciousness about form, genre, and the act of writing itself. Notwithstanding their other evasions, a number of romances, melodramas, and genial comedies of reconciliation from 1865 to 1900 do raise Whitman's question of how to get the real war into books. They do so never more than fleetingly and in most cases (one must assume) only unwittingly. The old familiar styles are still in evidence, glamorizing sectional rivalries and softening agony into mere heartache, but not every chord assimilates to the dominant harmony. The occasional dissonance suggests a chronic strain—one felt by the playwrights themselves, skeptical of the conventions they help ratify even though they lack the critical perspective to say so, much less the new ideas necessary for reform. The result is a strange, unstable genre. Indeed, Civil War drama lacks the cohesiveness essential to any genre, undone by an anxiety over style that makes its soldier-protagonists' nobility and their families' optimism seem self-conscious, in some plays even quoted—a sentimentality willed rather than spontaneous (as it would have been in earlier plays) and thus unreliable even at its most rousing.

The temporal distance dividing most of these playwrights from their subject is one cause of this instability. They are not close enough to the war to write about it with any immediacy, even if they could or wanted to—the vogue for Civil War plays, like that for Civil War novels, didn't begin until the 1880s—but neither are they far enough away to be analytical, much less self-critical. (One of the only Civil War plays produced during the war itself, a crude piece of Confederate agit-prop by James D. McCabe called *The Guerillas; or, The War in Virginia* [1862], deserves reading if only for its unsparingly graphic depiction of sectional violence and audacious portrait of its motivating racism. No later, more refined Civil War play is as frank about the war's causes and effects.)[9] Most playwrights participate as vigorously as any selectively forgetful veteran in the campaign for reconciliation between the sections. David W. Blight's *Race and Reunion: The Civil War in American Memory* (2001), while it doesn't discuss drama, eloquently describes the literary, political, and popular culture of calculated moral compromise that made such drama inevitable. "The tragedy of Reconstruction," he writes, "is rooted in this American paradox: the imperative of healing and the imperative of justice could not, ultimately, cohabit the same house. The one was the prisoner of memory, the other a creature of law." As a result, "Civil War memory fell into a drugged state, as though sent to an idyllic foreign land from which it has never fully found the way home."[10]

In keeping with the wishful thinking of this culture, the era's best-known plays begin in turmoil but always end happily, with once-frozen opponents melting together from rekindled compassion. The process seems simple because of its artificially small scale. Vast cultural differences are invariably personalized, shrunk to the dimensions of romantic or domestic drama so as to be manageable. Lines from Clyde Fitch's *Barbara Frietchie, the Frederick Girl* (1899) encapsulate a typical plot. "Yes," breathes the southern heroine to her northern lover, "in 1776 [North and South] were betrothed. This war's a lovers' quarrel; after it they'll *wed* for good, like you and I today."[11] William Dean Howells's famous words of sympathy to Edith Wharton — "What the American public always wants is a tragedy with a happy ending" — describe exactly the cultural expectations that discourage those writers who could advance radical, even blasphemous ideas of theatrical form from ever writing a play.[12]

Of those who do write plays in these years, the most subversive (necessarily a relative term) signal their understanding of Howells's mordant paradox by the ease with which they combine seemingly antithetical tones and demeanors. Beneath their plays' surface charm, they fall in and out of different keys in quick, sometimes manic succession: pathetic one moment, farcical the next, witty in one speech, tendentious in the next. They are unable to resist conventions of narrative suspense and romantic intrigue, but are also unwilling to employ them without making us notice that we're being manipulated. There is every reason to expect that by testing the nature of theatrical enchantment these playwrights will break it. The fact that they don't — that, in fact, they create a form of theater unlike anything in the imaginative literature about the war — is as much their subject as any cross-sectional battle, romance, or betrayal. Seducing us with the trappings of melodrama, these writers honor their tradition even as they lead us past its schedule of sensation and sentiment toward the very opposite of escapism — a commentary on nostalgia's undertow, romanticism's narcosis.

Of course they are no less resistant to realism. Working among writers beginning to agitate for greater imaginative credibility in other genres (a desire that, when it reaches the theater, culminates with James A. Herne's manifesto calling for "Art for Truth's Sake in the Drama" [1897]), Civil War dramatists establish just enough surface authenticity to render scenes familiar, but not so much that a character's primal, outsized emotions or anomalous impulses can't find room for expression. (The extremity of war can make the cartoonish seem truer than the realistic.) Their theater also invites spectators to acknowledge that even the most detailed rendering of experience can fail to account for behavior whose deepest sources resist *any* mode of representation. Bierce's complaint about the typical realist's slavish attention to "probability" is pertinent. "All men and women . . . act from impenetrable motives and in a way that is consonant with nothing in their lives, characters, and conditions. . . . Nothing is so improbable as what is true."[13] To audiences hoping for a convincing theatricalization of the Civil War, the lesson is even sharper. Those playwrights approaching the war realistically raise unrealistic expectations when they preach the gospel of objectivity, leading the faithful to think they can reach the bottommost truth of what is in fact a labyrinthine, persistently self-clouding subject. Looking at the war, or looking at it again in memory, however graphically, isn't enough to understand it — or so these writers imply at those frequent moments when their plots recede and the trial-and-error process of fitting form to content becomes its own drama. In these passages, they give up even the pretense of dramatizing what happened during the war and instead address how the war's lessons are taught, learned, and used — something a Reconstruction- or post-Reconstruction-era audience can identify with more than with this or that battle.

Indeed, these plays are best read as studies of their audience. Each play's war narrative, in this view, becomes the background for a more complicated drama among the war's onstage witnesses, interpreters, mythologizers, and mere bystanders — all surrogates for ourselves — as they and we persist in habits of thinking and seeing that grow harder to justify in the face of experience. The playwrights themselves recognize that they are just as guilty. Their best scenes exploit the tension between an idealizing theater culture, wanting the war to look picturesque and meaningful, and their own awakened spirit of inquiry. One can make the case without too much special pleading that when this tension tips, invariably, in the culture's favor, the memory of the alternative's allure remains to qualify our enjoyment. It's not without leaving evidence of the compromises they've made, in other words, that some of these playwrights retreat from life to art, from truer unpredictability to consoling convention. By failing to streamline their subject just as they fail to confront it honestly, they produce a vivid portrait of the ambivalence complicating every effort to get the real war on the stage.

An image of that equivocating artist hovers over William Gillette's *Held by the Enemy* (1886) and, by implication, over all plays about the war. A secondary character, a zealous newspaper illustrator named Tom Beene, patrols the margins of every battlefield and comes late to every advance, hoping to find marketable material without endangering himself by actually having to experience the war. Usually, he saves time and avoids risk altogether by sketching dramatic tableaux in advance, publishing them when he hears that a similar event has in fact occurred. Real life does resist his attempt to romanticize it. A protective southern aunt, sensing the aggression and proprietary motives behind any act of imagination, stands between Beene and her niece, saying to her, "I don't wish to have you illustrated!"[14] In another scene, an impatient colonel disabuses Beene of the idea that a particular battle involved a picturesquely burning mill, horses with their nostrils flaring swept down the river, or a driving rain ("Rot!" "Nothing swept down!" "Beautiful day!" [60–61]), leaving the illustrator crestfallen only for as long as it takes him to draw another, less egregiously dishonest picture. Gillette's satire targets any number of the era's real-life journalists — all those who overdramatize the story because they are underinformed about its particulars — but it is Gillette himself who potentially stands most embarrassed. Melodramatists are no less tempted to substitute ready-made versions of behavior for the less shapely facts of observed experience (a point driven home to those seeing Gillette himself play Beene in the premiere production). By exposing his illustrator as a fraud, Gillette pulls his own spectators back from the brink, past which they could only surrender to his art. The romance and intrigue of his main plot are no less stirring for being understood as manufactured. If anything, Gillette's critical distance from his action enables us to recognize how deeply we need the fantasy — one way an end-of-century melodramatist can answer the challenge put by the then-emergent realists and still honor his own tradition.

It is another anomaly in *Held by the Enemy,* however, that puts more pressure on the theater's complacencies. A loyal slave character, Rufus, is old, fragile, and nearly blind, breathing too hard to say much after he enters, groping the air when he exits. Often, he stands still, focusing on nothing, his face blank even when he is summoned. After one such petit-mal episode, he doesn't so much recover as merely recede into an indistinct, enveloping darkness. Although it is hardly surprising that Gillette's slaves are relegated to the margin in this as in all Civil War dramas, Rufus, in his few startling appearances and disappearances, manages to reach beyond its confines to make an eloquent display of desolation. He challenges more than the theatrical convention that would have him be obsequious or, at best, colorful. Disquieting in his silence and unsettling in his stillness, he troubles the entire play as well as the culture whose expectations the play tries to satisfy. The certainties of prewar life — and theater — crumble as he crumbles. (One can't help thinking of another emblem of passing theatrical and social convention, Chekhov's Firs.) Rufus also, more pointedly, reproaches postwar audiences for failing to reckon with him as they respond to this otherwise consoling account of the war. When he is onstage, a yawning space opens up in Gillette's otherwise tightly structured production. The witty banter falters; romantic narratives go cold; the suspense sags — and the real war gets into the books. Not as comprehensive reportage or cogent analysis: no extant drama of the period achieves that. The confusion in Rufus's sightless eyes is the visible sign of a trauma deeper than any caused by violence, out of reach to the softening light of sentimentality, unmastered and unmasterable, and lasting longer than a mere war.

The other dramatists who write under the sign of Rufus's perplexity reflect it in their own styles. Shaken by the excesses, distortions, and collapsing assumptions of a time out of joint, they try to keep their characters consistent and their narratives seamless, even as they recognize that prewar ideals are no longer reliable. In such an unsupported world, characters who have lost faith in a shared code of conduct find it impossible to gauge anyone's sincerity. They expose falsehood without believing that something more authentic lies underneath. Those who no longer respond to the restraining force of decorum submit to instinct and atavistic appetite. One reads or sees all these plays expecting a valedictory tone — the tone one wants from the postwar era as a whole, defining itself against what it has outgrown, survived, or sacrificed. These playwrights, however, distrust such knowingness as thoroughly as they see through outmoded illusions. Instead, they remain standing at the place where the past pulled away from the present, roused from their complacency but as yet unable, or unwilling, to settle back into a new emotional and intellectual security.

Such is the very image that opens Augustin Daly's *Under the Gaslight*, first produced two years after the war ended. "Good night," calls out the hostess of a glittering dinner party, standing with her back to us at the threshold of her front door, snow and darkness visible in the background. "Now they're gone," she adds as she turns back into the room, facing us for the first time, "and the holiday's gone with them."[15] Before a spectator can assign too much symbolism to the scene, Daly deliberately undercuts it. The character who seems to be bidding farewell to a whole holiday era, sobered as she might be by the war, refuses to find any greater seriousness or authenticity in the experience of loss. "I hate mourning," she says, chafing at having to remember her mother's death, "though it does become me" (137).

Her superficiality introduces a theme consciously developed throughout *Under the Gaslight*. The value of mourning, and of memory in general, isn't the only sacred principle that Daly strategically profanes. His plot — a complicated yet slight story about lost parents, broken engagements, and revoked status — exists to reveal the more compelling picture of a society uprooted from all ethical and moral foundations, scornful of the old sentimental values without yet subscribing to any new, compensatory faith. (Here, too, one hears the voice of Whitman's "Years of the Modern.") Some of Daly's targets are familiar. High society is exposed as hypocritical, promoting ideals of rectitude and orderliness that it can't fulfill itself. Stranger malformations occur at the other end of the social spectrum, where principles that, in another kind of play, would stand unquestioned instead lose credibility with alarming speed. Characters parrot "family values" for devious ends; their victims seek justice from a corrupt, derisive court. In a world gone this awry, inflexible virtue can be just as destructive as vice. A minor character, a signalman, has a sense of propriety so hypertrophied that he locks the heroine in a shed as she waits for a train, hoping to protect her from molestation—a weirder, more surprising act than the sensational rescue from the train tracks that follows. (To a contemporary viewer, the latter event also upsets expectations: in this, the first instance of what would become a trusted melodramatic cliché, it is the woman who rescues the man tied to the tracks.) One looks, finally, to that heroine herself for unequivocal endorsement of an ideal, any ideal—to be an embodiment of balance and transparency capable of offsetting the myriad dissolutions and inversions all around her. Yet she is the least supported by tradition. "The past has forgotten me," she says, confused by her murky biological and cultural parentage. "I know not who I am" (154, 159).

Neither, one can't help thinking, does the postwar American theater. The ignorance, however, is valuable—a theatrical opportunity. Daly, for his part, seizes it by creating variations on this blankness throughout *Under the Gaslight:* aural, visual, and narrative lacunae in the play's structure that, when taken together, disturb a viewer far more effectively than anything a character says or does. These varieties of erasure are, in fact, tangential to the plot— exactly Daly's point (one wants to think), for like craters in the track of our spectatorship, they interrupt the sedating flow of imagery. Eventually, a newly alert spectator begins to see nothing so clearly as the unseeable. In one scene, the stage grows dark as if to comment ironically on the heroine's sunny yet formulaic rhapsody on love and duty. Her fiancé, for his part, is indelibly identified with his desertion from the army when the Civil War began, information that can be taken not simply as proof of his weakness (Daniel C. Gerould's reading) but as a rare truthful admission of fear in a world of pretense.[16] It is also a form of absence that qualifies one made visible by another character, a veteran who lost an arm in battle. Other voids encountered by those who never came near the war are equally haunting. When the surviving aristocrats go to Delmonico's, the tony restaurant, they complain that "the rooms are almost empty" (145) and that they haven't enough men for a quadrille. (The women dance with one another instead.) It is one final absence that makes unignorable the uneasiness of all theater produced in the wake of the war, even when Daly tries his hardest to keep up the melodrama: in a last act that runs only four pages in one edition, Daly hastily wraps up numerous plot lines, omitting the explanations that would make credible the heroine's vision of "the long sought sunlight of our lives" (181). Truer are the words spoken just before this curtain line. "It is night! It is night always for me," says the army deserter, before sinking into definitive silence, one that withholds assent from what would otherwise seem to be Daly's own optimistic view. In this, as in all the play's gaps, Daly succeeds in summoning the war by *not* staging it, pointing instead to arenas populated only with characters doing nothing but withstanding the war's aftershocks.

One need look no further for an illustration of Whitman's belief that "the old wars [have] played their parts" and "the acts suitable to them [have] closed." After Daly calls attention to the literal emptiness underneath his form's excesses, it becomes harder to imagine Civil War playwrights sounding sincere about such abstractions as valor, self-sacrifice, and fidelity. Many continue to do so, of course. Those still readable, however, turn instead to the only form capable of exploiting, rather than suffering from, the fluidity of a culture in transition. Satire, in its brutalizing charms, keeps the postwar culture from erecting mythologies (including theater mythologies) no more authentic than those the war demolished. Yet these satires lack the genre's typical confidence and aloofness. They pursue a moving target—a society unsure about its articles of faith and code of manners, so battered by recent trauma that no truths are self-evident—and move unpredictably themselves. They disregard plausibility in narrative and an established sense of scale in character psychology. They upset more social structures than they create. They push comedy into slapstick and pathos into opera buffa.

Some of the most effective of these playwrights claim not to be satirical at all. Writing of his *Mulligan Guard Ball* (1879), the best known in a popular series of comic musicals intended to pay tribute to the optimism, vigor, and multifariousness of New York's immigrant communities, Edward Harrigan insists that he set out to take "a series of photographs of life to-day in the Empire City" and to be "truthful to the laws which govern society"[17]—an aim that, naturally, brought him to the attention of William Dean Howells, who called him "part of the great tendency toward the faithful representation of life which is now animating fiction."[18] Yet to audiences unable to shake off their Civil War inheritance so easily, Harrigan's theater may seem less a celebration of a vibrant present than a critique of the inflated expectations and romantic delusions of the past—especially of art's part in maintaining them.

It is no less entertaining for that. Indeed, at this distance, Harrigan's implicit metatheatrical commentary is much sharper than either his genial comedy of manners or his pretensions toward realism. Photographic neutrality is nowhere to be found in the action of the play itself. He may write with palpable fondness for the languages, domestic customs, and social rituals of his intersecting Irish, German, Italian, and African-American characters — many of whom are members of pseudo-military groups doing mock battle in their neighborhood streets and lodge halls — but such panoramic range doesn't limit him to tepid endorsement of social norms. Normativeness of any kind is alien to Harrigan's theater, unless it survives in our memory of other playwrights' idealized characters, whose grace and nobility these weekend guardsmen never rival.

That is Harrigan's point. Soldiering in this post-Romantic world is just recreation. The armies, such as they are, are buffoonish, drunk, prone to pettiness and self-aggrandizement. Even their regalia establishes how far they have fallen from the military ideal. Cut off from any arena in which to prove their valor and earn acclaim, they wear a mishmash of ribbons, medals, and sashes bought from neighborhood pawnshops; one "soldier" uses a sausage as his revolver. The merely theatrical nature of heroism to the Mulligans and their neighbors diminishes the few real ambitions they do have. One regiment calls it a day after marching to Avenue A; a rival group declares war "to Prevent de Irish from Riding on Horse Cars" — the closest possible contemporary substitute for the Civil War's noble principles.[19]

Yet in other ways the civil wars fought among the families of New York's Sixth Ward are more complex and deeply engrained than anything depicted in more rousing war plays. The fighting never ends here, even though it never inflicts more than superficial wounds. In fact, it has become to its combatants a satisfying way to impose structure on a society that would otherwise be overwhelming in its density and heterogeneity. Harrigan's play resounds with passionately held prejudices. Few characters go longer than a few minutes without merrily slandering other, alien immigrants. Their victims pick up their rhythm and slander still others in turn. In these relay races of suspicion and envy — the African-Americans mocking the Irish, the Irish mocking the Germans, the Germans mocking the Italians — Harrigan disillusions those who want to believe that all forms of American social friction subsided with the Peace of 1865.

Ethnic difference isn't the only source of tension. Harrigan's characters are also divided by moral boundaries, economic status, family insularity, even slang and tempo, their way of staking their claim to the urban landscape. Without mentioning the war, or even depicting a southerner, Harrigan's comedy makes the serious point that the ideology of reconciliation and reunion, so

Figure 5: Edward Harrigan (right) and Tony Hart (left) as the Mulligan Guards (1874). The Harvard Theatre Collection, Houghton Library.

dear to postwar reformers, is weaker than the underlying habits of animosity — weaker, too, than the pleasure to be had in declaring individuality. Harrigan also rejects the oversimple, binary view of sectional conflict structuring actual Civil War melodramas. The strife in these crowded streets is both wider and, when the Mulligans begin fighting among themselves, deeper and more self-consuming than conventional narratives allow — and than we are taught to believe. Even when characters divide for a seemingly decisive face-off, as when a dispute over the use of a ballroom prompts the African-American regiment to invade an Irish dance, the clarity it provides is short-lived. The ironies crowd upon us in such rapid succession as to confuse all distinctions between right and wrong, victor and victim, hero and enemy. A black "army" marching on white territory: it's an inviting Civil War scenario that lasts only until the black regiment agrees to segregate itself upstairs. The futility of this rush to social harmony is clear when the ceiling falls in, bringing black society crashing down onto, and into, the whites' space again. In this and in one final melee, Harrigan's vision of society — improvised, spontaneous, and rough, its borders temporary and its contracts forever renegotiated — triumphs over both the ward's proud separatists and, no less completely, over the well-meaning ambitions of Harrigan's original audiences, some few of whom, in the wake of

Reconstruction, may still have hoped to control the uncontrollable energies of their own fractious, seething communities.

"Such was the war. It was not a quadrille in a ball-room" (779). By now we don't need Whitman, in these typically acerbic sentences from *Specimen Days,* to remind us how pointless it is to impose decorum on instinct. More theatrically complicated is the no less instinctive compulsion that keeps dramatists and their characters trying anyway. In the first scene of one of the era's most celebrated plays, *Shenandoah* (1888), Bronson Howard literalizes the search for interpretive frames for the war's legacy. His scene also reads as an explicit comment on Whitman's words. The play opens after a ball where Charleston high society has gathered to view, like Howard's own audience, the long-awaited attack on Fort Sumter, the war's own first act. Developing the meta-theatrical preoccupations of earlier playwrights, Howard is as interested in the appetites and aversions of spectatorship as he is in the spectacle itself: we watch a scene of watching, as the characters array themselves before a set of French doors mimicking the real stage's proscenium arch. In the foreground, the men, soon to be soldiers, lounge around in tuxedos, drunk and self-satisfied, while in the background we hear and see the signal rockets of regiments gearing up for battle. The characters' readiness to theatricalize war isn't lost on them. "It is to be a gala day," one of them explains. "The preparations have become a part of [Charleston's] social life — of their amusement. . . . The ladies . . . hurried away to watch the 'spectacle' from their own verandas."[20]

Howard's central situation — two couples, each comprising a northerner and a southerner, thrown together and divided by the war — is itself a drama-turgical quadrille, and the narrative makes much of the symmetries and shuf-fling among characters, ending as the couples put their differences behind them, their anticipated weddings presaging a truce and reconciliation among military combatants as well. As the genre demands, both martial and marital affairs are diminished by such patterning. On Howard's stage, the war can literally be seen only through a crowd of squabbling lovers, all of whom seem to believe that, by casting themselves as spectators, they can simply choose not to attend the history unfolding around them and thus be spared its disturbing implications for their own fate. The romantic plot, for its part, seems no more genuine and spontaneous when set against the background of battle. The lovers' animosity — obviously skin-deep, more acted than actual — is sched-uled to vanish at the war's own curtain. Indeed, in his eagerness to absolve his characters as well as the sections they represent, Howard has the northern and southern lovers signal their true affection for one another even before the first scene is over. He further argues that no one is to blame for initiating the real war. One side may be "wrong," as one of the men says, but both are "honest" (381). This war will indeed be civil.

If Howard had let his play simply confirm these premises, it would have been no more challenging than the dozens of other war fantasies produced in the 1880s and 1890s. Yet in performance, the moment-to-moment action is bolder than this summary suggests, as the characters test the strength of the familiar patterns. *Shenandoah* doesn't advertise itself as anything other than a "military comedy," but its levity will comfort only those who ignore its undercurrent of mania. It is as if Howard hadn't anticipated how quickly the germ of comedy would multiply in his dramatic system. The center of his quadrille will not hold. Characters try to focus on only the most trivial aspects of situations they recognize as serious, tamping down instinctive and potentially disabling responses in favor of those approved by custom, directing strange sensations into familiar channels — and in every case succeed only in making more destructive the inevitable eruption of anxiety. It may be, as Jeffrey D. Mason writes in his discussion of *Shenandoah*, that Howard hoped to "rationalize the apparent chaos of the conflict" with his tightly constructed plot and transparent characters.[21] His play deserves reading now, however, as welcome evidence that he failed to do so, a failure that allows us to imagine the war's psychological effects.

Libido, equally resistant to politics and sentimentality, does conclusive damage to his theater's rationalizing aspirations. Howard's airy romance is in fact a hothouse in which everyone is absurdly overaroused. The quartet of lovers can't keep their emotions from spilling over onto unlikely objects. The women, Gertrude and Madeline, kiss one another more passionately than they kiss their fiancés. The men, Kerchival and Ellingham, are seen to "grasp each other's hands warmly" even as they confide in one another their just-kindled love for the women. ("We understand each other," says one of the men, meaningfully, making it hard to resist a camp reading [386].) Surrounding them are characters no less feverish. A general worries more over his wife's fidelity than the day's battle strategy. Another would-be military hero, ironically named Heartsease, loses his composure whenever he encounters one particular ingénue. A third soldier is a dirty old man out of Plautus. The character most aglow with sexual desirability is literally animalistic. Gertrude's horse, Jack, rivals her fiancé in her affections. The horse interrupts the couple's intimacies, elicits from the heroine the avowals of love she withholds from her human paramour, and surrenders to a frankly suggestive scene in which she feeds him bonbons. When she observes, in a line worthy of Mae West, that her horse is "impatient for me to be on his back," Kerchival masters his jealousy enough to say, "let me assist you to mount" (387, 389). With that, a classic narrative triangle is complete, the hero enabling his own humiliation with unconscious ribaldry, the heroine, tapping her riding crop against her jodhpurs here and in almost every scene, parodying sentimental formula with her erotic restlessness.

Gertrude's equine love invites us to read the play as a parody of *A Midsummer Night's Dream* as well. In other scenes, Howard turns to another Shakespeare to acknowledge the dangerous consequences of his characters' apparently trivial doings. "My fair Desdemona," says an unfairly suspicious general to his wife, brandishing another soldier's monogrammed pocket square. "I found Cassio's handkerchief in your room" (391). Of course Howard never approaches true tragedy: the characters bend but don't surrender to its gravity. More surprising is the play's refusal to settle into a comic mode either. At any point it can be seen as lighthearted or serious, depending on where one looks. In welcome contrast to the era's strenuously patriotic drama, *Shenandoah* continuously makes whiplash-causing shifts from silly sex-play to cloak-and-dagger intrigue to scenes of domestic sentimentality to displays of selfless heroism—and in each case it does so with a fullness and sincerity that lasts only until Howard loses faith in a particular mode of representation. The rhythm of his inconstancy eventually changes the subject from the story to its writer. Mimesis itself, inevitably betraying its object even as it immortalizes it, is Howard's concern—or more precisely, it can become our concern, enabling us to find unity in Howard's eclectic approaches and to bridge the distance between them and our own more complicated understanding of the play's subject.

Howard's successive attempts to find frames capable of enforcing attention to the war have a cumulative force greater than anything depicted within them. It is only when he cannot contain the war within either an aesthetic tradition (romantic comedy), narrative structure (quasi-Shakespearean plots), or the literal frames of decor and proscenium that we are allowed to face it directly. In a chilling sequence at the peak of Howard's action, a crowd of wounded soldiers from Cedar Creek appears in the background and crosses the stage—silent, dirty, bandaged, and limping, "swell[ing] in volume" (a stage direction says) until it threatens to obscure the protagonists (429). A human tide breaks through *Shenandoah*'s dam of charm, figures insisting we remember Whitman's "dead—*our* dead . . . all, all, all." But before we can finish thinking that here is a glimpse of the Civil War play no one else is writing, Howard changes his tone yet again and questions the hubris of sight itself. An actor meant to represent General Sheridan gallops across the stage in a blur of motion, hard to identify, much less identify with—a real-time entrance and exit that defeats his timeless stature.[22] Moreover, he is as easily displaced as the wounded fugitives: Sheridan's—and Howard's—pretenses to heroic drama

Figure 6: *Shenandoah* by Bronson Howard (1888). In the play's last scene, Barket (right) reenacts the battle at Cedar Creek. The Harvard Theatre Collection, Houghton Library.

don't survive the loudest cheer. "Jack! Jack!! Jack!!!" calls Gertrude to the horse carrying Sheridan, every additional exclamation mark pushing its rider from the celebrity spotlight and unsteadying further the genre over which he would preside (430).

Given Howard's own frenzy — a gallop through dramatic styles as he calls out for our attention — it is inevitable that he should put himself onstage, implicitly, after Sheridan's dust settles and we are left staring at empty space. In a coda, an old veteran named Barket haplessly seeks the right language for memorializing the events we just witnessed. He tries narrative, beginning a stirring account of the battle at Cedar Creek four times, but gets no further than the first sentence before one or another insufficiently enthralled character cuts him off. If language alone no longer can command attention, perhaps imagery and action will. He next uses a tea service as props in a staged re-creation, setting out cups, saucers, and slices of bread to represent the Union and Confederate regiments — like every playwright, diminishing the things he means to exalt. Sheridan makes his charge when Barket swings his cane through the arrangement, sending china flying everywhere. In an instant, Howard has himself shattered his play's sensation scene of an hour earlier, ridiculing his susceptibility to military romance in the effort to recapture it and embarrassing us, too, by pointing out our own need to glorify the merely human.

The shared embarrassment is productive and predictive, setting the stage for later writers to examine their own complicity in sustaining the culture's fantasy life. Like the heroic soldiers that shrink to Barket's banal things, Civil War playwrights themselves recover their human scale. Their surrogate in *Shenandoah* lacks the stature of the mythologizer or omniscient historian; he is instead a mere marginalized observer, trying to come to grips (literally) with resistant reality and indifferent audiences. Such humility controls our interpretive zeal as well. One wants to see Howard's last scene as punctuating an entire era's drama, but in fact it evades all forms of conclusiveness in order to pose a new challenge. The centrifugal force of *Shenandoah,* accelerating as both Howard and his characters don and doff attitudes, can be imagined as dissociating theatrical form itself: pieces of broken tea service litter the stage at the final curtain, leaving characters, writers, and spectators alike to pick up the pieces, unable to reassemble an antique genre. *Shenandoah* atomizes before our eyes, and we find ourselves back at the scene of composition, before recourse to a writer's proven craft can soften the memory of traumatic experience.

Howard's conventionalism doesn't allow him to do more than hint at the self-doubt accompanying such acts of recovery and imagination. It would take a playwright seemingly much more of a showman to expose the mechanics of illusion. The self-awareness William Gillette exhibited in *Held by the Enemy* is more consistent and, as a result, more psychologically penetrating and theatrically visionary in a better play, *Secret Service* (1895). Here, Gillette picks up where Howard leaves off, studying the means by which playwrights and directors control emotional pressure, arrange actors in space, manufacture narrative, and coin their characters' very language. To do so, Gillette submits himself to scrutiny. *Secret Service* is the inevitable work with which to conclude any survey of Civil War drama — not because it probes with unique sophistication the war's moral ambiguities and political costs but because, in failing to do so, it successfully shifts our attention to a reachable subject, the difficulty faced by the artist charged with mediating our encounter with the war's participants and witnesses. Seen this way, *Secret Service* may appear the smallest of Civil War plays, its field of action no larger than Gillette's consciousness. But it can, without distortion, equally be seen as the largest, for it delves so aggressively into the givens of performance — presence, speech, movement, time — that they lose their familiarity and begin to seem like vast stretches of undiscovered country.

Such a transformation in our attention is especially apparent as Gillette probes the nineteenth-century theater's dependence on feeling. After *Specimen*

Days, inherited ideas of emotion seem so debased as to humiliate those still organizing drama around their vague composition and unreliable, often indulgent expression. Their most spectacular variant, the awe felt before a *coup de théâtre,* is no less formulaic (especially after Barket's unintentional parody and the many intentional ones that will become staples of late-century burlesque). As an emotion that numbs rather than stimulates attention, awe will seem a cowardly escape from ambivalence, self-consciousness, any kind of nuanced response. Gillette recuperates both generalized feeling and acute sensation by approaching them clinically. His stage resembles a delicate filament sensitive to the slightest fluctuation in motion or emotion. His text is a seismograph recording such activity with obsessive precision. His actors are specimens enabling us to see the effect of such stimuli on behavior. Gillette focuses less on his plot's many surprising leaps and reversals than on the physiological reactions they trigger in those witnessing them. That the protagonist of *Secret Service,* one Captain Thorne, was made famous when Gillette himself played the role affirms the play's larger metatheatrical significance, developing a theme announced with the similarly strategic casting in *Held by the Enemy,* and transforming what could have been a mere science experiment into an intimate act of self-reckoning. *Secret Service* prolongs and magnifies every playwright's effort, after beholding a subject, to step out of the flow of time and compose a response in art.

Stepping out of time is hardly an obvious strategy for the writer of an espionage thriller, a form dependent on narrative momentum and its audience's tightening anxiety. Indeed, Bernard Shaw, reviewing the play's London production, complains that its climax "takes a huge deal of leading up to, and leads to nothing itself," as if he fears that Gillette's analytic temperament put him at odds with an audience's self-surrendering desires.[23] But what to Shaw is a flaw can seem a virtue to others. At least it can to a present-day viewer, weary, perhaps, of the way typical melodramas stream along with narrative inevitability and melodious sentiment, and ready for the fractured, even static procedures of modernism. *Secret Service* may owe its reputation to its relentless action — the publicists would call it nail-biting — but in fact it's a play of multiple delays, deferrals, and often complete stoppages as the impulses of a given moment are dissected and discussed. This style causes sensations more extreme than mere suspense. That is its rationale, but without violating his pact with those viewers expecting to be enthralled, Gillette himself takes distance from his story, the better to perfect his rendering of its affective structures. *Secret Service* manages the seemingly contradictory feat of being both more emotionally involving and more formally sensitive than other plays of the era. In its presence, Gillette's audiences better understand the procedures of an aging form — melodrama — just before it collapses under the challenge of ascendant styles.

The modernist who saw beyond sentiment to the imagistic, kinetic logic of *Uncle Tom's Cabin*, Gertrude Stein, also rescues *Secret Service* from those ready to dismiss it as mere escapism. (It is fitting that a former medical student would admire Gillette's scientific approach to psychology.) Her memorable assessment of it in her essay "Plays" (1935) is the place to begin any discussion of its achievement. "Gillette had conceived a new technique," she writes, "silence stillness and quick movement."[24] It is an exact description. By ignoring the plot, Stein teaches us how to pick up the play's complex rhythm, one that is nonetheless occasioned and controlled by the action. That action — a Union spy, Thorne, conspires to cause the downfall of the Confederate forces at Richmond — supports Gillette as he catalogues his characters' versions of expectation, alarm, suspicion, and connivance (many of which respond to events unrelated to his central story). As characters shift from one to another, or discover new styles, poses, and arrangements to denote different gradations of the same anxiety, or lose their composure altogether when the narrative abruptly changes course, the play's excitement is as choreographic as it is melodramatic.

A particularly angular choreography: nothing about *Secret Service* is fluid. Even a character doing something as simple as crossing the stage is likely to interrupt himself or herself with several motionless pauses for observation and second thoughts before getting to the other side. On almost every page, the stage directions keep the play to a spasmodic rhythm. One character, Edith, "stops — a moment's pause . . . stops, pauses, stands erect, looks about, motions Mrs. Varney to go."[25] Later, "after Edith is motionless, Captain Thorne walks briskly . . . stops an instant where he is, and then goes directly to her." At the scene's end, he "turns quickly . . . hesitates an instant . . . walks rapidly to window — a slight hesitating there, without stopping. Exits at window" (413). One can put these and the play's many other protracted sequences alongside Sheridan's blur of motion in *Shenandoah* and neatly summarize nineteenth-century American drama's effort to come to terms with changing ideas of speed in the modern world. It is as if Gillette were expanding and testing the possibilities of theatrical tableaux. Instead of staging them only at the ends of scenes, Gillette fills his play with dozens of them, each of which lasts no more than a few seconds before breaking, the actors reengaging with the crisis that made them stop in their tracks. The dissolution of these tableaux is as significant as their formation. Even when characters want to arrest the action long enough to master it, they are at the mercy of Gillette's unforgiving hurry-up-and-wait schedule. Hoping to seize control of their individual fates — and history in general? — by looking and listening intently, his characters instead help us to see only the impersonality of time.

Gillette's successive tableaux recall the efforts of a fellow protomodernist to master time. Eadweard Muybridge's "instantaneous photography," breaking down an animal's or person's fluid movement into a series of linked tableaux, springs from the same analytic, conservationist impulse motivating the playwright's choreography. Both artists subject to scrutiny what, away from the theater or the photographer's studio, is taken for granted — the collaboration among the different parts of a body as it works its way across space and through time — and rescue nuances of expression lost when history's unimpeded flow erases them. To those reading *Secret Service* alongside Muybridge's near-contemporaneous portfolios (his human figure studies, made in Philadelphia from 1884 to 1886, were published in 1887), the playwright's ostensibly fast-paced action reveals its internal composure just as the photographer's ostensibly neutral documents acquire unexpected pathos. More generally, the pictures offer themselves as models of the controlled dramaturgy needed to do justice to the war's stark history.

Of course one looks in vain through the 781 plates of *Animal Locomotion* for explicit depictions of wartime experience. Most scenes show men and women doing mundane tasks, athletic exercises, and such simple actions as climbing stairs, getting dressed or undressed, and lying down. But several sequences study more emphatic forms of expression that invite equally bold interpretations. Throughout the portfolio, Muybridge returns periodically to men (and, in one remarkable sequence, a woman) traveling through the stations of various rites of violence. Men pair off to box, wrestle, and fence. Solitary individuals practice punches, throw spears, charge with bayonets, kneel and fire rifles, and go through the codified stages of carrying and displaying arms.[26] Domestic violence is analyzed just as closely. One of the most harrowing plates consists of eighteen frames showing a woman spanking an infant from multiple perspectives (527). (The absurd counterpoint to this scene is one in which a woman hits another with a broomstick [464].) In all cases, the figure's coolness, ensuring the poise of situations that would seem explosive in other contexts, helps one register the momentousness of even familiar, seemingly innocuous forms of brutality.

It takes little effort to see these plates as cameos of larger, organized, and communal forms of aggression. (The war was, of course, still a living memory as Muybridge was taking his photographs.) Several plates, in fact, depict the wages of violence in familiar postwar terms. An amputee walks on crutches, one difficult step per frame (537). Another figure, with "partial paraplegia," walks with a cane (559). Two more seem to suffer convulsions (544–45). Yet these are no more pitiful than the pictures of gunplay and fistfighting are threatening. Muybridge's modernist impersonality — his banks of electrically triggered cameras indifferent to the psychological source, moral value, or ideological justification of a person's actions; the resulting print cropped to eliminate all traces of social and personal history — slows and disciplines his viewers' own behavior. As Muybridge segments our seeing as thoroughly as he segments a figure's movement, we no longer speed through a spectacle to its narrative conclusion, unaware of the procedures by which we respond to its sometimes grim imagery, much less take refuge in symbolic meaning. Muybridge's strict attention to the manner of violent expression ensures that we won't merely sympathize with, thrill to, or recoil from scenes whose atavistic origins and destructive consequences demand sober-minded analysis. (Rebecca Solnit, in her recent study of Muybridge, envisions the photographer turning animate bodies into "specimens" [as she calls them], plucking them from the stream of time and freezing them for recurrent study — an analogy that, as Whitman has already implied in *Specimen Days,* is just as useful to the writer resisting the no less powerful streams of sentiment and of consciousness animating imaginative literature.)[27]

The theatrical applications of this approach are anticipated in Muybridge's work itself. Marta Braun has persuasively argued that the motion studies can be read as dramas or narratives rather than scrupulously scientific demonstrations, their often nude protagonists incompletely stripped of the emotions that would elevate them to characters, their versions of behavior marked by peculiarities of style that even the most stoic model cannot repress.[28] Indeed, in this regard it is helpful to recall that Muybridge once wanted to photograph professional actors at work, using the same technique with which he photographed horses galloping and figures walking.[29] The deliberate stages by which a performer embodied, say, Lear raging on the heath would become apparent to a spectator hitherto enthralled only by the broad strokes of the character's ordeal. Muybridge never executed these studies, but one of his most celebrated plates can't help but appear exemplary to a theater-minded viewer. The series entitled "Turning Around in Surprise and Running Away" (73) shows a naked woman covering her eyes and genitals as she twists her body away from the camera. One frame catches her as she leans down on one bent leg, extends the other, and holds her left arm at a right angle over her eyes — a textbook melodramatic pose (indeed, it wouldn't look out of place as an illustration in such nineteenth-century acting manuals as *The Thespian Preceptor*) here reduced to the geometry delineating its shame and panic. The same geometrical style controls another plate with obvious melodramatic po-

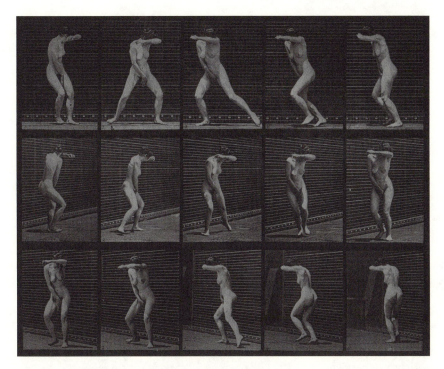

Figure 7: "Turning Around in Surprise and Running Away" by Eadweard Muybridge, from *Animal Locomotion* (1887). Collections of the University of Pennsylvania Archives.

tential: "Walking and Turning Around: Action of Aversion" (55). As in many Muybridge pictures, these models pose in front of grids, making explicit the photographer's spatial approach to character. A figure's trauma is charted — plotted — not just suffered.

The genre blurring suggests how Gillette emulates Muybridgean formalism while simultaneously fulfilling his obligation to tell a story fueled by characters' emotions. Readers attuned to the "silence stillness and quick movement" of *Secret Service* watch him follow through on Muybridge's instincts, extending the photographer's technique to subtler emotions, segmenting the stages of response that ordinarily we combine and give the name of a single unified feeling. (Present-day readers will no doubt have already recognized that Gillette, in turn, offers one prototype for the similarly segmented motion and emotion of much Robert Wilson and the dissociated logic informing both movement and writing in Richard Foreman.)[30] In *Secret Service*, sensations of grief or relief, delight or confusion, are shown to accumulate in stages rather than arrive fully formed and at peak intensity. Yet even as Gillette magnifies and fractures a figure's action or emotion, he also never lets us forget his controlling form of attention, one sustained by an insatiable desire for mastery as psychologically complex (and as theatrical) as anything onstage. His anxiety mirrors that of his characters.

The text of *Secret Service* attests on every page to this obsessive need for control. Its readers see what spectators can't: epic stage directions sprout in the cracks of dialogue and wrap around scenes like vines. They specify the actors' placement and flight patterns; the position of their arms, legs, fingers, and eyes; and the quality and timing of all the accompanying sounds and sights — prolix annotations not to be seen again until Eugene O'Neill. We should pause over them even at the risk of slowing our reading of an exciting scene. The directions are valuable not so much because they help us stage the play in our heads, nor because they pay tribute to Gillette's mastery of all the languages of performance. As we regularly break off from the dialogue to work through the differently paced prose of the stage directions, then move back again to speech, we experience something of the same stop-and-start rhythm controlling the actors themselves as they step in and out of Gillette's sequential tableaux. Reading becomes its own syncopated performance, as suspenseful and fraught with frustration as anything onstage. At the same time, Gillette's own frustration is palpable. The stage directions, for all their lavish specificity, describe nothing so vividly as the playwright's resentment of his art's inherent variability. His most emphatic instructions appear in a preface, intended perhaps as program note as well, that ties the action to a strict schedule. Act 1 opens at "EIGHT O'CLOCK" at night (the hysterical capital letters are Gillette's); act 2 at 9:00, act 3 at 10:00, and act 4 at 11:00.[31] Time's inevitable linearity, perhaps the one thing a playwright doesn't have to worry about, seems only to exacerbate his self-consciousness. Of course any decent thriller exploits the drama of a ticking clock; here, though, one can't help thinking that Gillette watches it more than his characters do, as if he fears that with every passing minute he is losing another opportunity to master his subject, or at least to synchronize the progress of his narrative (as well as of the larger history it reflects) to the analytic minds charged with understanding it. We can, if we choose, see self-criticism in such self-scrutiny. By monitoring the dramatic action so closely, Gillette offers himself as an image of his culture's futile attempt to contain the challenges surfacing in Civil War memory.

Gillette's desire to subdue time matches an equally strong need to landscape space, preventing its meanings from taking root anywhere unexpected. Here the playwright's zeal for containment is literal. Gillette sets all but one of his acts in a lavishly appointed living room of a Richmond mansion, but what we don't see, or see only partially, makes a stronger impression, as characters try to keep the war at bay. Upstage, a door leads to a parlor where women wrap bandages and sew bedclothes for the hospitals. We see this Greek chorus of active compassion whenever the door opens; if someone neglects to close it, their industry makes a silent, ongoing commentary on the often superficial action in the foreground. (One of the women, we learn later, is the relative of a soldier killed at Cold Harbor. With rare understatement, Gillette places an embodiment of mourning onstage from the beginning, rarely seen whole and given little to say but ever-present, working unobtrusively behind those who, thus far, are less haunted.) The back parlor isn't the only space that comments critically on the visible stage. Above the living room, we're told, is a bedroom where the family's oldest son, Howard, lies dying from battle wounds. We never see him, but his suffering literally hovers over the action belowstairs. Finally, from the left and right of the stage come the sounds of cannonading, as Union troops approach Richmond's border.

Gillette's theatrical geography is treacherous for seeming so well ordered. Behind, above, and to either side of the playing area, the war is suffered or resisted. By this exclusionary logic, emblematic of his theater's own resistance to his difficult subject, Gillette makes us register more clearly than we might otherwise do so the dimensions and condition of his stage — a small, improbably immaculate space where any expression of romanticism, domestic complacency, confidence, or humor seems willful or, at worst, ignorant. *Secret Service* finds the pathos in what Henry James (in his preface to *The Awkward Age*) calls the theater's "denial of expansibility," its remaining "shut up in its own presence" (as opposed to the novel's "perfect paradise of the loose end").[32] Yet although Gillette's stage may not be able to expand, it does contract, its borders closing in around the actors as the action proceeds. Every time one of the bandage-makers emerges from the back room, or a doctor descends from upstairs with bad news about Howard, or a soldier tramps in dust from the front, Gillette's ideal spectator measures what little space remains untouched by their dark knowledge. As death pushes against the stage's outer sides, back wall, and ceiling, the life lived inside the proscenium seems to grow more and more deliberate, staged with an awareness of the new limits being imposed on spontaneity. The living room begins to seem the last remaining space for fantasy and nostalgia — a transformation that invites historically minded spectators to see it as an emblem of the melodramatic American theater about to be contaminated by an imminent, fast-approaching realism.[33]

Gillette's dramaturgy of contraction leads him to tighten his focus on the characters' bodies (when a woman scissors away at a pair of ill-fitting military trousers, one can't help thinking of the soldier's own vulnerability to disfigurement) and, ultimately, on the characters' dialogue. Here Gillette is at his most radical, reducing ideology and desire to the language used to express them, then anatomizing language as he anatomized bodies until we see the parts of speech. Every act of verbal expression and reception — speaking and writing, as well as listening and reading — submits to such Muybridgean scrutiny, slowed until its separate impulses and responses are audible and visible, a process that, by directing attention to a character's consciousness, heightens the effect of the encroaching space and inexorably passing time. Such a procedure isn't only formal. The perils and deceptions of communication are at the heart of the plot. As a way, perhaps, of training audiences in the acute spectatorship appropriate to his climactic event — a long scene in which Thorne tries to telegraph a phony message to the enemy — Gillette magnifies the significance of all other, earlier exchanges, no matter how incidental. Private notes, official communiqués, a doctor's report, a messenger's announcement, even the charged looks and tentative nods passed between lovers: all these transactions stop the action, pull and narrow our focus to the point where information is exchanged, and draw from the characters themselves their fiercest attention.

To a degree perhaps only notable after an era of sensation melodrama, things happen to these people in language alone. Events that in a less austere play would inspire the most histrionic, emotionally lavish treatment — someone's suffering, another's betrayal, still another's defiance — are here experienced only as messages. Gillette stages one such scene — a face-off between father and son, that staple of many melodramas — without the expected anger and shame, without the father himself even present. It is only when the son writes a telegram to his father that we perceive the difficulty of their relationship, a difficulty Gillette prevents us from sentimentalizing by showing us the composition of the son's defiance, the individual parts of pride, when he and his girlfriend edit a draft. As they try to decide what to cut — the telegram office charges seven dollars a word — we feel each word's emotional cost, too. (Tellingly, the only line they can part with describes another man's death.)

Words become objects in this scene, inviting speakers to handle and position them, to consider them as phenomena no less active and substantial than the phenomena they signify. (In this light, one of Gillette's earliest admirers, Walter Prichard Eaton, seems exactly wrong, or at least unnecessarily restrictive, when he writes that "a study of this play becomes a study not of . . . the arrangement of words, but of how Gillette planned the actions . . . of his characters.")[34] In the wake of a theatrical era celebrated for pictorial acting and directing — performers forming their bodies into signs of emotional conditions, directors compensating for hackneyed dramaturgy with spectacular scenic effect — Gillette experiments with a kind of pictorial writing. Spectators who once read emotion in an actor's poses and gestures now see language.

Nowhere more so than in the suspenseful third act, set in the telegraph office itself: as Gillette designs it, it is a landscape of language. Bunched transmission cables crisscross the stage. Men come and go carrying text. Others cut and paste sentences for new messages. Dispatches pile up in boxes. On long tables, lines of Morse code machines, another of Gillette's choruses, keep up a constant chatter, speaking before anyone else does at the curtain's rise, interrupting human dialogue, having the last word. The whole room talks. In yet another fulfillment of Gertrude Stein's schedule of "silence stillness and quick movement," characters endure an often agonizing interval between thinking of something to say and being able to write it down, or between sending code and getting an answer. That delay isolates and thus heightens the clarity of characters ordinarily blurred by their relationships; it also helps Gillette maintain his skepticism toward emotional transactions usually taken for granted.

Showing the same severity with which he dissected filial rebellion, Gillette here analyzes declarations of love. "I've got to spell out every word," says a telegraph operator to a woman after she urges him to transmit an effusive note to her beloved (435). When Gillette reduces passion to a procedure, and puts between the lovers an intermediary punching in the words of love, he restores the true deliberateness and self-consciousness to sentiments other playwrights insist are spontaneous. Speaking in this scene requires the body's collaboration: the hand does the true work of expression, a shift in focus that wrests feeling from abstract, inviolate, and thus easily romanticized interiority. (The sequence also returns us to Muybridge to recover some of his least heralded pictures, those depicting hands manipulating various writing implements. In one, a hand draws a circle on a piece of paper; in another, a pair of hands changes the lead in a pencil [532, 536]. When placed alongside Gillette's hand studies, these plates remind viewers that stage action is not just embodied but written — a proposition that, as we'll see, Gillette not only acknowledges but makes theatrically legible.)

Gillette's love-scene-with-telegraph recuperates more than clichés. Every decision to disclose once private thought now seems properly momentous; all dialogue sounds telegraphic. Numerous dashes break up conversations in the published text, imposing lurching pauses at the ends of statements and in some cases fracturing sentences from within, causing speakers to jump from noun to noun, or exclamation to exclamation, and to dispense with all but essential thought. The rhythm is set in earlier acts: "Oh — I couldn't — for my whole — it's only you in the — Your mother — I'll say goodbye to her," says Thorne (392). Later, his beloved says, "Mama — he loves me! — Yes — and I — Oh — let someone else do it!" (423). The sputtering urgency of these and many other passages reaches its height when in the telegraph office another character comes out with, "Do — you — mean — to — say —" (435). Radical actors and directors will make us hear the dashes and see what rushes into the gaps in action they measure: pivots of intention, flashes of insight, a sudden uprush of passion or drain in confidence, a slow degradation in the adhesive that bonds speakers to listeners. Soon, characters are as unsupported as the words they utter. Their plight, rendered convincing by Gillette's minute attention to the form of panic (rather than just its cause and effect), illuminates the play's broadest social context. In an environment where all romantic, familial, political, and historical scaffolding is under siege, characters grab hold of the means of representing such a collapse—clutching dispatches, pasting words, fingering letter-keys—if by doing so they can also seize control of their uncertain future. (The only inevitable action on Gillette's third-act set is the effortless revolution of a wall clock's second hand.)

As Gillette affirms that his own writing is also an affair of hands, he takes on the last remaining illusion in an exposed landscape. In the face of his characters' workmanlike patience, the mythology of an artist's surrender to inspiration is no more supportable than that of a lover's fall into passion or a soldier's effortless rise to heroism. The ramifications of this merger of artist and subject are dizzying. *Secret Service* puts forward an image of writing the war, not just writing about it—writing as an image of waging or at least intervening in its battles, as its participants script rather than submit to its narrative. Yet the play also guards against the analogy's false promise of mastery: the smaller field of action, the page, magnifies the anxiety of covering it, as writing involves Gillette in a task as disorienting and tortured as any experienced by his subjects.

This enactment of an artist's private ordeal, embedded but easily ignored in a scene that seemingly owes its power to external events, recalls the similarly self-interrogatory, nervous attention to writing that Michael Fried, in *Realism, Writing, Disfiguration* (1987), finds in the near-contemporaneous work of Thomas Eakins and Stephen Crane. In their art, too, the visible scenes seem to argue for the sovereignty of their narratives and characters—the "realism" of the surgeon's procedure depicted in Eakins's *Gross Clinic* (1875), for instance, or the haunting "upturned faces" of the war dead in Crane's fiction—but in fact such tableaux, along with critical convention, may be screens obscuring private dramas unfolding far from any external experience and prohibiting detached observation. In *The Gross Clinic,* argues Fried, the artist wavers between the competing attractions of writing and painting, or what Fried calls (in words of special relevance to those arbitrating between a visual and literary theater) the "graphic" and the "pictorial": the surgeon's scalpel neatly invites comparisons to both the artist's brush and writer's pen. In Crane's fiction, a similar tension between overt and covert meaning reaches a near-debilitating extreme. Crane's act of writing—marking the page—takes on such visceral, magnified importance that he cannot see through the means to the subject of expression. "His attempt, before all, to make the reader *see*," writes Fried, "at least intermittently led Crane himself to see . . . those things that, *before all,* actually lay before Crane's eyes: the written words themselves, the white, lined sheet of paper on which they were inscribed, the marks made by his pen on the surface of the sheet, even perhaps the movements of his hand wielding the pen in the act of inscription."[35] One need only imagine the psychological distress implicit in these gestures—an anxious encounter with a reproachful blank page, regret or cathartic release as ink stains the sheet—to recognize their dramatic potential. (Fried himself acknowledges it, fleetingly, when he calls the text "the site, almost the theater, of an incessant becoming-visible and disappearing both of aspects of the scene of writing and . . . the text's reality as writing" [127–28].) If, in fact, Fried's theater-minded readers stress the indecision embodied in Crane's agon with the page (something Fried does not)—the writer contemplating but not making a choice of words, just as Eakins's Dr. Gross stands poised before making his next incision—they approach the experience of arrested or protracted consciousness dramatized in *Secret Service*.

Here, too, as another hand draws focus (inevitably, in a play that has been forcing attention into ever-narrower arenas from the beginning), we can envision the writer's self-doubt as he considers, makes, and retracts choices, something more pervasive and ambiguous than the anxiety occasioned by the narrative. It cannot be accidental that Gillette's stage directions are at their most obsessive when describing Thorne's gestures. In the telegraph office, Thorne "picks up [a cigar] with [his] left hand and lights a match with [his] right" (443). Later, he snatches the cigar out of his mouth with his left hand. At a decisive moment, his "right hand slowly slips off the telegraph key and toward his revolver" (446). With his left, he turns off the lights. Once our eyes are trained to view the stage this microscopically, we're sure not to miss the drops of blood on his left hand when the lights come on after a gun goes off.

These and other, similar sequences (Gillette is attentive to all his characters' handplay) strain against theater's fixed perspective to simulate the emotional power of a cinematic close-up. Remarkably, this internal tension between forms isn't destructive, perhaps because it isn't just a formal matter. In asking one to notice the structure and compressed energy of a hand in the seconds before it moves, Gillette asserts that every action originates in an actor—a self-evident truth, but one easily obscured by a Civil War mythology that prefers its opponents abstracted into good and evil, fulfilling a plan ordained by impersonal fate. Distance would have enabled one to recall only the grand sweep of battle, the pattern instead of the individual player who makes it, and to blur

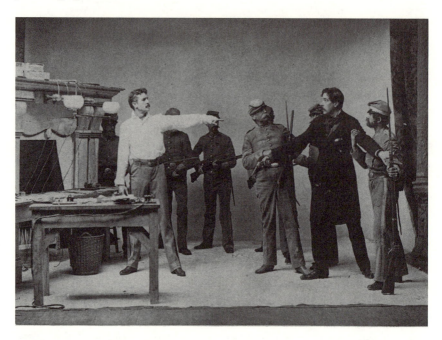

Figure 8: *Secret Service* by William Gillette (1896). In act 3, set in the War Department Telegraph Office, Captain Thorne (Gillette) orders guards to arrest Arrelsford (Campbell Gollan). Photograph by Pach Studio, Billy Rose Theatre Division, The New York Public Library for the Performing Arts, Astor, Lenox and Tilden Foundations.

choices of a moment into general principles. Rejecting distance in favor of cinematic intimacy, Gillette strips history of its grandeur and, most important, of its air of inevitability. With disarming literalness, he asks who has a hand in history's own plot.

Yet Gillette's moving hands wave one away from this promise of knowledge with equal force. It is possible to attend so closely to an actor's sequential motions (or to imagine a production that, in emphasizing them, slows our attention to the same pace) that readers or spectators can never extract themselves from the visual field to think about meanings or even to see its images whole. The Muybridgean analysis in this scene, divided into ever smaller units of movement, risks never adding up to a completed action. If we think of each of these actions — lighting a cigar, fingering a revolver, pressing a telegraph — as always a stand-in for the gestures of playwriting, then we will find it even harder to see his play's action. Shaw's lament that the play "takes a huge deal of leading up to, and leads to nothing itself" is unexpectedly useful, now, in calling attention to the nonlinear, durational, and often inconclusive logic of every artist's imagination. It is during these sequences that one especially envies *Secret Service*'s 1896 spectators, seeing the playwright's own hands at work when he took over the role of the protagonist. (Gillette himself acknowledged, in more general terms, the kinship between actor and writer. In his essay "The Illusion of the First Time in Acting" [1915], Gillette writes that superior actors give the impression that they themselves "search for and find words by which to express . . . thoughts.")[36] Like Bronson Howard at the end of *Shenandoah*, Gillette allows us to imagine that he is writing his play as we see it — or, more precisely, that his play is forever incomplete, held during performances in an agonizing hiatus before the playwright lowers his hand to the page. In this context, it's important to recall Gillette's most surprising reversal: moved by his love for a southern woman, Thorne chooses not to telegraph his fiction, an anticlimax that lets us imagine a playwright able simultaneously to create and withhold his own art.

These elaborate conclusions drawn from a seemingly banal play cast a retrospectively sharp light over the assembled series of earlier Civil War dramas, exposing the severity with which their playwrights trouble, unmoor, or eliminate elements of style once thought essential to theater. Their plays, as we've seen, tell a history of deliberate self-impoverishment that to the present-day reader or spectator can seem the formal equivalent of the war's own progressive devastation. The many images of absence and loss in *Under the Gaslight,* the rejection of norms of conduct in the leveling antipathies of *The Mulligan Guard Ball,* and the continuous evasion of tonal stability and emotional consistency in *Shenandoah* make inevitable Gillette's more severe economies. After he fences in the playing areas of *Secret Service,* isolates ever-subtler gestures of its characters, and stops the flow of speech to study its tiniest impulses — all part of an anti-illusionist critique initiated with the blind servant and corrupt illustrator in *Held by the Enemy* — spectators are left staring at a stage evacuated by skepticism and now charged with anticipation.

What do we wait for? The question remains unanswered as Gillette exploits the suspense form to make us rethink the purpose of theater itself. He directs attention away from events — this or that personal milestone, tragic fall, or heroic triumph — and toward the dull agony of awaiting their sequels. The fact that such an unsensational condition may remind readers of what Melville calls "the horror of the calm" felt by soldiers waiting out a lull in battle (so different from the less anxious postwar silence he calls "the after-quiet") prepares us to recognize this theater's largest achievement.[37] Gillette's actor on the verge of moving a limb or uttering a syllable mirrors not only the self-doubting writer on the verge of marking a page. Both actor and writer also show us to ourselves in multiple contexts. In the theater, we, too, slowly move from confusion to knowledge and finally to an opinion about what we see. Writer and actor also stand in for an art form that awaits, and gropes for, melodrama's successor. Finally, most meaningfully, they embody a society where the ruin of war has yet to be ameliorated by a durable reconstruction. If we ground all these varieties of expectation in the patrolling soldier's own mingled fear of and longing for the future — a visceral aversion to uneventfulness — then we can discover the true harrowing quality of what otherwise might seem a mere blank state or empty stage. Gillette's theater allows us to see the psychic and physical strain of contending with the unseen. All the wide-eyed figures acknowledged in *Secret Service,* those onstage and those they represent, hang in the air like a Muybridgean horse or high jumper, awaiting the moment when the ground — the stage and page, but also the battlefield, the enveloping culture, and history — leaps up to claim them.

Finally, Thorne's (and Gillette's) hand hovering above his writing instrument returns us to Whitman's "Years of the Modern," where we may continue to move away from the visionary confidence that dominates the poem. Questions rather than assertions of national, cultural, and personal destiny acquire theatrical clarity as Whitman describes himself looking at an unclear "space ahead" (by now one can't help thinking of both a stage and a page) and "vainly try[ing] to pierce it." The distance is unbridgeable. The "august dramas" occur only in the future, where the "horizon rises." Such a condition of permanent imminence is the essence of a theater that would be true to the withheld certainties of contemporary life — a drama of the not yet. Whitman's first line — "Years of the modern! years of the unperform'd!" — makes such an equation explicit.[38] In the face of Gillette's ability to theatricalize states of suspended expressiveness, it is no longer adequate to conclude that the Civil War is, in Daniel Aaron's famous phrase, the "unwritten war," unless one hears the words not as an indictment of failure but as a compositional strategy.[39] Of course all writers concede that writing, once written, diminishes its subject. The war's least compromising artists resist the narrative conventions by which we ordinarily deem a work finished, lest we also think its subject has been mastered. "The unperform'd . . . advance, advance upon me." Such an atmosphere of melodramatic foreboding, experienced by all the era's playwrights more acutely than their characters, serves them well as long as it never lifts. The simplest line in "Years of the Modern" freezes suspense at its peak: "No one knows what will happen next."

It may be that the theater of the Civil War achieved profundity only once, years before most playwrights began writing about it, during a single, never-repeated performance, far from any city, for an audience of only a few specially invited guests, starring an actor who would be dead in days. The actor was Lincoln and the performance, on April 9, 1865, was a spontaneous marathon reading of Shakespeare on board the *River Queen* as it returned to Washington from City Point, Virginia. Lincoln had traveled down the Potomac to mark the fall of Richmond, touring ravaged neighborhoods where black freedmen crowded the streets to cheer him while above their heads fashionable white Virginians ostentatiously shuttered their windows. The visit was a feat of considerable imaginative dexterity, Lincoln asserting victory even while identifying with the victims. After paying tribute to Union troops as they attacked a picket line, he visited an army hospital to shake the hands of wounded Confederates. Joining his generals to devise a peace plan, he insisted on the least punitive terms for the defeated. Just before leaving City Point, he asked a band to play "Dixie," declaring, "That tune is now Federal property; it belongs to us, and, at any rate, it is good to show the rebels that with us they will be free to hear it again." Perhaps the most compelling display of Lincoln's even-handed allegiance was as physical as it was psychological: at the Confederate White House in Richmond, he sat in one of Jefferson Davis's chairs, settling into an ambiguous mix of sympathy and hubris.[40]

Returning to Washington, Lincoln relied on these same techniques of identification — the self-transcendence necessary to the actor and spectator alike — to guide his performance on the *River Queen*. Of the many plays by Shakespeare he had all but memorized, Lincoln chose *Macbeth*, using it (we can imagine) to give meaningful shape to the often meaningless ruin he had just seen and, as he recited passage after passage, borrowing speech to reconcile the contradictory instincts in his response. He once wrote that *Macbeth* was his favorite of the tragedies, but more than taste makes it inevitable that he would reach for this play as the Civil War was ending. Opening with the news that its own rebellious uprising has been quashed, *Macbeth* warns against the debilitating effects of victory on an ever-hungrier victor — a long, sleepless night in which one wades into a deepening pool of blood, surrenders to doubt on fields primed for leadership, and resurrects the reproachful dead when one means to christen a new regime. Read with these stresses, Lincoln's *Macbeth* isn't only a reflection of the strife just ending, although of course there are many passages that we want to imagine him reciting as he sought names for and perspective on what he has seen. (One such is Rosse's act 4 speech that begins, "Alas, poor country!/Almost afraid to know itself," a lament for a landscape "where sighs, and groans, and shrieks that rent the air/Are made, not mark'd; where violent sorrow seems/A modern ecstasy . . . and good men's lives/Expire before the flowers in their caps.")[41] The play is also, for Lincoln as for war-torn America generally, a cautionary tale orienting one to the future, and it is that quality that may have drawn Lincoln to the one speech we know he did recite that day. Macbeth is speaking to his wife shortly after murdering Duncan:

> We have scorch'd the snake, not kill'd it:
> She'll close, and be herself; whilst our poor malice
> Remains in danger of her former tooth.
> But let the frame of things disjoint, both the worlds suffer,
> Ere we will eat our meal in fear, and sleep
> In the affliction of these terrible dreams,
> That shake us nightly. Better be with the dead,
> Whom we, to gain our peace, have sent to peace,
> Than on the torture of the mind to lie
> In restless ecstasy. Duncan is in his grave;
> After life's fitful fever he sleeps well;
> Treason has done his worst: nor steel, nor poison,
> Malice domestic, foreign levy, nothing
> Can touch him further! (3.2.13–26)

One of Lincoln's guests on the *River Queen*, the marquis de Chambrun, wrote about Lincoln's rendition of this speech, emphasizing its "vague presentiment" of the assassination six days later, especially as Lincoln "began to explain to us how true a description of the murderer that one was; when, the dark deed achieved, its tortured perpetrator came to envy the sleep of his victim."[42] But it is more interesting when read in a less limited context — as a text with which Lincoln addresses the present, certifying what he knows, and (like the Whitman of "Years of the Modern") strains toward what he has yet to see.

Scrutiny is as much his theme as it is his technique. (Lincoln's performance contributes one more instance to the nineteenth century's archive of parables about seeing.) The wariness of the king who thinks he may have only "scorch'd the snake" and now awaits the collapse of "the frame of things" is Lincoln's, too: the condition of a man prey to his own "terrible dreams" shaking him awake with the prospect of more catastrophe. (On his way to burnt-out Richmond, Lincoln twice dreamed that the White House was on fire.) He can only measure the breadth of uncertainty, for he is as yet unable to know either the value of the war or the nature of its sequel — an ungrounded, fluid state of thought nicely emphasized by the riverboat setting for this performance. Lincoln may look back to the departed shore with as much disbelief as relief, and with equal ambivalence may look ahead to the other side, understanding that a different crisis begins now that scheduled, structured violence has ended. As in *Macbeth*, only the sleeping dead will be spared.

In such a current of conflicting thoughts, Lincoln reaches for any rock. Indeed, the speech is remarkable for the continuously changing demands it places on the speaker's sympathies. After playing the aggressor, he puts himself "with the dead," an alliance to be expected from the Gettysburg elegist, his admission here that "both the worlds suffer" continuing an identification begun onshore and fulfilling this actor's civic duty as he prepares for future reconciliation. Less expected is his surgical probing of the killer's psyche. Lincoln may want to project himself past the rancor of his own nation's "malice domestic," but he first looks frankly at what has been done to "gain our peace," stripping the nobility from the Union cause to expose the primal and often homicidal drives it depends on. His scrutiny — incisive, indecorous, even unfair — is directed inward as much as outward, and as such ensures that his method in recitation will be experimental, not prosecutorial, this speaker trying out approaches that may launch him toward fresh knowledge of a familiar moral landscape. Speaking through Macbeth, he can confront otherwise inaccessible aspects of his own sovereignty, the equivocal motives and consequences of actions he has hitherto needed to consider decisive. Are these the "deep ambiguities" that Robert Penn Warren sees in this particular tableau of Lincoln?[43] The shock of Lincoln's choice of role — the epitome of probity taking on the guise of reckless evil — muddies easy, self-justifying distinctions between right and wrong, the same dichotomies on which melodrama relies for its normative power. They can't survive self-analysis this unsparing. Lincoln does similar violence to received notions of heroic drama. He shines light on the "torture of the mind" often obscured by heroic acts, even at the risk of soiling that heroism or seeing duty as simply malevolence rationalized. He shrinks himself to a mere "perpetrator" (to use the marquis de Chambrun's word) and recasts — resees — his deeds as "dark" to reach the chthonic source of acts committed in the name of his high office.

If he succeeds, it is by continuing to push theatrical technique past the boundaries set by nineteenth-century convention. Like any actor, he improves upon ordinary compassion by risking the humiliation of role-playing, shaping himself against the bodies and assuming the voices of his subjects so to effect a thoroughgoing submission to alien experience. Yet the context for Lincoln's impersonations leaves him exposed to a degree unknown to actors in any "real" Civil War drama. Whatever self-chastening Lincoln accomplishes is indelible at least in part because of the "theater" where he performs. The stateroom's privacy, redoubling the riverboat's distance from the public life lived onshore, is the condition for the spectator's ardent focus on Lincoln, an approach that even the self-scrutinizing actor cannot control. His listeners, gathered close about him, join him in identifying the human being unprotected by national symbolism — a form of attention that would be transgressive were it not authorized by performance. Seeing is especially invasive at a closet drama denied theater's usual visual distractions. One imagines Lincoln's auditors roused to the same kind of zealous interest in a performer's presence that we ascribed to Gillette's audience: the president's hands turning the pages of his volume of Shakespeare most likely create the only action to accompany his readings — action now as momentous as every bend of a finger in *Secret Service*. (That this manual emphasis is particularly appropriate to *Macbeth* need not be stressed. Don E. Fehrenbacher depicts a Lincoln haunted along with the king by hands stained by the blood they have shed.)[44]

The challenge put to an audience that sees nothing but the act of reading differs only in degree from that put to an audience that, in other theaters, sees little but the act of writing. If Gillette asks us to think about how a play is made, Lincoln asks us to think about how one is interpreted. The moments aboard the *River Queen* when, according to the marquis, Lincoln pauses after reading a speech to "explain [it] to us" and applaud its acuity, then to coax his listeners to the same conclusions as he recites the speech again, are as significant as the performance itself. By multiplying its meanings and associations in what the marquis calls a wide-ranging "conversation . . . upon literary subjects," Lincoln is able to pull the text around him more tightly, thinking aloud as a way of thickening the intimacy, and seeking his listeners' assent to his hermeneutic proposals as a way of rehearsing the larger, more obviously political acts of persuasion to be staged onshore. This theater is an arena less for embodying action than for mediating it, less for erecting ephemeral lyric structures and images than for testing them against permanent history.

One still marvels at the marquis's report that Lincoln read aloud this way for "several hours." The information suggests that his audience's attention may have narrowed even further during the performance — from the actor's body to the actor's voice, as over time its high tenor marked the boundaries of the listeners' world, a comfortable confinement known to any child being read to. When the reader is the nation's symbolic father, and the story, however displaced onto Shakespeare, is the Civil War, the "child's" longing for the voice's reassuring storytelling timbre has deeper and also more pathetic meaning. Only reluctantly does one relinquish the illusion that the war occasioning the reading can be resolved as inevitably as any narrative. The same disillusionment awaits those aboard the *River Queen* who, as the hours pass, let themselves imagine that the war, rubbed into the grain of Lincoln's voice, begins and ends as speech. Lincoln's reading denies auditors as much security as it creates. His imperfect impersonation — the analyst sharing space with the performer, breaking the spell to show how it is cast, forestalling his listeners' surrender to both the narrative's melodramatic terrors and the borrowed elegance of his diction — forces spectators to emulate his self-interrogatory model. At least one wants to imagine that it does, and it is as a proposal for a potential form of spectatorship that, ultimately, this small scene on the margins of Civil War theater stays in the mind. In the presence of a nearby performer, by his own fascination with a text becoming his listeners' peer rather than their idol, and of an annotated production that foregoes theatricality the better to depict a culture's disillusionment, an audience's eyes are open to a degree unrewarded in other nineteenth-century theater, if only because, in the end, it has only itself to see.

Realism against Itself

You embrace a whole world without once caring
To set it in order. That takes thought.

— James Merrill, "Mirror"

The abstract part that represents nothing . . . is the part that stands for
reality, for the object, for being awake.

— Fairfield Porter, "What Is Real?"

In his story "Manacled" (1899), Stephen Crane distills to a single harrowing image the American theater's uneasy relation to realism. The sketch is
usually read as an attack on the cult of authenticity limiting artists' (and
spectators') imaginative freedom. Such confinement, in this narrative, is literal. Crane's protagonist is an actor bound in handcuffs and anklets during the
climactic prison scene of a hoary melodrama. The play's archaism—the hero
says "curse you" with a straight face—contradicts its allegiance to the so-
called Theatre Nouveau producing it. No less confusing is the realistic stagecraft imposed on an unapologetically artificial narrative. The manacles are
made of steel and truly immobilize the actor, a choice that fulfills the promise

of an earlier farm scene "wherein real horses had drunk real water out of real buckets, afterward dragging a real wagon off stage, L.," but that proves fatal when a fire breaks out backstage and everyone flees, leaving the enchained actor to die alone.[1] "What a fool I was not to foresee this!" says the hero as he breathes his last. "I shall have Rogers furnish manacles of papier-mâché tomorrow" (162).

As a satire of realism's excesses, "Manacled" is brutally clear: the truer the life, the truer the death. Playwrights coming to the style long after novelists and painters asserted its viability make up for their belatedness with absurd zeal. The objects with which they weight a play's evanescent action in a concrete environment end up obstructing and then smothering the people who handle them. In an unanticipated turn more alarming than any plotted reversal, the objects end up handling the actors. ("If this tendency is logically followed out," Henry James once wrote about a similarly dogmatic production, "we shall soon be having Romeo drink real poison and Medea murder a fresh pair of babes every night.")[2]

Yet after its immediate pleasures have passed, "Manacled" remains open to a reading less certain about realism's sins. Crane's own attention to detail at times so far exceeds the norm as to appear obsessive. The manacled hero can take steps only "four inches long." Later, "each jump advanced him about three feet." When he tries to climb a flight of stairs, he faces the daunting reality that each step "arose eight inches from its fellow" (161–62). One can't help thinking that here, too, Crane is lampooning realist fussiness. But he also exploits it. Mock-pedantic when he describes the wagon dragged "off stage, L.," Crane later releases genuine pathos by similar attention to the actor's placement. A convincing picture of desperation emerges when Crane tracks the hero as he "dropped to a seat on the third step," then "pulled his feet to the second step," and finally "lifted himself to a seat on the fourth step" (162).

Crane's patient surveillance, remaining steady against the story's eventfulness, locates his protagonist in an environment so intimate and enveloping that it no longer seems mere background. The "intricate passages which mazed out behind the stage," the nightmarish vision of Piranesi-like stairs leading nowhere, the theater building as a whole that "hummed and shook . . . like a glade which holds some bellowing cataract of the mountains," the "crevice-like streets" outdoors, silent but for the eerie scraping of snow shovels: Crane erases the border between inside and outside, and town and country, compressing the bustling circulation of an entire landscape into the labyrinthine spaces through which spectators rush to safety (160–61). His attention to movement—its prods, currents, and consequences—unsteadies his setting metaphorically as much as physically. As the theater building resembles, in turn, a city whose urban grid is replicated in the building's corridors, a natural landscape (the scene of "mad surf amid rocks" and the "howl of a gale"), and finally a human body itself, shaking with a "palsy" as fever rushes through it and spectators gush like blood through its arteries, Crane assimilates the realist's three recurrent subjects to the very space meant to frame them.

To a degree that has implications for contemporaneous drama, Crane aggressively marks the boundaries of realism in "Manacled" in order to better transcend them. The "real horses" have their more convincing counterpart in the menagerie of animal metaphors with which Crane reveals his characters' primal instincts. Men "clawed like cats" (161). An actress is recalled going "at a canter" up a stairway. The manacled actor "pant[ed] with rage" and later "raved like a wolf." His last words — "they've left me chained up" — are the complaint of a lonely dog left in a yard (162). (Earlier, as he deliriously bites the handcuffs, one can't help thinking of a fox caught in a steel trap.) Doomed by the realist theater's lust for objects, he also becomes an object himself — and here, too, the figurative thing commands more attention than any of its truly inanimate equivalents. At the foot of the stairs, he lies "with his mouth close to the floor," intimate with the theater space to a degree known only by its furniture (162). Halfway up, he loses his balance and rolls back down, gravity establishing "presence" more definitively than actorly technique. Crane turns waspish when he links the realist's addiction to things to the spectator's own materialism. "Most of the people who were killed on the stairs," he writes, "still clutched their play-bills in their hands as if they had resolved to save them at all costs" (160). The image indicts more than the confused priorities that lead spectators to "save" a souvenir before the actor it memorializes. Crane envisions an entire culture of consumption consumed by flames, one in which such absurd fetishism is only the most obvious sign of a broader dissatisfaction with any encounter — affective, sensory, social, or aesthetic — that doesn't end in possession. The irresistible pun with which Crane opens "Manacled" identifies the procedure, and the price, of this longing: before the fire breaks out, the theater audience is "consumed with admiration" of the play (159).

The grace with which Crane moves between concrete and symbolic idioms, and between panoramic and microscopic points of view, prevents one from trusting any style. The vulnerability is useful. By the end of "Manacled," Crane's reader understands the protagonist's fate viscerally: both are unsupported by the structures of genre. The inexorable sequencing of events has penetrated so deep into Crane's scene ("inch by inch"), and then deeper still into the hero's consciousness, that representational imagery approaches abstraction. The writer and reader's claustrophobic intimacy with their subjects frustrates the realist desire to see figures and landscapes whole. Once the fire breaks out, Crane's world rapidly thickens with sound: screams "more shrill than whistles," humming, bellowing, scraping shovels, cries, howls, thundering fire engines, roaring hose carts, "hoarse shouts," crashing wood, galloping horses. The denotative meanings of such sounds, while available to those listening for them, are less significant than their participation in a symphonic tone poem. Crane expands the significance of color just as radically. The closer he looks at his scene, emulating realist fastidiousness, the further objects and figures retreat behind their surfaces. Colors float in front of the patterns they illustrated, grow so lurid as to disrupt the surrounding landscape, or acquire such radiance, lighting up hitherto undetected nuances, as to render familiar phenomena alien and fantastic. Pigments that were once mere attributes of a thing now become things in themselves and then forces, animate after long service to an inanimate landscape. The black of snow and the blue of asphalt, the "yellow plum-like reflection[s]" left by streetlights, a firebox's red beacon, the surging spectators' white faces, rhyming later with the hero's "chalk-color" rising up behind his "manly bronze" makeup: readers of Crane's better-known fiction will recognize the fever-dream style and palette. Most spectacular, the fire itself escapes its status both as melodramatic convenience—the centerpiece of countless sensation scenes—and faux-realism's scourge. After destroying the theater, it becomes purely "beautiful" (162). Of its flames, Crane writes, "some were crimson, some were orange, and here and there were tongues of purple, blue, green"—the discerning testimony of a connoisseur itemizing daubs on a canvas (162).

Aestheticism this unapologetic does more than correct the realist's overcautious sense of fidelity. (The artist who sees only red in fire conforms less to nature than to the catalogue of its simplified representations.) Crane asks whether any style can do more than treat the surfaces of experience. As we track the hero's long march, we also follow the writer's own progress. He staves off the panic of writing beyond the reach of convention with an eager sampling of existing styles—naturalistic density of detail, expressionistic clarity of emotion, and a fauve palette; the dramatic character's melodramatic dialogue giving way to the actor's drawing-room-comedy fluency; the farce of his plight and the slapstick of his movements tempering his tragedy; the drollery of Crane's tone leavening his brutal plot; the mingled languages of music (in the dissonant streetscape) and dance (in the corps' massing movements and soloist's agonized gestures), a synthesis enriched further by Crane's painterliness, itself a variable attribute, as he combines the procedures of landscape painting and portraiture, simultaneously hovering over a scene of urban anonymity and probing a single figure's body with unseemly fervor. "Blood started from under his fingernails. Soon he began to bite the hot steel, and blood fell from his blistered mouth" (162). Crane pushes against the mediations of craft itself in these unrelenting sentences from his story's penultimate paragraph. Is this a realism beyond realism, imagery that saves the style by testing its idea of decorum? The depleted tone of the next sentences extinguishes any such optimism. The parti-colored fire he deemed "beautiful" is now just a collection of "charming effects." The hero repeats his complaint that "they've left me chained up." Between the deliberately hackneyed adjective and redundant utterance are two sets of ellipses. They do more than measure the hero's slow slide toward insensibility and death. Such enforced silence marks the writer's resignation to the futility of art. In these blank spaces, style itself is exhausted. No language serves him here, before his narrative's starkest tableau. Undescribed, its own "charming effect" is uncontained. Unreadable, its reality survives undiminished. In his abstention from writing, Crane insulates his subject from literary (and by extension theatrical) consumption.

Readers turning from Crane's story to the theater he satirizes may be surprised to encounter narratives as mercurial as his own. As targets, American realist plays are elusive when we expect them to be easy, unpredictable instead of complacent, contradictory and opaque when realist dogma demands transparency. Alongside such theater, Crane's story seems less an indictment than a guide. The forceful intervention of objects, the eroding border between animate and inanimate life, the surprising ease with which representational technique slides toward abstraction, and the impenetrable lacunae in an otherwise explicit genre: all these features of "Manacled" appear in more elaborate form in the major works of American realism. (So, too, more generally, does the genre confusion, something Crane captures in the famous theater scene in *Maggie: A Girl of the Streets* [1893], where Maggie thrills to a melodrama about a "brain-clutching heroine" as if it were "transcendental realism.")[3] Upon individual plays one can also see traces of a struggle affecting the era as a whole. Realism's attraction to stable contexts and comprehensive explanations can seem at odds with theater's constant change, partial views, and uncaptioned presences. The relentless pace of performance neither encourages the spectator to pay sustained attention to visual detail (as does realist painting) nor grants the writer time to disclose as many psychological nuances as in realist fiction — liabilities that make for an agitated mode of presentation, as characters plant themselves in an art persuasive only insofar as it is incomplete and impermanent.

This contradiction is only the most enveloping of many that complicate a supposedly direct style. Theatrical realism, more than its literary or painterly equivalents, can confound spectators who dare to pause over its premises and procedures. Givens of theatrical craft suddenly seem irreconcilable when real objects stand out from artificial settings, or real actors argue for the authenticity of their imaginary characters. The double perception required to hold these opposites in the balance also directs audiences to subtler sources of uneasiness. The realist's partiality toward unremarkable aspects of private life must compromise with the inescapably public nature of performance. Any stage mirroring the spectator's own world is at once accessible and inaccessible, cordoned off by the very illusionism that forges our bond to its characters — an intimacy available only to those who keep their distance. The paradox causes what Philip Fisher, in a discussion of the city in American realist fiction, calls "the torment of proximate worlds that one can never enter," a torment more visceral in an art where spectators can measure the distance between their seats and the stage.[4]

William Dean Howells recognized as much in a famous scene from *A Hazard of New Fortunes* (1890). A magazine editor, Basil March, and his wife take a nighttime ride on a New York City elevated train and look out their windows into those of the tenements on Third Avenue. Mrs. March comments on the view: "She now said that . . . the fleeting intimacy you formed with people in second- and third-floor interiors, while all the usual street life went on underneath, had a domestic intensity mixed with a perfect repose. . . . He said it was better than the theater, of which it reminded him, to see those people through their windows: a family party of workfolk at a late tea, some of the men in their shirt-sleeves; a woman sewing by a lamp; a mother laying her child in its cradle; a man with his head fallen on his hands upon a table; a girl and her lover leaning over the windowsill together. What suggestion! What drama! What infinite interest!"[5]

This passage is typically read as a statement of literary doctrine ("the Howellsian aesthetic of realism in miniature," Eric Sundquist calls it) in its refusal of the melodramatic and its honoring of the quotidian, even though, as Sundquist and others point out, March eventually learns the price of his detachment, the presumptuousness of his voyeurism, and the incompleteness of his knowledge.[6] Late in the novel, fifteen years after their arrival in New York, the Marches congratulate themselves for seeing the city "more now as a life," whereas "then they only regarded it a spectacle" (276). The ambiguous value Howells assigns to spectatorship — it is both the prerequisite and impediment to what he calls "inquiry" — is only one of many sources of instability in the novel's vision of theater. His description of the Marches' view from the train hums with unresolved contradictions. "Intimacy" is "fleeting." "Intensity" throbs within "repose." The domestic interiors have all the authenticity of unconscious disclosures, yet they are also two-dimensional — lifelike scenes from an advent calendar. Moreover, these living rooms and bedrooms simultaneously expose and shield their inhabitants: the windowpanes and the white noise of the intervening street preserve silence; the tightly cropped window frames enforce discretion. The most exciting "drama," here, can be only "suggestion." Its "interest" may be "infinite," but the train's pause at this station is not.

As the train's departure smears the drama once visible through its windows, additional reasons for theater's intractability come into focus. On any realist stage, objects and figures slip the yoke of narrative and even mise-en-scène. They elude a playwright's or director's attempt to control our access to them as they radiate magnetic power unharnessed by dramatic structure. What Roland Barthes (in an essay on the French new novel) calls "adjectival film" never has a chance to build up on phenomena whose very presence renders irrelevant the writer's descriptive energies.[7] (Barthes envisions such an unmediated object being "kept open, available to its new dimension, time" [20] — an observation even more pertinent to the temporal art of theater.) To those accustomed to fiction's protocols, there's something alarming about these wayward objects and also about the unchaperoned spectators looking at them and drawing their own conclusions. Despite theater's best efforts to sedate the liveliness of objects so to improve their usefulness as props, and to bind individual spectators with a common mode of seeing, both subject and object of attention remain autonomous, stronger than the occasion bringing them together, indifferent to the realist theater's desire for proportionality.

Before the heat of such exchanges between spectator and stage, neutrality, too, seems a distant if not irrelevant ideal. The principles of realist doctrine — antiromanticism, scientific coolness, skepticism — lose their allure to audiences beguiled, instead, by sensuous artifacts. One need only consider one's actual experience (rather than idealized projection) of realist drama in performance to recognize how severely realist theory underestimates the hypnotic power of staged milieux. Writers may style themselves "mighty destroyer[s] of idols," charged with the "repudiation of the graces and enchantments of fine art" and of "theatrical romance" (such are the terms with which Bernard Shaw praised realist playwrights), but once their unsparing scenes are framed by the proscenium and bathed in light, all claims of objectivity seem powerless against the seductions of style.[8] The most degraded object turns numinous in such a context. The invisible history preceding its appearance — the artist choosing it from among countless alternatives, the care with which he or she placed it onstage to harmonize with its surroundings — supplies it with an aura unqualified by its actual importance or triviality in the action. By its newfound clarity alone, it masters spectators who are themselves expected to master (as witness, prosecutor, or judge) the world it furnishes.

Edgar Allan Poe's story "The Oval Portrait" (1842) captures well the deviousness by which realism can render helpless its most responsive audiences.

The titular object enthralls the narrator as he prepares for bed in a strange, abandoned chateau. His bedroom is frankly theatrical: the portrait is hung in a proscenium-like niche; the curtains of his four-poster bed further frame the image; light cast upon it from a candelabra heightens the scene's melodrama. For all this, though, the source of the portrait's power over him remains obscure until he realizes he has been looking too hard. "I fell back within the bed. I had found the spell of the picture in an absolute *life-likeliness* of expression, which at first startling, finally confounded, subdued, and appalled me."[9] In the extremity of his reaction — "appalled"? — he only incidentally echoes the typical antirealist offended by a style that has no use for flattery. Poe reminds us of realism's radical, violent zeal when he discloses the portrait's history. Its subject had slowly withered away as she sat for a painter unwilling to settle for anything but the strictest verisimilitude. Only when he could say, after many weeks of work, "This is indeed *Life* itself!" did he realize that his model had died (484). From Poe's tale an anxious theater-minded reader may turn to realist drama wondering if its own procedures are less a tribute to than a vampiric theft or violation of reality, and if the cost of the intensely pleasurable sensation of recognition inside the theater is some portion of our ability to engage with the life outside it.

The twin forms of compulsion Poe describes — the artist in thrall to his subject, the spectator to the art — are correctives to the commonplace that temperance alone ensures the continued vitality of realist practice. Harry Levin, in his study of French realism, understands the consequences of continuing to insist upon this point: "Man cannot be completely objective without becoming indifferent."[10] Poe's painter keeps indifference at bay by keeping his eye on a nearby horizon: enchanted by his model, he is even more consumed by his craft. "Life-likeliness" derives from obsessive attention to artifice; his materials disappear into the figure they form only after exacting their own tribute. By inviting us to imagine the painter's obsessive handling of paint — his appetite for revision fed "from hour to hour and from day to day" until he grows "wild with the ardor of his work" — Poe exposes the even more lifelike imbalance preceding the eerily poised image (483).

Another painter, not only realist but real, and another scene of revision provide one last, skeptical comment on the drive toward verisimilitude in American theater. Thomas Eakins's best-known works are, as many have pointed out, studies of audiences, qualifying the assertions of realist composition with the variety of modes of receiving them. *Salutat* (1898) literally turns its back on the stage, showing a boxer from behind as he greets his audience before exiting the ring. Eakins's attention to a space meant to remain in the dark and to figures usually protected by anonymity exposes a surprising variety of attitudes. For every jubilant fan, there are others who are skeptical, oddly resentful, or even menacing; one is on his way out altogether, uninterested in the denouement of this particular drama. The same uncertainty over how to respond to the realist spectacle tests the coherence of the celebrated *Gross Clinic* (1875) and *Agnew Clinic* (1889). In both paintings, a scientific view of life controls the foreground, where surgeons, anesthesiologists, and nurses encircle a patient's flayed body, yet it is the less controlled action in the background that fills more canvas space. Scattered among the engaged medical students in the amphitheater of *The Agnew Clinic* are two who bend their heads against each other like songbirds, one who leans against the railing as if trying to stay awake, and a third who violates all decorum by lying down — the class delinquent. In *The Gross Clinic,* the atmosphere of steady inquiry is broken most famously by a female figure who twists away in revulsion from the operation; she covers her eyes with clawlike hands, tensing them as if about to scratch back at the affront to her sensibility. The pose could have been copied directly from *The Thespian Preceptor,* the early nineteenth-century manual of melodramatic acting. (Michael Fried calls the painting "a melodrama of visibility.")[11] The very structure controlling the scenes of this and other paintings clarifies the debt that realism owes to the form it seemingly overturns. Eakins's situations depend on the oppositions familiar from narratives in which good triumphs over evil — the heroic doctor saves the helpless victim, the strong boxer defeats the weak — and yet simultaneously drain them of suspense, deflecting attention to an audience where multiplicity of emotion and action is the rule.

It was in a painting far less familiar than these that Eakins made the strongest case that true realists are always contending with their nonrealist instincts. The painting's history also comments, silently, on the ambiguous effects of spectatorship. Eakins never exhibited his only painting on an explicitly theatrical theme, *An Actress (Portrait of Suzanne Santje)* (1903) — a surprising choice that seems a deliberate check on the publicity-seeking instincts of its subject, a onetime member of Augustin Daly's company, and of her profession in general. This contradiction lights up further sites of ambivalence within the painting itself. Although it is true that, as those critics eager to confirm Eakins's realist bona fides argue, the great actress is shown in private, far from the stage where ordinary life is sentimentalized, she hasn't fully shed melodramatic habits of self-presentation. Languid, mordant, dressed in a flowing scarlet gown, she fixes the viewer with a dissolute and quizzical gaze, much like, as Marc Simpson notes, the tubercular title character of the script lying at her feet, *Camille.*[12] No one can doubt that the actress's disheveled appearance is carefully arranged: Santje manages to be at once glamorous and ugly, an oxymoron that exaggerates many performers' public form of privacy and that unsteadies the site as much as the sitter.[13] The room's furnishings also resist unity: the chair, carpet, and vase have reminded Eakins scholars of various other paintings by him in which the same things appear, yet on the wall hangs a portrait of Santje's father and on the floor lies an opened envelope bearing her address.[14] Are we in Eakins's studio or Santje's home, on or off a set? That Eakins is unwilling (rather than unable) to choose — or, more precisely, unwilling to treat opposites as mutually exclusive — is the implicit meaning of the strangest detail in the portrait. One may read a succinct summary of the painter's unresolved internal debate about style on the cover of the playscript lying face-down on the floor. Eakins seems to have first titled the play *Hamlet* then later settled on *Camille*, adding or painting over letters on the cover. He does what seems to be a purposefully sloppy job of revision, leaving both titles visible in a palimpsest, allowing us to imagine a sequence of second and third thoughts in the studio but preventing us from establishing its chronology with any certainty. Indeed, a viewer looking at the painting for the first time might reasonably think that *Camille*, not *Hamlet*, was his first, rejected choice.

Of course, the two plays themselves trigger contradictory associations. Confusion results not simply from the blurring of tragic and melodramatic art (and the elite and popular audiences supporting them). Neither play, in fact, fits easily into a culture edging toward realism. But has this script of *Camille* — an emblem of a bygone era's sentimental manipulations, the dramatic equivalent of everything Eakins supposedly rejected in his own art — in fact been discarded or just temporarily set aside, as if the painter himself were taking a break from resisting its seductions? *Hamlet*'s ghostly presence in the painting sends its own cross signals. Eakins may mean to suggest that Santje is rehearsing the title role — this was the era of famous female Hamlets, as Theodor Siegl reminds us — and thereby challenge his viewers to reconcile two more contradictory images.[15] As this Hamlet hovers between male and female, this *Hamlet* negotiates between Dumas's histrionics and Eakins's reserve. Here, too, dwells a self-referential allegory, unlocking new, personal meaning in the prince's fabled agony of indecision. The painter's similar affliction may explain why he signed the canvas, as if he had finished it, yet never let it leave his studio, as if he wanted to keep working on it forever.

Set against all these self-interrogations, a key principle of theatrical realism looks idealistic, if not naive. W. B. Worthen distills (without questioning) the essence of a widely accepted view when he writes that realist practice "argues that . . . reality can only be shown on the stage by effacing the medium — literary style, acting, mise-en-scène — that discloses it."[16] American theatrical

Figure 9: *An Actress (Portrait of Suzanne Santje)* by Thomas Eakins (1903). The actress's script lies face down to her right. Philadelphia Museum of Art. Gift of Mrs. Thomas Eakins and Miss Mary Adeline Williams, 1929.

realism doesn't depreciate when it can't fulfill this definition. On the contrary, the plays that bear rereading on the far side of modernism are compelling to the degree that they fail at "effacing the medium," a failure that directs spectators to the drama of "disclosing" as much as to anything disclosed. It falls to Theodore Dreiser to school us in the skepticism necessary to appreciate the tension between stage world and real world. Even though "dramatic art . . . is at once the most natural as well as the most understandable of the graces," he writes in *Sister Carrie* (1900) as Carrie prepares to make her acting debut in *Under the Gaslight,* "it scarcely occurs to the inexperienced onlooker that it must be difficult to be natural."[17]

The earliest examples of American realism are about that difficulty more than anything else — more than the hothouse environments, economic humiliations, and sexual volatility that typical realists depend on to pull our attention away from the scene of their representation, the stage itself. It would be rash to ascribe a sophisticated metatheatricality to these fledgling realists (although, as we'll see, many of them incorporate scenes of performance and spectatorship in their plays), but it would be no less imprudent to dismiss as mere incompetence the awkwardness afflicting those trying to seize a still fluid style. Despite realism's interest in determinism, these plays move unpredictably among tones and through models of structure, transforming attitudes that look sincere in one scene into irony or outright parody in the next. Yet the slipperiness is of more than merely formal interest. Those seeking evidence of a larger cultural uncertainty can find it here, as realist dramaturgy reflects the Gilded Age at the moment it loses trust in long-established social structures. The longing to preserve that trust, and prolong the innocence fostering it, can be felt as certain characters still submit to typology and hierarchy, as emotion flows in well-worn grooves of expression, and as narrative affirms inflexible codes of justice and morality. Yet these reassuring tropes exist in these plays only to be compromised. Many playwrights also find room for the sexual and economic aggression that would undermine such comforts — urges addressed with a candor that itself overflows grooves and strains against types. In another sign of the ambivalence maintaining this theater's febrile energy, some playwrights who claim for drama ordinary domestic negotiations and business procedures, realism's stock-in-trade, end up treating them with melodramatic breathlessness or sentimental piety. The contradiction gives their plays an air of permanent belatedness: in a culture changing rapidly, a playwright's style can never catch up with his or her curiosity.

James A. Herne's *Margaret Fleming* (1890) stands, shakily, as the embodiment of this condition. Despite Herne's status as one of his century's chief polemicists for dramatic realism (his 1897 essay "Art for Truth's Sake in the Drama" is the genre's sole American manifesto), he doesn't present us with a self-assured model of the form. Rather (and one wants to believe intentionally), he lets us watch him in the troubled process of working toward his chosen style. There are few attributes of older modes he's ready to reject outright. Any plot summary of *Margaret Fleming,* indifferent to its handling in performance, would include such instantly recognizable markers of sentimental melodrama as the domestic setting framed tightly around the relationship between mother and child; the temperance moralizing of a family friend; the husband's self-indictment for adultery and for fathering an illegitimate child; and the schedule of deception, comeuppance, and atonement with which Herne paces his action. Yet in context, the meaning and function of these elements are more ambiguous than they seem in this account. Herne has retained clichés to interrogate them, to clarify for himself and his viewers just how drama may change when realism enjoys a surer footing.

Herne's technique is especially apparent in his careful handling of the most volatile emotions, as actors trained by theatrical tradition to accelerate past nuance toward hysteria instead submit to the braking pressure of the playwright's sense of decorum. Whenever Margaret cries, for instance, Herne calls equal attention to the moment she stops—a swift shutting off of sentiment, followed by decisive action. As if Herne feared that degree of restraint weren't enough, he describes Margaret as suffering from a "blockage of the eye ducts," the cause of the glaucoma that later blinds her and, more suggestively, an impersonal means to control unpredictable sentiment: her body won't let her cry freely even if she wants to. Other characters who start operatic apologies—a loyal maid dropping to her knees is one—are cut off by pragmatic listeners impatient to move on. ("Get up, Maria," says Margaret, "don't go on like that!")[18] Margaret is just as intolerant of Maria's melodramatic brandishing of a pistol in a later scene, disarming her in the no-nonsense way a parent would discipline a misbehaving child. (It's as if Herne were disciplining melodrama itself.) In still another show of Herne's cautious radicalism, the typical scene of forgiveness—a satisfactory ending to earlier plays—is here only the prologue to a more substantial and open-ended scene of negotiation. As in *A Doll House* (performed in New York a year earlier and often considered a strong influence on *Margaret Fleming*), Herne's couple sits down to work out new terms of their relationship after their marriage crumbles. While the melodramatist in Herne can't resist including a suicide attempt—by the husband, Philip, when he feels powerless against his guilt—the realist in Herne controls its presence and significance. The attempt is kept offstage; it fails; it is mocked. (Philip says a nurse at the hospital "told me not to be a fool" [267].) Even its telling is incidental to the real, unsensational subject of the discussion scene: the responsibility of parenthood.

The discussion confirms changes to the iconography and meaning of parenthood visible throughout the production. Mother-child scenes that would seem mawkish if they were painted or narrated are, here, contested, gently burlesqued, and even overturned. Herne dispenses with any gauzy idea of maternity in the first scene, where the characters' frank talk of abortion recalls the financial and social pressures of pregnancy. In the next act, a form of visual counterpoint further controls the emotions aroused by Herne's imagery: Margaret sits in a rocking chair as she finishes nursing her baby while nearby her maid stands weeping—the source of her grief less important, for now, than the efficient way it opens up the stage to prevent Margaret's presence from becoming emblematic or even reassuring. As the play continues, maternity as a whole loses its sacred aura as characters adjust and readjust to the demands of fast-changing situations. They may still insist that the gestures of mothering spring from mysterious instinct, but they act with more deliberation and, at times, calculation, fulfilling their seemingly circumscribed role in order to seize unexpected power. At these moments, parody is more convincing than piety. Margaret playfully reproaches Philip in one scene by taking away his cigar and watchpiece—attributes of the man of the world—and replacing them with a rattle and ball: "You can play with these" (251). The infantilized Philip sitting on the floor with his new toys not only undoes the sentimentality typical of childhood scenes but also defeats the adult masculine sexual bravura lingering after the earlier report of Philip's affair and illegitimate child.

Other objects also change on this revisionist stage, gaining (or regaining) practical uses and simple meanings. A tell-all letter that accidentally falls into Margaret's hands—that staple of the well-made play—loses its exaggerated significance when Margaret recycles it, tearing off the blank bottom half to write a note of her own. Her utilitarianism continues in the next scene. After surviving humiliation, grief, and illness, she arrives onstage carrying a huge bouquet of just-cut flowers. It's hard to resist the image's obvious symbolism —her garden's renewal affirming her own spiritual rebirth—but Herne limits its pretensions. Margaret immediately discusses the nuisance of rose bugs and the virtues of insecticides. Her horticultural digression is not without underlying relevance to her domestic situation—"don't you know that the [way] to prevent trouble is to look ahead?" she says (261)—but it's more significant as evidence of Herne's struggle to fulfill realism's pledge of scientific impartiality without betraying melodrama's obligation to teach morality. That ambivalence is neatly encapsulated in another character, one Dr. Larkin. One might expect him, as a man of science, to affirm the precepts of realist drama, and to some extent he does, insisting on honesty and pointing out how environment determines character. Yet more than any other character, he also frets over moral contamination and inveighs against sin — refusing a cigar from a man whose conduct he censures, arguing that Margaret's emotional torment caused her glaucoma. The doctor has it both ways. He won't blame the play's "other woman," Lena, seeing her environment as the cause of her "fall" into pregnancy, but he will puritanically inveigh against the adulterous husband. Margaret vents her own anger at Philip's conduct in an equally confused hybrid of moralizing and scientific language: "I, too, cry 'pollution' " (265).

Neutrality does triumph, however, in an unlikely arena. Herne's most elegant adjustment of melodramatic dramaturgy changes the function of the tableau. Like earlier nineteenth-century plays, *Margaret Fleming* invites a director to arrange its actors in telling compositions at key turns in the narrative — occasions for spectators to study emotions in their most distilled form. Departing from tradition, however, Herne's tableaux do not serve as exclamation marks at the ends of scenes, nor do they trace the distribution of power among characters, nor stress the ethical significance of the action. Instead, they are muted and recessed, which doesn't make them any less compelling than typical, histrionic tableaux. If anything, we read them more closely because we're uncoerced toward their meanings.

A composition near the end of act 3 is representative and especially beautiful. Margaret, having just learned her husband's secret, stands stunned but tranquil in the sunlight of her rival's living room. She has also just noticed the first signs of what, by the end of the scene, will be her total blindness. Herne's vision of this transition is precise. The stage is silent. The light gathers around her as all else falls into shadow. She stands motionless, her right hand resting on a table, her left hand at her cheek. As Herne describes it in a stage direction, she "is lost in spiritual contemplation of the torment she is suffering" and "gaz[es] into space, the calmness of death upon her face." Near her are the two other components of the tableau — a Mrs. Burton, sitting in a rocking chair, and Maria, sharing the same space but like the others immersed in isolating meditation, sitting on a sofa "with clasped hands, her arms lying in her lap, her body bent" (258). This is a tableau of thinking, not of declaring, emoting, or even showing. All three actors turn in on themselves rather than out to the audience. No spectator is needed to ratify sensations that they alone experience; their own looking matters more than ours. It's not just Margaret's blindness that makes one think of Maeterlinck.[19] It's possible that only here, in this realist effort, has a nineteenth-century American dramatist benefited from the key symbolist discovery about character psychology — that at moments of greatest distress the body acquires unnatural poise and the face freezes under a glaze of introspection, sealing others off from private, untheatrical sorrow. (Only by seeing the scene as true to subjective rather than objective reality can one explain the implausibility of Margaret going blind in a matter of lines.)

Regardless of the manner of its presentation, the mere fact of Margaret's blindness reaches beyond the confines of character and narrative to test assumptions underlying all realist works. As several critics have reminded us — most recently Bill Brown in *A Sense of Things* (2003) and Peter Brooks in *Realist Vision* (2005) — realism is predicated on the acts of showing and beholding.[20] Vision commits viewer and exhibitor alike to the maintenance of the material world, as if the eye has power beyond that of mere acknowledgement to rescue and confer dignity upon all manner of experience. It frames the telling gesture or object in precincts dense with other phenomena demanding attention. Pushing back against the onrush of chaotic daily activity, it picks out traces of ephemeral feelings that would otherwise be lost. Yet the heroism of this project masks its naiveté. Since when has vision saved anything? Can mere seeing grant us the same knowledge as other, more rigorous forms of engagement? Herne doesn't ask these questions himself — they probably don't even occur to him — but his blind protagonist prompts us to face them ourselves. Margaret's vulnerable presence exposes a vulnerability in the style she heralds. The confidence projected by other realists drains away here, and in rushes hesitation and doubt, self-scrutinizing impulses that a realist's outward-directed curiosity usually represses.

Of course repression of any kind is anathema to realists already scornful of the demurrals of rival, more refined styles. Yet realists more secure than Herne have felt it necessary to avoid all questions about their premises and techniques, lest their art fail to convince us that their versions of life are authoritative. It is the continued awareness that such failure is possible — even inevitable — that distinguishes *Margaret Fleming* from other examples of the genre. Herne synchronizes the gradual dilation of our vision, an expansion that lets us see both the transgressive and banal aspects of a marriage, with the progressive contracting and dimming of Margaret's own sight. The juxtaposition keeps our pride in check. We can't congratulate ourselves for looking unflinchingly at hitherto sanitized human behavior when sight is coded as inadequate and embattled. Margaret's blindness also suggests that some part of Herne himself recoils from what he dramatizes. Her involuntary retreat from the visible world allows him to confess his desire to withdraw as well from its starkest truths (despite his assertions to the contrary in "Art for Truth's Sake in the Drama"), a confession that, if made openly, would of course be realist apostasy. Before Herne, Thomas Eakins proved the value of such ambivalence:

the painter's self-blinding mothers, dozing medical students, and distracted sports fans — along with the embedded self-portraits in which Eakins surfaces only to sink into shadow or hug the margins of the scene — populate a realism that gains authority by admitting the anxiety of confronting the real. Herne, for his part, turns such an admission into a challenge. His blind protagonist implicitly asks us to see what she (and he?) cannot.

We try to do just that in the play's most notorious scene. The delicate tableau in which Margaret senses the first threat to her eyesight shatters when Lena's baby starts crying. Margaret snaps out of her reverie, gropes her way toward the sound, and (as a stage direction puts it) "suddenly, with an impatient, swift movement . . . unbuttons her dress to give nourishment to the child, when the picture fades away into darkness" (259–60). One wants to regard this depiction of breast-feeding as an unqualified triumph of visibility and therefore of realism. (Most theater historians do.) Yet it would be misleading — and less interesting — to be so optimistic. While Herne succeeds in getting onstage a reality hitherto prohibited by his squeamish or overdecorous predecessors, he can't keep it there for more than a moment, allowing only a glimpse before darkness (or the curtain) falls. Herne cannily changes the subject here, from Margaret's embattled sight to our own.

Our seeing is now as potentially transgressive as any act committed by Herne's characters. It betrays desires stronger than mere interest and flickers with self-consciousness as such desires encounter inevitable resistance — our fear of censure for crossing the border of tact, say, or our regret at having to acknowledge the plainness of once-idealized scenarios. As we wait out the isolating blackout or face the impassible curtain after this scene, Herne advances his argument about realist attention still further. If we treat the darkness as a presence rather than an absence — the phenomenon Wallace Stevens has in mind when he famously directed readers away from the "nothing that is not there" to "the nothing that is" — we may recall other blind spots in Herne's play.[21] Many of them are even more deliberately scenic. A room stands empty for a long moment before actors enter to begin a scene. French-door curtains described as "filmy" blur our view of Philip's return home: he stands behind them as if embedded in opaque ice before finally opening the door. Gathering clouds extinguish the first act's "flooding" sunlight; eventually, rain veils the landscape once visible through the window. The room in which Lena lies dying, its door shut to us, is oppressive for being visually unreachable. The fathomless darkness around a living room fireplace (the brightest source of light in this scene) shrouds characters trackable only by their voices. Reports of the play's first production tell of a final manipulation of negative space: after Margaret utters the play's last line and is "left standing in tragic isolation on the stage" (writes Hamlin Garland), "the lights were turned out one by one" and "her figure gradually disappeared in deepening shadow."[22] With each click of a switch, Herne reclaims a section of the stage from hungry-eyed spectators. (The 1891 production also attuned spectators to the play's aural lacunae. In a circular mailed to potential ticket buyers, the title carries the tagline "An American Play without a Soliloquy!")[23]

Taken together, these various vacancies and absences are the scenic confirmation of Margaret's demeanor, the restraint that asserts itself only after she tamps down what one early stage direction calls a personality "overflowing with animation" (251). The inwardness of the tableau she forms on learning of Philip's betrayal proposes a general approach to embodying a role, one that proceeds by erasure, the steady elimination of affect, instead of the Stanislavskian notion of "building a character." Over the last two acts (if stage directions stressing her "suppressed emotion" are fair indication), Margaret becomes deliberately less distinct, flatter and duller, her presence seeming to dwindle in inverse proportion to the plot's escalating tensions. One reviewer tells how the original Margaret, Herne's wife Katharine, barely moved during the narrative's eruptions; another observer complained that she spoke "so low that you lose more than half of what she says."[24] A performance that Howells praised as "common," "pitilessly plain," "ugly," "but . . . true" rebuffs a spectator's gestures of empathy, that habit of realist spectatorship, and recalls us to the distance between stage and audience.[25] This gulf becomes yet another blank space, cleared of the supplications that corrupt much theatrical expression.

By remaining immaculate of the markings that would limit meaning, Herne's blank spaces invite spectators to ponder alternatives to the realist milieu and to imagine unstaged, unembodied aspects of characters. At the very least, they give us room to pivot our attention — away from the effaced center of the spectacle and toward marginal figures or other phenomena placed beyond the jurisdiction of realism's visual sovereignty. It cannot be accidental, for instance, that Herne stresses sounds when sights grow scarce or short-lived: the baby's wail, a moan from Maria, whispers beyond a threshold, another character's voice sharp enough to "arrest" an exiting Margaret, a letter read aloud to patient auditors, and Margaret and Philip's long concluding discussion, Herne's most sustained show of visual chastity, a scene in which speech expands until spectacle recedes entirely. All these aural performances would be unremarkable did they not add to our sense that, in this theater, ungraspable phenomena will always be testing our faith in the expressivity of the material world, of everything thought essential to what Bert O. States in his definition of realism calls "an art of pinning things down."[26] States is of course thinking of the playwright's art, but in the presence of works as deliberately evasive as Herne's the responsibility for "pinning things down" also falls to the spectators. Our frustrated attempts at productions of *Margaret Fleming* to see into the opaque patches of stage and character can seem, in this light, to emulate Herne's own efforts toward stylistic legibility, matching the energy of his hairpin turns from melodrama to symbolism to realism as he keeps the play in a constant state of reinvention.

That reinvention is more elaborate than Herne himself could have anticipated. The *Margaret Fleming* we read today is a memorial stone to an irretrievable original. Herne rewrote the last act after the disappointing premiere, buckling under a new producer's pressure to add a trace of hope to what earlier had been a wholly pessimistic ending. (While Margaret still insists the "wife-heart has gone out of me," she allows herself to imagine that it "would be a wonderful thing" if Philip won her back.)[27] Both the old and new versions were lost in 1909 when fire destroyed Herne's home; the play existed in legend more than fact until Katharine Herne rewrote the play from memory. (James died in 1901.) Her version, however, proved no more stable than the original. She responded to the promptings of friends, editors, potential producers, and her own sense of what would be "acceptable to the modern audience" (as she put it to Hamlin Garland) as she completed a series of revisions between 1914 and 1929.[28] The resulting texts shape new absences even as they mask old ones. Lines have been forgotten or purposefully omitted. Revisions equivocate on sensitive subjects or soften opinions once openly declared. Narrative threads are cut. The writer himself — or is it herself? — is obscured along with the writing. Hamlin Garland speaks of "producing" the play together with Katharine as they compared notes on the original. Arthur Hobson Quinn requested (and received) changes before consenting to publish it in *Representative American Plays*. As Katharine continued to widen the circle of collaboration she was only fulfilling an implicit policy set by Herne himself: long before the fire, he willingly diminished his own authorial presence by inviting Katharine to take what, in Quinn's words, was "an active part in the original creation of the play."[29] In light of this cumulative history, the act of writing seems as scandalous as the act of nursing on which Herne dropped so quick a curtain. First thoughts, bold first drafts, and the startling, unsoftened first production are glimpsed for only a moment before revision closes them off from view, their radicalism relegated to the safety of history.

The corrupt status of the published *Margaret Fleming* would disqualify it from our serious attention were it not a condition so true to — and reinforcing of — the play's subject matter and self-questioning method, its hesitating realism. The plot's preoccupation with blindness predicts the history of effacement afflicting the script. Moreover, the textual unreliability that audiences must reconcile themselves to on seeing *Margaret Fleming* fosters a flexibility that suits Herne's larger, ethical project. During the Flemings' final discussion, Margaret objects to Philip calling Lena's son "our dear child." "No," Margaret says, "not our child. . . . Your son" (265). Her verbal adjustment is an instance of *Margaret Fleming* revising itself before our eyes. A play stocked with images of maternity now reveals itself as concerned more deeply, and surprisingly, with paternity. All the "paraphernalia of the nursery" that the critic William Winter complained "make people sick in public" have been put in place so that here they can be reassigned.[30] Even more significant is the manner in which such responsibility is borne. The play ends with a simple action, among the simplest theater knows — Philip exiting, walking toward the garden where his two children are playing — that speaks of more than his new attitude as a parent. Before Philip reaches his destination, the curtain falls, another strategically timed descent. By choosing to end the play with movement, Herne (or rather, the Hernes) help us track a still developing realist dramaturgy. It's not just that here, as earlier, the rhetorical fixity of the typical tableau is no longer available. Philip's blur of motion also keeps us from prematurely trusting his change of heart. An ongoing moral evolution is embodied, literally, in his progress toward a garden that is itself shedding its associations with Edenic perfection to become a place for meeting real-world demands. Philip is changing, not yet changed, in a not-yet-realist theater that shares his uncertainty about identity, style, method, and future.

The many varieties of motion in *Margaret Fleming* — the free play of thought permitted by the blank spaces on the page and stage, the ever-more-pliant text revised continuously over forty years, the competing styles trumping one another, the reassignment of sentimental markers until they turn parodic or progressive, the stage aperture opening and closing as it offers and rescinds visual information, and finally, the uncompleted movement with which the play ends — are the seeds of an approach to stage composition that would only be realized, in spectacular form, with an otherwise unrelated artifact of American realism, *Salvation Nell* (1908). Edward Sheldon's title suggests he will be organizing his action around a single figure, arousing our sympathy by giving us a steady object of attention. Yet while much does depend on Nell's emotional development (she grows from an abused, patiently suffering barmaid and single mother to a vigorous missionary), narrative is the least important thing about the play. Sheldon writes with choreographic, musical buoyancy. Indeed, commentators have often forgotten that his first act is accompanied by a three-piece band playing popular songs under the action. His style invites us to scan the stage even when the distress of the heroine draws focus.

Spectators familiar with the cityscape plays of the previous generation — Benjamin Baker's *A Glance at New York* (1848), for instance — will doubtless see in *Salvation Nell* an heir. Here, as there, characters stimulate interest less for what they say than for how they move, as they mass like birds or fish, then scatter, only to gather again in new combinations, asserting a changed hierarchy. Yet Sheldon's picture plane is deeper and denser than Baker's; the figures of *Salvation Nell* are harder to track and their terrain is less mappable, as if his milieux were seen from the inside, in keeping with realism's disorienting intimacy instead of with the tourist's detachment and short attention span. Sheldon favors porous but nonetheless circumscribed spaces — a barroom, an intersection of streets hemmed in by tenements — that cause the action to churn instead of flow. The New York of *Salvation Nell* doesn't offer the ambulatory freedom available in Baker's city, where characters tick off a list of landmarks and addresses as they shape a narrative of seemingly endless linearity. Sheldon explores simultaneity instead. He describes his opening as "kaleidoscope-like," its "first scenes . . . to be played easily and swiftly, for a purely atmospheric effect."[31] The disclaimer diminishes the significance of his form. Treasured assumptions about dramatic structure, and about the ideology, psychology, and sentiment that such structure upholds, dissolve in the swirl of Sheldon's action. Much of that activity eventually proves to be insignificant, but the play refrains from making such distinctions for as long as possible, forcing us to decide for ourselves what is important or, even better, to relinquish our need for hierarchies of value altogether. (Here, too, Sheldon departs from his predecessors' example. Characters of an earlier era point us, sometimes literally, in narrative, emotional, or geographical directions, and expect we'll follow loyally behind them.)

Over a long opening scene (one can think of it as a single cinematic take), Sheldon alights upon several characters with the realist's strict neutrality, compiling a raw record of experience that awaits interpretation. Two drunks get obstreperous over the quality of the saloon's free lunch. A streetwalker secures the patronage of a gullible john. A policeman accepts a free drink as a bribe. A fight breaks out over a pool game. A girl wrapped in a threadbare shawl wanders in to buy a pitcher of beer for her penniless mother. Any one of these events could trigger the action of a whole play; each character could evolve into a protagonist. (Some, like the waif in the shawl, tease us into thinking we're about to see an old-fashioned melodrama. It's one of Sheldon's better jokes on our theatergoing habits that we never see her again.) The fact that all of them turn out to be supernumeraries changes the way we eventually see the principals. The latter characters' status also never appears stable, even when it has become clear that their emotional turmoil and moral quandaries are meant to have first claim on our sympathies. At any moment, these sentimental characters could be interrupted or simply reabsorbed by an indifferent society.

That possibility functions as skeptical counterpoint to every sincere declaration. Each of the three momentous disclosures and crestings of emotion in this first scene is cut short by the entrance of another character, one who pulls to himself or herself a spectator's affective loyalties. Nell's acknowledgment of her pregnancy never gets the sympathy it deserves after a crowd of pool players bursts onstage preening and bragging. Her reconciliation (the first of several) with her estranged lover, Jim, kindles but doesn't burn because a street tough's entrance draws away all the air in the room. A missionary's eloquent attempt to convert Nell peaks only to fall abruptly the moment a casino hostess makes her own flamboyant bid for attention. These battles between sentimental and unsentimental action aren't fatal. On the contrary, Sheldon's depictions of grief and tenderness, and of characters struggling to devise a workable personal morality, are stronger for having to fight their way to visibility, emerging even as characters try to meet a plethora of more immediate demands. One of the simplest reasons for Nell's delay in looking like the protagonist of the play that bears her name is that in this first act she is always working. Washing tables, scrubbing the floor, rinsing glasses, hanging holly on the windows, tending the pickle vat: Nell doesn't stand still long enough to be exalted, to seem noble in her oppression. The prosaic world of labor trumps the ideal world of lucid emotions and exemplary behavior, or at least Sheldon implies that moral purity and self-knowledge, no less than any other thing of value, have to be earned and maintained.

Such an assertion is news only after a century in which most theatrical depictions of virtue or vice were suspended in amber, impervious to contingency or even the particular social weather of the times. With this play, the tyranny of typology begins to loosen its grip on dramatic structure. The loosening is slight: Sheldon's whores with hearts of gold, vulnerable brutes, and charismatic missionaries are hardly departures from the norm. But (in an extension of a challenge previously restricted to comedies and burlesques by Edward Harrigan, John Brougham, and others) the norm — normativeness in general — can no longer be depended on for moral guidance. "God, why didn't ye help me?" asks Nell at a particularly low point. "Where did ye go?" (129). Characters exist in a world past trusting any models or countermodels of behavior. They treat determinism, the guiding principle of much realism, with resentment. "If I'm a thief," Jim complains to Nell, "it's 'cause the Gawd yer always gassin' about's made things so I can't be anythin' else" (128). Nell, for her part, resists her fate as defenseless victim. In this context, Sheldon's self-dissolving dramaturgy is appropriate to characters challenging a society that fixes their worth at its lowest level, on the easiest-to-read scale. Moreover, as we watch characters renegotiating their identity (or merely chafing at its limits) within a compositional structure that itself seems open to revision, we are made to acknowledge the variable intentions behind our own work of spectatorship. Faced with the apparent centerlessness of Sheldon's stage, it's left to us to impose structures both moral and compositional. Here, too, pragmatism wins out over didacticism. As we make decisions about what to look at (or think about), following certain characters while letting others merely cross our line of vision, we, like Nell, are simply too busy to bother with ideals.

If we pause in this work and step back from the stage, we may decide that Sheldon is unwittingly furthering James Herne's commentary on realist vision. Spectators coming to *Salvation Nell* after an encounter with blind Margaret Fleming may grow even more self-aware of the difficulty and consequences of an act that had once seemed automatic. In a series of throwaway lines, Sheldon explicitly declares his interest. "Look at me — look at me jus' once!" Nell says to Jim early on, a plea that sounds at the desperate far end of generalized self-consciousness about exposure and display (97). In this environment, effective vision needs more than good intentions. Other, less agitated customers in the crowded bar remark on Nell's fluctuating visibility ("thought I seen her over there a minute ago" [96]) while others acknowledge the fragility of all relationships by measuring the time between sightings ("Hello boys! Hain't seen ye fer a month" [97]). Serving private emotional needs, vision can turn aggressive. One of Nell's suitors kisses her with unwelcome force once he realizes he has an audience ("You just watch!"). When a rival assaults him, a chorus of shocked witnesses verifies the horror by variously denying, marveling at, or simply trying to control its visibility: "Would ye look at that!" "You've all seen what happened?" "I didn't see nothin'." "Pull down them shades" (102–4).

This last attempt to fortify the borders of the viewing space is the most emphatic gesture by an ensemble acutely sensitive to how the eye penetrates or fails to penetrate its landscape. "Bring down a candle! Think I can see in the dark?" complains a bartender as he descends to the cellar, one of many partitioned spaces on a warren-like stage that keeps anyone, including spectators, from seeing it all in a single glance (106). In the next act, Nell's eventual protector, a Salvation Army major, spends a long silent scene looking over the objects in her room, seeming both to violate and secure her privacy as he does so. By the last act, set outdoors, characters are complaining that they can't read in the gathering dusk even after the streetlights come on or, alternatively, are taking advantage of the shadows to avoid unwanted attention.

The same eye that challenges spatial limits also asserts its power of surveillance over individuals. One woman, eager to win Nell's trust, reports Jim's
infidelity after she "watched him from my winder" (105). Another woman, a
Salvation Army preacher, makes a competing bid for Nell's loyalty by insisting
"yer hain't got her yet! I've seen [Nell's] man at the Station" (106). Characters
who are unable to enthrall Nell also measure their affective power in visual
terms, feeling their weakness first as a kind of myopia. By the last act, the
desperate plea for attention with which Nell opens the play ("Look at me!")
finally has its answer. In a series of hammering, variously syncopated repetitions, Sheldon makes audible Jim's matching desperation and, more important, the desperation usually repressed in our own less urgent acts of seeing. "I
want ter see her!" "I want to see — her!" "I'll go, after I've seen — after I've seen
that she's all right!" "She was my girl before you ever laid eyes on her" (141–
42). In the last of these lines, he's addressing the major, who himself wants Jim
to "come out here where we can see each other," even as he urges him "never
to let her see you again" (142). Sheldon's denouement is both the triumph and
final defeat of vision. For even as Nell exults that she can "see things clear
now" and burns with "God's light in [her] eyes," it is a singing battalion of
Salvationists that gets the last word, asking their Savior to "Hold Thou Thy
Cross before my closing eyes" (144–48). Spectators following the contradictory prompts of their own vision can't share Nell's epiphany without speculat-
ing on the possibly greater insight available to those who, like her supporting
chorus, turn away from the visible world altogether — an irresolution, sustained to the final curtain, that is typical of Sheldon's endlessly self-qualify-
ing style.

Taken together, these many instances of vision beckoned or resisted enhance
the significance of a spectacular (but, it's important to note, largely unseen)
event early in the first act. A vice squad raids a nearby casino to the mingled
alarm, scorn, and schadenfreude of bystanders and the barroom clientele. The
raid itself is less important than its allure — the seductiveness of seduction's
suppression. At the first siren, characters gather far upstage at the saloon's
entrance to see how the raid plays out. Plays out indeed: their attentiveness,
mirroring our own, underscores the theatricality of moral reform long before
a character says, "Nothin' like furnishin' free vaudeville t' all the neighbors"
(100). For us, however, unticketed to the offstage vaudeville, it is the saloon's
front window that bears the heat of our own curiosity. It dominates the set.
Photographs from the first production reveal that it spans most of the back
wall. Sheldon's stage directions describe it as a "large, rather deep show window." It is "brilliantly lighted" and (lest we still miss the point that this show
window mimics the one framing the stage) is papered with "theatrical posters
which face the street outside" (90). Those inverted posters suggest that we

ourselves populate a performance visible to the street's pedestrians, or that at the very least Sheldon's characters are bound by spectators on two fronts. (Or more: it's significant that the other dominant element of decor is "an arrangement of mirrors" behind the bar.)

Sheldon's design illustrates Robert Alter's description of urban space in nineteenth- and twentieth-century fiction: "The city is a place of many windows facing other windows, in which human figures are imperfectly seen, and also look out."[32] Alter's recognition of the "imperfection" of such vision is especially pertinent to *Salvation Nell*. This window doesn't only literalize a common metaphor for realist practice. (Zola's transparent screen is the urversion from which all others descend.) It also complicates and critiques it. After cropping out what we expect to see, Sheldon's show window pulls us toward everything that realism usually keeps invisible. (And here one recalls the modernist answer to Zola, Ortega y Gasset's famous viewer at another window, having admired a garden in the distance, "withdrawing the ray of vision" until he sees only "a confused mass of color which appears pasted to the pane.")[33] The complacency of much realist perception dissolves when Sheldon's spectators, onstage and in the audience, encounter the hard reality of his own seemingly transparent glass. It becomes as much a barrier as an aperture — a point that returns us to Howells charting the currents of attention passing from subway windows to tenement windows in *A Hazard of New Fortunes*, relishing the paradox that the very structure enabling visual consumption also limits it.[34]

Sheldon's version of this trope looks fresh when imagined in the context of performance. All theater's necessary fluidity restores the complexity to commonplaces about Gilded Age consumption — its culture embodied for several critics and historians by the proliferation in the 1890s of the department store display window.[35] The stage's own display window whets appetites it can't satisfy, not only because of the illusoriness of its offerings or because decorum keeps us in our places. More fundamentally, a production's objects and figures — its goods — won't themselves stay in place. Sheldon makes this clear by almost cruelly lengthening the distance between his spectators and the raid, hiding the tantalizing event behind layers of attention. Consumers ourselves, we see consumers onstage (those at the window and door frame) look at other consumers (those who left the bar to get a better view from the street), who themselves watch consumers of the casino's pleasures get their comeuppance. Sheldon's many nesting frames only prove their inadequacy as they proliferate. "Drama," in this theater, eludes their capture, overflows their borders, or occurs only in what seems an ever receding distance. As if to underscore his point that in this world the spectacle of consumption is an object of desire in itself, the one thing Sheldon does let us see through the bar window is the satisfied, self-congratulatory crowd leaving the raid on their way to the inevitable next act at the station house. "Look at the pink one!" shouts one of the many gawkers about someone we can't see (101). He and his fellows are the audience's antisurrogates, taunting us as much as they taunt the vice squad's prey.

Sheldon's interest in the rhythm of change peaks in the third and final act, set in front of a Salvation Army meeting hall, where he subjects his own achievements to the acid of self-mockery. The shift outside is itself significant. Philip Fisher, in a discussion of Dreiser, treats the "open space of the street" as "the antithesis of the room — that classic space of drama and the novel, with its fixed and interrelated set of characters, its single unifying action, and its consecutive development."[36] Sheldon, having undermined those qualities from within drama and finding the conditions of Fisher's streetscape — "temporary," "disconnected," its views "partial," its action plagued by "interruption" — flourishing indoors, now heightens the distractedness until, by design, it threatens his own ability to sustain a dramaturgical premise. By merely placing us outside windows that once kept us inside, Sheldon declares that the browser's avid, sometimes arbitrary, and often self-canceling gestures of selection and rejection are ascendant.

At curtain's rise, we face the glass storefronts of delicatessens, pawnshops, groceries, and other businesses, as well as the exteriors of saloons and the Salvation Army headquarters, all these competing lures ensuring the ensemble's continuous circulation. Such a thriving field of play renders forgettable what by any conventional assessment is the heart of the play, its intimate second act, a series of pas de deux partnering Nell with those who would save her soul or win her body. To neglect it is to neglect sentiment, evolution of thought, narrative momentum, and the many accumulating details by which figures grow into rounded characters. But one discovers, as compensation, that such features, ordinarily deemed essential to realistic drama, in fact have more ambiguous, contingent value, their claim on us loosened by the play's far more vital clash of tones, images, and gestures. Indeed, the principle of competition — theatrical methods as much as subjects standing for only a moment before being knocked down and replaced — disrupts more than Sheldon's second-act scenes. The last act of *Salvation Nell* is, in many respects, a parody of the first, as if the bluster and busyness that were so refreshing in the saloon, overturning piety and undoing doctrine, had in the hour or so since the play began themselves become doctrine, already deserving of slander.

Evidence that Sheldon is rethinking his own premises from a skeptical distance is available before anyone says a word. This street is the domain of women, whereas the saloon belongs to men. In each site, the unenfranchised sex, while never absent, is never allowed to emerge from the margins. Here, the men reprise the macho struts, boasts, and bawling complaints from act 1, but they're lost in, or quickly absorbed by, the women hanging laundry, dandling infants, reading aloud from dime novels, gossiping, shopping, promenading, and calling home their families. Yet no sooner do the women seize control than Sheldon makes them cede it to the children. A little boy sidles up to a popcorn stand and says "Gimme two bags! An' put in plenty o' butter," a pitch-perfect imitation of the men ordering drinks at the bar in act 1 (132). When Myrtle, the casino hostess, enters, she is trailed by a group of girls copying her purposeful strut and self-aware flirtatiousness, using pieces of kindling as parasols. (One could see them as prototypes of Bill Brandt's famous *East End Girl Dancing the Lambeth Walk*.) Meanwhile, a group of boys breaks out fighting with a good-natured ferocity that matches the saloon's overreacting drunks and then exposes their silliness. Taken together, these and other burlesques do more than undercut earlier assertions of verisimilitude. Sheldon recodes authenticity itself as just an act, a style, a pose, a lingo — something that can be learned or questioned, deployed or withheld. It can also be exchanged. Just as characters seize focus only to relinquish it to others, so too do they claim and then transfer authority — the right to nominate their own behavior as the standard against which all else is judged artificial. The agility required to lay down a foundation of reality while simultaneously pointing out its vulnerability is exemplary. Those able to hold in the balance other contradictions without tipping to a single, eternal "truth" (one thinks again of this act's merciless children, young enough not to have been enlisted in one or another convention of behavior) seem most capable of responding to the realities of a fast-changing era.

"The new American," writes Henry Adams in the *Education,* "the child of incalculable coal-power, chemical power, electric power, and radiating energy, as well as of new forces yet undetermined . . . would need to think in contradictions." Adams is reflecting upon the first decade of the twentieth century (this passage is dated 1904), a period of "motion in a universe of motions, with an acceleration . . . of vertiginous violence," one in which "an earthquake became almost a nervous relaxation," the culmination of "the movement from unity into multiplicity."[37] Setting aside the uncontroversial fact that, in Adams's company, Sheldon looks especially crude and naive, the historian does recall us to the playwright's own milieu — *Salvation Nell* opened on Broadway the same decade, in 1908 — and helps us go beyond individual style in accounting for dramatic structure. What Adams calls the decade's "toss-up between anarchy and order" is replayed in the drama's own seeming indeterminacy, a dramaturgy best suited to representing states of transition (468). *Salvation Nell* succeeds in being of its time less for the lifelikeness of its decor or the plausibility of its characters' behavior than for its tenuous relation to time itself. Each shift in focus and tone can seem, to one who looks beyond the subjects occasioning them, the symptoms of the generalized and disorienting shift from one century's long untested security to another's still directionless youth. (Six years later, World War I would of course decisively bring the nineteenth century to an end.)

The closing sequence of *Salvation Nell* stages the difficulty of this transition in terms broad enough to show what's at stake for the audience's culture. All the action has been leading up to an ending in which Salvation Nell fulfills the promise of her name, winning over the tempted by the force of her belief in a more alluring God. In a long public prayer, Nell seeks communal absolution and implores her listeners to concede that "love saves the world" (148). The speech is to be staged, according to Sheldon's stage directions, with an awareness of its archetypal significance. Nell, "transfigured" as she speaks, stands on a platform and raises her face to light that falls, unrealistically, from above. The visual quotation of Little Eva's own transfiguration in *Uncle Tom's Cabin* must be intentional, but Aiken's certainties fall under Sheldon's skepticism. Nell may assure her listeners that they can escape degrading reality by launching themselves onto a spiritual, timeless plane, but once the hymn ends and the spotlight turns off, Nell moves into the crowd and asks for donations. *Salvation Nell* is no *Major Barbara* (the more sophisticated play was written three years earlier), but both protest religion's claims of exemption from material pressures. Nell's stepping down off her platform—a critical act in a production kept viable by its characters' crisscrossing movement—also pulls hypnotized viewers back to her speech's reality as performance. Despite its appearance of heartfelt spontaneity, the monologue is of course one this Salvationist has delivered many times. It has been scripted, rehearsed, lit with an eye to enhancing its seductiveness, set to music, and arranged on the miniature stage she now exits. None of which makes it any less sincere: the fact that it can be both artificial and genuine (one more contradiction in a play thriving on simultaneity) is a more surprising and important point than anything she actually says. Moreover, Sheldon's perpetual-motion machine ensures that Nell's pragmatism will itself be instantly displaced by her listeners' own material needs. "Naw! I'm savin' *my* dough fer my wife!" says one man Nell solicits, as others laugh their approval (148).

No single one of these moments matters as much as the overall sequence reasserting the contingency of all stage temperaments. Unearned emotion doesn't disappear entirely (there will soon be a heartwarming reunion of the lovers) but it does lose its unconditionality, its exemption from theatrical time's degrading effects. Likewise, Sheldon's embrace of impermanence doesn't discredit religion but merely adjusts its hold on believers, changing it from a force requiring submission—the passivity of Little Eva—to one conferring autonomy, economic power, and the confidence to move freely in the societies of the saloon and the street. *Salvation Nell* may end with a selection of every sentimentalist's favorite tropes—a tearful embrace, talk of returning "home," the prodigal spouse bowing his head in remorse—but Sheldon's ideal spectator tempers his or her empathy with mistrust capable of overwhelming all social, moral, and aesthetic orthodoxies. Everything could change.

The instability of early American realism is the proper context for any consideration of the form's most visible markers, its objects. They furnish public and private arenas, securing individuals within spaces that would otherwise seem limitless. Characters handle them obsessively to focus thought or still anxiety. Others use them as currency for intangible emotional transactions. All these services maintain gravity in the period before realism settles into a reliable genre: Gilded Age playwrights can be imagined stockpiling acquisitions from the material world in an effort to anchor wayward behavior and ensure its availability for scrutiny. The bond tying characters to their surroundings—the seam between foreground and background—is no less crucial to realism's credibility than any single aspect of action or decor. This is what J. M. Coetzee stresses in the chapter "Realism" from his novel *Elizabeth Costello:* "It is the embeddedness that is important, not the life itself."[38] E. M. Forster had already imagined the disastrous consequences of neglecting to lodge oneself in an environment: "We are reverting to the civilization of luggage," he famously writes in *Howards End.* (The novel's publication in 1910 coincides with the first flush of American dramatic realism.) "Historians of the future will note how the middle classes accreted possessions without taking root in the earth, and may find in this the secret of their imaginative poverty."[39]

The unrootedness Forster imagines found its theatrical equivalent in a newsmaking event of 1924, when the American Art Association in New York auctioned off the personal collections of the director and playwright David Belasco. In light of realism's dependence on objects, one wants to regard the auction as the purest performance in an often hybrid and, as we've seen, self-contradictory style. Consisting of more than 1,700 artifacts and lasting six days, the auction represented only a fraction of Belasco's ever-metastasizing collection of furniture, statuary, porcelain, books, jewelry, and textiles.[40] (An even larger auction would follow his death in 1931.) Here, curiosity seekers bid on French fans, Delft tiles, Japanese vases, German armor, and Bennington Potters doorknobs. Other lots featured ivory tusks, bronze cannons, silk tassels, egg cups, flip glasses, snuff boxes, and an early American rolling pin etched with "Forget Me Not." Shelves were lined with Staffordshire figurines of Shakespearean characters, a silver-plate statuette of the Hunchback of Notre Dame, a wax bust of Doctor Johnson, and a boxwood nutcracker carved as a squirrel. Galleries were hung with Genoese banners, Venetian shields, miniature pagodas, Dutch birdcages, and celestial globes. As one pages through the auction catalogues, one can't resist psychoanalytic questions. How should one interpret the compulsion of the Jewish-born Belasco to accumulate so many crucifixes, chasubles, and baldachins, as well as a cardinal's velvet dispatch bag, a prie-dieu, and a pulpit? What carnal need — it approaches necrophiliac intimacy — is met by the purchase of Edwin Booth's velvet coat, Sarah Bernhardt's snuffbox, Edwin Forrest's shoe buckles, and the entirety of Clyde Fitch's own collection of bric-a-brac? Does the collector of so much Napoleonia seek in the prints, busts, and documents validation of his own temperament? (Perhaps that's why the auction also includes many medieval daggers, dueling pistols, Revolutionary War shakoes, and a mace head.) What peculiar passion drove Belasco to keep acquiring miniature elephants carved in turquoise, amber, carnelian, malachite, aventurine, quartz, coral, and spinach jade, among many other substances?

The pleasure of listing these things is the pleasure of looking at them — a pleasure that is relived on stages equally dense with objects. One discovers an internal logic in heaps that at first seem accidental, or imposes a rhythm of perception on a series that would otherwise be monotonous. The discontinuity of that rhythm is inevitable. In a collection that resists unity as much as it strives for comprehensiveness, each striking object pulls one into an archaic or exotic world inhabitable only until one's attention is distracted by another odd thing, one no less urgent in its appeal than we imagine the milieu it once furnished. Belasco indulged the same chronically interrupted fantasies as he assembled his collection. The 1924 auction pays silent tribute to other, earlier auctions where Belasco first fell under the spell of the objects now returning to circulation. "Next to my work my greatest joy is in haunting auction-rooms," he once wrote, confirming the link between his twin theaters of objects. "I go to [them] as I would inspect the Coliseum at Rome. They are evidences of the fierce battles of a life. They speak of its victories and defeats. I am close to the heart of a man or woman, or of their household. It is a place of dreams."[41]

Such dreams have practical uses. Belasco wasn't only satisfying private desires as he bid on this or that curio. He was also acquiring props for upcoming

productions and seeking inspiration to continue work on texts still in progress. (He was two years away from finishing his play *The Return of Peter
Grimm* when he bought the antique Dutch furniture for its set.) Belasco encapsulated his materialist poetics in a famous aphorism, "plays are built, not
written," an approach illustrated in a photograph of the playwright-director
in his studio, working on a manuscript whose separate pages are tacked up on
a paneled screen surrounding his desk.[42] Words are things awaiting their ideal
arrangement in yet another new collection. Likewise, things become, or stand
in for, words in Belasco's dramas: one reads his elaborate opening descriptions
of decor and his internal stage directions (the latter as attentive to the relationships and movements of props as of people) with a growing awareness that the
material world communicates its own history, meaning, and even emotion in
counterpoint to the dialogue. If Belasco's scripts are best read as contributions
to the "art of the catalogue" (the phrase is Barthes's, writing in an unrelated
context), his ideal reader seeks in them the narrative told in their sequence of
display; the complex domestic, psychological, or cultural sagas recorded in
each thing's provenance; and the value appraised accurately only when one
considers an object's private, ambiguous, and highly charged relationship to
its possessor.[43]

Djuna Barnes captures that relationship vividly in a 1916 profile of Belasco,
qualifying and deepening our understanding not only of the artist but of theatrical realism as a whole. In her description of Belasco's filial attachment to
his objects, she also prepares us to see his plays (and their props) with a
matching intensity of attention. Barnes visits Belasco in what she recognizes is
a room "overcrowded with emotion" emanating not just from the collector
but from his collection.[44] "You see this table," Belasco says. "This table is
dying before my very eyes, and I love it as though it were a brother." Picking up
a Venetian tumbler, he adds, "Nothing lives forever, and everything changes —
yet out of it all will rise that terrible conqueror, worm." In this eschatology, he
includes writing itself, its materials betraying the conventional promise of
artistic immortality. "The sheet the author writes upon is maturing under his
pen," a perishable thing, like everything else in his studio (189). In this regard,
it's significant that Belasco secretes the pages of works-in-progress in a hidden
compartment of an antique chair — text enjoying more than merely figurative
intimacy with objects, the newborn never far from the dying or long dead.
Sobering as it is to see imagination thus reduced to the manipulation of objects, it is even more disarming to encounter objects that have all the animation and vulnerability of living beings. The life extracting a pledge of loyalty
from this realist flourishes beyond the borders of human conduct; the theater
hoping to do it justice treats things as protagonists with their own destinies to

Figure 10: David Belasco at work, with pages from a manuscript pinned to a folding screen (1909). The Byron Collection, Museum of the City of New York.

fulfill. One can see a cousin of Chekhov's Gaev in the Belasco ministering to his dying table. ("Dear old bookcase," Gaev says, caressing its side, "a hundred years have not dimmed your silent summons to useful labor.")[45] But with only a slight skewing of vision, one can also detect a more provocative kinship between Belasco's objects and surrealism's fur-covered tea cups and exhausted, expiring timepieces, things that in their playful resemblance to taxidermy and wilting plants join Belasco's table to assert that they had lives to lose. (The director-playwright who releases the actorliness, if not the animalism, of objects also ponders the objecthood of actors. In his memoir, *The Theatre through Its Stage Door,* Belasco relies on the same language of pursuit and capture to describe desirable props and performers alike. "I am hunting everywhere for my cast. . . . I ransack the varieties and the cheap stock companies. . . . I searched for some of my people in the theatres of the lower East Side."[46] The actors he eventually acquires are cherished as much for their diversity — "strangely variant types," he notes, after listing several favorite actresses in an essay published, tellingly, in a decorative arts magazine — as for their ability to harmonize with an evolving and perpetually restocked collection. "They come and go," he concludes. "I shall have another group of them before I pass on.")[47]

None of these details of Belasco's collecting passion and theatrical practice would merit such attention if they didn't illuminate a preoccupation of his plays themselves. *The Girl of the Golden West* (1905) is at once the most characteristic and most unsettling of his works, continually readjusting characters' relationships to their object worlds, erasing and redrawing the lines separating animate from inanimate matter. In the process, Belasco encourages us to be tougher analysts of the familiar sentimental appeals of nineteenth- and early-twentieth-century theater. The solace of home, the recuperative power of love, the potential for reform in even the most hardened sinner: Belasco never comes close to discarding these ideals from his narrative, but so severely does he ground them in the material world that he qualifies and even openly questions their promises. Each recalcitrant object contradicts the play's romantic conceit that its hero and heroine — the titular barmaid and a road agent traveling under the assumed name of Johnson — are "two people who came from nothing" (as the legend to one scene reads) and further troubles the idealism of the conviction that they, along with all inhabitants of this milieu, can "be all they ought to be" (as the Girl says), transforming themselves by escaping their environment.[48] This vision of character as something pliant and almost notional — a mere premise unbound by either past or present circumstances and always open to revision — sits uneasily amid decor whose own transformations come less easily, if at all. The emphatically present reality of Belasco's setting absorbs characters as another brand of stock, asserting a claim on them as forceful as that of their unvisited and unfurnished future. The two lovers may exult that "the promised land is always ahead!" (246), but that doesn't change the fact that Belasco's actual stage is always here.

It's hard not to see this tension between idealized "destiny" and plainer real-life outcomes figured in the play's narrative milieu. *The Girl of the Golden West* is set in a California mining camp during the gold rush of 1849, and while its plot has nothing to do with mining, its characters—prospectors and those who serve or regulate them—have the fervent tough-mindedness of those who are forever entertaining visions of spectacular wealth only to confront its poor substitute, the rock that remains after the glare of fantasy burns off. Rocks—or rather, surrogate objects that refer us to the possessive urge aroused by offstage gold—are everywhere in the production. A saloon is a display case for liquor bottles, containers of cigars and chewing tobacco, dice boxes, cans of food, garlands of red peppers and garlic, saddles and rope, barrels and scales. The Girl's cabin, for its part, exhibits woven baskets, strings of beads, a Valentine's card, a cologne bottle, a bunch of paper roses, a pincushion (among many other things), arranged carefully on shelves, bureau top, and mantelpiece, altars for private devotion. Sets this detailed ensure that characters engage with one another in terms of the things in their paths. When the Girl finally banishes her doubts about Johnson, she tells a miner to "bring in his saddle" (200). She further lubricates their relationship over a "special bottle . . . best in the house" (201). As the erotic temperature rises, she accidentally sits on her revolver, then restores the equilibrium (and checks the scene's potentially campy humor) by shaking hands with Johnson over an empty keg now used as a safe. Later, she gives him a lantern to guide his way to her cabin that night, thus confirming the sincerity of her invitation.

Subsequent scenes are no less dependent on things to seal allegiances or mark shifts in power. A cigar that Johnson carelessly leaves in the Girl's cabin betrays him to the sheriff. The miners, in offering the Girl oranges and berries, defer to her authority as teacher. An Indian couple agrees to marry not with a gush of sentiment but an inventory of goods: "Me marry you, how much me got give fatha?" asks Billy Jackrabbit in Belasco's crude dialect, quickly offering "one blanket" before his fiancée, Wowkle, insists upon "plenty bead" instead (211–12). A red handkerchief Billy gives their baby seems like both a compromise and a promissory note ratifying their engagement. Perhaps it shouldn't be surprising that, in a theater filled with so many lures to attention, greed colors love, commercial worldliness punctures the illusion of erotic abandon, and betrothal is classified as but a gentler form of possession. "You must be in the habit of taking things," the Girl says to Johnson, temporarily resisting the thief's own amorous advances. "You might have prospected a bit first" (214). She doesn't hold out for long, and the entire object world of *The Girl of the Golden West* collaborates in marking her surrender. When the couple kisses for the first time, a basket and flowerpot tip over, wall hangings and curtains flap, lamps flicker, and a mantel clock chimes the hour—all but the last ostensibly caused by a well-timed gust of wind, but more suggestive of a dramaturgy in which emotions overflow the borders of character to trigger environmental changes, and those changes, in turn, make manifest psychological aftershocks whose true severity would otherwise remain unmeasured. Belasco accords his objects the same status enjoyed by his characters: no longer mere accessories, they are agents of action in themselves. The chiming clock is only the most overt instance of their speech. ("The slogan for our times," writes W. J. T. Mitchell about other instances of animism, "is not 'things fall apart' but 'things come alive.'")[49]

On a stage where objects become characters, it is fitting that (as W. B. Worthen has argued about realism in general) characters become objects.[50] Such a transformation may seem counterintuitive in a play titled after its protagonist and powered by expressions of envy, romantic longing, and resignation. Yet even as this melodrama elicits our sympathy and excites our nervous energy, its characters cool the atmosphere by their growing intimacy with the material world. In a graphic realization of their status as objects of attention, Belasco's characters show that, however strongly they may express their passion for one another, they have forged a prior and stronger union with things. It's significant, for instance, that the Girl first appears by proxy, sending in a kettle of hot whiskey and lemon to the men ("Regards of the Girl," says her messenger) before she arrives in person. That the men call her "Girl" more often than Minnie, her given name, is just one of many confirmations that, on this stage, a character's phenomenological status determines identity more reliably than superficial labels. (The Girl herself isn't sure of her last name. Is it Smith or Falconer? It's not until the action moves to her cabin, where we can see a leather trunk with the initials "M.S.", that Belasco answers the question. Once again, only an object can unambiguously determine identity.)[51]

The Girl's customers also let objects speak for them or are silenced by an object's unauthorized assertions. Billy Jackrabbit is a collage of scavenged debris—"odds and ends of a white man's costume," reads Belasco's description, and "a quantity of brass jewelry"—and is forever enhancing his ambulatory collection with the junk he picks up off the floor or steals when no one is looking (188). When a character known as the Sidney Duck is caught cheating at poker, he is forced to wear the two of spades on his lapel, a badge of dishonor reducing him to the cause of his shame. One of the play's most powerful characters, a rival for Johnson's affections, is never seen, her menace palpable only in an inscribed photograph confiscated from her home. All these object-dramas save the Girl's highest praise of Johnson from sounding throwaway: "I seen from the first you was the real article" (206).

The distance between character and thing shortens further as one looks around a set decorated with taxidermy and other animal talismans. Claims we unthinkingly make for the autonomy and spontaneity of characters (and perhaps even for the humanism at the core of drama in general) grow harder to sustain amid the mounted elk antlers, bird wings, antelope heads, bearskin rugs, and wildcat pelts — to say nothing of a buck horn used as a coat hook, a deer's foot turned coat hanger, and a whole fawn carcass hung like mistletoe over the saloon entrance. Lest we overlook how thoroughly Belasco is dismantling the hierarchy separating humans, animals, and objects, a life-sized stuffed grizzly bear stands rampant at the bar, the same height as the men, a filial bond affirmed by a top hat on the bear's head and a parasol in one paw. There is even less to distinguish this figure from those who invade the Girl's cabin in the next act, the Sheriff and his men wrapped in thick, all-encompassing bear and buffalo coats, their humanness further obscured by fur-covered ear-muffs, hats, and gloves. A photograph from Belasco's original production makes them look like the saloon's taxidermy restored to life. Again the director relies on juxtaposition to add complexity to his argument: at the men's feet in one tableau lie numerous animal pelts, their less fortunate kin.

In the Girl's cabin, a horseshoe, a china dog and cat "of most glaring colors," and an embroidered portrait of a lamb join with the other animal effigies and synecdoches to complete this rival cast.[52] As artifacts that refer to life but don't embody it, they all insist upon the difference between realism and reality: don't theatrical characters — Belasco's or anyone's — have more in common with these inert facsimiles of life than with real people? This is nowhere more striking than in an otherwise insignificant bit of stage business when the Girl wobbles, literally, between the animate and inanimate world. After she tries on a pair of new slippers that are too tight for her, she rises "with difficulty" (as a stage direction puts it) and walks stiffly around the room, as if she were about to join the other figurines fated to immobility (213). (The presence in this scene of her Indian servant's papoose, the baby so completely swaddled in blankets as to be a mere piece of baggage, suggests what happens to those unable to resist such entropy.) It's not inappropriate to use the language of suspense to describe this balancing act upon the border separating characters from objects. Spectators who find its perils as thrilling as those of the narrative proper will respond with doubled force to the plot's decisive turn: a drop of

Figure 11: *The Girl of the Golden West* by David Belasco (1905). In this scene from act 1, the Girl behind the bar (Blanche Bates) is flanked by Rance (Frank Keenan) and Johnson (Robert Hilliard). The Byron Collection, Museum of the City of New York.

blood falls from the Girl's loft, arresting the Sheriff's attention just when he thinks he has lost Johnson. It does more than reveal the fugitive's where-abouts. It also asserts his humanness in an object-filled landscape. Things, including taxidermic things, don't bleed.

A minor character who never leaves the scenographic and narrative fringes of *The Girl of the Golden West* extends Belasco's essay on realism in directions the playwright no doubt didn't imagine and wouldn't sanction. Aggressive spectators may linger over the fact that, as Belasco writes, the "camp minstrel" confined to an upstage platform in the saloon has a "face half-blackened" (190), the odd imperfection of his mask making sense only as an invitation to consider the procedures by which we impose an identity upon neutral matter. In this case, as with the characters sporting nicknames or generic names, Belasco challenges us to locate the "true" self beneath contingent personality. Yet the minstrel, by exhibiting a flawed visual emblem of his role (and an ambiguous one: does the half-black face refer us to burnt cork or coal dust?), reaches toward a more fundamental understanding of self-presentation, one that is hands-on in the most concrete sense. Viewers who might otherwise be ready to surrender to the singer's illusory persona — or for that matter to those of Belasco's other characters — must first reckon with the smeared surface of his skin.

Those who do so may later pause over another of Belasco's surfaces with another imperfectly applied layer of "character." The minstrel's face can be seen as one part of a diptych that acquires its other half in the Girl's cabin. In the interest of verisimilitude, Belasco specifies that wallpaper covers only part of the cabin's walls — "as though the owner had bought fancy paper in Sacramento and the supply had fallen short."[53] The stage direction is typical of Belasco's fastidiousness, his obsessive search for the decisive detail that will clinch our belief, yet it also pulls us up short, insisting we remain self-conscious in our surrender to deception. What would be a seamless illusion is literally torn at the wallpaper's edge, and we are recalled to the set's identity as a set. Its maker's mark (the cabin owner's standing in for the set designer's) is visible where the paper ran out. The entire wall emerges from the background to assert itself, an entity as present as the actors standing in front of it, at once familiar and defamiliarized.

These two flawed surfaces acknowledge the same history of creation we encountered in Thomas Eakins's portrait of Suzanne Santje, where the palimpsest of inscribed, effaced, and incompletely reinscribed letters on the actress's script vouches for the reality of the artist's own work, if not of his scene. Indeed, visual art may seem a more natural frame of reference than theater for Belasco, an artist whose stage directions exploit the expressive capacities of color, texture, size, and light, as well as of the proscenium frame itself, its variable depth and breadth controlling the dimensions of our relationship to his characters. Of course a spectator risks sabotaging the illusion by paying too much attention to such formal devices and procedures. That danger is itself revealing. When does an artist's zeal for realist appearances prevent him or her from probing realist depths? What transforms an arrangement of surfaces — walls, floors, furniture, faces — from an abstract composition to an inhabited world?

Such questions can't help but preoccupy Belasco's present-day students. After a generation of twentieth-century visual artists have sharpened viewers' awareness of the nonrepresentational, material density of their art, it's hard not to pause over the overtly worked surfaces of Belasco's mise-en-scène, even if one eventually lets them recede in deference to the action in front of them. It's only Belasco's own history of connoisseurship that justifies such readings and saves them from anachronism: the collector's eye models the spectator's gradually discriminating attention. To read Belasco's script — especially the acting version, with its ampler descriptions of decor — is to encounter Belasco-the-storyteller continually managing an ambiguous, volatile alliance with Belasco-the-designer, one in which it is always unclear who is using whom to advance his own interests. At any moment, the set can leave off serving Belasco's story and begin telling its own. The slightest adjustment of our angle of vision will bring the background to the foreground, challenging us to take in patterns, chromatic studies, and topographies composed with far more sophistication than the narrative. The change opens *The Girl of the Golden West* to readings whose limits are only those heeded by the most rigorously sensuous advocates of abstraction. One dares introduce Clement Greenberg into a discussion of David Belasco — bishops of seemingly opposed aesthetic parishes — only in order to reacquaint us with a formal complexity easily overshadowed by narrative. As Greenberg puts it in "Towards a Newer Laocoon" (1940), "realistic space cracks and splinters into flat planes which come forward," or to put it another way, the scene frustrates "efforts to 'hole through' it for realistic perspectival space."[54] But one needn't leap generations to recover the impenetrable surfaces of theatricalized experience. In *The American Scene* (1907), a title that nods to theatrical composition, Henry James describes New York City as "all formidable foreground," a city where "the custom rages . . . for nipping the interior in the bud . . . for ignoring and defeating it in every possible way."[55] (It falls to yet another writer to reconcile "realistic space" and "flat planes." In *The Great Gatsby* [1925], a party guest awed by Gatsby's enormous library calls its owner "a regular Belasco" — less because the books are "bona fide piece[s] of printed matter" than because the pages are uncut. "Knew when to stop," he says, reminding us that realism can collapse if the integrity of its surfaces is violated.)[56]

The inexpert wall-papering job in *The Girl of the Golden West* is only one way in which Belasco draws us to surfaces meant to create the illusion of depth. The Girl's cabin is furnished with flowered curtains; colored prints; pieces of lace, silk, and embroidery draped over furniture; patchwork quilts; intricately woven Navajo blankets (the latter unfolded and hung from the rafters); and even stockings hung out to dry. Together they form a purposefully clashing ensemble of brilliant color and lively pattern, rendering irrelevant their various ordinary uses. As if to explicitly ratify this theater's membership in visual culture, the cabin becomes a gallery where spectators can travel spectrums of color, compare textures, trace geometry, and detect the logic of repeating series. The patience required for such viewing is at odds with the agitation stirred by the narrative, a tension that is in keeping with Belasco's desire throughout the production to make us read closely milieux that we might otherwise be in the habit of scanning.

Belasco thinks of such reading literally. Alongside the textiles, he hangs signs, magazine pages, and lettered posters, thereby exciting yet another, third mode of attention on a stage already integrating ways of seeing appropriate to theater and visual art. Both the saloon and the Girl's cabin are dominated by signs that make audible the characters' muffled expectations and disappointments. One can read them as captions to the scenes. "A Real Home for the Boys" declares a huge placard behind the bar. Over the Girl's window is a framed motto asking, "What Is Home without a Mother?" In a third interior space, a dance hall doubling as a schoolroom, still other signs spell out "Live and Learn" and "God Bless Our School" in wood or embroidery. Less didactic text awaits attentive readers elsewhere in these rooms. In the saloon, a "reward" notice demands Johnson's arrest, although its bottom half is "in smaller type which cannot be read from the front" (as a stage direction explains). An advertisement for "Espaniola cigarros" featuring a Spanish model in short skirts is similarly enticing and frustrating. Sheets torn from *Godey's Lady's Book* and tacked to the Girl's walls promote current fashions in detailed drawings and captions. As we strain to make out many of these signs, we press up against the walls, caressing them (or worrying them) with our attention, hoping to verify their presence. Words become additional exhibited images or palpable objects—collector's pride. (Indeed, they may remind us of the photograph of Belasco's screen of manuscript pages.) In this respect, the signs and posters are also kin to another piece of saloon printed matter: a newspaper delivered by pony express is (Belasco is careful to note) two months old. Stripped of its function, the paper reverts to sheer matter, but as compensation acquires an emotional aura it never had when its value depended on the things it referred to. Its happy recipient cares less for up-to-date information about life beyond his camp than for proof that such life exists at all.[57]

In Belasco's most emphatic attempt to denaturalize his walls, he directs us from the signs to the items holding them in place. A note on the decor reads, "here and there a picture is nailed on the walls with large nails which show."[58] The nails "which show" stand in for the hand which doesn't. Or does it? A recurrent decorative motif is of a hand itself. A sign shaped like one points from the saloon "to the dance hall" (so it reads); its opposite number, visible when the action shifts to the adjacent room, shows the entire arm, its own hand pointing "to the bar!" There is also, on the wanted poster, a hand pointing to the details of the offered reward. (Given that these lines are illegible to the spectator, this is a particularly taunting finger.) When the actors mimic these gestures with their own histrionic pointing, as the Girl does in almost every photograph of Belasco's own production, they take melodrama's approach to character-as-sign to its literal extreme. So, too, during the play's many poker games: we look to hands for the disclosures we ordinarily get from faces. The payoff to all these visual rhymes occurs when the Sheriff extends his hand to the Girl and notices a drop of blood fall on it. "Look at my hand . . . my hand," he says, and then looks himself toward the loft above his head, where the wounded Johnson is hiding (227).

Even if we didn't choose to treat all these hands as surrogates for Belasco's own, his staging of *The Girl of the Golden West* has other ways to keep us from forgetting that it is the result of human invention. The Girl's kitschy piece of framed embroidery in fact asks a good question: what *is* home without a mother? — or director? or designer? The dominant saloon sign — "A Real Home for the Boys" — is just as pertinent, insisting that we look critically at assertions of the "real" (as well as of "home") in a setting doubly deficient in authentic domesticity: Belasco's saloon is of course neither home nor, as even spectators most susceptible to its realism must admit, real. (It's fitting that the only lasting embodiment of home is a sign.) When a vocal quartet breaks into "I'll Build Me a Little Home," the stage finally makes explicit its identity as fabricated space.[59] The production itself is an object that forestalls any effort to turn it into a symbol, layer it with ideology or myth, or see it as more than an assemblage of its materials. No longer can we repress our knowledge that the realist milieu, for all its seeming naturalness, remains dependent upon a maker.

Such knowledge deepens as Belasco encourages us to scrutinize his production's other surfaces. The same materialist sensibility that treats walls less as backdrops than as palimpsests of wallpaper, signage, and media lavishes attention upon other parts of the stage. The materiality of the Girl's door — its doorness — is underscored, literally, by the horizontal plank placed across it for security. Characters continually manipulate and reposition interior partitions formed by an army blanket and a flimsy bedroom curtain, unable to trust in their durability. Belasco completes this articulation of the Girl's space by specifying that the loft's floorboards are widely spaced. Not only do the gaps allow Johnson's blood to drip through; they ensure that we'll never take for granted this or, for that matter, any stage floor. Elsewhere, light seeps through the similarly "rough cracks" of the saloon doors, striating their surface and thereby offsetting their banal function with more compelling abstract form. No longer just something to pass through on the way to "important" rooms, the doors demand attention as expressive spaces themselves. Likewise, the floor's pine boards "[are] to be the real thing" so that the knotholes are convincing and the audience can confirm what it sees with what it smells. In places, this surface is covered with a thin layer of sawdust — material further drawing us to the ground beneath the actors' feet. (Does each step leave a footprint, one to complement the set's various handprints?) The area above the actors' heads, space that other theaters sometimes leave to a spectator's imagination, is no less designed. Belasco asks for a visible ceiling in the saloon and dance hall (it, too, "must appear real") that seals in the inhabitants and firmly locates their action. Hinged to walls of matching pine and mirroring the floor, it becomes the lid of a box. Its contents, animate and inanimate, even more closely resemble treasured possessions stored for safe-keeping. (It's tempting to locate the source for this box in a childhood memory recounted in Djuna Barnes's article: Belasco once set up a large packing crate in his parents' cellar, lined it with velvet hangings that set off treasured objects, and then climbed inside what had become a custom-fitting jewel-box theater, simultaneously seeking escape from home and a surer form of enclosure.)

Indeed, for all the pleasure to be had in studying the highly worked surfaces of Belasco's sets, it would be wrong to accord them only formal significance. Spaces this vigilant about their edges and membranes, especially those formed by Belasco's unnervingly prominent ceilings, floors, and walls, confess a fear of loss: if the container isn't strong enough, might its contents slide into a void? The source of such a threat remains abstract, although at the start, in a series of painted drops that function as a visual overture to the action, Belasco provides glimpses of a ruptured landscape whose wounds are deep enough to suggest more metaphysical lacunae. A "deep sheer ravine" contains "purple mists rising up from the bottom." Elsewhere, bright moonlight "contrast[s] oddly with the cavernous shadows."[60] As a new painted drop settles into place, one can make out the entrance shaft to a mine positioned near — too near? — the saloon's own portal. That this particular abyss is easily named doesn't weaken its magnetic pull or neutralize its menace. Nor can one escape its dangers by going indoors. In the saloon itself (if a photograph from Belasco's production is accurate), the entrance to the dance hall is lit so brightly from within that its dimensions and depth are obscured. Miners in the mood to dance descend into an abyss of white light.

This environment — where negative space laps up against and erodes the edges of positive space, and where vanishing points are as psychological as they are scenographic — is the proper context in which to place Belasco's narrative preoccupations. Johnson's need for anonymity and a secure hiding place, the Sheriff's desire to expose deceit and extract his fugitive prey, the Girl's attempt to recover a private life in a culture dependent on her public role, and the miners' laments over their deracination are legible versions of themes that have their most elemental expression in the setting. So contested is the dividing line between exposed and enclosed space, and so thin the membrane between presence and absence, that characters take extreme measures to lodge themselves securely in place — nowhere more so than when suspense peaks in the Girl's cabin. Johnson wedging himself in the crawl space is only the most memorable exploitation of a stage so compartmentalized it defies the pursuing attention of spectators as much as of characters. Behind windows doubly covered — by frost and by wooden shutters — the Girl penetrates ever more deeply into her room as she goes about her otherwise unremarkable business, secreting herself at different moments inside a walk-in pine ward-robe, behind the calico curtains of a canopied bed, and on either side of a hanging army blanket dividing her room in half. These homes within homes, efforts toward a more durable privacy, cast into relief the cabin's other, less obvious compartments, enclosures that seem to proliferate once we start look-ing for them. A vestibule, a standing cupboard, the separate rooms formed by curtains in the loft, a table draped with a cloth that reaches almost to the floor (a detail Belasco stresses, for the tablecloth will later be whisked off to prevent cheating during a poker game) — to say nothing of the trunks, hatboxes, pack-ages, barrels, canisters, and jugs that Belasco lists in his stage directions: these all are boxes within the set's larger box, its own dimensions affirmed when a blizzard drives snow up against its walls, socking in the inhabitants to a degree unattainable by any man-made enclosure.

As characters wait to be dug out and snow blows in whenever the door opens, the domestic and natural landscapes merge — a development anticipated every time the Girl adjusts a hanging lamp to cast more of the room in shadow. This additional form of compartmentalization — electric light pooling in newly fath-omless darkness, the stage contracting elsewhere around candles and a fire-place — recalls the equally deep shadows, gullies, and ravines created by "moonlight" in Belasco's opening landscapes. Once a spectator permits the visual idioms of inside and outside (or floor and ground) to mingle, it's hard to resist an even more seductive analogy. The Girl's pigeonholed room becomes a landscape of mineshafts in the eyes of spectators still haunted by the opening glimpse of the terrain just beyond the saloon door — an allusion that would be a mere shadow upon the scene's domestic action were the characters themselves not so conscious of their attraction to the recesses between them. The pur-posefulness with which they go in and out of the stage's many holes prepares us to see enhanced significance in a poker game that the Girl and the Sheriff play to decide Johnson's fate. At a decisive moment, the Girl buries one set of cards in her bosom and extracts — mines? — another, winning hand from her stocking. She also recalls us to the figurative landscape enfolding her when she invokes a precedent for her romance: "What have you been reading lately?" asks John-son, making small talk. "Oh, it's an awfully funny book, about a couple," says the Girl, rising to get her copy of *The Divine Comedy* (215). In Dante's depths as in their own, characters forsake the certainties of the visible world for the knowledge available only in radical, near claustrophobic intimacy. "You can't see an inch ahead," says the Girl as meteorological and emotional storms shrink her environment (219).

Her complaint could be our own as Belasco foils our attempt to see the entirety of his curtained, boxed, and variably lit stage. At these moments, its observers and occupants alike must contend with ambiguities made especially troubling by the materialist clarity satisfying us everywhere else in the production. (One confusion among many: in a theater preoccupied with the fate of objects, are these many lacunae sites of loss or refuge — pockets or holes in pockets?) Once again, spectators run up against an exception to realism's promise of total revelation and explanation. We peer from the edge of a settled, inventoried world into zones of blankness, reminiscent of the omissions and blind spots in *Margaret Fleming* and *Salvation Nell*. Belasco's skill in creating a plausible milieu can't allay the uncertainty about one's ability to lay claim to it. Looking out on the blizzard's measureless, undifferentiated whiteness — an image of complete effacement — then back to her artificial space, the Girl describes a condition she shares with her spectators: "You don't know where you are" (215).

"I can't figger out jest exactly what you are" (206). The serendipitous rhyme of the Girl's two lines — widely separated but both directed to Johnson — suggests that, in this drama of torn and reinforced surfaces, the most treacherous gaps affect consciousness. Ignorance, confusion, ambivalence, or simply suspension of thought can be as threatening as literal holes in a style sustained by empirical knowledge. When consciousness is thus occluded, it is easy to imagine the erasure of character altogether — effacements of self that match effacements of space. That's just what happens when Johnson passes out soon after descending from the Girl's loft. As he falls in a heap, so too dissolve all vestigial claims of sovereign humanity — his status as anything more than one object among many. Slumped between the Girl and the Sheriff during their poker game and ignored to the point of absurdity, he seems to cap Belasco's argument for a strictly materialist realism. But he could, with equal justification, be seen as opening up unmarked space on this otherwise thoroughly inscribed and decorated stage. His inexpressive, inert form reclaims blankness as forcefully as the blizzard does. Amid characters taught by theatrical tradition to voice every thought and fan every flicker of feeling into raging emotion, he imposes no affect on us, nor demands a response. (In this, he seems the perfect, if unlikely, embodiment of one class of objects in Heidegger's famous taxonomy: "The unpretentious thing evades thought most stubbornly.")[61] Moreover, as one of many characters who once sustained the plot's accelerating momentum, he now establishes a zone of stasis—a roadblock around which characters must move if they are to keep up the suspenseful pace. Together with the stage's other sites of erasure, withdrawal, and concealment, Johnson's indistinct body is a place where what Montrose Moses calls Belasco's "relentless realism" finally relents.[62]

The retreat he foreshadows is definitive at the end of *The Girl of the Golden West*—a last act that to those reading for the plot will seem merely the inevitable resolution of the protagonists' romance, but to those tracking Belasco's essay on realism may appear a surprising renunciation of his articles of faith. There's nothing in itself remarkable in the action moving outdoors as the Girl and Johnson begin their journey out of California toward a life together in the East. Yet as the coda to a production lodging characters so thoroughly in their worlds that they seem to have geological permanence, the act of leaving an interior is radical. In what shall they now embed themselves (to recall Coetzee's verb)? The teepee they've set up on the prairie—a sad, rickety cluster of three branches and a blanket—couldn't be a more definitive rejection of the obsessiveness that drove Belasco to pad his walls, roof his stages, and thicken the atmosphere with objects, textiles, paper, and other debris. Unable to count on past or present decor, the Girl turns to her beloved and names him "my home" (247). The domestic sphere is now less a bounded and furnished place than a pledge of affiliation.

Imagery of any kind seems on the verge of dissipating on such an airy landscape—an impression reinforced by the unnatural brevity of this act, two pages in the standard edition, over in a few minutes: the theater's extensive resources for rendering experience are powerless to stop time. Belasco confesses as much when his characters exultantly greet the dawn and agree that "we must look ahead . . . not backwards," an assertion that also challenges the realist practice of consulting a character's history to understand his or her present (246). As the rising sun wipes clean the sky and presents a fresh, unmarked backdrop—another blank space—the dissolution of all but these two figures is explicit. "Only a few days ago, I clasped their hands," says the Girl, stressing the tangible proof of her friends' reality in language she might more appropriately direct to the things she also left behind. "And now they are fading" (247). When she refers to her forsaken world as "shadows in a dream," one can't help reading the phrase metatheatrically. After consorting with deceptive images of people and places, is she now awakening to a reality truer than realism? The fade-out is complete when the stage itself disappears—something that happens before the curtain falls. Once the foundation for carefully constructed facsimiles of home (or arenas in which to long for it), it becomes a platform for adieux. "Oh, my mountains, I'm leaving you," the Girl says. "Oh, my California, I'm leaving you. Oh, my lovely West — my Sierras! — I'm leaving you!" (247).

It's only partly satisfactory to see this turn to the unknown as the largest of the many visual and hermeneutic voids opening up throughout the production. While the play's self-eviction and self-dispossession neatly anticipates the auction, nineteen years later, of Belasco's home furnishings, an event marking the end of the first wave of realism, it also anticipates the birth of a style he pejoratively and misleadingly called "impressionism." In his memoir, Belasco relentlessly disparaged the nonrepresentational decor and fluid rhythms of the New Stagecraft, calling the advanced scenography of the 1910s and 1920s "freakish" and "eccentric," an "outbreak" against which no theater is "immune."[63] Belasco's medicalization of aesthetics is revealing. One is tempted to treat it as the panic of one who has good reason to fear catching the disease himself, for in his sensitivity to color, light, and texture he has already shown a predisposition to the formalism he deplores. Indeed, the countless times he rails against the New Stagecraft's "abnormality" and insists that his own approach is "healthy," "virile," and the expression of "normal tastes and desires" suggests he protests too much.[64] (In his sexual obsession, he also validates Michael Davitt Bell's argument that "claiming to be a realist or a naturalist in this period was to provide assurance . . . that one was a 'real' man rather than an effeminate 'artist.'")[65] Belasco may have sensed what the guardians of theatrical taxonomy are reluctant to admit: that realism incubates nonrealism; that studies in color and line are the origin of narratives of behavior and feeling; and that if we stare at a true-to-life stage milieu long enough, its references recede behind abstraction and thereby cease to console us.

During the years of realism's ascent, a parallel drama was unfolding in the shadows and on the margins of American culture, and one need only pause at its denouement to recognize the fragility of the realist's authority. Five months before his death, the director, playwright, and inventor Steele MacKaye accompanied his sons to the 1893 Chicago World's Fair, where they capped a week of sightseeing with a tour of the ghostly, rundown site intended for MacKaye's most ambitious project, the Spectatorium. A newspaper described a massive, half-built structure that "glowered down upon the dainty state and foreign pavilions . . . the most conspicuous object in the whole World's Fair territory . . . looking like the skeleton of some great extinct animal cast up by Lake Michigan on the antediluvian shores of Jackson Park."[66] Here, MacKaye led his family up an iron stairway "to nowhere" (as his son Percy writes in his biography of his father), until unable to climb any further, lacking a floor to step onto, and teetering on the "edge of air," MacKaye stopped and said, "this is where it was to have been" (425).

The mawkishness of the son's account shouldn't be allowed to obscure the significance of the father's encounter with nothingness. Before the 1893 stock market panic disabled its financing and brought construction to a halt, the Spectatorium was to have been both the triumph of realism and its most hubristic challenger. Six stories high with a seating capacity of ten thousand; a proscenium frame 150 feet wide and 70 feet high; seventeen million cubic feet of lighting; six miles of railroad track to move twenty-five "telescoped" stages; a 400-foot-long cyclorama; machinery to simulate rain, fog, and cyclones; and a stage capable of being flooded with six feet of water: MacKaye's theater aspired to global proportions in order to represent a global drama. The Spectatorium's inaugural production was to have been *The World Finder,* a re-enactment of Columbus's voyage to the New World (and fitting accompaniment to the fair's celebration of its four hundredth anniversary), complete with life-size, seaworthy replicas of the *Niña, Pinta,* and *Santa María*; a cast of twelve hundred, including seven Columbuses; and specially commissioned music by Dvořák and Victor Herbert.[67] (Dvořák's contribution eventually formed the core of his New World Symphony.) MacKaye's ambition quickly soared past the Columbian theme. He sought to represent not just the New World but the whole planet, not just the planet but the universe. (The overreaching is characteristic of a director who, in 1886, scripted and staged Buffalo Bill's *Drama of Civilization.*) Continents rivaled characters for pride of place in the mise-en-scène. Behind them, a night sky depicted the aurora borealis, meteors, the moon and dawning sun, the Milky Way, and a zodiac of constellations — these last arranged with such painstaking fidelity to their actual placement in the Southern Hemisphere that MacKaye dubbed his technique "light realism" (347). Even in his design of the proscenium, MacKaye sought an impossible identity with nature. The frame curved to match the curve of the Earth, giving spectators the illusion that a panoramic spectacle encircles them, its one visible portion stimulating the imagination to summon up all that remained out of sight.

As the MacKayes stood amid the ruins on that day in 1893, they may have sharply felt the consequences of this attempt to push back the border dividing visible and invisible worlds. The director's desire to represent everything to audiences yearning to see everything in a theater consecrated to sight (as the Spectatorium's very name declares) ends by enforcing irremediable blindness. Yet even earlier, when nothing seemed capable of mocking MacKaye's ideals, he himself sought to temper figurative expression with abstraction, formalized gesture, and an idea of time and space indifferent to human presence. The characters in *The World Finder* were to have been silent. Their physicality was to have been controlled by "harmonic gymnastics," an acting technique akin to the Delsartean style MacKaye introduced to America years earlier — regimented movements subordinating feeling to deportment, eliminating individual quirks, and transforming characters into iconic figures. Music elaborated a narrative with greater flexibility and ambiguity than language ever could. (It was also, as Percy MacKaye notes, as important as visual imagery in setting the scene: *The World Finder* was dubbed a "spectatorio.") Despite the work's title and MacKaye's own breathless description of "the steadfastness of purpose, the patient endurance, the stern determination, the benevolent nature, the religious faith, and the dauntless courage of the man to whom civilization is indebted for a new world" (409–10), in practice the depicted world would have overwhelmed the man who "finds" it. (Elsewhere MacKaye more accurately says, "I have sought to substitute the sheer grandeur of nature for the defective organism of man" [371].) Even that landscape's presence was unreliable: a "curtain of light" (as MacKaye called his invention) effaced the stage whenever there was a scene change.

The blank white spaces formed by such excessive wattage — considered not as mere hiatuses in the spectacle but as objects of attention in their own right — do suggest how MacKaye fuses the seemingly contradictory principles underpinning his idea of realism. "I [have] devised a new order of theatric art," he writes, "the aims of which [are] to unite the mystic with the realistic . . . and to awaken even the most ordinary minds to the ideal value of the real and the real value of the ideal."[68] His son describes the same goal more succinctly when he writes that MacKaye "paused on the threshold of symbolism — without passing beyond it" (354). (As he held himself on that border, MacKaye fulfills an ideal Walt Whitman expressed in *Democratic Vistas* [1871], where the poet envisioned an antidote to "the growing excess and arrogance of realism" in the "elevating and etherealizing ideas of the unknown and of unreality [that] must be brought forward with authority, as they are the legitimate heirs of the known, and of reality.")[69]

In light of this search for a rapprochement between the visionary and the visible, it's tempting to conclude that the collapse of the Spectatorium was the best thing that could have happened to MacKaye — that he succeeded by failing. Staring out at empty space from the top of his skeletal theater, he sees the "ideal" with a clarity and purity that would have dissolved once he translated his visions into prosaic objects, all-too-real decor, and inevitably overexplicit scenarios. The failure is fortunate for another reason: it helps one see that the most affecting drama of the Spectatorium—one that would have been invisible behind the emanations of the "nebulator," "colorator," and "luxauleator"; drowned out by the symphonic tone poems; and lost amid the hundreds of animate and inanimate figures—is that of MacKaye himself, the "executive dreamer" (as his son calls him) awakened to reality just when he thought he was free of geographical and temporal limits.

The stubbornness of such limits and the pathos of an artist undeterred in his desire to transcend them attracted even more attention several months after the Spectatorium was sold to a wrecking company, when MacKaye staged a shrunken version of *The World Finder* in a new theater he named the Scenitorium. Here, miniature models stood in for the original buildings and ships. Landscapes that once strained against the horizon contracted to manageable proportions. The cast of hundreds was nowhere to be seen, replaced by a single narrator, MacKaye himself, positioned alongside the stage in a box. This last component of the new *World Finder* made for a parallel spectacle—primitive when set against the vision of the Spectatorium, but for that reason even more compelling—in which spectators could register the price of trying to impose a new style upon a recalcitrant art. The concrete meaning of that act of will would have been obvious to all who watched MacKaye when they should have been letting him guide their eyes with his lecture. A theater manager recalls MacKaye "conducting" an invisible ensemble of technicians in a symphony of visual and aural effects. At times he played his own instrument, manning a console on which he executed light and sound cues.[70] Yet this image of an omnipotent creator wars with another, far less magisterial reality. MacKaye's speech points to an absence and concedes an inadequacy as he describes both what audiences see and (had the Spectatorium been completed) what they would have seen. Critics at the first performance recall that he also apologized for the "busted cyclone and erratic machinery" (443)—setbacks that, once remedied at later performances, enabled an undistracted view of another, insoluble breakdown, that of the infirm director himself. Dying of stomach cancer, MacKaye had to be carried into the theater each night and arranged at his table. He hunched over his manuscript and control board, visibly exhausted and near collapse, accompanied by a physician at all times. This spectacle of decrepitude provided a sharply critical counterimage to *The World Finder*'s celebration of an unstoppable Columbus. It also complicated the meaning of the play's title: MacKaye's stage world remained undiscovered. Unlike his surrogate-protagonist, this visionary was stopped in the midst of his pursuit. Spectators, too, were stopped well short of their promised reward. Unable to lose themselves in all-enveloping imagery and an ecstatic experience of spectatorship, they instead contended with the excruciating allure of images and landscapes that remained wholly speculative. The only reliable object of attention was a figure shaped by his yen to see, and to make others see, a performance permanently locked within his imagination.

W. B. Worthen, surveying unrelated developments in theatrical realism far from the Spectatorium and Scenitorium, unwittingly names both MacKaye's ambition and its frustration when he writes of stage designs that "signify an absence, an unattainable elsewhere that seems to have been forced out of the picture by the weight of the material world."[71] Unattainability as the condition of theatricality — the premise insults the reasonable expectation that art available for viewing consist of realized achievements. That MacKaye persisted in trying to reconcile presence and absence — and to retrain spectators accustomed to contained works of art to find nourishment instead from immanence and incompletion — may seem less eccentric when one puts his work in the proper context. The ghostly Spectatorium and Scenitorium join the proscenium-like window disclosing nothing in *Salvation Nell,* the unseeing Margaret Fleming figuring her play's many other occlusions, and the holes in *The Girl of the Golden West* hastening its deaccessioning of its objects. One can choose to read MacKaye's failures, along with these other voids, as emblematic of the representational tradition strained to the breaking point. But that would be to overlook the new tradition they herald. Together they reach toward the uncharted, impalpable "elsewhere" that Worthen names. They literally open up space for new forms of expression to take shape. MacKaye's friend Oscar Wilde (MacKaye taught Wilde Delsartean acting) stated plainly the change in priorities he hoped American artists and audiences would pursue. During his thirty-four-state American lecture tour in 1882, Wilde promoted an alternative to the strenuous gospel of the true and the real. As he told listeners in Bangor, Fort Worth, Salt Lake City, and Leadville, Colorado (among many other cities), "the visible world is dead" in this "dull, materialistic age." "The real life is the life we do not lead."[72]

Another of MacKaye's contemporaries (and a boyhood friend), Henry James, also uncouples authenticity from representation and embodiment, and pushes dramatists even more forcefully into an embrace with nothingness. He gives this new style a name, or several names, in *The Spoils of Poynton* (1897): Fleda Vetch describes "the impression in which half the beauty resides — the impression somehow of something dreamed and missed, something reduced, relinquished, resigned: the poetry, as it were, of something sensibly *gone."* "Ah," she concludes "triumphantly," "there's something here that will never be in the inventory!"[73] She is speaking, of course, in the aftermath of a devastating house fire, one that Bill Brown reads as the end of literary realism.[74] Yet in a novel begun after the disastrous opening of James's play *Guy Domville*

(1895), when James seeks in fiction a more malleable "drama-quality" (as he calls it) and compares his chapters to "acts," he also offers a model.[75] He suggests how theater can exploit its frustrating ephemerality, finding a deeper expressiveness only after time has rescinded the visible offerings of a performance. Not until the first stirrings of American theatrical modernism more than a decade later does a coherent style result from the past participles Fleda lists: "reduced, relinquished, resigned" and "missed" — less actions than anti-actions, hardly the gestures associated with creation, but essential to the revelation of everything upstaged by what James (in another post-*Domville* novel, *The Other House*) calls "the agony of the actual."[76] In the modernist American theater to come, the "inventory" (to borrow more of Fleda's language) will elude all attempts to hold it, and "poetry" will find a form for what is inaudible in explicit or discursive utterance. The "something dreamed" and the "something here" will both consist of a gap made visible by what's "gone." It will be felt, "sensibly" perceived, as ground solid enough to support this new, more penetrating imagination, as it asserts an idea of theatrical presence that has nothing to do with what is present.

4

The Borders of Modernism

So, as to the wonderful scene, they just stood at the door. They had the sense of the presence within — they felt the charged stillness; after which, their association deepened by it, they turned together away.

— *Henry James*, The Wings of the Dove

A play is scenery . . . not identity or place or time.

— *Gertrude Stein*, The Geographical History of America

A little-noted exhibition of stage designs that opened at New York's 291 Gallery in December 1910 didn't convince anyone that "human character changed" — Virginia Woolf's famous verdict on that month's cultural significance — but it may have been the first sign of changes to dramatic character and of other theatrical upheavals to come. The show, sponsored by an indifferent Alfred Stieglitz under pressure from Edward Steichen, displayed etchings by the visionary English director and designer Gordon Craig, of which the most important were a series of twelve "movements" — abstract, idealized settings for unnamed plays, populated by performers unaffiliated to recognizable characters. Most of those actors are dwarfed by looming geometric forms, impassive buildings that pull the eye up and away from the human activity unfolding in the shadows. The actors who do demand attention emulate the poise and reserve of the landscape. Their faces seem masked, their bodies cloaked and indistinct, if not in fact turned away from the viewer. Often, the etchings themselves seem to retreat. Frames nested within frames deepen the stage in one drawing. In another, a receding row of tall rectangles ushers us to a distant horizon. Craig's distaste for the theater's usual extroversion is most explicit in, oddly, his most ingratiating drawing. A realistic view of an open-air commedia-style performance troubles its apparent subject by devoting most of the picture to the action backstage. Not, despite one's probable first impression, to enhance the quaintness of his scene, nor simply to expose illusion: nothing, in fact, is exposed. On the side of the picture representing backstage, an inchoate dark mass shores up against the flimsy backdrop strung between the stage and the players' wagon. In its indistinctness it is more dramatic than the familiar scenarios presented to the villagers massing at the other end of the picture. A drawing that, at first glance, argues Craig's belief that theater's renewal will come from reclaiming its lost simplicity also suggests, obliquely, that such simplicity masks reservoirs of emotion resisting direct expression.

A note by Craig in the exhibition catalogue announces the ambition of these little pictures. After insisting that they "in no way have anything in common with the modern style" but rather record his "dream of an ideal theater," Craig writes, "we must translate movement through the medium of inanimate forms and thereby produce once more an impersonal art which shall take its place by the side of its two sister arts — music and architecture."[1] He elaborates on this interest in impersonality and turns even more decisively to inanimate form in the essays and dialogues that make up *On the Art of the Theatre,* published in the United States a few months later, in 1911. Against a culture notable for its fluency, charm, modishness, and sensationalism, Craig asks for theater to project a cooler, more taciturn demeanor. (One page of his book carries the running head "Art of Showing and Veiling.")[2] Indeed, "projecting" is too emphatic a verb. Only Craig's prose style is theatrical — a kind of fervent skepticism. His very subject is the tamping down of emotionalism in the interest of preserving the integrity of the self beneath the self — an entity undiminished by other people's attentions and expectations. By resisting all that theater has hitherto depended on — eventfulness, confession, passion, the magnetism of personality — Craig finds unexploited opportunities for privacy within a public art.

Such an interest will seem to contradict his devotion to impersonality only to those with an impoverished idea of interior life. Although the grandeur and inscrutability of Craig's settings may inspire mystical playwriting — the Euro-

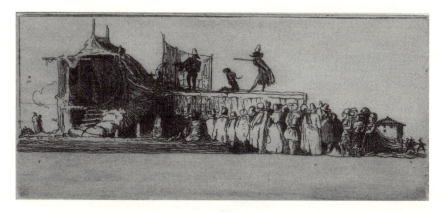

Figure 12: "Drama" from *A Portfolio of Etchings* by Edward Gordon Craig (1907), exhibited in New York at Alfred Stieglitz's 291 Gallery, 1910. Beinecke Rare Book and Manuscript Library, Yale University. Reproduced with permission of the Edward Gordon Craig Estate.

pean symbolists, Yeats most of all, claimed him — to more earthbound writers Craig offers a more radical model. "It is bad art to make so personal, so emotional, an appeal that the beholder forgets the thing itself" (79). In this pronouncement from *On the Art of the Theatre,* we hear the materialist Craig correcting those who would call him a mere visionary. Here is the Craig perhaps most attractive to American modernists: objective, empirical, pragmatic, wary of unjustified abstraction even more than of slavish realism. Yet Craig's notion of "the thing itself" is conditioned as much by what it conceals as by what it reveals. If, in his theater, "passion and pain" can be "caught by [the] hands, held gently, and viewed calmly" (as he writes), that is only because the artist refrains from reaching for emotions irreducible to exact form (83). His actors, emulating the poise of "machines," "statues," and, famously, "übermarionettes," do more than arrest and give shape to ordinarily fluid and imprecise behavior. They also stand in for aspects of the self resisting any kind of representation. Likewise, the mask is so suggestive a metaphor for Craig not only because it is "the only right medium of portraying the expressions of the soul" (13). It also shields that "soul" and rebuffs those who would presume to plumb its depths.

It would be wrong to overestimate the immediate influence on American theater of Craig's exhibition or the publication of *On the Art of the Theatre*. In December 1910, Eugene O'Neill, still three years away from writing his first play, was a sailor bound for Buenos Aires. Gertrude Stein, soon to initiate her own reform of drama, was of course in Paris and indifferent to theater in performance. The third instigator of American theatrical modernism, Thorn-

ton Wilder, was twelve years old and living with his family in China. But they
and other playwrights needn't have seen the twelve "movements" or read their
creator's book to have absorbed their lesson. As all the arts evolved toward
modernism, Craig's ideals were being echoed throughout the culture. Other
artists enjoying Stieglitz's patronage were equally impatient with emotionalism, moving instead toward the mute authority and reflective surfaces of objects. Personality, when it did emerge, was scrubbed of its merely contingent
qualities and set at a distance, obedient to the logic governing the composition
as a whole. Human forms were absorbed by machines, diagrams, and texts,
dwarfed by urban landscapes, atomized and dispersed in a vortex of social
energy, or effaced by the artist's self-reflexive argument about representation
itself.

At the 291 Gallery, the Intimate Gallery, and An American Place, and in the
journals *Camera Work* and *291,* Stieglitz and his protégés introduced Americans to Francis Picabia's peopleless, mechanical-age portraits — a "young
American girl" as a spark-plug; Marius de Zayas as various automobile parts
fused to a corset; Stieglitz himself as a hybrid of camera, gearshift, and brake.
Charles Demuth's own portraits substitute words and things for faces: the word
"Dove" stands in for Arthur Dove; "Love," "1, 2, 3," and a mask represent
Gertrude Stein. Paul Strand's monolithic office buildings, skeletal viaducts, and
stark clapboard housefronts render trivial the individuals in their shadows. His
famous *New York (Wall Street),* with its anonymous businessmen set against a
façade of tall black rectangles, even directly echoes Craig's scenography. (An
altogether different director, Harold Clurman, may have sensed a corrective to
theatrical habit when, in 1929, he praised Strand's photographs as "too far
aloof to lend themselves to our needs or to yield to the pressure of our desires.")[3]
Strand's portraits of the blind and aged are of a piece with these photographs,
transforming faces into façades as impenetrable as those of his buildings. One
may think of their hard surfaces when recalling another show at the 291
Gallery, Stieglitz's one apparent departure from modernist aesthetics. The actual masks in his 1914 exhibition of African art chasten those seeking emotional disclosures from carefully sculpted, stoic "character."

The theatrical appeal of African masks is unsurprising — according to Travis
Bogard, Charles Sheeler's photographs of them inspired *The Emperor Jones*[4]
— but it fell to another Stieglitz protégé, Marsden Hartley, to argue explicitly
for a performance style as withholding as modernist painting and photography. In a 1918 essay for *The Dial,* Hartley uses the occasion of a forgettable
play to imagine an ideal theater, its qualities thus far visible only in this production's leading man, John Barrymore. The frequency with which Hartley
resorts to analogies from the visual arts to describe good acting itself argues his

point. Silverpoint, aquarelle, chiaroscuro, Ingres, "drawing on stone": Hartley prizes the masters and methods of freezing, anatomizing, or shrouding emotion. The inherent discretion of the nontemporal arts disciplines the theater. The best actor is a "draftsman" able to "feel the value of reticence . . . the need for complete subjection of personal enthusiasm . . . [and] untoward excitement of nerves." Barrymore's "cold method" produces our own intellectual and affective heat, as spectators must rouse themselves to engage with art that declines to do the feeling for them. Such performance achieves what Hartley calls, in a phrase suggestive of the ways theater might one day equal modernist painting, a "degree of whiteness."[5]

One can dig out remarkably similar proposals for a new theater lodged in the writings of the literary modernists as well. That two of the most prominent, Ezra Pound and Marianne Moore, declare their affinity with Gordon Craig suggests that well before the American theater attained its own modernist maturity, it had become a figure for anxieties about intimacy in the other arts. One wants to imagine that the poets, photographers, and painters confronted these problems first, recoiling from a forwardness most easily imagined in a metaphoric theater, then offering their work as models to the dramatists writing in their wake.[6] How else to explain Marianne Moore in 1919 listing Craig as one of the only four artists with "direct influence bearing on my work"?[7] (The others were James, Blake, and Hardy.) Craig had already appeared as a presence in her poetry—he is the brave, uncowed title figure, rightly convinced of his artistic originality in "To a Man Working His Way Through the Crowd" (1915) and a model of "inclinational and unashamed" taste in "Picking and Choosing" (1920)—but to readers familiar with Craig's aesthetics, his role as a presiding spirit in Moore, and thus in American modernism in general, goes beyond embodying the confidence to "know what he likes" (as she puts it in "Picking and Choosing") even as he "need not know the way / To be arriving" (as she writes in "To a Man . . ."right).[8] The recurrence of the verb "to know" is one clue to Craig's deeper value to American modernists. He exemplifies evenhanded respect for both the concreteness of the known and the integrity of the unknowable. In "To a Man . . . ," he "unspells / Some mysteries" in order to preserve others, the latter made safe by the tact of their presentation—something Moore names obliquely in yet another theater-related poem, "The Hero" (1932), in which a figure is "speaking / as if in a play—not seeing her; with a / sense of human dignity / and reverence for mystery, standing like the shadow / of the willow" (188). (The description makes him seem like a figure in one of Craig's etchings.) Here, too, a single word, "mystery," echoes across two poems, qualifying its value as it does so in order to make Moore's point. The "mysteries" that survive will be unseductive, non-narcotic, truly remote. The distance that the actor in "The Hero" maintains — from emotional display, from expository discourse, from other figures, and from us — exemplifies an aesthetic control Moore prized throughout her career. "You cannot stand in the middle of this," she writes in one poem (145). Like "the Greeks" (reads part of another), one profits by "distrusting what was back / of what could not be clearly seen" (170). One wants to hear references to the stage in both passages — and an invitation to the American theater to reconsider its low opinion of repression.

Moore had pledged her allegiance to Craig in a letter to Ezra Pound, a friend whom she must have known would share her enthusiasm for the director's austerity. Three years earlier, in *The Classic Noh Theatre of Japan* (1916), Pound had drummed up interest in his subject by asserting that "it is a theatre of which both Mr. Yeats and Mr. Craig may approve."[9] Yet Pound's vision of an ideal theater is only ratified by, not derived from, the English director's example. Pound's particular complaint about "merely mimetic" theater — "the dominion of Belasco and the chews," he writes in a typically bilious letter — as well as his more general impatience with artistic "feeling" spring from his longstanding respect for the outer walls — the apartness — of the art object.[10] "Clean the word, clearly define its borders," he writes in *Polite Essays,* certain that if a text's materials are durable, its reader won't presume to claim its narrative or emotions as his own.[11] Pound scorns such possessive, invasive attention — what Hugh Kenner calls the "transfusion of personality rather than of perception" by which "writer and reader strive more or less desperately to get inside one another" — in the interest of the greater insight available at a distance.[12] That such insight should be (but rarely is) readily available in the theater — an art in which the distance between viewer and artwork is usually inflexible, and in which an inherent materialism translates every abstraction into image — may account for Pound's vituperative disappointment in it. Yet he doesn't stop courting it, if only indirectly. His poetics depend in part on theatrical figures and are most easily understood in a theatrical context: not just his frequent reference to the mask (the poems in *Personae,* he writes, are "complete masks of the self") but also his readiness to subject the static medium of poetry to the temporal and decentering pressures traditionally associated with performance. As Marjorie Perloff and Hugh Kenner remind us, Pound revives the Aristotelian idea of *poiesis* as "the imitation of an action" and opens his poem to multiple voices contesting one another in a play of thought.[13] His famous definition of "vortex" as "a radiant node or cluster . . . from which, and through which, and into which, ideas are constantly rushing" could also serve as a description of the stage's own bright arena filled with imagery in motion.[14] Most provocative, to a theater-minded reader, is his treatment of character as a spatial, not psychological, phenomenon. In a 1918 essay on Henry James, Pound salutes the master for his "respect for the peripheries of the individual."[15] Character, as thus conceived, is a zone that only tactless writers trespass upon.

When these oblique considerations of spectatorship are set alongside Pound's few explicit statements about performance, a complete theatrical aesthetic takes shape. In a 1916 essay published in the American magazine *Drama,* Pound recognizes (and applauds) the Noh-like control in Sarah Bernhardt ("she created an image . . . as durable as that of any piece of sculpture"), in the plays of Marivaux and Musset ("Passion veiling itself, restraining itself through a fine manner, through a very delicate form"), and in Joyce's play *Exiles,* its characters "drawn with that hardness of outline which we might compare to that of Dürer's painting."[16] In all cases, the theater is authentic to the extent that it preserves the inviolability of its surfaces and shuns the spectator. Aloofness ensures accurate and unsentimental appraisal of the art and keeps audiences from confusing stage life with real life.

A passionate summation of these principles appears in Pound's "Notes for Performers" (1918). Its subject is the reform of musical performance, but one wants to imagine American playwrights, directors, and actors prompted to make similar corrections to the course long followed by their own art. As the most complete description of the withdrawing and self-sealing gestures capable of establishing a new decorum in American theater, it is worth quoting at length.

> No performer can rely on emotionalizing the audience. Music in a concert-hall must rely on itself and the perfection of its execution; it is, as it were, under glass. It exists on the other side of the footlights, apart from the audience. With apologies to the language, the audience are spectators, they watch a thing of which they are not part, and that thing must be complete in itself. They may be moved by the contemplation of its beauty; they are not moved — or at least can be moved only in an inferior and irrelevant way — by being merged into the action of the stage. Hundreds of musical careers have been muddled because performers have not understood how entirely the music must lead its own life; must have its own separate existence apart from the audience; how utterly useless it is to try to mix up audience and performance.
>
> A concert in a concert-hall is a performance, a presentation, not an appeal to the sympathies of the audience. It is, or should be, as definitely a presentation or exhibition as if the performer were to bring out a painted picture and hang it before the audience.[17]

One risks looking foolish in trying to bridge the gap between this ideal and the comparatively less disciplined work of Eugene O'Neill. For one thing, many American modernist poets and painters — figures who, as we've seen, were far from indifferent to theater's expressive potential — openly made fun of him. Pound dismissed him as a "post-Shavian derivative" and was appalled when he won the Nobel Prize.[18] Marianne Moore wrote to a friend that she "somewhat mistrust[s]" him, and when asked by a magazine which play "has seemed to you dismal, disastrous, and distasteful," named *Desire Under the Elms,* citing it for "a gigantic inability to proceed."[19] In a letter to Alfred Stieglitz, Charles Demuth tried to be charitable about *Strange Interlude* before finally giving up: "So far as having any real quality (or whatever you want to call it), it hasn't! — any at all."[20] One can easily understand their mockery. As the rest of the advanced culture was moving away from sentiment, O'Neill seemed to say and show too much. Unable to match other writers' verbal precision, he specialized in approximate men — characters groping toward a cohesive presence and a secure context, repeating themselves in a desperate attempt to break through barriers to self-knowledge.

But perhaps one can recuperate O'Neill, aligning his work with other strains of American modernism, by shifting one's focus toward those very barriers. They include the crust of personality, hardened by convention and habit; the wayward or mechanized body, alien-seeming to its possessor; and the reticence of the surrounding environment. One can accept the characters' claims of psychological depth only by ignoring the surfaces comprising and enclosing them. They inhibit a spectator's own hunger for intimate access to O'Neill's milieux. If properly managed in performance, they control the pathos and neutralize the psychodrama, redirecting attention to the theater's more challenging modes of evasion and resistance. What isn't seen and said, in this view, assumes as much if not more importance than any lyrical outpouring or even the playwright's justly admired sense of visual composition. An O'Neill whom his fellow modernists might embrace is less a mythologizer of suffering and deliverance than a cartographer drawing (and drawn to) the border between known and unknowable psychological states, measuring his distance from regions of private life that neither his nor any theater can make us see.

Three images from O'Neill's writing life underscore the boundary between the seen and the unseen in his theater. A famous photograph of the Wharf Theater in Provincetown, Massachusetts — first home of the Provincetown Players — at first suggests that O'Neill's early plays resulted in permeable productions. The old fishing shack stood on stilts at the end of a rickety dock suspended over the Atlantic Ocean. During performances, ships' bells and foghorns competed with the dialogue. Rain, when it fell, could be heard on the roof. Fog engulfed the building. Large windows and skylights framed the horizon. Inside, the floorboards were perforated with open knotholes. If the tide was in (and it was, Susan Glaspell writes, for *Bound East for Cardiff*, a play set on a ship), "it washed under us and around, spraying through the holes in the floor, giving us the rhythm and the flavor of the sea."[21] This blurring of the line between the real and represented landscapes wasn't mere ingenious, serendipitous stagecraft — wasn't the triumph of realism, as more than one historian has called it.[22] If anything, the typical spectator may well have thought that theater fails when it competes with a reality this proximate. Yet any failure or success of verisimilitude orients us to a larger question O'Neill asks in many of his plays: what lies just beyond the artist's reach, behind the created world? With a clarifying literalness at Provincetown, O'Neill leans toward yet also shields the Platonic origin of his play's action; it stays just under the floor and behind the back wall. To reach these sources, we'd have to renounce the theater and reclaim our place in the landscape. We don't, of course, and it remains separate during the play — a separateness that accounts for its power. What we do see is shadowed by our knowledge that we're not seeing everything.

In 1917, after the Provincetown Players moved to New York, another theatrical margin concealed another, even more potent source for O'Neill's dramatic action. In his autobiography, William Carlos Williams describes standing in a hall alongside the stage of the company's new playhouse on MacDougal Street, watching rehearsals of O'Neill's *Fog*. Standing with Williams was O'Neill's father, James, the actor whose fame in *The Count of Monte Cristo* was only now waning. Bluster that no longer carried on his own stage filled the wings of his son's. He was "yelling out directions and suggestions to his son and the actors," Williams reports.[23] "Very moving" — a conclusion that leaves open whether Williams is describing the play or the Oedipal battle to shape it. If the latter, Williams moves us to a conclusion of our own: the scene becomes more interesting when seen not as a battle but as a collaboration. Most critics insist on reading the son's career as a rejection of the father's. Closer to the truth, as Virgil Geddes and others have argued, is a theater history that blurs the line between the two generations and two theatrical styles, just as the Wharf Theater blurs the line between sea and "sea."[24] The playwright still seeks the moral clarity and catharsis of melodrama, even though he won't approve its machinery, still seeks them because behind the walls of *this* set presses — yells! — a familial landscape that can neither be fully confronted, no matter how vigorously he writes toward it, nor escaped, no matter how strongly he renounces it. The James O'Neill that Williams remembers is close enough to touch, and strains at the decorum keeping him in the wings, but can't appear onstage. This picture complicates another familiar reading of O'Neill: interest in his work's autobiographical sources must take into account their remoteness and vexing intangibility. O'Neill's theater no more succeeds in plumbing them than it plumbs the sea. The more obviously he yearns to do so, the more he reminds us of the surface sealing him off from his past. The "failure" is compelling. His obsessive memories are alive — and theatrically satisfying — to the degree that some part of them is unrepresentable.

A final image, from the end of his writing life, confirms O'Neill's attraction to offstage landscapes. One of the private drawings he made while writing *Long Day's Journey into Night* seems the work of a playwright indifferent to the usual restrictions and practicalities of theatrical production. In fact, it represents the difficulty of reconciling theater's public nature with private life, some large part of which cannot be disclosed, no matter how ruthless the writer. The sketch, a floor plan of the Tyrone house, depicts many rooms spreading out in a warren of secret space behind and alongside the walls of the actual set. Back parlor, front parlor, dining room, kitchen, pantry: O'Neill rendered them all painstakingly, down to such details as the chairs placed against the dining room wall, the windows in the kitchen, the number of back steps — all theatrically irrelevant to a play that never leaves the living room. Of course, they aren't personally irrelevant. The drawing, which reproduces the layout of O'Neill's New London home, no doubt grounds the playwright in his subject, preparing his imagination to make its own designs. But as an accessory to a narrative that itself depends on the power of unseen space, the drawing has more than incidental value.

In production, its presence is felt immediately. The first act begins in clear morning light, but the characters enter from darkness — the cave-like upstage parlor, its lights kept off at James's insistence — a void made visually significant by its proximity to and sharp contrast with the bright foreground. This crucial adjustment to the popular impression of the play's structure clarifies its action. Despite its title, *Long Day's Journey into Night* actually begins in darkness. An emblem of the night is always present, enfolding the illuminated stage. Moreover, both dark and light spaces have distinct values: the play's classical decorum keeps most "action" out of sight, save a brief eruption of fisticuffs between the brothers, quickly absorbed and providing no catharsis. The living room is the place for recovering from unseen, unstaged insults and embarrassments. Here, the Tyrones steel themselves for future encounters with an uncomprehending world or prepare to retreat into an even thicker solitude. They prowl the space in a state of continuous inquiry and doubt, occupying this little room as if always about to be swept back into that dark space behind

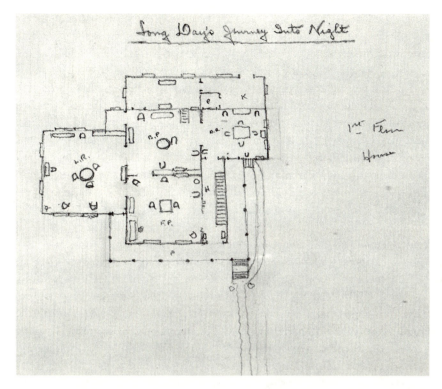

Figure 13: Eugene O'Neill's floor plan of the Tyrone house, *Long Day's Journey into Night* (1940). The Yale Collection of American Literature, Beinecke Rare Book and Manuscript Library, Yale University.

them, one that seems to expand without end. It looks more and more like a precipitous drop-off or a waiting, hungry maw. The four unseen rooms are his starkest image of the irretrievability of family history and the inchoate core within the self. In the face of our own desire to reach that core, they also assert his theater's right to privacy, qualifying the promise of the confessional style O'Neill did so much to establish.

These three theatrical landscapes — O'Neill's stages engulfed by unseen nature, kinship, or memory — help us see that his theater moves toward nothingness. As a mode of theatricality, this tendency at first seems not only undesirable but inappropriate to an artist as ostensibly archaeological as O'Neill. His rhetoric, echoed by his collaborators, leads us to expect access to subjects other artists shy away from or fail to reach. "We have endured too much from the banality of surfaces," he wrote in a program note for the Provincetown Players' 1924 production of *The Ghost Sonata,* one of what he called Strindberg's "behind-life" plays.[25] That last clumsy phrase recurs in a letter about his own earliest plays, in which he confesses his hope to "faintly shadow" at "the impelling, inscrutable forces behind life."[26] To George Jean Nathan he declares, "I want to dig at the roots of the sickness of today," and in his famous "Memoranda on Masks" outlines a strategy for unearthing "those profound hidden conflicts of the mind which the probings of psychology continue to disclose to us."[27] Kenneth Macgowan, O'Neill's close friend and colleague, heralded an avant-garde that would "get back of realism to reality — which is in art nothing but the exploration of the unconscious mind below the appearance and pretense of man."[28] As Joel Pfister points out in *Staging Depth: Eugene O'Neill and the Politics of Psychological Discourse*, this language — "probing," "disclosing," and "digging" for experiences that are "below," "behind," and "hidden" by the "surface" — also cues almost all biography and criticism of O'Neill.[29] A list of selected titles betrays their assumptions: *A Drama of Souls, Ritual and Pathos, The Haunted Heroes of Eugene O'Neill,* "The Secret of the Soul." Chapters of Arthur and Barbara Gelb's biography are titled "Birth of a Soul" and "Haunting Ghosts." Stephen Black's more recent biography claims to go "Beyond Mourning and Tragedy" (as its subtitle puts it) but is in fact unapologetically psychoanalytic. Even Pfister's *Staging Depth,* an important revisionist work exposing the cultural, economic, and political reasons for the emphasis on interiority, never doubts that "depth" is what the playwright sought and achieved.

What if O'Neill wasn't seeking — or staging — depth? What if, on the contrary, he wanted to indict such an ambition as presumptuous and such an idea of character as sentimental, even fallacious — wanted, most important, to locate the point beyond which the spectator cannot venture further into stage life? Of course, the idea pits O'Neill the self-exegete against O'Neill the practitioner. To accept it means accepting that the "banality of surfaces" is the platform for the most profound revelations in his theater. Repression, self-blindness, paralysis, latency, diffidence — all the obstacles O'Neill's characters seem fated to overcome are, in performance if not in print, far more durable than their rhetoric would have us believe. The failure to weaken them is fortunate. The idealist in O'Neill may hope to get "behind life," but the pragmatist knows that, in an art as hostile to abstraction as theater, exteriors are all he has and all he can show.

From his earliest plays, when the young writer might reasonably be imagined seizing every opportunity for expression, O'Neill resists the theater's conventional imperative of full disclosure. At first it seems that the four one-acts comprising the S. S. *Glencairn* cycle (1914–17), along with his other sea plays, do reach toward those "inscrutable forces" exactly as O'Neill says the

best theater must. In each, O'Neill catalogues varieties of interiority, emphasizing the psychological spaces separating a tortured individual from a group
of hearty, deceptively kindred sailors. But only sentimental habit sees those
spaces as veins of emotion waiting to be mined. As they prove resistant to
excavation, blankness appears not a sign of failed expression but an unequivocal statement in itself, pushing back against inquiry — an attitude that the
Melvillian in O'Neill might think of as a preferring-not-to.

The array of impediments to perception are in themselves visually and aurally attractive — or can be treated as such, a paradox that renders us always
alert to our point of view, if only because the plays never let us move beyond it.
The fog that blankets several sea plays is only the most obvious screen before
the action, thickening the ordinarily transparent space between actor and
audience, insulating the former from the latter's depredations. *Bound East for
Cardiff* adds more layers to the spectacle. The opening stage directions carefully describe the corner of a steamer's forecastle, the walls of which "almost
meet at the far end to form a triangle."[30] Bunk beds line this vortex-like space; in
front of them are wooden benches for a chorus of sailors. When actors sit down
(as they often do), they block the view of the ostensible protagonist, Yank, an
injured seaman dying in the uppermost corner of the triangle. (Conventional
playwrights would have put him front and center.) Air "heavy with rancid
tobacco smoke" further obscures our view (21). Light from a single bracket
lamp barely penetrates this interior fog. The polyglot accents of the crew —
Swedish, Irish, Cockney, Scottish, Norwegian — are themselves screens placed
in front of language, in their variety ensuring that we'll never accept a single
standard of expression. (The sailors also snore, further rebuffing audiences.)

The Moon of the Caribbees adds West Indian to this catalogue of tones and
rhythms; no less prominent and opaque in this sea play are nonverbal sounds
— tolling ships' bells, lapping waves, bursts of laughter, a sailor's accordion, a
woman's wordless lament — and silence. Many utterances are preceded by
deliberately shaped pauses, each an aural no-man's land — or dialogic fog —
delaying access to the familiar territory of speech. Language degrades further
in *In the Zone,* a play in which silence is as layered as sound. Dialogue is
regularly broken by a "pause," "a thick silence," "a deep silence," "a moment
of silence," or periods in which the men are "listening intently."[31] These variously worded stage directions invite us to assign a distinct quality to each
interval, to color them with particular emotions. Better to regard each instead
as Hartley's "degree of whiteness." We can't bore through the play's blank
spaces to explicit psychological expression. Even an interpretive stage direction — "each man is in agony with the hopelessness of finding a word he can
say" (66) — tells us nothing about the sources of such distress.

Engulfed by such blankness, the narratives (such as they are) are important for the stories they *don't* tell. The last sequence in *In the Zone,* in particular, supports readings sensitive to O'Neill's larger dramaturgical priorities. Interiority that was merely passive in *The Moon of the Caribbees* turns resistant here, as one character, Smitty, defends himself against his overinquisitive fellow sailors, the latter convinced they have a spy in their midst. With the shift comes a cautionary tale. At the start of a career in which it seems O'Neill will probe numerous psyches, he warns us — and himself? — against the violence of such ambitions. The sailors tie Smitty to a chair, gag him, break open his strongbox, and read aloud his private letters as he crumples from the embarrassment of being exposed not as a spy but as a rejected lover. The action provides a countermodel for any writer or spectator driven to know a character. "If we on'y had the code!" says one sailor, certain that there's more to be learned from intimate letters he takes to be messages to the Germans (65). No code, no glamorous conspiracy, no secrets within secrets. The anticlimax doesn't mock just the melodramatist; it also mocks the would-be reformer of melodrama. Psychologizing this reckless still won't get far below the surface; what is revealed seems in the light of our attention an inadequate explanation of suffering. Identity survives untouched, and all the tactful playwright can do is turn away from it, as O'Neill does here, through the final action of his ashamed sailors. They turn to the walls of their bunks as one of them switches off the compartment's only light, establishing a darkness stronger than any attempt to illuminate it.

In the major plays that immediately follow the one-acts — *The Emperor Jones* (1920) and *The Hairy Ape* (1921) — O'Neill extends his cautionary lesson to a broader social context. The move outward coincides with a renewed push inward. These protagonists seek their elemental selves, a core where instinct flourishes uncompromised by social conditioning; where "natural man" enjoys the sovereignty denied him by "culture"; where a character's individuality is strong enough to nullify, or at least render trivial, his presumed obligations to this or that class, race, or other collective. These are plays ruled by a fantasy of "before" — before maturity, civilization, modernity, induction into this or that social situation; before being seen, named, and judged by others; before consciousness shriveled into self-consciousness; before spontaneity ceded authority to consensus notions of grace and decorum; before habits of reasoning, behavior, and moral discrimination inhibited one's responsiveness. O'Neill's severest critics blame him for not recognizing the fantasy as fantasy — for himself endorsing the ideal of a presocialized or "primitive" self, supposedly the only repository of authenticity. A close look at the plays themselves will void that criticism.

If only because the "interior" is so overdetermined in the racial and geographic landscape of *The Emperor Jones,* it is easy to resist admitting that O'Neill closes it down long before Brutus Jones closes the circle of his journey. The play's scenic practice is distinguished by its austerity, O'Neill spoiling as many visual pleasures as he offers, if only to force us to look skeptically upon the relation between seeing and having. The vibrant color scheme of the first scene — a throne painted "eye-smiting scarlet" with a "brilliant orange" cushion, bright yellow sunlight, Smithers's red nose and "washy-blue" eyes, Jones's blue coat and red pants — gives way in all subsequent scenes to blacks and whites, a reversion to an impersonal mode of presentation, as if individual taste, even individual will, drained away with color.[32] At his severest, O'Neill uses black as a means of interdiction or outright erasure rather than inscription. One scene is backed by "a wall of darkness dividing the world" (278). Another contains "a massed blackness . . . like an encompassing barrier" (280). In their presence, spectators may feel they are viewing a grudgingly declassified document, whole passages of sensitive material inked over, access denied to spaces deemed for someone else's eyes only. Lest we think these masses are mere negative space, they can be effaced themselves. "Enormous pillars of deeper blackness" — tree trunks — obscure part of the "wall of darkness" (278). In another scene, "black, shapeless" figures — Brutus's "little formless fears" — emerge from and stand before the black forest (279). No sooner has a spectator's eye adjusted to this carefully modulated spectrum of blacks, dark grays, and midnight blues (one may think of Ad Reinhardt) than O'Neill seeks a still more radical visual economy, challenging us to make do with even fewer objects of attention. Whenever Brutus fires his gun into the murk, "the walls of the forest close in from both sides" (as the stage directions in one instance describe it) and everything is "blotted out in an enshrouding darkness" (284). *The Emperor Jones* proceeds by canceling an already cancelled landscape, erasing the very evidence of erasure, as if over the play's eight scenes, O'Neill were pursuing with Jones's own hopelessness a hermeticism and self-sufficiency purified of even the gestures of refusal, a zero-degree theater beholden to no referent.

This drive toward simplicity may help one recognize that in many scenes the stage glimpsed before the blackouts obeys classical decorum. Hardly an unruly and mysterious jungle, the playing spaces of the middle scenes — the play's own interior, enclosing Brutus at his most disoriented — are triangular (a clearing in the forest), diagonal (a path), circular (another clearing), and arched (trees reaching up and over the stage). Their formal restraint should give pause to those classifying the play as expressionist. Seemingly spontaneous, individual behavior conforms to principles of organization held in common across the culture. Indeed, the space teaches us how to view its occupant. Typically, we look to Jones to reveal more of his "authentic" self as he plunges deeper into the jungle. Yet as Jones regresses from tin-pot dictator to Pullman porter and convict to bare unaccommodated man, he also sheds individuality. He is returned to cultures he tried to deny — those of the American slave and African ancestor, emblems of oppression and "blackness" — but these categories are too broad to set him apart from the millions of others they also subsume. Superficial attributes were all that distinguished him from mere biological presence; the body thus exposed in fact shields its owner's most distinctive self.

Lest we still cling to the romantic expectation that O'Neill's corrosive dramaturgy (and our own invasive spectatorship) can reach below a character's habitual modes of self-presentation, Jones's penultimate lines reinforce the bedrock level of his identity. When he comes face-to-face with the Witch Doctor and Alligator God, he blurts out "Lawd, save me! Lawd Jesus, heah my prayer!" (290). The exclamation is enough to discredit any reading of the scene, or the play as a whole, that imagines it bequeathing to us some fundamental, "primitive" vision of its hero. Jones's Baptist socialization survives exposure to the theatrical elements. In the wake of this realization, spectators may reasonably wonder after the fate of character in general in O'Neill. If the playwright believes in the existence of a private self, unmediated by culture, he declines to grant it theatrical form. Or perhaps he values it so deeply that he refuses to demean it in the unavoidably simplifying medium of theater. Either way, Smithers's closing words over Brutus's corpse — " 'e'd lost 'imself" (292) — challenges orthodox interpretations of the play: we conventionally assume that Jones *discovers* himself. Moreover, by the end of *The Emperor Jones,* we, too, have "lost" him, and with him long-held assumptions about the availability of stage life in general.

The Hairy Ape arrives at the same conclusions about its own title character. Struggling just to name a sensation he feels but has yet to grasp, Yank talks around a gaping hole in understanding. "Dis ting's in your inside, but it ain't your belly. Feedin' your face . . . dat don't touch it. It's way down — at de bottom. Yuh can't grab it, and yuh can't stop it. It moves. . . ."[33] The man who glories in being "part of de engines" must also acknowledge motion's capacity to scatter, blur, and even eradicate him (364). Yank is at his most commanding only when he is most dispersed. He measures his energies only as they animate iron, gold, and coal. He tracks his narrative only as it sustains those of trains and ships. He recognizes his substantiality only as it dissipates into "smoke . . .

and factory whistles." "I'm de ting in noise dat makes yuh hear it" (365). Caked in coal dust, he appears blotted out, as if his creator had second thoughts about granting him presence and left us with only the evidence of his ambivalence — another incompletely censored document. From here, it's only a short step to complete abstraction. This self-appointed source of the modern landscape and soundscape becomes a standard for modernity's rate of exchange: "I'm de ting in gold dat makes it money!" (365). Character transforms into pure agency, the agent himself distant or veiled, implying that the only way to embody modernity is to be disembodied.

In such a context, the many moments when Yank poses as Rodin's *Thinker* seem counterefforts at self-consolidation. Yet the statuesque Yank is no more accessible than the scattered Yank. Rodin may exalt interiority — thinking or, as Yank quaintly puts it, "tinkin' " — but the sculpture's hard materiality keeps spectators on its surface. Leaping art forms, the lively stage character becomes the deadened icon, a transformation that collapses the sentimental scale of value informing most readings of the play's generating conflict. The brutal but "true" Yank conventionally opposes the two-dimensional Mildred and her aunt. The latter are classified among things rather than people — "lump of dough," "cold pork pudding," "a stiff" — when they aren't denied materiality altogether: their "stock had been sapped" (366–67, 377). That such inertia and shallowness form a direct challenge to theatrical orthodoxy is obvious in the aunt's memorable advice to her daughter: "Be as artificial as you are. . . . There's a sort of sincerity in that" (368). To early twentieth-century theatergoers just emerging from melodramas thick with their own declarations of "sincerity," it must have been disarming — and ultimately refreshing? — to encounter a new stage world recommending a retreat from nature and modeling skepticism toward nature's promise of transparency.

O'Neill confirms this when he unveils the third exemplary figure on his spectrum of behavior. The gorilla, for all his seemingly undomesticated, uncensored naturalness, is no less inaccessible than any other character. He is walled off behind a language unintelligible to O'Neill's other characters. To spectators resisting the illusion, he is also reduced to a mere theatrical costume. This facsimile of selfhood has a literal interior, unlike the Rodin sculpture in which Yank also seeks his reflection, but it's empty, site of an evacuated identity — another mockery of those readers or spectators hoping to plumb O'Neill's psychological depths. Here, as elsewhere, theatrical materials form a protective sheath around such impalpable and thus unstageable phenomena as thought, emotion, memory, and point of view. O'Neill's neatest trick is to write an expressionist play without an expressive subject — a play, moreover, that dramatizes the pathos of not "belongin' " (as Yank says) in the spectator's own struggle to penetrate the spectacle. Yank need not go to the zoo to see himself reflected; he need only look past the proscenium. His simplest complaints, vague in their contexts, gain resonance and specificity when heard as our own. "I can't see — it's all dark," he says in one scene (392). In another: "I couldn't get *in* it, see?" (394).

O'Neill's claim to modernist identity depends on his ability to sustain the paradox enclosed in these lines. By stripping spectators of their rights of spectatorship, O'Neill only makes them more importunate. The recurrent dramatization of our desperation — sailors interrogating the unforthcoming Smitty, Brutus castigating the indifferent forest, Yank bellowing at invisible masters — culminates in an emblematic scene from *The Iceman Cometh*. Every time Don Parritt buttonholes Larry Slade, it's hard not to see in their aggravated minuet another reflection of the relationship between spectator and stage: Parritt (and we) always want something, while Slade (and O'Neill) remain cold — distant but not absent. It's significant that Slade is the only character to remain both visible and awake throughout the play. He puts forward an articulate rejection of conversation, a powerful abdication of power, and an intensely confidential rebuffing of intimacy. In this and many other plays, O'Neill visibly sustains the vigor of depletedness. We are always arriving just as he retracts what seems to be on offer.

Only O'Neill's metastasizing dialogue keeps one from calling this style minimalist, for in many respects his impassive characters anticipate broader aesthetic convictions. A style that its most articulate exponents describe as seeking "intentional anonymity" and rejecting "romantic egoism," that regards a preoccupation with interiority as a form of violation ("mutilating the paint," one called it) has an unlikely predecessor in the O'Neill valued by those spectators happy to be stopped at his surfaces.[34] That his defenders dwell on his visual idiom is itself revealing — not only because, as many have argued, it is more sophisticated than his language, but because it forces spectators to acknowledge the work as an indivisible whole, to resist the temptation, so often indulged in other theaters, to contract one's focus on a character and relegate his or her context to the background. Indeed, as Ronald Wainscott shows in *Staging O'Neill,* his valuable account of original O'Neill productions, the very idea of "background" is embattled if not altogether absent in these plays.[35] The barriers estranging spectators from characters grow simpler, thicker, and plainer. What O'Neill famously called the "incongruous white mask" of the Mannon house in *Mourning Becomes Electra* opens to equally flat, shallow, and aggressively horizontal interiors.[36] In *Desire Under the Elms,* one quadrant of the Cabot house's exterior wall remains in place for much of the play, forbidding visual access until, in one brief scene, it finally slides open to reveal a "repressed room like a tomb in which the family has been interred alive."[37] Similar slabs rise and fall systematically over the upstairs and downstairs rooms of the four-square house in *Dynamo,* asserting a geometric logic as O'Neill works every possible combination of open and closed spaces. In *All God's Chillun Got Wings,* the walls and the ceilings threaten to efface dramatic action more definitively, literally closing in on a trapped couple in a horrific contraction of the stage aperture. (Their total effacement, while not shown, seems inevitable.)

Most illuminating of O'Neill's flattening aesthetics is the decor of an otherwise negligible play, *The Great God Brown.* Each of its interiors projects only the facsimile of depth, as backdrops painted with crude images of furniture or garish abstract patterns hang close to the curtain line. The actors, given little room to stand, cannot sit on the two-dimensional chairs. It is as if the production were pushing the characters out of the play. O'Neill implicitly affirms this triumph of surface over depth with particularly lacerating wit in one such room, an architect's office, where a floor plan is the only decorative element on an otherwise monochrome, oppressively flat and proximate back wall. As spectators attracted to the drawing let their eyes wander from "room" to "room," O'Neill teases us with the prospect of an interiority that the production refuses to fulfill. O'Neill acknowledged the architect in himself again near the end of his career. In one room of *More Stately Mansions,* a "large architect's drawing in perspective of a pretentious, nouveau-riche country estate" hangs on the wall, a picture that, like the others, demands that we recognize the two-dimensionality of the surrounding illusion of depth.[38]

These various approaches to space can be (and have been) read metaphorically, of course. An unforgiving society squeezes out an interracial couple. Denial inures a grim secret. A legacy of historical, cultural, and familial repression flattens individuals. But the thoroughness with which O'Neill shutters his mise-en-scène threatens also to efface such limited narrative and psychological contexts, along with their tendentious, all-too-explicit meanings. As we gaze helplessly at clapboard, stone, brick, canvas, or paper surfaces, we must come to terms with an even more disturbing form of blankness. Nonreferentiality doesn't seem possible in dramas this promiscuous in their citation of classical myth, Freudian iconography, and Nietzschean narratives (among other sources O'Neill favored), but all these cultural markers quickly prove inadequate and unsatisfying guides to interpretation. Less arid, because less derivative, is a reading that takes seriously the decor's prohibition on reading of any kind — that instead measures the change in perception and emotional temperature caused by the persistent neutrality of these impassible, often featureless squares and rectangles. They solicit no interest, offer no information, clarify no mysteries, exert no pressure on us whatsoever. They may at first seem to extend the purposefully self-contradictory methods of O'Neill's early plays—the writer visually crossing out what he inscribes or deploying a tangible image of absence to counter abstract, because verbal, claims of presence. But now even this analysis presses its points too emphatically for an artist pursuing a purer form of restraint. It creates just another narrative of conflict—another drama—where O'Neill means to abstain from all expression. Green shutters close over the eyes of the masklike Mannon façade. The backroom windows of *The Iceman Cometh* are "so glazed with grime one cannot see through them."[39] In *A Moon for the Misbegotten,* cardboard replaces glass in each window frame of the Hogans' own decrepit façade. Window shades in *Strange Interlude* are "the color of pale flesh," and when they are pulled down they look like "lifeless closed eyes."[40] After we have exhausted the language of rejection or defiance to describe such imagery, we are still left with the shapes themselves—panels baffling our approach—and even if we follow O'Neill in anthropomorphizing them, these closed eyes are expressive only insofar as they suggest a sleeping (or dead) person's obliviousness.

It is revealing that O'Neill shows the same care in closing the borders of both interior and exterior space. Outside characters can't see in; inside characters can't see out. Distinctions between indoors and outdoors disappear, flattening space further. The care with which O'Neill establishes the setting for *The Iceman Cometh* is characteristic: the men prefer the intermediate space of the saloon's backroom over both the oppressively public street and the claustrophobic, self-interrogating privacy of their upstairs bedrooms. In *A Moon for the Misbegotten,* O'Neill controls another form of depth. The action takes place in front of a house recently uprooted and moved across town. Set on timber blocks, it undermines any promise of reliable interiority, a condition O'Neill underscores by keeping his characters outside for all but one scene. Having thus evicted them, O'Neill prevents them from planting themselves in the ground as well. A "big boulder with a flat-top" (one of many in this nonarable farm) dominates the narrow strip of stage in front of the Hogan house.[41] It is like a second, even less hospitable stage, frustrating those trying to burrow toward a subterranean interior. To be an O'Neill character is to be pressed between equally unavailable elsewheres—the strangest of interludes in a theater that tests if only to discover the surprising permanence of spaces that, at first, seem mere way stations or channels en route to more secure ground. Bars, hotel lobbies, ship decks and cabins, piers, a narrow horizon line, the contested line between neighbors' properties, a strip of beach, a country highway: in O'Neill's theater, they are the only available spaces. Is this why O'Neill stresses the prepositions or prefixes of penetration in his titles—*in,* into, inter-, beyond, under—as if his words alone could compensate for a changeless here and now?

These many varieties of scenic interdiction are the proper context for any discussion of O'Neill's best-known effort to control access to his vision. In 1945, the playwright theatrically sealed a new manuscript under red wax in a "ceremony" (as his editor, one of the celebrants, called it) and then mandated its burial in the Random House vault until twenty-five years after his death.[42] The attempt to embargo *Long Day's Journey into Night* captures well the unresolved ambivalence over visibility that pervades all of O'Neill's work. Just as on his stage theatricality strikes an uneasy compromise with interiority, so, too, on the page does O'Neill seem to beckon us to his autobiography only to immediately cordon it off or renounce it altogether. The result is a kind of ostentatious diffidence. That paradoxical attitude was even more apparent when Carlotta Monterey O'Neill, the playwright's widow, prematurely exhumed the play in 1955. The revealed manuscript, accompanying notes, scenarios, and early drafts further demonstrate the playwright's style of radical will-lessness. A minor but telling instance: a draft of Mary Tyrone's long third-act speech about her wedding dress is in Carlotta's hand—explanation for the play's sudden tonal shift from its dominant asperity and self-pity to this passage's lusher descriptions of "duchesse lace" and "shimmering satin." (According to Arthur and Barbara Gelb, O'Neill delegated its writing to his wife on realizing how ill-suited he was to describing fashion.)[43] Traced back to Carlotta, the speech now stands less as an efflorescence of writerliness than its deliberate smothering—the playwright ceding control to another as he pursues a less exposed and less personal form of authorship. (Of course, it's appropriate that this instance of hiddenness is itself hidden, invisible to readers who know only the published text.) O'Neill further confesses his attraction to absence in a plot summary capped with three working titles for the play: "Long Day's Insurrection," "Long Day's Retirement," and "Long Day's Retreat." Read as a series, the titles dramatize the playwright's initial desire to move up and out from his family story (presumably serving this desire with an equally eruptive dramaturgy) before he seems to think better of such theatrics and opts for silence instead.

The most forceful—and most poignant—sign of O'Neill's calculated self-diminution is visible throughout the drafts. Few biographers have failed to note the remarkably small handwriting in which O'Neill wrote all his late plays—writing that grew smaller as the playwright's degenerative nervous condition worsened and he could control its most acute symptom, a persistent tremor, only by radically curtailing his hand's range. Yet nothing prepares one for seeing his actual pages. Many are scored with inscriptions legible only with a magnifying glass, arranged in dense blocks justified to form a left margin and reaching all the way to the right-hand edge of each page, as if O'Neill hoped to avenge the insult of his illness by ruthlessly colonizing the page and imposing upon it martial discipline. Only the most devoted students will have patience for them. To others, they are silent save for the hostile message communicated by their appearance: "Do not read." We've faced such prohibitions before. The slabs of text recall us to the slabs of stone, clapboard, and fog that earlier blocked the view of his stage. Now one can't help seeing each early mise-en-scène as anticipating the future scene of writing.

Like the settings, the pages approach abstraction — each line a drone sounding across the page or the faint signal of an EKG just barely rising above a flatline. Indeed, the author's viability seems doubtful; he is hardly present, if presence is achieved by expressive gesture. Penmanship itself irons out personality for this modernist. The hand, instrument of self-announcement and even self-glorification for artists in other disciplines, is here besieged, betraying a writer who, like the painter or musician, feels able to answer aesthetic impulse only kinesthetically, pulling at what the imagination pushes to the surface of consciousness. (Asked why he never used a typewriter, O'Neill said his thoughts "flowed from his brain, through his arm and into his pencil.")[44] Soon after completing *Long Day's Journey into Night,* he would try wearing a long metal plate belted against his spine in hopes of controlling his shaking. In making the transition from writer to writing machine, O'Neill regularizes gestures that the romantic wants to imagine are spontaneous and natural. Moreover, his self-binding provides another context for the various references to architecture in his theater. The hands of the architect and playwright alike, both draftsmen, are directed by instruments and a sense of measure, not by anything so imprecise and irrelevant as emotion.

This preoccupation with hands is reflected, of course, in *Long Day's Journey into Night,* where Mary's self-shaming body is the correlative of O'Neill's own. Both writer and character fear playing a hand, or being played by one, that gives away too much. Humiliated by her compulsively shaking body, Mary sounds an equally repetitive refrain: "Why are you staring, Jamie?"[45] "You really must not watch me all the time, James" (17). "So you pretended to be asleep," she says to Edmund, "in order to spy on me!" (48). Hovering over them all is an equally attentive Virgin Mary: "You can't hide from her!" (109). Mary resists this claustrophobic landscape — vision closing in just as walls and ceilings do in earlier plays — by mirroring it: "She watches us watching her," says Jamie (38). It's not just for their prurience that the monitors are themselves monitored on O'Neill's panopticon stage. The family scrutinizes Edmund for the onset of tuberculosis, Jamie for the slow slide beyond the point where he might reverse his dissipation, Tyrone for the cracks in the bravura performance with which he tries to win over all comers. When we read O'Neill's text, we realize that the playwright, too, is hoping to control what he sees. His coercive stage directions, mandating line readings more than merely telling actors where to move, suggest a writer reluctant to let the actors out of his sight. Bound to an equation of seeing and being seen, all four Tyrones force us (once again) to look critically at our own acts of seeing. By showing characters flinching when they are looked at, rushing into the shadows to hide like animals, or fighting back with insults or defiant stares of their own, O'Neill points out the violence in an act we'd like to think of as benign.

The metatheatrical commentary is inevitable, given the play's sources. In this last major play, O'Neill settles accounts with his father's melodramatic tradition as embodied in James Tyrone, mourns the squandered promise of his actor-brother, and ironically memorializes his own more elevated artistic aspirations in the voice of Edmund. But it is the disoriented, cringing Mary, fumbling for eyeglasses that both enable and defend against sight, who offers an image of the anxieties over attention that theater artists usually repress. By choosing not to repress them himself, O'Neill transforms *Long Day's Journey into Night* from a mere family drama into an essay on aesthetics — its confessionalism a cover allowing him to confess a deeper, more interesting insecurity about his responsibility toward his auditors. The obligation to marshal "pity and understanding and forgiveness" for "the four haunted Tyrones" (as O'Neill famously put it in his dedication) is, in this view, but a metaphor for the equally pressing need to establish a viable relation with the spectrelike forms haunting the darkened audience — the other "house" (7).

As O'Neill comes forward to confront the burden of our own expectation and judgment, he also battles an undertow pulling against every image and incident he brings to the surface. To locate the source of this conflict in mere shame is sentimental and diminishes its formal significance, one that transcends the ultimately irrelevant narrative of O'Neill confronting his past. Far more suggestive is O'Neill's implicit proposal that the best art gains vitality in the effort to subdue its own self-annihilating energies, that it wins our attention less for what it shows us than for successfully resisting the temptation not to show, not to appear at all — to fall silent or hide. Writers as self-skeptical as O'Neill are always on the verge of turning away from the scene of writing, or seem ready to blot out its traces, or simply leave unbroken the seals over the subjects they seize. What Susan Sontag (in "The Aesthetics of Silence") calls a "leading motif of modern art" — "ambivalence about making contact with the audience" if not the outright desire to "sever the dialogue" with it — informs

O'Neill's own modernism so thoroughly that the very fullness of this, his fullest work, results in "opaqueness" (to borrow another of Sontag's terms).[46] *Long Day's Journey,* no less than more obviously "silent" works of modernism, yearns to be "unviolable in [its] essential integrity by human scrutiny" (191), a virtue it could achieve only if it could renounce presence altogether.

Lest such ambitions seem merely theoretical, O'Neill indicates them concretely in his text. The "ambivalence" that Sontag sees as fundamental to an aesthetic of silence — the modernist performing his resistance to attention when he could simply refrain from writing altogether — surfaces early in a pair of morbid jokes. O'Neill sets the action in 1912, the year of his suicide attempt. He further flirts with absence by giving the Tyrones' dead infant his own first name. Against the perhaps too accessible self-portrait in Edmund, he balances this counterimage or, rather, nonimage of nothingness, mocking those readers and spectators seeking transparent autobiography. "Eugene" is less a cipher (that would imply he contained information to be decoded) than a gap in O'Neill's otherwise tightly knit family and densely verbal text. It offers the real Eugene a refuge where he can imagine momentary relief from writing. O'Neill teases us again in the text's cast list. It divulges Mary's maiden name, Cavan, but nowhere in the play itself does anyone utter it. A play ostensibly dedicated to mining family history leaves undisturbed one accessory to a past self. In keeping with his habit of following many disclosures with retractions, O'Neill exploits something as banal as script-formatting to expose a character's core identity only fleetingly, and at the margins of our consciousness, before rapidly reinterring it.

Spectators confront the most unsettling consequence of O'Neill's ambivalence when they move beyond the psychological meaning of his characters' mutual surveillance to ponder the practicalities of its enactment. O'Neill's notations of the exact angle and quality of almost every glance are at odds with the broadly public nature of performance. By magnifying the tiniest details of performance, O'Neill suggests that the only appropriate place to watch *Long Day's Journey into Night* is amid it — that the implied perspective on the action is onstage, near enough to the actors to actually see all the glances he describes so carefully. In this act of withdrawal, O'Neill silently declares that the audience isn't just unwelcome but superfluous. (The circumstances of the play's first production confirm this. Carlotta O'Neill famously denied permission to its potential American producers, granting it instead to the Royal Dramatic Theater of Stockholm, where a sequestered but muchpublicized production elaborated on the characters' own anxiety over being looked at. The necessary modernist gulf between viewer and artwork had become an ocean.)

Situated on remote or reachable stages, indifferent to or openly scornful of audiences, *Long Day's Journey into Night* nonetheless indulges its characters' addiction to performance — the strongest of their many addictions. That their habits of self-dramatization flourish here, in a house meant to be a refuge from the theater, doesn't undermine O'Neill's skepticism about theatricality. Far from it: the same turns enacted before a bored, bitter, or absent audience elicit few of the reactions that would bolster the performers' sense of self. We see thin facsimiles of once-spontaneous behavior or, rather, facsimiles of facsimiles, second editions of originals that were, like all performances, themselves re-enactments. As C. W. E. Bigsby puts it, the characters' rites of accusation and forgiveness echo dialogue we imagine spoken months and maybe years ago.[47] Only the weaker, hopeless tone distinguishes them from the first run-through. The redundancy of Tyrone's career — twenty-nine years in the same role — is also the model for the eternal recurrence of the family's own performance. This is a theater that, by design, never seems "as if for the first time."

The moment Mary and Tyrone make their first entrance through a set of portieres, O'Neill asserts the artificial, purposefully diminished quality of his stage. The Tyrones begin quoting feelings, manufacturing motives, and chore-ographing family interactions that can no longer be trusted to unfold easily. Even purely functional gestures and insignificant comments show how deeply engrained is the habit of controlling what others see. "I'm glad . . . Mary, when you act like your real self," says Tyrone, as if realness were available only to those who perform it (114). Illusionism fools no one, of course, least of all Mary: "I'm so sick and tired of pretending this is a home!" she says at another point, downgrading her environment to mere decor and confirming what has been obvious all along (69). Being "sick and tired" is itself a condition that, on O'Neill's stage, requires a performer's dedicated energies. Passivity must be worked up. "Make yourself not care," Mary says to Edmund (62). "All we can do," says Tyrone after Mary's latest relapse, "is try to be resigned — again," a startling line that captures the contradiction between liveliness and depletion sustaining the whole play (134). (No less challenging to an actor is an oxy-moronic stage direction describing Mary's "detached motherly solicitude" [94].) One hears all the characters long for a true resignation or detachment, one so definitive that it couldn't happen "again" — and so wouldn't be theater.

As the Tyrones direct what little energy they have to its suppression, they become more recessive — "bored with [their] quarrel." As they do so, they fulfill the latent meaning of the opening character descriptions, in which their faces are envisioned as colored panels — "reddish" for Jamie, "deep brown" yet "sallow" for Edmund, white for Mary — as artificial as O'Neill's early settings, rebuffing all attempts at surrogation (19–20). Of course, there are narrative explanations for the growing affectlessness. By the fourth act, the characters have been up all night. They are also drunk. More subtly, O'Neill early on casts a skeptical eye on any kind of zeal or even ambition. "Will-power" had been Doctor Hardy's inane mantra, spoken over Mary's inert body whenever she came seeking relief for her addiction. Its bankrupting seems to have made all forms of initiative suspect.

O'Neill's radicalism is to put the writer's own "will" — his readiness to impress his vision on the world — under the same suspicion. In doing so, he grants readers (and directors) permission to imagine a mode of production nourished by entropy. An acting style distinguished for its apathy does more than trouble the common view of *Long Day's Journey* as a play powered by blame and bristling with resentment. (Richard Sewall, among others, also speaks of the Tyrones' "stamina" as they "resist" and seek to "transcend" their fate.)[48] Their actual dullness is but one of many forms of abstention that nearly usher the play out of the theater altogether. On the simplest level, O'Neill strips the last act of its allegiance to place. Fog and darkness have erased the outer world. Inside, Tyrone turns out all lights save a single bulb above a central table, an island floating free of any context, as if the whole stage had fallen off the map. It falls out of time, too. The fourth act is set at midnight, poised between two days but belonging to neither — the ambivalent hour forming a black hole into which disappear notions of linearity (including the one narrated in the title) or any change thought essential to a temporal art such as theater. A basic tool for marking time — progressive dialogue — also loses prominence. The men frequently set aside their own language in favor of quotations. These often-long passages from Baudelaire, Swinburne, Dowson, Shakespeare, Rossetti, Kipling, and Wilde — blocks of verse obstructing the flow of all action save their display — shield their speakers as effectively as do the gathering night and fog. That the men's texts can all be found in the books shelved onstage, as the opening stage directions tell us, reinforces the impression that the characters are walling themselves up behind literature, just as O'Neill's earlier characters took refuge behind clapboard and stone facades. O'Neill himself is hiding, posing as other writers to escape his own authorial identity. *Long Day's Journey,* shadowed by the story of its painful composition and resistant autobiographical sources, has long been seen as a play about its own writing. But in its fourth act, it shows itself to be a play of reading, an anthology compiled by one who enjoys every reader's invisibility and self-forgetfulness as he plunges into other people's stories.

As writing changes from a force of expression to one of concealment, acting itself gains a new function. O'Neill recodes it, too, as a way to deflect, not solicit, attention. To embody a character, now, is to be a conduit for other

Figure 14: *Long Day's Journey into Night* by Eugene O'Neill, world premiere at Royal Dramatic Theater, Stockholm, 1956. Mary (Inga Tidblad) and Edmund (Jarl Kulle). Photograph by Beata Bergström. The Yale Collection of American Literature, Beinecke Rare Book and Manuscript Library. Reproduced with permission of the Sveriges Teatermuseum.

voices, not an amplifier of one's own. Tyrone quotes, and thus fleetingly becomes, Prospero and Cassius. Jamie plays Iago and Clarence. (He will also cast
Mary as Ophelia upon her final entrance.) Other acts of citation and recitation
enable them to transfer their vices to other sinners. Men who would ordinarily
be exposed in their frailty hide behind Dowson's consumption and Baudelaire's drunkenness. When Edmund quotes Rossetti—"a dope fiend!" says
Tyrone—he is flushing out someone to serve as Mary's decoy, a target the
Tyrone men can bear to hit (138). When Jamie quotes Wilde, he tries on a
glittering form of pathos that momentarily blinds us to the banality of his
own. O'Neill's stage rapidly fills with all these phantom speakers, the Tyrone
men conjuring a crowd in which they can lose one another and their larger
audience.

In this last scene, Mary self-scatters as well. The woman who earlier divided
herself in two—"they're far away," she had said of her hands (106)—now
more thoroughly disperses under the pressure of a family that moves beyond
mere surveillance to identification. Even before her final entrance, the men
show that they have been reading Mary as closely as they've read their favorite
poets—so closely that, like all sentimental readers, they no longer heed the
border between them. They disappear into her story as she, in turn, surrenders
to the obliterating power of their kinship. Tyrone's first speech to Edmund—
"I'm glad you've come, lad. I've been damned lonely"—appropriates Mary's
signature theme (128). He continues to do so when evaluating his career. In
almost the same cadences in which she regretted not being a great pianist, he
regrets not being a great actor, going so far as to say, "and for a time after that I
kept on upward with ambition high," a pre-echo of Mary's last line, "I fell in
love . . . and was so happy for a time" (153). When Tyrone wonders where he
stored a treasured note from Edwin Booth—"I remember I put it away carefully"—he helps us see that it serves the same function for him as Mary's
wedding dress, also stored away, does for her. Both bolster self-esteem, stave
off insecurity, mark the fork in their biographies where what could have been
departs from what is.

Edmund assumes other aspects of Mary's identity. First *he* complains that
Tyrone never gave Mary a home, dragging her through dirty hotel rooms,
then, in his long monologue about the sea, voices his own frustrated desire to
belong to something larger than himself, to hold a meaningful vision of God
and, finally, to free himself from being "a stranger who never feels at home"
(157). All are near quotations of Mary's own longings. It is only when it is
Jamie's turn to merge with his mother that one realizes how punitive are the
consequences—not solidarity with one another but mutual imprisonment. He
doesn't just parrot her themes. ("Doctors lot of fakers . . . all con men," he says

[168]). He entwines their destinies. "I'd begun to hope, if she'd beaten the game, I could, too." Since she can't, "I can't forgive her" (166). Unable to see himself apart from her, he condemns himself to her fate, a choice that O'Neill explores fully in *A Moon for the Misbegotten*. (Jamie also merges with Edmund in this fluid act: "I made you!" he rages at his brother, "You're my Frankenstein!" [167].)

Gestures go even further than speech to erode a character's individuality. As the bodies mirror one another, it becomes difficult to isolate any single figure, enabling Mary to elude her would-be judges. During the fourth act's card game, for instance, while the men take turns telling stories meant to explain their idiosyncrasies, their bodies are making us think of Mary. Their hands — picking up and putting down cards, botching the job of shuffling, delaying the deal — attract attention as much as Mary's hands did. Unsteady like hers, they also prompt our ridicule. (The elaborate business of Tyrone changing a light-bulb — hand reaching up mock-heroically to a hanging lamp — has the same effect.) The rest of the male body assimilates Mary's presence upon her entrance. After she bestows her wedding dress on Tyrone, he holds it (O'Neill writes) "with an unconscious, clumsy, protective gentleness" (176). The action causes many different adjustments to our vision. Holding the dress, Tyrone seems to assume the burden of her past and responsibility for the loss of her identity. In the Pietà-like composition of the tableau, he also holds *her,* as O'Neill's deanimating style reaches its logical end: a character becomes a thing. But the most suggestive meaning of the image is the least overt. Tyrone looks like a parent cradling a child with "protective gentleness." It's not only the girl in Mary that is revived by this tableau. It is also the lost boy, Eugene. More effectively than in all the memory-filled monologues earlier in the play, the dead return, saved. (As are, briefly, Mary's hands: since Mary wasn't yet addicted to morphine when the baby was alive, it follows that her surrogate, Tyrone, is able to "pour a drink" [as a stage direction says] "without disarranging the wedding gown he holds carefully" — his hands recovering *her* unembarrassed grace [178].)

"It's not her" (142). Tyrone was speaking, earlier in this act, about the effects of "the damned poison," but he could be describing the effects of O'Neill's dramaturgy. Instead of making his characters more familiar over the course of a production (as most playwrights do) and sinking their roots ever more deeply into their milieux, he erodes them until they nearly blow away. Jamie summarizes O'Neill's renunciatory style when he recites Swinburne's "A Leave-Taking." The relevant lines sound like a knell at the end of each stanza: "She would not know." "She would not hear." "She would not see" (176–78). The words reach beyond Mary to encompass all the characters. They should also make us doubt our own faith (one as persistent as Mary's is embattled) that mere looking and listening in the theater will grant us knowledge. *Long Day's Journey into Night* elevates the unarticulated (both the "stammered cry" that Edmund calls his "native eloquence" and its antiphonal silence), the unseen (Mary moving heavily in the attic during most of the last act), the unengaged (Mary rattling her fingers on the table, memorable as the play's one wholly private gesture), and, finally, the unalive ("Eugene" placed center-stage for the play's final tableau). O'Neill brings theater as close as he can to oblivion without extinguishing it altogether. That he stops just before that irremediable, definitive blankness is the most devastating blow cast in a play that, by suppressing almost all violence, magnifies pain. His characters long for total withdrawal, but a panoply of forces — theater itself subsuming all the others — denies it to them. They are brutalized by the minimum requirement of art — presence — more than by one another or their own accusing selves.

While O'Neill was troubling the givens of theater, another revolution was unfolding a continent away, sparked by a writer whose style, on the surface, seems antithetical to his. The fact that O'Neill and Gertrude Stein both began writing plays in 1913 has long seemed the only thing they have in common. Her theater — alternately imperious and silly — looks especially remote when set alongside his pathos. "Can you imagine any one today weeping over a character?" Stein asked in a 1946 interview.[49] Yet closer to the truth may be a theater history that puts them on a continuum. Stein's procedures are more daring than O'Neill's, of course, but they spring from a related skepticism toward the promises of conventional narrative. As he obstructs access to a character's innermost self and limits the revelations available from literal and figurative backgrounds, Stein refuses even to acknowledge the past as a temporal category, much less indulge a character's personal memories. "We in this period have not lived in remembering," she writes, "we have lived in moving."[50] Such movement isn't progressive. "I wanted to write a drama where no one did anything," she told Charlie Chaplin, "where there was no action."[51] ("The atom is dissociated," T. S. Eliot once said of her approach to theatrical presence and language.)[52] To O'Neill's students, such an ideal may recall his own dramaturgy of circularity, entropy, and stasis — plays narrowing to a point where characters fracture, disperse, or retreat altogether. Here, too, one can imagine the two modernists working from a common ambition. As O'Neill calls attention to the spectacle of speech in his early experiments with dialect and later collages of quotation, Stein goes further and treats words as ends unto themselves, finding in grammar, syntax, and sound everything she needs to know about a speaker.

The O'Neill we saw patrolling the border between his stage and spectator, erecting screens to keeps us at a distance, prepares us for the most persistent theme in Stein's theater. "She always was, she always is, tormented by the problem of the external and the internal," she says of herself in *The Autobiography of Alice B. Toklas.*[53] The problem takes numerous forms. Stein describes how she tries to reconcile the demands of public and private life, smooth the transition between inchoate idea and explicit utterance, and maintain the distinction between what she calls Human Mind (or "entity," the autonomous, unself-conscious self) and Human Nature (or "identity," the self conditioned by others). But she feels this "torment" with particular intensity at the theater. It is an art that, as she writes, makes "an outside inside existence for me, not so real as books, which were all inside me, but so real that it . . . made me real outside of me."[54]

This passage is from "Plays," an essay that, tellingly, is as much about being a spectator as being a playwright. Its argument begins with the death of a commonplace: an art presumably dependent on our identification with characters and involvement in their action in fact only enforces our difference. The "only thing I noticed" on seeing Edwin Booth's Hamlet, she writes, "is his lying at the Queen's feet during the play" (114). A spectator who watches other, onstage spectators, she treats theater not as a conduit to fantasy worlds but as a closed, at times even claustrophobic box that forces audiences back upon themselves. Such a rebound also occurred when, as a teenager, she saw Sarah Bernhardt in San Francisco. Not knowing enough French to follow the play closely, she could only listen to the trilling, burred sound of the actress's voice — a highly pleasing experience, it turns out, to one who hated the tedious job of "getting acquainted" with characters. Of that voice, Stein says, "I could rest in it untroubled" (115). The conventions controlling Bernhardt's physical presence were equally alluring: out of the vague attributes of personality, they "created a thing in itself and it existed in and for itself" (116). Shut out of one "interior" of this production, Stein instead probed this gestural language, verbal music, and visual imagery for meanings unqualified by linear story, simplistic psychology, social context, or any other threat to their independence.

These objects of attention decorate, and make palpable, what Stein famously calls the "continuous present" — itself an image of a border, a forcefully asserted here-and-now keeping spectators from wandering off to the there-and-then imaginable on each scene's far side. When Stein began writing her own plays, she sought to recreate this spectatorial experience and held herself to a shallow, infinitely widening present tense, resisting the longing for the "relief" (as she calls it) of climaxes. Hers is an intransitive idea of dramatic action: naming a principle underlying her dramaturgy, she said, simply, "writing should go on."[55] She qualifies this idea in "Plays," envisioning a theater that "moves but . . . also stays" (131). The phrase's seeming contradiction captures exactly the nature of stage space and time that dilates rather than scrolls onto new destinations. Such a theater submits to scrutiny but does not solicit it. It maintains its integrity — "the thing itself" — by maintaining its indifference to hierarchical structures of perception and composition. There may have been no precedent for this style in American theater, but Stein found one in nature: "I felt that if a play was exactly like a landscape then there would be no difficulty about the emotion of the person looking on at the play being behind or ahead of the play because the landscape does not have to make acquaintance. You may have to make acquaintance with it, but it does not with you, it is there. . . . The landscape has its formation . . . as after all a play has to have formation and be in relation one thing to the other thing . . . the landscape not moving but being always in relation, the trees to the hills the hills to the fields the trees to each other any piece of it to any sky and then any detail to any other detail" (122, 125).

The skittering exuberance with which Stein checks off sights in this passage confirms that nature has taught her how to resolve the "problem of the external and the internal." As she moves across this vista, she has access to only its empirically verifiable features. No imaginary interior tempts her; none exists in a space barring abstraction, mystification, and supposition. It is easy to imagine a similar form of attention before theatrical landscapes. As Stein plots them, they demand the same openness to simultaneity and multiple focus, the same ability to see (and think) horizontally rather than vertically. In *Byron A Play,* she put this idea concisely: "A play is when there is not only so but also."[56] A mode of spectatorship that takes "also" as its motto shuns a long-held ideal — viewers transfixed by single images, in thrall to mesmerizing characters and engrossing situations, boring into a field of view until its vein of pleasure is exhausted. Instead, they set out in many directions, touching lightly over incidents and keeping all possible meanings in play at once. Such flexibility isn't merely analytical. Each "so" exemplifies the same materialist, anti-abstract integrity that she admired in the trees, hills, and fields. As if Stein fears we will persist in treating her theater as merely a platform for illusion, she frequently interrupts "Plays" to restate first principles: "A play was a thing" (122). "A play is just there" (131). "I put into the play the things that were there" (129). The deliberately naive sentences reawaken theatergoers on the verge of surrendering to the narcotic pleasures of suspense or drifting into symbol-mongering. They keep dramatic action from softening into allegory, from becoming a pointer to something else. A character in *Listen to Me,* a play about the search for "words of one syllable," summarizes a view Stein expresses throughout her theater: the sentence "it is," he declares, is superior to "what is it about."[57]

Such self-consciousness affirms an even more basic reality. Stein reminds us what a play "is" every time she embeds the word "play" or "opera" in a work's title, or has a character announce the act number, or assigns lines to the acts themselves. Theatergoers hoping to enter characters' lives encounter Stein instead; she blocks our view by dramatizing her own manner of seeing the stage and manipulating her protagonists. Yet spectators thus held in place shouldn't expect any greater intimacy with Stein herself. As the titles of *Everybody's Autobiography* and *The Autobiography of Alice B. Toklas* suggest, this author carefully controls how much of the private woman is on display. (A scene in Stein's *The Mother of Us All* illustrates this mix of self-display and self-erasure particularly well: the Stein-like character Susan B. Anthony hides behind a statue of herself.) Throughout her theater, we see only the writer writing, or thinking about writing—a figure who discloses only those aspects of personal life that bear upon or are consumed by her work. Even passages alluding to Stein's erotic life are hardly intimate. They are as much "about" the puns, private slang, and secret language in which Stein codes them (and thus acknowledges a public readership) as any activity awaiting discovery behind closed doors.

It's fitting that a writer "tormented" by the relation of interior to exterior worlds would scrutinize the boundaries between art and life. Stein's commitment to "also" complicates the widespread impression of her hermeticism and forces us to redraw, if not remove, the borders around her plays. She continuously chafed against them. When she visited museums, as she writes in "Pictures," she studied the view out the windows more closely than the adjacent paintings—framed life besting framed art.[58] "Windows in a building are the most interesting thing in America," she writes in *Everybody's Autobiography* (157). Yet even they exclude too much, and before long Stein rebels against all structures that crop perception. Elsewhere in that work, she writes, "I am always hoping to have it the picture . . . not live in its frame, pictures have been imprisoned in frames. . . . Now that I have let them out . . . they want to get out by themselves" (272).

This vision of the canvas would powerfully influence her approach to the page. Stein's autobiographies describe the many times she unframed her texts, opening them up to what less confident writers would call distraction. "She was much influenced by the sound of the streets and the movement of the automobiles," she tells us in the *Autobiography* (206). In the country, she forged a similar kinship: "She wrote *Lucy Church Amiably* wholly to the sound of streams and waterfalls," reports Virgil Thomson in his autobiography.[59] Intimate landscapes were no less influential. Stein credits her poodle for teaching her about the nature of paragraphs in the way she lapped water. *A Circular Play* acknowledges her domestic drama even more directly: "I can hear Alice," a character says, apropos of nothing, as if Toklas were rattling around the kitchen while Stein wrote, or had just come in the door, interrupting her.[60] It is a scene like this that an impatient Richard Bridgman has in mind when he compares certain Stein works to "an interminable tape recording made secretly in a household."[61] As texts absorb interruptions, writing becomes indistinguishable from the scene of writing. The history of a text *is* the text. Her plays are, in this view, the evidence left behind after a long, fluid, and ultimately unrepresentable process that includes daydreaming, conversation, flanerie, and chance acquisitions, along with the acts of drafting, reading, and revision that overshadow the writer's ostensible subject. Such an approach can seem an extreme version of what Richard Poirier means by modernism's "primary" purpose: "to expose the factitiousness of its own local procedures." "Meaning," for such texts, "resides in the performance of writing and reading, of reading in the act of writing."[62]

Our own reading as much as Stein's: as we grow more conscious of the effort to move through her sentences, we may begin to feel that her various forms of autobiography (each the autobiography of the writing more than the writer) instruct us in our own conduct — that each text, once read, stands most prominently as a record of our reading it. Such a sensation returns us to the borders of Stein's art — sites where both reader and writer face a choice between external and internal landscapes. The same Stein who wrote to the sound of nature and her drinking dog also liked "to set a sentence for herself as a sort of tuning fork and metronome," as she herself admitted in the *Autobiography,* "and then write to that time and tune" (206). What William Gass calls Stein's "geography of the sentence" is as alluring as natural and theatrical landscapes.[63] Tenses beckon toward horizons or fence them off. Grammar domesticates the linguistic wilderness. Verbs clear space. Nouns reforest it. Syllables pace a speaker's journey. Punctuation slows them down at turns of phrase. For Stein, the way one talks about the world maps the world.

No part of speech is beneath notice to the naturalist happy to itemize hills, trees, and fields. Stein recounts how at a barbershop she realized that if she wanted to read a magazine while getting a haircut, she would have to hold her eyeglasses in her hand, using them like a magnifying glass. Reading sentences word by word, she discovered, "makes the writing that is not anything be something."[64] In the crevices of the fractured text, words are visible as if in three dimensions, recovering the wholeness they sacrificed on enlisting in expository or explanatory prose. Readers inside sentences are expected to respect the exteriors of words—the same respect for the integrity of the object and the clarity of the surface that we have seen in other versions of this modernist discipline. In her own writing, Stein hopes to control the collaboration among the parts of speech. "Renounce because and become," she declares in *The Geographical History* (184). The two words channel all generative power in a single direction, whereas she sought an egalitarian, multicentered, and multivalent verbal world. For the same reason, "Of should never be introduced" (223). Stein banishes the preposition for insisting on dependency, and for asking us to treat certain nouns as only the function of others. In their place, Stein substitutes "and" or "with." Juxtaposition is the more humane form of bondage.

When one imagines how to apply these ideas to life on or off stage, one sees that Stein's poetics are, among other things, a repository of metaphors with which to address matters of conduct. Her antipathy to hierarchical or interdependent sentences is a more decorous way to assert her equally staunch refusal to tolerate hierarchical societies, the culture of celebrity, and involuntary self-effacement. Many ethical dimensions of Stein's literary principles are enclosed within a perplexing, seemingly throwaway line from "Plays." "Strauss' Electra made me realize that . . . there could be a solution of the problem of conversation on the stage" (117). What problem? She doesn't say, but one can guess that conversation troubles her because each line of dialogue is, by necessity, *of* the others—responding to or provoking a listener's statements and thus not fully itself. How can *Elektra* help? Was Stein encouraged by the fact that Hofmannsthal's libretto is mostly monologues? More interesting is how he handles the rare dialogue. Characters alternate between private and public registers of expression within single conversations. When they emerge from self-contemplation to sing to one another, they remain partly isolated by fear, suspicion, anger, or despair; or they seem to have left behind some part of themselves or to be thinking about something else altogether. This is no less true at the opera's emotional peak. Strauss's characters are exposed, yet strangely remote; emotionally lavish yet also austere—withholding something, so never to be "of" the other characters. "She does not say / what she means," says Klytämnestra's confidante of Elektra, a quality that fortifies the opera's own border between inside and outside.[65]

One should already be hearing the larger implications of this formal strategy. It's not insignificant that "with" is the most frequently uttered word in *Four Saints in Three Acts*. The play's vision of spiritual devotion subtly refuses to endorse the disciple's typical subservience to God in favor of a more egalitarian union. So, too, with secular marriages. "Can two saints be one?" she asks. "No one is one when there are two," says a woman to her seducer in *Doctor Faustus Lights the Lights*.[66] (Faustus made his own error of exchanging independence for ephemeral power.) This theme is sounded yet again, its phrasing only slightly altered, in *The Mother of Us All*, Stein's opera about Susan B. Anthony. "I am not married . . . I could never be one of two I could never be two in one" (75). That Susan *is* married, in a way, to Anne is the very contradiction Stein hopes we'll linger over, here and in her other plays. What causes the need for solitude to arise simultaneously with the need for companionship? Does sexual communion compromise one's intellectual detachment? In the nervous, defiant title of *Three Sisters Who Are Not Sisters*, Stein voices the desire to break loose from biological fate even as she dramatizes how hard it is to renounce lifelong loyalties. *A Lyrical Opera Made by Two* celebrates creative unions, as its title suggests, but midway through the otherwise happy paean to Stein and Toklas's relationship, it stops dead to pose an uncomfortable, unanswerable question: "Who has whom."[67] Has consensuality degenerated into ownership? A darker image of commitment flashes briefly in another otherwise sunny play, *Say It with Flowers*: "They will be joined in hurts."[68] The darkness deepens in Stein's late works as she considers ambiguous political allegiances. *Yes Is for a Very Young Man*, set in Occupied France, depicts characters trying to decide just what to say "yes" to — the Vichy regime or the Resistance. In *Listen to Me*, from 1936, Stein implicitly resists the pathology of crowds and other coerced alliances: "Now very earnestly," a stage direction says, "all the characters do not come together" (403). Finally, in the memoir *Wars I Have Seen*, Stein forces us to rethink cultural bonds we take for granted or distort by sentimentality. Writing of her forsaken homeland in the wake of a war promoting a united front, Stein strives not to lose sight of its separate pieces: "After the last war I wanted to write a long book or poem . . . about how Kansas differed from Iowa and Iowa from Illinois and Illinois from Ohio, and Mississippi from Louisiana and Louisiana from Tennessee and Tennessee from Kentucky, and all the rest from all the rest, it would be most exciting, because each one of them does so completely differ from all the rest including their neighbors."[69] Only by listing the states — one by one, word by word — does she honor the complex meaning of nation and discover how to ensure a more perfect union.

The cumulative effect of all these passages argues in favor of what might seem, to the doctrinaire Steinian, critical heresy: to read even her early, landscape dramas for content as much as form. A closer look at one such play, *Four Saints in Three Acts*, will prove that Stein's work is resilient enough to withstand such scrutiny.[70] Recovering the saints in *Four Saints* does not usher in scenes of unequivocal piety. Nor must we muffle our interest in Stein's secular aesthetics. If anything, the historical models for her stage saints clarify the attractions of worldliness; they also instruct us in Stein's poetics with a visceral immediacy, and from a position of vulnerability, that Stein rarely allows herself. Three descriptions of writing and reading, from three separate writers, suggest the most obvious of many points of contact:

> One says the word . . . staying with this word for as long as one finds meanings, comparisons, relish and consolation in considerations related to it. One should do this for each word.[71]

> I also found it helpful to look at fields, water, or flowers. . . . They woke me, and brought me to a recollected state, and served me as a book.[72]

> She wrote without stopping or to erase or correct. . . . She had only to place her paper over her mind as it were, and make a tracing of the inspired script she found already engraved there.[73]

The first passage is by Saint Ignatius, from the *Spiritual Exercises;* the second is by Saint Teresa, from her autobiography, and the third, about Saint Teresa, is by Vita Sackville-West, from *The Eagle and the Dove.* Of course all could be by, and about, Gertrude Stein. Her identification with the historical saints would have tightened further when she encountered their own way of handling "the problem of the external and the internal." No disembodied mystic, the real Teresa was a hungry reader, an eager friend, a shrewd tactician, and an epicure. In her *Life,* she writes, "I seem to have wanted to reconcile two opposites as completely hostile, one to another, as the spiritual life and the joys, pleasures, and pastimes of the senses" (57). The supposed condition of saintliness — solitude — was impossible for her: "I could not shut myself inside myself — which was my whole method of procedure in prayer — without shutting a thousand vanities in with me" (57). Agony of a more fundamental kind confirmed Teresa's place on the border between spiritual and worldly experience: chronic illness fed the desire for spiritual deliverance even as it bred skepticism toward its promise. Religious submission, for its part, left her vulnerable to primal sexual pleasure — the latter surprisingly violent in spite (or because) of its sacred purpose. (Such is the premise of Bernini's famous, and famously graphic, sculpture of Teresa's transverberation.) It's customary to imagine these oppositions ending in stalemate or, no less absolute, happy union. Closer to the truth, and more pertinent to Stein's vision of life and theater as movement, is a drama in which the saint perpetually adjusts her position between them. We should renounce conventional affection, Teresa advises, but not the open heart needed to "marry" God. We should forsake will — never strain, she said — but not single-mindedness. We should guard against self-absorption, but still try to gather up the self's "scattered pieces." ("It is absurd to think that we can enter Heaven without first entering our own souls.")[74] In that work of consolidation, we must shake off the "restless little moth of the memory," but once safely in the present, we must also resist the false authority of the intellect (127). There seems to be no end to Teresa's narrowing, qualifying energies. Not even what she calls the "interior castle," a vision of seven concentrically arranged rooms that organize one's progress toward God, promises relief. When she reaches the seventh, innermost room, the saint must still remain "alert," as she writes, to the potential incursion of devilish snakes and toads from the outer chambers. The labor of "going in" matters more than its ultimate and long-sought destination. So, too, in the writing of her journey: "I'm so terrified as I'm writing this that I don't know how I can write it, or even live," she confesses, confident only in the painful, exquisite sensation of "going in" to prose.[75]

Gertrude Stein is everywhere in Teresa's account of her passion. It isn't just the saint's writing habits that recall the playwright's. Stein's own readiness to embrace difficulty is the sign of a deeper kinship. In *Four Saints*, she stages Teresa's many struggles — to reconcile opposites, to be simultaneously part of and apart from the world, to monitor one's commitments to others so to remain available for the more durable union with God, to resist the "moth of the memory" in favor of the continuous present, to make one's most reliable home in oneself, and, finally, to be able to write lucidly about one's journey. "I think I have got St. Therese onto the stage," Stein writes to Virgil Thomson while she works on the play. "It has been an awful struggle and I think I can keep her on."[76] Stein proposes a concrete equivalent for the act of entering the interior castle in the deceptively simple business of entering the stage. The first third of the opera depicts this laborious process, as Stein marks its stages with such lines as "Saint Therese has begun to be in act one," until finally a character makes an unequivocal announcement: "Saint Therese in an act one."[77] One can almost hear the play exhale a sigh of relief. The remainder of the opera depicts ever more challenging entrances — penetrations of buildings, temporal space, communities, conditions, individual psychologies, and ultimately language. Through it all, however, Stein never lets us forget her antipathy, in "Plays" and elsewhere, toward the spectator's habitual attempts to penetrate the stage. Theatrical visibility — making an entrance — is simply the prerequisite for a gradual recession toward invisibility. Or, as Stein herself puts it more gnomically in the play itself: "Saint Therese comes again to be absent" (448).

The innerness of *Four Saints* should be apparent even to readers unschooled in the saint's writings. The theme is literally on the text's surface — announced by the many words prefixed with "in" that recur like a nervous tic, each utterance tinged with hope that speech alone will admit speakers to interior landscapes — or at least drill into the aural space of the production. "Saint Therese in in in Lynn," reads one especially desperate line (458). Other words and phrases are no less freighted with emotion. Some connote seriousness verging on zeal: inclined, intending, intently, insisting, industriously. Others express frustration: interruption, intermittence, inability. Most resonant are those words confessing to ambivalence: intermediately, in between, indeterminately. Do the "individuals" of *Four Saints* live in dividedness? Therese may suggest that only by going "in" will one be "complete," but when Stein's characters speak the two words in sequence, they raise the specter of incompletion. A happier implication accompanies every appearance of "within." The historical Teresa may resist worldly relationships inside her castle, but the two syllables of "within," when Stein's Therese utters them together, hold out hope for an eventual reconciliation of solitude and sociability, if only in — within — language.

Subliminally coercive, the dialogue makes us experience movement even though, when it comes to actual activity, the play is static. It also makes stasis itself more substantial than it usually is in performance, returning us to the literal meaning of common phrases: all in all (460), once in a while (461), in a minute (465). We see that the actors shifting in and out of groups are, in fact, "all in all"; that, moreover, they are really "in a minute" — enclosed by the temporal space of the performance — and that each one of those moments, labeled as "once," is embedded in "a while." Lest we think Stein can't examine the particulars of stage presence any more microscopically, St. Therese, speaking of a fellow saint, says, "Settlement and in in" (464). If we hear the second "in" as a noun rather than a preposition, this self-burrowing play enters interiority itself. (Readers of *The Interior Castle* may recall Teresa's description of an "interior dilation" within the castle's innermost room, where one encounters a "thing so secret that God will not even entrust our thoughts with it" [82, 99].)

Just word games? Just one idea reiterated compulsively? *Four Saints* will seem so only to those who stop their ears to the continuo of worry playing beneath its minuets of going in and going out. Something seems wrong as soon as one reads the title. If there are only three acts for four saints, maybe one will be left out, not allowed into a play where life depends on interiority. "Who settles a private life," asks Therese as if fearful of being exiled from herself (446). The anxiety recurs in many direct and indirect ways. One saint is "sad," another "hurt," one "forgotten," still others "deceived." When someone describes a saint "begin[ning] to thin," one may think first of a wasting disease

(452). Therese herself is described as having lost her mother and later is widowed; she is "in pain" (452). Personal suffering quickly becomes global. Many words scattered throughout the text, unelaborated and thus ominous, refer to "violence," "attacks," a "plight," "miseries," "panic" — an escalating series that peaks early when we hear that it's "possible to kill five thousand chinamen by pressing a button" (445). Therese worries they "might be invaded" (464). As heard in the original 1934 production, such lines can be imagined as speaking to local fears. Later, when Stein writes there is "no peace on earth," we know it is our Earth she's talking about (451).

Fleeting and inchoate moods have the most power to darken the play. Certain lines could be captions to tableaux that illustrate some imminent but inexplicable danger. "Saint Therese in a storm," reads one stage direction. "He was hurrying," reads another, and only after five pages comes a possible reason: "if to stay to cry." Saints are "wary" and, later, "in doubt." They sense people "lurking"; they themselves "crept across" and "come to this brink" — not the only time they live "perilously," as if in a melodrama or silent movie. "Did she want him dead," reads one intertitle-like line. Another — "wed dead" — condenses countless domestic melodramas to their two essential plot turns. One of the strangest utterances in *Four Saints* — strange because the word is so much fancier than the others — is especially suggestive. "Rectify" appears in an otherwise innocuous list of other verbs, and it might occur to us that the word would only be there if something were wrong.

What *is* wrong? In *The Interior Castle*, the historical Teresa writes, "the soul has been wounded with love for the Spouse and seeks more opportunity of being alone" (126). In echoing this passage, Stein typically (and deceptively) adopts a sunnier tone: "It is very easy to love alone" (470). The riddle — just how does one "love alone"? — betrays her desire to complicate conventional definitions of solitude. It's not surprising that a writer who seeks autonomy within secular unions would, as we've seen, look carefully at the saint's marriage to God. Yet here Stein's intensity leads her beyond the issue of one's fidelity to a partner or obedience to authority. She is most preoccupied with one's commitment to a vocation. Work is another, perhaps purer form of "love." If one concedes that it can inspire the passion, loyalties, and obsessive dedication typical of social bonds, one will understand how one can (indeed, must) "love alone."

"Easy," though, it is not. In *Four Saints*, the work of prayer stands in for the work of writing, and both are distinguished for their arduousness as much as their ardor. The Stein who probes the interiors of sentences devotes the same attention to the experimentation that precedes a finished text — the aimless patterns of thought, groping for adequate forms, and trial-and-error assembly of paragraphs in the face of self-doubt—everything she approvingly calls "shoving the language around."[78] The single-mindedness of this work is as much Stein's concern as the work itself. *Four Saints* is a record of the effort to sustain the concentration, questioning, and self-questioning upon which all good writing depends. Stein affirms her seriousness with typical indirection: "singularly," "principally," "parted," "not attached," "selfish," "we do not care to share"—no single word or phrase, or any of the others on this theme that speckle her text, makes her case alone, but as they accumulate, their urgency increases and purpose clarifies. We can imagine the writer tightening her engagement with the page as she writes them, each the preamble to original expression. ("Let me listen to me," she tells herself in one of her *Stanzas in Meditation*.)

Roland Barthes helps us see further links between prayer and writing in his essay on the historical Ignatius, model for Therese's companion saint in *Four Saints in Three Acts*. The essay makes no reference to Stein, but everywhere it lights up the opera's obscurities—not least because for Barthes saintliness is a form of theatricality, and theatricality a function of language. "What is theatricalization?" he asks. "It is not designing a setting for representation, but unlimiting the language."[79] In Ignatius's *Spiritual Exercises*, Barthes shows, the saint restores to worship its identity as speech, and then asks of speech that it be more active and productive than usual—not merely to honor phenomena but to breed them. Before the worshipper, or "exercitant," can contemplate the abstract values enshrined by religion, he or she must probe the language that names them. That process involves believers in an all-consuming act of identification. Reimagining for themselves the life of Christ, they "live out scenes," Barthes writes, "as in a psychodrama" (61). "The most abstract things . . . must find some material movement where they can picture themselves and form a *tableau vivant*" (62). All the while, Barthes continues, "the exercitant must not hurry, must . . . do each Exercise without reference to its successor, not allow to arise too soon . . . the emotions of consolation, in short, he must respect the suspense of feelings, if not of facts" (61).

Readers coming to this passage after Stein will no doubt recognize a version of her continuous present. Ignatius won't rush ahead of or lag behind the sequence of affect in his prayer. Speech and writing—Ignatius's "definitive horizon"—enclose him even when spiritual passion lifts him out of everyday landscapes. The Steinian terms in Ignatius's own prose—repetition, composition, discernment—are his starting point for a description of writing that prizes the writer's ongoing, interrogatory engagement with his materials over any conclusion he might reach about his subject. The author of the *Spiritual Exercises* scrutinizes, on a gradually expanding field, the components of a prayer, the subjects they consecrate, and the universal conditions such subjects illustrate — or as Ignatius himself puts it, one makes "an account of one's soul . . . first about thoughts, then about words, and finally about deeds."[80] Ignatius's instruction for reciting the Lord's Prayer — "one stays with the word ['Father'] for as long as one finds meaning" before moving on to the next word — is but one manifestation of an experimental temperament that takes the whole world for its text. This saint moves from the inside out, mirroring Therese's opposite journey (and, with her, modeling the tension essential to Stein's purposefully static, self-contradictory theater).

Ignatius is such a valuable adjunct to Stein not only because he elevates procedures that could seem purely literary to a spiritual plane. (Nowhere is Stein more Ignatian than when she reads word by word in the barbershop chair.) The saint, for all his remote authority and principled "indifference" — like Stein, he wrote his autobiography in the third person — also asks us to acknowledge the strong emotion in this kind of reading. (Was this why his eyes, according to legend, were always "veiled with weeping"?)[81] He enhances his attractiveness to theater artists by thinking spatially and temporally about processes habitually considered abstract or wholly internal. In a passage on the rhythm of prayer, he locates the "interval between each breath" where one can measure "the distance between the other's greatness and one's own lowliness" (333). Lest one think this "interval" is too humbling, one need only recall Stein's own handling of the word in *Four Saints*: "An interval. Abundance. An interval" (465). The actual space between the repeated phrase in this passage — between the verbal signs of betweenness — is a land of plenty.

It is especially abundant in yearning — the striving toward knowledge and the expressiveness that is the fruit of such labor. A third and final variation on this trope appears in Barthes, who envisions an "anterior space" that separates the "new language" from "the other, common, idle, outmoded language, whose 'noise' might hinder it" (4). In all three images, it is transitional ground that hosts the greatest creativity — the progress toward vital speech. In Stein, conditions of uncertainty outshine, and are more theatrical than, the complacency that follows — when thought congeals into doctrine. In almost every play, we witness the playwright thinking about characters who themselves think about thinking. As Stein embraces the theater for its ability to widen the "anterior space" between self and the world and to prolong the "interval" between past and future, she consecrates sites of experimentation pursued without faith in the existence of a worthwhile discovery. What we do discover is a less regal, more humane artist. "I used not to understand but I am beginning to now," she writes in *Wars I Have Seen*.[82] Only beginning: committed to a spirit of inquiry, it's not surprising that she claims as one source of her dramatic structure the detective story.[83] She writes amid — between — possibilities. She prefers "choosing" rather than "using" words (as she says in "What Is English Literature") and retains the right to change her mind even after making a choice, if she can thereby defer hated climaxes.[84] A character in *Listen to Me* sums up Stein's aesthetic in a phrase that, like the word "also," captures the provisional, self-renewing nature of all her theater: "And everybody said nevertheless" (403). The line calls back readers who have ventured deep inside a scene, character, or sentence and thrusts them into the stage's open air, where they can consider something new, tease out the implications of once overlooked events, and, happily, redirect their forever incomplete and self-contradictory spectacles of interpretation.

Darmstadt, April 1946. The city was still in ruins after air raids in 1944 left more than 12,000 dead and 70,000 homeless. Germans were scrounging for clothes, shoes, and usable things behind the few walls still standing, none more than shoulder-high. People cooked what food they could find over open fires, made new homes in wet cellars, covered their faces against the stench of decay emanating from every crater. Desperation, here, was habitual, ingrown, and most of all, unhistrionic. In many accounts, observers remark on the overwhelming silence in the typical postwar "necropolis" — no cars, electricity, commercial or political networks; a pervasive "lassitude" and "lethargy" that blunted the force of even extreme emotions.[85] It is hard to imagine that there was enough leisure, much less energy, to mount a production of Thornton Wilder's *The Skin of Our Teeth* (1942), or that it was so successful that audiences crowded the bombed-out, unheated theaters here and (when it toured later that year) all across the country. The play's German title gave it the urgency of news: *Wir sind noch einmal davongekommen* — We Have Survived.

The many possible inflections one might give that title reveal the ambiguities of the play itself — and of Wilder in general. Triumphant? Defiant? Exhausted? Germans, we're told, couldn't agree about whether Wilder was being optimistic or pessimistic. Does the play view survival as only accidental and temporary, one stop on a cycle of destruction no less continuous than the cycle of creation? (Their evocative word for the play's tone — *Katastrophenoptimismus* — suggests a compromise between dark and light interpretations.)[86] Even darker, more particular meanings awaited those willing to acknowledge them at the start of the long period of self-scrutiny following Germany's surrender. One need only stress the word "we" in *We Have Survived* to feel the first stirrings of guilt over the six million who didn't.

However one settles the question of tone, one is already approaching the play with far greater subtlety than one usually associates with Wilder. The "enthusiast," as one of his biographers calls him, is nowhere to be found in a postwar landscape where enthusiasm would be blasphemous, if not impossible. Neither is the writer whom Dwight Macdonald used as exhibit A in his 1960 *Partisan Review* discussion of "Midcult" — a category under which he grouped Wilder with Pearl Buck, the Book of the Month Club, collegiate Gothic, and the common-language Bible. Macdonald's essay set the standard for the still-current embarrassment among sophisticated readers and spectators at the mere mention of Wilder. For Macdonald, as for many who followed him, Wilder forfeits serious respect, to say nothing of canonicity, by his supposed evasiveness. He "has the best of both tenses," writes Macdonald of *Our Town*, "the past is veiled by the nostalgic feelings of the present, while the present is softened by being conveyed in terms of a safely remote past."[87] Of course, the Germans who staged Wilder in 1946 (and in 1945, when Erich Engel mounted a production of *Our Town* for spectators wrapped in blankets) couldn't have softened their present or taken distance from their past even if they wanted to. W. G. Sebald, in *On the Natural History of Destruction* (a title that Wilder would have found attractive), describes a scene that models the practical-minded seeing Wilder dramatizes and invites from his audience. In a Hamburg apartment house miraculously left standing after air raids had razed every other structure surrounding it, a woman can be seen washing her windows — as if the sun had just risen on another day, as if no apocalypse had disrupted, or could disrupt, her routine.[88] None had: clear windows themselves won't restore normalcy but the act of cleaning them can. She affirms her still-intact ability to see a need and, by meeting it, begins to see the world around her. Wilder's plays, themselves systems for seeing as much as collections of things seen, may also have equipped their postwar spectators to approach what appears most dreadful — to see their lives for the first time cleansed of romanticism and malevolent national mythologies.

One wants Americans to make a similar correction — to cleanse Wilder's work itself of our own cultural assumptions and see it as we imagine the Germans did, if only to make it more urgently our own. If successful, we will reread and resee plays that are neither small and sentimental (as has been our habit with *Our Town*), nor overgeneralized and fabulistic (as with *The Skin of Our Teeth*). Yet it's easy to overcorrect — to make such a strenuous case for Wilder's "darkness" that one loses sight of what is valuable about him. (The same syndrome afflicts those who, uneasy with Wilder's "easiness," insist on his philosophical bona fides and love of Joyce.) No less dangerous than softening Wilder is hardening him. The sources of distress in his narratives — and they are plentiful — attract characters determined to understand them, to meet the plays' many private and public apocalypses not with rage or despair but with clear vision, direct language, common sense, and respect for fact — a vigorous, flexible simplicity, disarming to the degree that it is undeterred: "we have survived."

Such pragmatism is the strongest plank in Wilder's dramatic structure. *The Skin of Our Teeth* is typical in the persistence with which it challenges its own metaphysical consolations. A properly balanced production stresses the cycle of destruction and renewal no more than the practical business of getting through a single day. "I keep the home going," says Mrs. Antrobus, her stamina supported by long experience: "I've starved before. I know how."[89] Tasks fill countless minutes in Wilder — dusting, cooking, stoking fires, stringing beans, mowing the lawn, delivering papers and milk, packing and unpacking luggage, knitting a stocking, feeding chickens, sorting debris, righting overturned furniture, reinforcing walls and doors, and replenishing water in the car radiator, among many others. (Of course, in Wilder's anti-illusionistic theater, the actors who do these things take on the additional job of arranging and rearranging the stage.) Wilder reserves time for tasks not to give his plays the aura of authentically observed small-town or domestic experience (as directors often assume), but to illustrate his characters' attentiveness to their world — the one they find before them, not the one they hope for or mourn. That spirit of engagement serves them especially well in resisting the allure of moral and ethical abstractions. Testing every ideal against experience, they keep busy knocking down facile premises and looking coldly at habitual sentiment. As always, they side with the feasible over the perfect. Marriage, insists Mrs. Antrobus, is based not on love but on a contractual agreement. "Two imperfect people got married and it was the promise that made the marriage" (201). Mr. Antrobus subjects "freedom" to the same scrutiny. If it sanctions brutal disregard for others ("I'm going to be free, even if I have to kill half the world for it," says his son Henry [238]), then it, too, must be exchanged for a more careful conception of individual liberty. By the end of the play, the Antrobuses' tougher new ideals are credible for being as yet unrealized.

This kind of critical inquiry, sustained by the faith that sight, if clear-eyed enough, will lead to knowledge, had of course also been Gertrude Stein's project, and its appearance in Wilder's theater is only one of many obsessions they share. In the first of a series of page-long "autobiographies" dedicated to Wilder and included in *The Geographical History of America* (1936), Stein recalls that, as "a little one," "I did not see what I was seeing" (172–73). Wilder himself voices the same sentiment in the earlier *Pullman Car Hiawatha* (1931) — a character reaches the limits of her life upon saying, "I see now. I see now. I understand everything now" — and develops it in *Our Town,* admitting its full force of regret and frustration as he does so.[90] "I can't look at everything hard enough," complains Emily, returning home after her death. "Mama, just look at me one minute as though you really saw me. . . . *Let's look at one another.*"[91] (Is it to forestall the regret of learning this lesson too late that Gladys's newborn baby, in *The Skin of Our Teeth,* already "notices everything very well" [224]?)

Such attention, for all its passion, is nonetheless subject to strict discipline: Wilder's characters are careful not to envision what they cannot see. He writes as if to second Stein's warning, "Be careful of analysis and analogy. . . . Define what you do by what you see never by what you know" (93, 162). Here and elsewhere, Stein sounds like the "serene and didactic" Ma Kirby driving to her daughter in *The Happy Journey to Trenton and Camden* (1931), unable to "rest easy in my mind without I see her" with her own "firm and glassy eye."[92] We hear the same notes of insistence from Hawkins in *The Wreck on the Five-Twenty-Five* (1957), who declares "there is no 'away.' There's only 'here' ";[93] from the Stage Manager in *Our Town,* where "we like to know the facts about everybody" (8); and from Mrs. Antrobus, who throws into the ocean a letter correcting the misinformation about women in books, plays, movies, and advertisements: "We're not what you're all told and what you think we are: We're ourselves" (202). Throughout his work, Wilder purifies behavior of cultural distortions and rescues shared experience from local bias. "What's left when memory's gone, and your identity, Mrs. Smith?" asks the Stage Manager in *Our Town,* his question a conscious tribute to Stein's thinking about "identity" and "entity." The latter will be known only to those able to wait patiently for the "eternal part" of a character to "come out clear" (82).

Theater is the ideal arena in which to cultivate such attentiveness. There, "it is always 'now,' " Wilder writes in a preface — the commonplace sounding fresh because he joins it to an ambitious program for restoring shock to recognition and rigor to sympathy.[94] He's more than just the "remover of obtrusive bric-a-brac" from the stage (as he calls himself [xiv]). He puts forward concrete images, purposefully limited in reach, to stand in for states of mind that others might express in vaporous generalities. A repeated phrase in *The Long Christmas Dinner* is typical. Lucia is the first to look outdoors and marvel that "every last twig is wrapped around with ice," and with each recurrence of the line (four characters say it in all, with minor variations), it grows more transparent, shimmering, its style exactly adequate to both its modest subject and the sharp consciousness of mortality that underlies it — a fit rare in any drama.[95] It is a demonstration of what Glenway Wescott calls Wilder's unhurried style[96] — one that seems the playwright's own response to his many characters who lament, with Emily, that "it goes so fast" (100).

The directness of such a line recalls Stein's "ode to Thornton," in which she writes, "Nature is what it is. / Emotion is what it is" (192). In still another passage, she is simplest of all: "Thornton Wilder is" (89). The emphasis on "is" echoes a phrasing that occurs throughout Wilder's works, his much-consulted sources, and his broader cultural context. Asked by the *Paris Review* to define his approach to playwriting, he said he hoped to exploit the theater's ability to say "Behold! These things are" rather than the less declarative and succinct "This moral truth can be learned from beholding this action."[97] Readers of Wilder's lecture on Thoreau, "The American Loneliness," as well as his many journal entries on him and frequent approving citation, in other prose, of Thoreau's demand for "simplicity, simplicity, simplicity!" may recall a passage from *Walden* in which the author urges fellow writers to "work and wedge our feet downward through the mud and slush of opinion, and prejudice, and tradition, and delusion, and appearance . . . till we come to a hard bottom and rocks in place, which we can call *reality,* and say, This is."[98] As Wilder's brother, the theologian Amos Wilder, has suggested, an even stronger kinship exists between the playwright and American Puritan writers.[99] "To know a thing *as it is,* is to know it in its *Essence,* and comprehend it in its definition."[100] This New England schoolhouse motto hovers over all of Wilder's laconic, deliberately unimpressed assertions of place, identity, and feeling. Like the divines, Wilder "lets fly poynt blanck" with his characters' unfussy sentences. He aims "to see the simples in things" (as one Puritan writer put it) and seeks a style composed of words "stript" of "gilt" and sentences cut from mere "cloth to go warm." Only thus can he uphold the distinction Perry Miller makes between "substantials" and "accidentals" in speech and in the world speech commemorates.[101] (For all these reasons, Wilder can be regarded as our best early American dramatist.)

Yet Wilder seeks Puritan clarity with eyes wide open to modernist ambiguity, and asserts the simplicities of presence against a culture of increasing illegibility and perishability. Every unvarnished and complete statement in Wilder cannot be seen apart from those that are flawed, partial, and occluded. To hear the emphatic, even brazen tone of his theater's many variously worded assertions that "it is," one need only tune in to their broader context, one humming with sotto voce claims that "it isn't," "can't" or "won't be." Unsurprisingly, these are most audible at his plays' endings. Wilder takes care to mark the point at which an art that had granted presence rescinds it and evicts its passive and hidden observers. The last or penultimate lines are strikingly similar: "Good night," in *Our Town* and *The Skin of Our Teeth;* "Turn out the lights when you come" in *The Wreck on the Five-Twenty-Five;* "Shut your eyes . . ." in *The Happy Journey;* "All out" in *Pullman Car Hiawatha.* Such lines recall the even more definitive evictions enacted at the ends of other plays. Ermengarde walks through the portal of death in *The Long Christmas Dinner.* A personified Death welcomes a wounded knight in *Childe Roland to the Dark Tower Came.* The title character of *Leviathan* swallows a drowned prince. Mozart works feverishly on his *Requiem* in *Mozart and the Gray Steward,* dying before it (and the play?) are finished. One is hard-pressed to name a Wilder play not set in a necropolis. His bright visible world is backed by, flanked by, and built on a larger darkness, capable of swallowing the stage if he and we don't maintain the luminous power of our attention.

In some plays, suffering is more compelling for being thinned out to the point of imperceptibility — "death by regret," as the fortune teller calls it in *The Skin of Our Teeth* (172). In others, it affects us only when averted altogether. Characters in *The Wreck on the Five-Twenty-Five* contemplate, even wish for, a fatal train accident and a suicide, but neither occurs. The watchman in *Pullman Car Hiawatha* assures us that the train signals are working and that he's wide awake. In *The Happy Journey,* a neighbor's baby is choking until a backslap makes it spit up; Pa takes the car to the mechanic to allay Ma's worry about its safety; and a dog darts into the road, just barely avoiding traffic. In *Our Town,* death is omnipresent long before the third-act funeral, kept out of sight as if by classical decorum yet so compulsively acknowledged as to make absence itself permanently associated with menace, fear, and uncertainty. The Spartan and well-ordered stage seems only temporarily exempt from turmoil as the Stage Manager points to the surrounding offstage world. The morning star, he says, flares before it goes out. He itemizes all the dead Grovers, Cartwrights, Gibbses, and Herseys, telling us of Dr. and Mrs. Gibbs's own future death as they enter and of Joe Crowell's as he exits. All this retrospective and anticipated history arrives simultaneously with the news of the twins that Dr. Gibbs has just delivered. This giver of life often seeks out the landscapes of death: Dr. Gibbs is "never so happy" (reports Mrs. Gibbs) as when he's visiting Civil War battlefields (20).

Other unseen territory is similarly marked with ominous history and silently rebukes the equanimity of the landscapes close at hand. Against the fecundity of Mrs. Gibbs's and Mrs. Webb's gardens ("corn . . . peas . . . hollyhocks . . . heliotrope"), Wilder positions Silas Peckham's nearby cow pasture studded with fossils; the Cotahatchee tribes "who entirely disappeared" from their own land; the residents of "Polish Town" who drank too much and nearly froze to death in a snowdrift; Crawford Notch, where Wally Webb's appendix burst; the area "up that part of town" where people are locking their doors against a vague menace; and even French and Belgian battlefields, which may spring to mind when the Stage Manager announces at the start of act 3 that the year is 1913. Devastation that is beneath, beside, and just beyond the stage is coming closer. Rain worried about in act 1 pours in acts 2 and 3. Rebecca fears the moon has come unmoored and is hurtling toward earth, where "there'll be a big 'splosion" (41). The absurdity of her scenario doesn't make it any less terrifying. Wilder often mocks anxiety to affirm its pervasiveness: when the Stage Manager says that Mrs. Gibbs and Mrs. Webb have "never [had] a nervous breakdown," he makes us realize one is possible (47). George melo-dramatically slitting his throat as he says he has "five more hours to live" and, later, his genuine terror at the altar are two versions of the same psychosis.

In a theater where suffering is registered elsewhere, deferred, or memori-alized as safely "back then," it's significant that the one visible scene of pain, and the most chilling vision of mortality, is the most minor. Editor Webb enters the play wounded. Having cut himself while slicing an apple, he has a handkerchief wrapped around one finger. He twists the makeshift bandage more and more tightly as he recites statistics, demographics, cultural likes and dislikes — particularities that fade away quickly, unable to deflect our atten-tion from the speaker's more immediate experience. Here, too, we face a question of seeing: the editor invites us to take a panoramic or long view, but we can't help staring at his hand. It is as if he participates in a kind of sacrificial ritual, by his blood invoking that of others (and Others) near and far: Gibbs and Webb kin, ancestors, unacknowledged neighbors, first settlers, Cotahat-chee, Union, and doughboy dead. The wound encapsulates the vulnerability of all Wilder characters — their "porcelain life" easily broken, as Emily Webb's namesake, Emily Dickinson, puts it.[102] One slip of the hand tips a delicate balance between life and death.

To those thinking visually, the spurt of blood also threatens to stain the immaculate and carefully maintained surfaces of Wilder's mise-en-scène. The prospect of failed repression and the fear of subsequent disarray don't disap-pear when Editor Webb exits. His stanched wound is a key image not just for *Our Town* but for all Wilder. The finger points to an error that should have been avoided, or must be corrected, and to an experience of pain that must be restrained. In this light, the common complaint among those who dislike Wilder — that he hasn't just simplified experience but expurgated it — reveals a source of his theatrical energy. The "flaw" is the point. Wilder *wants* us to feel that something is being withheld, with frequent difficulty and variable success, and sets his plays in the volatile zone between disclosure and silence. There he exploits the conflict between his theater's equable tone and its unsettled ac-tion, his various stage managers' retrospective calm and the other actors' quivering presentness, the narrative's exegetical deliberateness and his charac-ters' subjection to mysteries they cannot penetrate. The very manner in which Wilder is forthcoming controls our presumptions: characters whose emotions are declarative, capacious, and undiluted rebuff further inquiry. Often Wilder eliminates protestations of sincerity to restore a sentiment's authenticity. He also dispenses with equivocations if they would reduce strong emotion to mere feeling. *Our Town* depends on "nervous compression," he once wrote.[103] With *The Skin of Our Teeth*, he told Gertrude Stein, "I tried to write a tragedy without tears, real *sec* knowing and telling."[104] To the producer of the film version of *Our Town*, he said, "New Hampshire wouldn't even go solemn slow" to the third-act funeral; "they just go."[105]

A "styleless stylist" (as Truman Capote called him), Wilder uses neutrality to draw attention to — and, as we'll see, to defend — a play's borders.[106] There are countless moments in which his theater averts its eyes, stops its ears, and bites its tongue. In *Bernice*, a man about to die obeys his maid's suggestion that he "go upstairs and hide youself" rather than subject us to his melodrama.[107] Mrs. Hawkins in *The Wreck on the Five-Twenty-Five* wishes her bottled-up husband "would complain once in a while," yet she also puts limits on intimacy and candor: we're "not supposed to *see* one another," she insists, as if aware of what disorder might result if they did (142, 151). In *Our Town*, Mrs. Gibbs swallows her disappointment at never traveling. Simon Stimson, harried by private furies, cannot or will not disclose the sources of his despair. When George Gibbs asks his future father-in-law whether or not he believes in marriage, Mr. Webb too quickly says, "Oh, yes; *oh, yes*" (57) — an attempt to conceal doubt that falters until he changes the subject to chicken-raising. Other plays unfold under the quizzical, diffident, or helpless eyes of characters whose inhibition may be culturally enforced. The Stage Manager in *Pullman Car Hiawatha* says to a black porter, "it's your turn to think. . . . You have a right to," but elicits from him only a sentence about Chicago and life insurance — impersonal subjects hiding the private man (45). Ivy and Hester, the black ushers who play the Hours at the end of *The Skin of Our Teeth*, are equally opaque. They jump from anonymity to allegory without stopping at humanity. We may, out of long habit, at first treat his characters' blank surfaces as invitations to interpretation, and in some instances it would be perverse not to imagine the emotions we think a character must be suppressing. Yet more often than not, we're left frustrated by a character who refuses to be forthcoming. We must reconcile ourselves to treating the absence of explicit motive or expansive reaction *as* an absence. (This is a particularly useful corrective to readings of Simon Stimson founded on a theory of his "true" sexuality.)

It's indicative of Wilder's commitment to ambiguity that the one character who knows the most is the one about whom we know the least. From one perspective, Wilder's many stage managers are the epitome of frankness. A usually invisible figure in the theater is now visible. But his presence can also be played as another form of absence, as if the author of this world has fled, leaving it in the hands of a faceless deputy, charged only with executing someone else's plan. The question is unspoken but persistent: why didn't Wilder assign pride of place to a "Playwright" character? Onstage only because someone else isn't, the stage manager never lets us forget we're not seeing everything. Are there other American plays whose main characters are so anonymous? (In his *Journals,* Wilder sides with those artists who depict "de-individualized" emotions and events, and insists that good acting "is not experiencing but describing and indicating a reality" — an unwitting echo of Perry Miller's description of the Plain Style as "indicative.")[108]

By making his theater's "voice" anti-authorial, Wilder does more than set the standard against which to measure all the other repressions in his theater. The stage managers' putative aura of control in fact concedes the existence of still more sources of uneasiness. As they chalk the borders of the stage space, check their stopwatches, and consult their promptbooks, they point to an unpredictable, error-prone world in need of constant supervision. It's not simply that they preside over characters fearing death or worlds on the edge of apocalypse. The aesthetic principles supporting these plots are equally unstable. "A play is what takes place," writes Wilder in "Some Thoughts on Playwriting." "A novel is what one person tells us took place."[109] Wilder's stage managers occupy neither genre — or both. Moving between fiction and theater, they report events and then fall silent, stepping back to let lives "take place." (In this respect, a hostile, if discerning, review of Wilder's novel *The Woman of Andros* is apposite. "The book is not written," says R. P. Blackmur, "it is written about."[110] The detachment that Blackmur takes as a failing in Wilder's fiction determines the achievement of his drama.) Genre slippage accounts for our own vertigo. Watching his plays, we can't trust either the intimacy of fiction — one voice talking in our ear — or the enfolding communality of theater. An energizing immediacy abruptly ends, and Wilder yanks us back to the stage manager's cooler, external perspective. But just when distance becomes its own pleasure, bringing the no less energizing freedom for scrutiny and analysis, Wilder pushes us back into the fray. Equally disturbing is the lack of clarity about time. It may well be that, as Wilder says, onstage it is always *now,* but his stage managers also live in a world where it is always *then.* Back then — when the production we are watching was conceived, rehearsed, and finally set, existing now under the stage manager's supervision. The stage we look at — enclosing a repetition of the now-inaccessible first performance, and before that, first rehearsal, and still further back, first draft — recedes even as the play asserts, no less vigorously than in any other theater, the irreproducibility of the performance we're watching. Here, too, as with his ambivalence over genre, Wilder purposefully declines to reconcile the contradiction. He tells us, with equal conviction, that his play is finished and unfinished, grown and growing, inanimate and animate, written and being written.

Robert Lowell, in his own variation on this theme, argues that a work of art "is an event, not a record of an event."[111] Undoing the neatness of the dictum, Wilder shows that recording can be an event in itself and as such is prey to all the fevers, hidden agendas, mistakes, and regrets of more spontaneous action. His theater reserves privileged places for the record-keepers — not just stage managers, but also journalists, geologists, historians, accountants, book collectors, and librarians — as well as for those awaiting the record-keeper's recognition: prophets, weather forecasters, and fortunetellers. They keep (or consult) the books in a culture indifferent, if not outright hostile, to such archival consciousness.[112] A book that records the relationships among all the characters in *The Long Christmas Dinner* is "somewhere upstairs" (18). No one knows exactly where, and no one goes to look. "The first thing to do is to burn up those old books," says Henry in *The Skin of Our Teeth* (228). We needn't think of the Nazi pyres to recognize how vulnerable to degradation all "immortal" text is in Wilder's world. All it takes is a case of food poisoning to sabotage the same play's philosophers' pageant, leaving the stage manager to hastily rehearse understudies in the words of Aristotle, Spinoza, and Plato. (The memory of these passages' near erasure, if upheld, will keep them from sounding like Bartlett's entries when finally spoken.) Here, too, the uneasy relation between prose and theater helps Wilder complicate (and stress the hard-won value of) his seeming simplicity. Characters stay "on" book, clinging to it, as Mr. Antrobus does when he unpacks his library at the end of *The Skin of Our Teeth*, in an irremediably temporal — and mortal — art. No matter how successful they are in finding security in print, they must remain on guard for speech's lapses and missteps. We sense that Wilder himself shares this anxiety when, in *Our Town*, he has the citizens of Grover's Corners inter his own playscript in their time capsule. The Stage Manager says they do so to inform future generations about themselves. More interesting is to see the gesture as Wilder's attempt to grant mercurial, volatile oral culture the poise of a document.

This staged negotiation between speech and text brings to mind Foucault's beautiful image in "Fantasia of the Library" of "the indefinite murmur of writing."[113] Not just in its most obvious illustrations — the Hours cycling across the stage in *The Skin of Our Teeth*, speaking words that Mr. Antrobus reads from the books salvaged below them, and the passengers of *Pullman Car Hiawatha* descending from public, theatrical speech into what Wilder calls "their thinking murmur" (54). Wilder is everywhere conscious of the "indefinite" even as he commemorates the definite, and finds in self-directed, self-shielding "murmur" meanings as resonant as those in clarion, declarative prose. Of the many Wilder stage managers standing on the much-breached border between writing and speaking, the one in *The Happy Journey,* the only one Wilder asks to hold his script in hand, reminds us with particular force that what we hear actors say was first written and read by its author. The audible rendering of Wilder's words (and visible enactment of his directions) can only be an imperfect approximation of the authoritative, ideal version printed on the page and held to the Stage Manager's chest, tantalizingly unavailable to the audience.

Errors of speech suggestively mar Wilder's plain style in almost every major play. None is significant, or even noticeable, in itself, but taken together they suggest a theater that understands the peril of its necessary allegiance to the present tense — how little room there is to maneuver, how each instant of performance involves total dissolution of the mise-en-scène and nimble repositioning of its occupants. It is as if, like the family en route to Camden, the plays themselves were just barely escaping disabling accident or total breakdown at every stage of their progress. Wilder's interest in a character's memory lapse, or his ear for the music in lines only half-completed, or his choice to let stand the wrong first passes at lines later corrected ensure that we keep in mind alternatives to what we hear — or, more precisely, acknowledge the fact, suppressed in any work by a strong artist, that there *are* alternatives. These many errata preserve in a seemingly frozen text the energy given off during the ordeal of composition. The Field, in *Pullman Car Hiawatha,* gets the source of a quotation wrong: "William Cullen — I mean James Russell Lowell" (50). Later, the characters of Ten O'clock and Twelve O'clock can't remember their lines and must be prompted. Mrs. Antrobus tells the convention in the second act of *The Skin of Our Teeth* that she "regret[s] every moment" of her marriage when she means to say the opposite (166). Mr. Antrobus loses his train of thought during his own speech, looks to his wife for help, and then botches the lines she whispers to him: "I think I can prophesy, . . . with complete lack of confidence, that a new day of security is about to dawn" (164).

Other tears in Wilder's smooth surfaces reveal more disturbing truths. One can calculate the cost of repression when Ma Kirby bursts out and says of her son, "I don't want him" (93). The vitriol courses through Wilder's oeuvre. Emily Webb says, "I *hate* him" before she marries George (75). Roderick, in *The Long Christmas Dinner,* says, "I hate this town and everything about it" (21). Harriet, in *Pullman Car Hiawatha,* hates herself: "I want to be punished for it all" (56). Mrs. Antrobus calls her daughter "detestable" and slaps her (131). Mr. Antrobus follows up by striking their son. When it's Sabina's turn to lose control, she directs her rage to a bigger target: "I hate this play" (115). After such violence, we watch the productions as much as the characters try to recover. Wilder tests, with ever mounting severity, his texts for their ability to withstand blows to the decorum he had worked equally hard to establish. The outcome of these experiments is especially ambiguous in *Our Town,* when the Stage Manager ends a speech about the many weddings he has performed by saying, "once in a thousand times it's interesting" (78). In a play urging us to see and value the complex detail in ostensibly ordinary lives, the admission is especially disconcerting. Indeed, Wilder feared he had inadvertently sabo-taged his narrative—committed his own error. In a letter to Malcolm Cowley, he worried that he was being "chilling and cynical" and tried to soften the line by recommending that the actor smile broadly as he says it.[114] Luckily, he didn't succeed. The smile only heightens our discomfort at a play itself un-nerved by a sudden outbreak of truth.

Correct errors, the right wrong steps: every breach undermines the assur-ances of cultural, societal, and familial cohesiveness that credulous readers think they hear in Wilder's theater. This challenge to received wisdom is ex-plicit in *Pullman Car Hiawatha.* The ghost of a workman speaks his lines in German, including a passage from the Gettysburg Address, yet the Stage Man-ager mistranslates Lincoln's opening lines as "Three score and seven years ago" (51). The mistake seems pointless unless one imagines that the Stage Manager, inattentive to the workman's recitation, is unwittingly casting doubt on the ideals it enshrines. No wonder that he cuts off the worker before the phrase about "integrating all peoples." Unvoiced, the ideal is unfulfilled. As it is throughout Wilder: the voice by its commissions and omissions puts up the first obstacle to the various forms of union commemorated in Wilder's titles—the echoed "our" in *Our Town* and *The Skin of Our Teeth,* the even more obvious optimism of *The Matchmaker*—and fostered by his household dinner tables, stacked train berths, and the close quarters of the family car.

His characters compensate for the revelations of error by taking refuge in various forms of code. Wilder's polyglot stage world may seem at first glance the image of a peaceable kingdom, but more often than not it is Babel, atomiz-ing its inhabitants and keeping spectators from assuming unearned intimacy with his theater. Like the Insane Woman in *Pullman Car Hiawatha,* who laments that "no one understands me," we, too, are pushed up to the limits of our comprehension at critical moments in a typical Wilder play. The plain style betrays its promise of transparency, and we now can see the opacity it strug-gles against. The language of the planets in *Pullman Car Hiawatha* consists of hums, "thrums," "whistles," and "zinging" sounds awaiting listeners sensitive to their urgent meanings (54). In *The Skin of Our Teeth,* only those characters fluent in the language of different black discs will know when they must flee an oncoming storm. (One disc means "bad weather"; four mean "the end of the world.") Different only in degree is the code of Bingo played while the clouds gather. "A-9 . . . C-24 . . . B-15": it is a language allowing its speakers to track the advance of pleasure just as the discs chronicle the advance of devastation. Those not in the game—a majority that includes ourselves—will hear these chants as only so many numbers and letters. We have felt our exclusion before. In act 1, Homer and Moses speak untranslated Greek and Hebrew, lines that register only as generalized "antique" speech to many listeners. No less frustrating is the play's first speech, in which an announcer tells of a wedding ring engraved with sentences from Genesis 2:18. He doesn't quote them, and spectators unable to recall them without consulting a Bible are left pondering the citation *as* citation. It is expressive less of the importance of marriage—such is the gist of the passage—than of the inhibitions in a culture that veils its most intimate sentiments in impersonal bibliographic style.

Our Town displays the same aversion to display in an utterance that (to recall Gordon Craig's phrase) encapsulates Wilder's own "art of showing and veiling." The epitaph on Simon Stimson's tombstone consists only of musical notes, their source unknown to the characters who visit his grave. "What is it?" asks Sam Craig—a line that, as we're discovering, hangs over Wilder's theater as stubbornly as "it is." Joe Stoddard answers no less meaningfully, "I wouldn't know" (85). The two men are, presumably, less deprived than readers and spectators, for Wilder declines to tell us which notes are on the stone. It is an apt memorial to a life conditioned by repression and knowable only to those versed in its social codes.

From these abstentions, it's only a short step to total silence, the other kind of Wilderian empty space. The ellipsis is a frequent ornament on Wilder's page. Open his texts to almost any place and they pop out like Morse code, scars left after candor's violent suppression. Theatrical dead air pervades Wilder's necropoli. "Roderick! My dear! What . . . ?" says Lucia in premature terror in *The Long Christmas Dinner;* when she does die, she merely moves her lips in an inaudible whisper (10). In *Our Town,* Mrs. Webb refuses to tell Emily the truth about her looks and later can't "bring [herself] to say anything" about sex on the eve of her daughter's marriage (72). Ma Kirby ends *The Happy Journey* by singing "The Ninety and Nine," the hymn about a lamb lost far from "the shelter of the fold," but the curtain falls before she gets to the stanza about God intervening to guide the lamb home. An opposite kind of omission qualifies the assertion of security in *Pullman Car Hiawatha.* Repressing her own voice, Harriet borrows her last words from Cardinal Newman's hymn "The Pillar of the Cloud." But she skips over the lines about being "far from home" on a "dark" night, surrounded by "moor and fen" and "crag and torrent," leaving only anodyne lines about being led peaceably out of the past.[115] One omitted line, "Lead, Kindly Light, amid the encircling doom," captures precisely the way in which, throughout Wilder's art, present perceptions lie nested within absence. Finally, spectators at *The Skin of Our Teeth* may not think much of the fact that Gladys never gets to recite the Longfellow sonnet she boasts of having memorized, but its absence communicates Wilder's meaning more faithfully than the poem itself would have. "The Evening Star" (the schoolroom standard whose title, in another error, Gladys gives as "The Star") describes the descent of "the star of love and rest," figure for the speaker's beloved who herself "retire[s] unto thy rest at night" as "from thy darkened window fades the light."[116] Wilder prevents Gladys from describing this trajectory not only out of compassion for readers lacking the taste for Longfellow's particular sweetness. The empty space where the recitation should be allows him also to withhold the poem's assurances of an orderly end, to postpone that end indefinitely.

"Skip to the end, Hester," says the stage manager in *The Skin of Our Teeth*, cutting off an actress reading Plato (219). Her quoted sentiment maintains its potency for being abbreviated—a truth Wilder demonstrated in *Pullman Car Hiawatha*, where ellipses follow the partial quotations from Kipling, Plato (again), and Augustine. One wants to imagine speakers recoiling not just from these authors but from Wilder himself, from any artist who violates the impersonality a stage figure enjoys when not subjected to action and dialogue. (Of course, as we saw in O'Neill, the act of quotation is itself an evasion of character.) Striking the same note, Sabina yells out, "Don't play this scene" (238). She stops *The Skin of Our Teeth* when she fears Henry and Mr. Antrobus will kill each other. (She had done so earlier, too, out of respect for the presumably delicate feelings of spectators offended by frank talk about infidelity.) In the stunned silence that follows Sabina's outburst, one can hear the questions Wilder asks of his art, and of us, in every play. What flickering image, ambiguous sensation, or penetrating insight is obscured when the theater strenuously asserts its presentness, seeks to prove its unflagging viability? Might not its failure to thrive—the larger fate predicted by these seemingly minor pauses and stoppages—elicit from us a livelier response? Sabina had to stop the play lest it stop for good—one possible consequence implied in Henry's mortal combat with his father. By keeping their fate undetermined, the play itself stays open. It may have to stop at "good night," but "the end . . . isn't written yet" (250).

As Wilder's plays circle the clock, or shuttle forward on tracks that imply a return and repeat journey, he proposes a final variant on the modernist virtue of aloofness. Not coming to rest; not saying everything; not always providing correct quotations, intelligible discourse, and reliable information; not allowing actions and speeches to unfurl without interruption — each strategy for undermining the authority of his text deprives his reader of authority as well. We can't pin down and enjoy the satisfaction of mastering it; it remains mercurial even as it grows more familiar. Looking at his naked stages, we may think we can see everything, but Wilder controls our presumptuousness and possessiveness. By withholding even small pieces that would complete the design of a play, he keeps us from seeing it whole, and from holding onto it. The play we do grasp is haunted by the play-not-there, the one composed of all the lines deferred, stifled, or botched. Wilder's best readers and spectators continually revise their expectations of him, trust no image or utterance as definitive, redefine what would constitute their own "knowledge" in a stageworld alive with characters themselves desperate to "understand everything now." An exhausted but wide-awake Mr. Antrobus speaks for us when, in a characteristic act of self-revision that snatches the opportunities of the present-tense back from elegiac contemplation of the past, he says, "We've learned. We're learning" (248).

Wilder includes himself among the still learning. In the Samuel French acting version of *Our Town,* a record of the play's first production, the Stage Manager asks of marriage, "Do I believe in it?" His answer — "I don't know" — is one we've heard at other hesitant turns in Wilder's theater. It hangs in the air, painful in its irresolution, imprecision, and equivocation. Too painful, it seems — for in the original production the Stage Manager adds, "I suppose I do," relieving spectators of any uncertainty about the outcome of his internal debate and about the value of the action before our eyes.[117] We can be grateful the relief didn't last. When Wilder published a definitive edition in 1957, that last line was gone.

5

Between the Acts

. . . he nevertheless sought, when people were beginning to feel surfeited with works that were too complete, in which everything was expressed, to satisfy an opposite need.

— *Marcel Proust,* Cities of the Plain

Weightless, austere, and remote, Wallace Stevens's play *Three Travelers Watch a Sunrise* seems, on a first reading, hardly capable of holding its own in performance, much less of anticipating and distilling a generation's theatrical obsessions. Despite its brevity — seventeen pages when it first appeared in 1916 in *Poetry* magazine — it moves among many places, periods, and styles. The setting is eastern Pennsylvania; the title characters are Chinese who arrive in "European" clothes; their attendants are black; a corpse, revealed at the end, is Italian. A stage direction places the action in the present, but when the three travelers put on brightly colored silk robes and recall life at court among warriors, hermits, and the emperor, the archaism blocks the view of 1916 or any other present. The plotless action and the aphoristic transparency of the verse approach ritual — or at least the ritualistic tranquility of, say, a Noh play. Characters chronicle rather than execute action. They cede the foreground to objects — a book, a porcelain water bottle, a candle, a jug, lanterns, baskets, tea things, fruit, and a percussive musical instrument. All events assume the simplicity and deliberateness we associate with parables. Yet for all these measures, Stevens can't resist melodrama. The diffuse action constricts when the travelers come upon a body hanging from a tree, the lover of a farmer's daughter (we're told), hunted down by her hostile father. The shift in tone and substance corresponds to a visual change. The half-light of dawn that had shrouded the stage at the start gives way definitively to morning, and once-indistinct shapes declare themselves as trees, bushes, and a firm horizon line.

The geographical, temporal, and stylistic confusion is inevitable. Narrative and character, object and landscape, exist in *Three Travelers* only insofar as they help Stevens locate the more interesting "indeterminate moments" (as the third traveler calls them) — "before [the sun] rises," before "one can tell / What the bottle is going to be," or more generally, before speculation gives way to knowledge.[1] Poised between the two, Stevens refrains as long as possible from choosing sides. He acknowledges the pleasures available to the imagination: sampling all the arts, the travelers read aloud from books, sing ballads, even (like "sweaty tragedian[s]") don costumes and impersonate the very characters whose story unfolds behind them. But as the play (and their play) proceeds, Stevens confronts the imagination with the eye's starker truths. The hanged man pulls the three travelers from the "seclusion of porcelain" — the utopia of art — and deposits them in the very world their private dramas had been designed to resist (151). "It is the invasion of humanity / That counts," admits the second traveler (153). "Poverty and wretchedness . . . suffering and . . . pity" render insignificant their "maxims," "jade," and "Venetian glass," and evict them from their "windless pavilions" (151–52). The change in attitude causes numerous changes in the landscape. The first traveler drops the musical instrument in the dirt, where it lies until the third traveler kicks it away. The jar, once symbolic of Earth, dwindles down to its plainer identity. So, too, the candle: as the sun rises, real light replaces the stage's weak substitute. The shift isn't only humbling. Against abstraction and disembodied aesthetics, Stevens sets forth nature, human suffering, and individual perception. "Nothing is beautiful," says the third traveler, "except with reference to ourselves" (154).

In the two decades after Stevens published his play, other American playwrights joined him in negotiating between "the seclusion of porcelain" and the "invasion of humanity." To reduce that process to an argument between art and life would be misleading — and unsatisfying. Art's value is secure; less certain is its autonomy. How sovereign is the imagination — how sovereign should it be — in a society undergoing rapid transformations and demanding of its citizens vigorous, imaginative declarations of commitment? The question — or rather, the uncertainty behind it — prompted some of the era's most vital theater. Dramatists between the two world wars replicated their intermediacy in numerous other divisions. They alternately engaged and resisted the surrounding culture, seeking principles of human conduct coded in an exuberant vernacular or lodged on levels of expression beneath mere behavior and expository talk. Their characters balance self-interest against fellow feeling or, alternatively, seek relief from both solitude and the equally obliterating absorption by a group. Formal tensions are just as severe. The decades' most rewarding drama isn't confident of its identity *as* drama: it exists between genres and, within single genres, between registers of expression. To counter the exposure of performance, some writers employ procedures drawn from poetry and fiction, removing both character and audience to a meditative zone typical of these more private arts. Other playwrights emulate the poise of painting or, at the opposite extreme, simulate the eruptive energies of burlesque, music hall, the circus, cinema, and other forms of popular culture. In each of their works, even the most esoteric, these playwrights testify to the pressures mounting outside the theater with their efforts, inside the theater, to evade, match, or overwhelm them.

Stevens himself summarized the argument between public and private models of the artistic life in "Of Modern Poetry" (1940), a work that, despite its title and metaphorical ambitions, allows a literal-minded reading of its early lines:

> Then the theatre was changed
> To something else. Its past was a souvenir.
>
> It has to be living, to learn the speech of the place.
> It has to face the men of the time and to meet
> The women of the time. It has to think about war
> And it has to find what will suffice. It has
> To construct a new stage.[2]

As a rallying cry, this seems uncomplicated, a convincing summation of the era's growing attraction to spirited practicality and engaged idealism. Yet the rest of the poem disappoints those expecting lessons in resolve. Having envisioned a public art, Stevens hesitates to commit to it. The actors in his theater speak not to an undifferentiated public but to "the delicatest ear of the mind." The audience listens "not to the play, but to itself." The opposing attractions — pulling the artist out toward the brightly lit "place" and "time" and simultaneously back to solitude — leaves Stevens's theater artist in an aesthetic no-man's-land. The fact that Stevens calls that intermediate space "the mind" —

his favorite landscape—suggests that it is hardly purgatorial. An artist who "cannot descend" to street-level entanglement in civic life and "has no will to rise" to disembodied metaphysics guarantees his effectiveness. He avoids generalities about both the people and the age, eschews moralism, and resists seductive utopias. Instead, he writes of "a man skating, a woman dancing, a woman / Combing" (as Stevens puts it at the end of his poem), scenes that are undramatic, introspective, isolating. (Even the dancer is unpartnered.) By a later theater poem, "As at a Theatre" (1950), the move away from public, communal life would be complete. In language reminiscent of *Three Travelers Watch a Sunrise,* he calls the theater "the candle of another being" and "the artifice of a new reality." The sun doesn't rise over this stage: "The curtains, when pulled, might show . . . a universe without life's limp and lack." Spared imperfection and compromise, this aestheticized world also lacks people—a liability that doesn't trouble the poem's speaker: "What difference would it make, / So long as the mind, for once, fulfilled itself?"[3]

The other American playwrights who themselves follow the trajectory traced in these three works can't be so smug. A theater that would allow the mind to fulfill itself must exist in a majority culture that recognizes only more measurable forms of accomplishment. The interwar period drew, and continues to draw, the most attention toward its earnest or angry works, especially the engagé plays of the 1930s—works that, in the words of Harold Clurman, one of their principal sponsors, "lead to the creation of a tradition of common values, an active consciousness of a common way of looking at and dealing with life."[4] The very name of the institution in which Clurman sought such commonality, the Group Theatre, like that of the contemporaneous Federal Theatre Project, asserts the supremacy of a corporate sensibility against singular, hermetic modes of imagination, artistic practice, and reception. (Hallie Flanagan, director of the Federal Theatre Project, insisted that artists no longer "huddle in the confines of a painted box set" but instead join together to "find visible and audible expression for the tempo and the psychology of our time" and dramatize "the search of the average American today for knowledge about his country and his world.")[5]

Yet the era's most probing dramatists, most of whom came of age theatrically in the 1920s, have a skeptical view of the "common," and their work, if assigned a secure place in American theater history, forces a more critical reading of the largely extroverted culture. These artists—E. E. Cummings, T. S. Eliot, Djuna Barnes, Zora Neale Hurston, and Jean Toomer—detain spectators eager to live vicariously through the high-spirited romps or sweeping urban panoramas stretching across the other stages of the 1920s. (The plays of Philip Barry and George S. Kaufman are polished examples of the genre.) They also ask spectators to pause before subscribing to the ideals of kinship and public spiritedness that emerged in the drama of the 1930s. (Clifford Odets is their most eloquent spokesman.) That all of them are better known for their work in nondramatic genres (and as important for their theater theory, however casually presented, as for their plays) is pertinent. From a marginal position, they see what others more centrally located in our theater overlook — modes of composition and definitions of theatricality obscured by tradition, as well as the status of marginality itself. Their definition of that status transcends matters of social membership, runs deeper than mere identity. They stage forms of estrangement and isolation from which they have cut all threads to the outside world. Intimacy, as experienced here, has no use for its usual accessories — secrets, embarrassments, and avowals, the sentimental idea that masks can fall from the "real" self. The skepticism that keeps these playwrights from endorsing a utopian vision of the public sphere remains sharp when they come indoors. No romantic loners or noble exiles, no easy solidarity with the outcast, no expectation that strong emotions, once recovered, will cushion solitude. Such pathos would compromise these writers' commitment to stage the most rigorous form of self-consciousness, guarantee of a mode of privacy that acknowledges the root it shares with privation. The privation is ours, too. The boldest of this work is unforthcoming. When measured by ordinary standards, it is undramatic, its speech ineptly distributed among contrasting voices and its action suppressed, internal, imminent, or lodged deep in the past, accessible to us only in the characters' cloudy recollections. Some of these plays are envisioned but incompletely executed, or finished but left to languish in a longer piece of prose, or staged but quickly reabsorbed into a willfully distracted culture. All these challenges to our idea of a "proper" theatrical event train us in a new form of spectatorship. In their presence, we learn to look to the peripheries for the central dramatic event or, more often, reconcile ourselves to the fact that decisive turns in stage lives and narratives often go undramatized altogether, leapt over in accordance with a dramaturgy suspicious of major statements, attuned instead to the subtler sound of the self-conscious, often self-doubting thoughts and actions flanking them. By retracting the markers of eventfulness and articulateness, these plays reach unexpectedly deep into our consciousness. Claims for their crucial importance in American theater (such as I'm making) must be balanced against their structural and thematic resistance to centrality of any kind. They are embodiments of minorness — minor in the types of incidents or figures they dramatize, minor in their key, or minor in their cultural status — but this very quality can stimulate in sympathetic spectators an urge to attend to them with more force than we show in the presence of more assertive works.

Henry James captures precisely the nature of this theatricality — and implies that there is particular value in the difficult, even stymied spectatorship it elicits — in a passage from *The American Scene*. Traveling through Florida near the end of his 1904–5 tour of the United States, his first visit since leaving for Europe twenty-one years earlier, he imagines that his Pullman is a "great moving proscenium" populated with "wayside imagery": "something that had been there, no doubt, as the action or the dialogue are presumably there in some untoward drama that spends itself at the back of the stage, that goes off, in a passion, at side doors, and perhaps even bursts back, incoherently, through windows; but that doesn't reach the stall in which you sit."[6] Haunted by what he intuits or too briefly sees, and driven to see more of it, James experiences the kind of conflict that his hypothetical drama, in deflecting attention away from its center, presumably has no use for. He is the protagonist in a struggle with the theater itself, longing to enter its entertainment but instead thrown back onto himself. This narrative of seeing becomes a parable for more general challenges of cultural and social participation. James the returning exile and James the tourist, like James the train car spectator and, finally, James the writer — all must choose how much distance to take from the worlds they observe. Too close or too far and blindness results. Theater, to this citizen, offers an ideal middle ground between self-obliterating public life and immobilizing private life.

One senses the uncertainty of interwar culture when one looks critically at those performance styles meant to relieve a spectator's self-consciousness. The fact that burlesque, vaudeville, music hall, and the variously arranged "follies" don't always do so, at least not to their most astute observers, forces us to rethink the role played by popular culture in the development of American art generally. It's customary to see that relation as symbiotic — "high" and "low" culture drawing imagery, languages, rhythms, and structures from one another, in the process blurring the lines between their audiences.[7] In the interwar era, high culture stood the most to gain from this exchange. Edmund Wilson spoke for many when he asked, "Can New York Stage a Serious Play?" — the title of a 1925 article contrasting most contemporary theater's "vagueness" and "lack of energy" with the "emphasis," "swiftness," and "headlong quality" of vaudeville, musical revues, and movies.[8] Wilson's connoisseurship of the latter forms, and his commitment to treating them on a level equal to that of drama, is evident throughout his peripatetic, propulsive chronicle of the twenties, "The Follies," part of *The American Earthquake*. He moves with happy prejudice from formulaic plays by Philip Barry, early Maxwell Anderson, and late Arthur Wing Pinero to the caustic pleasures or bracing effrontery of the Ziegfeld Follies, Bert Savoy and Eddie Cantor, Alice Lloyd and Far-

fariello, Texas Guinan's nightclub, *Gold Rush,* and animal acts at the circus. Between the reviews are descriptions of the urban landscape—its bookshops, construction sites, ferries, fashion advertising, billiard parlors, department stores, and public dance halls. The mix of art and commerce, real and theatrical "scenes," supports Wilson's conviction that popular culture won its patrons' loyalty by "concentrat[ing] the pulse of the city" (as he says of the Ziegfeld Follies)—its best productions "the expression of [New York's] nervous intensity to the tune of harsh and complicated harmonies." "When, afterwards, you take the subway home, it speeds you to your goal with a crash, like a fast song by Eddie Cantor; and in the roar of the nocturnal city, driven rhythmically for all its confusion, you can catch hoarse echoes of Gilda Gray and her incomparable *Come Along!*"[9] Elsewhere, Wilson speculates that urbanites respond to the "inconsecutive" art forms because "that is the way . . . their own minds are beginning to work."[10]

Yet the fullest understanding of an "inconsecutive" aesthetic acknowledges those moments when spectacle and spectator don't align, or when the gap between the ethos promoted by the popular culture and the temperament of its individual consumers is too wide to bridge. Some of Wilson's most haunting, if least heralded, passages suggest he is drawn to these brief flarings of need as much as to the entertainments that hope to smother them. He sees through the "pretense of enthusiasm" that can stand in at such events for genuine pleasure and discernment; lingers over the black performer who dispenses with the usual comedic song-and-dance in favor of pantomimes of disappointment and confusion; keeps taking notes after another show ends, so to capture the bewilderment of the "dingy city audience" as it tries, futilely, to retain the memory of an actor's tour-de-force before it must reenter banal daily life. In a particularly useful corrective to received wisdom, Wilson reports that burlesque's typical spectator doesn't hoot and holler at the lascivious displays but rather "remain[s] completely stolid." Men "may have come to the theater . . . in order to have their dreams made objective," but "they sit there each alone with his dream." The "vision of erotic ecstasy . . . frightens them and renders them mute."[11]

What Wilson doesn't acknowledge is that these moments when popular forms close in on themselves leave an opening for drama. Standing apart from the drawing-room comedies, ham-fisted social tracts, and other formulaic plays he disdains—separate, too, from the few plays that effectively, but merely, absorb and replicate the styles of the popular arts—are more challenging works that engage popular culture in order to argue with it, or that succumb to its seductive rhythms the better to resist them. These are works that go beyond celebrating the vitality of public life to dramatize the effort to negotiate among its competing, often overwhelming appeals. They work clever variations on themes originating in mechanized, commercial, and spectacular culture, but then reserve space for representations of all that cannot be sung, danced, or joked away. Unlike the artists enchanted by the era's vernacular, a few playwrights give voice to states of mind that no existing language—high or low—has yet succeeded in naming.

No American playwright of the 1920s and 1930s was more enchanted with the possibilities of popular culture than Wilson's friend (and occasional Virgil in his descent to its theaters and arenas), E. E. Cummings. Circus, vaudeville, burlesque, sports, and cabaret did more than merely inspire his art. They helped him judge it. Has he risen to the challenge they implicitly pose? Can he retain a spectator's attention in the face of these other temptations? Will he be able to keep up with the tempo accelerating around him? The foreword to his 1926 poetry collection *Is 5* declares his readiness to try: "Like the burlesk comedian, I am abnormally fond of that precision which creates movement. If a poet is anybody, he is somebody to whom things made matter very little— somebody who is obsessed by Making. . . . It is with roses and locomotives (not to mention acrobats Spring electricity Coney Island the 4th of July the eyes of mice and Niagara Falls) that my 'poems' are competing." His art, he concludes, always betrays his "ineluctable preoccupation with The Verb."[12]

Gertrude Stein's own commitments are audible in this last line, of course, and Cummings helps us recognize more of the cultural, social, and environmental sources for her interest in the kinetics of grammar and the aerodynamics of sentences and paragraphs. It's inevitable that Cummings would turn to the theater to test these principles; indeed, it's odd that he wrote only one major drama. (He also wrote a short morality play about Santa Claus, a ballet scenario based on *Uncle Tom's Cabin,* and several speeches for unfinished plays.) The unreliability of performance—words, things, actors, and time itself refusing to stay put—is invigorating in a culture that, to Cummings, has settled into complacency. So high are his expectations of theater that his disappointment with most plays is inevitable. In 1926, the *Dial* hired Cummings to review theater; instead, he spent most of his time at boxing matches and the National Winter Garden, New York's leading burlesque house. Only there, he argues, were spectators roused from passivity, encouraged to feel proprietary about the entertainment, and taught to engage the performers as well as one another. These supercharged modes of spectatorship respond to flexible modes of performance. The blur of action in a fight, constantly testing the boundary between controlled and chaotic violence; the disarming directness of burlesque; the improvisatory looseness of variety-show comedy — these forms seem vulgar only because they refuse to patronize their audiences, presenting elemental drives of aggression, lust, and vanity stripped of explanations. (They all share what Gilbert Seldes calls burlesque's "complete lack of sentimentality in the treatment of emotion and its treatment of appearance.")[13] On these platforms, strategies for seduction or domination multiply, centers of power shift continuously, performers assume an attitude only as long as it serves the goal of putting others off guard. The lightness of manner begets a dense spectacle. There's too much to see in too little time; no one shows restraint; the goal is always surprise — to teach spectators to be as alert as the performers are, both sides of the spectacle thinking not only about what's happening now but also about what's coming next.

A different kind of "nextness" — Cummings's word for juxtaposition — becomes for him another theatrical ideal. He recognizes it in a touring production by Nemirovich-Danchenko. Like a "pussy-café," Cummings writes, this kind of theater layers events, images, and techniques drawn from other arts without "violating the discreteness of any one of them . . . the principle at stake being not an agglomeration of ingredients but that spontaneous sequence of elements which inevitably is the expression of their respective densities."[14] Nextness ensures that no single incident or character — more important, no single style — can beguile audiences, deadening their senses with familiarity. Watching works that obey Cummings's ideal, the spectator must greet each segment, perhaps even each moment, with the same productive confusion usually experienced only in the first scene. Who's who? Where are we? What's at stake? What code of manners controls the action? We ask the same questions over and over, exercising our senses and tightening our hold on the production as we answer them. The result, ideally, is an overall response as layered as the production itself. We think in discrete, juxtaposed segments, aware that the conclusion we reach in one scene won't be valid in the next, nor will the emotions we feel in the presence of one constellation of characters be indulged when those same characters rearrange themselves. (Before long, we may even learn to drop a feeling as soon as it forms.) At the end of such a production, we emerge with a chaptered narrative of attention.

Cummings's prose is exuberant with his vision of such reform. The ideal theater production would be "an aesthetic continent, throughout whose roamable depth and height and breadth" spectators could move freely, adventurously, content with no particular discovery if others are beckoning in the distance. The most expressive language and most flexible narratives would derive from the "out-of-Spontaneous-by-Inevitably idiom." The best space would eliminate the flat backdrops and stable set—the "pennyintheslot peep show parlor"—in favor of a "mobile theatre."[15] The best actor would emulate June St. Clare, star of the Irving Place burlesque, who "propagates . . . a literally miraculous synthesis of flying and swimming and floating and rising and darting and gliding and pouncing and falling and creeping and every other conceivable way of moving."[16] Theatrical time itself, and our way of experiencing it, must also change. One learns to ignore the "measurable when" and instead plunges into the "illimitable now."[17]

But limits do exist. Cummings is at his best when acknowledging them, something he does to surprisingly poignant effect in his play *Him* (1927). The imagination is inhibited by fears, taboos, shame, or simply the kind of zeal that blinds itself to everything that doesn't feed a particular interest. On a more basic level, Cummings must reckon with the frustrations accompanying any attempt to realize ideals that are intoxicating on paper. "The IS or Verb of Coney Island escapes any portraiture," he concedes in his tribute to one model for his theater.[18] The requirement of reproducibility and legibility in the theater is a further reason for Cummings to qualify his enthusiasm. If one is trying to "see everything"—a goal Cummings announces in *Him*—is one actually seeing anything?[19] Or anyone? Do an artist's efforts to rouse the senses from their customary torpor prevent him from cultivating the kind of patient, generous interest in other people—alien experiences and ways of seeing—that expands knowledge? When the jocularity of Cummings dies down, we hear this debate over commitment. Like a dissonant undertone in his rhapsody on popular culture, or a quaver in his exhortation that we keep pace with his own mercurial spectacle, Cummings's afterthoughts are audible to those willing to read him skeptically. His most convincing tributes to the protean imagination include an indictment of its solipsism. His most passionate protagonists contend with their own selfishness, asking or being forced to ask themselves if, in their tours of circus tents, burlesque halls, sporting arenas, and Niagara Falls, they are able to respond deeply to anything other than their own hunger for more sensations.

Him puts this question in elaborate form. Cummings's title character is relentlessly playful, unable to resist riddles and childish puns, answering nonexistent invitations to recount his dreams and confess his fantasies, delivering himself of non sequiturs as if each were the one true word. His dialogues with a woman named "Me" are purposefully meandering, the couple confident that they will reach understanding whatever route they take. They consider one another's opinions with the same detached curiosity one might show before a shop window or museum vitrine—interested, possibly even acquisitive, but also wondering what's on display nearby. This spectator-like form of attention

Figure 15: "Frankie and Johnnie" by John Sloan (1928). Sloan's etching depicts act 2, scene 5 of E. E. Cummings's *Him,* as first staged at the Provincetown Playhouse. Reproduced with permission of the Kraushaar Galleries, New York.

is literal in the play's long second act, in which the couple watches a series of skits parodying then-current theatrical styles, and in the play's penultimate scene, in which a carnival barker directs us to the Queen of Serpents, the Human Needle, the Missing Link, and 600 Pounds of Passionate Pulchritude, among other "freaks."

The preoccupation with performance is inevitable: Him is a playwright uncertain about his talent, testing the possibilities of his imagination against Me's grounded skepticism. The scenes they watch in the second act are excerpts from his own play, submitted for her judgment. Their "inconsecutiveness" is but an extreme demonstration of the short attention span evident everywhere in *Him.* In an elliptical note to himself about the play, Cummings writes, "line = plot (sense). Not / to write play via a plot [which] = melodic line, but to let a play create itself by counterpoint . . . i.e.: that the succeeding of tableaux or incidents ('les plans'; the 'touches' of Cézanne modeling a volume) → Motion."[20] By replacing "plot" with presumably less teleological "motion," Cummings taunts those hoping to summarize his play's action. Many have tried. Edmund Wilson calls *Him* a lover's "ether-dream" before childbirth; another critic wonders if the dream may not precede an abortion instead; a third imagines the woman as torn between her doctor and her husband; yet others track such vague narratives as the hero's "quest for reality," "search for vocation," or "advent of self-consciousness." In an "imaginary dialogue between the author and a public," Cummings mocked all these readings. "What is *Him* about?" asks the Public. "Why ask me?" says the Author.[21]

Narrative isn't the only changeable aspect of the play. The first and third acts occur in a rotating room: with every new scene, the perspective shifts ninety degrees, revealing a once-invisible wall and demanding that we orient ourselves anew to furniture and objects suddenly made unfamiliar. Only thus does Cummings relieve what Him describes as every playwright's frustration: "patiently squeezing fourdimensional ideas into a twodimensional stage" (344). By this periodic restimulating of our attention, Cummings also changes the way we look at his characters: they, too, resist stable, unified identity. Cummings upsets convention with the very names he gives his protagonists. We expect that in a play about playwriting the character named "Me" will speak for the writer. Assigning that responsibility to "Him" instead (and assuming the point of view of the writer's antagonist, "Me"?), Cummings executes the first of many escapes—hiding from spectators who might desire blanket access to his private consciousness. Preserving identity by dispersing it, he writes what Him calls "a play . . . all about mirrors" (357)—many drawn from the funhouse—multiplying and scattering the self so continuously that it's never clear who the "real" Him is and where he really stands. Cummings's playwright-protagonist could be talking about this form of alienated self-consciousness when he says, "the nearer something is, the more outside of me it seems." Him goes on to define character as something uncontainable and contingent—potential rather than present. "There are no entities, no isolations, no abstractions; but there are departures, voyages, arrivals, contagions." A character's consciousness, he adds, is "a kinesis fatally composed of countless mutually dependent stresses, a product-and-quotient of innumerable perfectly interrelated tensions" (356). In practice, this means that Him will appear in various guises, including "O. Him," or Other Him, inviting intimacy so promiscuously that he actually prevents it. The author of nonlectures writes antiautobiography, succeeding as he makes it impossible to consider his surrogate self with undivided attention.

This very multiplicity of the self is also the cause of Cummings's eventual despair. "You have made me realize," Him says to Me, "that in the course of living I have created several less or more interesting people—none of whom was myself" (402). The speech, and the psychological shift it marks, are crucial to understanding *Him* as something more than a free-wheeling vaudeville. Critics have treated the play as a document of American surrealism or proto-absurdism, but neither label does justice to the emotional fluctuations of its two main characters.[22] Their conversations are in a different key than that controlling other scenes — muted, hesitant, as if the players were seeing their score for the first time. That the subject is the couple's own relationship accounts in part for the tentativeness. One watches Him, in particular, search for the right language for unfamiliar sensations — sensations that don't derive from Cummings's beloved mass culture, situations that aren't variations on popular types — and vent frustration that he can't script the conversation alone. The pair is locked in a difficult interdependence, one that affects their language and comportment so thoroughly that the dramaturgy itself changes. Their scrutiny of one another is exhausting — jazz-age Bergman. Even as they grow embarrassed — retracting a confession, adding second thoughts, fluent only when they talk of their shyness — they don't break from one another.

That's the point: Him and Me are discussing degrees of attention as they move through them. More precisely, Me demands from Him a quality of engagement far stronger than he, in his autonomous creativity and cultural sightseeing, prefers. He slows down in her presence, and with the change the play itself seems to make room for observations about human behavior that wouldn't surface in a busier landscape. ("I couldn't go carefully enough," laments Him at one point [420].) Single gestures stand out from what had earlier been a blur of movement, their specificity amid the otherwise dreamlike action lending them pathos. "A hand. Accurate and incredible," says Him as he holds his wife's wrist (397). Elsewhere, he wipes his sweaty forehead with a handkerchief. She pulls at her dress, moves her fingers absently to her head, puts stray hairs in place; later, she asks Him to "touch me a little" (403). In one particularly evocative stage direction, Cummings notes that "his shutting face whitens" (403). Throughout *Him*, Cummings writes of faces, hands, whole bodies "folding," closing, and opening again, at the same time as the characters note how darkness falls, wraps around them, and enforces an intimacy they might not be capable of on their own. In that hushed dusk, the entire play contracts, and Him's claims for the supremacy of his imagination, and of the fictions it creates, collapse before Me's more palpable reality.

Starting with a standard lover's complaint — "you fell in love with someone you invented, someone who wasn't me at all" — Me coaxes Him back to a world where acts, even acts of imagination, have consequences, and where intellect cannot overpower instinct (400). She shares in the impatience that follows his puns, points to the empty spaces between the play's entertaining acts, and helps us imagine a time when the room will stop revolving and the characters will stop mutating. "Beauty has shut me from truth," Him admits, finally, after conceding that he was wrong to think that mere ardor for the former is all one needs to grasp the latter (427). To those convinced by the standard précis of *Him*'s plot, there is an even more fundamental assertion of "truth" (and beauty): while Him writes his play, Me prepares to give birth to their child. But the narrative parallelism (pointed out by Daniel Gerould and Eric Bentley, among others) is misleading. The child matters more. Cummings's ideal of a mobile theater may foster protean characterization, fluid plotting, and exuberant language, but finally Him realizes that "in all directions I cannot move" (428). The line is devastating and eye-opening. If he chooses one direction, he might just get somewhere.

In the 1920s, T. S. Eliot—the anti-Cummings on matters of authorial demeanor and poetic decorum—shared with the writer of *Him* a vision of theater. As David E. Chinitz shows in his valuable study *T. S. Eliot and the Cultural Divide,* Eliot's miscellaneous prose of the decade returns over and over to the fertilizing service of popular forms. Charlie Chaplin, the music hall performer Marie Lloyd, the comedienne Ethel Levey, the circus star Enrico Rastelli: Eliot salutes them not only for their virtuosity in their separate arts but also for the example they set for the stiff and overcautious playwright. "It is the rhythm," Eliot writes, "which makes the juggling of Rastelli more cathartic than a performance of *A Doll's House.*"[23] Rhythm: Eliot's idea of this essential attribute goes beyond every poet's private, intuitive musicality to acknowledge public sources. "Think how large a part is now played in our sensory life by the internal combustion engine!" he exults in one essay.[24] It also embraces phenomena beyond language, everything that runs alongside speech in counterpoint when a text leaves the page for the stage. Songs, nonverbal sounds and noises, choreographed gestures, and even the syncopated presentation of scenic imagery: "We may say that the less 'realistic' literature is, the more visual it must be," writes Eliot in 1917, simultaneously anticipating the theater of images by half a century and recalling melodrama's own allegiances.[25] (Eliot directly, if unconsciously, echoes Pixérécourt's supposed desire to write for the illiterate when he says, "I myself should like an audience which could neither read nor write.")[26] Eliot's surprising populism reaches even further back for historical precedent. In an argument for a livelier modern verse drama, he cites the Elizabethan commitment to entertainment over "poetry" (the scare quotes are his own), and in a letter to Ezra Pound, he concludes that if his own era's audience "gets its strip-tease," it, too, "will swallow the poetry."[27] Eliot reminded himself to maintain a similar balance throughout his career: in his Faber and Faber office, he hung a photograph of Groucho Marx next to one of Paul Valéry.[28]

Eliot applied his principles to his own efforts in verse drama only once, in *Sweeney Agonistes* (1926–27), by far his best play and one of the more chilling dramas of the interwar period. That he also deemed it unfinished and grouped it with his poems rather than with his other plays says much about the particular strains placed on his imagination by the demands of theater and, more particularly, by his susceptibility to popular culture. He may aim for a seamless transition from "low" to "high" in the theater, eliding tired prejudices and simplistic oppositions, hoping thereby that spectators themselves will treat art with fewer inhibitions. ("Fine art is the *refinement,* not the antithesis, of popular art," he once wrote.)[29] But in practice he discovers a more spasmodic movement between styles — less "refinement" than uncertain negotiation, one that leaves this dramatist alert to the rumbling anxiety and unvoiced anguish from which popular culture, in its ebullient rhythms, may hope to distract us. To attentive readers of Eliot's reviews, this sobriety won't be wholly unexpected. In scattered articles, he implicitly objects to his fellow spectators' practice of finding meaning (and taking pleasure) in only the brightest and loudest aspect of a performance. Marie Lloyd created effective music hall routines not from hilarity or "exaggeration" but from "concentration."[30] An acrobat, he writes elsewhere, "appeals to the mind rather than to the senses."[31] Ethel Levey "plays for herself rather than for the audience."[32] The inwardness Eliot identifies in all these performers, seemingly at odds with the demands of their extroverted arts, expands in *Sweeney Agonistes.* One can approach it in the same spirit in which one left the nearly contemporaneous *Him.* Like Cummings, Eliot seems to dramatize both the moments of succumbing to and of awakening from the seductions of popular entertainment; if anything, he goes further than Cummings in looking skeptically at its promise to deliver us from earthbound preoccupations and private hauntings. Spectators who share Eliot's conviction that a Levey or a Lloyd (or others like them) respond to promptings they alone hear may discover in *Sweeney*'s recesses the underexplored — but contiguous — other side of mass culture.

There are structural reasons for the dominance of the implicit over the explicit in *Sweeney:* as a pair of shards — "fragment of a prologue" and "fragment of an agon," he calls them — negative space shadows positive space. The unwritten controls the appeal of the written. Silence is always engulfing sound, however jaunty or insidious the latter may be. Moreover, the play's narrative, for all its sensationalism, invites us to join its characters in confronting the self-conscious questions that impede any easy surrender to its spectacle. *Sweeney Agonistes* returns obsessively to the problem of knowing. The two women at its center, Dusty and Doris, worry over the trustworthiness of an obscure, absent man, Pereira, and over the meanings of the Tarot cards with which they pass the time, hoping to distract themselves from the vague threat Pereira represents. The Tarot's codedness vexes them even when it seems all too clear: "I'd like to know about that coffin," Doris says twice, willing herself into protective ignorance.[33] Sweeney's arrival in the second scene forces on her even less welcome knowledge. He enters with a threat to carry Doris off to "a cannibal isle" and "gobble you up," then tells of "a man once did a girl in . . . kept her there in a bath / With a gallon of lysol in a bath" (118, 122). His grisly anecdote, even as it confirms the Tarot's prediction and itself predicts further horror, also opens new mysteries that quickly envelop the stage. As before, the unknown is more alarming than the known. The murderer, Sweeney says, can't tell if his victim is dead or, for that matter, if he himself is. Certainty about the simplest things is not only hard to come by; it's irrelevant, Eliot implies, to the drama that goes on beneath vision, feeling, and thought—all the instruments with which one presumes, naively, to engage experience. (In fact, they only enable one's retreat.) Language itself is no help. "That dont apply," says Sweeney, "but I've gotta use words when I talk to you" (123). Words, like the ghastly scene they describe, are mere screens in front of a second world governed by primal demands—visions as yet unorganized into memories, compulsions too aggressive to be called mere needs, intuitions so uncanny they flood the mind and disable the will. The persistent mood of this whole extraordinary work is clarified in its final chorus.

> When you're alone in the middle of the night and you wake in a sweat and a
>   hell of a fright
> When you're alone in the middle of the bed and you wake like someone hit
>   you in the head
> You've had a cream of a nightmare dream and you've got the hoo-ha's
>   coming to you.
> Hoo hoo hoo
> You dreamt you waked up at seven o'clock and it's foggy and it's damp and
>   it's dawn and it's dark
> And you wait for a knock and the turning of a lock for you know the
>   hangman's waiting for you.
> And perhaps you're alive
> And perhaps you're dead
> Hoo ha ha
> Hoo ha ha
> Hoo
> Hoo
> Hoo
> KNOCK KNOCK KNOCK
> KNOCK KNOCK KNOCK
> KNOCK
> KNOCK
> KNOCK (124)

Dread is too familiar a term for what Eliot depicts here—an infinite and incurable form of expectation. Any event that might end the waiting instead implies more events to come, another Tarot card to turn over, the postponed arrival of Pereira, another knock at the door. (It matters that Eliot omits a final period.) One of the play's epigraphs, from *The Libation Bearers,* encapsulates this state of suspension, in which Orestes peers out to what is absent or eclipsed, just out of reach, impalpable but always imminent: "You don't see them, you don't—but *I* see them: they are hunting me down, I must move on" (111).

The best education in the play's purposefully unsettled and open-ended dramaturgy is Eliot's recitation of "Fragment of an Agon," recorded in 1947.[34] The cool, urbane voice, easy in its acquired English accent, is deliberately at odds with the subject matter, lulling us so to catch us off guard. Soon, Eliot is adjusting his pacing and volume to darken the scene. Repeated words and phrases that at first sound singsong now turn taunting, nowhere more so than in the petulant line "That's all, that's all, that's all, that's all"—nails hammered into the coffin Doris fears (119). The same progress characterizes Eliot's rendition of two popular songs that, deceptively, promise an escape from the narrative. He turns the chorus of "Under the Bamboo Tree" ("Under the bam / Under the boo / Under the bamboo tree") into a low, unnaturally steady threnody (120). After the death knells of the next song, "My Little Island Girl"—"Morning / Evening / Noontime / Night"—he delivers the play's remaining lines to an ominous marching beat, getting louder and more forceful in the final chorus, the "Hoo's" sounding first like a car horn, then like a footballer's grunts; the "Knock's" getting more desperate and implacable, until he stops short to allow horrible silences to answer back between his last three repetitions of the word. The spaces separating each knock seem impenetrable, hollow, dead at last.

Eliot's performance helps us see the other forms of vacancy in the play. Many gaps are left by the "inconsecutive" progress through incidents and speeches. Scenes start with a sudden eruption of talk and end just as abruptly. Within them, characters jump over chasms in the dialogue and narrative. Their accompanying emotions are equally spasmodic. Some figures consist of a single attitude that seizes them in recurrent attacks; others make only strong, unpredictably spaced stabs in the direction of complex feelings. Convulsiveness of a different order affects the play's relation to genre. *Sweeney Agonistes* retains the dissonances, dropped impulses, and torn edges left by a writer perpetually deferring the moment when he must commit to and develop a single style. Eliot's interest in mass culture is as distracted and heterogeneous as urban life itself. As Rachel Blau DuPlessis notes, he cites in rapid succession music hall, vaudeville, and minstrelsy (a rejected subtitle was "Fragments of a Comic

Minstrelsy"), managing to resist each form even as he exploits it. (Such strategic ambivalence "keeps the work mobile . . . difficult to fix or pin down," DuPlessis writes, unwittingly recalling Cummings's ideal of a "mobile theater.")[35] Yet none of the "low" forms dispels or replaces the allure of "high" art: Eliot also emulates the example of Noh theater, Athenian comedy, Christian and pre-Christian ritual. Happily dividing and subdividing his loyalties, he proposes many outrageous hybrids. In keeping with the play's actual subtitle, "Fragments of an Aristophanic Melodrama," characters quote stock dialogue ("Who pays the rent?" "Yes he pays the rent"), but wear Greek half-masks (111). They narrate raucous events from behind a refectory table, asserting a ritual formality in their motionlessness and expressionless speech. Only a few elements achieve consistency among these many contradictions. In a letter to Hallie Flanagan, who directed the play's American premiere at Vassar College in 1933, Eliot asks that a steady drumbeat underscore the action, as in *The Emperor Jones*. He also writes that the recurrent choruses "ought to have a noise like a street drill" and that the knocking should sound "like the angelus."[36] Yet these, too, refer us to three irreconcilable contexts: primitivism, modernity, and Christianity.

Eliot had also urged Flanagan to read Francis Cornford's *Origin of Attic Comedy* as preparation — its description of fertility rites the source of Eliot's conviction that *Sweeney Agonistes*, for all its preoccupation with death, actually envisions rebirth. This belief explains one of his strangest instructions to Flanagan: that Sweeney should be scrambling eggs in a chafing dish throughout the final scene, a gesture that, in keeping with Eliot's interest in unrhymed images, is at once banal and ceremonial, welcoming and (the longer it goes on) menacing. Flanagan disregarded most of his suggestions and staged the play on a wholly abstract set. At the other extreme, one need only look at a photograph from a 1934 production by London's Group Theatre, the British premiere, to realize that the text can support those who see it as pure melodrama: Sweeney lunges at Doris, a straight-edge razor in his hand, while she leans back, her body arched in a C, arms extended in front of her, fingers splayed, her features arranged in an expression of horror.[37] In fact, this production seems to have been a hodgepodge of styles — melodramatic acting, realistic decor (carpets and lamps, gramophones and telephones, liquor bottles and glasses), and expressionist (or classical?) masks on the women. Its reception suggests links to still other theatrical styles: Bertolt Brecht, reports the Group Theatre director, said the production was the "best thing he had seen for a long time" — perhaps because it persuasively suggested more ways to apply his ideas about "jumps" in dramatic structure ("each scene for itself") and the "separation of the elements" in production.[38] Like Brecht, Eliot jerks us away

Figure 16: *Sweeney Agonistes* by T. S. Eliot, as first staged by Hallie Flanagan in a production titled *Now I Know Love,* Vassar Experimental Theatre, 1933. Photograph by Margaret De M. Brown. Billy Rose Theatre Division, The New York Public Library for the Performing Arts, Astor, Lenox and Tilden Foundations.

from his culture's dominant rhythms before their narcotic effect can take hold. We see more sharply as a result of seeing less.

Just as Brecht insisted that his innovations must have more than formal value — fragmentariness, for him, opposed monolithic ideology and deterministic notions of history — Eliot, for his part, stresses his own disjunctiveness in order to expose psychological, cultural, and even creative needs. Perhaps nothing is communicated so emphatically by his work's varieties of incompletion than the longing for its opposite: Eliot recalls a lost unity and acknowledges the appeal of completeness whenever his characters cite the reliable patterns of popular entertainment. Each formulaic song or routine once kept away doubt about social cohesiveness. Now that ideal seems to break apart into the play's scattered allusions — each quotation an artifact from a buried culture. (The desire for security comes through explicitly in Eliot's original title — *Wanna Go Home, Baby?* — its tone less nonchalant than one might think.) Such a desire can be taken as personal: Eliot, in this view, doesn't pay tribute to the many

arcane or popular forms he samples so much as he vents frustration that none of
them is a perfect fit for his imagination. In the afterglow of each brilliant burst
of song or speech comes the realization that some large crucial part of his vision
remains lodged within him, unreleased into art. If one organizes Eliot's purposefully centrifugal dramaturgy around this core of dissatisfaction, *Sweeney
Agonistes* becomes a parable for this, or any, writer's ordeal of composition—
one that, like the characters' own ordeal, is by turns ritualistic, melodramatic,
tragicomic, and farcical. *This* play's nervous energy comes not only from
Doris's fear and Sweeney's mania but also from an artistic obsession that no
style can allay, a writer's impulses that no form can stabilize. Like Orestes, Eliot,
too, keeps moving, pursued by protagonists of a private drama, as yet unable to
make others see them whole. He wanders among different schools of art and
registers of expression, petitioning for admission as one exiled from form itself.
Such a fate isn't wholly pathetic. His distance from the common culture presents an opportunity. The conventional reading of *Sweeney Agonistes* treats it
as an accumulative work, one that stitches together scraps of high and low
culture. More accurate to see it as peeling off allusions and borrowed approaches as prelude to writing in an exposed condition, unsupported by a
shared idiom or an artistic precedent. Could this be the true "strip-tease" we get
before encountering a "poetry" authentically his own?

What would that new poetry look like? That Eliot doesn't say is the most
haunting of his play's many forms of omission. An epigraph Eliot appended to
an early typescript scenario of *Sweeney Agonistes* suggests a reason for his
restraint. (He later removed it, leaving yet another mark of indecision in the
play's progress toward completion.) Eliot quotes *Julius Caesar*:

> Between the acting of a dreadful thing
> And the first motion, all the interim is
> Like a phantasma or a hideous dream.[39]

The "interim" Brutus describes, and lives in, is Eliot's stage. He takes from
Brutus the understanding that the hesitation to act can be more eventful than
any action, just as silence can be more substantial than speech: all possibilities
of gesture and utterance are present to his characters, not yet winnowed by
choice. So, too, as we've seen, for Eliot himself. In keeping with the interwar
artist's fascination with intermediacy itself, he expands the space between the
artist's intuition—the "motion" he makes in a debate over compositional
approach—and his created image. He hears his own form of knocking—the
bid for attention made by this or that externally derived style—but he declines
to answer the door. (No clearer image of Eliot's commitment to intermediacy
is the mere fact of the play's publication: why else make public an unfinished

and thus presumably still private work? For this reason, it's best to see *Swee-ney Agonistes* as a play of incompletion rather than an incomplete play.) Those who recall Gertrude Stein's interest in the "interval" between words, scene of "abundant" invention, will sense what's at stake in Eliot's fascination with the "interim."[40] If anything, he hopes to isolate an even earlier stage of composition. In the dilating pause at the end of the play, we await Eliot's next word, or even his next deliberately shaped silence, and don't get it. Eliot himself seems to be waiting for an image to surface into his imagination—an expectation as harrowing as the one he names in his characters' final chorus. Like Doris, he has wanted to "know what you want to know" (114). Like Dusty, he had hoped to determine "what comes next" (114). Yet like Sweeney, he now concedes that "if you understand or if you dont / That's nothing to me and nothing to you" (123). Their—our—shared anticipation isn't idle. We arrive at the origins of expression, or at least a vision of them far more immediate and authentic than anything in Eliot's ur-text, *The Origin of Attic Comedy*. The origin of Eliot's dark comedy is far from any social, historical, and theological context. No public culture exerts a pull equal to the compulsions rooted in depths wholly his own—"something peculiar to himself," as a mystified Virginia Woolf said of the play's atmosphere after attending the London premiere.[41] The real agon Eliot dramatizes in "Fragments of an Agon" precedes and follows the one pitting his vulnerable and belligerent characters against one another. He works to hold onto his onetime sense of himself as master of a unique voice and cultivated student of others' voices, even as perceptions never before encountered—"hideous" for being as yet unwritten—demand new imagery, words, techniques of composition. If *Sweeney Agonistes* must be seen as a rebirth fable, its reach is secular, pragmatic, and formalist. A new playwright, acting on behalf of an American theater that never quite welcomed him, hastens the collapse of familiar dramatic structures in order to free up space—openings suggested by his play's many caesuras—for cultural renewal.

T. S. Eliot's "interim" is Djuna Barnes's "hiatus." In her preface to a late play, *The Antiphon* (1958), Barnes writes of the two protagonists, a long-estranged mother and daughter, that "their duel is in hiatus, and should be waged with style."[42] Spectators who expect their hostilities to resume at any moment thus have one explanation for the play's brittle, agitated nature. In Barnes's other, earlier plays, her characters also tread lightly, as if aware that any untoward intimacy or outburst of candor might detonate a psychic explosion. Their exquisite control over diction and deportment, in this context, seems less a mark of confidence than of resistance. They hope that by edging around the perimeters of dramatic "action" and artfully manufacturing oblique, detached commentaries on themselves and others, they can prolong the pause before spontaneous life engulfs them anew. Barnes elevates this anxious decorum to an aesthetic principle in the novel *Nightwood* (1936), her best-known work: "An image is a stop the mind makes between uncertainties."[43] The sentence describes another hiatus—this one inviting us to imagine the theater (or any image-based art) defying the lack of clarity flanking it. Since such an art can't vanquish ambiguity—its images come "between," not triumphantly after, bouts of the outside world's uncertainty—it embodies a pathos more resonant than any individual's separate (and often sentimental) distress. It also, ideally, cultivates in us a nervous attentiveness that itself breaks from the blurred, merely instinctive reactions with which we greet most experience. Like this theater, we are "between" less incisive, shaped modes of response—amid but not of the public when we become her spectators.

Barnes was drawn to her culture's flux even as she sought relief in a coterie theater and the "certainty" of an inimitable "style." Like Cummings and Eliot, she was an avid student of the commercial entertainments of the teens and twenties, contributing dozens of articles about singers, dancers, actors, and impresarios to New York periodicals. Her tropism toward scenes of performance led her to boxing matches, dance hall and roof garden openings, circuses, a raucous courtroom, Coney Island's Luna Park and Steeplechase, fashion shows, suffragette demonstrations, street-corner orators, and a dentist, Twingeless Twitchell, pulling teeth in a public square. Read together, the articles commemorate a city that is all distractions and no center, all outside and no inside. They also tacitly promote a form of citizenship appropriate to such a landscape—alert, questioning, daring, irreverent, and mobile, individuals finding their only security in the many temporary communities gathered around a particular spectacle. Barnes is as attentive to those ad hoc societies as to the objects of their attention, identifying the unspoken pacts that hold together partners on a dance floor, riders on a Ferris wheel, denizens of a coffee shop, and patrons of a vaudeville house.

Barnes's awareness of the fragility of such clusters draws her, in several articles, to moments when the entertainment can't distract her from untheatrical tableaux—scenes of actual interiority or isolation, temperaments that dissent from the cultural imperative of brightness, transparency, and harmony. What Edmund Wilson later senses intermittently, Barnes names first. Her survey of Chinatown begins eagerly, as Barnes and her fellow tourists hope to be titillated, but she soon concedes that the district's decadent aura is unsupported by its somber and gray reality. As the title of one of her several essays on her own neighborhood, "Greenwich Village as It Is," suggests, she is equally determined to correct Bohemian mythology. The Village's reputed eccentricity doesn't disturb "those lost places that are twice as charming because of their reticence."[44] So, too, a landscape that deserves its theatrical reputation: Coney Island lures Barnes, in one article, away from its "showy side"—with "the garish-colored Japanese lanterns and the sideshow with its fat lady," its "merry-go-rounds with their ring-grabbing, fully elated, abruptly consequential society of riders"—and toward a remote garden where an old couple eats lunch in near-total isolation.[45] (Later, returning to the sideshow, Barnes takes less interest in an "islander's" performed fierceness than in his unostentatious skill in chewing gum.)

As the self-subverting sideshow suggests, there are implications for the theater in Barnes's divided attention. Performers as much as places can convey authentic feeling in their "reticence." In an essay on the tango craze, Barnes finds herself focusing on what the dancers *can't* do under the censorious eye of the chaperone. (Is this self-consciousness the origin of another popular dance Barnes describes—the "Hesitation"?) Her article on a prizefight seems at first to anticipate Cummings's own tributes to the sport, but Barnes transforms what could have been a mere celebration of "vitality" into a complex and subtle description of the undersides of both the fighter's bravura (she recognizes "isolation" and "loneliness" in the losing boxer's fall) and the audience's own machismo: the few women in the arena, she writes, are interested "not in strength but in beauty"—the unspectacular virtuosity implied by "a certain curve of the chin, a certain line from throat to brow."[46] Even in her survey of the performing animals at the Hippodrome, she looks beneath conventional stage personas. A lion, she insists, is no "king" or "man secreter." "I will not allow my typewriter to put down more in a million times the statement that . . . his eyes pulsed with a purple or green doom," she writes, and instead slips away to look at the animal offstage, alone—"no longer before the public, no longer in the limelight or the footlight"—where true pathos can surface.[47] She recognizes the same qualities in her later profiles of biped theater personalities: Lillian Russell, Florenz Ziegfeld, Billy Sunday, and other celebrities of prewar and interwar mass culture. She lingers over the showman's despair and peevish fatigue; admires the pragmatism of the aging sex symbol undeceived about her status; and catches the usually radiant evangelist in private—silent, placid, vacant, a "slumbering night light."[48]

A theater manifesto emerges, in pieces and with none of the typical manifesto's braggadocio, from these articles. Joined to the actual drama criticism Barnes contributed to *Theatre Guild Magazine,* they are essential reading—not just as a guide to her plays, nor just as a dissent from the prevalent tone of the era. They itemize the principles of an idiosyncratic style of performance: tense, indifferent to attention, and, recurrently, mute. Barnes argues for the aesthetic by citing its successful exponents. Marlene Dietrich deserves acclaim for recognizing that "human experience" is best "served up with a little *silence* and Restraint." "Silence makes experience go further," Barnes explains, "and, when it does die, gives it that dignity common to a Thing one has touched but not RAVISHED."[49] In a similar spirit, Barnes praises Alla Nazimova's "overtones and underacting" and quotes the actress approvingly on the seismic effects of minimal expression: "When one wants something terribly, there is only a motion of the hand."[50] Even stricter minimalism comes from a now-forgotten Greek actress: in her performance "the world is told *off* without a gesture."[51] Another equally stringent performer conveys a "dry passion drained . . . of any *of the Oil* which usually clogs the *keenness* of Emotion."[52] The actors who win Barnes's approval attract attention to what isn't visible — the workings of minds — more than to heaving, agitated bodies caught up in intrigue, romance, villainy, or suffering. The passions that do surface have acquired lyrical poise: if they must forgo silence, they will be known only by highly stylized, artificial words — "great and beautiful dithyrambs, swung up from the innermost coil of [their] emotional nature."[53]

As this last demand suggests, Barnes's vision of acting requires a reform of playwriting. In her own plays and in her candid confession of the struggle to write them, Barnes pushes back against the sunlight-seeking pressures of theatrical form, just as she writes her way behind the dazzling facades of urban landscapes and mass-culture diversions. She unwittingly names her preferred theater space in her essay on Greenwich Village: "Even a basement has its basement."[54] Barnes seeks a style that acknowledges but does not defer to the public assumed essential to performance. "What on earth I am doing in [this] medium I have not the slightest idea," she writes to a friend as she works on a new play. "Action, plot . . . exactly *not* what I am suited for."[55] Edwin Muir, helping Barnes edit *The Antiphon,* told T. S. Eliot, "We talked a good deal about the 'exposition', which she thoroughly detests."[56] Her detestation does not spring from mere spite. Exposition requires faith that something can be exposed — a faith to which Barnes, wise about the human capacity for repression, never subscribes. "Why are not playwrights happy without exposing something, without pointing up and down?" she asks in a 1929 essay.[57] In her own plays, Barnes points emphatically only to the impediments to perception — the procedures that establish but also control the intimacy between spectator and spectacle. It is as if she draws a taut wire from audience to stage along which vibrate, in one direction, the spectator's desire for confidential information and, in the opposite direction, the artist's uncertainty over just how much of this prize she should relinquish. Barnes chooses to leave the uncertainty unresolved. She may "dislike . . . parading, or 'telling on' the innermost secret," as she writes in another letter, but she allows that it can be revealed in fiction and drama, if only because art's decorum ensures that it will remain coded and aloof — "given back to itself," as she says, rather than given over to the spectator.[58]

Barnes isn't only trying to prevent our voyeurism, as one critic argues.[59] Rather than rebuff us, Barnes retrains us, schooling us in a more patient kind of attention, one capable of registering just those nuances of psychology that get swept away when playwrights and performers hold nothing back. The discreet spectator that Barnes envisions — someone as restrained as the writer and performers are themselves restrained — treats her narratives' many undivulged secrets not as problems to be solved but rather as entities to be marveled over — compelling for their structure and, especially, for the style in which their possessors keep them. It's only fitting that the way they resist allure is itself alluring. The complicated clothing of the protagonist of *Two Ladies Take Tea* (1923) is described as "rebellious" and "desperate," but she herself is "fearfully blasé."[60] The all-white decor and costumes of *Water-Ice* (1923) are themselves affectless but also seem, in the manner of a blank page awaiting desecration, visual equivalents of what Barnes elsewhere calls "a silence white and dumbfounding."[61] (Even the fire in the fireplace burns clear, as if to disappoint those hoping for emotional heat.) *The Antiphon* taunts us most memorably: its central scenic element is a huge dollhouse, closed on all sides, within which (we're told) lies evidence of a horrific crime. Only those characters who, turning spectators, press their faces up to the windows can see it. In this play, scenography rivals the achievement of the language. The latter is glittering to a blinding degree, dense in allusion, and layered with mannerist imagery — all attributes by which Barnes foils those expecting transparency. The style, here, is an apt demonstration of what Marianne Moore said about all Barnes's work: reading it "is like reading a foreign language which you understand."[62] One catches everything except the subject that the hyperarticulate speakers hope not to disclose. (In the case of *The Antiphon*, it is the family secret of incest and rape.) In all her plays, Barnes avoids sensationalism by redirecting our prurient curiosity toward the no less extreme practices of evasion or censorship. Her typical characters are wound up but unsprung; their default state is archness and catlike attentiveness. The result is neither narrative vacancy nor obscurity, but rather an electrified atmosphere in which we sense that appalling, unstageable incidents are beyond the edges of our sight, just barely restrained by her form. Violence is more devastating for being suppressed; even innocuous kinds of dramatic action depend on latency, just as spectatorship depends on inference. "She never removed, she covered over," writes Barnes of the walls in a character's apartment (and by implication of the character herself) in her 1928 novel *Ryder*. "Nothing erased but much submerged."[63]

The brevity of Barnes's best play, *The Dove* (1926), heightens our sense that much has been suppressed. In the one-act, two middle-aged sisters, Vera and Amelia, and the title character, a young woman, live together in an atmosphere so fraught with unrealized sexual desire that its only expression, for much of the play, is continual exhaustion. The women are spent from the work of not spending themselves on one another. Yet what some critics have misread as "ennui" and a "flaccid" structure is in fact a worked-up stoicism designed to cushion the potentially catastrophic consequences of sexual arousal.[64] Stimulants are comically omnipresent. The furniture "is all of the reclining type."[65] One sister reads French novels. Another sister, we're told, lies in bed ogling pictures of bathing beauties. Somewhere in the apartment, tantalizingly undisclosed, is "the album that no one ever sees" — presumably containing pictures even more erotic (158). The sisters keep animals — both their own and those that come in through the windows, creatures whose instincts are less sublimated than their own. Even the play's color scheme is a taunt. The wallpaper and upholstery, as well as the women's clothing and hair, are in various intensities of red, pink, and yellow, colors capable of awakening dormant sensual impulses. Acting on them would be easy. In her boldest, funniest mockery of conventions of dramatic "action," Barnes decorates her set with so many guns and swords that the imperative to reach a violent climax — Chekhov's famous rule about guns seen in the first act fated to go off in the third — is here so great that it pushes the play beyond melodrama into absurdity. (Indeed, we first see the Dove obsessively polishing an enormous sword — a camp combination of eros and menace.)

The exoticism and hermeticism of this milieu are so complete that it's shocking to recall that the women actually live in nothing more than a "long, low, rambling" flat at the top of an ordinary urban apartment house, or to hear, midway through the play, that one sister has been out buying something as banal as a stick of butter (148). In *The Dove*, as in Barnes's journalism, drama occurs in the negotiation between public and private cultures. The sisters are "two splendid dams erected about two little puddles" (as the Dove calls them); Vera herself acknowledges that she has been a bat who "never . . . hung over anything but myself" (157, 159). The Dove threatens this cultivated indifference in part by her livelier intelligence and erotic appeal. Even more disturbing, she also excels at the sisters' own art of restraint and in the process releases its subversive potential. In her tranquility and grace, she conjures up visions of their opposites. "Delicate as china" (as she is described), she threatens to break

(149). Her "dangerously transparent" skin awaits a stain or pull (149). Unnaturally poised, she makes the sisters' cramped actions seem reckless. Having "the expectant waiting air of a deer," she causes us to look for the hunter (149). When stillness is this exquisite — not self-punishing, as the sisters' practice it — it seems only to "prevent nothing . . . , [to] let everything go on, as far as it can go" (154). (That is Vera's appalled judgment on the Dove's indifference to decorum.) By her seemingly impossible combination of effrontery and reserve — or rather, by the effrontery *of* reserve — the Dove establishes a destabilizing new form of equilibrium. She is "fond of . . . the darkness underground" and of "the open fields, too" (153). When everything around her is lewd, and everyone else agitates strenuously to resist lewdness's call, she remains noncommittal, embodying deep sexuality by renouncing superficial desire. Her inscrutability confuses those who would draw a clear line between morality and immorality and know what constitutes crossing it.

The Dove's demeanor attunes us to the many other tensions vibrating just under the play's surface. The sisters may prefer "that imagination that is the growth of ignorance" (as the Dove says), but they also "have made it our business to know — everything" (150–51). They have their "suspicions of nature," but they also hope "to see something first-hand" (153, 150). Vera fears action but also laments that she will "never be perverse" (150). Amelia fears sin but at the end declares, "I don't want anything to be shut out. . . . Destroy all the tunnels in the city, leave nothing underground or hidden" (159–60). That Barnes is interested in more than just this or that character's particular self-division — that she is, rather, proposing a mode of dramatic structure that is itself seized by stillness — becomes apparent when the Dove itemizes the principles of a truly transgressive form of expression. They all share a distrust of progressive action. Neither psychological probability nor theatrical tradition prepares us to recognize passions that the Dove says are "causeless" (156). ("To have a reason is to cheapen rage," she explains.) So, too, beauty, which in its ideal form is beyond "logic." Meaningful change, likewise, disregards "necessary continuity" and "probable sequence" (157).

One wants to see the realization of these precepts in the play's startling climax. With no warning, the Dove sinks her teeth into Amelia's neck. (Is she hoping to prove that Barnes's characters are not bloodless after all?) Then, in a second puncturing of the play's surface, she shoots a bullet into an offstage painting, Carpaccio's *Two Venetian Women* (often called *Two Courtesans*). If one thinks that Barnes is providing catharsis after debunking "action," one should look at the actual painting. (Amelia brings it onstage just before the curtain falls.) It is a scene drained of eventfulness, bathed in dull gold, as if the figures were suspended in amber or the sun were setting just outside the frame.

One era has ended, another has not yet begun. In the interval — still another "hiatus" attracting Barnes's attention — life is at an impasse. The two title figures sit in profile and face off against a line of animals — two dogs, two doves, a peacock, a parrot — yet there is nothing confrontational about the arrangement. One dog has its paw in a courtesan's hand. Another dog pulls at her stick, looking more bored than fierce, peering out from under hooded lids, turning his mouth down as if only going through the motions of growling. The birds seem unusually earthbound. The courtesans' sexuality is weary and workaday, its fires banked. (Their only erotic prospect, as one critic points out, is an asexual young boy entering from the edge of the scene.) All the figures are penned in by a balcony railing but seem unlikely to try to flee. The transgressive urge has subsided under the stronger and more shocking force of the painter's commitment to compositional balance.

No less shocking is the mere presence onstage of a painting — any painting. At the end of a play in which Barnes emulates Carpaccio's example, she gestures toward an even more ambitious form of equilibrium, one between the performing and visual arts. Moreover, the strange collision of genres in the play's last seconds suggests an equally awkward transition between kinds of spectatorship. Barnes seems to acknowledge this by allowing so little time to pass between the hypertheatrical vampiric attack and the painting's appearance (or entrance, for in its inanimateness it does seem the ideal Barnes actor). When the Dove turns vampire, Barnes indulges our purely instinctive habits of response — surprise, alarm, revulsion, all the emotions appropriate to Grand Guignol or gothic melodrama. But then, with a violence matching the Dove's own, she suddenly pulls back to a second tableau demanding far more measured attention. Turning from theatergoers to gallery visitors, we hasten to join the actors and the playwright in practicing our own form of "silence and restraint" — looking now analytically and calmly at a newly two-dimensional stage spared the prospect of change, each spectator unlinked from the others and sunk, happily, in the public solitude available in an encounter with painting.

The excruciating experience of public solitude — and the political dimensions of the theater's interior and self-squeezing spaces — will be apparent only to readers who, before they leave the interwar period, seek out the best drama of the Harlem Renaissance. Even now, after a surge in scholarship, it's not easy to find: sympathetic yet discerning historians acknowledge that the Renaissance's theater lagged behind its music, dance, and literature. The better plays — relegated to the margins of their writers' careers, still unpublished, or

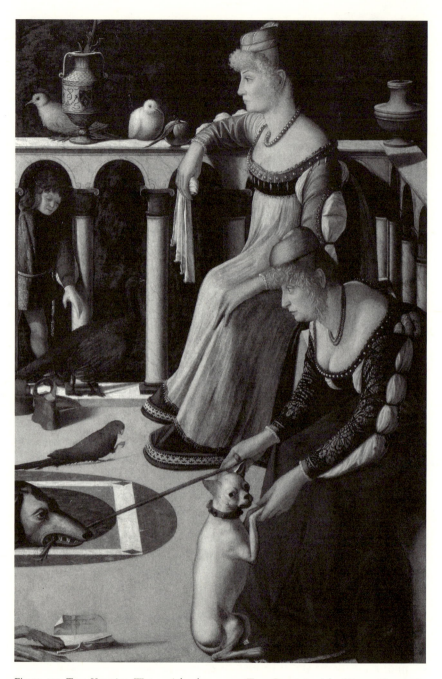

Figure 17: *Two Venetian Women* (also known as *Two Courtesans*) by Vittore Carpaccio (c. 1510), Museo Correr, Venice. The painting appears at the end of *The Dove* by Djuna Barnes (1926). Cameraphoto Arte, Venice / Art Resource, NY.

deemed "undramatic" in their time — seem to anticipate such neglect in their narratives. They unfold beneath and often in opposition to the confident popular culture of the Renaissance. At their center are figures obscured by their skepticism, sunk in the punishing but self-protective privacy Claude McKay recognized in "The Harlem Dancer" (1922). The well-known poem articulates a principle shared with other forms of Renaissance performance. McKay's title figure manages to be simultaneously present, indulging patrons who "devoured her shape with eager, passionate gaze," and even more shockingly absent: "But looking at her falsely-smiling face, / I knew her self was not in that strange place."[66]

If not there, where? Zora Neale Hurston, the Renaissance's best playwright, sets her work in the same gap between selves — yet another interwar "interim" — where characters deploy rather than merely embody personalities. "There are bound to be some in-betweens," she writes in a discussion of "the so-called races" in her memoir *Dust Tracks on a Road*.[67] For them, "character" depends less on passively inheriting the traits sanctioned by one's culture than on designing a new, close-fitting self in a series of public acts and utterances. "Being a Negro writer these days is a racket," says a character based on Hurston in Wallace Thurman's *Infants of the Spring* (1932). "Sure I cut the fool. But I enjoy it, too."[68] Sincerity and authenticity are doubtful attributes in a world so permeated by performance. Even one's most intimate transactions conform to — or resist — prevailing styles and assume the presence of spectators. "They know it's not courtship," writes Hurston of the "pushing, shoving show of gallantry" some boys perform for an audience of girls in *Their Eyes Were Watching God* (1937). "It's acting-out courtship and everybody is in the play."[69]

Everybody? In all her work, Hurston tracks the encroachment of various publics upon territory other writers would deem private. The very "concept of privacy," she suggests in her important essay "Characteristics of Negro Expression" (1934), recedes in African-American culture, as its "communal" societies "keep nothing secret" and "hold quarrels and fights in the open."[70] Yet in her own art, Hurston sees the relation between the "open" and "closed" regions of a character's life more ambiguously. She implicitly concedes as much by her emphasis on "quarrels and fights." Beyond any particular source of friction, Hurston's characters are also fighting to maintain or improve their standing in their societies. Some agitate for admission to its exclusive cliques; others ask for the merest sign of recognition from better-placed others. To readers and spectators who come to Hurston after encountering other interwar playwrights nourished by mass culture, her theater comes as a shock. Public life, for Hurston, is not the scene of unimpeded circulation of ideas and desires, nor of the gentle erasure of difference in the pursuit of a stronger union, nor of the effortless synchronization of individual will with broader cultural imperatives. Rather, even the most ordinary exchange between characters requires complex negotiation. "And how would you talk to me?" says one character in *Polk County* (1944), a question any Hurston character could ask — part playful come-on, part dare, part haughty territorialism, part genuine curiosity.[71] Here, as elsewhere, characters verify the terms of engagement before executing them. So, too, with nonverbal transactions. In the same play, a woman stops all visitors at her threshold, interrogating them until they disclose their backgrounds, sympathies, and motives, inviting them inside only after asserting her own rights of attention. Another play, *Cold Keener* (1930), finds a simple scenic image for the same diplomatic give-and-take: several scenes are set at the intersection of two streets.

As all these instances suggest, Hurston's recurrent subject is power. Her plays dramatize the machinations of those who want it, the anxieties of those who hope to keep it, and the shame of those who fail to resist it. Power's allure (and power's threat) motivate her characters' compulsive experimentation with modes of conduct, levels of emotional intensity, and degrees of self-exposure. Hurston's full-length plays — in addition to *Polk County* and *Cold Keener,* they include *Mule Bone* (1930, co-written with Langston Hughes) and *Spunk* (1935) — may speak in a symphonic voice and proceed in directions seemingly set by characters themselves as they arbitrate among one another's competing wishes. Yet it would be a mistake to underestimate the ferocity of that competition and the difficulty of the arbitration. In her panoramic views of Florida turpentine factories, parishes, and extended families, Hurston depicts cultures under construction, which often collapse just at the moment of their apparent completion. "They are ephemeral in every way," writes Hurston of the communities and relationships formed by the itinerant sawmill workers in *Polk County* (273). Many Hurston characters pledge allegiance to an ad hoc republic only after violently arguing over individual loyalties. They continuously revise their social contract with a flexible vernacular, redraw social boundaries by such communal rites as "jooking" and "woofing." Hurston respects the distinctions among kinds of affiliation. Fellowship demands a degree of conscious attention unnecessary to mere kinship. Kinship, for its part, signifies a deeper, instinctive attraction absent from clannishness. A character who shows devotion stops short of servitude. The loyalties between women declare themselves differently than those between men. Sexual bonds may be soluble, but certain friendships are not. Collegiality, partnership, obligation, need, and even ancient hatreds — these and other relationships inspire distinct languages, styles of deportment, and codes of conduct.

The "jook" — equal parts saloon, dance hall, casino, brothel, and boxing ring — provides Hurston with her theater's frequent setting and model of dramatic structure. Flux is its permanent condition. A jook's patrons continuously assert, test, and overturn social status; they shift in and out of one another's (and our own) field of view; narrative changes direction with every violation of territory, body, decorum, and trust. Readers of the "Characteristics" may regard the jook as one possible source for Hurston's interest in "asymmetry" in dramatic structure, "angularity" of theatrical character, and a style of behavior that obeys the nervous, eruptive "rhythm of segments" (834–35). The main plots of her longer plays — romantic rivals warring against one another — are far less significant than everything flanking them: fleeting encounters between ancillary characters, fragments of trivial discussions, ragged ends or beginnings of other possible, as-yet-untold stories tempting us to make a detour. Hurston's typical spectator is always making choices. Well into the long plays, every character is still a potential protagonist. Background and foreground continuously trade places, as do center and margin. Scenes churn restlessly as characters interrupt one another, change the rules of engagement, mock convention, cross the line. Protagonists are never unaware that they can be displaced at any moment. Even at their most confident, they remain on guard, always moving so as never to be pinned down, nourished by distrust. Hurston captured this quality in an oft-quoted attack on idle self-regard: "I do not belong to the sobbing school of Negrohood. . . . No, I do not weep at the world — I am too busy sharpening my oyster knife."[72] So, too, her typical theatrical surrogate — an unattached, mobile woman, propelled by impatience, disdain, and laughter (at herself as much as at others), kept on a self-chosen course by her far-sightedness, unsentimental (what Hurston calls "non-morbid"), unawed yet passionate.[73]

The brilliance of such emotions challenges convention with the same force as does Hurston's collapsing dramatic structure. "On Joe Clarke's porch," she writes in *Dust Tracks on a Road*, "there was open kindnesses, anger, hate, love, envy and its kinfolks, but all emotions were naked, and nakedly arrived at" (46). When Hurston recreates this threshold in *Mule Bone* (and establishes others like it in other plays), she goes even further. Her theater favors exultation over mere happiness, disgust over mere dislike, lust over mere desire, terror over mere fear. Speech grows bolder to capture such elemental feelings. "They do not say embrace when they mean that they slept with a woman," Hurston writes about the residents of the real Polk County. "A behind is a behind and not a form" (149). Hurston's characters are blunt, racy, and loud, euphoric in vulgarity, wary of ambiguity. (Clarity is the first among virtues for those who have learned by hard experience how euphemism and doublespeak can be used to exploit them.) They descend from, and extend, the post-Emancipation "era of tongue and lung."[74] For Hurston, speech is an aggressive, physical act, and the best words recall her to the moment of their coinage, when a speechless individual sought a word to answer a need and, not finding it at hand, made one. The memory of that action survives in the thrust and rhythm of the language — words that, serving lives, seem to live themselves, moving along with the experiences they name; retaining the sound or texture of the places, situations, and communities from which they sprang; enlivening speakers who can strengthen their grasp of abstract ideas by talking about them in gestural language. We hear them inching toward, lunging at, dancing around, or recoiling from the subjects under discussion. "So bumble-tongued! I felt like zotting him over the head." "You done put me on the linger." "You got me like a stepped-on worm. Half dead but still trying to crawl." "Squat that rabbit." "Rush your frog to the frolic." The body speaks even in words and phrases that don't describe movement: "vip," "vop," "oskobolic," "biggity."[75] Readers can find one precedent for this style in Emerson. The words he praised as "initiative" — "they are vascular and alive; they walk and run" — are echoed in what Hurston calls "verbal nouns."[76] The writers Emerson admired for "throw[ing] the weight of [the] body" into composition, and whose language furthers their engagement with wild and domesticated landscapes, have an heir in the Hurston whose "very words are action words."[77] "Every new relation is a new word," Emerson insists in "The Poet," sounding like Hurston in his awareness of community pressures on discourse.[78]

Yet Emerson is also useful as a counterexample. The secular playwright, working in a changeable and impermanent art, has none of the transcendentalist's faith that language will bring about a harmonious union with the world. Her itinerant characters, knowing true rather than merely verbal "walking and running," treat speech's claims as temporary. A verbal style that in one context seems high-spirited, in another is evidence of a struggle to hold onto — not just name — experiences, things, places, and people before they disappear. This kind of speech is a bid for social security: a campaign against the speakers' inevitable uprooting, audible to those who choose to hear it. One character's compulsive explaining and storytelling seem strategies to prevent her listeners from taking her subjects (and herself) for granted. Another character, master of baroque metaphors, similes, and compound adjectives, weighs down passing moments with heavy description. Still another speaker cultivates a bright and alert tone to deflect attention from unvoiced, embarrassing thoughts and unshaped emotions. In all these instances, Hurston's characters implicitly confess their fear of falling out of the broader community of talk. We encounter them often in sites that justify the anxiety over assimilation — on a threshold (as we've seen), but also outside a closed window; or in a room adjacent to, but set apart from, the main arena; or even (in *Cold Keener*) outside the pearly gates, trying to win admittance from a dubious Saint Peter. These are all forms of offstage in Hurston's theatricalizing world, where her actor-characters confront the prospect of a life lived without spectators or even fellow performers. (Others are enclosed no less definitively by jealousy, envy, spite, or mere longing.)

For all the conviviality of Hurston's theater, these sequestered characters set its tone. They are ready with one of Hurston's characteristically exuberant responses but await, sometimes futilely, a call. ("I hope you did call me, Eva-lina," says the title character in *Spunk* to his estranged girlfriend. "I needs calling" [259].) Hurston records her own experience of this condition. "I had a feeling of difference from my fellow men," she writes in *Dust Tracks on a Road*, recalling a youth filled with private visions. They gave her "a feeling of terrible aloneness. I stood in a world of vanished communion with my kind, which is worse than if it had never been. Nothing is so desolate as a place where life has been and gone. I stood on a soundless island in a tideless sea. . . . True, I played, fought, and studied with other children, but always I stood apart within" (43).

Apart within. No work of Hurston's dramatizes this contradictory state more sharply, or summarizes Hurston's aesthetics more succinctly, than *Color Struck* (1925). The one-act play begins on a Jim Crow train carrying contes-tants to a cakewalking competition. The black men and women, all from Jacksonville, Florida, sing, dance, parade up and down the aisle, scramble over seats, flaunt their elaborate outfits, and — with particular vigor — top one an-other's boasts, compliments, and put-downs. The theatricality of the train car, with every seat a stage, is so pronounced that the move, in the next scene, to the real stage of a weatherboard hall is inevitable. Here the circle of sociability widens. The characters encounter contestants from Ocala, St. Augustine, Palatka, Daytona, and Eatonville, and as they do so, the varieties of self-theatricalization multiply. Every exchange of pleasantries or food is an oppor-tunity to admire — and judge — one another. The performances proper — a parse-me-la and then the cakewalk — would seem to be afterthoughts if the crowd weren't so feverish in its rapidly accelerating interest. Indeed, the first half of *Color Struck* is as much a study of audiences as of performers. Individ-uals on both sides of the stage seem happily to lose themselves in roles autho-rized by a theatrical culture: the contestants obscured by their attitudinizing onstage and offstage, the spectators rendered impersonal by their communal enthusiasm.

Yet for all the obvious pleasure Hurston takes in memorializing this expres-sion of popular culture, she also senses its inadequacy. One of her characters, Emma, cannot lose sight of the ordinary selves beneath the finery, choreography, and the raillery known as "woofing." In the swirl of fluid social roles, Emma sees only what does not change. She focuses on skin: blackness cannot be acted out of sight or into something new. More precisely, its gradations, as the dark-skinned Emma obsessively remarks upon them, enforce divisions that survive the characters' vigorous campaigns for social cohesion and shared pleasure. Throughout the first three scenes, Emma monitors her brown-skinned date, John, in his encounters with a light-skinned woman, unable to beat back her jealousy of a potential rival. So omnivorous is her anxiety — it soon metastasizes to indict an entire culture in which "us blacks was made for cobble stones" — that it paralyzes her.[79] She sits out the cakewalk competition, unwilling to watch other women admire her boyfriend.

Her self-exile does more than remind us that role-playing brings only temporary relief from oppressive, or merely ordinary, conditions. It also tests theater's claim to be a mirror of its age. From the margins of the stage, Emma implicitly asks how complete are its representations. Our attention, divided between a theatrical panorama of confident public life and a meditative, motionless picture of private life, leads to a divided conclusion. *Color Struck* allows for the conventionally sympathetic response to individual suffering, but then prompts us to consider broader vulnerabilities of theater craft. Hurston is such a good student of folklore — she trained as an anthropologist under Franz Boas — that she recognizes what folklore *can't* explain. Emma's failure to participate in the contest and other ritualized forms of sociability suggests that whole regions of the interior life are beyond the reach of culture — beyond the reach of this play, too. Emma's anxieties may originate in the history of bias, but they result in an isolation so acute as to remove her from any explanatory social or aesthetic context.

Hurston dramatizes this apartness spatially and structurally. For much of the cakewalk contest, she keeps us behind the dance hall's curtain. As the characters move offstage (or, in the logic of the play, onstage) to begin competing, Emma stays in this anteroom, joining us in watching the dancers' shadows on the curtain, hearing the clapping, laughing, and music of a performance she need only cross the room to join. The stage arrangement is a concise expression of the play's anxieties over seeing. Wounded by sight — what she fears are others' judgments on her appearance — Emma rejects all forms of spectatorship.

The play's self-sequestering energies — moving us from a Jim Crow car where blacks and whites can't see one another to a dance hall ambivalent about self-exposure — push even deeper into unspectacular space in the last scene, set twenty years later. Its narrative surprise (Emma is now the mother of a mixed-race daughter) is less compelling than Hurston's elaboration of the solitude that had already seemed definitive behind the dance hall curtain. The one-room shack where Emma watches over her dying daughter seems to belong to another play entirely, one in which presence has nothing to do with character and in which time passes without reference to purposeful action. Dim light, wind blowing outside the door, "dead silence," an indistinct form (the girl) lying on a bed, her mother rocking monotonously in a rocking chair, transformed into an archetypal figure of vigilance: Hurston writes herself out of one kind of theater — the effervescent entertainments typical of the 1920s — and into another, its austerity a coterie taste in a culture beholden to eventfulness. Something does happen here — John arrives, hoping to marry Emma despite their decades-long separation, while her old, undiminished anxieties inadvertently hasten the girl's death — but Hurston underscores varieties of inertia. Emma does not move (she goes for a doctor only after great effort) and cannot change (she fears John is attracted to her blonde daughter) and won't be seen (she tries to keep John from lighting a lamp). Emma's own vision fails, her only explanation for her nonactions: "Couldn't see" (102). She accompanies the line, her last, with a vague gesture across her face, as if she were erasing herself. Similar erasures are carried out all across the stage as the play nears its end. The lamp blows out, plunging the stage back into near darkness. The other characters — John, the doctor, and, finally, the dead daughter — are absent. Dialogue also dies out and silence reasserts itself, broken only by the rocking chair's monotonous back-and-forth. Hurston systematically shuts off and closes down the elements of theater but leaves her protagonist behind, an unnerving and irremediable version of the play's many kinds of segregation. Emma is severed from the means of her representation. Seen thus, how inadequate it is to read *Color Struck,* as many do, as primarily about "identity." The play's depiction of authentic social oppression is preamble to a scene of abjection that no individual biography or societal narrative can explain. This pain is formal, not just psychological; its victim is the writer, not just the character. We are at the edge of the same abyss that fascinated T. S. Eliot in *Sweeney Agonistes.* Even after identifying the limitations of their theatrical languages, both writers refuse to relinquish their subjects — ones that resist the simplifications of art. The playwrights are also attached to the negative space that takes art's place — Eliot's silences, Hurston's darkness — and gather it around themselves as they wait for new imagery and new techniques to beckon from the void.

Only a romantic expects a cathartic end to this vigil. The lesson of *Sweeney Agonistes* toughens our response not just to *Color Struck* but to the unspoken principles of the Harlem Renaissance and of the interwar period in general. The promise of rebirth in any renaissance collapses here or is at least deferred indefinitely. Similarly, the premise underpinning an interwar culture — that the period's parenthesis must close — is in question: what if the hiatus ended not with a change but only a deeper interment in intermediacy? It's fitting that a playwright who is himself bracketed in most discussions of Renaissance theater theatricalizes such an impasse with audacity unseen elsewhere in the period. Jean Toomer's *Kabnis* (1923) is built around and leads toward a number of abysses — spatial, linguistic, aural, metaphysical — in which the title character confronts a buried and long-resisted racial inheritance. The play itself is buried in *Cane,* the collection of poems, prose sketches, and stories in dialogue memorializing Toomer's experience as a schoolteacher in Washington, DC, and rural Georgia. That literary context is only the most obvious reason the American theater ignored the play. In a letter to Kenneth Macgowan of the Provincetown Players, Toomer wrote, "I'm feeling, reaching out for my forms and for my esthetic. . . . Whether or not I am 'of the theatre' remains to be seen. . . . What I really want, I believe, (*Kabnis* may or may not be evidence of this) is a close-knit, deep-rolling, dynamic structure whose language tends more towards poetry than towards what is flat and commonplace."[80] Toomer's uncertainty — his parenthetical equivocations make him sound tentative even about his tentativeness — may have stimulated it in others. The Provincetown Players worried about the play's lack of "a general dramatic design" — an uncharacteristic response from a company committed to O'Neill's experiments in stasis and immobility — and other theaters were no more sanguine about its stageability.[81] A related confusion afflicts readers and critics. The different sections of *Cane* embody so many contradictory styles — melodrama, symbolism, naturalism, social allegory, and the pastoral — that only those willing to shake off programmed responses can move through it smoothly.

Such variety can be a virtue: Toomer's publisher, mindful of the public's appetite for popular entertainment, marketed the book as "a vaudeville out of the South."[82] But it can also be a form of evasion, as we've seen when other writers make a deceptively enthusiastic embrace of mass culture. In staging his own life, Toomer refashioned uncertainty as a positive rather than negative value, one gesture in a lifelong resistance to taxonomy. He famously renounced his African-American identity soon after *Cane*'s publication, asking his publisher to stop promoting him as a black writer. Later, he refused a place in a new edition of James Weldon Johnson's *Book of American Negro Poetry* (1931) and in Nancy Cunard's own anthology, *Negro* (1934). He gestured toward the same ambiguity in social and sexual identity: "I am of no particular class. . . . I am neither male nor female nor in-between," he wrote in *Essentials* (1931).[83] Toomer justifies all these evasions with soft tributes to vague fellow feeling: "Jean Toomer is an American." "I am of the human race." "I am of the earth."[84]

His overbroad pledges of allegiance are convincing only as a retreat from all "communities" — the very word implying compromises to a still evolving individuality. The Toomer of the autobiographical prose is dogmatically mercurial, guarding his fluid identity against those who would freeze it, insisting on multiple affiliations in — and against — a culture that demands irrevocable choice. "I have lived among Negroes," Toomer writes. "I have lived among Nordics and Anglo-Saxons. I have lived among Jews."[85] "I take the color of whatever group I at the time am sojourning in."[86] Stable loyalties, he implies, are easily exploited. The transparent self is too exposed. By assuming multiple personae, he effaces himself. By joining many publics, he preserves his privacy.

Toomer's militancy in these pursuits helps us see the radicalism of the era's other dissenting playwrights. Hurston's own impatience with identity ("there is no *The Negro* here," she once wrote),[87] Barnes's refusal to tell "the innermost secret," Eliot's fabled "impersonality," Cummings's shift from antic self-display to recognition of inner emptiness, even Stevens's argument with "humanity" from the twin "seclusion" of aesthetics and the autonomous mind: these varied styles of opting out and embracing nothingness, conducted by non-selves as they create what the broader culture calls non-plays, seem, after a reading of *Kabnis,* part of a large-scale, unwittingly collaborative revision of theatrical form and of the broader American theater culture. These playwrights are one possible context for Toomer's renunciation of context. In place of a larger frame of reference, he practices a radical self-sufficiency — eliminating distractions from self-scrutiny, dwelling with microscopic care on gradations of feeling and perception, sinking into plush old fears and unsatisfied urges. The play that results from this discipline — at once sensuous and self-abnegating — pushes American theater toward the kind of formal and psychological starkness it wouldn't fully embrace until the century's last decades.

Toomer's narrative offers a concrete version of this estrangement. Ralph Kabnis, northern-born, educated, hoping his "blue blood" will compensate for his black skin, is an outsider among the other black residents of a small Georgia town. He is scornful of the past — the lessons and burdens of slavery — yet unable to envision a future for his inchoate ambitions. Through a series of strippings or erasures, Toomer reduces Kabnis to a presumably original blankness, prelude to the inscription of a new, more legible character. He loses his home, then his teaching job, and finally his place in any kind of public life. The social denuding loosens the inhibitions on his rage. Discarding the measured language he usually speaks, he directs a stream of vitriol at himself and everyone around him until it, too, peters out. After "defiance" gives way to "acquiescence" (as Toomer charts it), Kabnis experiences even more acute stages of inertia — in his indifference plunging toward abjection and landing, finally, at insensibility.[88] The entropy is mesmerizing. Toomer's theater derives energy from leakage; Kabnis (and *Kabnis*) purify as they dissolve.

Toomer makes full use of the visual and aural resources of the theater to stage this passivity — an achievement worth stressing to those who judge *Kabnis* as incompletely weaned from prose. Indeed, in the absence of a character's commanding, centering will, Toomer lavishes attention on the coequal protagonists of sound, space, and light. His materialism provides concrete sources for Kabnis's fear, self-doubt, and emotional paralysis. The northerner's lack of cultural footing is explicit on a stage that caves in around him. Black cracks divide the wallboards of his cabin. "Powdery faded red dust" falls from additional cracks in the ceiling.[89] Behind the chimney lies the "perfect blackness" of a fathomless closet (93). A fireplace is another dark pit. When Kabnis goes to work in a wheelwright's shop, he finds no greater security. The outer walls are pocked with musket shot. The inner walls have shed enough plaster to reveal the lathing. Most of the windows are broken. An entrance to the cellar — "The Hole" — gapes open at the edge of the room, waiting for someone to fall in. The entire landscape, he says, is "a mud-hole trap" (93).

Deterritorialization also results from less obvious causes. After noting an oil lamp burning at Kabnis's bedside, Toomer writes, "The cabin room is spaced fantastically about it" (83). It is one of many sources of light that blur the borders of the stage. A valley under moonlight is "silvered gauze" (84). A fire makes a room "dance to the tongues of flames" (86). In another room, sunlight pools in magic circles and blinds us to the surrounding ordinariness. Toomer is a connoisseur of light, implicitly inviting designers to join him in distinguishing among its colors, strengths, and densities. He also ascribes to light emotional and even moral values usually reserved for the figures it illuminates. Dusk is not just "ashen" but "false" (93). Shadows are "menacing"; elsewhere they are "grotesque." Night "throbs" with unpredictable eros (105). When light breaks through — a match flares, coals heat up, daylight slips through a window — it rarely brings relief: weak and fleeting, it confirms the dominance of the larger darkness.

Toomer is equally attentive to the aural landscape. Sounds divorced from their sources — heard but hard to locate authoritatively in the night — create a world that closes in on its inhabitants. Lying in bed, Kabnis listens to a rat scuttling across the ceiling, a hen scraping its claws in an adjacent room, and wind rustling up through the floorboards. Later, a woman moans and shouts in an offstage church, an unseen preacher's own voice rises, someone shrieks nearby, and finally a brick crashes through a stage window, the outside world no longer kept at bay. No less violent is a contraction of stage space that begins with voices calling in the distance, moves to voices outside Kabnis's door, then culminates in a gunshot and a terrifying knock. The latter affects Kabnis "like huge cold finger tips" raising gooseflesh on his skin (97). "Things are so immediate in Georgia," Toomer writes, but in the theater the force of a sound (or an image) depends on Toomer delaying its arrival, if not muffling or squelching it altogether (86).

We wait in a silence with its own expressive, hypnotic power. A pause, seemingly unmarked, is "disagreeable" (96). As Kabnis lies in bed, "dead things moving in silence . . . come here to touch me" (86). The impalpable again becomes palpable when he later must "force through a gathering heaviness" simply to enter the stage (88). Another character's diffidence signifies "a muted folk who feel their way upward to a life that crushes or absorbs them" (106). It is in silence that Kabnis feels especially sharply the ever-narrowing culture of racist intimidation: one scene's tranquility resembles the atmosphere "where they burn and hang men" (86). (In addition to lynchings, there have also been an infanticide and multiple threats of further violence to interlopers such as himself.) Yet Toomer leaves many other forms of absence ambiguous. Like Eliot and Barnes, he is expert at dramatizing the state of expectation—waiting for the darkness to lift, the silence to break, a vacant street to fill with movement—and, like them, challenges us even more when he refuses to relieve it. The darkness thickens, the silence grows heavier, the stillness spreads until it saps even the energy needed to maintain a scene's lack of action. This particular form of effacement has no denotative function; it floats apart from characters and culture alike. "Close your eyes," says Kabnis to himself at the end of the first scene, rejecting the visible world, then canceling even interior projections and private texts with ever increasing severity. "Think nothing . . a long time . . nothing, nothing. Dont even think nothing. Blank. Not even blank. Count. No, mustnt count. Nothing . . blank . . nothing . . blank" (87).

How does Toomer move his play—and with it the American theater as a whole—from "blank" to "not even blank"? (Even an ellipsis, reduced here to two dots, seems too full for him.) We encounter nullity elsewhere in early twentieth-century drama—in O'Neill and Wilder, most prominently—but Toomer pushes beyond their shapely lacunae, visible emblems of asceticism. The better-known playwrights point us toward the presence of absence. Here we confront the absence of absence—"not even blank"—a definitive denial of our desire for spectacle. In this progression, Toomer rivals Beckett for demanding, satisfying ungenerosity. As in Beckett, the more severe the wasting, the more luminous the body. Devastation comes in the speed with which stasis reasserts itself after a defiant gesture or utterance. It seems impossible to diminish Kabnis any further than he does himself at the end of this scene, willing himself to a dreamless sleep (as Toomer writes) in a starless night. But the act of willing—the commands to himself to "think nothing . . dont even think nothing"—itself preserves some remnant of selfhood that Toomer eradicates over the next five scenes.

He does so, in part, by calling for a simple action. "They descend into the Hole" (105). Near the end of the play, Kabnis and three other characters surrender to the magnetic pull of the wheelwright shop's cellar, sinking below the surface of the theater floor as if to discover a purer form of passivity, one unresponsive even to the demands of stage presence. (One imagines the cellar inverting theatrical principles as well as theatrical architecture.) Toomer's hole once housed slaves grown too old and worn out to work. One elderly man, enslaved as a boy, lives there now. The hole's allusion to the grave is unignorable; Kabnis's own voluntary burial confirms his demotion to the status of mere matter, the inevitable conclusion to the many assaults on him in previous scenes. Throughout the play, bodies break into parts, are reduced to mere textures, or become settings for impersonal, organic change. Toomer scrutinizes the sweat gathering in Kabnis's armpits, notates the rhythm of his quivering lip, magnifies the violence of stones cutting through his pajamas when he falls. Hair pasted to a pillow, a thumb pressed against a chin, eyes lodged in a "lemon face"—they are detachable tokens of the larger self who rarely materializes (83). When he does, he is not quite animate. Kabnis burrows under the bedcovers in one scene, turning into a lump. Later, he "totters" as if on "artificial limbs" (85). In another scene, he is a "scarecrow replica" of himself, "fantastically plastered with red Georgia mud" (93)—parody of the rootedness he can't achieve, and of the "soil-ness" Toomer has said his play celebrates.[90] (It's revealing that Toomer refers to Kabnis as "it" rather than "he" in this scene.)

Now an object, Kabnis suffers the object world's characteristic insults. He is "thinning out," as if the elements were eroding him (98). Such a brutal cultural climate also leaves him "tarnished, burned . . . split, shredded: easily burned" (109). He is flattened by "the whole white South weigh[ing] down upon him. The pressure is terrific. . . . Chill beads run down his body" (102). Once it succeeds in pushing him underground, he flattens and erodes further—a process so thorough he almost disappears. The play itself almost does too. Illusionism that was convincing above ground is here exposed as phony. Figures and places that seemed substantial turn abstract. In the cellar, Kabnis puts on a garish robe and plays at regality, but he can't sustain the role. He collapses in a heap, his "character" a mere empty costume, his body lining the dirt floor he once lorded over. Renouncing the human privilege of verticality, he stays on his back to debate kinship with the ex-slave, as if pledging physical allegiance to the only institution he trusts. (Toomer's alter ego is "of the earth" after all.) Yet that space is itself dissolving. It "swims in a pale phosphorescence" (112). Objects and figures are "amoeba-like shadows" (112). Different shades of blackness slide across the stage, creating a world of an unbounded vagueness. (One wonders if Toomer, who wrote admiringly of *The Emperor Jones,* was making a conscious tribute to the inky landscape of the earlier play.)

"I get my life down in this scum-hole," says Kabnis after the degradation of all theatrical, characterological, narrative, and ideological platforms (115). What life? Tentative as always, Toomer imagines a receptive, deindividuated, spreading consciousness. (The word "self" suggests too coherent and contained an entity for a theater that is "not even blank.") Epiphanies, for a protagonist this liquid, aren't crystallizing or transforming. "I'm what sin is," says Kabnis at his most acute, coaxing us to imagine the attribute divorced from identifiable transgressions and from the standard narrative of individual guilt, punishment, and redemption (116). The sin consumes and replaces the sinner. Character is subsumed in waste, animate only in the gestures of abjection. So, too, with the new language native to the "scum-hole." Kabnis describes its genesis: a "form ... burned int my soul is some twisted awful thing that crept in from a dream," shaped to accommodate only "misshapen, split-gut, tortured, twisted words" — the elements of a new poetics appropriate to an antilyrical world (111). Kabnis's intimacy with his language far exceeds the decorous norm. Speech and speaker merge; words imprint themselves upon or fill the character. No longer can we uphold a quaintly humanist mode of speech (or writing) — each individual the master of a private style. Toomer's speaker is powerless against a biological imperative that has nothing to do with individual expressiveness. "White folks" feed words to his hollowed-out consciousness; "black niggers" and "yallar niggers" feed it with words of their own; "this whole damn bloated purple country" feeds it until the speaker is consumed by his inherited language — buried under a "holy avalanche of words" (111).

In another letter to Kenneth Macgowan, Toomer describes Kabnis as crushed by a "crude mass" with "friction and heat and sparks."[91] After such a denouement, the protagonist's ascent from the Hole as the curtain falls seems anticlimactic, even unearned, as does the sun's own rising after such irremediable darkness.[92] Only a sentimental reader would read the ending as redemptive, yet only an impatient reader would dismiss it as false. Toomer allows for a more nuanced third interpretation. Rebirth may well take hold in the broader culture — Toomer calls the sun a "gold-glowing child" who "sends a birth-song" down to the streets — but such optimism doesn't heal the beaten, spent form of Kabnis who "stumbles over [a] bucket," "trudges upstairs," and disappears without a word (117). This renaissance, as Toomer envisions it, excludes or overlooks as many as it sanctifies. Those not touched by its gold-glowing sun cast shadows over the larger public; that public, in turn, extends privileges of security and well-being only to those willing to subsume their individuality in a corporate body. After Kabnis's dissent (or, at best, abstention) from such a scenario, it is hard to look upon any resolution uncritically. The margin will always pull focus from the center. The double vision required to see such a stage in full will continue to serve us well after the interwar era ends. The strongest postwar playwrights position themselves off center, cultivate irony and archness, remain bent, and delay their assimilation by any culture hurrying to claim them.

Changing Decorum

When he's painted himself out of it
De Kooning says his picture's finished
   — Edwin Denby, "Sonnets"

The play demands coming to the surface.
      — Virginia Woolf, Diary

Historians seeking the hallowed ground of postwar theatrical experiment could do worse than start at the former Central High School of Needle Trades in New York City. The virtues suggested by the school's name — practicality, respect for patterns, stoicism before the pinprick of danger and pain — underpinned the performances it hosted for a single night in November 1946: two new ballets by George Balanchine, the more radical of which was the now-landmark *Four Temperaments*. The ballet's protagonists suggest rhythmic and gestural correspondences to the humors — melancholic, phlegmatic, sanguinic, and choleric — yet a skeptical, affectless corps, intercepting the soloists at their most expressive, keeps them (and us) from wallowing in any single emotional state. The dancers populate a ballet of continual displacements. One humor fails to prevent the onrush of the others. Within a particular temperament, partners extend themselves in opposite directions, betraying an ambivalence even strong feeling can't subdue. Together they establish coordinates of the stage only to see them wiped clean by the equally convincing patterns traced by other pairs.

The company's own multiple displacements as it sought a permanent theater affirmed this aesthetic of temporariness. It wasn't until 1948, after residencies in numerous inappropriate halls, that it finally settled into City Center, a former fraternal lodge and masterpiece of Moorish kitsch, where any pretensions to otherworldly grace and haute style couldn't survive the cramped seats, inconsistent sight lines, and an orchestra pit that one occupant compared to "a men's lavatory."[1] The ballets that the company, now named the New York City Ballet, performed after this move depended on additional tensions for their clarity. Igor Stravinsky, Balanchine's frequent collaborator in these years, praised classical dancing as "the triumph of studied conception over vagueness, of the rule over the arbitrary, of order over the haphazard."[2] City Ballet presented its audiences with many such victories, but its most audacious works argued that vagueness, the arbitrary, and the haphazard are all more persistent than Stravinsky suggests. Balanchine's dancers are shown in the struggle to subdue threats to their poise; the outcomes of these agons are often left unresolved.

One need only look at *Agon* (1957), another landmark work and one of the postwar era's most bracing Balanchine/Stravinsky collaborations, as an example. Its starting point may be the reassuring symmetries of seventeenth-century French court dancing, but its core is a contemporary landscape of violent encounters and separations—a vision of disequilibrium so unsparing that even when structure reasserts itself at the end, an unsentimental spectator won't trust it to last. The turbulence is nowhere more severe than in its celebrated pas de deux, a reimagining of ballet's fluid intimacy as a series of near collisions, off-balance tableaux, and whiplash turns freezing abruptly into deformed poses. This variety of grace makes one wince. A woman's head nearly brushes the floor during one plunge. She looks crucified, briefly, as she flattens herself against her partner's back. With no lack of tenderness, he handles her limbs possessively, lifting legs past the point they could move themselves, seeming to twist them out of their sockets. As originally cast, this frankly sexual duet held another element of risk: the man is black, the woman is white, a pairing that in 1957 may have pushed some audiences themselves off balance.

A spectator accustomed to the practices of American drama, especially as it was being codified in these decades by the Actors Studio (founded in 1947, a year before City Ballet's inaugural season) and other centers of the American Method, might expect an earnest psychological confrontation with all these dangers. Yet the deeper satisfaction of Balanchine's tightly coiled dances is in their coolness. There is no melodrama to the menace, no overt passion to the eros. To some observers, such as R. P. Blackmur, the landscape is barren: Balanchine's dancers, he complains, have "magnificent technique for expunging the psyche."[3] But to others this is the very source of their credibility — and of Balanchine's preeminence in American modernist performance. The critic Edwin Denby, an important figure in both dance and theater in these years, observes of *Agon* that "right after a climax, [there is] an inconsequence like the archness of high comedy."[4] The ballet may take its name from the competitions of Greek tragedians, but its own contemporary American conflicts deliberately lack tragic stature. Their outcomes are, if not irrelevant, provisional — one of many possible patterns in which any show of individual hubris or shame would limit the pertinence of the whole exercise. The qualities Denby singled out for praise in his other Balanchine reviews of the 1940s and 1950s — "irony in [the] tenderest pathos," "a certain dryness," "anonymity of style," "a simple statement" over "an emotional suggestion," and "disinterested" expression that "leaves the choreography unsoiled" — ensure that feeling, when it does emerge from fluid movement, will continue to move, reaching beyond personal situations to reflect the temperament of the age.[5]

The age was awkward. *Agon* is merely the most candid admission of a growing inability to fulfill old models of decorum and deportment. The resulting self-consciousness should be sensed every time Denby speaks of the "dignity" in other Balanchine works of these years (or every time Lincoln Kirstein, City Ballet's cofounder, speaks of their "courtesy" and "consideration").[6] Dignity, maintained by technique, may rein in actorly excess, but it also concedes the proximity of other, more humiliating forms of formlessness. The spectator who regards each highly patterned performance as a refuge from less shapely, less consoling reality has noticed only half the art. The dancers may offer themselves as "safeguards from streets outside swarming with chaos, anarchy, and despair," as Kirstein writes.[7] Yet the swarm isn't held at bay for long. Blackmur could have been replying to Kirstein when, in the same review of a City Ballet performance, he writes: "There is . . . no order which is complete . . . which does not invite, for its life, the constant and random supply of fresh disorder. Chaos is not what we must exclude; it is what we do not know, or ignore, of the behavior which . . . forms our lives."[8]

The critic is wrong to assume the choreographer himself ignores this. Balanchinian dignity isn't complacent. It pushes back against real foes — its opposite numbers that we call foolishness, lumpen idleness, a failure to stay alert.

Yet it also finds a way to accommodate them. Dancers embodying this idea of dignity remain firmly planted on the ground, often literally. A woman falls inelegantly in *Serenade* (1934). Another nearly tips over in *Symphony in C* (1947). (Her partner catches her just before the floor does). A man drags a woman to the wings in *The Four Temperaments*. In a later work, *Ivesiana* (1954), a group of men carry a ballerina as if she were an infirm animal or inanimate bundle, never allowing her to touch the ground—a mockery of ballet's typical floating world. We dispense with the ideal of weightlessness and instead register the effort it takes to keep her aloft. Balanchine further complicates the illusion of effortlessness in *Episodes* (1959), when his performers totter instead of glide on pointe, submit to partners who turn them unceremoniously upside down, and in one sequence, edge forward nervously in near darkness, like figures on a tightrope or window ledge, longing for terra firma. In an additional subversion of convention, Balanchine ensures that the beau ideal of partnering is most legible when it is violated. In some ballets, there is too much intimacy: two dancers in *Episodes* render themselves immobile after knotting their limbs together. In others, there is not enough. Paired dancers guard their individuality, pledge their support to one another on the verge of separation, cultivate outwardness (the principle of *en dehors* taken to an extreme) in order to prevent claustrophobic communion.[9]

In all these instances, audiences are present at an argument with stakes that transcend this particular art. In the literary theater, the debate between grace and ruin competes for attention with plots, characters, scenery, and language. The comparative starkness of Balanchine's work—especially the so-called black-and-white ballets, performed in practice clothes on bare stages—reveals a skeletal structure supporting the postwar culture as a whole. (In a much-quoted riposte to those who wanted more narrative intricacy and characterological interest from his work, Balanchine said, "there are no mothers-in-law in ballet.")[10] This theater's lack of cushioning itself suggests the bruising conclusion of every artist's flight toward fiction. We are always brought back to the brute certainties of performance as performance—this stage, these bodies, their physics indifferent to their personalities—and to the equally stark uncertainties of life outside the theater.

If we reread the very few lasting American dramas of the 1940s and 1950s after an encounter with Balanchine's modernism, the formal decisions that produced them, ordinarily effaced by their narratives, become as prominent and expressive as they are in the choreographer's art. In part, we simply grow attuned to basic questions every theater artist asks and answers. How has the playwright plotted the space (not just the action)? How large a surface will the figures be covering? How much room should separate them at any given moment? The answers to these and other technical questions can illuminate a network of affiliation — the dramatic equivalent of what Denby has in mind when he speaks of ballets that are "luminous in their spacing."[11] A performer's corporeal space is just as legible. To spectators in the habit of evaluating a dancer's deportment, an actor's surface, line, and volume will seem also to preoccupy the era's playwrights.

Yet more arresting than these aspects of a figure's (or a scene's) poise are the forces that threaten it. Spectators who moved to drama from dance in the New York of the 1940s and 1950s may have found themselves automatically reading plays as studies in motion. What was a habitual way of seeing to them can, if adopted by present-day spectators, reveal the kinetic complexity — the physics — of deceptively "natural" action. Narrative reversals and emotional tensions become reducible to gestural patterns, rhythmic changes, reconfigurations of the stage, and new dispositions of the figures. A stage picture that may at first seem inert, a reliable background, will itself appear vulnerable to change, its components delicately balanced against one another, its images sequenced in a scannable rhythm. The choreographer's most fundamental decision — when to have his performers move and when to have them stay put — can, if imagined as equally compelling to the playwright, reveal the essential, unifying strain in seemingly diverse psychological or social conditions.

In this regard, a recent discussion of American culture in the immediate postwar years is especially suggestive. Nicholas Jenkins develops the notion of "liquid modernity" — art seeking "a shape for shapelessness" in the brief, uncertain "hinge" period between 1945 and the start of the cold war. He points to the recurrence of oceanic imagery in much of the era's poetry, prose, and painting (his prime examples are Jackson Pollock, Robert Lowell, and Elizabeth Bishop) as evidence of a culturewide "confrontation with a formless, mutating social immensity," an attempt to represent in stable literary or visual form the lack of moral or psychological fixity, the experience of dissolution, and the sovereignty of chance.[12]

Performance isn't Jenkins's subject, but one can easily imagine theater in these same years exploiting its inherent changeability to reflect similar anxieties and desires. Three of the era's best plays stand in for the theater as a whole, finding emotional value in the different kinds of movement available in interior and exterior spaces. Stillness is debilitating to the restless inmates of *The Glass Menagerie* (1945) — a restlessness that, as Thomas Postlewait argues in his discussion of Tennessee Williams's "spatial order," fulfills "both a naturalistic and a choreographic function."[13] The characters in Arthur Miller's *Death of a Salesman* (1949) resist the humiliations of even closer, more immobilizing spaces — bodies and memories — by pursuing the self-forgetting available in travel, athletics, exploration, even wandering. Interiors serve as refuges from chaos in *In the Summer House* (1953), as Jane Bowles's title suggests, yet they also close off their occupants from the imaginative opportunities available only in flight. All three plays obey ideas of dramatic structure dependent on dissolution and of character dedicated to evasion. Protagonists fragment under the pressure of self-consciousness, sink beneath affectless surfaces, or foil would-be analysts with archness, self-mockery, and skepticism of the very sentiments to which they are susceptible. Even at their most candid, one senses a harassing force at their backs, pushing them toward the next speech and the next action. "The woods are burning!" Willy Loman says, impatient for an escape he doesn't know how to achieve.[14] "The cities swept about me like dead leaves," says Tom Wingfield in *The Glass Menagerie*. "I would have stopped, but I was pursued by something."[15] Molly in *In the Summer House* says, "I want to go out. . . . I'm going . . . I'm going out. . . . Let me go."[16]

Yet as these and other characters worry about what they may suffer if they root themselves in any single place, relationship, or even identity, they also calculate what they'll lose if they don't. Some characters believe that only in continuous change will they be less obvious targets for derision and exploitation. To others, the prize they seek — grace — is winnable only by recomposing a self designed according to someone else's plan. All manner of emotional and moral states — ambition, idealism, and newly aroused passion; or shame, self-doubt, impotence, and guilt — can be classified as forms of moving or standing still. (If they are, they may be described without the sentimentality that often clouds sympathetic analyses.) Equilibrium isn't just an abstract psychological ideal; it is an actual challenge to figures knocked off balance as soon as they come to rest. Collapse, too, isn't a figure of speech. What Matthew Roudané has noted about *Death of a Salesman,* that the play is rich in scenes of falling, is equally true of the other two plays.[17] All these protagonists drop out of social and family structures that no longer sustain them, or drop into identities they've long hoped to resist — the unwilled movement of those who dangerously slow down or pause over the courses they've charted.

It takes the subtlest writer on dance, Paul Valéry, to detect even more resonant meanings in any performing art's agon with stillness. In his dialogue "Dance and the Soul" (1921), a speaker imagines that audiences experience something sharper than mere satisfaction or disappointment at the end of a ballet. When a performer's exhilarating whirl of movement can be prolonged no longer, he says, a spectator can no longer evade "things as they are" inside or outside the theater.[18] To Valéry, this kind of forced attention to a constant object is unbearable — clinical when, to him, seeing should be agile and enchanting. The unwelcome "murderous lucidity" following a ballet's life-giving blur is a "state of pure disgust" (53). The observed is no luckier than the observer: "The universe cannot for one instant endure to be only what it is" (52). The dances we see, Valéry implies, reflect this impatience. Beneath their superficial narratives or geometric procedures lie more pressing motives for a dancer's actions. Self-aversion, dread of habit, boredom with precedent, or fear of being wholly known may prompt his or her sharp surprising changes. Performers stand in for any individual appalled at "being a thing," as Valéry puts it (57). Unlike us, they may regularly "burst into events" and thus relieve the embarrassment of objecthood (57). That eruption is the only visible scene in a long private drama of self-interrogation and self-judgment. Valéry deems the very attributes by which we ordinarily recognize individuality onstage as immobilizing and even corrupting. The performers he admires don't merely flee such a constricting idea of self: each "atones for its identity," Valéry writes, "by the number of its acts" (57).

The implications for theater are dizzying. Following Valéry, we might imagine that character, too, is something a dramatic figure is guilty of and must "atone for," if not renounce. In such a punitive context, penance takes the form of flight from psychology, from biography, and perhaps even from presence; renewed faith obligates one to continuous self-erasure. At the highly charged moments when the postwar American theater seems consciously to forge a relation between stillness and movement, or to confront its long unexamined assumptions about its liveness, it moves us, too, beyond the immobilizing concerns of a single character, or domestic scene, or social situation. (We can also move beyond the reputations that popularity has forced upon its most famous plays — another form of immobility.) The charismatic pathos of a typical Williams or Miller (or even Bowles) character may make it especially hard to imagine that their creators aim to explore anything other than emotion. One needn't ignore it. Narrative, psychological, and social contexts for analysis remain viable, but they are also the scenes of a more demanding pursuit of theater's outer limits, borders far from any story. These playwrights, working with the materials of character and plot, seem to contemplate the possibility of a never-achieved ideal of their temporal art — an identity with time, a permanent fluidity. As the characters indulge fantasies of grace, rail against inhibitions, indict families and other normative pressures as the cause of their suffocation, one can imagine a more generalized bending toward an idea of theater in which, at every moment, the appeal of change overwhelms that of consistency.

An idea, but not a reality: the theater's failure to subdue its inherent materialism can also be seen as a comment on narrative themes. When these plays (like all plays) fall into thingness even as they lift aloft on the energy of live performance, they can seem to dash their characters' own hopes for other, more limited forms of release. The protagonists of the most demanding postwar plays resemble currents as much as entities, their flow impeded by the very elements that make them visible. Decor, costume, other characters, the stage itself, and even an actor's own physicality become obstacles to flexible presence. Certain forms of speech are equally confining. We can hear, beneath the ostensible subject of any given conversation, characters speaking toward new forms of talk, seeking an arena for ampler expression. Finally, these plays implicitly reappraise the value of even more fundamental aspects of the playwright's craft. To idiosyncratic or merely self-questioning temperaments, publicness — a work of art's availability to viewers — can itself seem an immobilizing force. Williams, Miller, and Bowles all explore forms of privacy, recognizing in it a challenge to a culture of compromise, cheapened, midcult standards, and superficial charm.

They also look critically upon a play's writtenness. This attribute cannot be neutral when characters, like Tom Wingfield, find themselves literally within landscapes of words or, like Willy Loman, are acutely conscious of the efficacy of dialogue or, like Molly (and like the uncertain writer she sometimes resembles), gradually emerge from self-consciousness to force their way through blocks on the imagination. Style alone, inherited or original, is the most dangerous (because most alluring) impediment in these plays. Characters in the work of all three writers seek a manner that will organize and elevate mere instinct. Yet more often than not, they fear that their chosen forms of self-presentation will dull emotion and inhibit spontaneity. It's not hard to imagine the formal implications of their narratives. One can see in the characters each playwright's own anxiety over style, as he or she calculates what is gained and what is lost when technique mediates expression and when form imposes grace on often awkward and hesitant responsiveness. Here is a final connotation of this theater's oscillation toward and away from stability. Finished works of art, for all their elegance, risk deadness and entrapment by spectators' attention, whereas works-in-progress preserve their vitality in the artist's potential to retract or even wholly erase them. As we'll see, the postwar American playwrights' unresolved contemplation of the equally attractive rewards of art and non-art runs silently, but electrically, beneath the action of their best plays.

✶ ✶ ✶

In a brief encounter with a peripheral figure in American ballet culture, Tennessee Williams opens up new perspectives on his own theater's revision of kinetic grace. George Platt Lynes, who had been photographing Balanchine's work since the 1930s, had agreed to take Williams's portrait in 1944. Lynes made his name as a fashion photographer and was considered "somewhat chi-chi" (Williams's phrase), but here he satirizes his own reputation by depicting the playwright in a torn sweater, its unraveling sleeves and woundlike holes mocking the sitter's soulful expression. One imagines Williams, having put on the pretense of decorum visible in his face, straining against it until it tears elsewhere. (Lynes had already mischievously used the same sweater in a por-trait of Cecil Beaton, the era's avatar of immaculate style.) In a letter to his mother, Williams apologizes for the picture and promises others by Lynes that are more "respectable" and "elegant."[19] But of course this one is the more faithful representation of the futile attempts at style among the figures in his drama.

Lynes's photograph manages to be both sincere and funny, to hover between qualities that if allowed to dominate the portrait would diminish its subject. Readers of *The Glass Menagerie* will encounter a more elaborate form of this same theatrically valuable ambivalence. In his production notes to the play, Williams insists upon "the unimportance of the photographic in art" (395). Yet in a separate statement he attributes the "depth and significance" of a "completed work of art" to its "arrest of time."[20] In the notes, he calls *The Glass Menagerie* a contribution to the "new, plastic theater," his phrase an invitation to approach his work with a visual artist's sensitivity to surfaces, dimensions, and materials (395). Yet, a few lines earlier, he argues that life can be accurately represented only "through changing into other forms than those which were merely present in appearance" (395). On a more general level, he names "nostalgia" as "the first condition of the play" (397) — an inert state, in which one sinks into known experience — yet in an article taking stock of his career after the play's success, he writes, "security is a kind of death."[21]

The Glass Menagerie theatricalizes this clash of opposites with an almost overwhelming sensual complexity. As Williams imagines it, the mise-en-scène is an intricate assemblage of objects, images, and texts within which the play's animate presences can't assume they'll have first claim on our attention. The pleasure we take in surveying Williams's cabinet of wonders gives way to uneasiness whenever a character acknowledges the dull reality surrounding it, or when a magical object promising emotional release in fact only impedes real movement. This is the context for Jo Mielziner's original scene design: he imagined the stage as a collection of nested boxes — vitrines for display in a drama examining, among other things, the pathology of collecting. The Wing-field dining room, framed by a small proscenium arch, sits deep within the family apartment. The apartment is wedged inside a tenement. The tenement is hemmed in by streets running along its sides. The set as a whole is framed by the true proscenium, which is, of course, lodged within the theater building. C. W. E. Bigsby has a version of this architecture in mind as he describes Williams's dramaturgy of "enclosure," although he elsewhere concludes that the playwright is "hostile to an art of surfaces."[22] The opposite seems true. Williams draws attention to the surfaces of the set's innermost walls by asking designers to project upon them a changing display of photographs, among them a bouquet of blue roses, a winter landscape, a glamour magazine cover, a ship flying a pirate flag, a crescent moon, a girl greeting callers from her porch, and an office worker at his desk.[23] Each photograph is a material sign of a sentiment, memory, fantasy, or aspiration; together they discipline the circulation of emotions in a play that, to those seeking meaning only in the play's dialogue (or accepting uncritically Williams's description of the play's "nostalgia"), can seem impalpable. (One might see the entire environment—boxes within boxes holding charged objects and pictures—as Williams's homage to his friend of the 1940s, Joseph Cornell, who returned the gesture in a 1948 prose work entitled "A White Crested Cockatoo [for Blanche DuBois].")[24]

The projections also complement the setting's other highly worked surfaces. A wall mirror persistently beckons to the play's most self-conscious characters, then flattens and boxes their otherwise restless faces. A huge framed photograph of the Wingfield father, the only form in which he continues to influence his abandoned family, dominates another wall, lighting up whenever the animate characters allude to him. Still other elements of the design draw our attention to surfaces we may have taken for granted. Two gauze curtains hang between the actors and the audience at the play's opening—a double distancing that transforms the stage into a palimpsest. The first, a scrim that serves as the tenement's fourth wall, gives material density to ordinarily empty space. The second, a set of translucent portieres dividing the living room and dining room, will seem to have woven into its fabric the people behind it—a further flattening.

The most suggestive indication of Williams's drive toward plasticity is his handling of text. The handling is literal. Characters wield, fondle, or cling to printed matter throughout the play, sometimes showing an obsessiveness that diminishes the strangeness of Laura's attachment to her own magical objects. These encounters—print intimacies—are often unnoteworthy in themselves but gain significance as they accumulate. Filial sentiment, sexual energy, and more general anxieties cluster around a theater program from a high-school production of *The Pirates of Penzance;* a yearbook (*The Torch*); a newspaper that Tom reads, emblazoned with the headline "FRANCO TRIUMPHS"; another newspaper Amanda spreads on the fire escape and sits on; a third, *The Post*

Dispatch, that Jim uses to catch the wax dripping from a candelabra. (Emulating the Wingfield tropism toward print, he had earlier glanced through the sports section.) Williams underscores the importance of these objects by shadowing them with several unseen texts, props in offstage dramas that compress a character's ambition or humiliation to a single scene of reading. Laura learns of Jim's engagement in the Personals section. Tom's abstract longing for change turns concrete when he gets a letter from the Merchant Marine. Amanda rails at Tom's "immorality" on catching him reading D. H. Lawrence. She concedes her own hopes for imaginative fulfillment, along with romantic and familial satisfaction, as she peddles *The Homemaker's Companion* and Bessie Mae Hopper's novel *Honeymoon for Three* — the titles alone promise relief from loneliness. The entire Wingfield family finally acknowledges the permanence of the father's absence on reading a postcard consisting of only two words: "Hello! Goodbye!"

Williams casts his spectators as readers, too. Further breaking down the divisions among literary, dramatic, and visual arts, he projects touchstone lines of dialogue on the set's walls, anticipating their utterance later in the scene. Actors seem to have been cued by the projected text. (Might they even appear to join us in reading it before speaking?) The charged question "What have you done since high school?" hangs, literally, in the air before Jim finally asks it (452–53). "Not Jim!" reads another projection, the disbelief it expresses an environmental force, something rippling through the space and briefly shared by all until Laura claims it as her own (435). When Amanda says "things have a way of turning out so badly" moments after we've seen a projected version of the line, her self-pity sounds especially self-dramatizing, unoriginal, or simply camp (463). As these and other fragments of script become decor, they stand out as additional precious objects on a fetishizing stage, luminous with the collector's pride in their presence. They further affirm the play's writtenness, its reality as arranged words rather than mere feelings, the playwright's crafted pages rather than the character's spontaneous speech. (One imagines Williams, having earlier plucked these sentences from his work-in-progress for special attention, now proudly unveiling them after revision is complete.)

How far this procedure takes us from Williams's writing persona — the open fountain of sincere lyric sentiment memorialized in a story, "The Important Thing," published the same year as *The Glass Menagerie*'s Broadway premiere. "I think the main thing is just expressing yourself as honestly as you can," says a would-be writer. "I am not interested in style. . . . I'd rather just scramble through one thing and then rush into another, until I have said everything I have to say!"[25] No "scrambling" among the characters and the writer of *The Glass Menagerie*. They are slowed, if not stopped, by a word's all too palpable appearance. "Style" is a check on "honesty." A truer indication of Williams's attitude toward craft appears in his *Notebooks*. "A sombre play has to be very spare and angular," he writes in 1942. "You must keep the lines sharp and clean — tragedy is austere."[26] The projected lines of dialogue in *The Glass Menagerie* allow us to imagine the "sharp and clean" contours of the play as a whole. Regardless of the credibility of individual performers or the pathos of particular turns in the narrative, the play's dominant drama occurs at the scene of its fabrication.

In production, the writer's deliberate engagement with his creation is explicit. Tom, Williams's surrogate, may want us to believe that the play is "sentimental" and "not realistic" (as he says in his opening speech), but about writing, at least, it is cold (400). On the Wingfield dining-room table is "an upright typewriter and a wild disarray of manuscripts," suggestive only of the unromantic trial-and-error successfully obscured by every other onstage text (413). The set as a whole is marked by the processes of writing; at times it can even seem like a writing machine. On one wall hangs a diagram of a keyboard; on another a chart of the Gregg shorthand alphabet; and at one point a projected slide depicts "a swarm of typewriters" (406–7). Laura's brief enrollment in a secretarial training program explains the presence of all these objects and images, but their more lasting significance has nothing to do with plot. The idea of writing they communicate — impersonal, automated, dependent on skills of inscription and manipulation more than imagination — further disabuses those expecting artless self-revelation from Williams's own typing. ("Maybe I am a machine," writes Williams in his *Memoirs,* "a typist.")[27] The play's obvious autobiographical sources shouldn't distract us from the spectacle of their mediation — the graphic process, another screen, acknowledged in the very word "autobiography." Narrative and dramatic structures, literary and theatrical conventions, oral and gestural languages — everything that grants presence to a character — interest Williams as much as character itself.

No less attractive are the limits on presence. On a stage easily mistaken for a page, both the oppressiveness of the plot's historical moment and the doubtful freedom of individuals to shape histories of their own are reducible to questions of reading and writing. The 1930s, Tom says, were a decade when the middle classes had "their fingers pressed forcibly down on the fiery Braille alphabet of a dissolving economy" (400). When, near the end, Tom prepares to escape the conditions of such coerced reading and declares himself ready to embark on an as yet unwritten future, "the incandescent marquees and signs of the first-run movie houses light his face" (440). It is a demonstration of a fundamental premise: writing literally enables us to see character. Is Tom already imprinted with the city's text, its illuminated manuscript all that, as yet, illuminates him? (Williams presents an even more explicit version of character-as-text in *Suddenly Last Summer* [1958]: the never-seen Sebastian Venable, a writer himself, exists only as a function of other people's narratives.)

The other arts are also prominent on Williams's stage. The playwright may recount his family history in *The Glass Menagerie* and show how it incubated his writerly self, but to detached spectators his play can more fruitfully be seen as a consideration of aesthetic processes. How does an artist in any discipline shape experience? How do such procedures condition our responses? Williams dramatizes a range of romances with and betrayals by art. The needs aroused by culture are, for one character, childlike; for another, erotic; for a third, egotistical. All the characters seem most comfortably themselves in the roles of fan, connoisseur, spectator, marketer, hobbyist, or student of the arts.

Williams surrounds them with the souvenirs of the artist's labor. As these relics shore up their possessor's stage presence (sometimes literally), we are reminded that naturalness, grace, or simple credibility, when they exist, are the result of the conscious manipulation of form. A shower of movie ticket stubs falls around Tom's feet when he empties his pockets, becoming ground to his figure. Stacks of Mr. Wingfield's LP records lie around the house as a "painful reminder" of their absentee owner: they, as much as the more obviously representational photograph, *are* him (409). (Laura, for her part, seems to recover her own sense of self when, at her most anxious, she winds up the Victrola.) The nearby Paradise Dance Hall tempts characters toward a third rival art. When Jim asks Laura to waltz, they move toward versions of themselves that dialogue denies them.

The Gentleman Caller is an ambassador from several other media as well. He promotes public speaking; he studies radio engineering; and he is a true believer in the future of television. Against these last two agents of modernity, the on-stage emblems of older, simpler arts seem especially humble. The Victrola records are "worn-out" (409). Photography, as represented by the father's huge portrait and the school yearbook, confirms the ordinariness of its subjects and thus seems quaint. Tom's "upright typewriter" looks antique, one step away from the printing press. Visual art exists only in the form of its poor relation, the glass menagerie. Theater, dwindling to a high-school program, is amateurish. Taken together, these arts can neither embody true style nor confer lasting dignity in a milieu mined with devices to mock, diminish, or distort its residents. Here even the most vital modernist art, film, is compromised by nostalgia or by the dubious motives of its spectators. Tom seems to hope less for aesthetic than sexual pleasure in darkened cinemas. ("You go to the movies *entirely* too *much!*" says Amanda [421].) Additional projections — silent-film-style intertitles that supplement both the spoken and projected dialogue—turn the characters' efforts at sincere emotion into melodrama. "Ah!" reads one title (443). Another shatters what might have been a convincing scene with the word "Terror!" (443). No organic feeling or sprawling experience is exempt from media's co-opting reach. Whatever frightening history isn't simplified in the newspaper headlines is condensed and repackaged in the newsreels Tom watches. The Gentleman Caller arrives among Laura's menagerie first in miniaturized and mediated form himself: his yearbook photograph has aroused such nervous excitement that Laura is immobilized when she finally reunites with the real, lively, and life-sized person. In all these instances, Williams stresses the mechanisms producing strong emotion. The implicitly present projector and camera, along with the visible typewriter and Victrola, populate a world where technology is always insinuating itself between characters and immediate experience. No wonder the Wingfield father, employed by the telephone company, "fell in love with long distances," not with another person (401).

One might expect Williams to elevate his own performance over the deferrals and interruptions of other, technology-dependent arts. His most surprising achievement is to refrain from doing so. He conducts a withering, if largely implicit, critique of his medium, indicting it for an inability to sustain illusion, reflect the flux of real life, and gratify the imaginative longings of both playwright and spectator. This depiction of failure is far more compelling than its diminished reflection in the Wingfields' own haplessness. Any pity they stimulate as they leap from and fall back to the suffocating mundane won't reach full strength until we extend it to the artist who remains faithful to an even more insidiously constricting form. The play's many images or gestures of deliberate destruction—Tom smashing a drinking glass, breaking one of Laura's animals, and overturning a chair in his inadequate dining-room study; Amanda tearing the typing and shorthand charts in two—stand in for renunciations Williams himself can't make against an art that betrays its promise. Yet while he stops short of openly venting his frustrations with the theater, he does relentlessly point out where it's vulnerable to attack. Long before Williams superimposes himself on Laura as she blows out the candles on her pathetic stage—another, final destructive gesture—he concedes the perishability of his own representations.

Amanda bears the burden of Williams's skepticism, if not openly embarrassed antitheatricalism, at its most overt. The arbiter of style, she indulges every melodramatic habit and turns even small talk into an occasion for ritual self-sacrifice. Her most lachrymose turn—an ode to her own gentlemen callers—is sarcastically stage-managed by Tom, who mimes carrying a prompt-book and nods cues to the booth. Amanda's staging of Jim's visit, only the most elaborate fiasco among many implausible spectacles, sets an unwelcome standard for measuring any dramatic achievement. The lighting is now diffuse, "lemony." No more authentic are the chintz slipcovers over the shabby upholstery. Laura herself has become a character in Amanda's drama, "not actual, not lasting" (as a stage direction puts it) — fair description of any theatrical presence (433). As Amanda stuffs "gay deceivers" into Laura's brassiere just before Jim's arrival, the lively mendacity of all performance is unignorable, even laughable.

Each of these attempts at seduction is a judgment on Williams's own charm. How far, he seems to ask, has his own performance fallen short of its original, ideal conception? Are his own illusions persuasive enough, durable enough, to survive a viewer's doubt? His verdict is harsh. No sooner does a character or scene set a tone than Williams undercuts it. To keep us from surrendering to the poignancy of Jim's and Laura's colloquy, Williams scores it with Amanda's coarse laughter: it spills out from the kitchen, where she is holed up with Tom, and transforms her into our fellow spectator, one less credulous and sentimental than we might be. Amanda suffers a correction to her own romanticism when she tries to turn the fire escape into a "Mississippi veranda" — Williams describes her sitting next to Tom "demurely, as if she were settling into a swing" — and coyly asks, "Is there a moon this evening?" Tom's dry reply — "It's rising over Garfinkel's Delicatessen" — returns her, and us, to the real, pedestrian landscape (425). He pulls us back from religious romance just as effectively when, on hearing the nearby church bells, he rattles a noisemaker in secular antiphony. Williams seems to debunk his own faith in his chosen style — "the play is memory," as Tom says — when in a later and unrelated context Tom suggests that he is only "valuable to [Jim] as someone who could remember his former glory" (432). Is all memory, even Williams's, equally corrupted by vanity?

A pair of early, rejected titles for *The Glass Menagerie* best expresses the contrapuntal style informing Williams's dramaturgy. In a letter to Donald Windham, the playwright says that he can't decide whether to call his work-in-progress "The Human Tragedy" or "The Not so Beautiful People."[28] The grandiosity of the first title elicits a corrective in the cattiness of the second. They serve the play best as a diptych: if we bear in mind both titles at once, we can sense how the play wavers perpetually between sincerity and sarcasm. We can also recognize our own ambivalence. Following the playwright's example, we, too, alternate between empathy and laughter before any given scene. (One is reminded of the perhaps apocryphal story of Williams cackling during rehearsals of the final "solemn" scene in *A Streetcar Named Desire,* as Blanche is taken to the asylum.) In *The Glass Menagerie,* the reverent and irreverent attitudes temper rather than cancel one another, preventing the inertia of a single emotion and stopping us from sinking irretrievably into his narrative. They also remind us that Williams's main concern is aesthetic. The competing responses illuminate the gulf between playwright and play, a space in which Williams tries out different, equally plausible points of view on his subject. If we wish, we can follow that drama — the artist's search for a mode — as much as the Wingfields' own experiments in self-presentation. (Williams's interest in style as the substance, not just the veneer, of a work of art seems confirmed when we remember that the French translator of *A Streetcar Named Desire* was Jean Cocteau. Is this the same quality Lincoln Kirstein had in mind when he called Williams "more mannerist than tragic"?)[29]

Now, decades after *The Glass Menagerie*'s premiere, when the play has settled into a tone of "yearning," it is easy to overlook other, even stronger causes of its permanent unsteadiness. Readers seduced by the playwright's lyricism may forget what spectators cannot — that the Tom who narrates and enacts the action is many years older than the Tom represented in it. The former is a middle-aged man thrust back into an infantilizing family drama. Of course, the conventions of the memory play justify such a gap between teller and tale, but Williams exploits its potential for defamiliarization, awkwardness, and even deflating comedy. Audiences at the first production would have encountered an actor (Eddie Dowling) who was fifty years old, balding, his face lined and body less than virile — a heavy obstacle to credibility. He would have been a freakish, disruptive presence: when he was onstage, everything must have seemed off, perhaps nowhere more so than in his scenes with Amanda, the actress looking to be his near contemporary, tipping between the maternal and the uncomfortably erotic. (Her son, now much older than "the very handsome young man" in Mr. Wingfield's photograph, has assumed the place of her husband.) Williams did complain in letters that Dowling was older than he expected, but such a strain on decorum is theatrically valuable in a play candid about its fears of inadequacy. We witness the enthralling spectacle of an artist risking loss of control over his art.

He risks it again, and one might think recklessly, in his handling of the title objects. The glass menagerie is kitsch, artifacts of "vicarious experience and faked sensations," as Clement Greenberg memorably defined the category in 1939.[30] Such falsehood should be anathema to a playwright who once said that his only criterion for artistic value was "truthful intensity of feeling."[31] Yet "feeling," of course, is kitsch's deepest source — imitative, diluted feeling, or feeling recognized only by effects that blind us to less sensational causes. As Laura worries over the fate of her too-symbolic bric-a-brac, Williams worries over his play. A vessel of private meanings and emotions, the play, too, could fall—into obviousness, banality, even vulgarity. Williams confronts such a danger openly. *The Glass Menagerie* is remarkable for absorbing the very excess it dreads, embedding an image of the art that, at any moment, it could become. (It is as if the playwright were inoculating himself with a strain of aesthetics he fears catching.) Here, as with the other tensions produced by Williams's contrapuntal dramaturgy, theatricality occurs at the scene of Williams's resistance to his own impulses. The menagerie is always visible, a warning or taunting presence. A subtle production allows us to imagine the parallel drama of a playwright trying to heed the figurines' warning. He shows himself to be dependent on but taking distance from a fellow artist, a repellant doppelganger—the menagerie's own absent maker. The agon suggests another kind of memory play. For all its grace and polish, *The Glass Menagerie* is always recalling Williams not only to his youth but also to his play's own past as a work-in-progress—to a draft that struck the playwright while he was working on it as "nauseous" and "sentimental" (as he writes in his letters and notebooks), lacking the "astringent quality" he admires in another writer's prose, his own excesses cautioning him to "work within my limits."[32]

Hermann Broch, in a lecture from 1950, imagines an anxious art that "always moves along a razor's edge" between authenticity and kitsch.[33] Broch's meditations, here and in a 1933 essay, suggest a further reason why Williams refrained from simply avoiding the cheap aesthetics of the menagerie. All kitsch, Broch argues, "soothes nostalgia," and nostalgia is "just another way of entering a sphere that already belongs to kitsch's sphere of influence."[34] By setting a play explicitly pledged to nostalgia (its "first condition") within kitsch's "sphere of influence," Williams enables us to think critically about its appeals—even as we respond to them. He also enhances the symbolic value of the play's environment and forms of movement. Broch thinks of kitsch spatially and kinetically: it is a "finite system," he writes, that prevents artists from "mov[ing] relentlessly forward . . . from one discovery to the next" toward an "unattainable goal"—he calls it "truth"—"suspended in infinity and at an infinite distance" (61–62).

These phrasings invite us to imagine metatheatrical implications in the Wingfields' own surrender or resistance to confinement. Even though Laura's vow of stillness has a forceful defender in Jim—the high-school star athlete, himself "always at the point of defeating the laws of gravity," admires her for having the courage to "just stay here" when others "walk all over the earth"— it is the prelude to humiliation for Laura and every other Wingfield (432, 457). Usually she can't answer the door, or lies prone on the couch. Her sole movement, roaming parks when she should be at school, is circular and pointless and also ends in shame. After Tom makes the mistake of leaving the fire escape for the living room, and then further entrapping himself by sitting down, his mother infantilizes him by brushing down his cowlick. Amanda dwindles to her true size whenever she can't keep a conversation moving along — moving *her* along — on her own terms. A lapsed subscriber hangs up on her, or she fails to steer intimate discussion away from a genuine confession, and we see self-deception collapse in the ensuing silence. (Her confession that she loved her husband comes when she herself has sat down — one of the few times she's not fluttering about the apartment.)

Williams points to the larger significance of all these stoppages when, in his opening stage directions, he speaks of the loss of (or unthinking resistance to) social "fluidity" among an "enslaved section of American society" (399). C. W. E. Bigsby, for his part, recognizes the metaphysical dimensions of this tendency: Williams's characters try to "negotiate a temporary reprieve from the progress of history and time."[35] Yet one can also find a personal, formalist meaning in the play's choreography. Williams depicts individual and social confinement in order to confront (and help us confront) the theater's resigned acceptance of its frame. The frame is figurative as much as literal; the passivity afflicts artists working in nonrepresentational and representational styles alike. Qualities that Williams's typical reader may think of as desirable (and for which Williams is usually praised) — lyricism, compositional grace, openness, "poignant" moments — are themselves forms of inertia. A more complex Williams emerges if we imagine him fleeing the sources of his writerly strength. It's pertinent that Broch opposes "beauty" to "truth," implying that the former is another "finite" system uncomfortably close to kitsch: it limits its votaries to the creation of "sensations" (61). Does *The Glass Menagerie* warn Williams away from not just kitschy art but all art, its own "security" a "kind of death"?

In the penultimate scene, Tom famously complains that movies are no substitute for "moving" (440). It's left to us to imagine the verdict on plays. Williams implies that theater will attain its Platonic ideal not by embracing a "new" style, much less by presenting new stories, but by never relaxing its resistance to stable form. Protagonist and playwright alike hope "to find in motion what was lost in space" (465). *This* space, the space of the stage (not merely of the apartment, city, or historical moment), a vitrine for objects, images, furniture, other people — everything that displaces the more valuable prize of ephemerality. The dining-room proscenium frames this aesthetic argument forcefully: it can be seen as a concrete image of Broch's finitude — theater as an agent of control rather than spontaneity or release. It marks limits rather than opens onto vistas; it grounds, crushes, and shrinks the figures that other arenas might have flattered. It's fitting that here, around the table on the dining-room stage, Amanda insists that "Christian adults" should have nothing to do with "instinct," and complains of the "filth" and "diseased mind" of Tom's beloved modernist novelists (412, 421). Does this spatial context imply that theater's limits are antithetical to modernism's freedom? When, after one argument with his mother, Tom "tears [open] the portieres" hanging like stage curtains between dining and living rooms, it's the most overt attempt to protest the sensory repression and mental stultification fostered by an art of closed form (413).

We can leave *The Glass Menagerie* with a souvenir of its unresolved formal anxiety by linking together all the scenes in which its characters try, often clumsily, to leave it themselves. Early in the play, an enraged Tom grabs his coat and heads for the door, but he can't get his arm through one sleeve. "For a moment," writes Williams in a stage direction, "he is pinioned by the bulky garment" until he "split[s] the shoulder of it" (415). In another scene, when he is running late for work, he tries to put on his coat with more grace: Williams tempers any satisfaction in his success by noting, again, that the coat is "ugly and bulky" (422). Laura looks foolish in her own coat when she prepares to run an errand for her mother. The coat, originally Amanda's, is "inaccurately made-over, the sleeves too short" for her (418). Here, too, the actor holds still, briefly, after putting on the coat and before moving. "Go now or just don't go at all!" Amanda shouts, when Laura delays her exit by talking to Tom (418). She slips and falls on her way out — no surprise when one is costumed for humiliation. At the prolonged moments of all these exits, the play as a whole is suspended between the fantasy of unimpeded motion and the dreaded possibility of permanent stasis (to recall Thomas Postlewait's terms) — or between an ideal and a failed theater. On a stage of nested boxes, here is the most intimate — an especially smothering milieu.

We have come full circle, back to George Platt Lynes, who showed his own awareness of clothing's disruptive power when he photographed Williams in a ripped sweater. We also return to Paul Valéry, who in describing a dancer's fall helps us make the leap to the genre implications in Laura and Tom's own stumbles. Dancing, as Valéry describes it, owes its allure to the ever-present possibility that it will fail or, simply, end. "We never see her but about to fall," says Socrates in "Dance and the Soul" (58). Phaedrus says, "she seemed sometimes to be hovering on the brink of ineffable catastrophes!" (47). The dancer herself, on recovering from her fall, may treat motion as a "refuge" — "I was in thee, O movement — outside all things" — but the logic of any spectacle, theatrical as much as choreographic, in fact doesn't allow its performers to be so complacent (62). They are always tipping toward objecthood before righting themselves with gesture, nourished by their anxiety about whether or not they can replenish the energy they spend in full at every moment. Valéry calls such performers "divine in the Unstable" — the best description of theater's delicate balance between excessive life and deadly restraint (58).

Williams pledges faith in the same divinity. *The Glass Menagerie* is also a study of "hovering on the brink." An imaginative production would stress the play's many variations of falling or near-falling: Tom staggering drunk down the alley and dropping his keys; Amanda dropping her hat and gloves, then "sinking" into the sofa when she learns that Laura quit school; Laura herself, continuously described as swaying, stumbling, catching hold of chairs when she's most distraught; and of course the glass unicorn's inevitable fall. When the lights go out during Jim's visit, everyone is at risk: "Be careful you don't bump into something," says Amanda. "We don't want our gentleman caller to break his neck" (445). What is Jim's emphasis on "social poise" but an admission that he dreads its opposite (439)? In such an incurably gravitational world, it's only fitting that after Jim discloses his upcoming engagement, the projected legend reads "The Sky Falls" (462).

With it comes another fall, of unsustainable fantasies and immaterial hopes, and the reappearance of the dense, dull, weighted reality — Valéry's "things as they are." The transparent, near-invisible figurine acquires real presence only when broken into pieces. Williams underscores the gestures by which Laura puts the unicorn "in the palm of [Jim's] hand, then pushes his fingers closed upon it"(460): what was a symbol is now a tangible thing. So, too, the playwright's own precious possessions. The ideal forms of expression he cherished when planning the play "fall" into ordinary words on the page — something the many textual surfaces of a production won't let us forget. With the curtain's fall, audiences are left in the same situation as their onstage surrogates. No longer needing to suspend disbelief, we, too, collapse into visibility. Only by moving ourselves — leaving the theater as Tom leaves the fire escape — and continuing to move in our daily lives can we recover the anonymity and unselfconsciousness we enjoyed during the production, when our presence was merely theoretical, the actors looking through us as we, and they, looked through the glass menagerie, the two scrims, and the stage's other transparent and necessary falsehoods.

Readers attentive to the clothes in *The Glass Menagerie* — especially to their ability to cause literal and figurative falls — will find that they speak as meaningfully in *Death of a Salesman*. Arthur Miller shares more than his fashion sense with Williams. The two writers also amplify one another's meditations on shame, failure, claustrophobia, and the friction between public image and private self. But all these matters find their most concise expression in the garments Miller's characters wear, wish they still wore, plan to wear one day, or brandish as substitutes for statements they cannot make in other languages. We might reasonably fear that we risk trivializing the play by focusing on a single, pedestrian element of production. The risk is worth incurring, if by doing so we avoid the no less regrettable fate of valuing only the metaphysical or ideological significance of its action. As Williams does in *The Glass Menagerie,* Miller devotes considerable attention to the material goods on display in *Death of a Salesman* (a fitting choice in a play set against a background of commerce) so that we, too, will seek meaning on its surfaces.

Miller was born speaking the language of fashion. His father, uncles, and grandparents all made coats for a living. In his autobiography, he describes how his father arrived in New York from Poland at age six and almost immediately took his seat in the family's two-room apartment furnished with numerous sewing machines.[36] The demands of such work, Miller implies, stitched the family together as well. A more modest, and less optimistic, scene of sewing lies at the heart of *Death of a Salesman.* Decades of theatrical production have invested Linda's torn silk stockings with especially high value. When contrasted with the new pair that Willy gives his mistress, they concentrate in a single image the play's many forms of humiliation, mendacity, and self-deception. Yet as Linda sits mending her pair, she prepares us to see how other characters grapple no less literally with the fate their own clothes impose on them. For them, getting dressed and undressed is an encounter with resistant antagonists, a reckless surrender to fantasy, or more rarely, an opportunity for candid self-appraisal. "Do I — I look all right?" Willy asks the waiter who helps him up and brushes him off after he falls down in a saloon (121). At one time or another, almost every character in the play silently asks himself or herself the same question.

Clothing — or more precisely, clothing's symbolic meaning — is particularly oppressive to Willy's eldest son, Biff, whom Willy would fashion as his successor. Biff's history, as he and others tell it, has been one of straining against a steadily narrowing future by constantly changing or even discarding clothes. He owes his teenage identity to the football pants, shoulder pads, and gold helmet that Happy carries onstage in one scene — brother as devoted valet. He anticipates college glory by stenciling a pair of sneakers with the words "University of Virginia." (When he doesn't get in, he burns them.) Soon thereafter, we're told, his self-hatred, blurring with hatred of his adulterous father, peaks when he steals a suit in Kansas City and spends three months in jail. When we meet him, he is hoping to redeem himself with a decent job and submits to tutorials on dressing for success. Wear a business suit, his father insists, not a sports jacket and slacks; Happy agrees to help his brother buy a new tie and a smart striped shirt. Yet it's obvious from the start, to those versed in the play's fashion system, that Biff won't find fulfillment in such a workaday world even if it did welcome him. "To suffer fifty weeks of the year," he says in an early conversation with Happy, "when all you really desire is to be outdoors, with your shirt off" (22). (Happy admits a similar desire when he fantasizes about "rip[ping] my clothes off in the middle of the store" where he himself works [24].)

All this attention to appearance has an obvious narrative justification. Miller's protagonists must maintain the decorum necessary to the salesman's appeal — or as Willy's neighbor Charley says, "you get yourself a couple of spots on your hat, and you're finished" (138). Yet that reason doesn't dispel the strangeness of Miller's clothing fixation. Deeper than the characters' professional or social aspirations lie private, prerational sources of anxiety. The link, in Biff's biography, between his theft of a suit and his imprisonment is only the most extreme expression of a logic informing the whole play — that one can be punished for what one wears; that getting dressed is the first, deceptively innocuous act determining future scenes of self-abasement. "Where are the rest of your pants?" says Willy, laughing, when Charley appears in knickers (51). The jab reminds us that mere presence, whatever its quality, risks foolishness, and that other people's attentions — even the respectful tributes that might have answered Linda's famous demand that "attention must be paid!" — more often than not strip away the comforts of self-regard.

Literal stripping is the other side of Miller's costume drama. Perhaps Charley's embarrassment on exposing his calves prompts him to teach Willy how fleeting is the glory owed to style. He tells his friend that even J. P. Morgan wouldn't be able to stave off degradation without "his pockets on." When the banker strips down in a Turkish bath, he looks "like a butcher" (97). The unnerving image of the nude plutocrat echoes that of the shirtless Loman brothers and is one of the many instances when Miller invites us to envision "inappropriate" forms of visibility. Minutes after the curtain rises, Willy exposes his feet. (Linda had taken his shoes off for him.) He urges an even closer look by complaining about his "goddam arch supports" (13). The prominence of his unshod flat feet can, if we linger over them, control the sentiments indulged throughout the scene (and the play as a whole). Nothing can be noble or even decorous in their company. Willy for a moment *is* his feet — just as Charley will later be reduced to his calves and Linda to the legs inadequately sheathed in her torn stockings.

Miller's attraction to the synecdoche controls his treatment of all characters, palpable and impalpable. When Ben, Willy's cocksure brother, invites his nephews to punch him in the stomach, all his bravura concentrates in that impressively hard target. Willy's father is also a sign: the only thing his son remembers about him is a "big beard" (48). Likewise, Howard's wife and children are present only as voices on his tape recorder. Finally, at Willy's grave, Linda pays tribute to her husband's reliability and resourcefulness by declaring "he was so wonderful with his hands" (138). Mere hearsay, it unsuccessfully counters an earlier, enacted moment when Willy's hands can't help him: he "dumbly fumbles for Biff's face" (reads a stage direction) as Biff breaks down, the father unable to grab hold of a new, truer image of his long-idealized son (133). Willy, here, is no better than the "disgusting" men (as he calls them) who "can't handle tools" (44). In this context, a hackneyed line — "his life is in your hands," Linda tells Biff — acquires new power (60).

Miller's anatomizing approach to character peaks when Linda appears out-doors carrying a basket of laundry. If we can assume that she next hangs her family's pants, shirts, underwear, and socks on a clothesline, the sequence disassembles the Lomans' carefully worked-up personae. Each character's cha-risma, chutzpah, or compassion falls apart and hangs inert, in ordinary pieces. The potential for embarrassment is there for dry-eyed directors to exploit. The sorry sight of "private" clothes exposed to public view advances a dramaturgi-cal strategy that earlier gave us the salesman's arch supports and later will show us Willy in his hotel room hastily buttoning his shirt over his paunch while his mistress worries about being kicked out in nothing but a black slip. "But my clothes, I can't go out naked in the hall!" she protests — a line that captures, in whiny form, every other character's anxiety about being looked at, "caught," in anything other than a socially approved carapace (119).

Whenever Miller dismantles his characters' poise, or prolongs the moments before they reassert it after a shock, he purposefully threatens the poise of his drama as a whole. His fondness for synecdoches alone seems an unwittingly self-subverting, and funny, comment on a claim he made in the preface to a later play — that "a drama rises in stature . . . [and] gains its weight as it deals with . . . the whole man."[37] In his performed ambivalence, Miller resembles the Williams who tempts fate by contaminating *The Glass Menagerie* with kitsch. Just as Williams seems aroused by the challenge to bring his play right up to the brink of spurious sentiment, so, too, does Miller edge toward the outer limits of his own premises. He can be imagined as testing various strengths of embarrassment: how severely can "attention . . . be paid" upon a stage figure before a spectator's interest turns clinical or falls away entirely, replaced by his or her own embarrassment? Are there dramaturgical conditions under which an actor fails to transcend the brute reality of his or her presence to participate in a character's narrative or discourse? Are we, too, stuck at a fundamental premise of performance, unable to get beyond the first sensation of alarm in any act of seeing (look at that!) to relax into the compassion and empathy Miller encourages elsewhere in the play? If we join Miller in dwelling on these questions, *Death of a Salesman* can be read and played as a meditation not only on modernity's degradation of its inflexible protagonist but also on an equally debasing theater culture.

Miller finds some answers to his questions after he puts all his characters into pajamas. They domesticate Biff's and Happy's reportedly caddish sexuality: would "Adonises" (Willy's term for his sons) wear them? Everything that is grindingly ordinary in Willy's life looms large when Linda says, "your pajamas are hanging in the bathroom!" (66). Charley wears them, too, having left his bed to check on Willy, then staying to play cards. It's worth pausing over the weirdness of that event — a character going outside to visit a neighbor in a state rarely shown beyond one's own domestic borders — and of the costuming logic in general. How can "tragic" pathos gather around such homely figures? The incongruity can't be resolved by citing Miller's famous essay "Tragedy and the Common Man," published soon after *Death of a Salesman* opened on Broadway. His stage, populated by people padding around in slippers and wrapping robes around their uncorseted, unshaped frames, begins to look more eccentric than "common," more absurd than "tragic" — a hospital ward or nursing home or, at the other extreme, a children's slumber party. The vulnerability one associates with such places always verges on the unseemly — and so, too, do Miller's figures when looking their shabbiest and least defended in this antiheroic regalia.

At times, they go beyond verging. It's customary to see in *Death of a Salesman* aspirations to the bodilessness of a memory play — Miller has suggested that all the subsidiary characters are projections of Willy's imagination — yet those same characters, following the example of the title itself, are forever stressing biological processes, bodily functions, and physical imperfections. The Lomans sweat: "Don't perspire too much," Linda says to Biff before his job interview (76). They smell: "I can't get over the shaving lotion in this house!" she twice remarks (15, 71). They get dirty: "Did you pack fresh underwear?" (87). They have sex: an unsentimental Happy tallies the women he has "ruined" (25). They age: Biff regrets that his mother's hair has turned grey, and Willy checks to be sure he has his glasses. They change shape: "I'm losing weight, you notice, Pop?" Happy says, repeating himself two more times without winning Willy's attention (29, 33, 50). Linda is the most eager to talk about the subjects that decorum forbids, yet when it comes to her own body, she directs our attention with gesture alone. As she manipulates the sexualized stockings, spectators may recall the long, mildly disreputable tradition of paintings and photographs depicting women putting on or taking off their own stockings. Anne Hollander, in *Seeing Through Clothes,* teaches us how to read them. In a passage on eighteenth-century French and English painting, she writes, "The motif of the seated woman viewed from the front, leaning forward over prominently crossed legs, makes the most of calves and ankles, of promising suggestions of inner thigh, and of further delights adumbrated beyond them."[38] As adapted in *Death of a Salesman,* the motif usefully unsettles Linda's dowdy and long-suffering demeanor.

Her husband shows no such coyness in assessing his own sex appeal: "I'm fat," he says. "I'm very—foolish to look at" (37). The simplicity of Willy's admission is as startling as its honesty—and saves it from self-pity. The line's formal restraint also recalls us to the larger subject that all these separate scenes are meant to illuminate—the value of form itself. The general postwar instability that, in 1945, made Amanda Wingfield's digressions on presentability and Jim O'Connor's on poise as much cultural as psychological expressions of anxiety is, if anything, more acute four years later, when V-Day euphoria has worn off. The era's indeterminacy may be what prompted Miller to consider calling *Death of a Salesman* "A Period of Grace," as if he imagined that his dying protagonist could embody grace only on the eve of losing it definitively.[39] In his commentaries on this and other plays, Miller returns repeatedly to the related notion of "dignity." (The word, familiar from Edwin Denby's near-contemporaneous discussions of Balanchine's own negotiations with awkwardness, turns up equally often in Miller's prose.) "The fateful wound . . . is the wound of indignity," he writes in "Tragedy and the Common Man."[40] Willy Loman's "sin" is "to have committed himself so completely to the counterfeits of dignity."[41] A character from another play "sacrifice[s] . . . himself for his conception, however misguided, of . . . dignity."[42] All these arguments recommend retreat—away from a falsifying social world where every transaction is an occasion for judgment, and toward an interior where the only judge is oneself.

Yet Miller may have in mind an even sharper retreat. Another of his discarded titles was "The Inside of His Head," an image Miller briefly thought of realizing literally: an "enormous face the height of the proscenium arch . . . would appear and then open up."[43] The oppressiveness of that image—the head overwhelming and imprisoning its possessor in the same way the play's other detachable body parts do—suggests a punishing idea of inwardness. Readers should keep it, along with the rejected title, in mind as they approach the play today. Cultural need and critical habit have turned Miller into a civic spokesman, the fabricator of the "important public statement" (in Richard Gilman's sardonic phrase), the arbiter of modern morals and analyst of American myths.[44] Miller's own statements about his project, prompted by what he takes to be the disengagement of his fellow playwrights, support a narrative in which he writes in and for his historical moment. ("It's an attempt to remake the West," he once said of *Death of a Salesman*.)[45] Yet this, his best play, is in fact his smallest play—small not in size, of course, but in range. Willy's recurrent attraction to his garden is an apt correlative to Miller's dramaturgy. The playwright, too, claims a discrete plot and, by working it intensively, makes absorption itself one of his subjects. Michael Fried's preoccupations are not irrelevant. A scene of Willy gardening, like one of Linda sewing, or Biff going outdoors at night to smoke, or Willy, "totally immersed in himself," drinking milk at the kitchen table, implicitly assumes the subject's solitude, or at least indifference to his or her environment (28). *Death of a Salesman* may never let us forget that it unfolds under three sets of watchful eyes—our own, mirrored when Willy "faces the audience" in one scene and acknowledges the "important people in the stands"; those of envious, anxious, or pitying characters; and those of the larger, relentlessly evaluative culture (135). Yet one of the things we see is the search—it seems to be the play's more than the characters' search—for impervious forms of privacy.

In a nice irony, it is the offstage world, beyond the borders of Willy's and Miller's plots, that is dedicated to performance—the football field, Bernard's courtroom, and especially the salesman's territory. The latter is part of a boundless landscape present only when the characters recount their own or others' itineraries—Texas, California, Alaska, Virginia, Massachusetts, South Dakota, Ohio, Indiana, Michigan, Illinois, among others. The roll call of states inspires Miller's best critics to reach beyond psychological or narrowly social concerns. (Elinor Fuchs's geographical reading is a model revisionist approach.)[46] Yet Miller strictly limits our recourse to allegory or myth. A spectator tempted to generalize about the "Americanness" or "modernity" of Willy's situation, or to speculate about places Miller deliberately doesn't let us see, must first come to terms with the things we *do* see—most of them of such resolute ordinariness that they repel symbolism and, like all domestic objects, serve as buffers between their possessors and the outside world. Only those who own and use them are privy to their meanings and interested in their value. Even obviously "important" objects, such as the rubber tubing hidden behind the gas heater, or Willy's sample cases, or Linda's stockings, project drabness and oppressive functionality so emphatically that, in another provocative test of Miller's artistic control, they threaten to drag down the playwright's aspirations for them. The non- or antistyle is itself functional, for Miller codes the opposite quality—allure, the salesman's instrument—as false or transient. No offstage landscape is vaster and more wondrous than the African "interior" that Ben celebrates, but its main purpose here is to shrink the already self-demeaning characters and to make painfully clear how unlikely they are to leave the play's own interior. Nobody can go very far in pajamas, after all, not even Charley.

Indeed, they seem headed only to their bedrooms, a house's innermost spaces, where, in sleep, they can enjoy the most uncompromising absorptive state. In this, the bedrooms are companions to the play's other zones for hiding: Willy's hotel room, Charley's and Howard's inner offices ("pull yourself together," says Howard, "there's people outside" [84]), the saloon's back room ("a lotta people they don't like it private . . . but I know you, you ain't from Hackensack" [99]), and finally Willy's grave. The nocturnal or twilight settings for many of the scenes, and the obsessiveness with which characters speak of sleep, seem, in this context, to further disappoint a spectator's expectation of dramatic action and theatrical display. "Let's go to sleep" (25). "Sleep well, darling!" (67). "Go to sleep, dear" (68). "You'll sleep better" (44). As these and similar lines accumulate, one feels the production agitate for its own withdrawal. Such self-obscuring tendencies complicate Miller's definition of his preferred theater. "The social drama . . . is the main stream and the antisocial drama a bypass," he writes in 1955. "The social drama . . . must delve into the nature of man . . . to discover what his needs are, so that those needs may be amplified and exteriorized in terms of social concepts."[47] The characters of *Death of a Salesman*, however, resist amplification, exteriorization, and all other mechanical practices. The sight of them recalls Philip Fisher's thoughts on sleep and the "radical singularity" of private life. The "eight daily hours" of solitary unconsciousness "limit any merely social account of existence," he writes in *The Vehement Passions*.[48] The self asleep is a "withdrawn self for whom others do not exist and cannot press their claims at any level of importance that can be compared to the claims from within" (68). Miller's characters, never far from their own beds, shut out our claims, too. Enlisted by virtue of the play's fame in any number of debates over the national "self," they revert from group identity to unclassified individuality. "I am the only one in my world," Fisher says in the voice of the "extrasocial" person (68). That's also an infant's claim. In an additional reversion, Miller's characters move from adulthood to childhood. Biff and Happy are again sharing their boyhood room, where they trade grown-up tales of sexual adventure from children's twin beds. An even more severe regression occurs at the end of the first act, when Willy, lying in bed, asks Linda to sing him a lullaby. Having shed along with his clothes the burdens of maturity, parenthood, marriage, career, and all other markers of developed personality, and all forms of affiliation save the most fundamental, he enfolds himself in a kind of privacy that, deep within a milieu that he feels has otherwise "boxed [him] in," for once isn't suffocating (17).

That tableau returns us one last time to Miller's title. He may have forsaken the particularity of "The Inside of His Head" to traffic in the types announced by *Death of a Salesman*, but his crucial subtitle betrays a contrary impulse. "Certain Private Conversations in Two Acts and a Requiem": the phrase is among the more graceful in this drama of otherwise embattled grace. Most readers overlook it; most spectators never learn it; but it deserves scrutiny. Each of the first three words announces a dramaturgical principle. "Certain" prepares us to listen for tentativeness in the authorial voice, a quality easily ignored now that *Death of a Salesman* is a "classic." The dignity of that status, like all forms of dignity to Miller, is ambiguous: it risks obscuring the play's more authentic (and theatrically compelling) indeterminacy and incompleteness. The subtitle informs us that we're going to see "certain" scenes, not all of them, as chosen by a playwright who, as we've seen in his attraction to character synecdoches, prefers the part to the whole. The scenes' chosenness is fundamental to their theatricality. We are inside Miller's head as much as Willy's: the subtitle asks us to imagine the criteria by which he selected his scenes, and to register the pressure bearing down on the stage from those he excluded. The visible and audible play is shadowed by a vast negative space — all the other scenes that form the theoretical whole — just as the Loman home huddles in a corner of the unshown continent of states and beneath the skyscrapers of the surrounding city in Jo Mielziner's original design.

Spectators who pause over Miller's embrace of partiality may sense its dizzying implications for both his form and his narrative. To them, *Death of a Salesman* now seems merely a version or a draft rather than a definitive statement. Any of the possible plays not written (or arrangements of scenes not selected) attracts its own share of attention. Such a divided mode of spectatorship further separates the play's most famous line — "attention must be paid" — from its own classic, if not platitudinous, status. We can now hear it even more skeptically: can one ever pay enough attention in a world that grants access only to "certain" of a character's thoughts, actions, emotions, body parts? Moreover, how does one properly value what one does see? Ever optimistic, Miller's characters remain faithful to the possibility of authoritative knowledge of their own and others' true selves. "Let's hold on to the facts tonight, Pop," says Biff (106), and later he declares that "you're going to hear the truth — what you are and what I am!" (130). At Willy's grave, he says, "I know who I am" (138). Yet Miller ensures that knowing — and "facts" and "truth" — are no more comprehensive or durable than his dramatic structure. The play's most accurate moment of self-perception is also an astute piece of dramatic criticism: a collapsing Willy says, "I still feel — kind of temporary about myself" (51).

The torment audible in that line — self-scrutiny muddying rather than clarifying self-knowledge, unmooring rather than securing its subject — adds urgency to the second word in Miller's subtitle. The private, for Miller, is not a refuge from contingency, disorientation, or shame. Far from it: characters denied the analgesic benefits of social performance feel more acutely the pain of self-spectatorship. Solitude exposes rather than shields those who seek it; its revelations are disordering, not fortifying. Willy's unsparing look at his fatness is one of many expressions of Miller's interest in brutal intimacy — his protagonist both the object and subject in a private sideshow.

A glance beyond *Death of a Salesman* to exactly contemporaneous trends in American acting is again instructive. Readers thinking about developments in theater craft may interpret Miller's unsentimental vision of private life as a critique of his era's fetishization of the actor's inner self. Of course the comparison is outrageous. Even if we can accept that Miller is as skeptical as he is sincere, and as interested in aesthetics as in politics, it is hard to imagine such criticism tolerated in a production originally staged by Elia Kazan, cofounder of the Actors Studio. Yet the play does provide a useful corrective to those who uncritically embrace the central tenet of Method instruction: that actors should seek in their own lives the foundation of their characters. On Miller's stage, as we've seen, the private self is atomized and dispersed. It loses coherence the deeper one plumbs it. Moreover, memory — so crucial to the Method actor's recovery of emotion — is, as Miller envisions it, less an organized catalogue of images and sensations than a vortex, sucking characters into its depths and stymieing their every attempt to see the past with detachment. Miller states his intentions directly in the introduction to his *Collected Plays*. "Nothing in life comes 'next' but . . . everything exists together and at the same time within us; . . . there is no past to be 'brought forward' in a human being. . . . [Willy's] memories [are] like a mass of tangled roots without end or beginning."[49]

This notion of personal history defies mastery. Its subjects can't "summon" memories. Instead, they surrender to and hope to survive them. Neither can they manage a particular memory's effect, nor, having consulted it, return it to a secure place in their consciousness. Rather, they endure the past's throbbing, persistent presence and unpredictable bids for attention — a haunting that imprisons them as much as anything else in this claustrophobic play, and that, like all hauntings, is impossible to explain believably to anybody else.

Including us: Miller's stress on the "private" implies a still more radical withdrawal from his own spectators (a recession we last saw in *Long Day's Journey into Night*). The third word in the subtitle confirms the sense that we are superfluous presences, if not unwelcome eavesdroppers or trespassers. "Conversations" orients the play's speech inward, away from arenas that amplify every utterance into a social or simply a theatrical pronouncement. Scenes composed of conversation rather than dialogue suggest a less programmed form of engagement. Their speakers are exploratory, willing to change direction as they listen to a partner, making continual adjustments that keep speech from congealing into dogma. This decentering of stage speech implies an obvious judgment on the salesman's language. On Miller's intimate stage, the spiel gives way to the nonaggressive, egalitarian exchange, as Willy himself recognizes when he says, "I haven't got a story left in my head" (107). That line also comments on the writer's own technique. An art emulating the flexibility of conversation can't rely on the seductive forms prized by artists as much as by other, more obvious salesmen.

Yet as Miller promotes conversation against speechifying, or against even writing, he disillusions those who expect it to be risk free. These conversations reveal their participants' mutual dependence; we see them worry over the procedures by which they bind themselves to one another. Miller's characters talk about talking before moving on to any other subject, as if to check unreliable connections or force intimacy where none would arise naturally. As he does with "sleep," Miller repeats the pertinent word over and over, each iteration sounding like someone knocking at the door, begging for acknowledgment. "Talk to them again," Linda says to Willy, hoping his employers will let him work closer to home (14). "I wish you'd have a good talk with him," Happy says to Biff (27). "Let me talk to you—I got nobody to talk to," Willy says to a grown-up Bernard, a confession he later repeats to Ben (93, 126). "You gotta talk to him," Biff says to Willy, after his math teacher fails him (118). These pleas for conversation often fail, too—or, if answered, fail to provide relief to intractable loneliness—and then characters are confronted with new versions of old disappointments. "Dad left when I was such a baby," says Willy, "and I never had a chance to talk to him" (51). Chances for conversation he might have seized—with a wife, for instance, who (as David Savran notes) he interrupts with comic frequency—he forsakes in favor of uselessly enthusiastic chatter.[50] "Will you let me talk?" he says to Linda during his ode to Biff's theoretical future success (65). At his most deluded, a protagonist deprived of a dialogue's stabilizing context is left talking to himself: "I never heard him so loud," a worried Happy says to Linda, as Willy holds forth in his yard (53). "Left him babbling in a toilet," says a shamefaced Biff many scenes later, after the arena for conversation has shrunk even further (124). When characters are humiliated by such fiascoes of conversation, only a willed silence can rehabilitate them. A ferociously protective Linda warns her sons away from her broken husband: "You're not talking to him!" (125).

As the play nears its end, another, more alarming form of silence tears an unmendable hole in Miller's dialogue. "Willy, you coming up?" asks Linda. When he doesn't answer, Linda tries again. "Willy?" And again, this time (a stage direction tells us) "with real fear": "Willy, answer me! Willy!" (135–36). The death of conversation is of course the prelude to the death of a salesman.

The one collapse is the most eloquent image of the other. Willy's muteness also caps the play's argument with theatricality. Willy doesn't merely abstain from dialogue in his last moments; he vigorously rebuffs it, unwilling to risk again the degradation that has come to him with every act of speaking. Yet he isn't entirely silent. In his last sounds — mockeries of a dying hero's fetishized last words — one hears him bat away approaches not just from Linda or from the ghosts in his head, but also from Miller himself and even from an American theater that expects its protagonists to be models of expressiveness on platforms for public debate. A lost and querulous Willy sums up the play's own resentment of its availability as, in carefully spaced bursts, he says, "Sh!" "Sh! Sh!" "Shhh!" (136).

"I think that you should be more of a conversationalist," says Gertrude Eastman Cuevas in Jane Bowles's *In the Summer House* after several attempts to talk to her daughter, Molly, have elicited only monosyllabic replies or reproachful silence (211). Molly retreats from more than conversation: as the play's title suggests, the most precious space in this theater is out of sight, behind the walls of a small vine-covered round cottage in a garden on the Southern California coast. Here Molly sits through most of the first scene, invisible to us, keeping her distance from a mother who is herself immobilized and uneasy with the stage's exposures. Gertrude sits enclosed by her balcony in the adjacent main house, unwilling, for now, to emerge from the privacy she feels essential to her own equilibrium. ("I avoid the outside world as much as possible," she says, unapologetically [211].) For much of this scene, the two women talk across a vast gulf, space that establishes the play's preoccupation with decorum — the first of its many revisions of intimacy as an expression not of relaxation and trust but of quivering, volatile formality. It's telling that, in a letter from Paris written soon after she finished the play, Bowles says she had been "wildly excited" by a production of *Phèdre* at the Comédie Française: "the only thing I have enjoyed thoroughly in years."[51]

In another letter, written a year later as she worries about finding a satisfactory director for the play's first production, Bowles laments that "probably no one is right for it, except . . . Charlie Chaplin."[52] Racine and Chaplin: spectators able to keep both artists in mind as they watch *In the Summer House* stand the best chance at grasping the play's elusive rhythms and spatial logic, its unpredictable bursts of giddiness and vitriol on an otherwise dry landscape. The self-possession essential to both Racine and Chaplin also animates Bowles's play: she shares with them the conviction that effective drama comes less from what characters say and do than from what, with often Herculean effort, they keep unsaid and undone. "I've never in my life shown my feelings," Gertrude declares, and she senses the same restraint in her daughter: "There's something heavy and dangerous inside you," Gertrude says to Molly, "like some terrible rock that's ready to explode" (249, 253). Release of another, subtler kind worries a third character: "If I tell my feelings to a person, I don't want to see them any more" (234). In all these cases, Bowles's characters recognize that their beneficial coexistence depends on discretion.

The lesson for playwrights who themselves traffic in "feelings" is self-evident. Throughout *In the Summer House,* appetites grow more consuming for being unindulged, opinions are stronger when they're laconic, violence is more devastating when total mayhem is averted. Bowles's achievement is to unlock the expressiveness in repression, and in the process to restore the tautness to so-called psychological drama. "You admit you relax too much," Gertrude says to Molly, an indictment that Bowles implicitly also directs to the era's theater (208).

Bowles keeps her own play in shape by regularly testing its ability to accommodate surprise. In the early scenes, the two houses are surrounded and invaded by various representatives of disorder. A Mexican family — its patriarch, Mr. Solares, Gertrude's indefatigable suitor — arrives for a picnic, singing, squealing, "hysterical with laughter," "bobbing around" with precariously balanced plates of spaghetti. From another flank comes a pair of tourists, the nervous Mrs. Constable and her daughter Vivian. Vivian is Molly's age and will soon be her rival. The girl is bright-eyed, high-strung, and overpowering, breaking through whatever remnant of decorum survived the Solareses' arrival in a bid for affection less suffocating than her mother's. Her seizure of the summer house at the scene's end is only the most direct of her many incursions on territory Molly thought hers alone. Between these two disruptions comes a quieter but, to Gertrude, more insidious guest. Lionel, an affable, visionary young man, arrives carrying a huge cardboard image of Neptune, an advertisement with which he hopes to lure patrons to his restaurant, the Lobster Bowl. The ludicrousness of his appearance (he is attended by a mermaid and channel swimmer and carries a toy lobster) conceals the subtler threat he poses to the play's fragile system of affiliation. Before long, he will try to lure Molly away from a mother who expects a lover's fidelity from her daughter, and out of a landscape that seems to narrow as both women's fears expand uncontrollably.

Readers of *The Glass Menagerie* will recognize what's at stake in this milieu. Bowles works variations on the earlier play's themes of constriction and the vine-like attachments between parent and child. Williams was a stalwart supporter of Bowles. He smoothed the play's path to production and defended it against those who would neutralize its characters, action, and tone. ("The efforts to motivate and clarify and justify the happenings in the play," he said of

Figure 18: *In the Summer House* by Jane Bowles, directed by José Quintero, New York, 1953. In act 1, scene 1, Gertrude (Judith Anderson, on balcony) and Molly (Elizabeth Ross, standing left) greet Lionel (Logan Ramsey, standing center) and Mr. Solares (Don Mayo, seated right). Photograph by Eileen Darby. Reproduced by permission of Eileen Darby Images, Inc.

its producers' intrusions, are "at the expense of its purity.")[53] Present-day readers who themselves reduce the play to a psychoanalytic case study of maternal envy (say) or filial rivalry or adolescent dread don't so much distort it—all those pathologies are present—as miss the point of its brittle style. Bowles cultivates her play's surface to control access to its depths. As Molly and Gertrude rebuff characters seeking admission to their domestic interiors, Bowles rebuffs readers who would dig out the "true" motives for the play's visible action and audible statements. She had already reached the logical development of this approach in *A Quarreling Pair,* her 1945 puppet play in which one of the wooden protagonists says, "I've come to believe that what is inside of people is not so very interesting."[54] In that play as in this one, Bowles's characters use frankness as a baffle: the antisentimental Gertrude and the impacted Molly deploy certain emotions so they don't have to concede others. A sudden confession disarms their listeners, a flaring of anger blinds onlookers, and in the ensuing discomfort the speakers are able to escape further prying. Throughout the play, Bowles's tone is quizzical and droll. Her perspective on the action varies unpredictably between extremes of alienation and oppressive intimacy. Speakers, too, seem either complacent, as if survey-ing their scenes from above and vaguely intuiting their future actions, or shockingly immediate, speaking with a rawness that implies the inadequacy of old notions of grief, dependency, or egotism. Such conditions—neither inert nor, to recall Gertrude's objection to "feelings," easily "showable"—are kine-tic, gestural. They are known by their effect on stage space and production rhythm. Those who experience them move—or, equally often, can't move— as they absorb shocks that are physical as much as psychological. Bowles's dramatic writing draws its fluctuating and unbalancing energy from her own effort to approximate in speech what are essentially somatic states.

In a foreword to Bowles's posthumous collection *Feminine Wiles* (1976), Tennessee Williams identifies a personal source for her interest in the kinetics of mental life. He writes of the "excited indecision" Bowles often showed in real-life social situations, a "true and dreadful concern that she might suggest a wrong move in a world that she had correctly surmised to be so inclined to turn wrongly."[55] Gertrude and Molly themselves seem to teeter on the edge of a precipice—the thin margin separating them from taboo passion, self-annihilating rage, and a bottomless abyss of shame and self-hatred. The stum-bling Wingfields and the fragmenting, overexposed Lomans have their equiv-alent in the women whose vigorous protests against other people's tactless-ness, ardor, or vulnerability can't break their own fall into indignity. Bowles literalizes the point in represented and reported stage action. The balcony from which Gertrude looks down upon the rising chaos is inadequate to stave off internal collapse. "Sometimes I wake up at night," she confesses, "with a strange feeling of isolation . . . as if I'd fallen off the cliffs and landed miles away from everything that was close to my heart . . . as if a shadow had passed over my whole life and made it dark" (210). When Molly and Lionel take in the view from the balcony, Molly can't get past the fact that "it all looks so different." Strangeness breeds fear—she requires a predictable point of view on her surroundings to feel secure in her view on herself—and she is impatient to get back on solid emotional ground. Scenes of such persistent vertigo ensure that the play's one sensational piece of news will come as no shock. Vivian, we hear, falls to her death from high rocks overlooking the ocean; a jealous Molly may have pushed her. Vivian's mother rings the last change on this theme as she tries to describe the depth of her subsequent grief: "You must be one of the fortunate," she says to an employee at the Lobster Bowl, "who has not yet stood on the edge of the black pit" (268). (In a later, unfinished play, Bowles abstracts even more metaphysical meaning from this precariousness: "She guards her false trust in order not to fall into her single heart," Bowles writes of one character. "The single heart is herself — it is suffering — it is God — it is nothing.")[56]

"Nothing," "a black pit," a place "miles away from everything," a "shadow" — what lies below the surface isn't authoritative meaning but non-meaning, vacancy. Gertrude speaks for all the major characters in describing a recurrent feeling of suspendedness. For her, it first arose in childhood, when she was expelled from what she mistakenly took to be her privileged kinship with her father. (In a revealing echo of her refusal to "show her feelings," she insists that her father preferred her, his "true love," to her sister, even though "he never showed it" [212].) Now, she often wakes up disoriented in the middle of the night (as she describes it) and says her name aloud, as if to call forth an intruder from the shadows or to reunite a foreign body with its racing mind. Yet that "doesn't hook things together," she says. Only after a literal grounding — going downstairs to sit at her kitchen table "with the light switched on" and drinking a glass of fizzy water — can she recover the reassuring context that shapes the self (210). Finally, she suffers a new form of self-severance after she consents to marry Mr. Solares and move with him to Mexico. "I've lost my daily life," she realizes. She "lie[s] awake in the night" — another form of suspension — "trying to think of just one standard or one ideal," surrendering to a paradoxical hope that such abstractions will provide solidity (282). All three experiences — sequential evictions from identity — lie behind her distaste for "wild women" who "break the bonds" and even for Lionel's huge Neptune placard: "I've always hated everything that was larger than life size," she tells him (210, 221). Life size is her size: any violation of scale, like any loss of "standards," "daily life," or "bonds," unsteadies one who feels only begrudgingly accommodated and unreliably rooted in her world.

A bereaved Mrs. Constable breaks bonds of her own — "I didn't really love them," she says of her husband and daughter — and learns that "my heart had fake roots" (263). It is a judgment her actual deracination upholds. No interior life remains open to her after Vivian's death: the domestic and maternal energies with which she sheltered her daughter now spend themselves in a void. She won't go home, preferring instead to sleep on the beach, in Gertrude's garden, or on the floor of the Lobster Bowl. Her days are filled with circular wandering, kinetic image of her futile attempts at forgetting. "I run after the waves," she says. "All along the way I think [my life is] beginning . . . and then . . . I see the hotel" (265). One can almost see her grind to a disappointed halt.

Mrs. Constable's constant, loitering presence onstage directs us to the choreographic patterns of the play as a whole. Bowles accompanies every decisive emotional turn with a physical one: characters lunge, dash, abruptly change course, grandly depart, or submit to another's ebbing tide. Lionel has to pull Molly outside after their marriage; later, after they've been living at the Lobster Bowl, he insists they make a break for a new city or "be shut in here forever" (273). Gertrude's elaborate move after her own marriage leads only to her sudden return. That, in turn, precipitates other forms of reversion. She reclaims Molly from Lionel, promising next to reclaim their old house, and implies an even deeper withdrawal when she offers Molly her own nightgown.[57] (Molly had earlier greeted her mother by descending the Lobster Bowl stairs in her wedding dress. The citation of the famous descent in *Long Day's Journey into Night* heightens the play's sense of withdrawal: it is as if *In the Summer House* is retreating into theater history.)

The desires turned up by these forward and backward movements are raw. One needn't dig deep for Bowles's devastating critique of familial pieties. Her recursive pattern reveals an unprogressive, self-consuming kinship: it is figured as something that parents and children enter violently or from which they are violently ejected. Kinship alternatively depicted as one of various kinds of mere adjacency—companionship, mutuality, respect, or even devotion—is inadequate to the needs of these ostensibly decorous, but in fact voracious, characters. Indeed, by the play's end, the earlier emphasis on discretion and the stage's once carefully measured distances seem utopian forms of détente, not evidence of stunted intimacy—an imposition of clarity upon impulses that, now unchecked, result in hysteria. The breakdowns that Gertrude and Mrs. Constable experience after both daughters' departures (Vivian's death merely a definitive version of the loss suffered on Molly's marriage) expose psychic cracks that had always been present, presumably dating back to the mothers' childhoods. The parents are revealed as no more able than their children to move beyond instinct. Incestuous longing, reflexive need, primal terror: Bowles's characters house themselves within states attractive only for their familiarity.

If Bowles had pointed to only these connotations of her dramatic structure, *In the Summer House* would not be as unsettling as it is. Her narrative of arrested development implies an idea of drama that is itself averse to change or even time, that burrows into itself when theatrical convention dictates greater and riskier exposures, and that evades our desire for surrogates by presenting characters who offer themselves only to each other. At times, even those approaches feel intrusive. "I like to be with you because you seem to only half hear me," says Lionel to Molly, a refreshing antidote to the passionate fusing in most love scenes (234). Does Lionel's momentary preference for a half-hearing lover (he later changes his mind) reflect Bowles's preference for a half-hearing spectator? Does Molly practice the form of attention best suited to her play? Perhaps Molly allows herself to "only half hear" her lover out of concern that any more interest would enlist her in his world, his way of thinking and feeling, and thus evict her from the fragile house of her own consciousness. Listening to him means not listening to herself. The carefully measured distance between the couple — matched by the many spaces between other characters — helps us recognize our own position, in any theater, between prurience and aversion. We know better than to lean toward either extreme: theatrical custom has taught us to temper curiosity with tact and to forestall self-absorption with an openness to surprise. As we strive for this balance, we experience something of the same ardent frozenness known to Bowles's protagonists. They and we are caught on one of the many thresholds between our own and another's experience.

So, too, is Bowles herself. Her characters' and spectators' ambivalence is an essential aspect of her writerly sensibility. From one perspective, she is an artist of infinite regression — a "writer's writer's writer," as John Ashbery famously called her, one whose portraits of "human apartness" (Truman Capote's phrase) gain credibility from her own detachment from postwar literary and theatrical culture.[58] That celebrity-driven world is only the most vulgar form of a more general public theatricality from which Bowles recoils. In a passage that recalls Gertrude's aversion to everything "larger than life size," her husband, Paul Bowles, reports that "nature in general horrified her. . . . The sea or storms frightened her. She'd say, 'Yes, yes, they're beautiful, but . . . let's go inside. It's almost the cocktail hour.' What was unknown, overpowering, not within human measure, geysers, tornadoes, thunderstorms, she hated."[59] Yet this Bowles is no sooner inside than she yearns to go outside, no sooner monastic than dissolute. Her husband also recalls a winter night she stayed out until dawn "wandering around the docks." "I had to," she explained, "or I couldn't face myself in the mirror tomorrow . . . because that was the one thing I was afraid of."[60]

Easy to imagine theater as another zone in which to confront fear of exposure. The Jane Bowles whom American literary culture has typed as nervous and recessive in fact hungered for public approval, especially the explicit, measurable show of interest available only in the theater. "There's no point in writing a play for your five hundred goony friends," she said to an interviewer when *In the Summer House* closed after a disappointingly short run. "You have to reach more people."[61] She refined her views on reputation in a letter, lamenting that she writes in a no-man's-land between the popular and the exalted: "I do not know how to write a commercial line, nor could I write *Waiting for Godot* if I was sitting with a million dollars in my pocket."[62] The complaint could be any playwright's, of course. What makes it relevant to a reading of Bowles is that it reflects an impasse that also exists on the level of sentences. The very act of writing, for the famously blocked Bowles, brought her up against the walls dividing her from a private theater — the page — and from an audience of one, herself, relieved of the responsibility of writing on becoming her own reader. Like one of her arrested figures, Bowles can neither go in or out. To plunge deeper into her imagination is to risk muteness and thus irrelevance — a fatal fall into a mental chasm akin to Mrs. Constable's "black pit." Yet its alternative, a fluid outpouring of well-wrought prose or dialogue, is equally impossible and may even be unacceptable. In a 1957 letter, written as she struggled with a new, never-to-be-completed play, she describes the constant challenge to find a middle ground between knowing nothing — "it is impossible to write a play in the dark without having some idea of where one is going" — and knowing too much: "I did get an idea but it was so definite that I couldn't go against it either."[63] A notebook entry describes with painful precision an equally impacted, immured state. For her, she says, writing origi-nates within two nested boxes: "A play. There comes a moment [in working on it] when there is no possibility of escape, as if the spirit were a box hitting at the walls of the head." Yet, she later says, "the only time I wrote well, when I passed through the inner door, I felt guilt."[64]

This language — writing as a form of "going," "going against," or "passing through"; an imagination enclosed by "walls" and a "door" — returns us to *In the Summer House,* of course, and with it comes an invitation to broaden our reading of its central symbol. A character taking refuge in the summer house is also "in" writing, or at least in the writing mind. Such a conceit aligns Bowles with Arthur Miller limning "the inside of his head" and Tennessee Williams designing the language-rich, image-dense decor of *The Glass Menagerie* on the model of the writer's memory. Bowles's predecessors themselves measure the currents pushing back against expression. After Miller opposes solitary talking to ampler conversation and Williams rejects dining-room writing for writing in the world, a reader may easily find a self-reflexive argument in Bowles's own narrative. Molly's struggle for independence is especially affecting as a meta-phor for seeking a style. Her mother worries that when Molly "get[s] inside that summer house," she is "plotting something," and reproaches her for being unable to "express an opinion [or] have an outlook" (210–11). Molly herself admits that she "waste[s] a lot of time day-dreaming" behind its walls (264). It takes little effort to see that such a condition corresponds to every writer's unbearable vagueness before the mental fog lifts and he or she can commit words to the page. Writerly common sense suggests that such a release is possible only under deliberately ascetic conditions: even as the house prolongs

Molly's immaturity, audiences can idealize it as the three-dimensional correlative of the focused mind, swept clean of lures to the writer's heightened senses. Its windows frame no distracting view, save that of the vines that cover its exterior. When Gertrude complains that Molly is "indifferent to the beauties of nature" (an echo of Paul Bowles's description) we may think of a writer who faces her desk to the wall, the better to see only the beauties of her own imagining (208). It is telling that, after Molly leaves home for the Lobster Bowl, she does little else besides read comic books, as if only antiliterary expression were possible in a landscape lacking the writer's usual protections.

Yet Molly's emergence from the summer house begins a sequence of departures that, in the end, allows Bowles to make a much sharper and more surprising point about the writing life. The phrasing with which Molly had greeted the view from Gertrude's balcony — "it's all so different" — recurs twice more in that scene; all three speeches are themselves echoes of Molly's response when Lionel first broaches the subject of marriage and moving from home: "I can't picture anything being any different than it is," she says. "I feel I might just plain die if everything changes" (235). Molly once again strikes this note when Gertrude returns from Mexico, telling her mother, "You look . . . different. . . . You're all changed" (289, 293). Now, on their third iteration, anxieties over difference and change overflow the borders of any single cause. Bowles hints that their significance transcends domestic matters when Molly, as if reacting to the visual shock of a changed Gertrude, rushes out of the restaurant as the play ends. "Molly's flight is sudden," the stage directions tell us. "She is visible in the blue light beyond the oyster-shell door only for a second" (295). It is a striking change of rhythm for a character who, till now, had often sat abstracted or "spellbound," refusing to engage the world around her. Her speed seems a long-delayed rebuttal to one of Gertrude's early judgments: "You seem to have developed such a slow and gloomy way of walking. . . . Don't you think you could correct your walk?" ("I'm trying to correct it," Molly answers [208].) The emphasis on "correct" style links the character's and the playwright's quests for grace. That Bowles often stressed her own difficulty moving (she had limped since childhood, irresistible physical correlative of her difficulty in composition) only throws into sharper relief every writer's ideal — what Virginia Woolf, accounting for the "incandescent" artist's confidence and ease in *A Room of One's Own,* calls a mind from which all quotidian obstacles have been "fired out . . . and consumed" so that writing may "flow . . . free and unimpeded."[65]

The rhyme of Woolf's and Bowles's titles has welcome but potentially misleading implications. To a spectator treating Bowles's play as an allegory of writing, the summer house will, as we've seen, present an especially attractive room of one's own. Yet in Bowles's last scene she moves us away from such romanticism. Only if a writer allows a cherished subject or scene of imagined action to "look so different"—only if he or she gives up familiar points of view, casts of mind, and even habits of concentration—can he or she acquire the sharper, fresher vision capable of breaking through seemingly permanent blockages. The attention Bowles pays to language in her final scene further suggests that she sees a writer's impasse in Molly's choice of suitors. Caught between Gertrude's wall of speech pleading for her return and Lionel's seductive argument for departure, Molly offers silence and stammering—"I . . . ," a weak "no . . . ," her voice "sticking in her throat," another speech lost when Gertrude "cut[s] in," ellipses serving as placeholders until words can be found (288, 292–94). Bowles also underscores the mechanics of composition in this last scene: "I have something to tell you," Gertrude says to Mrs. Constable, starting to expose Molly's presumptive role in Vivian's death (294). It is a threat of narration that, for a moment, seems to have overcome Molly's resistance to staying home: She is briefly immobilized. Moments later, another form of storytelling releases her and pushes her decisively toward change: "When I was a little girl . . . ," begins Gertrude, but she can't get past this formulaic prelude to autobiography before realizing that she, too, has been jealous of a rival (295). Only at the moment of recognizing their closest similarity can mother and daughter separate: when Molly leaves the Lobster Bowl, she leaves more than her mother's claustrophobic idea of kinship. She also escapes her idea of narrative and, in an implicit rebuke to the era's most celebrated form of theater, the memory that generates it.

In the Summer House ends with blurred action, an incomplete sentence (Gertrude's repeated "when I was a little girl . . ."), the protagonist's dispersal and self-erasure beyond the stage's "blue light." The title of a novel Bowles worked on throughout the 1950s, *Out in the World,* inverts the play's title to name a destination for writing as much as for the writer—out there, not in the imagination, or in the theater, or even on the page. (Bowles never finished the book, but the play succeeds in making the same point.) She argues that eviction from a room of one's own, expulsion from the Edenic garden enclosing it, and alienation from a sheltering idea of self are the truly necessary conditions of art.

One of Jane Bowles's most fervent admirers—he called *In the Summer House* "the best American play of our time"—embodies the alertness and impiety of artists able to leave their own summer houses.[66] Frank O'Hara stands as a monument to a restless postwar culture, or rather, he would if he trusted monuments or cared to stand still. As he implies in the title of his posthumous collection of prose, *Standing Still and Walking in New York,* stasis is merely the prelude to motion, a temporary pause to gather one's thoughts and focus one's eyes before greeting new opportunities for disorientation. That principle, as many have observed, underlies his canonical poems. Their most self-conscious lines urge us to be conscious of everything beyond the self. The poet who is "always tying up / and then deciding to depart," who tries to "live as variously as possible" and is purposefully "disloyal," and who is spent from "the ecstasy of always bursting forth" models an artistic life dismissive of everything that more meditative artists hold dear.[67] It may be that, as O'Hara puts it, "attention equals Life" — an equation that Marjorie Perloff and Richard Howard, among others, see as central to his poetics — but elsewhere he insists that "to move is to love."[68] Love lifts him higher than mere attention, and O'Hara welcomes the light-headedness and self-dispersal that results. He moves through his city — New York City, the crucial backdrop for much of his work — making sudden, crushing embraces followed by equally brisk, total renunciations; the cityscape itself suffers this fate as he pushes himself toward ever more capacious responsiveness (what Clark Coolidge calls the "peripheral vision" that expands the frame around his art).[69] "I know you love Manhattan," the Sun tells him in "A True Account of Talking to the Sun at Fire Island," "but / you ought to look up more often."[70]

To readers of *In the Summer House,* O'Hara's dilating effusiveness and strategic intemperance may come as a welcome antidote to Gertrude Eastman Cuevas's insistence on "controls." Indeed, O'Hara sounds as if he is responding directly to her boast that "I've never in my life shown my feelings" when he declares, in "To Edwin Denby," "feelings are our facts."[71] As the poem's title suggests, the feelings aroused by art are among the most pleasurable. Much of his work responds to other people's work, and those encounters, in turn, establish his frame of reference for life beyond the gallery, theater, or concert hall. "The wind sounded exactly like / Stravinsky." The "El Greco / heavens [are] breaking open." A ballerina helps him make sense of another sky in another poem: "the clouds are imitating Diana Adams." A questionable haircut makes him "look more Brancusi than usual."[72] As O'Hara deliberately fails to distinguish art viewing from other kinds of experience, he sets in motion a large-scale, if largely implicit, reconsideration of many givens of postwar artistic culture. His particular value to any survey of American theater lies here: not only in his theater work — although, as we'll see, he was a prolific if unfulfilled playwright as well as an occasional performer — but also in his call for more flexible definitions of playwriting, performance, and spectatorship.

Artworks, in his view, aren't discrete, remote, or unchanging entities.[73] Their makers, too, are not cut off from their environments, colleagues, or the unpredictable needs and emotions of their audiences. The poet who hears Stravinsky gusting between office buildings, and who refuses to restrict Diana Adams's grace to City Center, imagines his fellow writers also contending with cosmopolitan, metropolitan life as they compose their own work. The best art results from surrendering to rather than shutting out distraction. The finished work retains the unpredictable energy of its scene of origin even when it exudes poise and seems untouchable. Spectators and readers do it justice when they disregard the limits imposed by page, stage, or canvas and let their minds wander toward the uncontainable experience that occasioned it. That would include gossip, arguments, and in-jokes; planned visits, glancing encounters, and solitary flanerie; emotional debts incurred, repaid, or dodged; diversions, obstacles, and annoying interruptions; fondness, flirtation, or full-scale sexual obsession. Coming after all this, the work of art may seem ephemeral, only marginally important, purely a function of its circumstances — precisely O'Hara's hope. The devaluation is welcome if it means we will see the poem or play as an object of exchange, not reverence, occupying a landscape, not an abstract plane — an expression of one person's impulses, not an era's expectations. The change is especially beneficial to the theater. In a postwar period straining for a national culture, and near the end of an era of big plays that began with *The Glass Menagerie* and Arthur Miller's *All My Sons* (1947) and peaked with the belated premiere of *Long Day's Journey into Night* in 1956, O'Hara perversely insists on the value of situational, contingent, even disposable works. Against the homogenizing effects of "culture," he elevates private, at times even hermetic meaning. Resisting the call for "timeless" art, he affirms theater's loyalty to the circumstances of its creation and presentation.

The many scattered references to theater in O'Hara's poems, if strung together, express this aesthetic with deceptive casualness. His speakers stake claims on rather than simply read or attend plays, and assign them coded significance undecipherable to anyone beyond their circle. Theater buildings are similarly privileged, serving initiates as utopian spaces where they can register feelings too fragile or, at the other extreme, too outré for the outside world. Those emotions, in O'Hara's telling, are often unrelated to the play or performance. "ENDGAME WAITING FOR GODOT WATT HAPPY DAYS . . . means I love you," he writes in "Biotherm (for Bill Berkson)."[74] The notion that three plays and a novel can convey O'Hara's meanings along with Beckett's own is presumptuous but consistent with an idea of spectatorship that treats personal enthusiasms as valid only when they are shared. Art is an adhesive, capable of consecrating unions among its spectators, illuminating the hitherto unacknowledged complexity of their interdependence. "Leaning on you in the theatre," he writes later in the same poem—the free-floating image all that's needed to suggest the unself-conscious, stronger bond available to intimates who direct their attention past one another to a third beloved object (448). The value of O'Hara's friendship with Patsy Southgate crystallizes in "The Day Lady Died" as he lingers in a bookshop trying to decide whether to give her "Brendan Behan's new play or *Le Balcon* or *Les Nègres*."[75] A love affair commemorated in an untitled poem reaches a new, gratifying level when one partner says he thinks Ionesco is overrated and the other agrees.[76] At the "experimental theatre," O'Hara writes in another poem, the actors' "Emotive Fruition" sanctions the audience's own ardor, and when such onstage passion "wed[s] Poetic Insight," it tightens vows of fidelity offstage, too.[77] Kinship continues to deepen even after the curtain falls. A performance by the New York City Ballet fills him with anticipation of "more discussions in lobbies of the respective greatnesses of Diana Adams and Allegra Kent."[78] So all-consuming are these exchanges that the substance of this or any performance itself rarely concerns him. Few of his poems describe a play or ballet or explain what it is "about"; more important is the drama of its reception—a spectacle with its own agons, reversals, and denouements. "How I hate subject matter," O'Hara writes in a poem recalling his performances at the Poets' Theater in Cambridge, "and all things that don't change."[79]

When O'Hara turns from watching plays to writing them, he works to maintain the same sense of fellowship enjoyed in lobbies. Speaking about one of his plays, he once said, "it's really just the raw material for an experience."[80] He had in mind the rehearsal hall encounters among painters, poets, and performers, each adjusting his or her artistic procedures to accommodate the demands of other modes of creativity. Yet an equally rich part of the "experience" involves the modulation of longstanding friendships under the pressure of theater—the latter formalizes one's sociable instincts—as well as the reconsideration of long-held assumptions about theater under the pressure of friendship. O'Hara is a dedicative playwright: he writes for another person, an occasion, a setting, and even a set.[81] The characters of *Try! Try!* (1951, revised 1953) are named after their first actors—Violet Lang, John Ashbery, and Jack Rogers—O'Hara's close friends and Poets' Theater colleagues: their voices, O'Hara says in an "Epilogue to the Players," were "in my typewriter" and "in my ear" as he wrote.[82] When the Artists' Theater assembled a different cast for a New York production, O'Hara extensively rewrote the play. New actors, along with new decor by Larry Rivers, provided O'Hara with a new opportunity— more precious than any sentimental idea of originality—to respond to the circumstances of the present moment. Still other plays cite or caricature figures in O'Hara's New York circle. In one play, there is talk of Edwin Denby. New

York School painters and Beat poets appear in others. In *The Houses at Falling Hanging* (1953), a character mentions Judith Malina and Julian Beck, who first thought of producing the play at the Living Theatre. O'Hara himself is a character in *Shopping for Joe* — the extreme in a compulsive self-referentiality that sharpens distinctions between those spectators who are fluent in O'Hara's codes and those who aren't.

In all these cases, O'Hara refuses to pander to or even acknowledge a wider circle of potential spectators. The interest his work elicits from strangers is welcome but not pursued. As one might expect, this attitude leaves him vulnerable to accusations of cliquishness and to misunderstanding by even those who would defend him. (At the premiere of *Try! Try!* Thornton Wilder famously scolded the audience for laughing at what he mistakenly took to be a solemn play.)[83] Yet both hostile and naive responses fail to look beyond particular plays to the threat they pose to tired ideas of theater's "inherent" publicness. O'Hara seeks to retain his rights over his work even as it enters the culture, to keep its sentimental value from depreciating in the city square, and to ensure that private meanings don't disappear beneath others' interpretations of it. Some large part of an O'Hara play — larger than in many other playwrights' works — will always be off-limits to us. O'Hara envisions productions that establish the intimacy of texts, and writes texts that have the tentativeness and inscrutability of manuscripts — or, as we'll see, of letters.[84] With this ambition in mind, a reader should pause over the many unfinished works in his *Selected Plays*. Their variable quality and interest aside, they make explicit what is implicit in the completed plays: their status as writing, as works reluctant to cut the cord to their progenitor. The self-consciousness about writing that we observed in *The Glass Menagerie, Death of a Salesman,* and *In the Summer House* peaks with O'Hara and exposes the ambivalence at its core. This playwright may be "out in the world," but his plays are (to cite Gertrude Stein, another O'Hara passion) "half in and half out of doors."[85] O'Hara's possessiveness survives him and transforms his plays from commodities into fetishes. Those he parts with (only a handful were published or produced in his lifetime) are meant to be regarded as gifts, instilling in the reader or spectator an almost illicit pleasure at being present for the divulgence of secrets. This desire to reconcile confidentiality with the open forum of theater may seem, to readers of his poetry, the most provocative application of his theory of "Personism." The ideal poem, he notoriously argued, is positioned "Lucky Pierre style" between two people, writer and reader, "instead of two pages"; it "address[es] itself to one person."[86] Nowhere else in the American theater of this period is a playwright writing toward a "one-person" idea of spectatorship.

This mode of transmission accounts for his theater's perishability. After mailing the only copy of a play to a lucky chosen reader, he'd never ask for it back. Other "dramas *à clef*," as O'Hara's Cambridge friend Alison Lurie calls them, were "passed from hand to hand" in a network of the initiated (often the same people depicted in the plays themselves), rarely making their way back to the writer, much less onto a stage.[87] Questions of ownership were murky anyway when so many O'Hara plays were collaborations. He partnered with Kenneth Koch, John Ashbery, and Frank Lima for separate projects. On a flight from Rome, Bill Berkson and O'Hara passed a portable typewriter back and forth to write *Flight 115*. While O'Hara posed for Larry Rivers's famous nude portrait, the poet and the painter kept themselves amused by coming up with dialogue for *Kenneth Koch, a Tragedy*. Of course, one can't help thinking that many of these scenes of consensual writing authorize or clarify erotic contact. Alternatively, and more simply, O'Hara may be adapting ballet's custom of mutual support to the notoriously egotistical theater, or emulating the art of conversation, the model for all art he admires. The members of a ballet corps, he observes in a review, "extend each other's range of expression as in a Platonic dialogue."[88] The parts of one dancer's body (he writes in a poem about Tanaquil LeClercq) are equally integrated, as "when they conducted the dialogues / in distant Athens."[89] To this art (O'Hara writes elsewhere), Edwin Denby brings an idea of criticism as itself an "open dialogue of opinion and discussion between writer and reader which is nonaggressive."[90] O'Hara promotes this same egalitarianism in his poetry — "what really makes me happy is when something just falls into place as if it were a conversation" — but it is the theater, an art typically forcing extroverted performers toward hungry spectators, that stands to benefit the most from "nonaggressive" expression.[91] As we extend ourselves toward his plays, supplying the connective tissue that his often diffident characters withhold, our relationship to the playwright mirrors that of his collaborators. These relationships are themselves variants on the narratives of fidelity and betrayal among his characters. O'Hara — famous, we're told, for enlivening house parties with his readings from Chekhov's plays — himself dramatizes the crystallization and dissolution of domestic societies.[92] He won't insist on the larger implications of this subject and technique — that would be too "aggressive" — but they are easily imagined. "Open dialogue" among artists and between spectacle and spectator, along with concern for its breakdown among characters, enables him to pursue a utopian vision: art that "addresses itself to one person" at a time stands the best chance of reknitting a raveled postwar social fabric.

In *Kenneth Koch, a Tragedy* (the allusion to Mayakovsky's play is simultaneously reverent and irreverent), the title character finds another phrase for

O'Hara's "nonaggressive" dramaturgy. "Greatness in art isn't heavy, it's light."[93] (That the play breaks off moments after this line confirms the playwright's dread of excessive weight.) Here and in almost every play, O'Hara has little interest in narrative: his plots are banal and notional. Of more importance is the space between characters, where we can observe the tightening and loosening of friendships, family loyalties, or forms of erotic servitude. Such negotiations are cool and unforced, even when the stakes are high — bemusement in the face of volatile emotion. This style is in refreshing contrast to the hand-wringing and bluster of much postwar American theater — what O'Hara, in a letter to Koch, calls "The Bleeding Mouths School of Dramatic Significance."[94]

On his stages, exchanges are glancing, distracted, aphoristic sometimes at the expense of intelligibility, superfluous when circumstances demand seriousness. Characters are confident that they can speak most truthfully not by hammering points home or wrenching responses from one another, but by indirection and innuendo. When they do admit to a desire or grievance, they do so unostentatiously and seem to be partly talking to themselves, as if to marvel at their own "grace . . . to live as variously as possible." O'Hara, almost always writing in verse, permits his characters to speak in several registers over the course of a single play. Those who skate quickly over topics and situations, covering a subject with a spray of talk, can also relax to the point of lassitude and wait for narratively irrelevant, unpsychological, yet more expansively self-aware expression to surface. At still other moments, they speak telegraphically, cryptically: the structural cavities in their speeches allow for greater emotional resonance. O'Hara's protagonists are simultaneously engaged and insular. Even in the midst of action, they hover over themselves, mystified by the strangeness beneath them. Even as they seal themselves within airless private milieux, they wonder what is socially or culturally typical in their behavior. An aspiration that O'Hara eventually renounced for his poetry remains a useful description of his theater — to "make life's nebulous events tangible to me" and to "bring forth the intangible quality of incidents which are all too concrete and circumstantial."[95]

One precedent for this approach is the 1930s and 1940s film comedy of manners. Olivier Brossard has noted similarities between *The Houses at Falling Hanging* and Ernst Lubitsch's version of *Design for Living,* but the attraction goes beyond any single film.[96] In an entertaining annotated list of his favorite comedies of manners, O'Hara names the principles that, to a reader of his plays, will seem to have determined his own style: "Lines . . . handled like some spare, dry music" (in the *Thin Man* series), characters "mocking [their] own sexual aura" (in *Flame of New Orleans*), milieux that grant their inhabitants high style but threaten to revoke their humanity (a danger Loretta Young's character resists in *He Stayed for Breakfast*).[97] The genre's chastity and brisk, impatient intelligence also find a dedicated student in O'Hara. When he salutes the sublimation of passion in *Woman Chases Man* — "sexual attraction took its true place in the firmament of 'ideas' " — he could be describing his own theater's worldliness (168). Both the comedies he admires and those he writes insist on a restraining skepticism toward "natural" behavior, a highly polished surface to every character's demeanor, and an impersonality that makes even candor sound calculated. No wonder that prominent on his list are films that pay tribute to performance itself — *Trouble in Paradise,* with its thieves impersonating aristocrats, and *The Princess Comes Across,* its title character really a Brooklyn-born schemer seeking Hollywood riches. In them, and in any actor's manufactured ingenuousness, one can see a source for O'Hara's interest in the interdependence of deception and authenticity.

The category of "manners" distills this interplay to its essence. In O'Hara's plays, as in his favorite films, flexible codes control the characters' social intercourse, keeping them from rising to, much less lingering at, emotional extremes, lest they lose the ability to adjust their moods, change their minds, or respond to a new object of interest. Yet this discretion, a socially presentable form of repression, is also the most genuine testimony to the anxiety roiling under the surface or kept to the margins of consciousness. What O'Hara once wrote about Balanchine's *Western Symphony* is germane: "The ability to move and to think fast, to be gay and admired, takes away part of the pain of living."[98] The intricate choreography of social discourse has the same ameliorative function, numbing one's fear of fate by heightening one's sensitivity to circumstance. "Manners are the means by which society robs the individual of his sincerity," O'Hara writes in his article on film comedy (165). As adapted to his plays, the principle is theatrically viable insofar as O'Hara prevents us from knowing whether he regrets or celebrates the theft.

Indeed, O'Hara's revision of sincerity, that staple of much American acting and playwriting, reveals the ambiguities of a theater often considered merely arch. O'Hara opposes sincerity to his much-prized feeling — the former is performed, saccharine, and derivative; the latter is open, flowing, unrehearsed, fresh. (The transparency of even the strongest feelings explains why he calls them "facts.") His poems, as in so many other instances, condense this argument to an aphorism: "It is more important to affirm the least sincere," he writes, sincerely, in "Meditations in an Emergency."[99] (He makes the same point more directly in the essay "How to Proceed in the Arts": "Aren't we sick of sincerity?")[100] These sentiments seem, at first glance, our cue to admire the disinterested and decorous atmosphere of the plays — or rather, they would be, had O'Hara not admitted in another poem that he "loathe[s] disinterest . . .

and the decorum of the senses!"[101] His ambivalence deepens in one of his many poems inspired by Edwin Denby: "I seem intimate with what I merely touch."[102] We may at first hear the poet boasting of his skill in drawing full pleasure from fleeting encounters, but it shouldn't take long for us also to sense his regret at passing up deeper experiences.

Depth should repel a writer devoted, as many have noted, to the cultivation of surfaces: "Tell me," he says in a much-quoted letter to Larry Rivers accompanying some new poems, "if there are 'holes' in them, if the surface isn't kept 'up.' "[103] But in light of his ongoing self-debate over sincerity and feeling, this obsession, too, grows equivocal. O'Hara worries over rather than merely caresses a text's surface, aware of the subterranean pressures that might make it crack. In doing so, he makes another distinction between affective states: sincerity is controllable, while feeling is not. If he didn't practice "self-conscious bitterness . . . and admire it as technique," he writes in "The 'Unfinished' " (a memorial poem for his Poets' Theater colleague Bunny Lang), he'd be "perfectly truthful / and fall into the vat of longing and suffocate in its suet."[104] Much as he'd like always to project an air of knowingness, vulnerability breaks through, as happens in his poem "At the Theatre." O'Hara's ironic detachment seems secure when he names Pirandello in the first line and when, further on, he writes, "I'd read the program, knew who / was really acting and who was not." Nonetheless, sophistication is no protection against feeling: before long, he is "sobbing" while "people in niches / sneered at my intrusion."[105] ("You think your life is like Pirandello," he tells himself in "Lines for the Fortune Cookies," "but it's really like O'Neill.")[106]

The protagonists of O'Hara's plays also fail to resist the undertow of their acute sensitivity. It pulls them below the plays' chic surfaces toward an emptiness they had hoped to ignore. Three of O'Hara's most achieved plays are studies of attachment. Family life in *Change Your Bedding!* (1951), marriage in *Try! Try!* and the broader social scene in *The Houses at Falling Hanging* are all sites of resistance and self-questioning, where characters try to find a way to take pleasure from companionship without sacrificing their autonomy. The young son in *Change Your Bedding!* rebels against parents who believe that "manner is all" and against his own O'Haraesque habit of seeing all life as art. Only by succeeding at separating himself from them (and their idea of him) will he know "what's true," become "articulate" and "myself," and no longer fear (as his parents still do) confronting "real pain" instead of merely "apparent horror."[107] In *The Houses at Falling Hanging*, Miriam, a guest at a cocktail party, detects the boredom and anxiety beneath the glittering talk. ("I always feel terribly melancholy / at this time of day," one man admits, and another agrees: "That's why / we invite each other for drinks I guess.")[108] To save

Figure 19: Scene design by Edward Gorey for Frank O'Hara's *Try! Try!* as presented by the Poets' Theater, Cambridge, 1951. The Harvard Theatre Collection, Houghton Library. Reproduced by permission of the Edward Gorey Charitable Trust.

herself from falling into their melodramatic abyss—rendered especially frightening, Olivier Brossard notes, in the actual drop-off at the edge of the host's property (7)—Miriam chooses primitive over "civilized" pleasures: a Tarzan-like suitor swings on a vine across the stage at the end and promises to carry her away from self-involvement and predictable excitement. Miriam's counterpart in *Try! Try!* is quizzical and mildly anesthetized, suspended halfway between conviction and indifference. Parrying the claims of a lover and a husband (the latter a soldier returning home from war), Violet implements a strategy of "inattention," "passionately efficient distraction," "attractive distances," even "blessed boredom," if by such half-withdrawals she can keep "the blackness in me" tamped down. "I do think I / despise you," she says to one suitor, "but not as much as you would wish" (39).

The two versions of *Try! Try!* are studded with declarations that, when taken together, warn against the consequences of excessive introspection. (They also, not incidentally, seem to reproach American theater for many unexamined articles of faith, especially those promoting psychological depth: characters insist they "can't carry memory / everywhere" [27], that "it's not enough / to be thoughtful" [31], and that "it's not fun / to be understood" [20].) Most indicative of the crisis in which they find themselves, when the tensions of an adultery narrative should be stimulating the keenest of emotions and the most quivering alertness, is Violet's admission that "I don't know what I feel" (21).

At these moments O'Hara's art, usually propelled by his unequivocal, fluent opinions, his own "knowing what he feels," sinks into shadow. His speakers can no longer sustain the bright, smart personae we've grown accustomed to from the poems. Yet neither are they wholly dark. No such romantic posture is available to them. Violet's confession points to a confusion affecting the play as a whole. O'Hara succeeds in finding theatrical power in inchoate, mild, and thus, by conventional standards, untheatrical states. These protagonists are often slack, even helpless; their demeanors are pallid. "One season you're tan, you're happy, you're lying / beside an ocean," says Violet. "The next," adds her lover, John, "you're losing weight, you're cold, you're / getting bald" (40). The poet of motion shows himself to be a playwright of deliquescence, even inertia. This is the most suggestive meaning, beyond the obvious formal appeal, of an opening stage direction: "The movement is photographic rather than dramatic," O'Hara writes, explaining why he calls *Try! Try!* a Noh play (17). The title itself establishes his theater's intimacy with failure. The repetition of "Try" and the overenthusiastic, even crazed exclamation points are not so much rallying cries as admissions of futility. "We look / for abundance of feeling, to counteract / the sterility of war," John says in the 1951 version, when the sterility of 1950s America was itself beginning to encroach on O'Hara's own milieu (19). Yet he seems aware that his chances of succeeding are slim. The play unfolds in an aftermath, when the energies needed for renewal, long since depleted, have yet to be replenished. Excitement is something the characters experience only retrospectively—the frisson of adultery, the thrill of battle, a "dazzled time" that Violet wistfully commemorates. "Life went by so fast," she says as the play begins, implying that the theatricalized life we're about to see is, in some sense, posthumous (19).

The action opens after the last chance for "real" action has been revoked. O'Hara writes the only comedy of manners possible in a landscape being mapped in these same years by Beckett. (O'Hara had been reading him devoutly since college.) The American playwright deposits his own directionless characters in a shapeless, barren setting and strips them of all but the most local purposes. They, too, wait—"as when the subway stops / just before reaching a station," says John—and "breathe heavily / for a minute, all of a minute, though very sure / of the time, his hand on her lips; her eyes / stirring" (22). These trapped characters anticipate their own arrival in a new context, where there will be new prods to their ambition. In the meantime, they feel only the thickness of the present moment: "I feel like a tube of hot / cement," Violet says (33). Her husband, Jack, remembers the moment in battle when his courage gave way definitively to cowardice, a diminishment that defines him still. John, more prosaically, suffers the insult of being deemed "no gangster of the sheets" and, simply, not "interesting" (34–35). Together, the three are a satirical comment on the kind of theater their histories should have destined for them. The warrior, the siren, and the Casanova are, here, inmates of a shallow, ordinary room (a kitchen in one version, a studio in another). "I'm glad / you're back," says Violet when her husband returns from war. But before the expected heartwarming embrace, she adds, "Just don't / look at my fingernails" (23).

An explicit reference to the theater helps us sense the largest implications of O'Hara's mutating aesthetic principles. "It's not easy to be / spectator or audience," says John. "Always overruled by / someone else's plan / of what you really want" (21). The speech should surprise O'Hara's students. Doesn't he ordinarily relish the customs of spectatorship, look forward to the very surrender of autonomy that John regrets? Here O'Hara concedes what he elsewhere suppresses — that at the peak of stimulation, spectatorship can be enervating, if not masochistic in its passivity. The reality that one has been "overruled" in the presence of art reasserts itself after the egotistical fantasy of power that comes with acting on one's taste. The play's languid characters mirror their suppliant spectators more than any external reality.

Moreover, the characters' knowledge that true excitement faded long ago reflects a truth about art's own belatedness. The rapture of creativity also ended before the curtain's rise. In his poems, O'Hara embraces this fact so passionately as to suggest its pleasures rival those of art itself. "Wait / till the *Liebeslieder Walzer* are all / over," he writes of Balanchine's 1960 ballet in "Variations on Saturday," "and we'll have that regret too / to hold us and cheer us."[109] The lines turn on the paradox that a work of theater is only complete when time erases it, that the most exquisite pleasure follows the end of stimulation, and that the spectator's responsiveness sharpens when there is nothing tangible left to respond to. A more definitive loss shadows "Ode to Tanaquil LeClercq." New York City Ballet's wittiest ballerina (and Balanchine's then-wife) was stricken with polio in 1956 at age twenty-seven; dismay at her premature retirement keeps O'Hara from floating "upward into lilac-colored ozone" on a fantasy of her, or any dancer's, perpetual speed and weightlessness. He is "dropped . . . from way up there" when she herself stops moving. A beloved performer "disappear[s] in the wings," leaving "nothing . . . but . . . a decision about death" and an audience that "holds its breath / to see if you are there" (364). In that unrelieved state of waiting, facing a permanently empty stage, O'Hara gains time and space to confront a fact evaded during bouts of intoxicated spectatorship: arts of continuous motion doom their addicts to an experience of continuous mourning.

The awareness of death flickering briefly in this poem joins it to O'Hara's other poems marking a performer's catastrophic fall — Billie Holiday's in "The Day Lady Died," Lana Turner's in the untitled poem that begins "Lana Turner has collapsed!" In a lesser-known work composed before these meditations on mortality in dance, music, and film, O'Hara fleetingly imagines theater's own fall. A gnomic line in an untitled poem points to "the theater where my play is echoed by dying voices."[110] (The phrase itself is an echo of Beckett's "all the dead voices.") O'Hara's well-known aesthetic commitments, at once self-centered and collaborative, supply one meaning for the passage: a play's fullest life exists only in the writing of it and in the excited talk after his friends' first reading of it. Actors' voices, speaking later (another disappointing aftermath), are mere echoes that grow fainter and further from their source with every repetition.

Other meanings are available only to readers coming to the poem, or to the unnamed play it cites, years after its initial sounding. Now the texts are conditioned by the dispersal of the social circle they convened and commemorated, by the dissipation of the collaborative energies that executed them, and by the degrading effects of time itself. The plays, and torsos of plays, that dedicated editors, resourceful scholars, and pack-rat friends have salvaged are the only material traces of permanently lost moments in a history of affection. Their characters mark sites of now irretrievable pleasure. Their scenes are souvenirs of severed companionship and dried-up passion. "I have lost . . . the scene of my selves," he writes in the premonitory "In Memory of My Feelings," a title that suggests the deepest pleasure of any emotion occurs in a future (and thus detached) reexperiencing of it (257). (O'Hara's early death in 1966, at age forty, of course intensifies this desolation, but it would be there in any case.) O'Hara unwittingly writes ghost plays; they form a theater that, having measured degrees of liveliness in its own day, is now archeological. In his *Selected Plays,* the dramatic fragments join wholes of uncertain significance to conjure up a dead city. Coming to it belatedly, we piece together a culture's manner of kinship and its myriad social courtesies. We've already seen how O'Hara, in drawing attention to the work of writing, may have hoped to prevent just such a transformation of artworks into artifacts. Was he also hoping to postpone indefinitely their decay by neglecting to finish, publish, or stage so many of them? If a text won't be born, can it ever die? Time prevails, of course. The plays are now infused with regret for the transience of everything they represent and symbolize — the same regret O'Hara clings to after the end of *Liebeslieder Walzer,* itself a work gesturing to a lost empire of style nowhere to be seen in the America of 1960. "You were always changing into something else / and always will be," he writes of LeClercq (364). Upholding an O'Hara ideal in ways he couldn't have anticipated, the plays, too, have changed.

7

Returning to Neutral

There is no peace in images.
— *Roland Barthes,* The Neutral

I always find it advantageous to leave an empty space in each work; it has to do with not imposing.
                    — *Wassily Kandinsky, letter to Arnold Schoenberg*

In a series of articles published in the *Village Voice* after the 1961 New York premiere of *The Blacks,* the ground gives way beneath the American theater. Here the play's most prominent defender is no more able than its most eloquent detractor to accept Jean Genet's challenge to established theatrical practices. Norman Mailer, burning with conviction in the first essay, frequently interrupts himself to warn against the playwright's lack of conviction. He praises Genet for his "unrelenting sense of where the bodies are buried" in the "haunted canyons of the cancer-ridden city," yet mocks him for "adoring any perfume which conceals the smell of the dead."[1] The whiff of macho derision is predictable, given the source. It is present, too, when Mailer vents his frustration at the playwright's aloofness. "A line which is a universal blow is followed by a speech too private for his latest lover to comprehend" (14). By the end of Mailer's essay, his admiration is mixed with regret that Genet is not more sincere or (what amounts to the same thing) that he is too theatrical. To one who believes that only rough gestures can awaken the culture from complacency, Genet will seem a "Narcissist," his art a mere "pirouette." "How great a writer," Mailer concludes, "how hideous a cage" (15).

The surprise in Lorraine Hansberry's response to the play, published in the *Voice* two weeks later, isn't that she lampoons Mailer's "paternalism" (as she calls it) nor that she dissents from the popular, positive opinion of Genet. The author of *A Raisin in the Sun* owes her own theatrical authority to her characters' vulnerability and honesty — qualities alien, if not unintelligible, to Genet, a writer skeptical of all emotions save those accompanying betrayal. What readers may not expect, however, especially from a writer positioning herself as Mailer's antagonist, is that she expresses her distaste for indirection in terms that Mailer himself first proposes. The Mailer who insists that "White and Black in mortal confrontation are far more interesting than the play of shadows Genet brings to it" (14) has an unlikely ally in the Hansberry who argues that "the oppressed" have become mere "shadows upon the windows" in *The Blacks:* they "have been abstracted into 'the style.' "[2]

Shadowiness may be a particular affront to a writer who has labored to bring a hitherto unacknowledged culture to light. "Style" can seem an instrument of deception to one wary of euphemism and dishonesty in the larger world. Yet Hansberry's impatience with Genet's formal ingenuities reveals more than her desire to do justice to the society surrounding her. She also speaks for many other spectators, regardless of their own commitments, who are bewildered and irritated by a diffident mode of theatricality. The New York premiere of *The Blacks* was a commercial and critical success — it ran for four years and was a generative event in the history of Off Broadway — but in the process it exposed an aesthetic fault line. In her essay, Hansberry stands at its edge, naming exactly an attitude that is offensive to those artists and audiences still faithful, as she is, to a theater that invites our involvement by the credibility of its representations, and that delivers us from confusion into useful knowledge. She resents Genet's "refusal to honor our longings for communion" (10). The "absence of humanness" in *The Blacks*, she implies, renders its arguments about race trivial or specious (14).

Like Mailer, Hansberry is an astute diagnostician of techniques she can't abide. Genet does rebuff the prying viewer. Spectatorship at his theater is more isolating than the often forced fellowship available in other arenas. (Writing to *The Blacks*' first director, Genet pushed himself to go still further in future plays: "The action must be rather evasive — but not vague! — in order to leave the spectator confronted with himself alone.")[3] Those who expect to share in the "ultimate anguish" of "*man's* oppression of *man*," as Hansberry puts it, instead encounter only "theatrical" facsimiles of misery—the epithet used, again, in defense of a realistic and more sociable theater (14). There's no one behind these images, no "man" populates the landscape of oppression. Blacks, Hansberry rightly remarks, have been replaced by "The Blacks" (14), a substitution that, in the American theater of 1961, may have caused spectators to feel embarrassed by how credulous they have been before the "reality" of their own dramas.

Other Genet plays had appeared in New York before 1961—Julie Bovasso's Tempo Theater produced the American premiere of *The Maids* in 1955; *The Balcony* opened in 1960—but *The Blacks* seems, in retrospect, to have cut most deeply into American theatrical culture, so much so that today it reads as an American play. No doubt its social context sharpened its effect on us. As Edmund White, Genet's biographer, points out, a narrative opposing black subjects to white authority, precondition for a clash of rebellious and repressive energies, seduces audiences of the civil rights era and beyond with its familiarity (506). Yet this seduction, like many seductions, is deceptive. Genet's influence on a generation of American writers has more to do with his skill in escaping the confines of subject matter and ideology than in legitimizing them. Attentive readers give up any expectation of a race melodrama before the play begins. A prefatory note disputes what would seem to be such a plot's basic fact: "What exactly is a black?" Genet writes. "First of all, what's his color?"[4] Spectators, for their part, suffer the same correction upon the entrance of the "white" characters: they are played by black actors wearing white masks, caricatures of religious, legal, and political powerbrokers. Throughout the play, Genet demolishes sacrosanct ideas of theatrical presence and immediacy without recommending comforting alternatives. In such a void, he models resignation to a "stage where everything is relative," as one character says (41). "Dramatic" action—the rape and killing of a white woman, the trial of both her murderer and the white judges — and pronouncements about its moral consequences take shape only to dissolve, their value effaced by the anxiety over mimesis.

Effacement itself becomes Genet's subject. The literal masking of the actors (even the "black" actors smear their faces with burnt cork) is the visible sign of an attraction to invisibility. One character speaks of "stretching language . . . sufficiently to wrap ourselves in it and hide" (27). He later imagines his fellow actors "reflected in [the theater] . . . slowly disappearing into its waters" (38–39). All the performers maintain an unpopulated, ceremonial distance between themselves and their spectators; ensure that "the ultimate gesture" (here, the trial and execution of a black revolutionary) "is performed offstage" (84); and, finally, check the desire to resist their own erasure. "Every actor knows that at a given time the curtain will fall" (90). When the white figures disappear into "Africa," "sink into shame," and at the end submit to their "lyrical" execution, Genet completes the evacuation of his stage (115). What remains is what Genet began with — only the "architecture of emptiness and words" (126), a space in which are exposed the latent desires of an increasingly self-conscious audience. "We are what they want us to be," says one of the blacks of his white judges (126), pausing until the whites in Genet's own audience look from the stage toward themselves.

To playwrights oppressed by the unironic, unhesitant assertions of liveness on American stages, Genet's example teaches methods of resistance. Samuel Beckett teaches still others, and it's customary to credit him with even more forcefully determining the move toward absence in post-1960 American drama. Of course, any notion of movement inherited from Beckett betrays the term's promise of change. As Leo Bersani and Ulysse Dutoit note, the first line of *Endgame* (produced in New York in 1958) implies that the play is over before it begins: "Finished," Clov says, "it's finished, nearly finished."[5] One of Clov's last lines confirms that after a single long act the play has gone nowhere. "It ends, it changes" (81). Here, as in all his work, Beckett asks us to imagine a drama that changes after ending or that simultaneously ends and changes. Hamm later says, "moments for nothing. . . . Time was never and time is over" (83). The additional contradiction challenges American playwrights to break free of teleology while still providing the illusion of action. Ambitious writers postpone climaxes indefinitely as separate "moments" dilate and deepen. Equally ambitious audiences contemplate these scenes without referring them to external sources of meaning. They aren't "for" anything but themselves. They aren't about anything, not even "nothing." As Bersani and Dutoit argue, Beckett's "art of impoverishment" imposes austerity measures upon even the representation of poverty (14). We can't comfort ourselves that, in a landscape of "impotence" and "incompetence" (as Bersani and Dutoit describe it), at least the technique to communicate such a deficit survives. "I ask the words that remain," says Clov, seeking from them a way to name and thus understand the extremity of his state. "They have nothing to say" (81). Hamm echoes him: "You . . . remain," he tells himself, just before covering his face with the handkerchief that earlier quoted the stage curtain — and thus removing himself from the sphere of art (84).

Genet himself dwells on the word "remain" in his famous essay on Giacometti (written the same year as *Endgame*) and in the process sets up a tension that affects the American theater more than either playwright does alone. One imagines the two writers in debate: if what remains in Beckett is inert and has "nothing to say," in Genet that same residue is beguiling and mercurial. Genet imagines Giacometti asking, "what remains of man when the pretence is removed?" as the sculptor works upon his eroding, anorexic figures.[6] Another layer of clay, it seems. Writing of a set of finished sculptures, and again stressing the resonant verb, Genet asks, "while their image remains visible, where are they?" (43). Beckett may lead us to endings of irremediable exhaustion, but Genet reminds us that we haven't reached the end of performance. After what seems like extinction, the "image" survives—one that crystallizes only after other facsimiles of life dissolve. Genet's essay "The Tightrope Walker" (1958) puts the matter concisely, in terms that apply no less to other forms of performance. "Death . . . is not the one that will follow your fall," he says to the acrobat, "but the one that precedes your appearance on the wire."[7] The performer must banish his own identity if his stage persona is to be legible— "diminish" himself, as Genet puts it, "to let [his] image . . . sparkle ever more brilliantly. He should exist finally only in his appearance" (73).

As this passage makes clear, the death that Genet imagines enlivening theater bears only superficial similarity to the deaths that end certain narratives or ensure a character's pathos (although in his plays he depicts both). Genet has in mind a more pervasive, less anecdotal condition. His ideal theater challenges the facile charisma on other stages (and the vaunted immortality in other arts) by admitting the perishability of every personality, the contingency of every composition, and the ephemerality of every action. It also takes distance from dramas of proselytizing argument and earnest statements. His preferred theater—"in the catacombs," as he puts it in a letter, or "in the shadow" of a "cemetery"—would be the strongest possible antidote to a culture that "seems to be going so cheerfully toward the luminosity of analysis," where "science deciphers everything."[8] Throughout his writings on theater, he pulls his reader away from any art's seemingly necessary availability, through what he calls the "fissures" of spectacle and "interstices between words," down to a "subterranean life."[9] There, in an implicit rebuke to other artists unjustifiably confident that they have captured their subjects, lies "an appearance that shows the void."[10]

This idea of presence has profound implications for the American drama written in the shadow of its shadows. If the proliferation of necrophiliac plays since 1960 is any indication, Genet's metaphor continues to prove attractive to artists who share his simultaneous enchantment by and skepticism of illusion. One best approaches this work with Genet's sensibility in mind—moving past the narrative and emotional significance of death to the aesthetic and ideological value of nullity. Granted, the sheer theatricality of these representations (or the incantatory power of the language substituting for them) often makes it hard to do so. Drop down almost at random into the serious American theater and you're amid "catacombs" and "cemeteries," archeological sites, scenes of ruin and failure. In Sam Shepard's *Buried Child* (1978) the earth gives up a child's skeleton, an object shocking only in its inability to shock the family that discarded it. The protagonist of Wallace Shawn's *The Fever* (1990) tells us that a "fragment of bone . . . a piece — of a human brain — a severed hand" sit on his night table, an exhumation to counter the many forms of moral falling he experiences throughout the play.[11] Other bones surface in August Wilson's *Joe Turner's Come and Gone* (1988) — "a whole heap of them," says a character about the slave ancestors he sees in a hallucination. "They come up out the water and started marching."[12] Water is no more secure a grave in Wilson's *The Piano Lesson* (1990): a ghost of a landowner who drowned in a well haunts those who would themselves emerge from an airless, too-enclosing legacy of oppression. Still another grave opens at the start of Tony Kushner's *Angels in America* (1992) (it will hold one character's grandmother) and never closes: the nation's dead climb out of it to reproach or salute the living for their ethical choices; the living teeter on its edge, defiantly keeping their balance. Kushner's *Hydriotaphia* (1987) comes alive in the same argument with mortality. Its dying protagonist, Sir Thomas Browne, delays his own urn burial by seeking (as Kushner himself does in all his work) an ever clearer, more complete and specific, more historically grounded and morally resonant name for fate.

Maria Irene Fornes and Adrienne Kennedy pay especially obsessive attention to the membrane separating theatrical presence and absence. Fornes's *Enter THE NIGHT* (1993) is set around a pit ("as large as the space permits") in a warehouse.[13] Characters descend to and rise from its depths, or edge around its perimeter, as they conduct various rituals of self-abasement. Orlando, in Fornes's *The Conduct of Life* (1985), imprisons, rapes, and tortures a young girl in his sepulchral basement. In *Fefu and Her Friends* (1977), Fefu and Emma begin one scene by emerging from a root cellar. Another character, Julia, seems to sink into the earth — the floor of her room is incongruously covered with leaves — before surfacing from her memory of sexual violence. The scenic opposite of all these abysses is in *Mud* (1983), where a mound of dirt forms an antiheroic pedestal for her poor, unhealthy protagonists, as if a grave, having once claimed them, has thrown them up.

Adrienne Kennedy's *Funnyhouse of a Negro* (1964) echoes with the threnody "he is dead, but dead he comes knocking at my door."[14] This particular revenant is the protagonist's father, but all the characters have "highly powdered" faces "as in the face of death," and their stage is framed by a white satin curtain meant to "bring to mind the interior of a cheap casket" (11–12). Here, as in all these plays, depictions of death transcend individual experience: photographs of "Roman ruins" decorate the title character's room, where she futilely hopes for the sense of membership she can't enjoy in the outside, present-day world. She dwells in an entire culture's grave. So, too, does the protagonist of *The Owl Answers* (1965) who wants to bury her "Dead White Father" in the crypt of Saint Paul's Cathedral but is trapped in various sites of sacrifice—the prison at the Tower of London, an altar at Saint Peter's Basilica, a Harlem hotel room—each of which confirms her exclusion from both European and African-American culture. Kennedy traces similar cycles of longing and rejection in *A Movie Star Has to Star in Black and White* (1976). Clara, her alter ego, enlists Bette Davis, Jean Peters, and Shelley Winters to "star in her life" and submerges her family narrative in settings from their famous movies. Her self-annihilating form of identification exists on a spectrum of erasure that includes a suicide attempt, a miscarriage, and a coma in Clara's own family; Shelley Winters slipping beneath a lake's surface in *A Place in the Sun;* Bette Davis, in *Now Voyager,* burying her once-awkward identity beneath new glamour; and Kennedy herself sinking into her own theater history when Clara reads aloud from the earlier *The Owl Answers.*

Artists whom theater historians usually segregate from these playwrights join them in probing the ruins of illusion: this art of the beneath (as one might call it) is confined to no single school. The American theater's most uncompromising archeologist, Jack Smith, organized a number of his productions from 1970 to 1972 around a vast heap of plaster in his New York apartment. It presumably fell from the ceiling, where a huge hole revealed his living quarters on the loft's second floor—an arrangement that implied that we, along with Smith, were underground, or at least beneath the orderly world of domesticity. All his work, including the many productions Smith staged in future apartments up to his death in 1989, emerged from rubble. Smith's plays began with detritus—dead Christmas trees, plastic fish, stuffed animals, dolls, silks, LPs, signs, wigs—all assembled for "the final burial rites of the capitalist civilization" (as Jonas Mekas describes them) over which Smith presided like a "grave keeper."[15] They degenerated still further in separate performances and over the course of a run. Smith chose not to resist, and often triggered, numerous breakdowns in production. Performances typically began hours late. Scenery collapsed. Lighting never satisfied the tropistic star it illuminated. Effects fastidiously prepared ended up malfunctioning. Performers (Smith included) forgot, or seemed to forget, their lines. If Smith carried a script, he often dropped or misplaced crucial pages. Everything unfolded with excruciating slowness.

Writing of a 1940s film performance, Smith praises "the disintegration of its character—especially the leading man. . . . He is given every opportunity to disintegrate to the point of gilded splendor."[16] Smith's own ravishingly artificial productions also submit to nature's logic, embracing a biological identity (one that of course ends in death) to put forward a more authentic spectacle of life. Smith strove for the penetrating expressiveness that surfaces only in the experience of creative exhaustion. "Things would grow up around it," Smith writes, hopefully, of a giant junkyard he wants to establish in the center of his city.[17] "In this theater," he writes elsewhere, "the first consideration in every decision is good ecology."[18]

Smith's communion with the dead led to new life in the theater around him, too. Charles Ludlam emulated his recuperative ambition and scavenging technique, raiding theater history for plots, character types, models of dramatic structure, and styles of diction discarded in the culture's quest for originality. His rhetoric directly echoed Smith: "It's ecological theater," Ludlam writes in "Confessions of a Farceur." "We take the abandoned refuse, the used images, the shoes from abandoned shoe factories, the clichés, and search for their true meaning. We are recycling culture."[19] (That utopian project doesn't compensate for the hole now visible in Ludlam's plays after the death of their author and leading man.) Richard Foreman enacts burial rites of his own in a setting that, not incidentally, realizes Genet's hope of a theatricalized cemetery. Audiences attending his plays at St. Mark's Church, one of New York's oldest houses of worship, first walk through a garden filled with decrepit gravestones and other memorials (the Stuyvesants are buried here) before ascending to a tiny second-floor room. It's a journey that prepares them for dramas of spiritual seeking set against the gravitational pull of secular fate. The titles of Meredith Monk's music-theater pieces— *Quarry, American Archeology I, Recent Ruins, Volcano Songs*—name her own art's decaying, petrifying landscape and the compulsion for recovery that reanimates it. "I started thinking about the idea of residue," Monk has said about *Portable,* a work from 1966.[20] In later pieces, she gathers traces of Holocaust dead, Ellis Island ghosts, patients in a nineteenth-century smallpox hospital, inmates of a long-closed prison, and victims of Pompeii-like devastation—often using and dramatizing the use of photography, video, and film to stress her theater's battle with oblivion. Yet she also forestalls the preservationist's pride by insisting on the unbridgeable distance between present and past. At the end of *Quarry* (1976), her best work, her protagonist points to pictures of the dead and sings an agitated, vertiginous threnody, as if she were protesting not only the loss but photography's, or any art's, failure to compensate for it.

Elizabeth LeCompte measures these same distances, in a wholly different idiom, with the Wooster Group, a company whose offhand neutrality or (at the other extreme) obviously constructed expressions of emotion respect the privacy of bereavement, concede its unstageability, and open up space to confront more expansive, cultural forms of absence. Archeology remains the metaphor of choice. A 2007 production based on Richard Burton's 1964 "Theatrofilm" of *Hamlet* "reconstruct[s] a hypothetical theater piece from the fragmentary evidence of the edited film" (as the group puts it in a program note), "like an archeologist inferring an improbable temple from a collection of ruins."[21] Earlier works pull the company into ruins without the guarantee of deliverance. In *Poor Theater* (2004), the actors descend into a hole after completing a ceremony for the dead in their company (their fellow actors Ron Vawter and Spalding Gray), their city (a New York turned necropolis on September 11, 2001), and their century (the six million memorialized in Jerzy Grotowski's Holocaust play *Akropolis*, another "collection of ruins" that the group excavates, partly reconstructs, and then reinters). This burial ground recalls — and seems to expand — one that first opened in *Route 1 and 9 (The Last Act)* (1981). That production's last section is set within — not merely at — the graves of *Our Town*'s third act. The stage is shrouded in darkness; performers cough up "blood"; their clothes drop from their bodies; blackface that they wore at the start smears like dirt, as if they were freshly exhumed or recently interred corpses. "Dead people talking," an actor impersonating Clifton Fadiman had said near the start, summing up the action of *Our Town*.[22] Scenes from Wilder's play appear on video monitors hung from the ceiling, performed by actors who are pristine and brightly lit. We gaze up at the screens from the dead's point of view.

After one catalogues these plays and productions, one might think there's no further — or rather, no lower — the American theater can go in confronting absence. Yet this theater's preoccupation with last things is best seen as a prelude to an even more demanding notion of austerity, merely the image or (to recall Genet) the "appearance" of death that masks a nonreferential "void." There is a further withdrawal that many of these same artists make, a chasm deeper than the grave they sound. As they seek this purer blankness, they promise us no revelation, not even a new image or utterance. That's the point: on these stages, they await the theater that surfaces when they refrain from expression.

While she isn't speaking explicitly about American drama, Peggy Phelan seems to have just this elusiveness in mind when she points us to the "remains" of an artwork that "cannot be assimilated into an . . . object of . . . contemplation."[23] One might add that it can't be assimilated into an object of criticism. Several of the most searching recent critics — Marvin Carlson, Alice Rayner, Joseph Roach, and David Savran, among others — gravitate to sites where this art of presence and the present tense is shadowed by absence and the past.[24] Yet at their most suggestive these writers allow us to imagine their rhetoric's inadequacy before nonrepresentational recesses and hollows. A discourse of "mourning" or "memory," or a narrative of "haunting," falls silent before a theater where nothing awaits our remembering, where no entity ever registered its presence forcefully enough to be effaced and uncovered later. Theater enlisted in acts of commemoration — the stage serving as shrine — depends on narratives that move from possession to loss, and then from loss to restoration, if only in one's imagination. Yet discrete passages in certain American plays disregard that compensatory logic in favor of a longer, inconclusive engagement with depletion. They are among the most rewarding artifacts in our theater. Their value depends on their remaining immaculate, untouched by any artistic or interpretive mark, so clean as to blind all who approach them. The only action in such empty spaces is idleness. Characters themselves seem emptied out — affectless or, if forthcoming, so skeptical of their own disclosures that they revert to self-blurring ambivalence. The source of this style deflects any attempt to ally it to a particular cause, and shakes off metaphors if they impose too much meaning on a carefully maintained neutrality.

Roland Barthes's own commitment to what he calls "the Neutral" offers the best correlative for these artists' discipline. "I define the Neutral as that which outplays the paradigm," he writes in a lecture from 1978, "or rather I call Neutral everything that baffles the paradigm."[25] The "paradigm" is binary conflict (which Barthes elsewhere calls "too theatrical") and all that conflict requires: dogma, ideology, systems, "affirmation."[26] That which "outplays" it (one welcomes the theatrical allusion in the English verb) includes such states as weariness and sleep, such actions as retreat and "shirking," and such attributes as indifference and tact. The inspiration for Barthes's lectures, Maurice Blanchot, could be describing this theater's relation to its audience when he writes, "The neutral does not seduce, does not attract."[27] Reticence, diffidence, impassivity, invisibility — readers and spectators who, in other theaters, might impatiently pull aside these veils in search of more eventfulness or personality instead learn to distinguish among nuances of restraint. They consider them as they might look at a spectrum of whites, or hear distinctive tones of silence, or pass through a series of unoccupied, unfurnished rooms, each with its own particular resonance. Indeed, it's only through this abnegation that the American theater achieves the same stoicism animating contemporaneous visual art and dance. ("NO to spectacle," said Yvonne Rainer in post-1960 dance's fundamental manifesto, "no to transformations and magic and make-believe . . . no to style . . . no to seduction of spectator by the wiles of the performer.")[28]

A theater of "no" might strike us as fatally impalpable, and indeed some of these playwrights gaze into ruins where there is nothing to see or salvage. "I feel I am hollow," says a Fornes character in *Mud*.[29] "I feel sometimes that I am drowning in vagueness — that I have no character," says another woman in her *Abingdon Square* (1987).[30] Ma Rainey, in August Wilson's *Ma Rainey's Black Bottom* (1984), sings into what she calls her listeners' "emptiness," yet even as she "fill[s] it up" with the blues, she knows the appeal of her art depends on their emptying out again.[31] Yet other writers treat emptiness as an opportunity. Not an opportunity for replenishment: the harder task is to preserve openness after measuring loss. In these instances, theirs is a more rigorous practice than recovery. The typical responses to sites of deterioration — grief, piety, curatorial ardor — are sentimental and inert; they close the circle of one's engagement with the scene, when what's needed is purposeful uncertainty. Is there an alternative response that depends on duration, on both spectator and artist delaying their access to language, imagery, thought, emotion — all the elements by which we recognize a spectacle as a spectacle? A number of the same playwrights we've already encountered enclose caesuras, neutral screens, and other detheatrical-ized zones in their otherwise image-rich plays, thereby offering us versions of a gift available from other forms of minimalism — breathing room, unstructured time, freedom from explicit and even implicit meanings, an uncoercive rela-tionship with someone else's imagination. Rereading them, we are forced to revise conclusions we may have reached at their scenes of ruin and decay. The latter — intelligible substitutes for losses unsusceptible to narrative and uncon-tainable by character — are too enthralling to "leave the spectator confronted with himself alone" (to recall Genet's phrase). Despite the thoroughness with which these writers depict forms of individual or cultural erasure, they fulfill their ambition only in acts of self-erasure — when they depict the ruin of writing itself or, more simply, when they refrain from writing altogether.

Many of Sam Shepard's protagonists (for instance) begin and end as blank slates. "I'm looking forward to my life," says Jeep at the start of *Action* (1975). "I'm looking forward to uh — me."[32] By the end, that self has yet to arrive — or has come and quickly gone. "It's like I'm dismissed" (188). (His friend Shooter says, "Maybe I'm gone" [188].) Their confusion is shared by the many other Shepard figures who peel off inherited or inorganic personalities while simulta-neously discouraging us from thinking a "true" character exists at their cores. "You'd be O.K . . . if you had a self," Hoss tells a friend in *The Tooth of Crime* (1972). "So would I."[33] Near the end, the onetime rock star rejects all illusions of individualism with a desperate "IT AIN'T ME! IT AIN'T ME! IT AIN'T ME!!" (247). Niles, in *Suicide in B Flat* (1976), kills off roles he's been playing in his own music career "so I can start over" in a neutral state.[34] In *Curse of the Starving Class* (1978), Weston doesn't recognize himself one morning ("It didn't feel like me") and radically changes his appearance into something even less plausible. His daughter, declaring that "nobody looks like what they are," implies that authentic selves of any kind can't exist in the theater — an art of "looks." She runs offstage to her death with an exultant "I'm gone, I'm gone!"[35]

Adrienne Kennedy's protagonists are, if anything, excessively present, but here, too, their kaleidoscopic surfaces conceal abysses. They are best seen as a series of provisional statements rather than a comprehensive argument for an identity. The character in *The Owl Answers* known as "She who is Clara Passmore who is the Virgin Mary who is the Bastard who is the Owl" is at once all of these figures and none of them. Each of her roles deflects our attention to someone else; she eludes our possessive attention by flooding us with performances. Sarah in *Funnyhouse of a Negro* uses the same strategy. She calls upon an array of supporting characters — the Duchess of Hapsburg, Queen Victoria, and Jesus, among others — to serve as "herselves." Yet they, like the white friends Sarah cultivates, enable her only to "maintain a stark fortress against recognition of myself." It's important to note that Kennedy's protagonist treats whiteness not as compensation for her blackness, not as a positive value to her negative. On the contrary, it is the perfection of effacement. "I want to possess no moral value . . . I want not to be. I ask nothing except anonymity," she says, and adds, more prosaically, that she treasures white paper and her white glass table — correlatives to the white ancestors and friends she yearns for, of course, but also to an ideal transparency, neutrality, even nullity.[36]

Meredith Monk, Richard Foreman, and Elizabeth LeCompte, artists associated with the Theater of Images, seem to protest that classification as they envision scenic and compositional synonyms for nullity. The most chilling of reversals in Monk's *Volcano Songs* occurs when Monk, the only performer, lies down on sheets of photographic paper to imprint them with her silhouette, then allows the images to fade before we can finish admiring them. "The shadows disappear, but you have the traces," Monk says of this sequence and (one can assume) of her art in general. "Yet eventually even they disappear."[37] Near the start of Richard Foreman's *Pearls for Pigs* (1997), the artist-protagonist says, "Tonight, the play's canceled!" — a call to flee all manner of theatrical being.[38] He is "a man who runs out of stories" (235) and an actor who "erases lines of text from his sawdust-filled head" (237). The mise-en-scène should be just as vacant: "The curtain rises on nothing," says a Pierrot figure, naming a paradisiacal landscape of only potential artistry, where the imagination has yet to be compromised by visual and verbal signs (237). One imagines the playwright himself hoping for a vicarious return to this unfallen state whenever his characters tear out the pages from books (as they often do) and erase already erased blackboards. All these aggressive measures mean to bring about what Foreman calls the ideal (yet impossible) theaters of "sleep," of "doubt," of "missed opportunities," and of "hesitations." (Discussing his style with Elinor Fuchs in 1993, Foreman said, there's "always a delay. . . . So that more can be said. . . . I think my plays are always postulating a dream of presence, or a dream of transcendence . . . and then saying: But, not yet.")[39]

Elizabeth LeCompte employs her own self-canceling technique to shape (or, rather, unshape) expression, cultivating the very inhibitions most other artists feel they must overcome if they are to write anything. Static replaces certain scenes from *Our Town* on the video monitors in *Route 1 and 9 (The Last Act)*. The group's reconstruction of the old Clifton Fadiman television introduction to Wilder's play preserves the gaps in the poor dupe of the original broadcast. In *L. S. D. (. . . Just the High Points . . .)*, a buzzer cuts off actors midsentence during their recitations from 1960s-era prose. In *Brace Up!* (1991), a version of *Three Sisters*, some actors take cover behind folding screens, others never leave the upper reaches of the stage, one sits in the corner with his back to us. The play itself hides: the company omits passages of Chekhov's text and relegates the fourth act to another production altogether. *Hamlet* further develops this strategy of self-effacement. The Wooster Group performers sacrifice their own expressiveness to take on the English actors' rhythms and patterns. The production also advances an aesthetic of partiality. LeCompte uses a high-tech form of airbrushing to eliminate certain figures from the Theatrofilm (projected through most of the production). Occasionally the word "unrendered" appears onscreen, replacing an entire scene of Shakespeare. The opposite but identical image of an unrendered performance is one wholly spent: when the group presents any one of its productions as a work-in-progress (its standard practice), the action sometimes ends midscene after an actor says, "That's all for tonight."

The unlikeliest embodiment of writerly abstention is the contemporary theater's most voluble and digressive of artists. Tony Kushner answers his era's needs not, as many have said, by scoring its requiem; nor by mounting indictments against its failures of will, compassion, or imagination; nor even by showing how fear and shame corrupt analytic clarity (although he is expert in staging all these conditions). He is a more potent writer when he seems to neglect his gifts, stepping out of the light. The teeming historical stage on which he sets his plays — Weimar Germany, twenty-first-century Afghanistan, 1980s New York, the Jim Crow South — ensures that his personal withdrawal reads as his protest against the bullying dogma of the larger culture. A mute girl stands on the margins of *Slavs!* (1994), her silence a recommendation to those bereft of a viable ideology since 1989. *Homebody/Kabul* (2001/2004)

dilates around another absence: the Homebody, a woman of undeterred eloquence, vanishes after the first scene, and the rest of the play derives its urgency from our continuous and never satisfied expectation of her return. "The
ocean is deep and cold and erasing," she says just before she plunges into
Kabul's public sphere, where the play itself also erases her.[40] Her daughter,
looking for her mother in the remaining scenes, frequently appears in a burka
— another effacing of character, another present absence.

Yet it is in the gleaming final moments of *Angels in America*, a work that, like
its title figures, hovers over this era, that Kushner most fruitfully resists his
expressive urges and allows helplessness to replace a writer's pride. By this
point in his five-hour, two-part play, he has plumbed numerous forms of
emptiness — those created by the demise of ideology, abstraction, self-delusion,
facile idealism, and inflexible antipathies, as well as by the decay of cities,
institutions, facsimiles of benevolence and democracy, repressive ideas of the
"normal," pledges of loyalty, vows of fidelity, and — of course, everywhere —
bodies. (His New York updates Norman Mailer's "haunted canyons of the
cancer-ridden city.") On such a landscape, the damage is too great and the
wisdom gleaned from it too deep for survivors and their spectators to countenance the mere reconstruction of the ruin, or the mere replenishment of spent
energies. Instead, Kushner fulfills the promise in the title of his play's second
half — "Perestroika," the emphasis falling on the action rather than the accomplished thing, on "restructuring" rather than the "structure." At the end, his
character Prior makes his own a line uttered earlier by the Angel: "The Great
Work Begins."[41] Prior's last speech returns us to Clov's first: "Finished, it's
finished, nearly finished." The inversion — Beckett orienting us to the past,
Kushner to the equally inaccessible future — springs from the same skepticism
about art's consolations. Theater itself, like Kushner's protagonist, is merely
"prior." Kushner's play — as full as Beckett's is spare, of an all-enveloping
density of incident, language, emotional turmoil, and moral searching — places
real (not merely theatrical) action at some purposefully vague point in the
future. That "work," not the present dramatic work (Kushner implies), is more
properly seen as "great." To those of us reading Kushner in the context of other
post-1960 drama, the passage sharply revises our sense of the American theater's preoccupation with absence. Could other playwrights also create empty
spaces, ruined landscapes, and waiting graves less to mark deaths, or any less
literal end, than to signify an endlessly deferred beginning? In this view, the era's
best playwrights can be imagined as writing in, or of, a prelude, not an aftermath. We join them before a blank page and unoccupied stage — correlatives of
the empty, still neutral imagination — and await the first mark. Achievement is
nowhere in sight — a happy state of inadequacy, for it means that in a theater

and in a world where restless hunger, desire, and inquiry have yet to earn the deadly status of knowledge, there will be, as Prior says just before the stage lights go out, "*More Life*" (148).

More life in the theater, as it is envisioned by four playwrights who stand out on this crowded American landscape, means resisting mere liveliness. Edward Albee, David Mamet, Suzan-Lori Parks, and Wallace Shawn, for all their obvious differences, share a productive indifference to the elements of craft that keep plays going. Not just to plots so narcotic they dull the senses to other sources of pleasure, nor just to characters who with little prompting unburden themselves of implausibly coherent thoughts and pent-up passion. These writers also refuse the easy rewards of a compositional rhythm that overwhelms our own pace of seeing (and thinking about what we see), of a language that puts no obstacle before the things it signifies, and of images that claim infallible authority by their sheer visuality. Also of performative outwardness — if such an affect means only to indicate candor or "energy" — and even of inwardness, if it only beckons us, falsely, toward "real" selves, spaces exempt from contingency, or a standard of truth unsullied by the compromises art makes to be public. A close look at the work of these writers reveals the richness and variety of these many styles of renunciation. The alternatives they pursue are versions of neutrality — vibrant (rather than merely repressive) decorum (in Albee), durable codedness (in Mamet), a space apart from both a humiliating public sphere and an insecure private room (in Parks), and (in Shawn) a disarming absence of authorial ego, guaranteed by an idea of dramatic discourse that, even as it entrances us, discourages undivided attention. The world outside his plays threatens — or promises — to scatter the playwright trying to represent it.

"There are no mountains in my life . . . nor chasms," says Agnes near the start of Edward Albee's *A Delicate Balance* (1966).[42] Anyone coming to this play after Albee's other works knows it is only a matter of time before the chasms open. In much of his theater, characters fall from grace under various forms of pressure. Peter's dissolution before Jerry's provocations in *The Zoo Story* (1958) — literalized when he almost falls off "his" park bench into the dirt — is the first of a series of collapses, some unexpected, others self-willed or welcomed, that expose the fragility of poise and the factitiousness of ordinary decorum. "Portrait of a man drowning," Martha says in *Who's Afraid of Virginia Woolf?*

(1962), as her husband, George, can no longer float on the lies and self-deceptions he's been telling since childhood.[43] When, over his wife's objections, he exposes the lie of their "child," a sinkhole opens up that claims them both. In *Seascape* (1975), Charlie tells of sinking below the water's surface voluntarily, as he remembers a childhood pastime with the longing of an adult impatient to escape the socialized repression and compromises of life on the ground. "Under," he says — the word orienting us to much Albee.[44] "I would . . . let out my breath. . . . You sink, gently, and you can sit on the bottom. . . . One stops being an intruder, finally — just one more object come to the bottom . . . part of the undulation and the silence" (16–17). *All Over* (1971) is the most explicit about the meaning of all these descents. "He seems to have diminished every time I turn my head away and come back," says a doctor attending a dying patriarch while the family sits vigilantly in their living room. "There'll be precious little left for the worms."[45] A hospital screen shields the patient from view throughout the production: it is a neutral object that is ultimately more expressive than the "drama" occurring behind it. Like the noncharacter at the center of *Who's Afraid of Virginia Woolf?* the screen's nonimage and the man it effaces enable other forms of repression, most notably by the character known as "The Wife," whose grief erupts only after her husband is dead. Yet the screen, which no one ever moves, also suggests that even with the surfacing of "feeling," nothing is gained. Immediately after The Wife bursts out with a loud, sobbing "Because . . . I'm . . . unhappy" (someone asked her why she's crying), she stifles her emotion, repeats the line in what Albee calls an "almost conversational . . . empty, flat" tone, and the play is over (110).

The sequence directs us from individual to aesthetic endings. To watch this production is to witness another kind of "diminishing." Every time we, too, "turn [our] heads away and come back," more of the play is gone. Albee synchronizes his art's and his absent character's dying. The resisted reality of all spectatorship — that as the minutes elapse we aren't acquiring visions and experiences but losing them — is unignorable in a purposefully ascetic play, where the "all" of all theater — action, character, spectacle — is already "over." (The only activity in *All Over* is waiting, and talking about waiting; the life these characters call their own is elsewhere, as well as before and after the present suspended action.) The title's preposition is as important as "under" is in *Seascape*. "Over" combines in one word the conditions of being covered and being finished — not shown and no longer active — qualities fatal to a theater artist bent on expression. But to Albee, connoisseur of styles of unavailability and apostate from the faith that catharsis brings change, the bleakness frees him to consider ultimately more revealing sources of behavior and speech. No less theatrical than the many atavistic dreads, lusts, and angers that tear Albee's surfaces are the characters' efforts to reposition the screens of propriety, normativeness, unflappability, and even anonymity.

A Delicate Balance, as its very title suggests, begins with the knowledge that those screens are always prone to collapse. Albee lavishes attention on the many rituals and habits by which his main characters — Agnes and Tobias, an affluent suburban couple — try to preserve equanimity in the company of an alcoholic sister, a querulous and much-divorced grown daughter, and another couple, their inexplicably anxious best friends, all of whom take refuge under Agnes's and Tobias's roof. The lapidary, Jamesian style of Agnes's opening speech is a syntactical image of the control she tries to sustain throughout the play: "What I find most astonishing — aside from that belief of mine, which never ceases to surprise me by the very fact of its surprising lack of unpleasant-ness, the belief that I might very easily — as they say — lose my mind one day, not that I suspect I am about to, or am even . . . nearby . . . for I'm not that sort; merely that it is not beyond . . . happening. [. . .] It is supposed to be healthy — the speculation, or the assumption, I suppose, that if it occurs to you that you might be, then you are not; but I've never been much comforted by it; it follows, to my mind, that since I speculate I might, some day, or early evening I think more likely — some autumn dusk — go quite mad, then I very well might" (3–4). The measured pace, nice semantic distinctions, sideways approaches to a subject followed by a quick retreat, and clauses balanced against clauses all serve to defer the moment she must come to rest at the source of her anxiety. (It's a technique that many Albee characters favor.) Indeed, when Agnes re-peats, and extends, the same speech at the end of the play, one senses that the three intervening acts have occurred within a parenthesis — its two brackets shaping a hole into which Agnes and those near her tumble after trusting too much in style.

They had hoped that gesture would have saved them, too. Like the for-malities of conversation, the rituals of moving to and from the living-room bar, mixing and serving drinks, or, in other scenes, pouring coffee and tea, then passing sugar and cream, serve to establish a baseline of convention against which to measure deviation. At first, these activities will seem only so much filler, and to a certain extent they are. Yet their neutrality is the point. The characters execute this stage business meticulously, as if such routine choreog-raphy were their only way of resisting or inuring themselves to the disorder that frequently overtakes Albee's stage. When transgressions do occur — pre-sumptuousness, absurd or gauche behavior (Claire, Agnes's sister, yodels and plays the accordion), inappropriate confessions, unpresentable rage, or mere candor—Albee makes sure we pay equal attention to the haste with which other characters deflect attention or take distance from them. As decorum returns, it becomes clear that the scene's real scandal is less the outrageous act than the nervousness it exposes in onlookers. We see how tenuous is their perch above instinct, how groundless their faith in routine, and how temporary their reprieve from unbalancing memory. For all their self-consciousness, they are still unable to look into their own depths without suffering an attack of vertigo.

Albee is strategically vague about what his characters do see at the bottom of these chasms. Namelessness itself is one cause of discomfort. The neighbors, Harry and Edna, can't explain what has prompted their flight from home. *Something* has frightened them, but the anesthetic comforts of upper-class suburban life haven't prepared them to confront, much less combat, it or any disruption of habit. Agnes's and Tobias's daughter, Julia, is also at a loss to identify the reason for her own chronic disaffection. All she can say is "I want," the phrase's explosiveness and redundancy (she says it many times) confirmation that she nurses desires larger than any single prize. Want—and its close relation, need, another word uttered throughout the play—measure the distances between all the characters. Not all the gaps demand closing. Characters insist on certain forms and degrees of separation in order to forestall the more painful recognitions that come with proximity—that their longings can't, or won't, be met or that intimacy, taken for granted, has deteriorated beyond repair.

The landscape of *A Delicate Balance* is lined with these figurative trenches —between Tobias and Agnes, who no longer share a bedroom; between Agnes and Claire, who part ways on Claire's alcoholism and other matters of propriety; between Harry and Tobias, whose confidence in their friendship depends on their not asking too much of one another; and between all the characters and an invisible cast of servants. (It comes as a shock, halfway through the play, to learn that the latter have been in the house all along, additional causes of inhibition.) Characters do all they can to avoid trespassing into the murky, unoccupied zone between self and other. The action-lessness of the play—only confirmed when Julia ludicrously brandishes, but doesn't fire, a pistol—teaches us to appreciate varieties of caution. Albee's characters eschew happiness for the more decorous, less exposed state of contentment (a distinction Tobias makes about a cat he once owned). They are predictably skeptical of impulsiveness but also stop short of ordinary decision making (an objection Agnes lodges against her passive husband). They are, as Claire puts it, a "giving but not sharing" people (97)—the latter quality threatening the detachment that enables them "to view a situation objectively" (85).

(Subjective seeing would attach them, sentimentally, to the people seen.) They sense their belatedness — "it's too late, or something," says Tobias, a deliberately imprecise observation that Agnes varies without improving near the end (74, 171) — but don't ask what they might have discovered if they had moved faster. They notice but do not resist "the gradual demise of intensity" (86). They like one another "well enough" (168). They pull out during sex (Tobias's custom). They don't cry (Agnes's choice).

It's characteristic of Albee that he mentions the one external reason for all these forms of stifling casually, quickly — and so late in the play it seems like an afterthought or slip of the tongue. Tobias and Agnes had a son who died. (In infancy? Childhood? As in so many other instances, Albee won't say.) Like the imaginary son in *Who's Afraid of Virginia Woolf?* this child shapes a hole around which the living gather. There, they "teeter," as Agnes says in an unrelated context, believing that they're "on level ground" without daring to test their belief (86). The child's grave (if one can imagine such a thing) marks one point of entry to the action's subterranean level — space that, along with the margins populated with the ghostlike servants, is a seat of judgment upon the visible stage. The verdict is inaudible; simply to approach its source is to feel the shame of failure. Failed to obey the patterns of happy, bourgeois life, Agnes would say, thinking of the intact family, its members carefully spaced but still linked by what she calls the "string" (106). Claire speaks for her sister when she says, "we have our friends and guests for patterns, don't we? — known quantities . . . . We can't have changes. . . . The world would be full of strangers" (150). She means to mock this attitude and flies quickly past her own culpability. Even the "freest" characters — if Claire's drunken indiscretion or Julia's uncensored rage qualify as freedom — won't sacrifice the comforts of familiarity for unscripted expression. "The drunks stay drunk," says Claire (150). Julia, on her fourth return home after another failed marriage, can only replay a well-known scene.

Here is another reason that Albee makes sure we sense the writtenness of his plays. His characters need the certainty of formula, or the assurance that form exists, as much as the typical spectator does. Deviations from the norm that would be imperceptible or insignificant in other plays would be cataclysmic here, given the austerity of the milieu. Such shocks for these characters would include mutual recognition stripped of criticism and unconditioned by expectation; engagement that doesn't start the clock toward withdrawal; open, not necessarily "articulate," speech (Agnes: "I apologize for being articulate" [14]); undemanding touch; patient seeing. The rarity of such phenomena in all Albee, his biographer suggests, may help explain why he values two moments in Thornton Wilder — Mr. Webb in *Our Town* saying "Where's my girl?

Where's my birthday girl?" to an Emily returned from the dead, and Mrs. Antrobus in *The Skin of Our Teeth* finally acknowledging a repressed truth when she calls out to her son Henry: "Cain! Cain!"[46] Both are instances of naming—and by naming, claiming—a seemingly lost figure. Albee adds complexity to Wilder's interest in such restorative attention (an interest encapsulated in Emily's line, "*let's look at one another*") by finding ways to portray characters reluctant to be seen. "You sank to cipher," Julia says to her father, recalling the trajectory of *Seascape* and other plays (66). Later, Claire picks up the image and refines it: "We submerge our truths," she says disdainfully, "and have our sunsets on untroubled waters. . . . We live with our truths in the grassy bottom" (97–98). Agnes mourns the same disappearance in the same terms when she notes how "the individuality we hold so dearly sinks into crotchet" (86). These self-burials do more than speak for the unspeakable burial of Tobias's and Agnes's son; they are also the spur for a startling reversal —an attempt at forced restitution—in the play's last moments, when Tobias says to Harry, "I want your plague! . . . Bring it in! . . . You live with us! Stay! Stay!" (166–69). Tobias, by this embrace of disease, seems to protest the play's many other literal and figurative quarantines—not just those separating friend from friend but also the estrangement of husbands and wives, the alienation of inner from outer selves, and the loss of a child who also refused to "live with us." Yet his vision of fellowship is utopian, of course, and his gesture toward it, like so many others in the play, peters out.

The emptiness is more revealing than the preceding charge against repression—a hard truth to accept for spectators expecting progress before the curtain falls. *A Delicate Balance* ends with multiple failures. Whatever passion Tobias releases with his plea to Harry evaporates on contact with the air. In its aftermath, he is a far from exalted figure—mumbling, clearing his throat, asking for approval, apologizing—all small utterances getting smaller until he finally falls silent. The virtues that we might have thought would reverse his slow spiritual dying—sincerity and directness ("wasn't I honest?" he asks Claire [177])—seem, after their appearance, to be even weaker than what they oppose. They look like desperate clinging, acts of foolish passion, intense but unproductive pleasures. They make an unreliable foundation for a new domestic order. Albee has located the vacancy beneath his characters' placid surfaces—"the play is basically about these people who have accommodated to their weaknesses and compromises, the adjustments they've made," Albee has said—and he's too principled a realist to trust in any sudden access of substance.[47] It could be just as artificial, just as performed, as the characters' other carefully scripted exchanges. (Tellingly, Albee calls Tobias's big speech to Harry an "aria.") Moreover, presumably spontaneous interiors are as worrisome as affectless exteriors. "They say we sleep to let the demons out," Agnes says in the play's last speech, "to let the mind go raving mad, our dreams and nightmares all our logic gone awry, the dark side of our reason. And when the daylight comes again . . . comes order with it" (177).

Order. We've seen its stultifying variants — one of which Harold Pinter, in a letter to Albee about the play, calls being "caged in grace" — and it may be perverse to doubt that Albee pities those submissive to its discipline.[48] Yet a more complicated idea of the cage may occur to readers who remember that in no play does Albee depict release without skepticism, if not anxiety about its destructive consequences. Jerry's violence, George's and Martha's mutually assured destruction, even Martin's passion in *The Goat* (2002), where his sexual longing for the title character comes at the expense of his wife's dignity: in the context of the carnage that ends these plays, Agnes's efforts to re-establish equilibrium models a salutary alternative to both repression and unfettered instinct. As she describes it, the descent into instinct is valuable only insofar as it enables a stronger embrace of reason — one sustained by knowledge rather than dread of what lies beneath the surface. Characters who return from this underworld are alert, unsuperstitious, self-aware, ready: "Come now," Agnes says as the play ends, "we can begin the day" (178). (Her last line rhymes with other Albee endings: Leslie saying "begin" in *Seascape*; dawn breaking in *Who's Afraid of Virginia Woolf?*) Is Albee allowing us to entertain the possibility that the character who seemed the stiffest and most disapproving throughout the past three acts now appears, in this last scene, to be the best prepared to carry on, to emerge from the ruin and rebuild — to "begin"?

If we think so, the play's title, too, will suggest surprising new meanings. Characters who sought a delicate balance between spontaneity and inhibition, or between self-exposure and self-deception — all forms of the play's real war between life and death — at first looked merely weak, cowardly. Now this balance seems less a compromise than a pragmatic choice. Aware that "civilized" behavior is an inadequate mask over raw need, Albee's characters nonetheless learn that masks of one kind or another are all that ensures their legibility and availability to others. Albee himself upholds this truth. He underscores his theater's artificiality as if to debunk the myth that anything but structured feeling and plotted conduct is possible onstage. Such an attitude of course puts *A Delicate Balance* at odds with other newsworthy theater art of its decade: *Hair* (1967) opened several months after Albee's play closed on Broadway; a year later brought the premieres of the Open Theater's *The Serpent* and the Living Theatre's *Paradise Now*. Even as Albee also scrutinizes the very bourgeoisie these productions satirize more broadly, he implies that individual liberation matters less than social obligation. Marriage, partnership, friendship, parenthood, even the guardianship of animals — these forms of responsibility, preoccupying him throughout his career (and made explicit in such titles as *Marriage Play* [1993] and *The Play About the Baby* [1998]) qualify any sympathy Albee may have for private needs. Plumbing one's own depths may be therapeutic, but a more durable, enlightened, civic well-being comes only when one acknowledges — yet refrains from intruding upon — those of others. Against the accumulating calls of "I want" in *A Delicate Balance* and its characters' ever more urgent demands for full disclosure, Albee insists that there are some things one cannot have and will never understand. "It's sad to come to the end of it," Edna says on her way out the door, "and still not know" (170–71).

"I don't know." "We don't know." "You don't want to know." "I don't know what you mean."[49] There's nothing remarkable about the persistence of confusion in a play called *The Cryptogram* (1994). Yet David Mamet does more than merely present us with a puzzle to be solved or a code to be broken. For one thing, the code never breaks. We do learn a secret midway through the play — a husband, never seen, has been carrying on an affair; his best friend has helped deceive his wife — but its exposure doesn't relieve the pressure of the unknown. Characters say "I don't know" more, not less, frequently as the play unfolds, rebuffing questions about weekend plans and tea preferences (at one end of the spectrum of gravity) and (at the other end) moral rectitude and attitudes toward death. It's soon clear that Mamet is interested less in solving mysteries than in sounding them, redirecting our attention away from possible clues and toward the empty architecture of incomprehension. Mamet's signature traits — severed utterances, throbbing silences, subterranean rumblings of implicit meaning — arouse but do not reward the desire for content in what is at once his starkest and richest play. Other Mamet plays enable us to tolerate obscurity and codedness by establishing a recognizable context — business intrigue, masculine competitiveness, sexual games-playing, crime. There is no such situational scaffolding here. Although Mamet does tell readers of *The Cryptogram*, in a prefatory note, that the play is set in 1959, he keeps this modest piece of information from spectators. Nothing in the dialogue dates the action with such specificity, and there is little else to ground us — no clue as to its geographical setting, few markers of culture or class. Unlike *Glengarry Glen Ross* (1983), *Speed-the-Plow* (1988), and *Oleanna* (1992), where a character's power (or weakness) depends in large part on his or her status in a professional setting, here the characters have vague or nonexistent occupations. Their only job is to be on this stage. Even that occupation is radically curtailed: there isn't much for them to do. They worry over the meanings of a few objects — a book, a photograph, a knife, a letter — all of which grow less knowable and thus seemingly less present the more the characters scrutinize them. The stage world becomes even more austere in the last act as the betrayed wife, Donny, prepares to move out. "The room is denuded," Mamet notes (77). Boxes take the place of objects and furniture, and in the original production a large rug—correlative of the stage itself—is rolled up, leaving the stage's occupants even less confident in the ground they occupy.

Mamet secures *The Cryptogram*'s minimalism in his choice of protagonist. As he writes in a preface to the play's British edition, the adultery plot sets up expectations not just of emotional heat but of focus.[50] Betrayer and betrayed typically monopolize our attention, yet here their drama is muted, even smothered, as another character, unimplicated in the scandal, draws us to his own separate turmoil. In production, this other drama literally occurs in the background, on the upstage stairs and in the unseen reaches of the house's upper floors. That this figure is a ten-year-old child further controls the significance of his presence. By virtue of his youth, John lacks many of the attributes that enable spectators to place and know characters: occupation, autonomy, agency, full self-awareness, command of language. The knowledge he does have seals him off from the others, a further form of effacement. He picks up cues audible only to himself, or absorbs but cannot speak of the tremors of emotion originating beneath the adults' carefully composed surfaces. (One thinks of Henry James's Maisie, also present at the dissolution of a marriage. She is one of his "light vessel[s] of consciousness," as he calls her, whose "vivacity of intelligence . . . vibrate[s] in the infected air" and whose "vision is at any moment much richer, their apprehension even constantly stronger, than their prompt, their at all producible, vocabulary.")[51] Only an unfinished self seems capable of such acute responsiveness; an older, self-regarding figure would push back against outside influence. Yet Mamet's child, dissenting from the sentimental cliché, is opaque rather than transparent; his innocence, if it exists at all, is remote. What is open about him is empty—all expectation, inquiry, confusion, awe, need. What is closed is impervious to others' petitions: he stands at the center of an encircling, encroaching fear. To a playwright beguiled by coded behavior, as Mamet is, a character at this age must be an irresistible object of study. Not simply because latency itself prevents legibility; more challenging are the character's conscious obfuscations. Poised between childhood and adolescence, the ten-year-old achieves a delicate balance of accessibility and inaccessibility. He withholds a thought for every one disclosed, a disorienting shift for adults no longer able to count on old, automatic modes of intimacy. Mamet emulates his subject in order to challenge his spectator: he tempers our pleasure in what we hear and see with a continuous unspoken reminder that he has held back much more.

Yet it is pointless, Mamet also implies, to go looking for what isn't dramatized. *The Cryptogram* at once distills and strengthens his career-long prohibition on abstraction. The characters who "don't know" or "don't want to know" echo earlier Mamet characters who admit their ignorance before they trust to speculation or even feeling, if feeling cannot be verified in action. (*American Buffalo* [1976] is particularly insistent upon this empiricism.) Mamet aims to reconcile audiences, too, to the limits of their knowledge. In an interview with C. W. E. Bigsby, he speaks of hoping to offer "courage to look at the world around you and say I don't know what the hell the answer is but I'm willing to try to reduce all of my perspectives . . . to the proper place."[52] Even when Mamet isn't directly recommending such humility, the style in which he stages his plays keeps us from demanding intimate knowledge of his characters. (*The Cryptogram* is one of many he himself directed.) His actors are unfailingly controlled, even formal, barring the way to interiority. Some characters blind us with the force of their unblinking concentration. Others challenge us to keep up with their roving alertness. All are engaged so vigorously with present-tense life around them that they seem indifferent to their pasts. As closed experience, the past poses no challenge to characters brought to life in the attempt to keep pace with a constantly moving, ever-changing quarry.

This attentiveness to "the finer, the shyer, the more anxious small vibrations" of the present (to borrow again from James's preface to *What Maisie Knew*) is one cause of the many instances of failed remembering in *The Cryptogram* (149). Some lapses are fleeting and seem trivial. Donny forgets her lines in a bit of storybook dialogue that has always eased her son off to sleep. John forgets to pack his coat for a camping trip. Del, Donny's friend, loses the thread of a conversation ("Where were we?" [3]). Other failures are more sustained and trigger obsessive efforts to compensate for them. An old photograph that Donny finds in the attic won't give up its secrets even to those it depicts. Unlike most family snapshots — restorers of lost knowledge, supplements to imperfect memory — this one taunts its viewers. Looking at it, they see most clearly only the image of their ignorance, their alienation from experience they thought they owned. They can't verify even the most basic facts. Who took it? (It depicts Del, Donny, and Donny's husband Robert, and they can't remember a fourth joining them.) Whose shirt is Del wearing? (It seems to be Robert's, but why is it on Del?) When was it taken? Del asks the question on five separate occasions and is ignored until Donny finally, but vaguely, guesses "before the War" (38). The other inadequate responses — silence, a non sequitur, an attempt to change the subject, an interruption by John — are more revealing of this, or any, photograph's limited relationship to its subject.

It doesn't open onto the past but seals it. It confirms rather than closes the distance between now and then. It points toward but does not usher one into a lost realm of experience. What it commemorates is permanently unavailable to its viewers: it is a monument to an absence, a mute artifact from a now-vanished city, a gravestone, another "appearance that shows the void." "Can you make the pattern out?" Donny asks, referring explicitly to Del's shirt in the photograph but allowing the question to embrace the play as a whole (39). Frustration rises and falls in Del's voice as he looks more and more intently at the withholding image. "I don't understand this photograph," he says at first (17). "Who, who, what *is* this?" he says later (36). Then, finally, a resigned "I don't remember it" (37).

One might again consult Roland Barthes to gauge the ontological anxieties behind Del's responses. A passage from *Camera Lucida* uncannily anticipates the bewilderment Mamet dramatizes: "One day I received from a photographer a picture of myself which I could not remember being taken, for all my efforts; I inspected the tie, the sweater, to discover in what circumstances I had worn them; to no avail. And yet, *because it was a photograph* I could not deny that I had been *there* (even if I did not know *where*). This distortion between certainty and oblivion gave me a kind of vertigo, something of a 'detective' anguish. . . . I went to the photographer's show as to a police investigation, to learn at last what I no longer knew about myself."[53] It's doubtful he gained the education he sought. For Barthes, "oblivion" exerts a stronger pull than "certainty." While a photograph may confirm that something or someone existed — "that has been," as Barthes says, the photograph's *noeme,* or only authoritative statement (115) — it cannot disclose anything more, and by this poverty of meaning leaves viewers to contemplate only existence's opposite. The "image . . . produces Death while trying to preserve life," Barthes writes — an enveloping death that, staking its claim upon the subject, reminds viewers that the same fate awaits them (92). "Each photograph always contains the imperious sign of my future death" (97). It's in this way that the image — a surface that "cannot be penetrated" as we "sweep it with [our] glance" (106) — becomes a chasm.

So it is in *The Cryptogram.* Donny's photograph, impenetrable the way the milieu, situation, and character affects are impenetrable, is a puzzle that cannot be solved — or that the characters resist solving.[54] To do so would be to acknowledge the picture's authority ("that has been") and thereby tacitly to accept the equally authoritative fact of eventual nonbeing. It's more than mere wordplay that lodges "crypt" within "cryptogram." Mamet's minimalism makes it hard for spectators to ignore the ontological pressure bearing down on all theater — its proximity to nothingness, its victimization by time. "All plays

are about decay," he writes in a lecture collected in *Writing in Restaurants.*
"They are about the ends of a situation which has achieved itself fully, and the
inevitable disorder which ensues until equilibrium is again established."[55]

One doesn't need to wait long in *The Cryptogram* for mortality to make
itself felt. John introduces the subject of loss in the first line—"I couldn't find
'em," he says of his missing slippers, fixating on something trivial with the
insomniac's typical fervor (1). His wakefulness is itself open to dark readings.
Resisting sleep, he seems to resist sleep's double—the even more definitive
form of oblivion that Del acknowledges in speaking vaguely, ominously, of the
"thoughts . . . of what they're going *toward*" that haunt John on the eve of his
camping trip (6). Tangible, minor deaths also contribute to the play's nervous
atmosphere. Donny breaks a teapot; John worries he has torn a blanket. The
fragile fabric of theatrical presence is most threatened by Robert's absence.
Some spectators may think they've stumbled on a typical father-son colloquy
when, at the start, the curtain rises on a man reassuring an anxious child. Not
for another ten minutes (five pages in the standard edition) will it become clear
that Del is not who he seems. The subtle surprise leaves a gap that Mamet
refrains from filling—and an anxiety he refuses to allay. The absence of John's
actual father remains unexplained until the end of the act, a delay that magnifies it into another, more dire disappearance. "Why isn't he home?" asks John.
"We don't know," says Del (5).

After these many indirect allusions to mortality, the appearance of a real
threat may seem superfluous. Del gives John a knife—a "German pilot's
knife," he calls it, supposedly seized during World War II—and suggests the
boy use it to cut the twine on a box in the attic. That act of cutting (described
but, like so much else, not shown) retrospectively heightens the importance of
an earlier reference to "good heavy line" John insists on bringing along for
fishing; it also prepares us to hear more resonance in Donny's explanation,
later, of what she calls the "Meaning" of the knife: "The pilot would use it to
cut the *cords*. If his parachute snagged. . . . On a tree" (64–65). When Del
understands that the knife "released" the pilot, the security of a character's,
even an actor's, own presence becomes questionable (66). Is being onstage
itself a form of being "snagged," a condition awaiting "release"? Or the opposite? Mamet's figures seem at once bound and cut loose, caught by too little
information, there and not there.

The play's two strong gestures toward release are undramatized—Robert's
escape from the bond of marriage, before the narrative begins, and John's
decision to kill himself, implied as the narrative ends—but they attune us, on
rereading, to the many other forms of nonpresence, of life after the cords have
been cut, that Mamet does ask us to confront. They have nothing to do with

plot; indeed, that detachment from story and even from circumstance is the point. Mamet envisions a brutal form of autonomy—a state in which one cannot engage with, make a mark on, or root oneself in one's context. "Are you dead?" John asks his apparently living mother (75). "Things unfold . . . independent of our fears of them," Del says to John in an earlier scene, inviting us to imagine another, equally complete separation from the world and to ask if any emotion (or thought, or action) can influence "things" (31). Things— historical trajectories, moral and ethical consequences, and even physical surroundings—are no more susceptible to objective description. "We couldn't choose the pond . . . to observe," John says, rebuffing Del's suggestion that he "write down [his] *recollections*" of what he sees while camping: "It's chang- ing" (33, 36). John already understands what Del and Donny are discovering about the photograph: that it's impossible to arrest fluid life with acts of representation, and that the work of "recollection" is futile, another instance in which time erodes rather than shores up knowledge. Mamet decisively punc- tures illusions of mastery in a startling speech by his ten-year-old protagonist. John envisions a state of total, uncompromising absence—one heedless of the limits marked by an individual's life, unconfined by the contours of narrative —an evacuation not just of places and persons but of consciousness, and of the art that presumes to reflect consciousness. The child's perceptions gather force inexorably, blocking out more and more certainty as they do so. "I thought that maybe there was nothing there," he says as the second act begins, having come down from bed the next night, again unable to sleep. "I thought that nothing was *there*. Then I was looking at my *book*. I thought 'Maybe there's nothing *in* my book.' It talked about the *buildings*. Maybe there's nothing *in* the buildings. And . . . or on my *globe*. [. . .] Maybe there's nothing on the thing that it is of. We don't know what's there. *We* don't know that those things are there. [. . .] Or in *buildings* we have not been in. Or in *history*. In the *history* of things. Or *thought*. (*Pause*.) I was *lying* there, and maybe there is no such thing as *thought*. Who *says* there is? Or human beings" (53– 54). Unable to stop thinking about the pointlessness of thinking, he hovers over a void where the spectacle of death, presumably the only definitive phe- nomenon, is itself only theoretical. "How do we *know* . . . that we're *born*. . . . Or that dead people moan." He asks his question in the face of rising vertigo, absence itself taunting him with equivocation, and hearing no answer, under- stands that "all we do is *say* things" (54).

John's line is of course a fair description of a Mamet play. If the playwright's persona weren't one of supreme confidence, one might imagine that he himself suffered John's anxiety—that as he writes the boy's speech he gazes worriedly into the shadows of an art form that itself withholds assurances of the real.

"Maybe there was nothing there" onstage, too. That possibility sits in uneasy counterpoint to the Barthesian guarantee of Donny's photograph — "that was there" — before finally overriding it. Far from regretting this outcome, Mamet welcomes it. In each of his three acts, he undermines the authority of one of theater's supposedly essential elements — visuality, in act 1, as the photograph proves impenetrable; the actor, in act 2, when John asks if his mother is "dead"; and space, in act 3, when the curtain rises on a "denuded" room. These three erasures predict a fourth: language, the source of Mamet's writerly identity, collapses in the play's last scenes. "Saying things" itself becomes fraught with worry and difficulty. Words degrade. Voices peter out or simply go dead.

It wasn't always thus. Robert announces that he's leaving his wife in a letter discovered in act 1: it contains the one unambiguous utterance on a stage hazy with inferences, suspicions, fears, and feelings of envy. It matters that a declaration that ordinarily would permit a histrionic tour de force appears in print form — not ephemeral speech but something one can hold. Yet its seeming durability is powerless against the many varieties of impeded expression. Characters trying to talk about seemingly unimportant subjects discover that they don't speak the same language. An object's concreteness, in these cases, is no defense against the vagueness of the language describing it. The item Del calls a "lap robe" Donny calls a "*stadium* blanket" (18). Yet when John calls it a "blanket," Donny calls it a "coverlet" (44–45). A separate conversation between John and Donny idles and almost stalls as they can't decide whether to describe a coat as "melton," "fabric," "wool," or simply "blue" (18–19). This crisis of understanding on the level of individual parts of speech is the context for Donny's later rage at a minor transgression: "Do You Know What It Means To Give . . . to give your word?" she says when John comes downstairs once again, Mamet's eccentric capitalization emphasizing the object-like elements in a gust of speech (96). The same determination to hold onto language — and with it, to secure fluid experience and affirm one's claims on other people — characterizes Donny's sudden switch to formality in the questions she puts to Del late in the play: "Where's my son?" "How is my husband" (82). By now, however, such claims of ownership — relatives turned into objects — are hollow. The word "my" gets her nothing on a stage where all occupants are centrifugally spinning away from one another. Neither "son" nor "husband" can make their absent or receding referents any more accessible. (Her vitriolic name-calling of Del — "fairy," "faggot," "lad" — is an equally weak attempt at mastery.)

This breakdown of speech — another form of "decay" Mamet observes in all theater — has an inevitable end. Inexplicably, Del begins stuttering in the last act: he can't get past "Jjjj" to acknowledge John; "bbb" delays him from naming a book (84, 98). From syllables, it's a short step to silence. In one scene, he arrives having rehearsed "things . . . I have been longing to say," but after a theatrical beginning ("Here is what I think"), he pauses and never resumes (95). The void breeds others. John doesn't answer his mother ("I'm *speaking* to you. . . . I've asked you a question"); Donny retaliates by ignoring him (99). Yet it is the silence at the end of *The Cryptogram* that is far more alarming than these failures or renunciations of language. "I hear voices," John says. "They're calling my name" (100–101). To treat this admission as merely the sign of psychosis is to resist Mamet's challenge to theater form and to spectatorial complacency. The silence through which we strain to hear John's voices insulates a drama no one can witness: in these last moments, Mamet doesn't simply let his play dwindle — or decay — to invisibility. Instead, he removes the "significant" action and dialogue to a hypothetical arena, a character's consciousness, and bars access to it. The speech John hears, uttered by a nonspecific "they," is memorable for being unheard by others, just as the play's upstairs spaces, the photograph's image, and the letter's contents are alluring for being unseen and unread by us. The high value that Mamet accords to these nonplaces, nontexts, nonimages, and noncharacters should change our sense of everything we do see and hear. Ideally, as we sit in his theater, we will feel that we are confined to a kind of anteroom and are privy only to a secondary drama. Genet's terms are once again appropriate: the available play is a screen erected before experience impervious to this artist's appeals.[56] Mamet implies that his virtuosic craft if left unchecked would debase its object. In leading us to this conclusion, he performs an unexpected act of self-degradation. The legible, audible play — the published, staged play — depreciates when set against the one Mamet refrains from writing. His theater reaches its fullest strength only when it concedes, even embraces, its weakness.

Suzan-Lori Parks, playful and irreverent where Mamet is stoic, is nonetheless as wise as he is to the deceptions of style. Indeed, her mode of theatricality — delighting in gestural speech and in the outwardness, even outrageousness, of acting — seems calculated to make her sudden withdrawals to neutrality all the more disarming. At her theater's most spontaneous, she threatens to cancel its pleasures. A typical scene points to the desire that sustains illusion only to expose its powerlessness before an indifferent or hostile reality. Art, she concedes, can betray the experiences it means to honor; the same acts of spectatorship that exalt performers entrap them. Seeking an alternative to this fate, Parks establishes empty, silent, dark, and closed spaces in her theater, allowing their vagueness to contest our certainty about what we do see and hear.

Genet's readers will hear an echo of his disdain for those "going so cheer-fully toward the luminosity of analysis." Another passage from his prose an-ticipates even more explicitly Parks's dramaturgy. Amplifying his vision of a theater located where "graves are being dug all the time," Genet writes: "Be-fore burying the dead man, carry the corpse in his casket to the front of the stage; let his friends, enemies, and the curious sit in the section reserved for the audience; let the funeral-mime who led the procession divide and multiply; let him turn into a theatrical company, and let him re-create the life and death of the dead man, right in front of the corpse and the audience; afterwards, let the casket be carried to the grave in the dead of night; let the audience finally leave—the feast is finished. Until another ceremony, occasioned by another corpse whose life is worthy of a dramatic performance—not a tragic one. Tragedy must be lived, not played."[57]

This scenario lists many of the procedures and themes of Parks's *Venus* (1996), not least its own funeral mime in the person of the Negro Resurrec-tionist, overseeing a reenacted life of the Venus Hottentot after presenting her body and announcing her death. The passage also names the deliberately unresolved tension between exposure and concealment in many other Parks plays. It's an ambivalence for which Genet found a simple theatrical sign: in the stage directions to *Deathwatch,* he insists that the lighting be as bright as possible all the time in the otherwise tomb-like prison cell. The condemned men may be out of sight, buried alive in a hole, but they are not unseen. There is always a spectator monitoring their actions; the characters, denied privacy, are always onstage. The same harsh, unremitting light should fill both the stage and the house of *The Screens,* Genet wrote to Roger Blin, that play's first director, "because I should in some way like both actors and audience to be caught up in the same illumination, and for there to be no place for them to hide, or even half-hide."[58]

There may be no place to "hide or even half-hide" in Parks, either—so habitual is her characters' theatricality and so pervasive is the accompanying surveillance—yet she nonetheless recognizes the strength of an undertow pull-ing the action down and out of sight. The characters' response to this extraor-dinary force *is* the action. As many critics (Una Chaudhuri, Greg Miller, Alice Rayner, and Harry J. Elam, Jr., among others) have observed, Parks's theater occupies a perforated landscape.[59] Her stages are pockmarked with ditches, pools, and graves; the texts with lacunae; the bodies with wounds; the narra-tives with secrets and other recesses from which authoritative meaning won't emerge. This is a theater in perpetual retreat from visual, verbal, and physical presence, recoiling as readers and viewers reach toward it. We each have made our own lists of its hiding places: under a porch or in a slaveship hold in *The*

Death of the Last Black Man in the Whole Entire World (1992); under a bridge in *In the Blood* (1999); the "Great Hole of History" and, less obviously, Lucy's pledge of confidentiality in *The America Play* (1993); a cage, cell, and dark bedroom in *Venus;* a well, orchestra pit, and open mouth in *365 Days / 365 Plays* (2006); and in many works, the privacy of footnotes and the anticipatory silence before speech, or the helplessness after it.

These aren't always mere absences or omissions, as some have described them, but instead can be arenas of action. Here, in the spaces opened up whenever the plays sink below the surface of declarative language, social behavior, and expository action, Parks's characters engage with histories both individual and cultural, seize and sift the very matter supporting their presence, and confront aspects of themselves that can't be regularized into dramatically manageable form onstage or in spoken language. Not that these recesses are wholly divorced from Parks's relentlessly spectatorial culture. As in Genet, the idea of privacy exists only as a simulation, teasing characters with promises of a security it can no longer fulfill. "Yr only yrself . . . when no ones watching," Parks writes, optimistically, in *Topdog/Underdog* (2001) — welcoming the irony that the brothers are actually quoting one of their voyeuristic customers.[60] Is there ever true solitude in Parks's theater? A naturalist and, later, a photographer hover over the action in *Imperceptible Mutabilities in the Third Kingdom* (1989). Hester's bridge in *In the Blood* is regularly invaded by policemen, welfare officials, and vandals scrawling graffiti. The needy and the menacing burst in on the Hester of *Fucking A* (2000) just when she settles into the first private hour of the night. In *Topdog/Underdog,* the most intimate companion of one's seclusion becomes the most intrusive spectator. The action of that play exists in a state of permanent inhibition, as the brothers are always spying on one another or fearing discovery. One brother looks in, unnoticed, from the threshold or eavesdrops from behind a screen; the other hides his possessions — money, porn magazines, a weapon — from prying eyes or tries, futilely, to smother the shame that follows his own moments of self-consciousness.

In her recognition of the pull exerted by subterranean spaces — literal or figurative — Parks extends a tradition of concealment in African-American theater. The oldest hole swallowing her own is in William Wells Brown's *The Escape; or, A Leap for Freedom* (1858), the first play published by a black writer. Its most memorable image is a deep pit in which a slave is kept prisoner by a sadistic overseer. (That synonym for slave owner, as Parks recognized in *Imperceptible Mutabilities,* nicely captures the relation of spectatorship to possession.) Jean Toomer's *Kabnis,* the play buried in his 1923 work *Cane,* places the title character in a murky cellar where he must face a painful ancestry he thought he understood above ground. "I get my life down in this scum-hole," he says.[61] Marita Bonner's 1928 play *The Purple Flower* envisions a dimly lit level below the thin "skin of civilization," as she calls it — the stage on which most of the play's action occurs. The latter repeatedly cracks ("a thought can drop you through it," she says), and Bonner's characters plunge into an atavistic past.[62] More recent plays make Parks's imagery seem all the more inevitable. LeRoi Jones (later Amiri Baraka) sets *Dutchman* in what he famously called "the flying underbelly of the city" — a hot, cramped subway car.[63] Another subway car encloses the phantasmagoric action of Adrienne Kennedy's *The Owl Answers*. In her 1992 *Ohio State Murders* (near contemporaneous with Parks's major early plays), a Kennedy-like protagonist retreats to the underground level of a university library, a single window hung far above the stage, to consider why her theater is so preoccupied with violence. Of course, the best-known hole in American literature is in Ralph Ellison's *Invisible Man* (1952), and its protagonist's monologue sets the standard for all subsequent self-interrogations. In Ellison's novel, as in all this theater, characters who have had invisibility forced upon them use it to study their disguises, compromises, and inhibitions, if never wholly to shed them. They also surrender to elemental fear, anger, and longing — these emotions no longer cut to fit any landscape other than their own. (In *The America Play,* Parks writes that the Great Hole "gave a shape" to the character occupying it.)[64] Out of sight, all these characters hope to arrive at insights penetrating, candid, and self-surprising.

In Parks's theater, the pits, underbellies, and cellars of these earlier writers appear as replicas and echoes (to cite two forms from *The America Play*), or rather, throughout this theater history, each void can be seen as citing an earlier one, digging deeper into a shared absence.[65] In fact, the digging is as important as the hole. Parks makes the most of theater's temporality to confront the experience of losing, not just the subsequent recognition of loss — of retreat, not mere vacancy — and of the dynamic struggle either to resist it or, more often and more surprising, to welcome it and, by trying to control it, to turn it to one's advantage. (As Elizabeth Bishop advises in "One Art," "practice losing farther, losing faster.")[66] Images of falling or sinking recur obsessively in Parks's theater, as if each sequence advanced by a few segments one endless, metaphysical descent, the ground forever lowering just as the characters near it. (Is this a vision of the original Fall from grace as rendered by a playwright who acknowledges Catholicism's formative influence on her theater?)[67] In *The America Play,* the Lesser Known — a black man who, in the person of the Foundling Father, reenacts Lincoln's assassination at a penny arcade — slumps repeatedly in his chair after being "shot." The character Kinseer, in *Imperceptible Mutabilities,* sinks through the ocean after being jettisoned from a slave ship. An Icarus-like pilot in the same play falls out of the sky onto Sergeant Smith. The sky itself seems to fall on Hester during the eclipse in *In the Blood*, an experience that makes her feel (she says) as if "the hand of fate with its 5 fingers [were] coming down on me."[68] Miss Miss imagines (falsely, it turns out) her own drowning in the short play *Pickling* (1988). "Down down down," says Black Woman with Fried Drumstick in *The Death of the Last Black Man*. "Down down down down down."[69] Perhaps this is her account of Black Man with Watermelon, who tumbles through the experience of dying over and over but never reaches the bottom of death.

As characters fall, so too does the *idea* of character. The Foundling Father, already a fallen version of the real Lincoln, dwindles further over the course of the play, present only as a Lincoln bust early in act 2; then a Lincoln penny; then, even further reduced, an intangible face on the TV, which reruns the play's first act, now, in a final diminishment, played in silence. So runs down memory. As his widow Lucy and their son Brazil try to retrieve the past, it dissolves in their hands and before their eyes. This erosion of character has its equivalents in just about every Parks play. Bodies turn to maimed bodies, which fracture into body parts. The latter give way to facsimiles of body parts, which are themselves replaced, finally, by mere words for those parts. The glossary at the end of the printed version of *Venus* is meant to be read (and perhaps staged) as part of the body of the text, on par with its footnotes. (Here, of course, the corporeal associations of the word "footnotes" are hard to ignore.)

The regression doesn't stop here. The glossary asserts an authority that Parks deliberately withholds in other plays. This procedure involves more than interrupting speech with silence. As memorable in themselves as are Parks's famous "spells" (her term for the pauses that, on the page, are scripted as dialogue), equally important are the passages of falling toward the moment when silence reestablishes order. Recalling an image from Bonner's *Purple Flower,* we can imagine the thin ice of the play's verbal civilization cracking and the speakers plunging through a languageless chasm so horrifying that the silence at the bottom comes as a relief: at least *that* is stable. In sequences that parallel bodily dispersal and decay, writing itself slowly recoils from our attention, as characters burrow into private, coded modes of expression or pull back even further toward a time when they could not, or would not, express anything. Enacting a kind of reverse evolution of language over the course of several plays, Parks seeks ever stronger ways of troubling, if not wholly burying, expression. Each departure from established language initiates more extreme retreats. One step removed from the vernacular that enlivens her dialogue are the echoes of the vernacular, or in *Fucking A,* the still more remote, exclusive vernacular in an invented language Parks calls "TALK." The buried language of the written footnotes is more accessible than unwritten ones. (In *The Death of the Last Black Man,* Parks ornaments one character's speech with superscript numbers but omits their text.) The preverbal sounds of the glottal stops, quick intakes of breath, and tongue clicks in many plays subside to the shaped silences of the spells, which finally sink deeper toward the un-shaped silences in which characters hear themselves trail off into an unvoiced question or a dash (*The America Play* ends in one)—ways of marking the sudden failure of any dramatic structure, verbal or silent, to support its characters. A beautiful line from *The Death of the Last Black Man* captures this dissolution of language and the desperation to retain it before it rushes away. "My text was writ on water," says Black Man with Watermelon. "I would like tuh drink it down." Another character, Queen-then-Pharaoh Hatshepsut, adds, "My son erased his mothers mark," further asserting the perishability of writing (116).

Venus could be another text "writ on water." Parks labels its scenes in reverse order, starting at scene 31 and ending at scene 1, a structure that suggests the melting of a solid into fluid, or the shedding of skins: what once had bulk— presence—slowly disappears until nothing remains. Nothing? Or everything? Perhaps the play's structure is the inverse of the dying that goes on throughout Parks. Her theater, with this play, returns to its newborn state, or even to some earlier stage, in which (on which?) actors haven't yet turned into characters, haven't submitted themselves to our attention, a time when everything was still potential—a state of grace. (This trajectory recalls that of Tony Kushner's *Perestroika* and of Richard Foreman's own search for expressive origins— perhaps one reason why Foreman was eager to direct the premiere of *Venus.*) Parks's recursive dramaturgy is perhaps nowhere more pronounced than in *365 Days / 365 Plays.* A number of the cycle's short plays depict writing and the writing life, but the least representational episodes more suggestively comment on an artist's narrative. One can't help thinking of Parks at her desk every morning, waiting for a spark to kindle the day's play, when the lights go up on one of the cycle's many other forms of waiting. Parks works a dizzying array of variations on the theme. Characters wait for a train, a store clerk, a spouse's return, the barbarians' arrival, and Jesus' resurrection (among many other things). They typically muffle their frustration, impatience, and hopelessness, as well as their disappointment when the waiting ends anticlimactically in action or apparent reward.

The several plays in the *365* cycle that pay tribute to dead artists—Sarah Kane, Carol Shields, Barry White, Nina Simone, Gregory Hines, William Faulkner, and even John Ritter and George Plimpton—also recall us to Parks's process, illuminating a vast network of welcome and surprising influence surrounding the deceptively solitary writer. Starker absences fill still other plays. One play features a man known only as El Silencio Grande. Characters confront apocalyptic devastation in *Theres Nothing Here.* Another play is called (and is) *Empty.* Several more occur in total darkness or end in a no less blinding flash of light. Beyond their associations with the blank page (or empty imagination, or reclusive muse), these many emblems of inaction ensure we never forget a fundamental principle of the 365 project as a whole. Each visible stage is flanked by those recently vacated and those awaiting a performer's arrival. The small play we see or read one day sits in the shadow of the 364 others we can't reach. (Anyone can see part of the cycle, but no one can see it all.) When a play ends, some with obliterating finality, Parks returns us to the start of writing, a continually reinitiated, even optimistic process that accompanies the action of a single scene. The cycle's last images push this premise to its inevitable but still startling conclusion. The penultimate play, *The Blank Before the World,* displays a stage "which is completely blank" ("is this possible?" asks Parks) — a corollary to the Barthesian Neutral.[70] After the lights go out, they bump up "white-hot" to reveal the manuscript of *365 Days / 365 Plays.* Parks moves us from nothing to everything. Or has she in fact moved us from everything, all possible expression held in suspension, to nothing — her year-long, nation-scaled performance now subsiding to an inert, atemporal, depopulated, and portable thing?

By ending with an impermeable text rather than a porous scene, Parks furthers a debate about theatricality she has been arguing throughout her career. Does she preserve whole strata of experience and emotion that would be vulnerable to decay by refusing to show them in the theater? Venus is famously said to have died of "exposure." Hers is only the most obvious instance in which performance is manipulative and distorting. The three-card monte spectacle in *Topdog/Underdog,* the mountebank preacher in *In the Blood,* the phony Lincoln in *The America Play* (reminding us, further, that Lincoln was of course killed while watching a play): theater in Parks is always associated with fakery (one thinks of Sartre's superb phrase for Genet's spectacles — "patient fakings") and always a dangerous and unprotected space.[71] When her invisible men and women reject such duplicity and sink into their holes, they seek fact, not illusion, something more durable than a mere image of experience. They compulsively measure their surroundings, weigh and take stock of its contents — actions they believe are the first steps toward having a history and (as Parks puts it in *The Death of the Last Black Man*) hiding it "under a rock" (102). They honor pledges and keep secrets, save money, pickle things in mason jars. They take photographs, write and save letters, keep records and monitor those kept by others, balance the budget. In every case, Parks's characters are working to "Hold it. Hold it. Hold it," as all the characters say seven times in all at the end of *The Death of the Last Black Man* (131), thereby filling their voids with knowledge, however unexalted. As Lincoln insists in *Topdog/Underdog,* if "you dont know what is, you dont know what aint" (73). Sometimes the holding is simply a matter of usage. "You: is. It: be. . . . You: still is. They: be. . . . Remember me," says Black Man with Watermelon (126).[72] At other times, the same need is satisfied less articulately. During the spells, the characters are claiming moments of silence, not merely observing them; they mark them with their particular styles of refusal. The silence literally has their names on it.

This activity returns us to Genet's description of a funeral-mime. At the end of the passage, Genet makes a careful distinction. Lives enacted on this graveside stage are "worthy of a dramatic performance — not a tragic one," he writes, adding that "tragedy must be lived, not played." Parks also observes the difference between the playable and the unplayable — and cordons off territory for life uncorrupted by the theater. Every action, every aspect of character in her theater implies a world of incident and psychology saved from the fate of being shown. As she writes in "New Black Math," her 2005 essay proposing numerous definitions of a "black" play, "a black play aint playing."[73] Or as Venus says, "Loves soul . . . hides in heaven. . . . Loves corpse stands on show."[74] Up in heaven, or down in a hole. Parks presents us with the drama lodged between the two sites, but the tragedy flanking it remains obscured — "lived, not played." In her plays, we see the stereotypes, archetypes, variations on literary characters, facsimiles of historical figures — masks all. The people they stand in for cause anxiety by staying just beneath the surface — landmines (to borrow an image from *Imperceptible Mutabilities*) that might explode if we're not careful. Parks knows there is no way in the simplifying medium of theater to do justice to the "tragedies" of the woman in *Venus,* of the two men in *Topdog/Underdog,* of the family in *Imperceptible Mutabilities,* of the race in *The Death of the Last Black Man,* and, finally, of the nation in *The America Play.* (One is reminded of Brecht's complaint — or is it praise? — that theater "theaters everything down.")[75] She rejects her art to save her subjects. That she does so *within* her art preserves her own self-protective ambiguity: we can't pin her down. "Miss me. . . . *Kiss* me" says Venus (160, 162), sounding like Parks herself as she rejects and summons us in an unbroken circle.

It's fitting that the American play arguing most fluently against our claims on art appeared in an unadvertised short run on the outskirts of the cultural center in a nontheater seating no more than forty spectators. The many people who couldn't get a ticket to the 2000 New York premiere of Wallace Shawn's *The Designated Mourner* (1996) learned the play's lesson more viscerally than those who could. In his earlier work, Shawn tacitly indicts the passivity and blinkered vision of most theatergoers. A typical spectacle, he implies, dulls rather than sharpens the senses, dampens rather than arouses critical resistance. In *The Designated Mourner,* he goes further, demoting his own theater in a city and a historical moment crowded with other things having equal rights to our committed attention. The play — suffused with millennial stocktaking — redirects its spectators' possessive urges away from itself and toward a culture as threatened with extinction as any ephemeral production.

André Gregory staged *The Designated Mourner* first in apartments for invited audiences, then in a long-shuttered Gilded Age men's club in New York's Wall Street district. The neighborhood, pulsing with capitalist appetite during the day, falls dead at night. The streets are empty; few restaurants or shops are open; no one seems to live in the darkened, silent buildings. The club is a particularly ghostly place. Audiences walked up narrow dank stairwells barely illuminated by exposed light bulbs, down halls of crumbling plaster and peeling paint, and through once-ornate rooms where shabby, sagging wing chairs lay scattered in no discernable pattern, their regular occupants long gone. In one such room, the floor was also covered with mounted heads of deer, bear, and moose, as if these once noble effigies had reverted to their banal identity as corpses and now lay unceremoniously in a makeshift morgue. The "theater" was just beyond this room — another decrepit space that accommodated spectators in mismatched couches and armchairs scavenged from the rooms nearby. The coziness it provided was short-lived. After an intermission, spectators were escorted to a second, sterile space — it looked like an old squash court but could have been an interrogation chamber — and directed to bleachers beneath harsh fluorescent bulbs and a leaky skylight. (When it rained, water dripped steadily onstage.) In this act, it becomes clear that two of the three characters died before the narrative began. Their posthumous status is only the most palpable sign that *The Designated Mourner* presses up against the limits of theatrical presence. It is a burial rite played out in an insecure bunker forgotten in an emptied landscape.

It can also be seen as participating in — if only to subvert — an established dramatic genre. Like Shawn's *Aunt Dan and Lemon* (1985) and *The Fever* (1990), *The Designated Mourner* is a memory play presided over by a memoirist of ambiguous morality. Jack's vulgarity, pettiness, and scorn for all artistic

Figure 20: *The Designated Mourner* by Wallace Shawn, directed by André Gregory, New York, 2000. Pictured, left to right, André Gregory, Deborah Eisenberg (Judy), Larry Pine (Howard), Wallace Shawn (Jack). Photograph by Brigitte Lacombe.

and intellectual ambition leave him seemingly ill suited to be the one person charged with honoring an extinct culture. He is flanked by Judy, his wife, and Judy's father, Howard, a distinguished poet and essayist whose ethical probity marks him for both Jack's derision and, later, for greater and more devastating violence. Howard embodies both the strength and vulnerability of the comfortable world enclosing all three characters. His aesthetic and intellectual commitments set the standard for the life of the mind. Yet the life of the body encroaches on him and the others with ever-increasing force. Jack reports that when he first met Judy, then still living at home, she walked around the house topless, arousing no comment or any other discernable reaction from her father. Sex is merely theoretical amid so much literary beauty. Such equilibrium doesn't last long. Experiences that, to Howard and his kind, had once stayed securely within the bounds of writing as "mental phenomena" (in Jack's phrase) — poverty, oppression, power, revolution — become physical facts.[76] The characters describe a series of ever more aggressive intrusions of reality. First, a rock smashes through Howard's window. Later, demonstrators fill the streets. Then, in quick succession, gunshots break out at a concert, people are killed in nice restaurants, and "human remains" are dropped at "the carousel in the middle of the park" (52). When Howard again becomes a target, he is beaten to death. A full-scale uprising follows, in which Judy is rounded up and executed by what she calls "dirt-eaters," the poor she mistakenly thought would temper their rage once they noticed her sympathy for them. Before long, Jack says, "everyone on earth who could read John Donne [is] dead" (99).

The political naiveté of these "readers of poetry," as Jack calls them, is obvious (28). Less easy to mock is their faith in art. *The Designated Mourner,* like *The Fever* and *Aunt Dan and Lemon* before it, seduces its spectators with a vision of passionate, even erotic communion with culture. Characters surrender to their enthusiasms, seize opportunities to exercise their judgment, overflow with recommendations and dissents. They exude the particular well-being of those who find clarity, structure, and purpose in a daily regimen of spectatorship. To the characters in *The Fever* and *The Designated Mourner,* the sensuous surfaces of a cultural artifact matter as much as its contents. The unnamed protagonist of *The Fever* relishes the way "the bow of the violin *cut[s]* into the string."[77] Characters in *The Designated Mourner* fondle books, read aloud to enjoy the grain of the voice, marvel at the way a musician's "heels dig into the stage" (51–52). (In the film version, Judy languorously prolongs the act of refilling a fountain pen.) No less significant than these experiences are those establishing fellowship among spectators and readers. (Readers of Frank O'Hara will recognize the sensibility.) Culture fosters an intimacy unavailable in other kinds of intercourse. "I like to go out at night in a cosmopolitan city and sit in a dark auditorium watching dancers fly into each other's arms," says the protagonist of *The Fever* (179). Later he suggests that a glittering new production of *The Cherry Orchard* is mere curtain-raiser to the higher drama that follows: "Riding in a taxi home from the play, my friends were critical of one of the actors. His performance had been slack, inadequate, not thought through" (193). The act of reading is just as incomplete. It is only the preparatory stage in a broader initiative to relieve the customary solitude of both reader and writer: "I write little notes to people I like when I enjoy the articles they've written" (210).

Shawn's sympathy for this cultural commitment doesn't blind him to its limits and excesses. The impressionable Lemon, in *Aunt Dan and Lemon,* confesses that she has only felt compassion "reading a novel and . . . watching a film — 'Oh how sad, that child is sick! . . .' — but I can't ever remember feeling it in life."[78] In *The Fever,* the cultured protagonist easily and unthinkingly aestheticizes pain: "Yes — a beggar can be beautiful. . . . Her simple shawl seems elegant . . . the right way to dress" (202). The difficulty we sometimes have knowing whether *The Designated Mourner* is endorsing or lampooning its characters' aestheticism accounts for much of its own power. "So from an early age," Judy says of Howard, "he was always wondering, Why were certain people — the ones *not* from his background — systematically made to eat dirt and kept so far away from the songs of Schubert?" (24).

However the line is played — and whether or not it is met with assent or derisive laughter — it underscores the fact that *The Designated Mourner* contains no sustained discussion of any actual art. Shawn names particular artists or their works only in the context of introducing people who because of taste, education, or circumstance don't have access to them. Those with access either misinterpret art or ruin the pleasure others take in it. ("When she said those things," Judy says of a friend with whom she discusses a play they've both seen, "the performance that was sitting in my memory was poisoned" [96].) In this light, it becomes obvious that high culture was in danger long before the vaguely motivated uprising began. Cherishing art fails to preserve it from degradation or annihilation; those who take it for granted are in fact just as cut off from its deeper challenges as the untutored or unprivileged. *The Designated Mourner* owes its vertiginous quality in part to this uncomfortable truth: Howard's admirable principles don't save him from fatuousness; Jack's vulgarity doesn't entirely discredit his scorn for posturing. A model of conduct better than either man — one who practices slow, acutely observant engagement with all manner of sensation — is Shawn himself.

The formal austerity of *The Designated Mourner* makes it impossible to ignore his effort — effort that doesn't preclude grace. Nothing happens theatrically beyond the borders of discourse. Characters chronicle but do not enact horrific action. Pathos, such as it is, emerges as they impose narrative form on events that destroyed a culture of stories, or as they seek the right tone to describe the brutality of those indifferent to style. Shawn registers these contradictions in the rhythms of his sentences. He finds eloquence in hesitation. Characters speak an exploratory and meticulous prose, accumulating details of a meal, a holiday ritual, an invigorating fight, or a sexual encounter without pretending that speech alone can save these experiences from ephemerality. The archeological sensibility we see in Shawn's contemporaries is no less strong in his own work. With the tools of inquiry, exposition, and argument, his speakers probe the memory of events incompletely understood in their own time. Yet this style of restoration takes equal care to mark our present distance from its object. Shawn is a cold elegist. His tribute to material losses — artworks, artists, sensitive auditors for art — directs us even more forcefully to the immaterial and thus unrecoverable atmosphere they once occupied and in which they found meaning. It is an atmosphere composed of characters' glances, inflections, and the rhythms in which they approach or evade one another — all ways to exchange opinions that would lose their richness if voiced directly, and all unreadable to those outside their magic circle. Shawn finds a style that suggests he writes from the perimeter of this circle — neither inside nor outside, or looking both inward and outward — keeping his balance only by the persistence of his curiosity.

The New York production of *The Designated Mourner* found a literal image for this point of view. When audiences entered the theater space, they encountered Shawn himself strolling the margin between stage and house. He gazed quizzically out at the spectators who gazed back at him, seeming to invite friendly approaches only to mark intimacy's limit the moment he stepped back onto the stage and began the play.[79] He had cast himself as Jack. By taking on the role of pathetic jester and envious low-brow, Shawn wreaked havoc on conventional forms of artistic authority. Whatever moral high ground Shawn-the-playwright enjoyed was undermined by Shawn-the-actor, who on speaking words he himself wrote confused their critical intent. As speech battled writing for supremacy, audiences experienced another form of abandonment in this desolate theater and city. The author, obscured by his character, leaves us unchaperoned — or at least mistrustful of the guide standing before us. We can't subscribe to the odious point of view argued so cogently before us, yet also can't dismiss it as mere satire.

When *The Designated Mourner* was being developed in private performances, some spectators experienced an even sharper form of interpretive dislocation. At one reading, Arthur Miller played Howard opposite Shawn's Jack. The two playwrights, side by side, may have tempted observers to find a metatheatrical allegory in the play — a generational and aesthetic conflict, with the younger, more politically subtle writer favored to prevail. Yet as the representative of the new diminishes himself alongside an embodiment of American theater tradition, it becomes clear that Shawn's particular power as a writer depends on self-abasement, even self-cancellation. He writes against his own convictions — refusing to ally himself, here, with a fellow skeptic of liberal complacency; in earlier plays, granting the most persuasive skill to characters espousing noxious politics — and in the process alerts us to the ease with which any writer, failing to be vigilant, can lose authority over his or her subject.

As if to demonstrate the vulnerability of all writing in such a world, Shawn began the Wall Street production of *The Designated Mourner* by setting a match to a piece of paper—a tissue holding a pastry—and watching spellbound as ash rose above his head, floated for a moment, and disappeared. Are the pages of his play also turning to ash in this sequence, dying before beginning? The act, anticipating a passage at the end in which Jack describes doing the same thing in a park café, of course prepares us to see the evanescence of more durable institutions and communities, along with their principles and conventions. "A very special little world has died," he says as the play opens. "Someone is assigned to grieve, to wail, and light the public ritual fire" (5).

Yet *The Designated Mourner* is also an elegy for individuals—or more precisely, for the idea of individuality in a world unable to acknowledge the self except as it is allied to social categories, aesthetic schools, and intellectual positions. Shawn's most disarming passages aren't those in which characters lash out at boorishness (on one side) or snobbery (on the other), or in which they report on rage among the underclass and terror among the "civilized." He is a more surprising writer in scenes where characters fail to muster these, or any, emotions. The tragedy of a disappearing culture exposes the absurdity of an already departed self. One's inchoate impulses will no longer coalesce into legible identities. As Shawn returns over and over to moments of impeded expression, we learn how thin the veneer of any character's emotion, opinion, or attitude, and how fathomless the emptiness it attempts to cover. "I'd fallen out and gone down," Jack says, recalling the gravitational pull affecting the speaker in *The Fever* (as well as similar trajectories in Albee, a playwright Shawn admires).[80] "I was falling through a spiraling darkness," he continues, "blackness filling my lungs" (62–63). The descent strips him of everything inessential to his presence. "Why am I struggling every day to learn my lines, to once again impersonate this awful character?" he asks himself (70). Even his name, when uttered by a new lover, "rang so oddly in my ears" (74). He trusts only his primal responses and acts—treating us to descriptions of his eating, masturbating, defecating, and urinating—but can't, or won't, see them as conditioned by his history or predictive of his destiny. Once and future selves "mean exactly *nothing* to me, because none of these people actually exist" (40). Neither, he argues elsewhere, do symbolic or allegorical selves. Despite Judy's prodding, he refuses to put himself in other people's shoes or to consider playing a social role. "Do you see yourself now as just—what?" she asks impatiently. "I don't see myself 'as' anything at all," he replies, reaffirming only empirical truth and solipsistic authority (57).

Yet even they don't survive the play's entropic climate. The body, seemingly the only incontrovertible evidence of presence, "is simply a shell," Jack says (71). Its owner doesn't recognize it. "I saw my ass in the mirror [and] said to myself, 'What *is* that. . . . And what does it have to do with me?' " (54–55). Shawn charts a steep and rapid decline: self-disgust takes the place of self-absorption before itself giving way to self-destruction. "I threw it on its back," he says, imagining revenge on a hounding, taunting identity, and "kicked it smartly in the face . . . and strangled it and bashed its skull against the floor until it . . . was gone" (91). (This is one of many occasions on which Shawn stresses the word "gone.") But self-loathing still depends on the existence of a self. Rage dissipates, along with every other kind of passionate impulse, replaced by weariness. Jack's pornography collection now leaves him cold: "The pictures were dead . . . were paper. They were nothing." Looking at them, "I felt nothing" (94). Eventually, he implies, he won't even be able to remember earlier twinges of desire, much less, as he says in the play's last moments, what he once knew of higher cultural practices. "I was . . . forgetting his name," he says of Donne, "forgetting him, and forgetting all the ones who remembered him" (101).

These utterances, the issue of a rapidly ebbing consciousness, seem the protagonist's last possible offering. They mark the ascendancy of an idea of character — and of drama — that stands apart from expression. It's not just that libido and ego are exhausted. Commitment, compassion, and all related modes of imposing personality on others are irrelevant to Shawn's ideal zero-degree theatricality. This is perhaps the logical terminus for a playwright who in other works has shown the dangerous consequences of virtuosic reason. (In *Aunt Dan and Lemon*, rational minds excuse fascism; in *The Fever,* they justify killing the poor.) Throughout *The Designated Mourner*, deliquescence takes many forms. Jack's love for Judy "sputtered . . . bent its head, and turned into a vague little plume of smoke" (86). Howard tells himself to "stop struggling. Lie back. Put your head on the pillow. Close your eyes," before he finally dies (67). Judy's skin "grow[s] suddenly pale" one day and then she stops speaking — rehearsal for her own imminent death (60). A girl Jack meets in the park (he tells us) describes seeing herself "in a picture . . . and something smudge[s] it" (72). Throughout the city, he says elsewhere, "things were shrinking" or "had simply ended" (93, 62).

The strenuous passivity of some of these constructions — no sentence names a cause — ensures we'll continue to think about speech's often obscured role in shaping experience. One can't help notice the submissiveness of the prose here, when elsewhere Shawn uses language (this labored phrase seems, for once, an apt substitute for the simpler "writes") to control events and the feelings they arouse. Near the end of *The Designated Mourner,* Jack comes across a newspaper photograph of Judy's execution and says, "I happened to notice that the woman sitting in the very last chair with her head at that rather odd angle was obviously Judy" (98). The speaker — affecting casualness ("happened to") and adding adjectives and unnecessary intensifiers ("very," "rather") — does everything he can to delay facing his sentence's awful object, her name postponed one last time with the word "obviously." It's left to the actor to decide whether or not the playwright's jaded adverb successfully tempers the character's emotion.

This negotiation between actor and playwright returns us one last time to the circumstances of the New York production. In playing his own protagonist, Shawn bolsters his presence against the onset of theater's nightly disappearance. Yet a move that in another production would be seen as hubris here suggests its opposite. Just as Jack's protracted sentence confirms the greater strength of a fate no words can vanquish, so too does Shawn's deliberately excessive effort to impose himself on us look desperate — panic in the face of growing marginality and certain extinction. Doubly present, Shawn doubles the inevitable absence we know he will leave behind. His character, having contaminated both playwright and actor by his anti-aesthetic, aggressively pursues both the oblivion at the end of every text and the oblivion at the end of every performance. "I heard John Donne . . . plummeting fast through the earth on his way to Hell," he says near the end, minutes before Shawn also plummets through the thin skin of theatrical presence into unreliable memory (101).

And yet — it's typical of Shawn that a bit of wordplay suggests a more nuanced conclusion. Because Judy makes so much, early in the play, of the overdecorous phrase "human remains" — those that were dumped by the carousel in the park — we're primed to pay special attention to the recurrence of the word "remains" at the end. Here, though, it signifies survival, even rebirth, instead of death. "So much remains," says Jack, and among the many objects that arouse his connoisseurship is the same carousel once sullied by the dead (103). Fireworks will be set off above it after dark, Jack says, as he compiles a list of other, less emphatic pleasures: a lemonade stand, "twinkling yellow" light at dusk, "rose color" air, the "trembling sky," squirrels, birds, trees. He sits on a bench in the park, "lost — sunk deep — in the experience of unbelievable physical pleasure, maybe the greatest pleasure we can know on this earth — the sweet, ever-changing caress of an early evening breeze" (103). In these, the play's last lines, Jack gives himself over wholly both to the scene and to the pleasure to be had describing it.[81] Everything that precedes this passage urges us *not* to give ourselves over to it — this lyricist is corrupt — yet if we are at all susceptible to prose rhythm we won't entirely succeed. This tug-of-war ensures we ourselves won't settle tranquilly into the scene. The passage is beautiful even as, by its choice of subjects, it refuses to limit beauty to cultural achievement. What "remains" is indifferent to any artist. The natural landscape — dusk, air, sky, trees — reasserts its sovereignty over those who would cut it down to writing's size. That a writer, by the delicacy of his writing in these last pages, succeeds in arguing this point is a paradox Shawn expects us to address as we rethink the responsibility of art.

The paradox also illuminates a struggle Shawn seems to wage throughout his career. To the frustration of his admirers, Shawn is unprolific — three plays between 1985 and 2008, each widely spaced, the last two eschewing "action" for expository speech.[82] In the silent periods — and, in *The Fever* and *The Designated Mourner,* on the uneventful stages — one can see the playwright confronting and hoping to get beyond a seductive image of himself. Before *Aunt Dan and Lemon,* he said in an interview with Mark Strand, "I was so obsessed with myself and with trying to foist myself on the world that I didn't notice anything [else]. . . . And [now] I just am not as interested in myself as I used to be."[83] Jack, along with the speaker in *The Fever,* is the exaggerated result of this plummeting self-regard, of course. (Shawn's recent plays are about "myself" only insofar as, in Jack's words, he "kicks it smartly in the face.") But Jack also, perversely, practices a responsiveness that Shawn aspires to match on a larger stage. The playwright knows that each of his plays, even as it engages social and cultural "issues," blocks his view of the world in which they matter most — that his art reflects back to himself his own sensibility when he is desperate to escape the parochialism of any merely personal consciousness. (A journal in which Jack notes his many desecrations of art is called "Experiments in Privacy," a title that itself names both the achievement and limitation of most art.) "I consider myself an idiot," Shawn said to Strand. "It's idiotic to be talking about all of these things without taking any action" (194). The selfish protagonist of *The Designated Mourner,* tabulating the features of a world indifferent to human conduct in his last panoramic speech, enables Shawn to acquire a selfless vision. Theater — or any art — isn't everything. Only everything is everything. Can Shawn accept that conclusion without dooming himself to permanent inadequacy, without rendering himself superfluous? Can any writer write without egotism? We might imagine Shawn grappling rigorously, uncomplacently, with these questions during the years between plays in his career. As such, those periods no longer seem dead — unless one imagines the writer spending them in mourning what has become an obsolete idea of writing. The American theater's most restless playwright delays the act of writing; its ideal spectator is most responsive when waiting for something to see. We merely wait for a new play, but Shawn seeks a new kind of theater, one that marshals many theatrical elements — eloquence, narrative momentum, persuasive character, meticulous production — to assert that other things matter. Matter more? Shawn keeps his argumentative spirit alive — keeps the long-incubating plays from dying into mere statements on contact with the culture's air — by refusing to decide.

Notes

Introduction

1. See Sylvère Lotringer, "Robert Wilson: Interview," *Semiotext(e)* 3 (1978): 21, and Richard Foreman, "Directing the Actors, Mostly," in *Unbalancing Acts: Foundations for a Theater* (New York: Pantheon, 1992), 37–38. For a discussion of Foreman's links to melodrama, see James Leverett, "Old Forms Enter the New American Theater: Shepard, Foreman, Kirby, and Ludlam," in *Melodrama,* ed. Daniel Gerould (New York: New York Literary Forum, 1980), 107–22.

2. Stephen Crane, *Maggie: A Girl of the Streets, and Other Tales of New York* (New York: Penguin, 2000), 37.

3. Stanley Cavell, "The Avoidance of Love: A Reading of *King Lear,*" in *Disowning Knowledge in Seven Plays of Shakespeare* (Cambridge: Cambridge University Press, 2003), 102, 105.

4. T. S. Eliot, *Four Quartets,* in *Collected Poems, 1909–1962* (New York: Harcourt, Brace and World, 1970), 186.

5. T. S. Eliot, *The Family Reunion* (New York: Harcourt, Brace and World, 1939), 28.

6. Virginia Woolf, "Notes on an Elizabethan Play," in *The Common Reader: First Series* (San Diego: Harcourt, 1984), 57.

7. Ibid., 57. Also see Ezra Pound's letter to James Joyce, September 1915, in which he complains that theater, dependent on "feeling," forces cohesiveness upon its audiences. "There is no union in intellect, when we think we diverge, we explore, we go away. When we feel we unite." *Pound/Joyce: The Letters of Ezra Pound to James Joyce,* ed. Forrest Read (New York: New Directions, 1967), 46.

8. Djuna Barnes, "Playgoer's Almanac," *Theatre Guild Magazine* 8, no. 4 (January 1931): 35.

9. Ezra Pound and Ernest Fenollosa, *The Classic Noh Theatre of Japan* (New York: New Directions, 1959), 130.

10. Richard Poirier, *Poetry and Pragmatism* (Cambridge: Harvard University Press, 1992), 138, 149, 151–54.

11. Djuna Barnes, *Nightwood* (New York: New Directions, 1961), 111.

12. William Dunlap, *André* (1798), in *Early American Drama*, ed. Jeffrey H. Richards (New York: Penguin, 1997), 101. Future page references appear parenthetically.

13. Sacvan Bercovitch, *The Puritan Origins of the American Self* (New Haven: Yale University Press, 1975), 103.

14. William Bradford, *Of Plymouth Plantation, 1620–1647*, quoted in Bercovitch, *The Puritan Origins of the American Self*, 45.

15. Thomas Postlewait takes a skeptical view of realism's "triumph" over melodrama in "From Melodrama to Realism: The Suspect History of American Drama," in *Melodrama: The Cultural Emergence of a Genre*, ed. Michael Hays and Anastasia Nikolopoulou (New York: St. Martin's, 1996), 39–60.

16. Bert O. States, *The Pleasure of the Play* (Ithaca: Cornell University Press, 1994), 75.

17. John Brougham, *Columbus el Filibustero!!* (New York: Samuel French, 1858), 1. John Brougham, *Po-ca-hon-tas; or, The Gentle Savage*, in *Dramas from the American Theatre, 1762–1909*, ed. Richard Moody (Cleveland: World Publishing, 1966), 403. Future page references appear parenthetically.

18. John Brougham, *Much Ado About a Merchant of Venice* (New York: Samuel French, 1869), 17.

19. Charles Ludlam, "Confessions of a Farceur," in *Ridiculous Theatre, Scourge of Human Folly: The Essays and Opinions of Charles Ludlam*, ed. Steven Samuels (New York: Theatre Communications Group, 1992), 38.

20. John Brougham, *Metamora; or, The Last of the Pollywogs* (1847), in *Staging the Nation: Plays from the American Theater, 1787–1909*, ed. Don B. Wilmeth (Boston: Bedford, 1998), 123.

21. I am aware of the other firsts in American theater history: *Ye Bare and Ye Cubb*, the first recorded play performed in the English colonies (1665); *Androborus* by Robert Hunter, the first published American play (1715); and *The Prince of Parthia* by Thomas Godfrey (1759), the first American tragedy. Only the latter two survive, and they make for dreary reading.

22. Royall Tyler, *The Contrast* (1787), in *Early American Drama*, ed. Richards, 33. Future page references appear parenthetically.

23. John Howard Payne quoted in David Grimsted, *Melodrama Unveiled: American Theater and Culture, 1800–1850* (Berkeley: University of California Press, 1968), 99.

24. Jeffrey H. Richards, *Drama, Theatre, and Identity in the American New Republic* (New York: Cambridge University Press, 2005), 29. Don B. Wilmeth in his introduction to *Staging the Nation* also acknowledges the "bifurcation" of the "postcolonial nation in search of an identity" (2).

25. Kenneth Silverman, *A Cultural History of the American Revolution* (New York: Thomas Y. Crowell, 1976), 559.

26. Gordon S. Wood, *The Radicalism of the American Revolution* (1992) (New York: Vintage, 1993), 221. The quotation from Benjamin Rush is from his letter to James Beattie, August 1, 1786. Wood also cites John Adams: "Science and literature are of no party or nation." For discussions of other transatlantic exchanges animating American theater, see Elizabeth Maddock Dillon, *New World Dramas: Theater of the Atlantic, 1660–1860* (Durham: Duke University Press, forthcoming), and Joseph Roach, *Cities of the Dead: Circum-Atlantic Performance* (New York: Columbia University Press, 1996).

27. Richard Brinsley Sheridan, *The School for Scandal* (1777), in *The School for Scandal and Other Plays* (London: Penguin, 1988), 277.

28. William Dunlap, *The Father; or, American Shandyism* (1789) (New York: The Dunlap Society, 1887), 68.

29. William Dunlap, *The Voice of Nature* (New York: David Longworth, at the Dramatic Repository, Shakespeare Gallery, 1807), 43.

30. See Richard Moody, introduction to William Dunlap, *The Glory of Columbia: Her Yeomanry!* in *Dramas from the American Theatre, 1762–1909*, ed. Moody, 87.

31. *Early American Drama*, ed. Richards, 61.

32. For an influential discussion of masculine sentiment in other American and British literature, see Julie Ellison, *Cato's Tears and the Making of Anglo-American Emotion* (Chicago: University of Chicago Press, 1999), esp. 48–73.

33. Gordon S. Wood has described how Washington "used his natural reticence to reinforce the image of a stern and forbidding classical hero." (*Radicalism of the American Revolution*, 404)

Chapter 1: Envisioning the Nineteenth Century

Epigraphs from Ralph Waldo Emerson, "Nature," in *Selected Writings of Ralph Waldo Emerson*, ed. William H. Gilman (New York: New American Library, 1965), 188, and Barbara Rose, *Rauschenberg: An Interview* (New York: Viking, 1987), quoted in Walter Hopps and Susan Davidson, *Robert Rauschenberg: A Retrospective* (New York: Guggenheim Museum, 1997), 227.

1. Henry James, *Autobiography*, ed. Frederick W. Dupee (Princeton: Princeton University Press, 1983), 61–63, 91. Future page references appear parenthetically. Leon Edel cites some of these examples, along with several others, in "Henry James: The Dramatic Years," the introduction to Edel's edition of *The Complete Plays of Henry James* (London: Rupert Hart-Davis, 1949), 23.

2. Walt Whitman, "Song of Myself," in *Complete Poetry and Collected Prose* (New York: Library of America, 1982), 30.

3. William Wells Brown, *The Escape; or, A Leap for Freedom* (Boston: R. F. Wallcut, 1858), 1.

4. Pixérécourt's claim is mentioned in Peter Brooks, *The Melodramatic Imagination: Balzac, Henry James, Melodrama, and the Mode of Excess* (New Haven: Yale University Press, 1976), 89, and in Michael Booth, *English Melodrama* (London: Herbert Jenkins, 1965), 44. Daniel Gerould and Marvin Carlson have recently cast doubt on this durable piece of Pixérécourt lore. See their introduction to René-Charles Guilbert de Pixérécourt, *Four Melodramas* (New York: Martin E. Segal Theatre Center, 2002), x.

5. See Brooks, *Melodramatic Imagination,* 14–15, 43–44.

6. Booth, *English Melodrama,* 190.

7. Quoted in Marvin Carlson, *Theories of the Theatre* (Ithaca: Cornell University Press, 1984), 154. There are also many British precedents for the early American theater's interest in vision. The best overview of the subject is Martin Meisel, *Realizations: Narrative, Pictorial, and Theatrical Arts in Nineteenth-Century England* (Princeton: Princeton University Press, 1983). Meisel's discussion of the new "pictorial dramaturgy" is especially pertinent: "In the new dramaturgy . . . the play creates a series of . . . pictures, some of them offering a culminating symbolic summary of represented events, while others substitute an arrested situation for action and reaction. Each picture, dissolving, leads not into consequent activity, but to a new infusion and distribution of elements from which a new picture will be assembled or resolved" (38).

8. See Michael Fried, *Absorption and Theatricality: Painting and the Beholder in the Age of Diderot* (Chicago: University of Chicago Press, 1980), 79. Fried is citing Diderot's *Lettre sur les sourds et muets* (1751).

9. Garry Wills, *Inventing America: Jefferson's Declaration of Independence* (New York: Vintage, 1979), 318. A concise summary of Hutcheson's ideas of spectatorship appears on pages 195–96.

10. Lord Kames (Henry Home), *Elements of Criticism* (1762), quoted in Jay Fliegelman, *Declaring Independence: Jefferson, Natural Language, and the Culture of Performance* (Stanford, Stanford University Press, 1993), 16.

11. See, for instance, *The Thespian Preceptor; or, A Full Display of Scenic Art* (Boston: printed by Joshua Belcher, for sale by Elam Bliss, 1810). Walter J. Meserve quotes the instructions for rendering fear: The actor "opens the eyes and mouth very wide, draws down the eyebrows, gives the countenance an air of wildness, draws back the elbows parallel with the sides, lifts up the open hand (his fingers together) to the height of the breast," and so on. Quoted in Walter J. Meserve, *An Emerging Entertainment: The Drama of the American People to 1828* (Bloomington: Indiana University Press, 1977), 171–72.

12. For more on Edwin Forrest's self-emblematizing acting, see Richard Moody, *Edwin Forrest: First Star of the American Stage* (New York: Alfred A. Knopf, 1960); Bruce A. McConachie, *Melodramatic Formations: American Theater and Society, 1820–1870* (Iowa City: University of Iowa Press, 1992), 69–118; and Joseph Roach, "The Emergence of the American Actor," in *The Cambridge History of American Theater,* 3 vols., ed. Don B. Wilmeth and Christopher Bigsby (Cambridge: Cambridge University Press, 1998–2000), 1:352–56.

13. Dion Boucicault, *The Poor of New York* (1857), in *American Melodrama,* ed. Daniel C. Gerould (New York: Performing Arts Journal Publications, 1983), 39.

14. Roland Barthes, *Camera Lucida: Reflections on Photography,* trans. Richard Howard (London: Fontana, 1984), 55.

15. Edith Wharton, *The House of Mirth* (New York: Scribner, 1995), 194, 196–97.

16. Dion Boucicault quoted in *American Melodrama,* ed. Gerould, 11.

17. Dion Boucicault, *The Octoroon; or, Life in Louisiana,* in *Early American Drama,* ed. Jeffrey H. Richards (New York: Penguin, 1997), 464.

18. *Scenes at Gurney's: An Ethiopian Act,* as performed by the San Francisco Min-

strels, in *Darkey Plays,* vol. 1 (New York: Roorbach, 1870), 7. Future page references appear parenthetically.

19. Eric Lott, *Love and Theft: Blackface Minstrelsy and the American Working Class* (New York: Oxford University Press, 1993), 140.

20. The film is in the collection of the Museum of Modern Art, New York. Tom Gunning discusses *The Drunkard's Reformation* in detail in *D. W. Griffith and the Origins of American Narrative Film: The Early Years at Biograph* (Urbana: University of Illinois Press, 1991), 162–71.

21. Jeffrey D. Mason, *Melodrama and the Myth of America* (Bloomington: Indiana University Press, 1993), 77. John W. Frick reads the play alongside other temperance dramas in *Theatre, Culture, and Temperance Reform in Nineteenth-Century America* (Cambridge: Cambridge University Press, 2003), 112–27.

22. William Henry Smith, *The Drunkard; or, The Fallen Saved,* in *Early American Drama,* ed. Richards, 252. Future page references appear parenthetically.

23. Washington Irving, *Histories, Tales, and Sketches* (New York: Library of America, 1983), 23.

24. Fanny Trollope, *Domestic Manners of the Americans* (London: Penguin, 1997), 263.

25. Henry James, *The American Scene* (1907) (New York: Penguin, 1994), 148.

26. For more on the African Company, see Marvin McAllister, *White People Do Not Know How to Behave at Entertainments Designed for Ladies and Gentlemen of Colour: William Brown's African and American Theater* (Chapel Hill: University of North Carolina Press, 2003) and Shane White, *Stories of Freedom: Black New York* (Cambridge: Harvard University Press, 2002).

27. Robert Montgomery Bird, *The Gladiator,* in *Early American Drama,* ed. Richards, 187–88.

28. William Dunlap, *A Trip to Niagara; or, Travellers in America,* in *Dramas from the American Theatre, 1762–1909,* ed. Richard Moody (Cleveland: World, 1966), 178. Future page references appear parenthetically.

29. Richard Poirier, *A World Elsewhere: The Place of Style in American Literature* (New York: Oxford University Press, 1966), 51.

30. The experience recalls what Jonathan Crary says about the rise of another quasi-theatrical form, the camera obscura, in the 1820s and 1830s. These rooms, by simultaneously removing viewers from street life and engulfing them with its simulacra, "liberate" nineteenth-century vision, "blurring . . . the distinction between internal sensation and external signs." As in the theater, the spectator goes inside to attain (or enjoy the illusion of attaining) mastery over the outside. See Jonathan Crary, *Techniques of the Observer: On Vision and Modernity in the Nineteenth Century* (Cambridge: MIT Press, 1990), 38–39.

31. Stephan Oettermann, *The Panorama: History of a Mass Medium,* trans. Deborah Lucas Schneider (New York: Zone, 1997), 23–24, 31–32.

32. Quoted in *Dramas from the American Theatre,* ed. Moody, 175.

33. Charles Dickens, "The American Panorama," in *The Examiner,* December 16, 1848, reprinted in Stephan Oettermann, *The Panorama: History of a Mass Medium,* trans. Deborah Lucas Schneider (New York: Zone, 1997), 329–30.

34. For more on Henry "Box" Brown, see Cynthia Griffin Wolff, "Passing Beyond the Middle Passage: Henry "Box" Brown's Translations of Slavery," *Massachusetts Review* 37, no. 1 (Spring 1996): 23–44, and esp. Daphne A. Brooks, *Bodies in Dissent: Spectacular Performances of Race and Freedom, 1850–1910* (Durham: Duke University Press, 2006), 66–130.

35. Whitman quoted in Sean Wilentz, *Chants Democratic: New York City and the Rise of the American Working Class, 1788–1850* (New York: Oxford University Press, 1984), 258. For more on the city's theatricality, discussed below, see W. T. Lhamon, Jr., *Raising Cain: Blackface Performance from Jim Crow to Hip-Hop* (Cambridge: Harvard University Press, 1998), 25–28.

36. Benjamin A. Baker, *A Glance at New York*, in *On Stage America!* ed. Walter J. Meserve (New York: Feedback Theatrebooks and Prospero Press, 1996), 164. Future page references appear parenthetically.

37. Henri Lefebvre, "The Right to the City," in *Writings on Cities,* trans. Eleonore Kofman and Elizabeth Lebas (Oxford: Blackwell, 1996), 147–59.

38. Jane Tompkins, *Sensational Designs: The Cultural Work of American Fiction, 1790–1860* (New York: Oxford University Press, 1985), 122–46.

39. George L. Aiken, *Uncle Tom's Cabin; or, Life Among the Lowly,* in *Early American Drama,* ed. Richards, 404, 407. Future page references appear parenthetically.

40. James Baldwin, "Everybody's Protest Novel," in *Notes of a Native Son* (New York: Bantam, 1964), 14, 11. Future page references appear parenthetically.

41. Daniel C. Gerould, "The Americanization of Melodrama," in *American Melodrama,* ed. Gerould, 16. Future page references appear parenthetically.

42. Charles Baudelaire, "The Painter of Modern Life," in *The Painter of Modern Life and Other Essays,* trans. Jonathan Mayne (New York: Da Capo, 1986), 13. Baudelaire's essay was written in 1860.

43. Gertrude Stein, "Plays," in *Lectures in America* (1935) (Boston: Beacon, 1985), 113. Future page references appear parenthetically.

Chapter 2: Staging the Civil War

Epigraph from William Shakespeare, *Macbeth,* 1.3.137–38.

1. Walt Whitman, "Years of the Modern," in Whitman, *Complete Poetry and Prose* (New York: Library of America, 1982), 597. Whitman's poem first appeared in an earlier version in *Drum-Taps* (1865) under the title "Years of the Unperform'd." It was included in its present form in the 1871 edition of *Leaves of Grass.* Lines 11–24 are drawn from Whitman's essay "The Eighteenth Presidency!" (1856). For an insightful discussion of Whitman's relation to theater in general, see Alan L. Ackerman, Jr., *The Portable Theater: American Literature and the Nineteenth-Century Stage* (Baltimore: Johns Hopkins University Press, 1999), 42–88.

2. Among those reading the poem as optimistic prophecy are Roger Asselineau (*The Evolution of Walt Whitman*), James E. Miller (*A Critical Guide to Leaves of Grass*), and Gay Wilson Allen (*The New Walt Whitman Handbook*).

3. Walt Whitman, *Specimen Days,* in Whitman, *Complete Poetry and Prose,* 706. The war sketches were first published separately as *Memoranda During the War* (1876). Future page references appear parenthetically.

4. Alfred Kazin also discusses, with a different emphasis, the importance of numbers in the war sketches. See his introduction to *Specimen Days* (Boston: David R. Godine, 1971).

5. Stephen Crane, *The Red Badge of Courage* (New York: Modern Library, 2000), 65.

6. Ulysses S. Grant, *Personal Memoirs* (New York: Modern Library, 1999), 580.

7. Ambrose Bierce, "One Kind of Officer" (1892), in *Tale of Soldiers and Civilians and Other Stories* (New York: Penguin, 2000), 86.

8. Herman Melville, "A Utilitarian View of the Monitor's Fight," "Malvern Hill," in *Battle-Pieces and Aspects of the War* (Amherst, NY: Prometheus, 2001), 89, 93.

9. *The Guerillas* was first staged in Richmond on December 22, 1862. It was published in Richmond by West and Johnston in 1863. The text is also in *Fateful Lightning: America's Civil War Plays,* ed. Walter J. Meserve and Mollie Ann Meserve (New York: Feedback Theatrebooks and Prospero Press, 2000).

10. David W. Blight, *Race and Reunion: The Civil War in American Memory* (Cambridge: Harvard University Press, 2001), 57, 217.

11. Clyde Fitch, *Barbara Frietchie, the Frederick Girl* (New York: Samuel French, 1900), 63.

12. Quoted in Edith Wharton, *A Backward Glance,* in *Novellas and Other Writings* (New York: Library of America, 1990), 894.

13. Ambrose Bierce, "The Short Story" (1897), in *Tale of Soldiers and Civilians and Other Stories,* 257, 259.

14. William Gillette, *Held by the Enemy* (New York: Samuel French, 1898), 24. Future page references appear parenthetically.

15. Augustin Daly, *Under the Gaslight,* in *American Melodrama,* ed. Daniel C. Gerould (New York: Performing Arts Journal Publications, 1983), 137. Future page references appear parenthetically.

16. Daniel C. Gerould, "The Americanization of Melodrama," in *American Melodrama,* ed. Gerould, 21.

17. Edward Harrigan's comments appear in "American Playwrights on the American Drama," a series of statements by Harrigan, Augustin Daly, Bronson Howard, William Gillette, and others, published in *Harper's Weekly,* February 2, 1889, pp. 97–98.

18. William Dean Howells, "Editor's Study," *Harper's Monthly,* July 1886, pp. 314–17, reprinted as "Good Drama vs. Good Theatre," in *A Realist in the American Theatre: Selected Drama Criticism of William Dean Howells,* ed. Brenda Murphy (Athens: Ohio University Press, 1992), 29.

19. Edward Harrigan, *The Mulligan Guard Ball,* in *Dramas from the American Theatre 1762–1909,* ed. Richard Moody (Cleveland: World, 1966), 553.

20. Bronson Howard, *Shenandoah,* in *Representative Plays by American Dramatists,* vol. 3 (1856–1911), ed. Montrose J. Moses (New York: E. P. Dutton, 1921), 380. Future page references appear parenthetically.

21. Jeffrey D. Mason, *Melodrama and the Myth of America* (Bloomington: Indiana University Press, 1993), 175.

22. Mason reads this scene in an opposite way: "By showing Sheridan only in the midst of his ride rather than including him in the dialogue of the play, Howard avoids making him too familiar, and he appropriates for the play the general's potential for deification"

(*Melodrama and the Myth of America,* 184). As I suggest above and below, the war-wounded and the horse prevent us from seeing Sheridan at the heroic center of at least this scene of war.

23. George Bernard Shaw, "Ibsen Triumphant" (May 22, 1897), in *Our Theatres in the Nineties,* vol. 3 (London: Constable, 1931), 150.

24. Gertrude Stein, "Plays," in *Lectures in America* (Boston: Beacon, 1985), 116.

25. William Gillette, *Secret Service,* in *Staging the Nation: Plays from the American Theater, 1787–1909,* ed. Don B. Wilmeth (Boston: Bedford, 1998), 412. Future page references appear parenthetically.

26. Eadweard Muybridge, *Complete Human and Animal Locomotion* (a reprint of the 1887 *Animal Locomotion*), 3 vols. (New York: Dover, 1979), plates 329–50, 356–61, 520. Future plate references appear parenthetically.

27. Rebecca Solnit, *River of Shadows: Eadweard Muybridge and the Technological Wild West* (New York: Viking, 2003), 195.

28. See Marta Braun, *Picturing Time: The Work of Etienne-Jules Marey, 1830–1904* (Chicago: University of Chicago Press, 1992), 228–54. Robert Bartlett Haas suggests a link between Gertrude Stein and Muybridge in *Muybridge: Man in Motion* (Berkeley: University of California Press, 1976), 158.

29. In an 1883 prospectus, Muybridge announces a "new and elaborate work" that will include "photographs of actors performing their respective parts," among other subjects. Quoted in Braun, *Picturing Time,* 231.

30. Robert Wilson cites the pertinence to his work of the psychiatrist Daniel Stern's 1960s slow-motion film studies of mothers approaching crying babies. Writing of his own theater, Richard Foreman argues that "the text of any given work is a series of 'change of subjects'—which I believe becomes the subject of the work itself, as the continual change-of-subject, interruption, re-beginning, reflects the true shape and texture of conscious experience." See Laurence Shyer, *Robert Wilson and His Collaborators* (New York: Theatre Communications Group, 1989), 7, and Richard Foreman, "How I Write My (Plays: Self)," in *Reverberation Machines: The Later Plays and Essays* (Barrytown, NY: Station Hill, 1985), 238.

31. The note appears with the time breakdown in the edition of *Secret Service* printed in *Representative American Plays: From 1767 to the Present Day,* 6th ed., ed. Arthur Hobson Quinn (New York: D. Appleton–Century, 1938). In his introduction, Quinn writes that he "has reprinted the manuscript exactly as Mr. Gillette prepared it" for this edition (549).

32. Henry James, *The Art of the Novel: Critical Prefaces,* ed. R. P. Blackmur (New York: Charles Scribner's Sons, 1953), 111, 114, 115.

33. If one chooses, one can also find a personal parallel to this play's monitored spaces and self-conscious inhabitants: Gillette equipped part of his own home with a series of unobtrusive mirrors enabling him to maintain surveillance from his bedroom of his guests in the bar. Thank you to Joseph Roach for this information. Also see Brendan Gill, "Gillette Castle: An Actor's Folly on a Connecticut Hilltop," in *Architectural Digest,* November 1993, pp. 32ff.

34. Walter Prichard Eaton quoted in *Best Plays of the Early American Theatre: From the Beginning to 1916,* ed. John Gassner (New York: Crown, 1967), xxxviii.

35. Michael Fried, *Realism, Writing, Disfiguration: On Thomas Eakins and Stephen Crane* (Chicago: University of Chicago Press, 1987), 119–20. Future page references appear parenthetically. This emphasis on the visuality of writing recalls Gertrude Stein's belief that "a writer should write with his eyes" — perhaps one more point of kinship she found with Gillette. See "A Transatlantic Interview" (1946) in *A Primer for the Gradual Understanding of Gertrude Stein,* ed. Robert Bartlett Haas (Santa Barbara: Black Sparrow, 1971), 31.

36. William Gillette, "The Illusion of the First Time in Acting," in *Actors on Acting,* ed. Toby Cole and Helen Krich Chinoy (New York: Three Rivers, 1970), 565.

37. Herman Melville, "Apathy and Enthusiasm" and "An Uninscribed Monument on One of the Battle-fields of the Wilderness," in *Battle-Pieces and Aspects of the War,* 57, 175.

38. This version of the first line appears in the revised poem prepared for inclusion among the "Songs of Parting" in *Leaves of Grass.*

39. Daniel Aaron, *The Unwritten War: American Writers and the Civil War* (New York: Alfred A. Knopf, 1973).

40. Details of Lincoln's visit and of the *Macbeth* reading aboard the *River Queen* are in Marquis de Chambrun, "Personal Recollections of Mr. Lincoln," *Scribner's Magazine* 13 (May 1893): 26–38, and from David Herbert Donald, *Lincoln* (New York: Simon and Schuster, 1995), 571–80.

41. William Shakespeare, *Macbeth* [Arden edition] (Cambridge: Harvard University Press, 1957), 4.3.164–72. Future references appear parenthetically.

42. Marquis de Chambrun, "Personal Recollections of Mr. Lincoln," 35. For a discussion of the theatrical resonances of Lincoln's assassination, see Albert Furtwangler, *Assassin on Stage: Brutus, Hamlet, and the Death of Lincoln* (Urbana: University of Illinois Press, 1991).

43. Robert Penn Warren, *The Legacy of the Civil War: Meditations on the Centennial* (New York: Random House, 1961), 106.

44. Don E. Fehrenbacher, "The Weight of Responsibility," in *Lincoln in Text and Context: Collected Essays* (Stanford: Stanford University Press, 1987), 161.

Chapter 3: Realism against Itself

Epigraphs from James Merrill, "Mirror," in *Selected Poems, 1946–1985* (New York: Alfred A. Knopf, 1993), 35. (The lines refer to a window, the mirror's opposite number.) Fairfield Porter, "What Is Real" (1960), in *Art in Its Own Terms: Selected Criticism, 1935–1975,* ed. Rackstraw Downes (Cambridge: Zoland, 1993) 89. (The passage is from a review of paintings by Isabel Bishop.)

1. Stephen Crane, "Manacled," in *Tales, Sketches, and Reports,* ed. Fredson Bowers (Charlottesville: University Press of Virginia, 1973), 159. Future page references appear parenthetically.

2. Henry James, "The London Theatres" (1877), in *The Scenic Art: Notes on Acting and the Drama, 1872–1901,* ed. Allan Wade (New York: Hill and Wang, 1948), 107.

3. Stephen Crane, *Maggie: A Girl of the Streets and Other Tales of New York* (New York: Penguin, 2000), 37.

4. Philip Fisher, *Hard Facts: Setting and Form in the American Novel* (New York: Oxford University Press, 1987), 150.

5. William Dean Howells, *A Hazard of New Fortunes* (New York: Penguin, 2001), 64. Future page references appear parenthetically.

6. Eric J. Sundquist, "The Country of the Blue," in *American Realism: New Essays,* ed. Eric J. Sundquist (Baltimore: Johns Hopkins University Press, 1982), 16.

7. Roland Barthes, "Objective Literature," in *Critical Essays,* trans. Richard Howard (Evanston: Northwestern University Press, 1972), 20. Future page references appear parenthetically.

8. George Bernard Shaw, preface to Eugene Brieux, *Three Plays* (New York: Brentano's, 1911), ix, xxvii.

9. Edgar Allan Poe, "The Oval Portrait," in *Poetry and Tales* (New York: Library of America, 1984), 482. Future page references appear parenthetically.

10. Harry Levin, *The Gates of Horn: A Study of Five French Realists* (New York: Oxford University Press, 1963), 55.

11. Michael Fried, *Realism, Writing, Disfiguration* (Chicago: University of Chicago Press: 1987), 59. Elsewhere he writes, "her presence in *The Gross Clinic* may have been at least partly determined by a logic of feeling that had nothing whatever to do with strictly realist factors" (41).

12. Marc Simpson, "The 1900s," in *Thomas Eakins,* ed. Darrel Sewell (New Haven: Yale University Press/Philadelphia Museum of Art, 2001), 323–24.

13. Also see Stanislavski on an actor's "public solitude," as discussed by Joseph Roach in "It," *Theatre Journal* 56, no. 4 (2004): 567.

14. See Simpson, "1900s," 323, where he also cites research by Kathleen Foster.

15. Theodor Siegl, *The Thomas Eakins Collection* (Philadelphia: Philadelphia Museum of Art, 1978), 159.

16. W. B. Worthen, *Modern Drama and the Rhetoric of Theater* (Berkeley: University of California Press, 1992), 14.

17. Theodore Dreiser, *Sister Carrie* (New York: Penguin, 1994), 158.

18. James A. Herne, *Margaret Fleming,* in *Nineteenth-Century American Plays,* ed. Myron Matlaw (New York: Applause, 2001), 258–59. Future page references appear parenthetically.

19. Montrose Moses, in *The American Dramatist* (New York: Little, Brown, 1925), sees in Herne's own acting a realization of "Maeterlinck's conception of what static drama should be" (215). But John Perry, in *James A. Herne: The American Ibsen* (Chicago: Nelson-Hall, 1978), reports that Herne considered Maeterlinck "dishonest" (178).

20. Bill Brown, *A Sense of Things: The Object Matter of American Literature* (Chicago: University of Chicago Press, 2003), 149, and Peter Brooks, *Realist Vision* (New Haven: Yale University Press, 2005), 3ff.

21. Wallace Stevens, "The Snow Man," in *The Palm at the End of the Mind: Selected Poems and a Play* (New York: Vintage, 1972), 54.

22. Hamlin Garland, *Roadside Meetings* (New York: Macmillan, 1930), 77, quoted in Perry, *James A. Herne,* 155.

23. Quoted in Perry, *James A. Herne,* 151.

24. Quoted in ibid., 165.

25. William Dean Howells, "The Moral Reformation of the Stage" (1891), in *A Realist*

in the American Theatre: Selected Drama Criticism of William Dean Howells, ed. Brenda Murphy (Athens: Ohio University Press, 1992), 54.

26. Bert O. States, *Great Reckonings in Little Rooms: On the Phenomenology of Theater* (Berkeley: University of California Press, 1985), 61.

27. Differences between the two versions are detailed by Hamlin Garland in an article for *The Arena* (October 1891), quoted extensively in Myron Matlaw's preface to *Margaret Fleming,* in *Nineteenth-Century American Plays,* ed. Matlaw, 213–16. For the revision, Herne also cut the baby's death, Philip's turn to alcoholism, and the Flemings' decision to divorce.

28. Hamlin Garland, *My Friendly Contemporaries: A Literary Log* (New York: Macmillan, 1932), 52.

29. *Representative American Plays,* ed. Arthur Hobson Quinn (New York: D. Appleton–Century, 1938), 516.

30. William Winter, *New York Daily Tribune,* December 10, 1891, 7, quoted in Brenda Murphy, *American Realism and American Drama: 1880–1940* (Cambridge: Cambridge University Press, 1987), 85.

31. Edward Sheldon, *Salvation Nell,* in *Fifty Best Plays of the American Theatre,* 4 vols., ed. Clive Barnes (New York: Crown, 1970), 1:90–91. Future page references appear parenthetically.

32. Robert Alter, *Imagined Cities: Urban Experience and the Language of the Novel* (New Haven: Yale University Press, 2005), 113.

33. Jose Ortega y Gasset, *The Dehumanization of Art,* in *The Idea of the Modern in Literature and the Arts,* ed. Irving Howe (New York: Horizon, 1967), 84.

34. Other significant windows in American realism can be found in Frank Norris, who opens *McTeague* (1899) with a panoramic survey of street life viewed from the dentist's bay window; Theodore Dreiser, who, as Philip Fisher writes, draws the pedestrians of *Sister Carrie* (1900) to windows that "invite you to imagine being in while strongly reminding you that you are out" (Fisher, *Hard Facts,* 156); and — jumping eras and art forms — Edward Hopper, whose own figures are under glass like aquarium fish, at once on display and off-limits. In the theater, Bronson Howard set one precedent in *Shenandoah* (1888), where, as we've seen, he erects French doors between his protagonists and a Civil War that is visible but as yet unthreatening.

35. See Patricia McDonnell, "American Early Modern Artists, Vaudeville, and Film," in *On the Edge of Your Seat: Popular Theater and Film in Early Twentieth-Century American Art,* ed. Patricia McDonnell (New Haven: Yale University Press, 2002), 26–27, and Peter Brooks, *Realist Vision,* 138. Horatio Alger forges one link between theater and other forms of consumption in *Ragged Dick* (1890), when he moves seamlessly from a description of New York's "show windows with their multifarious contents [that] interested and aroused" his hero's appetites to, a few sentences later, a paean to the theater in Barnum's Museum, "most as good as the Old Bowery, only the plays isn't so exciting," and a connoisseur's description of one especially attractive melodrama (Horatio Alger, Jr., *Ragged Dick* and *Struggling Upward* [New York: Penguin, 1985], 24–25).

36. Fisher, *Hard Facts,* 135.

37. Henry Adams, *The Education of Henry Adams* (1918) (New York: Penguin, 1995), 467–70. Future page references appear parenthetically.

38. J. M. Coetzee, *Elizabeth Costello* (New York: Viking, 2003), 32.

39. E. M. Forster, *Howards End* (1910) (New York: Vintage, 1989), 156–57.

40. See the auction catalogue *The Private Collection of David Belasco* (October 20–25, 1924) (New York: American Art Association, 1924).

41. David Belasco, "Beauty as I See It," in *Arts and Decoration,* July 1923, p. 61.

42. David Belasco, *The Theatre through Its Stage Door* (1919) (New York: Benjamin Blom, 1969), 68.

43. Roland Barthes, "The World as Object" in *Critical Essays,* 7. For more on catalogues and collections, see Stanley Cavell, "The World as Things," in *Philosophy the Day after Tomorrow* (Cambridge: Harvard University Press, 2005), 251, and Susan Stewart, *On Longing: Narratives of the Miniature, the Gigantic, the Souvenir, the Collection* (Durham: Duke University Press, 1993), 156.

44. Djuna Barnes, "David Belasco Dreams," in *New York Morning Telegraph Sunday Magazine,* December 31, 1916, reprinted in Djuna Barnes, *Interviews,* ed. Alyce Barry (Washington: Sun and Moon, 1985), 188. Future page references appear parenthetically.

45. Anton Chekhov, *The Cherry Orchard,* trans. Paul Schmidt, in *Complete Plays* (New York: HarperCollins, 1997), 342.

46. Belasco, *Theatre through Its Stage Door,* 62–63.

47. Belasco, "Beauty as I See It," 61.

48. David Belasco, *The Girl of the Golden West,* in *American Melodrama,* ed. Daniel C. Gerould (New York: PAJ Publications, 1983), 210, 236. Future page references appear parenthetically. For a detailed account and analysis of Belasco's staging of his play, see Lisa-Lone Marker, *David Belasco: Naturalism in the American Theatre* (Princeton: Princeton University Press, 1975), 139–60.

49. W. J. T. Mitchell, "Romanticism and the Life of Things," in *What Do Pictures Want? The Lives and Loves of Images* (Chicago: University of Chicago Press, 2005), 172.

50. In *Modern Drama and the Rhetoric of Theater,* W. B. Worthen describes how "sociological" drama "transforms the characters into things" (73). He also briefly mentions that the protagonist of Belasco's *Return of Peter Grimm* is "fully identified with its productive environment" (18).

51. The monogrammed trunk is listed in the property plot printed in the acting edition of the play (New York: Samuel French, 1915), 140.

52. *Girl of the Golden West,* Samuel French edition, 58–62. Some items listed here are omitted from the PAJ edition.

53. *Girl of the Golden West,* Samuel French edition, 58.

54. Clement Greenberg, "Towards a Newer Laocoon" (1940), in *The Collected Essays and Criticism,* vol. 1, *Perceptions and Judgments, 1939–1944,* ed. John O'Brian (Chicago: University of Chicago Press, 1986), 34–35.

55. Henry James, *The American Scene* (1907) (New York: Penguin, 1994), 99, 125.

56. F. Scott Fitzgerald, *The Great Gatsby* (1925) (New York: Collier, 1992), 50.

57. See also Greenberg, "Sometimes this advance to the surface is accelerated by . . . drawing exactly printed letters, and placing them so that they destroy the partial illusion of depth" ("Towards a Newer Laocoon," 35).

58. *Girl of the Golden West,* Samuel French edition, 61.

59. See "Notes on Production" in ibid., 163.

60. Ibid., 12.

61. Martin Heidegger, *Poetry, Language, Thought,* trans. Albert Hofstadter (New York: Harper and Row, 1975), 31.

62. *Representative Plays by American Dramatists, 1856–1911,* ed. Montrose J. Moses (New York: E. P. Dutton, 1921), 709–10. Moses is speaking of another Belasco effort, his staging of Eugene Walter's *The Easiest Way.*

63. Belasco, *Theatre through Its Stage Door,* 224, 229, 232, 241.

64. Ibid., 230, 231, 235.

65. Michael Davitt Bell, *The Problem of American Realism: Studies in the Cultural History of a Literary Idea* (Chicago: University of Chicago Press, 1993), 6.

66. *Pittsburgh Dispatch,* February 28, 1894, quoted in Percy MacKaye, *Epoch: The Life of Steele MacKaye,* vol. 2 (New York: Boni and Liveright, 1927), 425. Future page references appear parenthetically.

67. *The World Finder* was also known as *The Great Discovery.* For additional details about the planned spectacle, and about the Spectatorium and Scenitorium in general, see Tim Fort, "Steele MacKaye's Lighting Visions for *The World Finder,*" *Nineteenth Century Theatre* 18, nos. 1–2 (1990): 35–51, and J. A. Sokalski, *Pictorial Illusionism: The Theatre of Steele MacKaye* (Montreal: McGill–Queen's University Press, 2007), 179–254.

68. Quoted in Percy MacKaye, "The Theatre of Ten Thousand: Steele MacKaye's Spectatorium," *Theatre Arts* 7, no. 2 (1923): 123.

69. Walt Whitman, *Democratic Vistas,* in *The Portable Walt Whitman,* ed. Mark Van Doren (New York: Penguin, 1977), 373.

70. MacKaye, *Epoch,* 442. Also see 439, where a journalist describes MacKaye as "manipulating the electric connections." Present-day readers familiar with the theater of Richard Foreman, a director-playwright who also presides over his creations, will recognize a predecessor in MacKaye.

71. Worthen, *Modern Drama and the Rhetoric of Theater,* 75.

72. Oscar Wilde, "The English Renaissance of Art," in *The Uncollected Oscar Wilde,* ed. John Wyse Jackson (London: Fourth Estate, 1995), 12, 18, 20.

73. Henry James, *The Spoils of Poynton* (1897) (New York: Penguin, 1987), 203.

74. See Brown, *Sense of Things,* 150. This fire of course also anticipates Stephen Crane's in "Manacled" two years later.

75. Henry James, *The Notebooks of Henry James,* ed. F. O. Matthiessen and Kenneth B. Murdock (New York: Oxford University Press, 1947), excerpts reprinted in appendix to James, *Spoils of Poynton,* 216.

76. Henry James, *The Other House* (1896) (New York: New York Review Books, 1999), 302.

Chapter 4: The Borders of Modernism

Epigraphs from Henry James, *The Wings of the Dove* (1902) (New York: Penguin, 2003), 469, and Gertrude Stein, *The Geographical History of America* (1936) (Baltimore: Johns Hopkins University Press, 1995), 230.

1. Edward Gordon Craig, brochure for exhibition at Little Galleries of the Photo-Secession, New York, December 14, 1910–January 12, 1911, unpaginated.

2. Edward Gordon Craig, *On the Art of the Theatre* (Chicago: Browne's Bookstore, 1911), 84. Future page references appear parenthetically.

3. Harold Clurman quoted in Sarah Greenough, *Modern Art and America: Alfred Stieglitz and his New York Galleries* (Washington: National Gallery of Art, 2000), 394.

4. Travis Bogard, *Contour in Time: The Plays of Eugene O'Neill* (New York: Oxford University Press, 1972), 135. Sheeler's photographs record a 1917 exhibition of these works at New York's Modern Gallery.

5. Marsden Hartley, "John Barrymore in *Peter Ibbetson*," in *Adventures in the Arts: Informal Chapters on Painters, Vaudeville and Poets* (New York: Hacker Art Books, 1972), 184–85.

6. Martin Puchner groups Craig with theater's other "antitheatrical" modernists in *Stage Fright: Modernism, Anti-Theatricality, and Drama* (Baltimore: Johns Hopkins University Press, 2002), 127–29.

7. Letter reprinted in *Marianne Moore: A Collection of Critical Essays,* ed. Charles Tomlinson (Englewood Cliffs, NJ: Prentice-Hall, 1969), 17.

8. Marianne Moore, *The Poems of Marianne Moore,* ed. Grace Schulman (New York: Viking, 2003), 80, 138. Future page references appear parenthetically.

9. Ezra Pound and Ernest Fenollosa, *The Classic Noh Theatre of Japan* (1916) (New York: New Directions, 1959), 4.

10. Ezra Pound to Homer Pound, 1916. Letter in Ezra Pound Papers, Yale Collection of American Literature, YCAL MSS 43, box 60, folder 2678, Beinecke Library. In expurgated form, the letter is quoted in Donald Gallup, introduction to Ezra Pound, *Plays Modeled on the Noh* (Toledo: Friends of the University of Toledo Libraries, 1987), i.

11. Ezra Pound, "We Have Had No Battles, but We Have Joined In and Made Roads," in *Polite Essays* (Norfolk, CT: New Directions, n.d.), 52. Quoted in Hugh Kenner, *The Poetry of Ezra Pound* (London: Faber and Faber, 1951), 49.

12. Kenner, *Poetry of Ezra Pound,* 72.

13. Ibid., 121, 57. Marjorie Perloff, *The Dance of the Intellect: Studies in the Poetry of the Pound Tradition* (1985) (Evanston, IL: Northwestern University Press, 1996), 22.

14. Ezra Pound, *Gaudier-Brzeska,* quoted in Hugh Kenner, *The Pound Era* (Berkeley: University of California Press, 1971), 146.

15. Ezra Pound, "Henry James" (1918), in *Literary Essays of Ezra Pound,* ed. T. S. Eliot (New York: New Directions, 1968), 296. I am indebted to Frank Lentricchia for this citation: *Modernist Quartet* (Cambridge: Cambridge University Press, 1994), 188ff.

16. Ezra Pound, "Mr. James Joyce and the Modern Stage," in *The Drama* 6, no. 2 (February 1916): 122–32, reprinted in *Pound/Joyce,* ed. Forrest Read (New York: New Directions, 1967), 49–56.

17. Reprinted in Ezra Pound, *Antheil and the Treatise on Harmony* (1927) (New York: Da Capo, 1968), 75–77.

18. Ezra Pound, letter to Eric Mesterton, December 1936, in *The Letters of Ezra Pound, 1907–1941,* ed. D. D. Paige (New York: Harcourt, Brace, 1950), 284.

19. Marianne Moore, letter to Bryher, May 5, 1923, in *Selected Letters,* ed. Bonnie Costello (New York: Alfred A. Knopf, 1997), 197. Marianne Moore, "Antidotes," in *Harper's Bazaar* 96 (July 19, 1963), reprinted in *Complete Prose,* ed. Patricia C. Willis (New York: Viking, 1986), 680.

20. Charles Demuth quoted in Louis Sheaffer, *O'Neill: Son and Artist* (Boston: Little, Brown, 1973), 287.

21. Susan Glaspell quoted in Louis Sheaffer, *O'Neill: Son and Playwright* (Boston: Little, Brown, 1968), 348. The photograph of the Wharf Theater is on p. 349.

22. See, among others, Brenda Murphy, "Plays and Playwrights: 1915–1945," in *Cambridge History of American Theatre,* ed. Wilmeth and Bigsby, 2:291.

23. William Carlos Williams, *Autobiography* (New York: Random House, 1951), 139.

24. See Virgil Geddes, *The Melodramadness of Eugene O'Neill* (Brookfield, CT: Brookfield Players, 1934). Other readings attuned to different aspects of O'Neill's debt to melodrama include Kurt Eisen, *The Inner Strength of Opposites: O'Neill's Novelistic Drama and the Melodramatic Imagination* (Athens: University of Georgia Press, 1994), Eric Bentley, "Trying to Like O'Neill," in *In Search of Theater* (New York: Vintage, 1953), 220–34, and Thomas Postlewait, "From Melodrama to Realism: The Suspect History of American Drama," in *Melodrama: The Cultural Emergence of a Genre,* ed. Michael Hays and Anastasia Nikolopoulou (New York: St. Martin's, 1996), 39–60.

25. Eugene O'Neill, "Strindberg and Our Theater" (1924), reprinted in Helen Deutsch and Stella Hanau, *The Provincetown: A Story of the Theatre* (New York: Farrar and Rinehart, 1931), 192.

26. Letter to Barrett Clark (1919) reprinted in *O'Neill and His Plays: Four Decades of Criticism,* ed. Oscar Cargill, N. Bryllion Fagin, and William J. Fisher (New York: New York University Press, 1961), 100.

27. Letter to George Jean Nathan, titled by editors "On Man and God" and reprinted in *O'Neill and His Plays: Four Decades of Criticism,* ed. Oscar Cargill, N. Bryllion Fagin, and William J. Fisher, 115. Eugene O'Neill, "Memoranda on Masks," in *O'Neill and His Plays,* 116.

28. Kenneth Macgowan, *The Theatre of Tomorrow* (New York: Boni and Liveright, 1921), 248.

29. Joel Pfister, *Staging Depth: Eugene O'Neill and the Politics of Psychological Discourse* (Chapel Hill: University of North Carolina Press, 1995), 4–5.

30. Eugene O'Neill, *Bound East for Cardiff,* in *Early Plays,* ed. Jeffrey H. Richards (New York: Penguin, 2001), 21. Future page references appear parenthetically.

31. Eugene O'Neill, *In the Zone,* in *Early Plays,* ed. Richards, 55, 58–59, 65–66. Future page references appear parenthetically.

32. Eugene O'Neill, *The Emperor Jones,* in *Early Plays,* ed. Richards, 267. Future page references appear parenthetically. In this context, a production of *The Emperor Jones* by the Wooster Group is especially satisfying. Ostensibly a radical departure from the text, the group's version (first produced onstage in 1993 and adapted for film in 1999) in fact ruthlessly fulfills O'Neill's own skepticism about authenticity and psychological depth. The surfaces are numerous: a white woman, Kate Valk, plays Jones in blackface; exaggerates O'Neill's dialect; adds squeals, roars, and glottal stops; and wears a costume assembled from clashing sources. In the film version, the film stock itself demands acknowledgment. It is blemished, seemingly about to degrade. The brown blotches that further obscure the already hidden actors expose how naive it was—is—to expect any stage figure to emerge from the theater's less obvious impedimenta.

33. Eugene O'Neill, *The Hairy Ape,* in *Early Plays,* ed. Richards, 392. Future page references appear parenthetically.

34. See Frank Stella in Bruce Glaser, "Questions to Stella and Judd," and E. C. Goossen, "Two Exhibitions," in *Minimalist Art: A Critical Anthology,* ed. Gregory Battcock (Berkeley: University of California Press, 1995), 159, 169.

35. Ronald H. Wainscott, *Staging O'Neill: The Experimental Years, 1920–1934* (New Haven: Yale University Press, 1988). Timo Tiusanen also discusses decor in a broad analysis of O'Neill's theatricality in *O'Neill's Scenic Images* (Princeton: Princeton University Press, 1968).

36. Eugene O'Neill, *Mourning Becomes Electra,* in *Complete Plays, 1920–1931* (New York: Library of America, 1988), 893.

37. Quoted in Wainscott, *Staging O'Neill,* 163.

38. Eugene O'Neill, *More Stately Mansions,* in *Complete Plays, 1932–1943* (New York: Library of America, 1988), 477.

39. Eugene O'Neill, *The Iceman Cometh,* in *Complete Plays, 1932–1943,* 565.

40. Eugene O'Neill, *Strange Interlude,* in *Complete Plays, 1920–1931,* 653.

41. Eugene O'Neill, *A Moon for the Misbegotten,* in *Complete Plays, 1932–1943,* 856.

42. Bennett Cerf quoted in Arthur and Barbara Gelb, *O'Neill* (New York: Harper and Row, 1973), 862.

43. Arthur and Barbara Gelb, lecture at Yale School of Drama, January 2006.

44. Arthur and Barbara Gelb, *O'Neill,* 848.

45. Eugene O'Neill, *Long Day's Journey into Night* (New Haven: Yale University Press, 2002), 20. Future page references appear parenthetically. In his introduction to *Eugene O'Neill,* Harold Bloom discusses what he calls a "grim ballet of looks" in one scene from the play (New York: Chelsea House, 1987), 12.

46. Susan Sontag, "The Aesthetics of Silence," in *A Susan Sontag Reader* (New York: Vintage, 1983), 183, 191. Future page references appear parenthetically.

47. C. W. E. Bigsby, *A Critical Introduction to Twentieth-Century American Drama,* vol. 1 (Cambridge: Cambridge University Press, 1982), 99.

48. Richard Sewall, *The Vision of Tragedy* (enlarged edition) (New Haven: Yale University Press, 1980), 161–74.

49. Gertrude Stein, "A Transatlantic Interview" (1946), in *A Primer for the Gradual Understanding of Gertrude Stein,* ed. Robert B. Haas (Los Angeles: Black Sparrow, 1971), 21.

50. Gertrude Stein quoted in Richard Bridgman, *Gertrude Stein in Pieces* (New York: Oxford University Press, 1970), 253.

51. Gertrude Stein, *Everybody's Autobiography* (1937) (London: Virago, 1985), 246.

52. T. S. Eliot, "Charleston, Hey! Hey!" in *Nation & Athenaeum* (London), January 29, 1927, p. 595.

53. Gertrude Stein, *The Autobiography of Alice B. Toklas* (1933) (New York: Vintage, 1960), 119. Future page references appear parenthetically.

54. Gertrude Stein, "Plays," in *Lectures in America* (1935) (Boston: Beacon, 1985), 114. Future page references appear parenthetically.

55. Gertrude Stein, "Poetry and Grammar," in *Lectures in America,* 217.

56. Gertrude Stein, *Byron A Play* (1933), in *Last Operas and Plays* (Baltimore: Johns Hopkins University Press, 1995), 336.

57. Gertrude Stein, *Listen to Me* (1936), in *Last Operas and Plays,* 389.

58. Gertrude Stein, "Pictures," in *Lectures in America,* 70. The passage is also discussed in Bridgman, *Gertrude Stein in Pieces,* 248.

59. Virgil Thomson, *Virgil Thomson* (New York: Da Capo, 1967), 170.

60. Gertrude Stein, *A Circular Play* (1920), in *Last Operas and Plays,* 151.

61. Bridgman, *Gertrude Stein in Pieces,* 149.

62. Richard Poirier, "The Difficulties of Modernism and the Modernism of Difficulty," *Humanities in Society* 1 (1978): 281.

63. William H. Gass, "Gertrude Stein and the Geography of the Sentence," in *The World within the Word* (Boston: David R. Godine, 1979). Jane Palatini Bowers calls the same phenomenon a "lang-scape" in *"They Watch Me as They Watch This": Gertrude Stein's Metadramas* (Philadelphia: University of Pennsylvania Press, 1991).

64. Gertrude Stein, *The Geographical History of America,* 143. Future page references appear parenthetically.

65. Hugo von Hofmannsthal, *Elektra* (1908), trans. G. M. Holland and Ken Chalmers, in Richard Strauss, *Elektra,* cond. Seiji Ozawa (New York: Philips Classics CD, 1988), 78.

66. Gertrude Stein, *Doctor Faustus Lights the Lights* (1938), in *Last Operas and Plays,* 108.

67. Gertrude Stein, *A Lyrical Opera Made by Two* (1928), in Stein, *Operas and Plays* (Barrytown, NY: Station Hill, 1987), 54.

68. Gertrude Stein, *Say It with Flowers* (1931), in *Operas and Plays,* 341.

69. Gertrude Stein, *Wars I Have Seen* (1945), excerpted in *Selected Writings of Gertrude Stein,* ed. Carl Van Vechten (New York: Vintage, 1990), 696–97.

70. Many critics downplay Stein's familiarity with, or even interest in, her historical sources, preferring to see the opera as about only text, or theater, or antitheater, or Stein's theater, or Stein herself. See Stark Young ("the words are . . . a very secondary part of it") and, more recently, Richard Bridgman ("the signs of her ignorance [of the saints] were manifold") and Jane Palatini Bowers ("Though this lang-scape purports to be about saints, it does not take its meaning from history or biography or from any temporal form of experience outside of the lang-scape itself"). Stark Young, "Four Saints in Three Acts," in Young, *Immortal Shadows* (New York: Hill and Wang, 1948), 138. Bridgman, *Gertrude Stein in Pieces,* 180. Jane Palatini Bowers, "The Composition That All the World Can See: Gertrude Stein's Theater Landscapes," in *Land/Scape/Theater,* ed. Elinor Fuchs and Una Chaudhuri (Ann Arbor: University of Michigan Press, 2002), 140. Harry R. Garvin does briefly discuss Stein's substance in "Sound and Sense in *Four Saints in Three Acts,*" *Bucknell Review* 5, no. 1 (December 1954): 1–11.

71. Ignatius of Loyola, *Spiritual Exercises,* in *Personal Writings,* trans. Joseph A. Munitiz and Philip Endean (New York: Penguin, 1996), 332. Future page references appear parenthetically.

72. Teresa of Avila, *The Life of Saint Teresa of Avila by Herself,* trans. J. M. Cohen (London: Penguin, 1957), 68. Future page references appear parenthetically.

73. Vita Sackville-West, *The Eagle and the Dove: A Study in Contrasts* (London: Michael Joseph, 1943), 47–48.

74. Teresa of Avila, *Interior Castle,* trans. E. Allison Peers (New York: Image, 1989), 53. Future page references appear parenthetically.

75. Teresa quoted in Cathleen Medwick, *Teresa of Avila: The Progress of a Soul* (New York: Alfred A. Knopf, 1999), 208. Also see Teresa of Avila, *Interior Castle,* 57.

76. Quoted in Bridgman, *Gertrude Stein in Pieces,* 179.

77. Gertrude Stein, *Four Saints in Three Acts,* in *Last Operas and Plays,* 453. Future page references appear parenthetically.

78. Stein, *Wars I Have Seen,* in *Selected Writings of Gertrude Stein,* ed. Carl Van Vechten, 705.

79. Roland Barthes, *Sade, Fourier, Loyola,* trans. Richard Miller (New York: Hill and Wang, 1976), 5–6. Future page references appear parenthetically.

80. Ignatius of Loyola, *Spiritual Exercises,* 293.

81. Barthes, *Sade, Fourier, Loyola,* 74.

82. Quoted in Janet Malcolm, *Two Lives: Gertrude and Alice* (New Haven: Yale University Press, 2007), 104.

83. See Wendy Steiner, *Exact Resemblance to Exact Resemblance: The Literary Portraiture of Gertrude Stein* (New Haven: Yale University Press, 1978), 191–95.

84. Gertrude Stein, "What Is English Literature," in *Lectures in America,* 25, 27.

85. See Douglas Botting, *In the Ruins of the Reich* (London: George Allen and Unwin, 1985), 93–104, and W. G. Sebald, *On the Natural History of Destruction* (1999) (London: Hamish Hamilton, 2003), 33ff.

86. Horst Frenz, "The Reception of Thornton Wilder's Plays in Germany," in *Modern Drama* 3, no. 2 (September 1960): 127.

87. Dwight Macdonald, "Masscult and Midcult," *Partisan Review* 27, no. 4 (Fall 1960): 605.

88. Sebald, *On the Natural History of Destruction,* 41. Sebald is citing reporting by Hans Erich Nossack.

89. Thornton Wilder, *The Skin of Our Teeth,* in *Three Plays* (New York: HarperPerennial, 1957), 120, 179. Future page references appear parenthetically.

90. Thornton Wilder, *Pullman Car Hiawatha,* in *Collected Short Plays,* vol. 1, ed. Donald Gallup and A. Tappan Wilder (New York: Theatre Communications Group, 1997), 58. Future page references appear parenthetically.

91. Thornton Wilder, *Our Town,* in *Three Plays,* 99. Future page references appear parenthetically.

92. Thornton Wilder, *The Happy Journey to Trenton and Camden,* in *Collected Short Plays,* vol. 1, 96, 87, 99. Future page references appear parenthetically.

93. Thornton Wilder, *The Wreck on the Five-Twenty-Five,* in *Collected Short Plays,* vol. 1, 151. Future page references appear parenthetically.

94. Thornton Wilder, preface to *Three Plays,* xi. Future page references appear parenthetically.

95. Thornton Wilder, *The Long Christmas Dinner,* in *Collected Short Plays,* vol. 1, 5. Future page references appear parenthetically.

96. Glenway Wescott, "Talks with Thornton Wilder," in *Images of Truth: Remembrances and Criticism* (New York: Harper and Row, 1962), 244.

97. "Thornton Wilder," in *Writers at Work: The* Paris Review *Interviews,* ed. Malcolm Cowley (New York: Viking, 1959), 109.

98. Henry David Thoreau, *Walden* and *Civil Disobedience* (New York: Penguin, 1986), 142.

99. Amos Niven Wilder explores his brother's "Puritan indebtedness" in *Thornton Wilder and His Public* (Philadelphia: Fortress, 1980), 36–50. A recent study, Lincoln Konkle's *Thornton Wilder and the Puritan Narrative Tradition,* closely reads Wilder's plays and novels alongside Puritan sermons, jeremiads, and other literature (Columbia: University of Missouri Press, 2006).

100. Quoted in Perry Miller, *The New England Mind: The Seventeenth Century* (Cambridge: Harvard University Press, 1954), 178. Emphasis in the original.

101. See Perry Miller, *The New England Mind,* 169, 342, 350, and *The Puritans: A Sourcebook of Their Writings,* vol. 2, ed. Perry Miller and Thomas H. Johnson (New York: Harper and Row, 1963), 673.

102. Dickinson's phrase, in a letter to Samuel Bowles, is quoted in Wilder's essay "Emily Dickinson," in *American Characteristics and Other Essays,* ed. Donald Gallup (New York: Harper and Row, 1979), 54.

103. Wilder in a note to himself during rehearsals for the 1938 premiere, reprinted in *The Letters of Gertrude Stein and Thornton Wilder,* ed. Edward M. Burns and Ulla Dydo (New Haven: Yale University Press, 1996), 376.

104. Wilder to Stein, March 25, 1942, in *Letters of Gertrude Stein and Thornton Wilder,* ed. Burns and Dydo, 305.

105. Wilder quoted in Gilbert A. Harrison, *The Enthusiast: A Life of Thornton Wilder* (New Haven: Ticknor and Fields, 1983), 203.

106. See "Truman Capote," in *Writers at Work,* ed. Cowley, 295.

107. Thornton Wilder, *Bernice,* in *Collected Short Plays,* vol. 1, 137.

108. *The Journals of Thornton Wilder, 1939–1961,* ed. Donald Gallup (New Haven: Yale University Press, 1985), 6–7. Miller, *New England Mind,* 356.

109. Thornton Wilder, "Some Thoughts on Playwriting," in *American Characteristics,* 125.

110. R. P. Blackmur, review of *The Woman of Andros,* in *Hound and Horn* 3, no. 4 (Summer 1930): 589.

111. Robert Lowell quoted in Seamus Heaney, "Lowell's Command," in *The Government of the Tongue: Selected Prose, 1978–1987* (New York: Farrar, Straus and Giroux, 1989), 129.

112. Wilder's nontheatrical works show the same obsession with the archive. *The Bridge of San Luis Rey* (1927) is a book about a book, Brother Juniper's "enormous book" "cataloguing thousands of little facts and anecdotes and testimonies" about the victims of the bridge collapse (New York: Harper and Row, 1986), 8. Wilder's screenplay for Alfred Hitchcock's *Shadow of a Doubt* (1943) sends Charlie to the library, where she discovers her uncle's true identity by looking through old newspapers. Ernest Hemingway was unwittingly insightful when he dismissed Wilder as one who "represents the library." Ernest Hemingway, *Selected Letters,* ed. Carlos Baker (New York: Charles Scribner's Sons, 1981), 30, quoted in Gilbert Harrison, *The Enthusiast,* 98.

113. Michel Foucault, "Fantasia of the Library," in *Language, Counter-Memory, Practice: Selected Essays and Interviews,* ed. and trans. Donald F. Bouchard and Sherry Simon (Ithaca: Cornell University Press, 1977), 93.

114. Quoted in Harrison, *Enthusiast,* 187.

115. John Henry, Cardinal Newman, "The Pillar of the Cloud," in *The Oxford Book of English Mystical Verse,* ed. D. H. S. Nicholson and A. H. E. Lee (Oxford: Clarendon, 1932), 135.

116. Henry Wadsworth Longfellow, "The Evening Star," in *The Complete Poetical Works of Longfellow* (Boston: Houghton Mifflin, 1922), 69.

117. Thornton Wilder, *Our Town* (New York: Coward-McCann/Samuel French, 1939), 64.

Chapter 5: Between the Acts

Epigraph from Marcel Proust, *Cities of the Plain* (1922), in *Remembrance of Things Past,* vol. 2, trans. C. K. Scott Moncrieff and Terence Kilmartin (New York: Vintage, 1982), 843. Proust is speaking of Debussy.

1. Wallace Stevens, *Three Travelers Watch a Sunrise* (1916), in *Opus Posthumous,* ed. Milton J. Bates (New York: Vintage, 1990), 152. Future page references appear parenthetically.

2. Wallace Stevens, "Of Modern Poetry" (1940), in *The Palm at the End of the Mind: Selected Poems and a Play,* ed. Holly Stevens (New York: Vintage, 1972), 174–75.

3. Wallace Stevens, "As at a Theatre" (1950), in *Palm at the End of the Mind,* ed. Stevens, 361–62.

4. Harold Clurman, *The Fervent Years: The Group Theatre and the Thirties* (1975) (New York: Da Capo, 1983), 72.

5. Hallie Flanagan, quoted in C. W. E. Bigsby, *A Critical Introduction to Twentieth-Century American Drama,* vol. 1 (Cambridge: Cambridge University Press, 1982), 212, 218.

6. Henry James, *The American Scene* (1907) (New York: Penguin, 1994), 319.

7. For recent discussions of this relationship, see, among other works, Christopher Innes, *Designing Modern America: Broadway to Main Street* (New Haven: Yale University Press, 2005).

8. Edmund Wilson, "Can New York Stage a Serious Play?" (1925), in *The American Earthquake: A Documentary of the Twenties and Thirties* (Garden City, NY: Doubleday Anchor, 1958), 64–65.

9. Edmund Wilson, "The Finale at the Follies" (1925) and "Bert Savoy and Eddie Cantor of the Follies" (1923), in *American Earthquake,* 47, 59.

10. Edmund Wilson, "The Seven Lively Arts" (1924), in *The Shores of Light: A Literary Chronicle of the Twenties and Thirties* (New York: Farrar, Straus and Young, 1952), 163–64. Also see Roland Barthes: "Whatever the theater, we experience time there as continuous. Time in the music hall is by definition interrupted; it is an immediate time." "At the Music Hall," in *The Eiffel Tower and Other Mythologies,* trans. Richard Howard (New York: Hill and Wang, 1979), 123.

11. Edmund Wilson, "Peaches — A Humdinger" (1926), in *Shores of Light,* 280–81.

12. E. E. Cummings, *Is 5* (New York: Boni and Liveright, 1926), vii.

13. Gilbert Seldes, *The 7 Lively Arts* (1924) (New York: Dover, 2001), 291.

14. E. E. Cummings, "The Theatre: I," *Dial,* April 1926, reprinted in *A Miscellany Revised,* ed. George J. Firmage (New York: October House, 1965), 142–43.

15. Cummings, "Theatre: I," in *Miscellany Revised,* 143.

16. E. E. Cummings, "Burlesque, I Love It!" *Stage,* March 1936, reprinted in *Miscellany Revised,* 295.

17. E. E. Cummings, *I: Six Nonlectures* (Cambridge: Harvard University Press, 1954), 79.

18. E. E. Cummings, "Coney Island," *Vanity Fair,* June 1926, reprinted in *Miscellany Revised,* 152.

19. E. E. Cummings, *Him* (1927), in *Avant-Garde Drama: A Casebook,* ed. Bernard F. Dukore and Daniel C. Gerould (New York: Thomas Y. Crowell, 1976), 346. Future page references appear parenthetically.

20. Quoted in Milton A. Cohen, *Poet and Painter: The Aesthetics of E. E. Cummings's Early Work* (Detroit: Wayne State University Press, 1987), 148.

21. See Edmund Wilson, "E. E. Cummings's *Him,*" in *Shores of Light,* 283; Eric Bentley, "Notes on *Him,*" in *From the Modern Repertoire,* series 2, ed. Eric Bentley (Denver: University of Denver Press, 1952), 487; Charles Norman, *E. E. Cummings: The Magic-Maker* (Indianapolis: Bobbs-Merrill, 1972), 204; Jacques Barzun, "E. E. Cummings: A Word about *Him,*" *Wake,* no. 5 (Spring 1946): 55–56; Paul Rosenfeld, "The Voyages," *Wake,* no. 5 (Spring 1946): 40; William L. Oliver, "*Him:* A Director's Note," *Educational Theatre Journal* 26, no. 3 (October 1974): 328; Daniel C. Gerould and Bernard F. Dukore, introduction to *Him,* in *Avant-Garde Drama,* ed. Dukore and Gerould , 335; and the booklet *Him and the Critics,* introduced by Gilbert Seldes, published by the Provincetown Playhouse, c. 1927–28.

22. Daniel C. Gerould links *Him* to surrealism in *Avant-Garde Drama: A Casebook,* 334. George J. Firmage calls the play "one of the first successful attempts at . . . 'the theatre of the absurd' " in his introduction to Cummings, *Three Plays and a Ballet* (New York: October House, 1967), vii.

23. T. S. Eliot, "The Beating of a Drum," *Nation & Athenaeum,* October 6, 1923, quoted in David E. Chinitz, *T. S. Eliot and the Cultural Divide* (Chicago: University of Chicago Press, 2003), 87.

24. T. S. Eliot, introduction to Charlotte Eliot, *Savonarola: A Dramatic Poem* (1926), quoted in Carol H. Smith, *T. S. Eliot's Dramatic Theory and Practice: From* Sweeney Agonistes *to* The Elder Statesman (Princeton: Princeton University Press, 1963), 51.

25. T. S. Eliot, "Noh and the Image," *Egoist* 4, no. 7 (August 1917): 103.

26. T. S. Eliot, *The Use of Poetry and the Use of Criticism* (1933), quoted in Chinitz, *T. S. Eliot and the Cultural Divide,* 95. For Pixérécourt's claim, see chap. 1, n4.

27. T. S. Eliot, "The Possibility of a Poetic Drama" (1920), quoted in Smith, *T. S. Eliot's Dramatic Theory and Practice,* 37. T. S. Eliot to Ezra Pound, letter of December 19, 1937 (titled "Five Points on Dramatic Writing"), quoted in Lyndall Gordon, *Eliot's New Life* (New York: Farrar, Straus and Giroux, 1988), 63.

28. See Phillip Herring, *Djuna: The Life and Work of Djuna Barnes* (New York: Penguin, 1996), 234.

29. T. S. Eliot, "Marianne Moore," *Dial,* December 1923, quoted in Hugh Kenner, *The Invisible Poet: T. S. Eliot* (1959) (London: Methuen, 1979), 175.

30. T. S. Eliot, "Marie Lloyd" (1922), in *Selected Prose of T. S. Eliot,* ed. Frank Kermode (London: Faber and Faber, 1975), 173.

31. T. S. Eliot, "The Ballet," *Criterion* 3 (1924–25): 442.

32. T. S. Eliot, "London Letter," *Dial,* June 1921, quoted in Chinitz, *T. S. Eliot and the Cultural Divide,* 120.

33. T. S. Eliot, *Sweeney Agonistes,* in *Collected Poems, 1909–1962* (New York: Harcourt, Brace and World, 1970), 115. Future page references appear parenthetically.

34. The recording, made in 1947 for the Poetry Room of the Harvard College Library and distributed by Harvard Vocarium Records, was reissued as part of the "Poet's Voice" series, ed. Stratis Haviaris (Cambridge: Harvard University Press, 1978). Hugh Kenner in *The Invisible Poet* calls it "a finer performance . . . than any cast on a stage is likely to manage" (182).

35. Rachel Blau DuPlessis, *Genders, Races, and Religious Cultures in Modern American Poetry, 1908–1934* (Cambridge: Cambridge University Press, 2001), 103.

36. T. S. Eliot, letter to Hallie Flanagan, March 18, 1933, reprinted in Hallie Flanagan, *Dynamo* (New York: Duell, Sloan and Pearce, 1943), 83. Eliot's request for drumbeats recalls his lament, in "The Beating of a Drum," that "we have lost the drum" once central to drama's ritualistic origins. (Quoted in Smith, *T. S. Eliot's Dramatic Theory and Practice,* 48–49.) David Chinitz argues that this merger of ritualistic and popular forms accounts for the play's failure (15, 124ff). But a close look at the history of the play in production, and a readiness to see the value of the merger's awkwardness and incompletion, can lead to the opposite conclusion, as I argue below.

37. The photograph appears in Michael J. Sidnell, *Dances of Death: The Group Theatre of London in the Thirties* (London: Faber and Faber, 1984), between pages 160 and 161.

38. Sidnell, *Dances of Death,* 103. Bertolt Brecht, "The Modern Theatre Is the Epic Theatre" (1930), in *Brecht on Theatre: The Development of an Aesthetic,* ed. and trans. John Willett (New York: Hill and Wang, 1964), 37.

39. William Shakespeare, *Julius Caesar,* 2.1.63–65, quoted in Gordon, *Eliot's New Life,* 60. Brutus's lines, as many have pointed out, recall "The Hollow Men" — "Between the motion / And the act / Falls the Shadow." See Kenner, *Invisible Poet,* 165, acknowledging Grover Smith.

40. See chapter 4, p. 198.

41. Virginia Woolf, *Diary,* November 12, 1934, quoted in Gordon, *Eliot's New Life,* 63.

42. Djuna Barnes, *The Antiphon* (1958) (Los Angeles: Green Integer: 2000), 5.

43. Djuna Barnes, *Nightwood* (1936) (New York: New Directions, 1961), 111.

44. Djuna Barnes, "Becoming Intimate with the Bohemians," *New York Morning Telegraph Sunday Magazine,* November 19, 1916, reprinted in *New York,* ed. Alyce Barry (Los Angeles: Sun and Moon, 1989), 240.

45. Djuna Barnes, "If Noise Were Forbidden at Coney Island, a Lot of People Would Lose Their Jobs," *New York Press,* June 7, 1914, reprinted in *New York,* ed. Barry, 145.

46. Djuna Barnes, "My Sisters and I at a New York Prizefight," *New York World Magazine,* August 23, 1914, reprinted in *New York,* ed. Barry, 171, 173.

47. Djuna Barnes, "Djuna Barnes Probes the Souls of Jungle Folk at the Hippodrome Circus," *New York Press,* February 14, 1915, reprinted in *New York,* ed. Barry, 197.

48. Djuna Barnes, "Billy Sunday Loves the Multitude, Not the Individual," *New York Press,* February 21, 1915, reprinted in *Interviews,* ed. Alyce Barry (Washington, DC: Sun and Moon, 1985), 115.

49. Djuna Barnes, "Playgoer's Almanac," *Theatre Guild Magazine* 8, no. 4 (January 1931): 35. Here and below, the eccentric capitalization and italicization are Barnes's own.

50. Djuna Barnes, "Alla Nazimova, One of the Greatest of Living Actresses, Talks of Her Art," *Theatre Guild Magazine* 7, no. 9 (June 1930), reprinted in *Interviews,* ed. Barry, 356, 358.

51. Djuna Barnes, "Playgoer's Almanac," *Theatre Guild Magazine* 8, no. 6 (March 1931): 26.

52. Djuna Barnes, "Playgoer's Almanac," *Theatre Guild Magazine* 8, no. 5 (February 1931): 34.

53. Lady Lydia Steptoe (Djuna Barnes), "Hamlet's Custard Pie," *Theatre Guild Magazine* 7, no. 10 (July 1930): 35.

54. Barnes, "Becoming Intimate with the Bohemians," 241.

55. Djuna Barnes to Emily Coleman, March 31, 1949, quoted in Herring, *Djuna: The Life and Work of Djuna Barnes,* 345, n24.

56. Edwin Muir to T. S. Eliot, January 13, 1956, in *Selected Letters of Edwin Muir,* ed. P. H. Butter (London: Hogarth, 1974), 176.

57. Djuna Barnes, "Why Actors?" *Theatre Guild Magazine* 7, no. 3 (December 1929): 43.

58. Djuna Barnes to Emily Coleman, November 30, 1937, quoted in Herring, *Djuna: The Life and Work of Djuna Barnes,* 263.

59. See Ann Larabee, "The Early Attic Stage of Djuna Barnes," in *Silence and Power: A Reevaluation of Djuna Barnes,* ed. Mary Lynn Broe (Carbondale: Southern Illinois University Press, 1991), 37.

60. Djuna Barnes, *Two Ladies Take Tea* (1923), in *At the Roots of the Stars: The Short Plays,* ed. Douglas Messerli (Los Angeles: Sun and Moon, 1995), 127.

61. Djuna Barnes, "Playgoer's Almanac," *Theatre Guild Magazine* 8, no. 6 (March 1931): 26.

62. Marianne Moore, quoted in Herring, *Djuna: The Life and Work of Djuna Barnes,* 298.

63. Djuna Barnes, *Ryder* (1928) (Normal, IL: Dalkey Archive Press, 1995), 13.

64. See, for example, Louis F. Kannenstine, *The Art of Djuna Barnes: Duality and Damnation* (New York: New York University Press, 1977), 135–36.

65. Djuna Barnes, *The Dove* (1926), in *At the Roots of the Stars,* 149. Future page references appear parenthetically.

66. Claude McKay, "The Harlem Dancer," in *Harlem Shadows* (1922), quoted in David Levering Lewis, *When Harlem Was in Vogue* (1981) (New York: Penguin, 1997), 55–56.

67. Zora Neale Hurston, *Dust Tracks on a Road* (1942) (New York: HarperPerennial, 1996), 191. Future page references appear parenthetically.

68. Wallace Thurman, *Infants of the Spring* (1932), quoted in Nathan Irvin Huggins, *Harlem Renaissance* (New York: Oxford University Press, 1971), 131.

69. Zora Neale Hurston, *Their Eyes Were Watching God* (1937) (New York: Harper-Perennial, 1998), 67.

70. Zora Neale Hurston, "Characteristics of Negro Expression" (1934), in *Folklore, Memoirs, and Other Writings* (New York: Library of America, 1995), 839–40. Future page references appear parenthetically.

71. Zora Neale Hurston and Dorothy Waring, *Polk County,* in Hurston, *Collected*

Plays, ed. Jean Lee Cole and Charles Mitchell (New Brunswick, NJ: Rutgers University Press, 2008), 322. Future page references appear parenthetically.

72. Zora Neale Hurston, "How It Feels to Be Colored Me," *World Tomorrow* (May 1928), reprinted in *Folklore, Memoirs, and Other Writings,* 827.

73. Zora Neale Hurston, "What White Publishers Won't Print," *Negro Digest* (April 1950), reprinted in *Folklore, Memoirs, and Other Writings,* 954.

74. Zora Neale Hurston, "Art and Such," written for the Florida Federal Writers' Project, *The Florida Negro,* 1938, first published in *Folklore, Memoirs, and Other Writings,* 906.

75. The quoted passages are from *Polk County* (285, 305, 328, 333) and *Spunk* (1935) (233, 234, 258) in Hurston, *Collected Plays.* Future page references appear parenthetically.

76. Ralph Waldo Emerson, *Journals,* quoted in F. O. Matthiessen, *American Renaissance: Art and Expression in the Age of Emerson and Whitman* (1941) (New York: Oxford University Press, 1974), 35. Zora Neale Hurston, "Characteristics of Negro Expression," in *Folklore, Memoirs, and Other Writings,* 832. John Lowe briefly links Hurston to Emerson on different grounds: Both writers, he argues, regard "words for natural things" as "spiritual." See *Jump at the Sun: Zora Neale Hurston's Cosmic Comedy* (Urbana: University of Illinois Press, 1994), 151, n23.

77. Emerson, *Journals,* quoted in Matthiessen, *American Renaissance,* 33. Emerson is referring to Dante, Byron, Burke, and Carlyle. Also see Emerson: "the words of Electra and Orestes are like actions," in *Journals,* quoted in Matthiessen, *American Renaissance,* 16. Hurston, "Characteristics of Negro Expression," in *Folklore, Memoirs, and Other Writings,* 830.

78. Ralph Waldo Emerson, "The Poet" (1844), in *Selected Writings of Ralph Waldo Emerson,* ed. William H. Gilman (New York: New American Library, 1965), 314.

79. Zora Neale Hurston, *Color Struck* (1925), in *Black Female Playwrights: An Anthology of Plays before 1950,* ed. Kathy Perkins (Bloomington: Indiana University Press, 1989), 97. Future page references appear parenthetically.

80. Jean Toomer to Kenneth Macgowan, letter of March 21, 1923, in *The Letters of Jean Toomer, 1919–1924,* ed. Mark Whalan (Knoxville: University of Tennessee Press, 2006), 150–51.

81. Kenneth Macgowan to Jean Toomer, letter of September 22, 1923, quoted in Darwin T. Turner, "The Failure of a Playwright," *CLA Journal* 10 (June 1967): 313. Hart Crane, in an October 2, 1923, letter to Toomer, writes that "the Neighborhood Playhouse crowd is waxing enthusiastic" about the play, but eventually it, too, decided not to produce it. *O My Land, My Friends: The Selected Letters of Hart Crane,* ed. Langdon Hammer and Brom Weber (New York: 4 Walls 8 Windows, 1997), 165.

82. See Nellie Y. McKay, *Jean Toomer, Artist: A Study of His Literary Life and Work, 1894–1936* (Chapel Hill: University of North Carolina Press, 1984), excerpted in *Cane,* ed. Darwin T. Turner (New York: W. W. Norton, 1988), 238.

83. See Henry Louis Gates, Jr., *Figures in Black: Words, Signs, and the "Racial" Self* (New York: Oxford University Press, 1987), 204–5, and Werner Sollers, "Jean Toomer's *Cane:* Modernism and Race in Interwar America," in *Jean Toomer and the Harlem Renaissance,* ed. Geneviève Fabre and Michel Feith (New Brunswick, NJ: Rutgers University Press, 2001), 30.

84. Jean Toomer, "The Crock of Problems" (1928), in *Selected Essays and Literary Criticism,* ed. Robert B. Jones (Knoxville: University of Tennessee Press, 1996), 59. Toomer quoted in Sollers, "Jean Toomer's *Cane:* Modernism and Race in Interwar America," in *Jean Toomer and the Harlem Renaissance,* ed. Fabre and Feith, 30.

85. Toomer, "The Crock of Problems," in *Selected Essays and Literary Criticism,* ed. Jones, 56.

86. Jean Toomer, letter to John McClure, June 30, 1922, quoted in Gates, *Figures in Black,* 204.

87. Hurston, *Dust Tracks on a Road,* 192. Also see Hurston, "How It Feels to Be Colored Me," in which she writes, "At certain times I have no race, I am *me*," in *Folklore, Memoirs, and Other Writings,* 829.

88. Jean Toomer, "The South in Literature" (c. 1923), in *Selected Essays and Literary Criticism,* ed. Jones, 15. Toomer charts one version of Kabnis's "downward" progression in this essay.

89. Jean Toomer, "Kabnis," in *Cane* (1923) (New York: W. W. Norton, 1988), 84. Future page references appear parenthetically.

90. Toomer, "The South in Literature," in *Selected Essays and Literary Criticism,* ed. Jones, 15.

91. Jean Toomer to Kenneth Macgowan, letter of March 15, 1923, in *The Letters of Jean Toomer, 1919–1924,* ed. Whalan, 141.

92. In her foreword to *The Letters of Jean Toomer,* Barbara Foley, citing a letter from Toomer to Waldo Frank, suggests that the optimistic ending may have been a last-minute addition. See page xii.

Chapter 6: Changing Decorum

Epigraphs from Edwin Denby, "Sonnets," in *Dance Writings and Poetry,* ed. Robert Cornfield (New Haven: Yale University Press, 1998), 23; Virginia Woolf, *A Writer's Diary,* ed. Leonard Woolf (New York: Harcourt Brace Jovanovich, 1954), 209. The entry is from the 1934 diary.

1. Bernard Taper, *Balanchine: A Biography* (New York: Macmillan, 1974), 241. Taper is reporting Igor Stravinsky's opinion.

2. Igor Stravinsky, *An Autobiography* (1936), quoted in Richard Sennett, "Watching Music," in *Dance for a City: Fifty Years of the New York City Ballet,* ed. Lynn Garafola and Eric Foner (New York: Columbia University Press, 1999), 125.

3. R. P. Blackmur, "The Swan in Zurich," in *A Primer of Ignorance,* ed. Joseph Frank (New York: Harcourt, Brace and World, 1967), 132.

4. Edwin Denby, "Three Sides of *Agon*" (1959), in *Dance Writings and Poetry,* 269.

5. Denby, *Dance Writings and Poetry,* 51, 96, 224, 223, 231, 226.

6. See, for instance, Denby, *Dance Writings and Poetry,* 154, 188, 237, 267, and Lincoln Kirstein, *By With To and From: A Lincoln Kirstein Reader,* ed. Nicholas Jenkins (New York: Farrar, Straus and Giroux, 1991), 167, 169, 185, 198, 215.

7. Lincoln Kirstein, "A Ballet Master's Belief" (1984), in *By With To and From,* 206.

8. R. P. Blackmur, "The Swan in Zurich," in *Primer of Ignorance,* ed. Frank, 143.

9. On outwardness, see Selma Jean Cohen, "Problems of Definition," in *What Is*

Dance? Readings in Theory and Criticism, ed. Roger Copeland and Marshall Cohen (Oxford: Oxford University Press, 1983), 341–42.

10. George Balanchine, quoted in *What Is Dance?* ed. Copeland and Cohen, 106.

11. Edwin Denby, "Serenade" (1944), in *Dance Writings and Poetry,* 118.

12. Nicholas Jenkins, "'Running on the Waves': Pollock, Lowell, Bishop, and the American Ocean," *Yale Review* 95, no. 2 (April 2007): 46, 82.

13. Thomas Postlewait, "Spatial Order and Meaning in the Theatre: The Case of Tennessee Williams," *Assaph: Studies in the Theatre,* no. 10 (1994): 54. Postlewait (and C. W. E. Bigsby) link Williams's studies in motion to psychological and thematic concerns—characters seeking freedom from claustrophobia. I read them as composing an essay in aesthetics, or to put it another way, I follow the playwright's, not just the characters', movement—out of forms, not just spaces.

14. Arthur Miller, *Death of a Salesman* (1949) (New York: Penguin, 1976), 41. Future page references appear parenthetically.

15. Tennessee Williams, *The Glass Menagerie* (1945), in *Plays, 1937–1955* (New York: Library of America, 2000), 465. Future page references appear parenthetically.

16. Jane Bowles, *In the Summer House* (1953), in *My Sister's Hand in Mine* (New York: Farrar, Straus and Giroux, 1995), 293. Future page references appear parenthetically.

17. Matthew C. Roudané, "*Death of a Salesman* and the Poetics of Arthur Miller," in *The Cambridge Companion to Arthur Miller,* ed. Christopher Bigsby (Cambridge: Cambridge University Press, 1997), 66–68.

18. Paul Valéry, "Dance and the Soul" (1921), in *Dialogues,* trans. William McCausland Stewart (New York: Bollingen Foundation/Pantheon, 1956), 52. Future page references appear parenthetically.

19. Tennessee Williams to Edwina Dakin Williams, May 10, 1944, in *The Selected Letters of Tennessee Williams,* vol. 1, ed. Albert J. Devlin and Nancy M. Tischler (New York: New Directions, 2000), 523. The description of Lynes as "somewhat chi-chi" appears in a letter to James Laughlin, April 2, 1944, in *Selected Letters,* vol. 1, 522. Further details about this and the Beaton sittings appear in David Leddick, *Intimate Companions: A Triography of George Platt Lynes, Paul Cadmus, Lincoln Kirstein, and Their Circle* (New York: St. Martin's, 2000). In *Communists, Cowboys, and Queers: The Politics of Masculinity in the Work of Arthur Miller and Tennessee Williams* (Minneapolis: University of Minnesota Press, 1992), David Savran links Williams to Lynes's "homoerotic surrealist" art photographs. See page 97.

20. Tennessee Williams, "The Timeless World of a Play" (1951), in *Where I Live: Selected Essays* (New York: New Directions, 1978), 49, quoted in C. W. E. Bigsby, *A Critical Introduction to Twentieth-Century American Drama,* vol. 2 (Cambridge: Cambridge University Press, 1984), 46.

21. Tennessee Williams, "On a Streetcar Named Success" (1947), in *Where I Live,* 21.

22. C. W. E. Bigsby, *Modern American Drama, 1945–1990* (Cambridge: Cambridge University Press, 1992), 36.

23. The original, Broadway production omitted the projections, as did the acting edition of the text.

24. Williams met Joseph Cornell at the offices of *Dance Index,* where Williams's friend Donald Windham was an editor and where Cornell worked as a cover artist and occa-

sional contributor. Diane Waldman points out that the two artists shared similar family backgrounds and suggests, fleetingly, that Cornell identified with the claustrophobic depiction of kinship in *The Glass Menagerie*. See Diane Waldman, *Joseph Cornell: Master of Dreams* (New York: Harry N. Abrams, 2002), 66. Cornell's "White Crested Cockatoo (for Blanche DuBois)" is in his 1948 diary, collected in the Joseph Cornell Papers at the Smithsonian Archives of American Art.

25. Tennessee Williams, "The Important Thing" (1945), in *Collected Stories* (New York: New Directions, 1985), 165.

26. Tennessee Williams, *Notebooks*, ed. Margaret Bradham Thornton (New Haven: Yale University Press, 2006), 305.

27. Tennessee Williams, *Memoirs* (Garden City, NY: Doubleday, 1975), 84.

28. Tennessee Williams to Donald Windham, April 1943, in *Tennessee Williams' Letters to Donald Windham, 1940–1965*, ed. Donald Windham (New York: Penguin, 1980), 59.

29. Lincoln Kirstein, "Marilyn Monroe, 1926–1962" (1962), in *By With To and From*, 304. On Cocteau's translation of Williams, see Francis Steegmuller, *Cocteau: A Biography* (Boston: Atlantic Monthly Press, 1970), 478.

30. Clement Greenberg, "Avant-Garde and Kitsch" (1939), in *Collected Essays and Criticism*, vol. 1 (Chicago: University of Chicago Press, 1988), 12.

31. Tennessee Williams, "Preface to My Poems" (1944), in *Where I Live*, 6.

32. Tennessee Williams to Margo Jones, March 2, 1944, in *Selected Letters*, vol. 1, 514, and Williams, *Notebooks*, 413, 419.

33. Hermann Broch, "Notes on the Problem of Kitsch" (1950), in Gillo Dorfles, *Kitsch: The World of Bad Taste* (New York: Universe, 1969), 52. Future page references appear parenthetically.

34. Hermann Broch, "Evil in the System of the Values of Art" (1933), excerpted in Dorfles, *Kitsch*, 73.

35. Bigsby, *Critical Introduction to Twentieth-Century American Drama*, 2:45.

36. Arthur Miller, *Timebends: A Life* (New York: Grove, 1987), 9.

37. Arthur Miller, "On Social Plays" (1955), in *The Theater Essays of Arthur Miller*, ed. Robert A. Martin (New York: Penguin, 1978), 54.

38. Anne Hollander, *Seeing Through Clothes* (New York: Viking, 1978), 220.

39. Christopher Bigsby examines other meanings of the working title in *Arthur Miller: A Critical Study* (Cambridge: Cambridge University Press, 2005), 112.

40. Arthur Miller, "Tragedy and the Common Man" (1949), in *Theater Essays of Arthur Miller*, 4.

41. Arthur Miller, "Introduction to the *Collected Plays*" (1957), in *Theater Essays of Arthur Miller*, 147.

42. Ibid., 166. Miller is speaking of Eddie Carbone in *A View from the Bridge*.

43. Ibid., 135.

44. Richard Gilman, "Miller's *Incident at Vichy*" (1964), in *The Drama Is Coming Now: The Theater Criticism of Richard Gilman, 1961–1991* (New Haven: Yale University Press, 2005), 109.

45. Arthur Miller quoted in Bigsby, *Critical Introduction to Twentieth-Century American Drama*, 2:173.

46. Elinor Fuchs, "Reading for Landscape: The Case of American Drama," in *Land/*

Scape/Theater, ed. Elinor Fuchs and Una Chaudhuri (Ann Arbor: University of Michigan Press, 2002), 31–34.

47. Miller, "On Social Plays," in *Theater Essays of Arthur Miller,* 57, 61–62.

48. Philip Fisher, *The Vehement Passions* (Princeton: Princeton University Press, 2002), 67–68. Future page references appear parenthetically.

49. Miller, "Introduction to the *Collected Plays,*" in *Theater Essays of Arthur Miller,* 136, 138.

50. See Savran, *Communists, Cowboys, and Queers,* 37.

51. Jane Bowles to Paul Bowles, January 17, 1950, in *Out in the World: Selected Letters of Jane Bowles, 1935–1970,* ed. Millicent Dillon (Santa Barbara, CA: Black Sparrow, 1985), 148.

52. Jane Bowles to Libby Holman, February 18, 1951, in *Out in the World,* ed. Dillon, 168.

53. Tennessee Williams to Brooks Atkinson, January 14, 1954, in *The Selected Letters of Tennessee Williams,* vol. 2, ed. Albert J. Devlin and Nancy M. Tischler (New York: New Directions, 2004), 510.

54. Jane Bowles, *A Quarreling Pair* (1945), in *My Sister's Hand in Mine,* 416.

55. Tennessee Williams, foreword to Jane Bowles, *Feminine Wiles* (Santa Barbara, CA: Black Sparrow, 1976), 8.

56. Jane Bowles quoted in Millicent Dillon, *A Little Original Sin: The Life and Work of Jane Bowles* (New York: Anchor, 1990), 415.

57. Gayle Austin has argued that Molly and Gertrude symbolically marry one another in an earlier scene when Bowles puts them both onstage in their wedding dresses but keeps the grooms offstage. See Austin, *Feminist Theories for Dramatic Criticism* (Ann Arbor: University of Michigan Press, 1990), 70. David Savran explores the play's elaborate displacement of homosexual and homosocial desire (and recognizes the summer house's service as a closet) in "A Different Kind of Closet Drama or, The Melancholy Heterosexuality of Jane Bowles," in Savran, *A Queer Sort of Materialism: Recontextualizing American Theater* (Ann Arbor: University of Michigan Press, 2003), 155–69.

58. John Ashbery, "Up from the Underground," in *New York Times Book Review,* January 29, 1967, quoted in *A Tawdry Place of Salvation: The Art of Jane Bowles,* ed. Jennie Skerl (Carbondale: Southern Illinois University Press, 1997), 11. Truman Capote, introduction to Bowles, *My Sister's Hand in Mine,* ix.

59. Paul Bowles quoted in Dillon, *Little Original Sin,* 133.

60. Dillon, *Little Original Sin,* 74.

61. Jane Bowles interviewed in *Vogue,* May 1, 1954, quoted in Dillon, *Little Original Sin,* 235.

62. Jane Bowles to Libby Holman, January 16, 1957, in *Out in the World,* ed. Dillon, 187.

63. Jane Bowles to Paul Bowles, February 1, 1957, in *Out in the World,* ed. Dillon, 189.

64. Jane Bowles quoted in Dillon, *Little Original Sin,* 238–39.

65. Virginia Woolf, *A Room of One's Own* (1929) (New York: Harcourt Brace Jovanovich, 1957), 58–59.

66. Frank O'Hara quoted in Brad Gooch, *City Poet: The Life of Frank O'Hara* (New York: Alfred A. Knopf, 1993), 246.

67. Frank O'Hara, "To the Harbormaster," "In Memory of My Feelings," and "Meditations in an Emergency," in *The Collected Poems of Frank O'Hara*, ed. Donald Allen (Berkeley: University of California Press, 1995), 217, 256, 197.

68. Frank O'Hara, introduction to Edwin Denby, *Dancers Buildings and People in the Streets* (1965), reprinted in Frank O'Hara, *Standing Still and Walking in New York*, ed. Donald Allen (Bolinas, CA: Grey Fox, 1975), 184. O'Hara, "In Memory of My Feelings," in *Collected Poems*, 256. Marjorie Perloff, *Frank O'Hara: Poet among Painters* (New York: George Braziller, 1977), 1–30. Richard Howard, *Alone with America* (New York: Atheneum, 1969), 396–412.

69. Clark Coolidge, "FO'H Notes," in *Homage to Frank O'Hara*, ed. Bill Berkson and Joe LeSueur (Bolinas, CA: Big Sky, 1988), 184.

70. Frank O'Hara, "A True Account of Talking to the Sun at Fire Island," in *Collected Poems*, 307.

71. Frank O'Hara, "To Edwin Denby," in *Collected Poems*, 287.

72. Frank O'Hara, "Ode to Michael Goldberg ('s Birth and Other Births)," "Avenue A," "Variations on Pasternak's 'Mein Liebchen, Was Willst Du Noch Mehr,'" "A Warm Day for December," in *Collected Poems*, 292, 356, 339, 376.

73. Marjorie Perloff makes the point succinctly: "We can now understand why O'Hara loves the *motion* picture, *action* painting, and all forms of dance—artforms that capture the *present* rather than the past, the present in all its chaotic splendor." *Frank O'Hara: Poet among Painters*, 21.

74. Frank O'Hara, "Biotherm (for Bill Berkson)," in *Collected Poems*, 444. Future page references appear parenthetically.

75. Frank O'Hara, "The Day Lady Died," in *Collected Poems*, 325.

76. Frank O'Hara, "Poem (Khrushchev is coming on the right day!)," in *Collected Poems*, 340.

77. Frank O'Hara, "To the Film Industry in Crisis," in *Collected Poems*, 232.

78. Frank O'Hara, "Poem Read at Joan Mitchell's," in *Collected Poems*, 266.

79. Frank O'Hara, "To Hell with It," in *Collected Poems*, 275.

80. Frank O'Hara, interview for the film *USA: Poetry* (1966), in *Homage to Frank O'Hara*, ed. Berkson and LeSueur, 215.

81. In this, of course, O'Hara is extending to playwriting a long-held and much-discussed principle of his poetry. Joe LeSueur traces the origins of many poems in *Digressions on Some Poems by Frank O'Hara* (New York: Farrar, Straus and Giroux, 2003). See also Perloff, *Frank O'Hara: Poet among Painters*, 117.

82. Frank O'Hara, *Try! Try!* (1951 version), in *Amorous Nightmares of Delay: Selected Plays* (Baltimore: Johns Hopkins University Press, 1997), 30. Future page references appear parenthetically.

83. See Joe LeSueur, introduction to O'Hara, *Amorous Nightmares of Delay*, xvii. LeSueur later writes, "Some of these plays are so personal, or private . . . that I wonder how they seem to readers who never moved in Frank's circle" (xxii).

84. Perloff doesn't touch on the plays in this context but opposes the view of the poems as letters, *Frank O'Hara: Poet among Painters*, 27–29.

85. Gertrude Stein, *Four Saints in Three Acts*, in *Last Operas and Plays* (1949) (Baltimore: Johns Hopkins University Press, 1995), 445.

86. Frank O'Hara, "Personism: A Manifesto" (1959), in *Collected Poems,* 499.

87. Alison Lurie, "V. R. Lang: A Memoir," in V. R. Lang, *Poems and Plays* (New York: Random House, 1975), 14.

88. Frank O'Hara, "Roma" (1955), in *Standing Still and Walking in New York,* 69.

89. Frank O'Hara, "Ode to Tanaquil LeClercq," in *Collected Poems,* 364. Future page references appear parenthetically.

90. O'Hara, introduction to *Dancers Buildings and People in the Streets,* in *Standing Still and Walking in New York,* 182.

91. Frank O'Hara quoted in Edward Lucie-Smith, "An Interview with Frank O'Hara" (1965), in *Standing Still and Walking in New York,* 21.

92. William Corbett, in his edition of *The Letters of James Schuyler to Frank O'Hara* (New York: Turtle Point, 2006), writes that O'Hara, Schuyler, Arthur Gold, and Robert Fizdale "read Chekhov aloud" during gatherings at Gold's and Fizdale's house in 1953. Schuyler, in a letter, praises O'Hara for his "great Chekhov performances." See page 18.

93. Frank O'Hara and Larry Rivers, *Kenneth Koch, a Tragedy,* in O'Hara, *Amorous Nightmares of Delay,* 132.

94. Frank O'Hara to Kenneth Koch, quoted in Olivier Brossard, introduction to Frank O'Hara, *The Houses at Falling Hanging, Yale Review* 92, no. 1 (January 2004): 5.

95. Frank O'Hara, untitled statement for *The New American Poetry,* ed. Donald Allen (New York: Grove, 1960), reprinted in *Collected Poems,* 500.

96. Olivier Brossard, introduction to O'Hara, *Houses at Falling Hanging,* 6.

97. Frank O'Hara, "Comedy of Manners (American)" (1962), in *Standing Still and Walking in New York,* 165–67. Future page references appear parenthetically.

98. O'Hara, "Roma," in *Standing Still and Walking in New York,* 71.

99. O'Hara, "Meditations in an Emergency," in *Collected Poems,* 197.

100. Frank O'Hara and Larry Rivers, "How to Proceed in the Arts" (1961), in Frank O'Hara, *Art Chronicles, 1954–1966* (New York: George Braziller, 1975), 94.

101. Frank O'Hara, "The Afternoon," in *Collected Poems,* 174–75.

102. Frank O'Hara, "Two Variations," in *Collected Poems,* 134. A note on page 528 explains that the poem was originally titled "To Edwin."

103. Frank O'Hara to Larry Rivers (1957), quoted in Perloff, *Frank O'Hara: Poet among Painters,* 22. For a discussion of O'Hara's commitment to theatrical surfaces, see Charles Altieri, "Varieties of Immanentist Expression," excerpted in *Frank O'Hara: To Be True to a City,* ed. Jim Elledge (Ann Arbor: University of Michigan Press, 1990), 189–208. Alex Katz, Bill Berkson, and Kenneth Koch also discuss what one of them calls the "surfacey" quality of the poems in their contributions to *Homage to Frank O'Hara,* ed. Berkson and LeSueur, 99, 162, 207.

104. Frank O'Hara, "The 'Unfinished,'" in *Collected Poems,* 317.

105. Frank O'Hara, "At the Theatre," in *Early Writing,* ed. Donald Allen (Bolinas, CA: Grey Fox, 1977), 71.

106. Frank O'Hara, "Lines for the Fortune Cookies," in *Collected Poems,* 466.

107. Frank O'Hara, *Change Your Bedding!* (1951), in *Amorous Nightmares of Delay,* 58–60.

108. O'Hara, *Houses at Falling Hanging,* 21.

109. Frank O'Hara, "Variations on Saturday," in *Collected Poems,* 378.

110. Frank O'Hara, "Poem (I watched an armory combing its bronze bricks)," in *Collected Poems,* 216.

Chapter 7: Returning to Neutral

Epigraphs from Roland Barthes, *The Neutral* (lecture course at the Collège de France, 1978), trans. Rosalind E. Krauss and Denis Hollier (New York: Columbia University Press, 2005), 57; Wassily Kandinsky, letter to Arnold Schoenberg, October 16, 1911, quoted in Annabelle Henkin Melzer, *Dada and Surrealist Performance* (1980) (Baltimore: Johns Hopkins University Press, 1994), 17.

1. Norman Mailer, "Theatre: *The Blacks,* cont.," *Village Voice,* May 18, 1961, p. 14. (Mailer's essay appeared in two parts. The first part was published in the May 11, 1961, issue, pp. 11, 14. Also see "Mailer to Hansberry," June 8, 1961, pp. 11–12.) Future page references appear parenthetically.

2. Lorraine Hansberry, "Thoughts on Genet, Mailer, and the New Paternalism," *Village Voice,* June 1, 1961, p. 14. Future page references appear parenthetically.

3. Jean Genet to Roger Blin, quoted in Edmund White, *Genet: A Biography* (New York: Alfred A. Knopf, 1993), 499. Future page references appear parenthetically.

4. Jean Genet, *The Blacks* (1958), trans. Bernard Frechtman (New York: Grove, 1960), 3. Future page references appear parenthetically.

5. Leo Bersani and Ulysse Dutoit, *Arts of Impoverishment: Beckett, Rothko, Resnais* (Cambridge, Harvard University Press, 1993), 39–40. Samuel Beckett, *Endgame* (1957) (New York: Grove, 1958), 1. Future page references appear parenthetically.

6. Jean Genet, "The Studio of Alberto Giacometti" (1958), in *Fragments of the Artwork,* trans. Charlotte Mandell (Stanford: Stanford University Press, 2003), 41. Future page references appear parenthetically.

7. Jean Genet, "The Tightrope Walker," in *Fragments of the Artwork,* 71. Future page references appear parenthetically.

8. Jean Genet, "Letter to Jean-Jacques Pauvert" (1954), and "That Strange Word . . ." (1967), in *Fragments of the Artwork,* 39, 104, 110.

9. Jean Genet, "Jean Cocteau," in *Fragments of the Artwork,* 17.

10. Genet, "That Strange Word . . ." in *Fragments of the Artwork,* 107.

11. Wallace Shawn, *The Fever* (1990), in *Four Plays* (New York: Farrar, Straus and Giroux, 1998), 228.

12. August Wilson, *Joe Turner's Come and Gone* (New York: New American Library, 1988), 53.

13. Maria Irene Fornes, *Enter THE NIGHT* (1993), in *Plays for the End of the Century,* ed. Bonnie Marranca (Baltimore: Johns Hopkins University Press, 1996), 123.

14. Adrienne Kennedy, *Funnyhouse of a Negro* (1964), in *The Adrienne Kennedy Reader* (Minneapolis: University of Minnesota Press, 2001), 24. Future page references appear parenthetically.

15. Jonas Mekas, "Jack Smith, or the End of Civilization" (1970), in *Movie Journal: The Rise of the New American Cinema, 1959–1971* (New York: Macmillan, 1972), 392–94. Also see Stefan Brecht, *Queer Theatre* (Frankfurt: Suhrkamp, 1978), 10–27, and J. Hoberman, "The Theatre of Jack Smith," in *Theatre of the Ridiculous,* ed. Bonnie

Marranca and Gautam Dasgupta (Baltimore: Johns Hopkins University Press, 1997), 1–11.

16. Jack Smith, "Taboo of Jingola," *Village Voice,* December 21, 1972, reprinted in *Wait for Me at the Bottom of the Pool: The Writings of Jack Smith,* ed. J. Hoberman and Edward Leffingwell (New York: Serpent's Tail, 1997), 103.

17. Jack Smith, "Uncle Fishook and the Sacred Baby Poo Poo of Art" (interview with Sylvère Lotringer), *Semiotext(e)* 3, no. 2 (1978), reprinted in *Wait for Me at the Bottom of the Pool,* 115.

18. Jack Smith, *What's Underground about Marshmallows* (1981), in *Wait for Me at the Bottom of the Pool,* 140.

19. Charles Ludlam, "Confessions of a Farceur," in *Ridiculous Theatre: Scourge of Human Folly: The Essays and Opinions of Charles Ludlam,* ed. Steven Samuels (New York: Theatre Communications Group, 1992), 32.

20. Meredith Monk, "Process Notes on *Portable,* May 10, 1966," in *Meredith Monk,* ed. Deborah Jowitt (Baltimore: Johns Hopkins University Press, 1997), 18.

21. The Wooster Group, program for *Hamlet* (New York: St. Ann's Warehouse, 2007), unpaginated.

22. The Wooster Group, *Route 1 and 9 (The Last Act), Benzene,* no. 5/6 (Spring/Summer 1982): 5. For a suggestive discussion of the Wooster Group's preoccupation with death, see David Savran, "The Death of the Avantgarde," *TDR: The Drama Review* 49, no. 3 (Fall 2005): 10–42.

23. Peggy Phelan, *Mourning Sex: Performing Public Memories* (New York: Routledge, 1997), 10.

24. Joseph Roach, in *Cities of the Dead* (New York: Columbia University Press, 1996), treats the actor as a "medium" whose virtuosity depends on his or her ability to "impart the gestures of the dead to the living" (78, 80). David Savran, in the chapter entitled "The Haunted Stages of Modernity" from *A Queer Sort of Materialism: Recontextualizing American Theater* (Ann Arbor: University of Michigan Press, 2003), reads ghost plays against a history of imperialism, decolonization, and neocolonialism, spectators and artists haunted by history they hope to bury (98–99). Alice Rayner, in *Ghosts: Death's Double and the Phenomena of Theater* (Minneapolis: University of Minnesota Press, 2006), sees the performer "unconcealing" and "unforgetting" the experiences he or she represents, in the process "measuring an absence" as compelling as the presence that screens it (xvi). Marvin Carlson, for his part, imagines an infinite regression of such false fronts. In *The Haunted Stage: The Theatre as Memory Machine* (Ann Arbor: University of Michigan Press, 2001), he argues that actors both summon and mask the memory of earlier interpretations of their roles. Texts echo earlier soundings of their themes. Spaces are marked by previous claims on their clarifying services. There is no "as if for the first time," Carlson shows, in a theater that betrays its supposed allegiance to the present by its bottomless interment in the past. The idea itself harkens back to the past: Herbert Blau (as Carlson and others acknowledge) was among the first to chronicle what he calls the "disappearance of origin." At the theater, Blau writes in *Blooded Thought: Occasions of Theatre* (New York: PAJ Publications, 1982), we are beckoned toward but never reach "the phantom or vanishing source of all behavior, every sound" (84). "Something is slipping away. . . . The theatre confronts this fact" (109) — even if it can't reconcile us to it.

25. Barthes, *Neutral,* 6.

26. Roland Barthes, *Roland Barthes*, trans. Richard Howard (New York: Farrar, Straus and Giroux, 1977), 132. Barthes, *Neutral,* 16, 29, 37, 41, 70–71, 137.

27. Maurice Blanchot, *The Infinite Conversation,* trans. Susan Hanson (Minneapolis: University of Minnesota Press, 1993), 311, quoted in Barthes, *Neutral,* 69.

28. Yvonne Rainer, "Some Retrospective Notes on a Dance for 10 People and 12 Mattresses Called 'Parts of Some Sextets,' Performed at the Wadsworth Atheneum, Hartford, Connecticut, and Judson Memorial Church, New York, in March 1965," *Tulane Drama Review* 10 (Winter 1965), quoted in Sally Banes, *Terpsichore in Sneakers: Post-Modern Dance* (Hanover, NH: Wesleyan University Press/University Press of New England, 1987), 43.

29. Maria Irene Fornes, *Mud,* in *Plays* (New York: PAJ Publications, 1986), 24.

30. Maria Irene Fornes, *Abingdon Square* (1987) (Los Angeles: Green Integer, 2000), 22.

31. August Wilson, *Ma Rainey's Black Bottom* (New York: New American Library, 1985), 83.

32. Sam Shepard, *Action* (1975), in *Fool for Love and Other Plays* (New York: Bantam, 1984), 169. Future page references appear parenthetically.

33. Sam Shepard, *The Tooth of Crime* (1972), in *Seven Plays* (New York: Bantam, 1981), 225. Future page references appear parenthetically.

34. Sam Shepard, *Suicide in B Flat* (1976), in *Fool for Love and Other Plays,* 216.

35. Sam Shepard, *Curse of the Starving Class* (1978), in *Seven Plays,* 185, 197.

36. Kennedy, *Funnyhouse of a Negro,* in *Adrienne Kennedy Reader,* 14.

37. Marc Robinson, "New Frequencies" (interview with Meredith Monk), *Theater* 30, no. 2 (2000): 53.

38. Richard Foreman, *Pearls for Pigs* (1997), in *Paradise Hotel and Other Plays* (Woodstock, NY: Overlook, 2001), 194. Future page references appear parenthetically.

39. Elinor Fuchs, "Today I Am a Fountain Pen: An Interview with Richard Foreman," *Theater* 25, no. 1 (Spring/Summer 1994): 86.

40. Tony Kushner, *Homebody/Kabul* (rev. version) (New York: Theatre Communications Group, 2004), 28.

41. Tony Kushner, *Angels in America: A Gay Fantasia on National Themes. Part Two: Perestroika* (New York: Theatre Communications Group, 1994), 148. Future page references appear parenthetically.

42. Edward Albee, *A Delicate Balance* (1966) (New York: Plume, 1997), 9. Future page references appear parenthetically.

43. Edward Albee, *Who's Afraid of Virginia Woolf?* (1962) (New York: Signet, 1983), 139.

44. Edward Albee, *Seascape* (New York: Atheneum, 1975), 13. Future page references appear parenthetically.

45. Edward Albee, *All Over* (New York: Atheneum, 1971), 21. Future page references appear parenthetically.

46. See Mel Gussow, *Edward Albee: A Singular Journey* (New York: Simon and Schuster, 1999), 15.

47. Edward Albee quoted in Gussow, *Edward Albee,* 256.

48. Harold Pinter quoted in Gussow, *Edward Albee,* 266.

49. David Mamet, *The Cryptogram* (New York: Vintage, 1995), 89, 5, 73, 31. Future page references appear parenthetically.

50. David Mamet, *Plays: 4* (London: Methuen, 2002), xi.

51. Henry James, *The Art of the Novel* (New York: Scribners, 1934), 143, 145, 149. Future page references appear parenthetically.

52. David Mamet quoted in C. W. E. Bigsby, *David Mamet* (London: Methuen, 1985), 133.

53. Roland Barthes, *Camera Lucida: Reflections on Photography,* trans. Richard Howard (London: Flamingo, 1984), 85. Future page references appear parenthetically.

54. "The Photograph [is] an image without code." Barthes, *Camera Lucida,* 88.

55. David Mamet, "Decay: Some Thoughts for Actors" (1986), in *A Whore's Profession: Notes and Essays* (London: Faber and Faber, 1994), 187.

56. See also Jean Genet: "If we go to the theater, it is to penetrate into the hall, into the anteroom of that precarious death that sleep will be" ("The Tightrope Walker," in *Fragments of the Artwork,* 81).

57. Jean Genet, "The Strange Word *Urb* . . . ," trans. Bettina L. Knapp, in *Genet/Ionesco: The Theatre of the Double,* ed. Kelly Morris (New York: Bantam, 1969), 114–15.

58. Jean Genet, *Letters to Roger Blin: Reflections on the Theater,* trans. Richard Seaver (New York: Grove, 1969), 69.

59. See Una Chaudhuri, *Staging Place: The Geography of Modern Drama* (Ann Arbor: University of Michigan Press, 1995), 262; Greg Miller, "The Bottom of Desire in Suzan-Lori Parks's *Venus," Modern Drama* 45, no. 1 (Spring 2002): 125–37; Alice Rayner and Harry J. Elam, Jr., "Unfinished Business: Reconfiguring History in Suzan-Lori Parks's *The Death of the Last Black Man in the Whole Entire World," Theatre Journal* 46 (1994): 447–61. Also see Steven Drukman, "Suzan-Lori Parks and Liz Diamond: Doo-a-diddly-dit-dit" (an interview), *Drama Review* 39, no. 3 (Fall 1995): 56–75, and Marc Robinson, *The Other American Drama* (New York: Cambridge University Press, 1994), 191–92.

60. Suzan-Lori Parks, *Topdog/Underdog* (New York: Theatre Communications Group, 2001), 34. Further references cited parenthetically in the text.

61. Jean Toomer, *Cane* (1923) (New York: W. W. Norton, 1988), 115.

62. Marita Bonner, *The Purple Flower* (1928), in *Black Female Playwrights: An Anthology of Plays Before 1950,* ed. Kathy Perkins (Bloomington: Indiana University Press, 1989), 192.

63. LeRoi Jones, *Dutchman,* in *Dutchman* and *The Slave* (New York: Morrow, 1964), 3.

64. Suzan-Lori Parks, *The America Play,* in *The America Play and Other Works* (New York: Theatre Communications Group, 1995), 162. Future page references appear parenthetically.

65. Daphne A. Brooks suggests still other variations on this theme in her discussion of the "epistemological cavities" and "spectatorial opacities" in the theaters of Henry "Box" Brown, Bert Williams and George Walker, and other late nineteenth- and early twentieth-century African-American performers. See Daphne A. Brooks, *Bodies in Dissent: Spectacular Performances of Race and Freedom, 1850–1910* (Durham: Duke University Press, 2006), 8, 101–12.

66. Elizabeth Bishop, "One Art," in *The Complete Poems, 1927–1979* (New York: Farrar, Straus and Giroux, 1984), 178.

67. See interview in David Savran, *The Playwright's Voice* (New York: Theatre Communications Group, 1999), 148. Also see Marc Robinson, "Liz Diamond" (interview with the director of Parks's early plays), in *Speak Theater and Film! The Best of* Bomb Magazine's *Interviews with Playwrights, Actors, and Directors,* ed. Betsy Sussler (New York: G + B Arts International, 1999), 218, and Joseph Roach, "The Great Hole of History: Liturgical Silence in Beckett, Osofisan, and Parks, *South Atlantic Quarterly* 100, no. 1 (2001): 307–17.

68. Suzan-Lori Parks, *In the Blood,* in *The Red Letter Plays* (New York: Theatre Communications Group, 2001), 77. Future page references appear parenthetically.

69. Suzan-Lori Parks, *The Death of the Last Black Man in the Whole Entire World,* in *America Play and Other Works,* 104. Future page references appear parenthetically.

70. Suzan-Lori Parks, *365 Days / 365 Plays* (New York: Theatre Communications Group, 2006), 376.

71. Jean-Paul Sartre, introduction to Jean Genet, *The Maids* and *Deathwatch,* trans. Bernard Frechtman (New York: Grove, 1962), 31.

72. The passage recalls dialogue between Vardaman and Darl in *As I Lay Dying:* " 'What is your ma, Darl,' I said. 'I haven't got ere one,' Darl said. 'Because if I had one, it is *was*. And if it is was, it cant be *is*. Can it?' ... 'But you *are*, Darl,' I said. 'I know it,' Darl said. 'That's why I am not *is*. *Are* is too many for one woman to foal.' " William Faulkner, *As I Lay Dying* (1930) (New York: Vintage, 1964), 95.

73. Suzan-Lori Parks, "New Black Math," *Theatre Journal* 57, no. 4 (December 2005): 578.

74. Suzan-Lori Parks, *Venus* (New York: Theatre Communications Group, 1997), 161. Future page references appear parenthetically.

75. Bertolt Brecht, quoted in Richard Gilman, "Jest, Satire, Irony, and Deeper Meaning: Thirty Years of Off-Broadway" (1985), in *The Drama Is Coming Now: The Theater Criticism of Richard Gilman, 1961–1991* (New Haven: Yale University Press, 2005), 304.

76. Wallace Shawn, *The Designated Mourner* (New York: Farrar, Straus and Giroux, 1996), 35. Future page references appear parenthetically.

77. Shawn, *The Fever,* in *Four Plays,* 179. Future page references appear parenthetically.

78. Shawn, *Aunt Dan and Lemon,* in *Four Plays,* 169. Future page references appear parenthetically.

79. Shawn begins his 2007 New York production of *The Fever* similarly, inviting spectators to join him onstage for champagne before the play begins. Only the naive think they're encountering an unperforming Shawn; only those unfamiliar with Shawn's typical subversiveness are surprised when his character later mocks the smugness of the "cultured."

80. *All Over* was "one of the great experiences I ever had in the theater." Wallace Shawn quoted in Gussow, *Edward Albee,* 285.

81. Jack also echoes lines spoken by the protagonist of *The Fever:* "I look out the window, and in the cool breeze I remember I once was a child in a beautiful city, surrounded by hope. And I feel such joy — the coolness of the breeze — I wonder if I could put down for a moment my burden of lies, of lying" (224).

82. In an April 2008 interview with Don Shewey, Shawn announced that he recently completed a draft of a new play, *Grasses of a Thousand Colors*. See Don Shewey, "Wallace Shawn: The Playwright Nobody (and Everybody) Knows," *American Theatre* 25, no. 4 (April 2008), 26–27, 81–82.

83. Mark Strand, "The Man behind the Voice: Interview of Wallace Shawn," *Interview* (March 1989), reprinted in W. D. King, *Writing Wrongs: The Work of Wallace Shawn* (Philadelphia: Temple University Press, 1997), 188. Future page references appear parenthetically.

Index

Aaron, Daniel, 100

Abingdon Square (Fornes), 320

Across the Continent; or, Scenes from New York Life and the Pacific Railroad (McCloskey), 46

acting techniques: Barnes on, 237; Gillette on, 99; harmonic gymnastics, 153; Method acting, 259, 285; in the nineteenth century, 32, 90, 94, 114, 358(n11)

Action (Shepard), 320

Actors Studio, 258–59, 285

An Actress (Portrait of Suzanne Santje) (Eakins painting), 114–15, 116(fig), 143

Adams, Diana, 297, 298, 299

Adams, Henry, 132

Adams, John, 357(n26)

African Company, 42, 47

African-American theater: African Company, 42, 47; Harlem Renaissance theater, 241–43, 249–50; subterranean

spaces in, 340–41, 388(n65). *See also* Baraka, Amiri; Bonner, Marita; Brown, Henry "Box"; Brown, William Wells; Hansberry, Lorraine; Hughes, Langston; Hurston, Zora Neale; Kennedy, Adrienne; Parks, Suzan-Lori; Toomer, Jean; Wilson, August

The Agnew Clinic (Eakins painting), 114

Agon (Balanchine ballet), 258, 259

Aiken, George L. *(Uncle Tom's Cabin)*, 2, 34, 35(fig), 53–64, 133

Akropolis (Grotowski), 318

Albee, Edward, 5, 324–31, 351, 389(n80)

Alger, Horatio, 365(n35)

All God's Chillun Got Wings (O'Neill), 175

All My Sons (Miller), 298

All Over (Albee), 325, 389(n80)

Alter, Robert, 130

The America Play (Parks), 340, 341, 343, 344, 345